CONTENTS

Tour of the book's features

Before starting to use the book, we invite you to come on a quick tour to show you some of the book's features and help you get the most out of it.

Working women's rally, Bangladesh.

Topic 3 Feminist Theories

Feminism sees society as male dominated and it seeks to describe, explain and change the position of women in society. It is therefore both a theory of women's subordination, and a political movement.

The roots of feminism, like those of other modernist theories, can be traced back to the late 18th century Enlightenment. This proclaimed universal principles of liberty and equality, along with the idea that human reason can liberate us from ignorance and create a better society.

Feminists argued that, since both sexes had the same power of reason, these principles should apply to women as much as to men and that women's emancipation must be included as part of the Enlightenment project.

A 'first wave' of feminism appeared in the late 19th century, with the suffragettes' campaign for the right to vote. The 1960s saw a 'second wave' emerge on a global scale.

Since then, feminism has had a major influence on sociology. Feminists criticise mainstream sociology for being 'malestream' – seeing society only from a male perspective. By contrast, feminists examine society from the viewpoint of women. Feminist sociologists see their work as part of the struggle against women's subordination.

However, although all feminists oppose women's subordination, there are disagreements among feminists about its causes and how to overcome it. In this Topic, we concentrate on those feminist theories that have had most impact on sociology:

- Liberal or reformist feminism
- Radical feminism
- Marxist feminism
- Dual systems feminism
- Difference feminism and poststructuralism

Learning objectives

After studying this Topic, you should:
- Know the main types of feminist theories.
- Understand the similarities and differences between feminist theories.
- Be able to evaluate the strengths and limitations of feminist theories.

Topics

Each chapter is divided into manageable sized Topics, each covering a separate issue in sociology.

The AQA Specification

At the start of each chapter, this tells you what you are required to study for the exam.

The AQA Specification

The specification is the syllabus produced by the exam board, telling you what you have to study. The AQA specification for Crime and Deviance requires you to examine the following:

- Different theories of crime, deviance, social order and social control.
- The social distribution of crime and deviance by age, ethnicity, gender, locality and social class, including recent patterns and trends in crime.
- Globalisation and crime in contemporary society; the mass media and crime; green crime; human rights and state crimes.
- Crime control, prevention and punishment, victims, and the role of the criminal justice system and other agencies.
- The sociological study of suicide and its theoretical and methodological implications.
- The connections between sociological theory and methods and the study of crime and deviance.

Synoptic links: theory and core themes

Left realist and neo-Marxist **theories** offer alternative views of whether black criminality is a fact or a social construct. However, both link ethnic differences in recorded crime to the relative lack of **power** and marginal position of ethnic minorities in the **stratification** system.

Synoptic links

These link the Topic you are studying to sociological theory, research methods and the core themes (stratification, differentiation and power, and culture, socialisation and identity) that run through the whole specification. These links are assessed in both the A2 exam papers.

Learning objectives

After studying this Topic, you should:
- Know the main characteristics of crime and deviance as a context for sociological research.
- Understand some of the problems and opportunities that researching issues in crime and deviance presents for sociologists.
- Be aware of some of the research strategies sociologists use to investigate crime and deviance.

Learning objectives

These spell out what you are going to learn in each Topic.

Is it possible for, say, twenty trained interviewers all to ask a set of questions in exactly the same way? Give your reasons.

Question panels

In each Topic there are short questions on what you are reading about for you to answer on your own or with others.

Boxes

These contain extra information, such as examples,
details of important sociological ideas or studies, or
relevant policies and laws. Some have questions to get
you thinking further.

QuickCheck Questions

These test-yourself questions come at the end of each Topic to
test your understanding of what you have read and reinforce your
knowledge of key ideas. You can check your answers on our website.

QuickCheck Questions

1 According to Weber, which is the area of sociology into
which values must not be allowed to enter?

2 True or false? Relativism argues that everyone's view of the
world is equally valid.

3 What is Gouldner's main criticism of modern positivist
sociologists?

4 Why do interactionists argue we should see things from the
point of view of the underdog?

5 Why might the military see anthropologists as useful to
them in Iraq and Afghanistan?

6 Explain what is meant by 'objectivity'.

7 Why do many sociologists wish to be seen as scientific?

Check your answers at www.sociology.uk.net

Summary

The early positivists and Marx believed that we could discover
objective scientific knowledge and use it to improve society. Weber
argued that values are essential in deciding what to research, in
interpreting findings and in determining how they should be used,
but must be kept out of the data-collection process. However, 20th
century positivists claimed to be 'value-free', leading Gouldner to
accuse them of being subservient to their paymasters. Becker argues
that sociologists should take the side of the underdog. The values
of those funding the research play a part in determining what gets
researched and published. Sociologists' own values influence the
kinds of research questions they ask, their methods and findings.

Summaries

Each Topic ends with a summary that picks out
the most important points. This at-a-glance
overview will help you consolidate what you
have learned and revise for the exam.

Activity   Gender and risk factors for offending

Go to www.sociology.uk.net

Activities

These develop your knowledge, understanding and skills by
giving you a task to carry out, either on your own or with
classmates. Some involve research outside class, carrying
our small surveys or searching the library and the Internet,
including the book's own website.

The examiner's advice

Every one of these questions
has its own examiner's advice
panel to guide you and help
you plan your answers.

Examining Marxist theories

Examine some of the ways in which Marxists explain crime.

(12 marks)

Exam questions

At the end of every Topic
there is a practice question
based on those you'll find
on the exam papers. At the
end of the chapter, there is
a full exam question for you
to try, plus a mock exam for
both units in Chapter 5.

The examiner's advice

This question carries 6 AO1 marks (knowledge and understanding) and 6 AO2 marks (interpretation, application, analysis and evaluation).

You should start with the idea that Marxists see capitalism as criminogenic because it creates the conditions for crime through exploitation
and competition. You need to examine both traditional Marxist and neo-Marxist approaches. The key ideas of traditional Marxists include
the power of the ruling class to make and selectively enforce the law, the ideological functions of the law, the way criminalisation is used to
divide the working class, and the idea that capitalism created crime in all classes but largely only convicts the working class.

You should evaluate this approach e.g. in terms of its determinism, and from this go on to consider neo-Marxism (critical criminology).
Key ideas to cover include the idea of crime as a political choice or act of rebellion, and the incorporation of ideas from labelling theory. To
evaluate it, you could use left realist criticisms that it ignores the reality of crime.

METHODS IN CONTEXT

The Research Methods chapter has special *Methods in Context* sections that show you how each method can be used to study topics in Crime and Deviance.

Methods Link: using official statistics

If Merton is correct in claiming that blocked access to legitimate opportunities such as paid work lead to crime, then we might expect to find that unemployment and crime are linked. When Tarling (1982) analysed official statistics for England and Wales, he found that the crime rate and the unemployment rate rose steadily together from 1950 to 1980 – findings that are compatible with Merton's theory.

However, showing that the two are correlated does not prove that one causes the other. Also, we have no way of knowing if the individuals who are unemployed are the same people who are committing the crimes.

Read more about official statistics and researching crime and deviance in **Methods in Context**, Chapter 3, Topic 7.

SPECIAL *METHODS IN CONTEXT* FEATURES

A big feature of the A2 exam is the compulsory *Methods in Context* question, where you have to apply a given research method to a topic in Crime and Deviance. This book has a series of unique features devoted to preparing you to tackle this question successfully.

- The Research Methods chapter has special *Methods in Context* sections that show you how each method can be used to study topics in Crime and Deviance.
- Each *Methods in Context* section has its own practice question just like those in the exam.
- All practice questions have the Examiner's advice to guide you.
- The Crime and Deviance chapter has *Methods Links* boxes throughout that deal with the way sociologists apply different research methods to educational topics.

ADDITIONAL FEATURES

Key concepts – a list of essential terms you need to be familiar with, defined briefly and clearly. Use it as a quick reference section to check the meaning of key terms. Also good when revising for the exam!

Preparing for the exam – Chapter 5 tells you what the Examiners are looking for. It gives detailed advice on exam technique and how to tackle questions effectively.

Mock exam papers for you to try, with advice on how to tackle the questions. And every chapter has a full exam question and student answer, with the Examiner's marks and comments, as well as advice on how to score top marks.

 www.sociology.uk.net This book has its own dedicated website where you can find additional activities, questions, answers and Examiner's advice – plus lots more to help you succeed.

Examining experiments in context

Item A **Researching the real rate of street crime**

Street crime includes acts such as demanding money or mobile phones with the threat of violence, bag snatching, and damage to vehicles. Unlike with some other crimes, people are usually aware that they are the victims of such crimes. Indeed, street crime can be an intense emotional experience for the victim and not something they can easily forget about.

However, many street crimes are not reported to the police. Victims may feel that the amount of time involved in going to a police station, giving statements and so on is simply not worth the cost of whatever loss had resulted from the crime. Other victims may feel that crimes such as these are one of the normal risks of everyday life. On the other hand, if the damage is substantial or an insurance claim could be made, victims are more likely to report the crime.

Structured interviews are useful for investigating the real rate of street crime because they can be carried out with a large sample of people, thus gaining a representative picture of the amount of such crimes. However, they rely on the accuracy of people's memories of street crime experiences.

Question

Using material from **Item A** and elsewhere, assess the strengths and weaknesses of using structured interviews to investigate the real rate of street crime.

(15 marks)

The examiner's advice

This question carries 6 AO1 marks (knowledge and understanding) and 9 AO2 marks (interpretation, application, analysis and evaluation). It requires you to **apply** your knowledge and understanding of structured interviews to the study of the **particular** issue of the real rate of street crime. It is not enough simply to discuss structured interviews in general.

You need to attach one or more of the strengths of structured interviews to the research characteristics of the real rate of street crime. A good place to start is Item A. For example, it states that one research characteristic is that many street crimes are not reported to the police, so the real rate of crime is not apparent from official statistics of reported crime. One strength of a structured interview is that their standardised nature means they can be replicated on a large scale, allowing the real rate of crime to be identified.

However, structured interviews are retrospective research and rely on the accuracy of interviewees' memory. Relatively minor episodes may be forgotten; equally, being the victim of a major street crime may have traumatised the individual and this may not be something they want to re-visit in an interview.

Other research characteristics not mentioned in Item A include defining street crime. For example, does the researcher include drug deals in which both sides consent to the act so there may be no immediately identifiable 'victim'? Most street crime, however defined, is unpredictable and swift, so a victim's awareness and subsequent recollection of events may not be accurate.

Try to keep a reasonable balance between the strengths and limitations of structured interviews. You can also refer to studies that have used this method (e.g. the British Crime Survey) and to any relevant research you have been involved in.

Beliefs in Society

CHAPTER 1

Introduction

Understanding beliefs is central to sociology because beliefs shape the way we see the world and influence how we live. In this chapter, our major focus is on religious beliefs, practices and organisations.

Sociologists are interested in the social role of religion. In Topic 1, we investigate the functions it performs for individuals, groups and society. Many sociologists see religion as performing a conservative function, helping to maintain the status quo, but others argue that it can also be a powerful force for social change. We examine this view in Topic 2.

Another major area of interest for sociologists is the future of religion. Some argue that modern society undermines religious beliefs and institutions, and that the ongoing long-term decline in churchgoing signals the end for religion.

By contrast, other sociologists argue that religion is simply changing its form – reinventing itself in a new postmodern era of consumer choice. Some see a shift taking place from traditional religion to a new, more personal spirituality, with new religious movements and New Age cults taking the place of the churches. We examine these debates and issues in Topics 3 and 4.

In today's increasingly interconnected world, it is clear that we need to examine religion in its global context – limiting our focus to Britain and the West will produce a distorted view of important issues about the future of religion and its social functions. A global perspective helps us to understand causes of religious fundamentalism and religious conflict, as well as the ways in which religion, development and modernisation are related. We look at religion in its global context in Topic 5.

Just as there are many kinds of religious belief, so too there are many kinds of religious organisations, such as churches,

sects and cults. These different beliefs and organisations tend to appeal to different social groups and to perform different functions for them. For example, the poor may turn to religions that offer an explanation for their poverty and promise a reward in the life to come. In Topic 6, we examine the different types of religious organisations and movements and the groups they attract.

Sociologists are also interested in other kinds of beliefs, not just religious ones. In Topic 7, we look at science as a belief system. For example, how do scientific explanations of the world differ from those put forward by religion or witchcraft? This Topic also examines the concept of ideology and the way in which ideas can serve the interests of particular social groups.

The AQA Specification

The specification is the syllabus produced by the exam board, telling you what you have to study. The AQA specification for Beliefs in Society requires you to examine the following:

- Different theories of ideology, science and religion, including both Christian and non-Christian religious traditions.
- The relationship between religious beliefs and social change and stability.
- Religious organisations, including cults, sects, denominations, churches and New Age movements, and their relationship to religious and spiritual belief and practice.
- The relationship between different social groups and religious/spiritual organisations and movements, beliefs and practices.
- The significance of religion and religiosity in the contemporary world, including the nature and extent of secularisation in a global context.

Totemic symbols such as carvings of animals and plants are sacred to Aboriginal clans.

Topic 1 Theories of religion

What do we mean by 'religion', and how does religion differ from other kinds of belief? Does it always involve a belief in the supernatural? Is it best to define religion in terms of particular kinds of beliefs, or in terms of its social role?

An important question for sociologists is the role of religion in society. What functions does it perform, and who benefits from them – society as a whole, or just the powerful?

Sociologists are also interested in how religion may meet individual needs, for example by giving answers to questions about the meaning of life and helping people to cope with misfortune.

In this Topic, we begin by examining how sociologists define religion. We then go on to focus on the main sociological theories of the functions of religion – functionalism, Marxism and feminism.

Learning objectives

After studying this Topic, you should:

- Understand different sociological definitions of religion.
- Understand how different sociological theories explain the role and functions of religion, and how religion contributes to social stability.
- Be able to evaluate different sociological definitions and theories of religion.

What is religion?

There are three main ways in which sociologists define religion: substantive; functional and social constructionist.

Substantive definitions

These focus on the content or substance of religious belief, such as belief in God or the supernatural. For example, Max Weber (1905) defines religion as belief in a superior or supernatural power that is above nature and cannot be explained scientifically. Substantive definitions are *exclusive* – they draw a clear line between religious and non-religious beliefs. To be a religion, a set of beliefs must include belief in God or the supernatural.

Substantive definitions conform to a widespread view of religion as belief in God. However, defining religion in this way leaves no room for beliefs and practices that perform similar functions to religion but do not involve belief in God. These are examined below. Substantive definitions are also accused of Western bias because they exclude religions such as Buddhism, which do not have the Western idea of a god.

Functional definitions

Rather than defining religion in terms of specific kinds of belief, functional definitions define it in terms of the social or psychological functions it performs for individuals or society. For example, Emile Durkheim (1915) defines religion in terms of the contribution it makes to social integration, rather than any specific belief in God or the supernatural. Another functionalist, Milton Yinger (1970) identifies

functions that religion performs for individuals, such as answering 'ultimate questions' about the meaning of life and what happens when we die.

An advantage of functional definitions is that they are *inclusive* – allowing us to include a wide range of beliefs and practices that perform functions such as integration. Also, since they do not specify belief in god or the supernatural, there is no bias against non-Western religions such as Buddhism. However, just because an institution helps integrate individuals into groups, this does not make it a religion. For example, collective chanting at football matches might give individuals a sense of integration, but this doesn't mean it is a religion.

Social constructionist definitions

Social constructionists take an interpretivist approach that focuses on how members of society themselves define religion. They argue that it is not possible to produce a single universal definition of religion to cover all cases, since in reality different individuals and groups mean very different things by 'religion'.

Social constructionists are interested in how definitions of religion are constructed, challenged and fought over. For example, Alan Aldridge (2007) shows how, for its followers, Scientology is a religion, whereas several governments have denied it legal status as a religion and sought to ban it. This shows that definitions of religion can be contested and are influenced by who has power to define the situation.

Social constructionists do not assume that religion always involves a belief in God or the supernatural, or that it performs similar functions for everyone in all societies. Their approach allows them to get close to the meanings people themselves give to religion. However, this makes it impossible to generalise about the nature of religion, since people may have widely differing views about what counts as a religion.

Box 1.1　Sikh schoolgirl wins 'bracelet' case

A school prefect of Punjabi parentage who was taught in isolation for two months and eventually barred from school for wearing a *Kara*, a Sikh religious symbol in the form of a steel bracelet, has won her case in the High Court that she was discriminated against religiously and racially. The school had told the student that wearing the Kara was against the school's no-jewelry policy.

The judge said the school had discriminated against her. He accepted that the Kara was essential to her religious identity and that she was disadvantaged in being forbidden to wear it. The Kara was a sign that a Sikh was 'handcuffed to God', the judge said. It was not to be regarded as a piece of jewelry, but as something to which the student attached exceptional importance and a defining physical symbol of being a Sikh.

Adapted from Church Times (2008)

Activity

In pairs, make a list of the similarities and differences between attending a football match and attending a religious service. How far is it fair to describe attending a football match as a religious experience?

Functionalist theories of religion

For functionalists, society is a system of interrelated parts or social institutions, such as religion, the family and the economy. Society is like an organism, with basic needs that it must meet in order to survive. These needs are met by the different institutions. Each institution performs certain functions – that is, each contributes to maintaining the social system by meeting a need.

Society's most basic need is the need for social order and solidarity so that its members can cooperate. For functionalists, what makes order possible is the existence of value consensus – a set of shared norms and values by which society's members live. Without this, individuals would pursue their own selfish desires and society would disintegrate.

Durkheim on religion

For functionalists, religious institutions play a central part in creating and maintaining value consensus, order and solidarity. The first functionalist to develop this idea was Emile Durkheim (1858-1917).

The sacred and the profane

For Durkheim (1915), the key feature of religion was not a belief in gods, spirits or the supernatural, but a fundamental distinction between the sacred and the profane found in all religions. The *sacred* are things set apart and forbidden, that inspire feelings of awe, fear and wonder, and are surrounded by taboos and prohibitions. By contrast, the *profane* are things that have no special significance – things that are ordinary and mundane. Furthermore, a religion is never simply a set of beliefs. It also involves definite rituals or *practices* in relation to the sacred, and these rituals are *collective* – performed by social groups.

The fact that sacred things evoke such powerful feelings in believers indicates to Durkheim that this is because they are symbols representing something of great power. In his view, this thing can only be society itself, since society is the only thing powerful enough to command such feelings. When they worship the sacred symbols, therefore, people are worshipping society itself. For Durkheim, although sacred symbols vary from religion to religion, they all perform the essential function of uniting believers into a single moral community.

Totemism

Durkheim believed that the essence of all religion could be found by studying its simplest form, in the simplest type of society – clan society. For this reason, he used studies of the Arunta, an Australian Aboriginal tribe with a clan system.

Arunta clans consist of bands of kin who come together periodically to perform rituals involving worship of a sacred totem. The totem is the clan's emblem, such as an animal or plant that symbolises the clan's origins and identity. The totemic rituals venerating it serve to reinforce the group's solidarity and sense of belonging.

For Durkheim, when clan members worship their totemic animal, they are in reality worshipping society – even though they themselves are not aware of this fact. The totem inspires feelings of awe in the clan's members precisely because it represents the power of the group on which the individual is 'utterly dependent'.

The collective conscience

In Durkheim's view, the sacred symbols represent society's *collective conscience* or consciousness (the French word 'conscience' means both conscience and consciousness). The collective conscience is the shared norms, values, beliefs and knowledge that make social life and cooperation between individuals possible – without these, society would disintegrate.

For Durkheim, regular shared religious rituals reinforce the collective conscience and maintain social integration. Participating in shared rituals binds individuals together, reminding them that they are part of a single moral community to which they owe their loyalty. Such rituals also remind the individual of the power of society – without which they themselves are nothing, and to which they owe everything.

In this sense, religion also performs an important function for the *individual*. By making us feel part of something greater than ourselves, religion reinvigorates and strengthens us to face life's trials and motivates us to overcome obstacles that would otherwise defeat us.

Cognitive functions of religion

Durkheim sees religion not only as the source of social solidarity, but also of our intellectual or cognitive capacities – our ability to reason and think conceptually. For example, in order to think at all, we need categories such as time, space, cause, substance, number etc (try thinking of an event that had no cause and that occurred outside time and space, for example). And secondly, in order to share our thoughts, we need to use the same categories as others.

In Durkheim's view, religion is the origin of the concepts and categories we need for reasoning, understanding the world and communicating. In their book *Primitive Classification*, Durkheim and Marcel Mauss (1903) argue that religion provides basic categories such as time, space and causation – for example, with ideas about a creator bringing the world into being at the beginning of time. Similarly, the division of tribes into clans gives humans their first notion of classification. Thus for Durkheim, religion is the origin of human thought, reason and science.

Criticisms

The evidence on totemism is unsound. Worsley (1956) notes that there is no sharp division between the sacred and the profane, and that different clans share the same totems. And even if Durkheim is right about totemism, this does not prove that he has discovered the essence of all other religions.

Durkheim's theory may apply better to small-scale societies with a single religion. It is harder to apply it to large-scale societies, where two or more religious communities may be in conflict. His theory may explain social integration *within* communities, but not the conflicts *between* them.

Similarly, postmodernists such as Stjepan Mestrovic (1997) argue that Durkheim's ideas cannot be applied to contemporary society, because increasing diversity has fragmented the collective conscience, so there is no longer a single shared value system for religion to reinforce.

Suggest two examples of societies where religion may have caused conflict between communities.

Psychological functions

The anthropologist Bronislaw Malinowski (1954) agrees with Durkheim that religion promotes solidarity. However, in his view, it does so by performing psychological functions for individuals, helping them cope with emotional stress that would undermine social solidarity. Malinowski identifies two types of situation in which religion performs this role:

1 Where the outcome is important but is uncontrollable and thus uncertain In his study of the Trobriand Islanders of the Western Pacific, Malinowski contrasts fishing in the lagoon and fishing in the ocean.

- Lagoon fishing is safe and uses the predictable and successful method of poisoning. When the islanders fish in the lagoon, there is no ritual.
- Ocean fishing is dangerous and uncertain, and is always accompanied by 'canoe magic' – rituals to ensure a safe and successful expedition. This gives people a sense of control, which eases tension, gives them confidence to undertake hazardous tasks and reinforces group solidarity. He sees ritual serving as a 'god of the gaps' – it fills the gaps in human beings' control over the world, such as being unable to control the outcome of a fishing trip.

2 At times of life crises Events such as birth, puberty, marriage and especially death mark major and disruptive changes in social groups. Religion helps to minimise disruption. For example, the funeral rituals reinforce a feeling of solidarity among the survivors, while the notion of immortality gives comfort to the bereaved by denying the fact of death. In fact, Malinowski argues that death is the main reason for the existence of religious belief.

In what ways might the birth of a new baby disrupt social relationships?

Parsons: values and meaning

Like Malinowski, Talcott Parsons (1967) sees religion helping individuals to cope with unforeseen events and uncontrollable outcomes. In addition, Parsons identifies two other essential functions that religion performs in modern society.

- It creates and legitimates society's central values.
- It is the primary source of meaning.

Religion creates and legitimates society's basic norms and values by sacralising them (making them sacred). Thus in the USA, Protestantism has sacralised the core American values of individualism, meritocracy and self-discipline. This serves to promote value consensus and thus social stability.

Religion also provides a source of meaning. In particular, it answers 'ultimate' questions about the human condition, such as why the good suffer and why some die young. Such events defy our sense of justice and make life appear meaningless, and this may undermine our commitment to society's values. Religion provides answers to such questions, for example by explaining suffering as a test of faith that will be rewarded in heaven. By doing so, religion enables people to adjust to adverse events or circumstances and helps maintain stability.

Civil religion

Like Parsons, Robert Bellah (1970) is interested in how religion unifies society, especially a multi-faith society like America. What unifies American society is an overarching *civil religion* – a belief system that attaches sacred qualities to society itself. In the American case, civil religion is a faith in Americanism or 'the American way of life'.

Bellah argues that civil religion integrates society in a way that individual religions cannot. While none of the many individual churches and denominations can claim the loyalty of all Americans, civil religion can. American civil religion involves loyalty to the nation-state and a belief in God, both of which are equated with being a true American. It is expressed in various rituals, symbols and beliefs; such as the pledge of allegiance to the flag, singing the national anthem, the Lincoln Memorial, and phrases such as 'One nation under God'.

▲ *The Coronation of Queen Elizabeth II: an example of civil religion?*

However, this is not a specifically Catholic, Protestant or Jewish God, but rather an 'American' God. It sacralises the American way of life and binds together Americans from many different ethnic and religious backgrounds.

Functional alternatives

Functional alternatives or functional equivalents to religion are non-religious beliefs and practices that perform functions similar to those of organised religion, such as reinforcing shared values or maintaining social cohesion.

For example, although civil religion in America involves a belief in God, Bellah argues that this doesn't have to be the case. Some other belief system could perform the same functions. For example, Nazi Germany and the Soviet Union had secular (non-religious) political beliefs and rituals around which they sought to unite society.

However, the problem with the idea of functional alternatives is the same as with functional definitions of religion that we saw earlier. That is, it ignores what makes religion distinctive and different – namely, its belief in the supernatural.

Activity

In small groups, list some examples of civil religion in the United Kingdom. Think of events, objects, and ceremonies etc that are similar to the American examples.

Evaluation of functionalism

Functionalism emphasises the social nature of religion and the positive functions it performs, but it neglects negative aspects, such as religion as a source of oppression of the poor or women.

It ignores religion as source of division and conflict, especially in complex modern societies where there is more than one religion – e.g. Northern Ireland. Where there is religious pluralism (many religions), it is hard to see how it can unite people and promote integration.

The idea of civil religion overcomes this problem to some extent, by arguing that societies may still have an overarching belief system shared by all, but is this really religion – especially if it is not based on belief in the supernatural?

Marxist theories of religion

Unlike functionalists, who see society as based on harmony and consensus, Marxists sees all societies as divided into two classes, one of which exploits the labour of the other. In modern capitalist society, the capitalist class who own the means of production exploit the working class.

In such a society, there is always the potential for class conflict, and Marx predicted that the working class would ultimately become conscious of their exploitation and unite to overthrow capitalism. This would bring into being a classless society in which there would no longer be exploitation.

Marx's theory of religion needs to be seen in the context of this general view of society. Whereas functionalism sees religion as a unifying force that strengthens the value consensus and is a feature of all societies, Marxism sees religion as a feature only of class-divided society. As such, there will be no need for religion in classless society and it will disappear.

Religion as ideology

For Marx, ideology is a belief system that distorts people's perception of reality in ways that serve the interests of the ruling class. He argues that the class that controls economic production also controls the production and distribution of ideas in society, through institutions such as the church, the education system and the media.

In Marx's view, religion operates as an ideological weapon used by the ruling class to legitimate (justify) the suffering of the poor as something inevitable and god-given. Religion misleads the poor into believing that their suffering is virtuous and that they will be favoured in the afterlife. For example, according to Christianity, it is easier for a camel to pass through the eye of a needle than it is for a rich man to enter the kingdom of heaven.

Such ideas create a *false consciousness* – a distorted view of reality that prevents the poor from acting to change their situation.

Similarly, Lenin (1870-1924) describes religion as 'spiritual gin' – an intoxicant doled out to the masses by the ruling class to confuse them and keep them in their place. In Lenin's view, the ruling class use religion cynically to manipulate the masses and keep them from attempting to overthrow the ruling class by creating a 'mystical fog' that obscures reality.

Religion also legitimates the power and privilege of the dominant class by making their position appear to be divinely ordained. For example, the 16th century idea of the Divine Right of Kings was the belief that the king is God's representative on earth and is owed total obedience. Disobedience is not just illegal, but a sinful challenge to God's authority. For another example of religion and legitimation see Box 1.2.

Religion and alienation

Marx (1844) also sees religion as the product of alienation. Alienation involves becoming separated from or losing control over something that one has produced or created. Alienation exists in all class societies, but it is more extreme under capitalism. Under capitalism, workers are alienated because they do not own what they produce and have no control over the production process, and thus no freedom to express their true nature as creative beings. Alienation reaches a peak with the detailed division of labour in the capitalist factory, where the worker endlessly repeats the same minute task, devoid of all meaning or skill.

In these dehumanising conditions, the exploited turn to religion as a form of consolation. As Marx puts it, religion:

> *'is the opium of the people. It is the sigh of the oppressed creature, the heart of a heartless world, the soul of soulless conditions, the spirit of a spiritless situation.'*

Religion acts as an opiate to dull the pain of exploitation. But just as opium masks pain rather than treating its cause, so religion masks the underlying problem of exploitation that creates the need for it. Because religion is a distorted view of the world, it can offer no solution to earthly misery.

Synoptic link: core themes

Marx's theory shows the relationship between religion and **social stratification**. In his view religion is an ideology that legitimates the class structure. Religious ideas help to maintain the existing distribution of **power** and privilege in society by compensating the poor for their deprivation; for example by promising rewards in heaven.

Box 1.2	Caste and the legitimation of inequality

Another example of religion justifying social inequality is the Hindu caste system. Caste is a system of social stratification based on ascribed status. You are born into the same caste as your parents and marriage between castes is forbidden. The highest caste is that of the priests, followed by a warrior caste, a merchant caste and the lowest caste of servants and labourers. Beneath these four groups are the untouchables who are not considered to have a caste at all.

The doctrine of *karma* teaches that if you behave well in this world by accepting and observing the rules of caste, after death you will be reincarnated (re-born) into a higher caste. These rules include strict norms about purity and impurity, governing what food may be eaten and what social contact allowed between members of different castes. Higher castes must maintain higher levels of purity. For example, touching someone from a lower caste may be seen as pollution and must be followed by elaborate cleansing rituals.

The doctrines of reincarnation and *karma* serve to maintain inequality by assuring those at the bottom of the caste system that their obedience will be rewarded or disobedience punished by reincarnation into a higher or lower caste. Meanwhile, higher castes perceive their privileged positions as a reward for their virtue in a previous life.

Instead, its promises of the afterlife create an illusory happiness that distracts attention from the true source of the suffering, namely capitalism.

Thus, Marx sees religion as the product of alienation. It arises out of suffering and acts as a consolation for it, but fails to deal with its cause, namely class exploitation. Religion also acts as an ideology that legitimates both the suffering of the poor and the privileges of the ruling class.

Evaluation

- Marx shows how religion may be a tool of oppression that masks exploitation and creates false consciousness. However, he ignores positive functions of religion, such as psychological adjustment to misfortune. Neo-Marxists see certain forms of religion as assisting not hindering the development of class consciousness.

- Some Marxists, such as Althusser (1971), reject the concept of alienation as unscientific and based on a romantic idea that human beings have a 'true self'. This would make the concept an inadequate basis for a theory of religion.

- Religion does not necessarily function effectively as an ideology to control the population. For example, Abercrombie and Turner (1978) argue that in pre-capitalist society, while Christianity was a major element of ruling-class ideology, it had only limited impact on the peasantry.

Feminist theories of religion

Feminists see society as patriarchal – that is, based on male domination. Many feminists regard religion as a patriarchal institution that reflects and perpetuates this inequality. Religious beliefs function as a patriarchal ideology that legitimates female subordination.

Evidence of patriarchy

Although the formal teachings of religions often stress equality between the sexes, there is considerable evidence of patriarchy within many of them. For example:

- **Religious organisations** are mainly male-dominated despite the fact that women often participate more than men in these organisations. For example, Orthodox Judaism and Catholicism forbid women to become priests. Karen Armstrong (1993) sees women's exclusion from the priesthood of most religions as evidence of their marginalisation.

- **Places of worship** often segregate the sexes and marginalise women, for example seating them behind screens while the men occupy the central and more sacred spaces. Women's participation may be restricted, for example not being allowed to preach or to read from sacred texts. Taboos that regard menstruation, pregnancy and childbirth as polluting may also prevent participation. For example, in Islam, menstruating women are not allowed to touch the Qur'an. Jean Holm (1994) describes this as the devaluation of women in contemporary religion.

- **Sacred texts** largely feature the doings of male gods, prophets etc, and are usually written and interpreted by men. Stories often reflect anti-female stereotypes, such as that of Eve who, in the Judaeo-Christian story of Genesis, caused humanity's fall from grace and expulsion from the Garden of Eden.

- **Religious laws and customs** may give women fewer rights than men, for example in access to divorce, how many spouses they may marry, decision making, dress codes etc. Religious influences on cultural norms may also lead to unequal treatment, such as genital mutilation or punishments for sexual transgressions. Many religions legitimate and regulate women's traditional domestic and reproductive role. For example, the Catholic Church bans abortion and artificial contraception. Woodhead (2002) argues that the exclusion of women from the Catholic priesthood is evidence of the Church's deep unease about the emancipation of women generally.

However, feminists argue that women have not always been subordinate to men within religion. Karen Armstrong (1993) argues that early religions often placed women at the centre. For example, earth mother goddesses, fertility cults and female priesthoods were found throughout the Middle East until about 6,000 years ago. However, from about 4,000 years ago, the rise of monotheistic religions saw the establishment of a single, all-powerful male God, such as the Hebrews' Jehovah, and male prophets such as Abraham/Ibrahim, the first prophet of Judaism, Christianity and Islam.

While religion may be used to oppress women, Nawal El Saadawi (1980) argues that it is not the direct cause of their subordination. Rather, this is the result of patriarchal forms of society coming into existence in the last few thousand years. However, once in existence, patriarchy began to influence and re-shape religion. For example, men reinterpreted religious beliefs in ways that favoured patriarchy. Thus religion now contributes to women's oppression. Like Armstrong, El Saadawi sees the rise of monotheism as legitimating the power of men over women.

Activity

In small groups, investigate two religions to find out their arrangements in relation to women holding positions of responsibility, participation in worship, laws or customs governing male and female behaviour and any other features related to gender.

Woodhead: religious feminism

Linda Woodhead (2002) criticises feminist explanations that simply equate religion with patriarchy and the oppression of women. While accepting that much traditional religion is patriarchal, she emphasises that this is not true of all religion. She argues that there are 'religious forms of feminism' – ways in which women use religion to gain greater freedom and respect.

Woodhead uses the example of the hijab or veil worn by many Muslim women. While Western feminists tend to see it as a symbol of oppression, to the wearer it may symbolise resistance to oppression. Woodhead argues that some Muslim women choose to wear the hijab to escape the confines of the home and enter education and employment. For them, the hijab is a symbol of liberation that enables them to enter the public sphere without losing their culture and history.

Women also use religion to gain status and respect for their roles within the private sphere of home and family. For example, belonging to an evangelical group can be empowering for some women. Despite the strong belief in traditional gender roles that such groups hold, women are able to use religion to increase their power and influence. For example, a strongly held belief among evangelicals is that men should respect women. This gives women power to influence men's behaviour by insisting that they practise what they preach and refrain from 'macho' behaviour. Similarly, women make use of activities linked to the church, such as Bible study groups, to share experiences and find support.

We should also note that the position of women within some religions is changing. For example, the Church of England has permitted women's ordination into the priesthood since 1992 and about a fifth of all its priests are now female.

Summary

Sociologists define religion in substantive, functional and social constructionist terms. Functionalism is a consensus perspective that sees religion performing positive functions for society and individuals. These include social solidarity and integration; provision of values and meanings, and psychological functions for individuals. Functionalists also identify functional alternatives such as civil religion. Marxism and Feminism are conflict perspectives that highlight the ideological functions of religion. Marxists see religion as dulling the pain of class exploitation and as fostering false consciousness. They see religion as a form of ideology and a response to alienation. Feminists see religion as an instrument of patriarchy – a set of beliefs and practices responsible for women's subordination. Some feminists argue that religion is not always patriarchal.

For more activities on Theories of religion...

 Go to www.sociology.uk.net

QuickCheck Questions

1 True or False? Substantive definitions of religion are inclusive.

2 How does Durkheim distinguish between the sacred and the profane?

3 Explain how religion may perform a cognitive function.

4 Explain what is meant by 'civil religion'.

5 Identify two criticisms of the functionalist view of religion.

6 According to Marx, what is the main cause of alienation?

7 Identify one way in which Hinduism may legitimate inequality.

8 Identify three examples of ways in which religions may be patriarchal.

9 Give one example of how religion may be empowering for women.

 Check your answers at www.sociology.uk.net

Examining theories of religion

Item A A common theme in functionalist approaches is the emphasis on religion's contribution to value consensus and social integration. For example, Durkheim and Parsons describe religion as integrating individuals into a community by instilling into them a set of shared beliefs that gives them a feeling of belonging and a common identity. Functionalists argue that this is beneficial both for society and for individuals.

Marxists and feminists take a different view. They emphasise conflict and inequality and they argue that some individuals and groups may benefit from religion at the expense of others.

Question

(a) Identify and briefly explain **one** advantage and **two** disadvantages of functional definitions of religion. (9 marks)

(b) Using material from **Item A** and elsewhere, assess the functionalist view that religion benefits both society as a whole and its individual members. (18 marks)

The examiner's advice

Part (b) carries 6 AO1 marks (knowledge and understanding) and 12 AO2 marks (interpretation, application, analysis and evaluation). You need to explain why and how functionalists see religion as beneficial both to society and to individuals. Link your explanation to key features of the functionalist perspective on society such as its emphasis on consensus. You should therefore consider the range of social and psychological functions they see religion performing, such as integration and solidarity, cognitive functions, coping with stress and uncertainty, offering answers to ultimate questions etc. Use the Item to help you develop some of these, and use other sources too (e.g. Malinowski, Bellah). Use Marxist and feminist views to question whether religion is beneficial for all members of society or only the ruling class or men. Consider cases where religion causes division rather than integration.

Martin Luther King ends his famous 'I Have a Dream' speech with the words, 'Free at last! Free at last! Thank God Almighty, we are free at last!' August 28, 1963

Topic 2 Religion and social change

In Topic 1, we examined functionalist, Marxist and feminist theories of religion. In different ways, these theories all see religion as maintaining the status quo, stabilising society as it is and preventing change. Religions have also often been supporters of traditional conservative values, especially in relation to the family, sexuality and personal morality. However, many sociologists argue that religion can also be a powerful force for social change, at least under certain circumstances.

In this Topic, we examine some of these circumstances. The evidence comes from four continents, ranging from the role of 17th century Calvinists in bringing about capitalism in Europe and the 'cargo cults' and anti-colonial movements of the Western Pacific, via the American black civil rights movement and the struggles of Kentucky coalminers, to liberation theology and political change in Latin America. We examine the theories sociologists have developed to account for the role of religion in bringing about change.

Learning objectives

After studying this Topic, you should:

- Be able to describe a range of examples of religion and analyse their role in social change.

- Understand sociological explanations of the role of religion in promoting social change.

- Be able to evaluate different sociological explanations of the relationship between religion, social stability and social change.

Religion as a conservative force

Religion can be seen as a conservative force in two different senses:

1. It is often seen as conservative in the sense of being 'traditional', defending traditional customs, institutions, moral views, roles etc. In other words, *it upholds traditional beliefs* about how society should be organised.

2. It is conservative because *it functions to conserve or preserve things as they are.* It stabilises society and maintains the status quo.

Religion's conservative beliefs

Most religions have traditional conservative beliefs about moral issues and many of them oppose changes that would allow individuals more freedom in personal and sexual matters. For example, the Catholic Church forbids divorce, abortion and artificial contraception. It opposes gay marriage and condemns homosexual behaviour.

Similarly, most religions uphold 'family values' and often favour a traditional patriarchal domestic division of labour. For example, the belief that the man should be the head of the family is embedded in the traditional marriage ceremony of the Church of England dating from 1602. The bride vows to 'love, honour and *obey*', but the groom is only required to 'love and honour'. Since 1966, the bride has been allowed to drop the vow to 'obey' her husband if she wishes.

Traditional conservative values also predominate in non-Christian religions. For example, Hinduism endorses male domestic authority and the practice of arranged marriage.

Religion's conservative functions

Religion is also a conservative force in the second sense of the phrase – it functions to conserve or preserve things as they are and maintain the status quo. As we saw in Topic 1, this view of religion is held by functionalists, Marxists and feminists. Although each of these perspectives sees the role of religion differently, all of them argue that it contributes to social stability.

Religion and consensus Functionalists see religion as a conservative force because it functions to maintain social stability and prevent society from disintegrating. For example, it promotes social solidarity by creating value consensus, thus reducing the likelihood of society collapsing through individuals pursuing their own selfish interests at the expense of others. It also helps individuals to deal with stresses that would otherwise disrupt the life of society.

By contrast, Marxists and feminists see religion as an ideology that supports the existing social structure and acts as a means of social control, creating stability in the interests of the powerful. This helps to maintain the status quo by preventing the less powerful from changing things.

Religion and capitalism Marx sees religion as a conservative ideology that prevents social change. By legitimating or disguising exploitation and inequality, it creates false consciousness in the working class and prevents revolution, thereby maintaining the stability of capitalist society.

Religion and patriarchy Feminists see religion as a conservative force because it acts as an ideology that legitimates patriarchal power and maintains women's subordination in the family and wider society.

Weber: religion as a force for change

We have seen how religion can be a conservative force, but sociologists have also shown it to be a force for change. Perhaps the most famous example of this view is Max Weber's (1905) study of *The Protestant Ethic and the Spirit of Capitalism*. In it, Weber argues that the religious beliefs of Calvinism (a form of Protestantism founded by John Calvin during the Reformation) helped to bring about major social change – specifically, the emergence of modern capitalism in Northern Europe in the 16th and 17th centuries.

Weber notes that many past societies had capitalism in the sense of greed for wealth, which they often spent on luxury consumption. However, modern capitalism is unique, he argues, because it is based on the systematic, efficient, rational pursuit of profit for its own sake, rather than for consumption. Weber calls this *the spirit of capitalism*. According to Weber, this spirit had what he calls an *elective affinity* or unconscious similarity to the Calvinists' beliefs and attitudes. Calvinism had several distinctive beliefs.

Calvinist beliefs

Predestination God had predetermined which souls would be saved – 'the elect' – and which would not, even before birth. Individuals could do nothing whatsoever to change this, whether through their deeds, as the Catholics believed (e.g. through pilgrimages, prayer or giving to the Church), nor through faith, as the Lutheran Protestants believed. God's decision is already made and cannot be altered.

Divine transcendence God was so far above and beyond this world and so incomparably greater than any mortal, that no human being could possibly claim to know his will (other than what he had chosen to reveal through the Bible). This included the Church and its priests – leaving the Calvinists to feel 'an unprecedented inner loneliness'. When combined with the doctrine of predestination, this created what Weber calls a *salvation panic* in the Calvinists. They could not know whether they had been chosen to be saved, and they could not do anything to earn their salvation.

Asceticism This refers to abstinence, self-discipline and self-denial. For example, monks lead an ascetic existence, refraining from luxury, wearing simple clothes and avoiding excess in order to devote themselves to God and a life of prayer.

The idea of a vocation or calling Before Calvinism, the idea of a religious vocation (a calling to serve God) meant renouncing everyday life to join a convent or monastery. Weber calls this *other-worldly asceticism*. By contrast, Calvinism introduces for the first time the idea of *this-worldly asceticism*. The only thing Calvinists knew of God's plan for humanity came from the Bible, which revealed to them that we were put on the earth to glorify God's name by our work. Thus for the Calvinists the idea of a calling or vocation meant constant, methodical work in an occupation, not in a monastery. However, work could not earn salvation – it was simply a religious duty.

For this reason, the Calvinists led an ascetic lifestyle shunning all luxury, worked long hours and practised rigorous self-discipline. Idleness is a sin; as the Calvinist Benjamin Franklin put it, 'Lose no time; be always employed in something useful'. The Calvinists' hard work and asceticism had two consequences.

Firstly, their wealth and success performed a psychological function for the Calvinists that allowed them to cope with their salvation panic. As they grew wealthier, they took this as a sign of God's favour and their salvation – for why else would we have prospered, they asked themselves. This of course was contrary to their original doctrine that God's will was unknowable.

Secondly, driven by their work ethic, they systematically and methodically accumulated wealth by the most efficient and rational means possible. But not permitting themselves to squander it on luxuries, they reinvested it in their businesses, which grew and prospered, producing further profit to reinvest and so on and on. In Weber's view, this is the very spirit of modern capitalism – where the object is simply the acquisition of more and more money as an end in itself. Calvinism thus brought capitalism as we now know it into the world.

Hinduism and Confucianism

It is very important to note that Weber was not arguing that Calvinist beliefs were *the* cause of modern capitalism, but simply that they were *one* of its causes. The Protestant ethic of the Calvinists was not sufficient on its own to bring modern capitalism into being. On the contrary, a number of material or economic factors were necessary, such as natural resources, trade, a money economy, towns and cities, a system of law and so on.

On the other hand, Weber notes that there have been other societies that have had a higher level of economic development than Northern Europe had in the 16th and 17th centuries, but that still failed to develop modern capitalism. In particular, he argues that ancient China and India were materially more advanced than Europe, but capitalism did not take off there. He argues that the failure of capitalism to take off there was due to the lack of a religious belief system like that of Calvinism that would have spurred its development.

Thus in ancient India, Hinduism was an ascetic religion, like Calvinism, favouring renunciation of the material world. However, its orientation was *other-worldly* – it directed its followers' concerns away from the material world and towards the spiritual world. In ancient China, Confucianism also discouraged the growth of rational capitalism, but for different reasons. Like Calvinism, Confucianism was a *this-worldly* religion that directed its followers towards the material world but, unlike Calvinism, it was not ascetic. Both Hinduism and Confucianism thus lacked the drive to systematically accumulate wealth that is necessary for modern capitalism. Calvinism was unique in combining asceticism with a this-worldly orientation to enable the spirit of modern capitalism to emerge.

Evaluation

Weber's work is often described as a 'debate with Marx's ghost'. Marx saw economic or material factors as the driving force of change, whereas Weber argues that material factors alone are not enough to bring about capitalism. As we have just seen, in Weber's view, it also needed specific cultural factors – the beliefs and values of Calvinism – to bring it into being.

Marxists have responded with their own criticisms of Weber. For example, Karl Kautsky (1927) argues that Weber overestimates the role of ideas and underestimates economic factors in bringing capitalism into being. He argues that in fact capitalism preceded rather than followed Calvinism.

Similarly, R.H.Tawney (1926) argues that technological change, not religious ideas, caused the birth of capitalism. It was only after capitalism was established that the bourgeoisie adopted Calvinist beliefs to legitimate their pursuit of economic gain.

Weber has also been criticised because capitalism did not develop in every country where there were Calvinists. For example, Scotland had a large Calvinist population but was slow to develop capitalism. However, Weberians such as Gordon Marshall (1982) argue that this was because of a lack of investment capital and skilled labour – supporting

Weber's point that both material and cultural factors need to be present for capitalism to emerge.

Others argue that although Calvinists were among the first capitalists, this was not because of their beliefs but simply because they had been excluded by law from political office and many of the professions, like the Jews in Eastern Europe. They turned to business as one of the few alternatives open to them. However, Weberians reply that other religious minorities were also excluded in this way but did not become successful capitalists.

How does Weber's view of social change differ from the Marxist view?

Religion and social protest

Like Weber, Steve Bruce (2003) is interested in the relationship between religion and social change. Using case studies, he compares two examples of the role of religiously inspired protest movements in America that have tried to change society: the civil rights movement and the New Christian Right.

The American civil rights movement

Bruce describes the struggle of the black civil rights movement of the 1950s and 1960s to end racial segregation as an example of religiously motivated social change. Although slavery had been abolished in 1865, blacks were denied legal and political rights in many Southern states where segregation was enforced, preventing them from using the same amenities (such as buses, shops and toilets) as whites. Schools were segregated and inter-racial marriages forbidden. Blacks were often excluded from voting by various legal restrictions and intimidation.

The civil rights movement began in 1955 when Rosa Parks, a black civil rights activist in Montgomery, Alabama, refused to sit at the back of a bus, as blacks were expected to do. Campaigning involved direct action by black people themselves, including protest marches, boycotts and demonstrations. Almost a decade later, in 1964, segregation was outlawed.

Bruce describes the black clergy as the backbone of the movement. Led by Dr Martin Luther King, they played a decisive role, giving support and moral legitimacy to civil rights activists. Their churches provided meeting places and sanctuary from the threat of white violence, and rituals

such as prayer meetings and hymn singing were a source of unity in the face of oppression. Bruce argues that the black clergy were able to shame whites into changing the law by appealing to their shared Christian values of equality. Although the impact on white clergy in the South was limited, their message reached a wide audience outside the Southern states and gained national support.

Bruce sees religion in this context as an *ideological resource* – it provided beliefs and practices that protesters could draw on for motivation and support. Using the civil rights movement as an example, he identifies several ways in which religious organisations are well equipped to support protests and contribute to social change:

- **Taking the moral high ground** Black clergy pointed out the hypocrisy of white clergy who preached 'love thy neighbour' but supported racial segregation.
- **Channelling dissent** Religion provides channels to express political dissent. For example, the funeral of Martin Luther King was a rallying point for the civil rights cause.
- **Acting as honest broker** Churches can provide a context for negotiating change because they are often respected by both sides in a conflict and seen as standing above 'mere politics'.
- **Mobilising public opinion** Black churches in the South successfully campaigned for support across the whole of America.

Bruce sees the civil rights movement as an example of religion becoming involved in secular struggle and helping to bring about change. In his view, the movement achieved its aims because it shared the same values as wider society and those in power. It brought about change by shaming those in power to put into practice the principle of equality embodied in the American Constitution that all men and women are born equal.

The New Christian Right

The New Christian Right is a politically and morally conservative, Protestant fundamentalist movement. It has gained prominence since the 1960s because of its opposition to the liberalising of American society.

The aims of the New Christian Right are extremely ambitious, seeking nothing less than to take America 'back to God'. They wish to make abortion, homosexuality and divorce illegal, turning the clock back to a time before the liberalisation of American culture and society began.

The New Christian Right believes strongly in the traditional family and traditional gender roles. It campaigns for the teaching of 'creationism' (the view that the Bible's account of creation is literally true) and to ban sex education in schools.

These campaigns have raised the profile of the New Christian Right since the 1970s. It has made effective use of the media and networking, notably televangelism, where church-owned television stations raise funds and broadcast programmes aimed at making converts and recruiting new members. The Moral Majority, a right-wing Christian pressure group founded in 1978, became the focus for political campaigning and for strengthening links with the Republican Party.

However, the New Christian Right has been largely unsuccessful in achieving its aims. Bruce suggests these reasons:

- The 'Moral Majority' was never a majority, but 15% of the population at most.
- Its campaigners find it very difficult to cooperate with people from other religious groups, even when campaigning on the same issue, such as abortion.
- The New Christian Right lacks widespread support and has met with strong opposition from groups who stand for freedom of choice, such as Planned Parenthood and People for the American Way.

Why might the New Christian Right campaigners find it difficult to cooperate with people from other religions, even when they are campaigning on the same issues?

Bruce describes the New Christian Right as a failed movement for change. Despite enormous publicity and a high profile in the media, it has not achieved its aim of taking America 'back to God'. In his view, its attempt to impose Protestant fundamentalist morality on others has failed because of the basically liberal and democratic values of most of American society. These values include a belief in the separation of church and state – very few Americans support the idea of a theocracy (rule by religious leaders).

Numerous surveys show that most Americans are comfortable with legalising activities that they personally believe are immoral, such as abortion, homosexuality and pornography, and unwilling to accept other people's definition of how they should live their lives. This poses an enormous problem for the New Christian Right, which believes in the literal truth of the Bible and insists everyone should be made to conform to its teaching. As Bruce points out, this is an impossible demand to make in a mature democracy.

Comparisons with the civil rights movement are interesting. They suggest that to achieve success, the beliefs and demands of religiously motivated protest movements and pressure groups need to be consistent with those of wider society. Thus in the American case, they need to connect with mainstream beliefs about democracy, equality and religious freedom, which the civil rights movement did but the New Christian Right has failed to do.

Activity

Opinion polls suggest many Americans are willing to accept that some behaviour they personally consider immoral should not be against the law. In small groups, write a list of pre-coded questions to use in structured interviews with fellow students. Ask whether they personally believe the following are immoral and then ask if they believe other people should be prevented from doing them: divorce, abortion, contraception, same-sex relationships, cohabitation, sex before marriage, extra-marital sex, eating meat, binge drinking, smoking tobacco, smoking cannabis.

Marxism, religion and change

Marxists are often thought of as seeing religion as an entirely conservative ideology – a set of ruling-class ideas that are shaped by and legitimate the class inequalities in society's economic base. However, this is not the case – Marxists recognise that ideas, including religious ideas, can have relative autonomy. That is, they can be partly independent of the economic base of society. As a result, religion can have a dual character and can sometimes be a force for change as well as stability.

For example, Marx himself does not see religion in entirely negative terms, describing it as 'the soul of soulless conditions' and the 'heart of a heartless world'. He sees religion as capable of humanising a world made inhuman by exploitation, even if the comfort it offers is illusory.

The idea that religion has a dual character is taken up by Friedrich Engels (1895), Marx's life-long collaborator. Engels argues that although religion inhibits change by disguising inequality, it can also challenge the status quo and encourage social change. For example, religion sometimes preaches liberation from slavery and misery. Also, although senior clergy usually support the status quo, lower ranks within the church hierarchy have often supported or even inspired and organised popular protest.

Ernst Bloch: the principle of hope

Ernst Bloch (1959) also sees religion as having a dual character. He argues for a view of religion that recognises both its positive and negative influence on social change. As a Marxist, he accepts that religion often inhibits change, but he emphasises that it can also inspire protest and rebellion. For Bloch, religion is an expression of 'the principle of hope' – our dreams of a better life that contain images of utopia (the perfect world).

Images of utopia can sometimes deceive people with promises of rewards in heaven, as Marx himself describes. However, they may also help people see what needs to be changed in this world. Religious beliefs may therefore create a vision of a better world, which, if combined with effective political organisation and leadership, can bring about social change.

In the next section we examine what some Marxists see as religion's dual character; that is, how religion can either encourage or discourage protest and change.

Liberation theology

Liberation theology is a movement that emerged within the Catholic Church in Latin America at the end of the 1960s, with a strong commitment to the poor and opposition to military dictatorships. Liberation theology was a major change of direction for the Catholic Church in Latin America. For centuries, it had been an extremely conservative institution, encouraging a fatalistic acceptance of poverty and supporting wealthy elites and military dictatorships.

The factors that led to the emergence of liberation theology were:

- Deepening rural poverty and the growth of urban slums throughout Latin America.
- Human rights abuses following military take-overs, such as false imprisonment, torture and death squads murdering political opponents, for example in Argentina, Brazil and Chile.
- The growing commitment among Catholic priests to an ideology that supported the poor and opposed violations of human rights.

The emphasis in liberation theology is on 'praxis' – practical action guided by theory. Unlike traditional Catholicism, which supported the status quo, liberation theology set out to change society. For example, priests helped the poor to establish support groups, called 'base communities', and helped workers and peasants to fight oppression under the protection of the church. Priests took the lead in developing literacy programmes, educating the poor about their situation, raising awareness and mobilising support.

During the 1970s, Catholic priests actively resisted state terror in Latin America. They were often the only authority figures who took the side of the oppressed when dictatorships used murder squads and torture to hold on to power. However, during the 1980s the Church's official attitude changed. Pope John Paul II condemned liberation theology on the grounds that it resembled Marxism, and instructed priests to concentrate on pastoral activities, not political struggle.

Since then, the movement has lost influence. However, as Casanova (1994) emphasises, liberation theology played an important part in resisting state terror and bringing about democracy in Latin American countries, most of which now have democratically elected governments. Although Catholicism in Latin America has become more conservative since the 1970s, it continues to defend the democracy and human rights that were achieved in part by liberation theology.

The success of liberation theology has led some neo-Marxists to question the view that religion is always a conservative force. For example, Otto Maduro (1982) believes that religion can be a revolutionary force that brings about change. In the case of liberation theology, religious ideas radicalised the Catholic clergy in defence of peasants and workers, making them see that serving the poor was part of their Christian duty. Similarly, Löwy (2005) questions Marx's view that religion always legitimates social inequality.

Both Maduro and Löwy see liberation theology as an example of religiously inspired social change but other Marxists disagree. Much depends on how social change is defined. Liberation theology may have helped to bring about democracy but it did not threaten the stability of capitalism.

Synoptic link: core themes

Liberation theology is an example of a religious movement that grew in response to hugely unequal systems of **stratification** and **power** in Latin America. The movement did not succeed in its aim of re-distributing wealth to the poor. However, it did help to bring about democracy in some countries.

Millenarian movements

Because religion raises the hope of a better world in the afterlife, it may also create a desire to change things here and now, for example to bring about the kingdom of God on earth. Millenarian movements are an important example of this desire.

Millenarian movements take their name from the word 'millennium', meaning a thousand years. In Christian theology, this refers to the idea that Christ would come into the world for a second time and rule for a thousand years before the

Day of Judgment and the end of the world. According to Peter Worsley (1968), such movements expect the total and imminent transformation of this world by supernatural means. This will create a heaven on earth, a life free from pain, death, sin, corruption and imperfection. The transformation will be collective – the *group* will be saved, not just individuals.

The appeal of millenarian movements is largely to the poor because they promise immediate improvement, and they often arise in colonial situations. European colonialism led to economic exploitation and cultural and religious domination, for example through the Christian missionaries and their schools. At the same time, it shattered the traditional tribal social structures and cultures of the colonised peoples. Local leaders and local gods lose power and credibility when their people are forced to work for colonists who live in luxury.

Worsley studied the millenarian movements in Melanesia (Western Pacific) known as *cargo cults*. The islanders felt wrongfully deprived when 'cargo' (material goods) arrived in the islands for the colonists. A series of cargo cults sprang up during the 19th and 20th centuries asserting that the cargo had been meant for the natives but had been diverted by the whites for themselves, and that this unjust social order was about to be overturned. These movements often led to widespread unrest that threatened colonial rule.

Worsley notes that the movements combined elements of traditional beliefs with elements of Christianity – such as ideas about a heaven where the suffering of the righteous will be rewarded, Christ's imminent second coming to earth, the Day of Judgment and punishment of the wicked. He describes the movements as *pre-political* – they used religious ideas and images, but they united native populations in mass movements that spanned tribal divisions. Many of the secular nationalist leaders and parties that were to overthrow colonial rule in the 1950s and 1960s developed out of millenarian movements. Similarly, from a Marxist perspective, Engels argues that they represent the first awakening of 'proletarian self-consciousness'.

Gramsci: religion and hegemony

Antonio Gramsci (1971) is interested in how the ruling class maintain their control over society through the use of ideas rather than simply through coercion (force). He uses the term *hegemony* to refer to the way that the ruling class are able to use ideas such as religion to maintain control. By hegemony, Gramsci means ideological domination or leadership of society. When hegemony is established, the ruling class can rely on popular consent to their rule, so there is less need for coercion. For example, writing in Italy in the 1920s and 1930s, Gramsci notes the immense conservative ideological power of the Catholic Church in helping to win support for Mussolini's fascist regime.

However, hegemony is never guaranteed. It is always possible for the working class to develop an alternative vision

Activity

In small groups, use on-line encyclopaedias to research millenarian movements. Try searching on these terms: millenarianism, John Frum, cargo cults, ghost dance, the Center for Millennial Studies.

of how society should be organised – that is, a counter-hegemony. Like Engels, Gramsci sees religion as having a dual character and he notes that in some circumstances, it can challenge as well as support the ruling class. He argues that popular forms of religion can help workers see through the ruling-class hegemony by offering a vision of a better, fairer world. Similarly, some clergy may act as *organic intellectuals* – that is, as educators, organisers and leaders. They can help workers see the situation they are in and support working-class organisations such as trade unions.

Religion and class conflict

Dwight Billings (1990) applies Gramsci's ideas in a case study comparing class struggle in two communities – one of coalminers, the other of textile workers – in Kentucky during the 1920s and 1930s. Both were working-class and evangelical Protestant, but they experienced very different levels of strike activity and industrial conflict. The miners were much more militant, struggling for recognition of their union and better conditions, while the textile workers were quiescent, uncomplainingly accepting the status quo.

Following Gramsci, Billings argues that the differences in levels of militancy can be understood in terms of hegemony and the role of religion. Billings identifies three ways in which religion either supported or challenged the employers' hegemony:

- **Leadership** The miners benefited from the leadership of organic intellectuals – many of them lay preachers who were themselves miners and trade union activists. These clergy helped to convert miners to the union cause. Textile workers lacked such leadership. This meant they were easily influenced by the views of clergy who identified with the employers and denounced unions as 'ungodly'.
- **Organisation** The miners were able to use independent churches to hold meetings and organise, whereas the textile workers lacked such spaces. They remained in 'company churches' that were under the control of the textile mill owners.
- **Support** The churches kept miners' morale high with supportive sermons, prayer meetings and group singing. By contrast, textile workers who engaged in union activity met with opposition from local church leaders, who branded them as communists.

Billings shows that religion was an important factor affecting the level of class struggle, but he notes that other factors played a role. For example, mining relies on teamwork and miners have to rely on each other for safety. This partly explains their stronger sense of solidarity in opposing their employers. Billings concludes that religion can play 'a prominent oppositional role'. His study shows that the same religion can be called upon either to defend the status quo or justify the struggle to change it.

For more activities on Religion and social change...

Go to www.sociology.uk.net

QuickCheck Questions

1 What was the Calvinist doctrine of predestination?

2 Explain what Weber means by 'this-worldly asceticism'.

3 Why does Weber argue that the Calvinists experienced 'salvation panic'?

4 According to Weber, why did Hinduism discourage social change?

5 Explain what is meant by 'hegemony'.

6 Identify two ways in which the churches were able to support the black civil rights movement.

7 Suggest one similarity between liberation theology and Marxism.

8 Identify three characteristics of millenarian movements.

9 Why do Marxists see religion as having a dual character?

Check your answers at www.sociology.uk.net

Summary

Some sociologists argue that religion does not always uphold traditional beliefs and function to maintain the status quo. For example, Weber argues the Protestant ethic contributed to the birth of rational capitalism. Weber is criticised by Marxists such as Kautsky who argue that economic factors are the main cause of change. In this view religion reflects but does not cause change. Other Marxists such as Maduro, who gives liberation theology as an example, argue that religion has potential to bring about change. Religious organisations have actively supported campaigns for social change. Some such as the US civil rights movement have succeeded. Others such as the New Christian Right have failed to gain popular support. Unlike functionalists, who see religion only as a conservative force, most others argue that whether religion helps to bring about or inhibits social change varies according to social or historical conditions.

Examining religion and social change

Item A   Sociologists have identified a range of examples, taken from different societies and historical periods, which show that religion can play an important part in bringing about social change. For example, religious ideas can be a powerful motivation for change, as Weber showed in his study of Calvinism. Similarly, religious organisations have sometimes supported protest movements and even taken the lead in campaigning for social reforms.

Question

(a)   Identify and briefly explain **three** reasons why the New Christian Right might have failed to achieve its aims.   (9 marks)

(b)   Using material from **Item A** and elsewhere, assess the contribution of religion to social change.   (18 marks)

The examiner's advice

Part (b) carries 6 AO1 marks (knowledge and understanding) and 12 AO2 marks (interpretation, application, analysis and evaluation). Begin by putting your answer into a theoretical context by starting with Weber's views on the role of ideas and material factors in change. Use the Protestant ethic to illustrate this. Make sure you use the Item, e.g. to consider examples of movements for change such as civil rights, liberation theology, millenarian movements etc. Give these a theoretical context, e.g. using Gramsci's ideas on hegemony. To evaluate, you can consider cases where religion tries but fails to bring about change (e.g. the New Christian Right). Remember this is a question about change, not change versus stability, so when evaluating, keep focused on specific criticisms rather than giving a lengthy account of religion as a conservative force.

Emergency touchdown in the Hudson River, New York City: a miracle – or a pilot who kept his nerve?

Topic 3 Secularisation

Having examined arguments about the role of religion and how far it encourages or inhibits social change, we now look at arguments and evidence about the extent to which religion has declined.

Secularisation refers to the decline in the importance of religion. There is much disagreement among sociologists about whether or how far religion has declined.

In this Topic we shall:

- Consider the arguments and evidence put forward by sociologists who support the theory of secularisation.
- Look at how secularisation theory has been applied to both the UK and the USA.
- Examine the claim that a spiritual revolution is taking place, contrary to the downward trend in religion predicted by secularisation theory.

Learning objectives

After studying this Topic, you should:

- Know the main trends in patterns of religious belief and practice in the UK and USA.
- Understand and be able to analyse the possible causes of secularisation.
- Be able to evaluate arguments and evidence for the view that secularisation is occurring.

Secularisation in Britain

Based on evidence from the 1851 Census of Religious Worship, Crockett (1998) estimates that in that year, 40% or more of the adult population of Britain attended church on Sundays. This is a much higher figure than today and it has led some sociologists to claim that the 19th century was a 'golden age' of religiosity. Whether this is a fair description is open to debate, but it is certainly the case that there have been some major changes in religion in the UK since then. For example:

- A decline in the proportion of the population going to church.
- An increase in the average age of churchgoers.
- Fewer baptisms and church weddings.
- A decline in the numbers holding traditional Christian beliefs.
- Greater religious diversity, including more non-Christian religions.

Sociologists have put forward different explanations of these trends and reached different conclusions about whether, and how far, religion is declining.

In 1966, Bryan Wilson argued that Western societies had been undergoing a long-term process of secularisation. He defined secularisation as 'the process whereby religious beliefs, practices and institutions lose social significance'. For example, church attendance in England and Wales had fallen from 40% of the population in the mid-19th century to 10–15% by the 1960s. Church weddings, baptisms and Sunday school attendance had also declined, leading Wilson to conclude that Britain had become a secular society.

Church attendance today

The trends Wilson identified have continued. Only 6.3% of the adult population attended church on Sundays in 2005. Churchgoing in Britain has therefore halved since Wilson's research in the 1960s and is projected to fall further, to 4.7% by 2015. Sunday school attendance has declined further and only a tiny proportion of children now attend.

The English Church Census (2006) shows that attendance and membership of large religious organisations such as the Church of England and the Catholic Church have declined more than small organisations, some of which are remaining stable or have grown. However, the growth of these small organisations has not made up for the decline of large ones, so the overall trend is still one of decline.

Similarly, while church *weddings and baptisms* remain more popular than attendance at Sunday services, here too the trend is downwards. In 1971, three-fifths of weddings were in church, but by 2006 the proportion was only a third.

Similarly, baptisms of children fell from 55% in 1991 to 41% in 2005.

Religious beliefs today

Evidence about religious beliefs from over 60 years of opinion polls and attitude surveys shows that:

- More people claim they hold Christian beliefs than actually belong to or go to church.
- Religious belief is declining in line with the decline in church attendance and membership.

For example, Robin Gill et al (1998) reviewed almost 100 national surveys on religious belief from 1939 to 1996. They show a significant decline in belief in a personal god, in Jesus as the son of God, and in traditional teachings about the afterlife and the Bible. When asked, 'Would you describe yourself as being of any religion or denomination?' only 23% replied 'no' in 1950, but by 1996 this had increased to 43%.

Religious institutions today

Not only have religious belief and practice declined, so too has the influence of religion as a social institution. Although the church has some influence on public life, (for example 26 Church of England bishops sit in the House of Lords, where they have some influence on legislation), this has declined significantly since the 19th century. In particular, the state has taken over many of the functions that the church used to perform. Thus, whereas religion once pervaded every aspect of life, it has increasingly been relegated to the private sphere of the individual and the family.

For example, until the mid-19th century, the churches provided education, but since then it has been provided mainly by the state. Although there are still 'faith schools', these are mainly state-funded and must conform to the state's regulations, such as teaching the National Curriculum. Similarly, although there is a legal requirement for schools to provide a daily act of collective worship of a 'broadly Christian character', a BBC survey in 2005 found that over half the secondary schools in Wales failed to comply with this.

One measure of the institutional weakness of the church is the number of clergy, which fell from 45,000 in 1900 to 34,000 in 2000 – at a time when the population almost doubled in size. Had it kept pace with population growth, the clergy would now number 80,000. A lack of clergy on the ground in local communities means the day-to-day influence of the church is reduced.

Summing up the overall trend, Steve Bruce (2002) agrees with Wilson that all the evidence on secularisation has now been pointing in the same direction for many years. He concludes that:

'Whether we measure church membership, church attendance, the popularity of religious ceremonies to mark rites of passage (such as weddings and baptisms), or religious belief, we find that there is a steady and unremitting decline.'

Bruce predicts that if current trends continue, the Methodist Church will fold around 2030 and by then the Church of England will be merely a small voluntary organisation with a large amount of heritage property.

> Suggest one fact or event that might contradict the conclusion that religion is declining in Britain today.

Explanations of secularisation

Sociologists have developed a variety of theories and concepts to explain the process of secularisation. A common theme is modernisation, involving the decline of tradition and its replacement with rational and scientific ways of thinking that tend to undermine religion. Secularisation theory also emphasises the effect of social change on religion. For example, industrialisation leads to the break up of small communities that were held together by common religious beliefs.

A major theme in explanations of secularisation is the growth of social and religious diversity. Not only are people increasingly diverse in terms of their occupational and cultural backgrounds but religious institutions are much more varied. Secularisation theorists argue that the growth of diversity has undermined both the authority of religious institutions and the credibility of religious beliefs. As a result of these changes religious practice, such as churchgoing, has also declined.

Max Weber: rationalisation

In relation to secularisation, rationalisation refers to the process by which rational ways of thinking and acting come to replace religious ones. Many sociologists have argued that Western society has undergone a process of rationalisation in the last few centuries. The most important of these is Max Weber (1905). He argued that the Protestant Reformation begun by Martin Luther in the 16th century started a process of rationalisation of life in the West. This process undermined the religious worldview of the Middle Ages and replaced it with the rational scientific outlook found in modern society.

For Weber, the medieval Catholic worldview that dominated Europe saw the world as an 'enchanted (or magical) garden'. God and other spiritual beings and forces, such as angels, the devil and so on, were believed to be present and active in this world, changing the course of events through their supernatural powers and miraculous interventions in it. Humans could try to influence these beings and forces

by magical means such as prayers and spells, fasts and pilgrimages, the wearing of charms etc, in order to ensure a good harvest, protect against disease and so on.

Disenchantment

However, the Protestant Reformation brought a new worldview. Instead of the interventionist God of medieval Catholicism, Protestantism saw God as transcendent – as existing above and beyond, or outside, this world. Although God had created the world, he did not intervene in it, but instead left it to run according to its own laws of nature. Like a watchmaker, he had made the world and set it in motion, but thereafter it ran according to its own principles and its creator played no further part.

This meant that events were no longer to be explained as the work of unpredictable supernatural beings, but as the predictable workings of natural forces. All that was needed to understand them was rationality – the power of reason. Using reason and science, humans could discover the laws of nature, understand and predict how the world works and control it through technology. In other words, there was no longer a need for religious explanations of the world, since the world was no longer an enchanted garden.

In Weber's view, therefore, the Protestant Reformation begins the 'disenchantment' of the world – it squeezes out magical and religious ways of thinking and starts off the rationalisation process that leads to the dominance of the rational mode of thought. This enables science to thrive and provide the basis for technological advances that give humans more and more power to control nature. In turn, this further undermines the religious worldview.

A technological worldview

Following Weber, Bruce argues that the growth of a *technological worldview* has largely replaced religious or supernatural explanations of why things happen. For example, when a plane crashes with the loss of many lives, we are unlikely to regard it as the work of evil spirits or God's punishment of the wicked. Instead, we look for scientific and technological explanations.

A technological worldview thus leaves little room for religious explanations in everyday life, which only survive in areas where technology is least effective – for example, we may pray for help if we are suffering from an illness for which scientific medicine has no cure.

Bruce concludes that although scientific explanations do not challenge religion directly, they have greatly reduced the scope for religious explanations. Scientific knowledge does not in itself make people into atheists, but the worldview it encourages results in people taking religion less seriously.

Structural differentiation

Talcott Parsons (1951) defines structural differentiation as a process of specialisation that occurs with the development of industrial society. Separate, specialised institutions develop to carry out functions that were previously performed by a single institution. Parsons sees this as having happened to religion – it dominated pre-industrial society, but with industrialisation it has become a smaller and more specialised institution.

According to Parsons, structural differentiation leads to the *disengagement* of religion. Its functions are transferred to other institutions such as the state and it becomes disconnected from wider society. For example, the church loses the influence it once had on education, social welfare and the law.

Bruce agrees that religion has become separated from wider society and lost many of its former functions. It has become *privatised* – confined to the private sphere of the home and family. Religious beliefs are now largely a matter of personal choice and religious institutions have lost much of their influence on wider society. As a result, traditional rituals and symbols have lost meaning.

Even where religion continues to perform functions such as education or social welfare, it must conform to the requirements of the secular state. For example, teachers in faith schools must hold qualifications that are recognised by the state. At the same time, church and state tend to become separated in modern society. Modern states increasingly accept that religion is a personal choice and therefore that the state should not be identified with one particular faith.

Social and cultural diversity

The move from pre-industrial to industrial society brings about the decline of community and this contributes to the decline of religion. Wilson argues that in pre-industrial communities, shared values were expressed through collective religious rituals that integrated individuals and

regulated their behaviour. However, when religion lost its basis in stable local communities, it lost its vitality and its hold over individuals.

Similarly, Bruce sees industrialisation as undermining the consensus of religious beliefs that hold small rural communities together. Small close-knit rural communities give way to large loose-knit urban communities with diverse beliefs and values. Social and geographical mobility not only breaks up communities but brings people together from many different backgrounds, creating even more diversity.

Diversity of occupations, cultures and lifestyles undermines religion. Even where people continue to hold religious beliefs, they cannot avoid knowing that many of those around them hold very different views. Bruce argues that the plausibility (believability) of beliefs is undermined by alternatives. It is also undermined by individualism because the plausibility of religion depends on the existence of a practising community of believers. In the absence of a practising religious community that functions on a day-to-day basis, both religious belief and practice tend to decline.

Criticisms

The view that the decline of community causes the decline of religion has been criticised. Aldridge points out that a community does not have to be in a particular area:

- Religion can be a source of identity on a worldwide scale. This is true of Jewish, Hindu and Muslim communities, for example.
- Some religious communities are *imagined communities* that interact through the use of global media.
- Pentecostal and other religious groups often flourish in 'impersonal' urban areas.

Activity The golden age of religion

Go to www.sociology.uk.net

Religious diversity

According to Berger (1969), another cause of secularisation is the trend towards religious diversity where instead of there being only one religious organisation and only one interpretation of the faith, there are many.

In the Middle Ages, the Catholic Church held an absolute monopoly – it had no competition. As a result, everyone lived under a single *sacred canopy* or set of beliefs shared by all. This gave these beliefs greater plausibility because they had no challengers and the Church's version of the truth was unquestioned.

This all changed with the Protestant Reformation, when Protestant churches and sects broke away from the Catholic Church in the 16th century. Since the Reformation, the number and variety of religious organisations has continued to grow, each with a different version of the truth. With the arrival of this religious diversity, no church can now claim an unchallenged monopoly of the truth.

Society is thus no longer unified under the single sacred canopy provided by one church. Instead, religious diversity creates a *plurality of life worlds*, where people's perceptions of the world vary and where there are different interpretations of the truth.

Berger argues that this creates a crisis of credibility for religion. Diversity undermines religion's 'plausibility structure' – the reasons why people find it believable. When there are alternative versions of religion to choose between, people are likely to question all of them and this erodes the absolute certainties of traditional religion. Religious beliefs become relative rather than absolute – what is true or false becomes simply a personal point of view, and this creates the possibility of opting out of religion altogether.

Bruce sees the trend towards religious diversity as the most important cause of secularisation. As he puts it:

'It is difficult to live in a world that treats as equally valid a large number of incompatible beliefs, without coming to suppose that there is no one truth.'

Cultural defence and transition

Bruce identifies two counter-trends that seem to go against secularisation theory. Both are associated with higher than average levels of religious participation.

- **Cultural defence** is where religion provides a focal point for the defence of national, ethnic, local or group identity in a struggle against an external force such as a hostile foreign power. Examples include the popularity of Catholicism in Poland before the fall of communism and the resurgence of Islam before the revolution in Iran in 1979 (see Topic 5).
- **Cultural transition** is where religion provides support and a sense of community for ethnic groups such as migrants to a different country and culture. Herberg describes this in his study of religion and immigration to the USA. Religion has performed similar functions for Irish, African Caribbean, Muslim, Hindu and other migrants to the UK.

However, Bruce argues that religion survives in such situations only because it is a focus for group identity. Thus these examples do not disprove secularisation, but show that religion is most likely to survive where it performs functions other than relating individuals to the supernatural. Evidence supports Bruce's conclusion. For example, churchgoing declined in Poland after the fall of communism and there is evidence that religion loses importance for migrants once they are integrated into society.

Synoptic link: core themes

The notions of cultural defence and cultural transition show the link between religion and **identity**. People may continue to identify with a religious tradition as a symbol of their cultural or ethnic identity even if they do not have deeply held religious beliefs.

Suggest three types of support that a religious community might be likely to give to recent immigrants.

Criticisms

Berger (1999) has changed his views and now argues that diversity and choice actually stimulate interest and participation in religion. For example, the growth of evangelicalism in Latin America and the New Christian Right in the USA point to the continuing vitality of religion, not its decline.

Beckford (2003) agrees with the idea that religious diversity will lead some to question or even abandon their religious beliefs, but this is not inevitable. Opposing views can have the effect of strengthening a religious group's commitment to its existing beliefs rather than undermining them.

A spiritual revolution?

Some sociologists argue that a 'spiritual revolution' is taking place today, in which traditional Christianity is giving way to 'holistic spirituality' or New Age beliefs and practices that emphasise personal development and subjective experience. Increased interest in spirituality can be seen in the growth of a 'spiritual market', with an explosion in the number of books about self-help and spirituality, and the many practitioners who offer consultations, courses and 'therapies', ranging from meditation to crystal healing. Table 1A identifies the key differences between religion and spirituality.

Activity

Working in pairs and using the Internet or Yellow Pages, compile a list of a dozen alternative or complementary therapies. What claims are made about the benefits of these therapies? How many refer to spiritual healing or other spiritual benefits? Briefly compare your findings with others.

In their study of Kendal in Cumbria, Heelas and Woodhead investigate whether traditional religion has declined and, if so, how far the growth of spirituality is compensating for this. They distinguish between two groups:

- **The congregational domain** of traditional and evangelical Christianity.
- **The holistic milieu** of spirituality and the New Age.

They found that in 2000, in a typical week, 7.9% of the population attended church and 1.6% took part in the activities of the holistic milieu. However, within the congregational domain, the traditional churches were losing support, while evangelical churches were holding their own and faring relatively well. Although fewer were involved in the holistic milieu, it was growing. Heelas and Woodhead offer an explanation for these trends:

1. New Age spirituality has grown because of a massive *subjective turn* in today's culture. This involves a shift away from the idea of doing your duty and obeying external authority, to exploring your inner self by following a spiritual path.

2. As a result traditional religions, which demand duty and obedience, are declining. As Heelas and Woodhead put it: *'Religion that tells you what to believe and how to behave is out of tune with a culture which believes it is up to us to seek out answers for ourselves.'*

3. Evangelical churches are more successful than the traditional churches. They both demand discipline and duty, but the evangelicals also emphasise the importance of spiritual healing and personal growth through the experience of being 'born again'.

In the spiritual marketplace, therefore, the winners are those who appeal to personal experience as the only genuine source of meaning and fulfilment, rather than the received teachings and commandments of traditional religion.

Nevertheless, Heelas and Woodhead argue that a spiritual revolution has not taken place. Although the holistic milieu has grown in popularity since the 1970s, its growth has not compensated for the decline of traditional religion. They therefore conclude that secularisation is occurring in Britain, because the subjective turn has undermined the basis of traditional religion.

Table 1A	Contrasts between religion and spirituality	
Religion	**Spirituality**	
Life as duty	Life as discovery	
Self-sacrifice	Personal development	
Deference	Autonomy	
Conforming with external authority	Connecting with your inner self	
Family life: traditional values and discipline	Family life: emotional bonds and self-expression	
Employment: service to an organisation	Employment: professional growth	
Future of religion: out of step and losing ground	Future of spirituality: growing and gaining ground	

Adapted from Heelas and Woodhead (2005)

Secularisation in America

In 1962, Wilson found that 45% of Americans attended church on Sundays. However, he argued that churchgoing in America was more an expression of the 'American way of life' than of deeply held religious beliefs. Wilson claimed that America was a secular society, not because people had abandoned the churches, but because religion there had become superficial.

Bruce (2002) shares Wilson's view. He uses three sources of evidence to support his claim that America is becoming increasingly secular: declining church attendance; 'secularisation from within' and a trend towards religious diversity and relativism.

Declining church attendance

Opinion poll research asking people about church attendance suggests that it has been stable at about 40%

of the population since 1940. However, Kirk Hadaway (1993), working with a team of researchers employed by major churches, found that this figure did not match the churches' own attendance statistics. If 40% of Americans were going to church, the churches would be full – but they were not.

To investigate their suspicion that opinion polls exaggerate attendance rates, Hadaway et al (1993) studied church attendance in Ashtabula County, Ohio. To estimate attendance, they carried out head counts at services. Then in interviews, they asked people if they attended church. They found that the level of attendance claimed by the interviewees was 83% higher than their estimates of church attendance in the county.

There is evidence that this tendency to exaggerate churchgoing is a recent development. Until the 1970s, the findings of opinion polls matched the churches' own estimates, but since then the 'attendance gap' has widened. For example, a study of attendance at Catholic mass in San Francisco found that in 1972, opinion polls exaggerated attendance by 47% but by 1996, the exaggeration had doubled to 101%.

Thus Bruce concludes that a stable rate of self-reported attendance of about 40% has masked a decline in actual attendance in the United States. The widening gap may be due to the fact that it is still seen as socially desirable or normative to go to church, so people who have stopped going will still say they attend if asked in a survey.

Secularisation from within

Bruce argues that the way American religion has adjusted to the modern world amounts to *secularisation from within*. The emphasis on traditional Christian beliefs and glorifying God has declined and religion in America has become 'psychologised' or turned into a form of therapy. This change has enabled it to fit in with a secular society. In short, American religion has remained popular by becoming less religious.

The purpose of religion has changed from seeking salvation in heaven to seeking personal improvement in this world. This decline in commitment to traditional beliefs can be seen in people's attitudes and lifestyles. Churchgoers are now much less strict than previously in their adherence to traditional religious morality, as Table 1B shows.

Table 1B	Moral attitudes of young American Evangelicals, 1951 and 1982

% agreeing that the following are always morally wrong

	1951	1982
Playing cards	77	0
Social dancing	91	0
Going to the movies	46	0
Smoking cigarettes	93	51
Drinking alcohol	98	17
Heavy petting	81*	45
Premarital sexual intercourse	94*	89

* 1961 figures

Adapted from Hunter (1987)

Religious diversity

The growth of religious diversity has also contributed to secularisation from within. Churchgoers are becoming less dogmatic in their views.

Bruce identifies a trend towards *practical relativism* among American Christians, involving acceptance of the view that others are entitled to hold beliefs that are different to one's own. This is shown in Lynd and Lynd's (1929) study which found in 1924 that 94% of churchgoing young people agreed with the statement, 'Christianity is the one true religion and all people should be converted to it'. However, by 1977 only 41% agreed.

The counterpart to practical relativism is *the erosion of absolutism* – that is, we now live in a society where many people hold views that are completely different to ours, which undermines our assumption that our own views are absolutely true.

Criticisms of secularisation theory

Secularisation theorists put forward strong arguments and evidence to support their claim that religious beliefs, practices and institutions have declined both in Britain and America. However, secularisation theory has been criticised in several ways. Its opponents highlight the following points, which we shall examine in detail in the next Topic:

- Religion is not declining but simply changing its form.
- Secularisation theory is one-sided. It focuses on decline and ignores religious revivals and the growth of new religions.
- Evidence of falling church attendance ignores people who believe but don't go to church.
- Religion may have declined in Europe but not in America or globally, so secularisation is not universal.
- The past was not a 'golden age' of faith from which we have declined, and the future will not be an age of atheism.
- Far from causing decline, religious diversity increases participation because it offers choice. There is no overall downward trend. Religious trends point in different directions and people make use of religion in all sorts of different ways.

Activity

In pairs, go through the criticisms of secularisation theory and identify the arguments and evidence that each criticism is aimed at. How might supporters of secularisation theory defend their views against these criticisms?

Synoptic link: methods

Questionnaires have been used in research on church attendance. However, one disadvantage of using questionnaires is the social desirability effect. People may give answers they think will show them in a favourable light and impress the interviewer, even if it means exaggerating or telling lies about how often they attend church.

For more activities on Secularisation...

Go to www.sociology.uk.net

Summary

Secularisation refers to the decline of religion. Statistics show church attendance in the UK falling. The number of baptisms and church weddings has declined. Meanwhile opinion polls show that religious belief is declining. Reasons include rationalisation, social and structural differentiation, social and religious diversity. Counter-trends are cultural transition and defence; for example where religion may be a focal point for preserving an ethnic minority's culture. The Kendal Project found growing interest in spirituality, including the New Age, but its growth does not compensate for the large numbers leaving traditional religion. Secularisation theorists argue that religion is also declining in America. Although church attendance is comparatively high, nevertheless it is declining. American religion is also experiencing secularisation from within; becoming less strict and having to accept religious diversity.

QuickCheck Questions

1   What percentage of the adult population of Britain attended church on Sundays in 1851?

2   What proportion of weddings now takes place in church: (a) a fifth; (b) a quarter; (c) a third; (d) a half?

3   Why did Weber think that the Protestant Reformation led to the 'disenchantment' of the world?

4   What term is used to describe a society containing a wide variety of religious groups?

5   What does Berger mean by the 'sacred canopy'?

6   Explain what is meant by 'disengagement'.

7   What is meant by the term 'cultural transition'?

8   Explain the difference between the 'holistic milieu' and the 'congregational domain'.

Check your answers at www.sociology.uk.net

Examining secularisation

Item A   Secularisation theorists argue that religion is declining in both Europe and America. For example, statistics for Britain show a steady increase in the average age of churchgoers over many years. On present trends, a majority will soon be over 65 years of age. Similarly, very few children now attend Sunday school or have parents who read Bible stories or teach them to say their prayers. Religion is also losing institutional influence. For example, schools are supposed to hold a daily act of collective worship but many no longer do so.

However, critics argue that secularisation theory paints too bleak a picture of the future of religion. They point to the popularity of evangelical Christianity and the growth of New Age spirituality as evidence of its continuing vitality.

Question

(a)   Identify and briefly explain **three** reasons that support the claim that American society is becoming increasingly secular.   (9 marks)

(b)   Using material from **Item A** and elsewhere, assess the arguments and evidence for the view that Britain is becoming a secular society.   (18 marks)

The examiner's advice

Part (b) carries 6 AO1 marks and 12 AO2 marks. Begin by defining secularisation and then present a range of statistical evidence on the decline of beliefs, practices and institutions. Remember that you must focus specifically on evidence about Britain. Then go on to explain the trends by using concepts such as rationalisation, structural differentiation, and social and religious diversity. Make sure you use the Item as a source of evidence that you can comment on. You should refer to alternative views and to counter-evidence in your evaluation, but remember that the question is not asking you for a lengthy account of the various alternatives to secularisation theory.

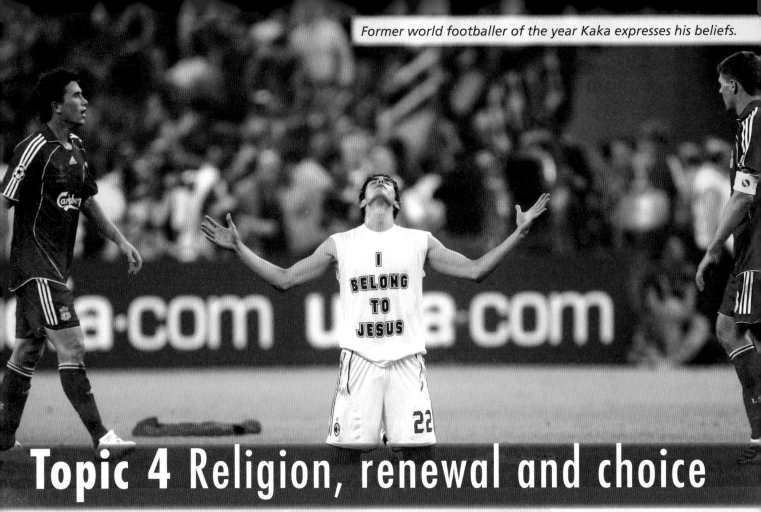

Former world footballer of the year Kaka expresses his beliefs.

I BELONG TO JESUS

Topic 4 Religion, renewal and choice

Critics have challenged secularisation theory's claim that religion is declining:

- They question whether religion is in fact declining rather than simply changing.
- They question whether church attendance statistics are a valid measure of religious belief.
- They reject the view that increased diversity and choice undermines religion's plausibility and claim that it encourages greater involvement in religion.
- They question whether religion is declining on a global scale, or only in parts of Europe.

In this Topic, we examine three main alternatives to secularisation theory:

- **Theories of late modernity and postmodernity** – these argue that religion is not declining but merely changing as society develops.
- **Religious market theory** – the view that secularisation is only one stage of a constant cycle of secularisation, revival and renewal.
- **Existential security theory** – the view that religion has declined in richer countries because they are more economically secure.

Learning objectives

After studying this Topic, you should:

- Understand the reasons why some sociologists reject the idea of secularisation.
- Be able to analyse alternative interpretations of the nature and position of religion today.
- Understand and be able to evaluate debates about the nature and extent of secularisation.

Postmodernity and religion

Some sociologists reject the secularisation thesis that religion must inevitably decline in modern society. In this section, we examine the idea that religion is changing rather than declining. In this view, changes in religion are largely the result of changes in wider society, such as greater individualism and consumerism, or even a shift from modern to late modern or postmodern society.

Believing without belonging

Grace Davie (2007) is one sociologist who argues against secularisation theory. In her view, religion is not declining but simply taking a different, more *privatised* form. For example, people no longer go to church because they feel they have to or because it is 'respectable' to do so. Thus, although churchgoing has declined, this is simply because attendance is now a matter of personal choice rather than the obligation it used to be. As a result, we now have *believing without belonging* – where people hold religious beliefs but don't go to church. Thus, the decline of traditional religion is matched by the growth of a new form of religion.

Vicarious religion

Davie also notes a trend towards 'vicarious religion', where a small number of professional clergy practise religion on behalf of a much larger number of people, who experience it at second hand. This pattern is typical of Britain and Northern Europe. In these societies, despite low levels of attendance, many people still use the church for rites of passage – rituals that mark a change of status, such as baptisms, weddings and funerals.

A similar finding comes from Reginald Bibby's (1993) Canadian survey, which found that only 25% of Canadians attended church regularly. However, 80% said they had religious beliefs, identified positively with religious traditions and turned to religion for rites of passage. Although they seldom went to church, they continued to be interested in the supernatural.

Davie compares vicarious religion to the tip of an iceberg and sees it as evidence of believing without belonging. Beneath what appears to be only a small commitment to religion is a much wider commitment. This can be seen when people are drawn to church at times of national tragedy; for example, following the death of Princess Diana in 1997. The same is true for individuals and families when they face tragedy and loss. Those involved may not normally go to church or pray, but they are attached to the church as an institution for providing ritual and support.

According to Davie, secularisation theory assumes that modernisation affects every society in the same way, causing the decline of religion and its replacement by science. Davie questions this assumption. Instead of a single version of modern society, she argues there are *multiple modernities*. For example, Britain and America are both modern societies, but with very different patterns of religion, especially in relation to church attendance – high in America, low in Britain, but accompanied by believing without belonging. Davie rejects the view that religion will simply be replaced by science. Her view is that they will continue to coexist.

Criticisms

Voas and Crockett (2005) do not accept Davie's claim that there is more believing than belonging. Evidence from British Social Attitudes surveys from 1983 to 2000 shows that both church attendance *and* belief in God are declining. If Davie were right, we would expect to see higher levels of belief.

Bruce adds that if people are not willing to invest time in going to church, this just reflects the declining strength of their beliefs. When people no longer believe, they no longer wish to belong, and so their involvement in religion diminishes.

Spiritual shopping

Danielle Hervieu-Léger (2000; 2006) continues the theme of personal choice and believing without belonging. She agrees that there has been a dramatic decline in institutional religion in Europe, with fewer and fewer people attending church in most countries.

This is partly because of what she calls *cultural amnesia*, or a loss of collective memory. For centuries, children used to be taught religion in the extended family and parish church. Nowadays, however, we have largely lost the religion that used to be handed down from generation to generation, because few parents now teach their children about religion. Instead, parents today let children decide for themselves what to believe. At the same time, the trend towards greater social equality has undermined the traditional power of the Church to impose religion on people from above. As a result, young people no longer inherit a fixed religious identity and they are ignorant of traditional religion.

However, while traditional institutional religion has declined, religion itself has not disappeared. Instead, individual consumerism has replaced collective tradition. People today now feel they have a choice as consumers of religion

– they have become *spiritual shoppers*. Religion is now individualised – we now develop our own 'do-it-yourself' beliefs that give meaning to our lives and fit in with our interests and aspirations.

Religion has thus become a personal spiritual journey in which we choose the elements we want to explore and the groups we wish to join. As a result, Hervieu-Léger argues, two new religious types are emerging – *pilgrims* and *converts*:

- **Pilgrims** follow an individual path in a search for self-discovery, for example exploring New Age spirituality by joining groups, or through individual 'therapy'. The demand is created by today's emphasis on personal development.
- **Converts** join religious groups that offer a strong sense of belonging, usually based on a shared ethnic background or religious doctrine. Such groups re-create a sense of community in a society that has lost many of its religious traditions. Examples include evangelical movements and the churches of ethnic minorities.

As a result of these trends, religion no longer acts as the source of collective identity that it once did. However, Hervieu-Léger notes that religion does continue to have some influence on society's values. For example, the values of equality and human rights have their roots in religion, she argues. Such values can be a source of shared cultural identity and social solidarity, even for those who are not actively involved in religion.

> Suggest two other values, apart from equality and human rights, that are held by non-religious people but that could be said to have their roots in religion.

Hervieu-Léger's views can be related to the idea of *late modernity*. This is the notion that in recent decades some of the trends within modern society have begun to accelerate, such as the decline of tradition and increasing individualism. This explains the weakening of traditional institutions such as the church, as well as the growing importance of individual choice in matters of religion. (For more on the idea of late modernity, see Chapter 4, Topic 5.)

Activity

In groups of 3–4, design a questionnaire about religious behaviour, beliefs and spirituality based on Davie and Hervieu-Léger's ideas. Include questions about attendance and beliefs; parental teaching; rites of passage; privatised religion such as praying in crisis situations; watching religious TV programmes; interest in spirituality and New Age beliefs. Collect answers from a wide range of students and then collate your findings.

How much of what you find is 'traditional' religion? How much variety did you find in people's beliefs? Do your findings support the ideas of Davie and Hervieu-Léger?

Lyon: 'Jesus in Disneyland'

David Lyon (2000) agrees with Davie that believing without belonging is increasingly popular. He argues that traditional religion is giving way to a variety of new religious forms that demonstrate its continuing vigour. As a postmodernist, he explains this in terms of a shift in recent decades from modern to postmodern society. In Lyon's view, postmodern society has a number of features that are changing the nature of religion. These include globalisation, the increased importance of the media and communications, and the growth of consumerism.

The relocation of religion

Globalisation refers to the growing interconnectedness of societies, which has led to greatly increased movements of ideas and beliefs across national boundaries. This is due to the central role played in postmodern society by the media and information technology, which saturate us with images and messages from around the globe, compressing time and space to give us instantaneous access to the ideas and beliefs of previously remote regions and religions.

These ideas have become 'disembedded' – the media lift them out of their original local contexts and move them to a different place and time. For example, the 'electronic church' and televangelism disembed religion from real, local churches and relocate it on the Internet, allowing believers to express their faith without physically attending church. Similarly, Lyon describes a Harvest Day Crusade held not in church, but at Disneyland – an example of how the boundaries between different areas of social life become blurred in postmodern society.

As a result, religion becomes de-institutionalised – its signs and images become detached from their place in religious institutions, floating and multiplying on television and in cyber-space. Removed from their original location in the church, they become a cultural resource that individuals can adapt for their own purposes.

Religious consumerism

Postmodern society also involves the growth of consumerism, and especially the idea that we now construct our identities through what we choose to consume. As Hervieu-Léger emphasises, this is also true of religion, where we act as 'spiritual shoppers', choosing religious beliefs and practices to meet our individual needs, from the vast range available in the religious marketplace. We no longer have to sign up to any one religious tradition; instead, we can pick and mix elements of different faiths to suit our tastes and make them part of our identity – until something more fashionable or attractive comes along. Box 1.3 has an example of an individualised religion.

In Lyon's view, religion has relocated to the *sphere of consumption*. While people may have ceased to belong to religious organisations, they have not abandoned religion. Instead they have become 'religious consumers', making conscious choices about which elements of religion they find useful. For example, the American Christian fundamentalists in Nancy Ammerman's (1987) study made use of a number of churches without giving strong loyalty to any of them. One family attended services at a Methodist church and bereavement counselling at a Baptist church, while taking their children to another church for day care.

One effect of having a great variety of religious products to choose from is a loss of faith in 'meta-narratives' – theories or worldviews that claim to have the absolute, authoritative truth. These include the traditional religions. Now that people have access to a wide range of different and contradictory religious ideas and beliefs, this weakens the claims of traditional religions, because exposure to many competing versions of the truth makes people sceptical that any one of them is really true. Thus, previously dominant religious organisations and traditions lose their authority and decline. In their place, many new religious movements spring up that we the consumers can 'sample'.

Re-enchantment of the world

Lyon criticises secularisation theory for assuming that religion is declining and being replaced by a rational, scientific worldview. Contrary to Weber's prediction of increasing rationalisation and disenchantment of the world, Lyon sees the last three or four decades as a period of *re-enchantment*, with the growth of unconventional beliefs, practices and spirituality. Although traditional forms of religion have declined, especially in Europe, Lyon points to the growing vitality of non-traditional religion in the West and its resurgence elsewhere in the world.

Criticisms

Postmodernists claim that the growth of religious media and the electronic church is evidence against secularisation. However, research shows that people choose to view programmes that confirm their *existing* beliefs. It is unlikely therefore that the religious media attract many new converts.

Lyon criticises the evidence used by secularisation theorists, such as church attendance statistics. However, the alternatives he puts forward – such as the idea of the electronic church – are not based on extensive evidence.

Bruce argues that consumerist religion of the sort Lyon describes is weak religion – it has little effect on the lives of its adherents. As such, he sees its rise as evidence of secularisation, not of the continuing vitality of religion.

Synoptic link: theory

Lyon's explanation of religion in today's society is an example of **postmodernist theory**. As a postmodernist, Lyon opposes secularisation theory on the grounds that it is a meta-narrative that claims religion will inevitably decline in all societies. Postmodernism rejects the idea that it is possible to identify general trends such as secularisation.

Box 1.3   Sheilaism

To illustrate the idea of individualised religion, Bellah (1996) gives the example of 'Sheilaism'. This is the response from Sheila, a nurse interviewed for his study about personal beliefs:

'I believe in God. I'm not a religious fanatic. I can't remember the last time I went to Church. My faith carried me a long way. It's Sheilaism. Just my own little voice... It's just, try to love yourself and be gentle with yourself. You know, I guess, take care of each other. I think He would want us to take care of each other.'

Bellah comments that if everyone saw religion in the same way as Sheila, there would be 220 million religions in America: one for every individual. He adds that when individuals have their own interpretations, they may hold religious beliefs without ever practising their religion.

What is meant by individualised religion and how does it differ from the sort of religion Durkheim describes among Aboriginal clans (see Topic 1)?

Religious market theory

The main advocates of religious market theory (also called rational choice theory) are Stark and Bainbridge (1985). They are very critical of secularisation theory, which they see as *Eurocentric* – it focuses on the decline of religion in Europe and fails to explain its continuing vitality in America and

elsewhere. In their view, it also puts forward a distorted view of the past and future. Stark and Bainbridge argue that there was no 'golden age' of religion in the past, as secularisation theory implies, nor is it realistic to predict a future end-point for religion when everyone will be an atheist.

Instead, Stark and Bainbridge propose religious market theory. This theory is based on two assumptions.

- People are naturally religious and religion meets human needs. Therefore the overall demand for religion remains constant, even though the demand for particular *types* of religion may vary.
- It is human nature to seek rewards and avoid costs. When people make choices, they weigh up the costs and benefits of the different options available.

According to Stark and Bainbridge, religion is attractive because it provides us with *compensators*. When real rewards are scarce or unobtainable, religion compensates by promising supernatural ones. For example, immortality is unobtainable, but religion compensates by promising life after death. Only religion can provide such compensators. Non-religious ideologies such as humanism and communism do not provide credible compensators because they do not promise supernatural rewards.

Activity

In small groups, use the Internet to investigate humanism. What are the beliefs of the Humanist Association? In what ways does humanism differ from religion? Based on your findings, how far do you agree with Stark and Bainbridge that humanism fails to provide credible compensators?

As an alternative to secularisation theory, which sees a one-way process of continuous decline, Stark and Bainbridge put forward the concept of a *cycle* of religious decline, revival and renewal. They describe a perpetual cycle throughout history, with some religions declining and others growing and attracting new members. For example, when established churches decline, they leave a gap in the market for sects and cults to attract new followers. From this point of view, secularisation theory is one-sided: it sees the decline, but ignores the growth of new religions and religious revivals.

According to Stark and Bainbridge, churches operate like companies selling goods in a market. Where secularisation theory sees competition between different religious organisations as undermining religion, religious market theorists take the opposite view. They argue that competition leads to improvements in the quality of the religious 'goods' on offer. The churches that make their product attractive will succeed in attracting more 'customers'. Meanwhile churches that are not responsive to the needs of their members will decline.

America vs. Europe

The demand for religion increases when there are different sorts to choose from, because consumers can find one that meets their needs. By contrast, where there is a religious monopoly – one church with no competition – it leads to decline. This is because without competition, a church has no incentive to provide people with what they want.

Stark and Bainbridge believe that religion thrives in the USA because there has never been a religious monopoly there. The Constitution guarantees freedom of religion and the separation of church and state, and there has always been a great variety of denominations to choose from. This has encouraged the growth of a healthy religious market where religions grow or decline according to consumer demand.

The situation in Europe is entirely different. Most European countries have been dominated by an official state church which had a religious monopoly, such as the Church of England. Competition has been held back and the lack of choice has led to decline.

Stark and Bainbridge conclude that the main factor influencing the level of religious participation is not the demand for religion, as secularisation theory suggests, but the supply. Participation increases when there is an ample supply of religious groups to choose from, but declines when supply is restricted. Also based on their comparison of America and Europe, Stark and Bainbridge argue that the decline of religion is not a universal trend happening in all societies, as secularisation theory suggests.

Supply-led religion

A range of studies support Stark and Bainbridge's view that demand for religion is greatly influenced by the quality and variety of religion on offer and the extent to which it responds to people's needs.

For example, Hadden and Shupe (1998) argue that the growth of 'televangelism' in America shows that the level of religious participation is supply-led. When commercial funding of religious broadcasts began in the 1960s, it opened up competition in which evangelical churches thrived. As a commercial enterprise, televangelism responded to consumer demand by preaching a 'prosperity gospel'.

Finke (1997) argues that the lifting of restrictions on Asian immigration into America in the 1960s allowed Asian religions such as Hare Krishna and Transcendental Meditation to set up permanently in the USA, so Asian faiths became another option that proved popular with consumers in the religious marketplace.

Another example is the growth of evangelical megachurches (churches with congregations of 2,000 or more). Most are in the United States but they are also found in South Korea and elsewhere. With such large congregations, they have lavish resources and are able to offer a vast range of activities to meet the diverse needs of their members. Miller (1997) compares them with hypermarkets.

According to Stark (1990), Japan is another society where a free market in religion has stimulated participation. Until 1945, Shintoism was the state religion and other religions were suppressed. However, after World War Two, religion was de-regulated, creating a market in which new religions such as Soka Gakkai (a type of Buddhism) have thrived. Japan's experience contrasts with that of post-war Germany, where religion was closely regulated by the state and as a result declined.

Criticisms

Religious market theory is the approach adopted by most American sociologists of religion. It highlights the supply side of religion and consumer choice, and can be useful for understanding the growth of new religions. However there are several criticisms.

Bruce rejects the view that diversity and competition increase the demand for religion. Statistics show that diversity has been accompanied by religious decline in both Europe *and* America.

Bruce argues that Stark and Bainbridge misrepresent secularisation theory. The theory does not claim there was a past 'golden age' of religion, or that everyone will become atheists. It simply claims that religion is in long-term decline. Nor does it claim secularisation is universal – just that it applies to Europe and America.

▲ *Evangelicalism is the fastest-growing branch of Christianity.*

Norris and Inglehart (2004) show that high levels of religious participation exist in Catholic countries where the Church has a near monopoly, such as Ireland and Venezuela. By contrast, countries with religious pluralism, such as Holland and Australia, often have low levels of participation. This contradicts Stark and Bainbridge's theory.

Beckford criticises religious market theory as unsociological, because it assumes people are 'naturally' religious and fails to explain why they make the choices they do.

Existential security theory

Norris and Inglehart (2004) reject religious market theory on the grounds that it only applies to America and fails to explain the variations in religiosity between different societies. For example, international studies of religion have found no evidence of the link between religious choice and religious participation that Stark and Bainbridge claim exists.

Norris and Inglehart argue that the reason for variations in religiosity between societies is not different degrees of religious choice, but different degrees of *existential security*. By this, they mean 'the feeling that survival is secure enough that it can be taken for granted'. Religion meets a need for security, and therefore societies where people feel secure have a low level of demand for religion:

- **Poor societies**, where people face life-threatening risks such as famine, disease and environmental disasters, have high levels of insecurity and thus high levels of religiosity. Poor people who live in rich societies also face greater insecurity and are therefore more religious than rich people in those societies.
- **Rich societies**, where people have a high standard of living and are at less risk, have a greater sense of security and thus lower levels of religiosity.

Thus the demand for religion is not constant, as Stark and Bainbridge claim, but varies both within and between societies. Demand is greatest from low-income groups and societies, because they are less secure. This explains why poor Third World countries remain religious, while prosperous Western countries have become more secular.

Norris and Inglehart note that global population growth undermines the trend towards secularisation. Rich, secure, secular Western countries have low levels of population growth, whereas poor, insecure, religious Third World countries have high rates. As a result, while rich countries are becoming more secular, the majority of the world is becoming more religious.

Europe vs. America

In Western Europe, the trend is towards increasing secularisation. Norris and Inglehart argue that this is not surprising, because these societies are among the most equal and secure in the world, with well developed welfare states offering comprehensive health care, social services and pensions. This reduces poverty and protects those at the bottom from insecurity.

By comparison with Europe, the United States remains much more religious. Norris and Inglehart argue that this is because America is also the most unequal of the rich societies, with an inadequate welfare safety-net and individualistic 'dog eat dog' values. This creates high levels of poverty and insecurity, which creates a greater need for religion.

Thus, although America is more religious than Europe, this is explained by Norris and Inglehart's general theory of religiosity as the result of insecurity. For example, they point out that although America is religious by the standards of other rich nations, it is less religious than poor ones.

Synoptic link: core themes

Norris and Inglehart establish links between religious participation, existential security and **stratification**. They found that religious participation is highest in poorer societies and groups where people lack security.

State welfare and religiosity

Norris and Inglehart's argument is supported by Gill and Lundegaarde (2004), who found that the more a country spends on welfare, the lower the level of religious participation. Thus European countries, which spend more than the USA, are also more secular than the USA.

Gill and Lundegaarde note that in the past religion used to provide welfare for the poor, and still does so in poorer countries. However, from the 20th century, the state in the West began to provide welfare and this contributed to religion's decline.

For more activities on Religion, renewal and choice...

Go to www.sociology.uk.net

Nevertheless, Gill and Lundegaarde do not expect religion to disappear completely, because although welfare provision meets the need for security, it does not answer 'ultimate' questions about the meaning of life, unlike religion. Thus although the availability of welfare reduces the need for religion, it does not eliminate that need completely.

Box 1.4	The case of Uruguay

Gill and Lundegaarde identify the interesting case of Uruguay, a small Latin American country which has religious diversity but low levels of religious participation. This goes against Stark and Bainbridge's claim that a free market in religion stimulates participation.

Uruguay is culturally very similar to neighbouring countries that have substantially higher rates of religious participation, but the difference is that Uruguay has more generous welfare provision. This supports existential security theory.

Evaluation

Vásquez (2007) accepts that Norris and Inglehart offer a valuable explanation of different levels of religious participation not only in Europe and the USA, but globally. However, he makes two criticisms:

They use only quantitative data about income levels; they don't examine people's own definitions of 'existential security'. Vásquez argues that qualitative research is also needed.

Norris and Inglehart only see religion as a negative response to deprivation. They ignore the positive reasons people have for religious participation and the appeal that some types of religion have for the wealthy.

Summary

Secularisation theory has various opponents. Postmodernists argue that traditional religion has been replaced by personal beliefs, spiritual shopping and the electronic church, for example. It has not declined but been disembedded, relocated and transformed. Individual consumption now replaces communal worship. Religious market theory argues that religion thrives where there is diversity and choice (e.g. in USA and most other countries) but has declined in Europe where the church has been a monopoly. In this view, there is a perpetual cycle – religious decline is followed by renewal and revival. The overall demand for religion remains constant because it meets human needs. Secularisation theory is Eurocentric and mistaken. Existential security theory is another view. Global trends show that religion declines when standards of living and welfare provision improve. However, global population growth is undermining the trend towards secularisation. Religion is declining in richer nations but growing in poorer nations as the population increases due to high birth rates.

QuickCheck Questions

1 Explain what is meant by 'believing without belonging'.

2 Explain what is meant by 'vicarious religion'.

3 According to Hervieu-Léger, how do 'pilgrims' differ from 'converts'?

4 What do Stark and Bainbridge mean by 'compensators'?

5 Suggest two reasons why patterns of religiosity in America and Europe are different.

6 Why do some sociologists criticise secularisation theory as 'Eurocentric'?

7 Identify two criticisms of religious market theory.

8 What is meant by 'existential security'?

 Check your answers at www.sociology.uk.net

Examining religion, renewal and choice

Assess the view that religious beliefs and practices are changing to reflect a new era of diversity and choice.   (33 marks)

The examiner's advice

The essay carries 15 AO1 marks and 18 AO2 marks (9 for interpretation and application, and 9 for analysis and evaluation). You need to consider the different ways in which religion may be changing in today's society, using concepts and issues such as believing without belonging, consumerism and spiritual shopping, converts and pilgrims, individualisation, de-institutionalisation and disembedding of religion, diversity and choice versus religious monopoly etc. You can also consider some of the material covered in Topic 3 here, such as the spiritual revolution. You should put these into a broader theoretical context using approaches such as religious market theory and postmodernism.

You should evaluate the view in the question, for example by reference to existential security theory as a criticism of religious market theory. You should use secularisation theory (e.g. Bruce) as an alternative approach to explaining some of these trends.

Topic 5 Religion in a global context

Religion has long existed in a worldwide context and it has been described as *the original globaliser,* because for centuries the major religions have spread across the world, through conquest, colonisation and migration.

The world today is more interconnected than ever before – a process known as *globalisation*. This has consequences for all areas of life, including religion:

- As societies and religions come into closer contact with one another, there is the potential for religious conflict and for religious diversity and change.
- When one society or state dominates another, people may use religion to explain and resist this domination.
- Cultural and social changes brought by globalisation may threaten cherished values and lead some to turn to the certainties promised by fundamentalism.
- Religious ideas lead some people to act in new ways that encourage economic development in less developed societies.

In this Topic, we examine some of the main ways in which religion and its international and global context affect one another:

- Religion and its relationship to economic development
- The nature of religious fundamentalism
- Religion as cultural defence against an external threat
- Religion and the 'clash of civilisations'.

Learning objectives

After studying this Topic, you should:

- Understand some of the different ways in which religion interacts with its global context.
- Understand the role of religion in economic development in a globalising world.
- Understand and be able to evaluate explanations of the nature of religious fundamentalism.
- Understand and be able to evaluate explanations of the role of religion in international conflict.

Religion and development

For secularisation theory, modernisation undermines religion. The importance of science and technology in economic development, and the rational worldview on which they depend, are seen as destroying belief in the supernatural. On the other hand, religion may contribute to development, as Weber argued in the case of the Protestant ethic. More recently, sociologists have examined what role religion may play in development in today's globalising world.

God and globalisation in India

Globalisation has brought rapid economic growth and has seen India become a more important player on the world political stage. It has also brought rising prosperity to some – notably India's new middle class. Meera Nanda's (2008) book, *God and Globalization*, examines the role of Hinduism, the religion of 85% of the population, in legitimating both the rise of a new Hindu 'ultra-nationalism' and the prosperity of the Indian middle class.

Hinduism and consumerism

Globalisation has created a huge and prosperous, scientifically educated, urban middle class in India, working in IT, pharmaceuticals and biotechnology sectors closely tied into the global economy. These are precisely the people whom secularisation theory predicts will be the first to abandon religion in favour of a secular worldview.

Yet, as Nanda observes, a vast majority of this class continue to believe in the supernatural. A survey by the Centre for the Study of Developing Societies (2007) found that Indians are becoming more religious. Only 5% said their religiosity had declined in the last five years, while 30% said they had become more religious. The survey also found that 'urban educated Indians are more religious than their rural and illiterate counterparts'. Increased interest in religion has also been reflected in a dramatic growth of religious tourism, such as visits to shrines and temples. Nanda notes that it is becoming fashionable to be religious and to be seen to be so.

Another feature of this middle-class religiosity is that they are attracted to what were once low-status village gods and goddesses worshipped by the poor. This is because these deities are seen as being more responsive to people's needs than the traditional Hindu 'great gods'.

Nanda examines what motivates the sophisticated, urban middle classes to continue to believe in miracles and supernatural beings. She rejects poverty and existential

▲ *Hinduism is a religion at ease with modernity.*

insecurity as an explanation, because they are not poor. She also rejects the idea that their religiosity is a defensive reaction to modernisation and Westernisation. On the contrary, the Indian middle classes are optimistic about the opportunities that globalisation brings them. Instead, Nanda argues, their increasing religiosity is the result of their ambivalence about their newfound wealth.

This ambivalence stems from a tension between the traditional Hindu belief in renunciation of materialism and worldly desires, and the new prosperity of the middle classes. This is resolved for them by the modern holy men and tele-gurus to whom they turn, who preach the message that desire is not bad, but rather a manifestation of divinity that motivates people to do things. Similarly, they dispense business-friendly versions of Hinduism and take the edge off guilt by teaching that middle-class consumerism can be 'spiritually balanced' by paying for the performance of appropriate and often extravagant rituals – which also serve as a way of displaying one's wealth. Modern versions of Hinduism therefore legitimate the position of the middle class and allow them to adjust to globalised consumer capitalism.

Hindu ultra-nationalism

Nanda also examines the role of Hinduism in legitimating a triumphalist version of Indian nationalism. For example, the Pew Global Attitude Survey found that 93% of Indians – more than any other country – agreed with the statement that, 'Our people are not perfect, but our culture is superior to others'. Nanda notes that India's success in the global market is increasingly attributed to the superiority of 'Hindu values', a view constantly promoted by the media and politicians, along with the idea that Hinduism is the essence of Indian culture and identity.

In this Hindu ultra-nationalism, the worship of Hindu gods has become the same as worshipping the nation of India, and Hinduism has become a *civil religion* (see Topic 1). However, as Nanda points out, this is creating a widening gulf between Hindus and non-Hindu minorities.

Hinduism has also penetrated public life, so that the supposedly secular state is increasingly influenced by religion. For example, in education 'Hindu sciences' such as astrology are being taught as an academic subject in public universities and being used supposedly to predict earthquakes and natural disasters. Meanwhile, the Ministry of Defence is sponsoring research and development of weapons and devices with magical powers mentioned in the ancient Hindu texts, and the Health Ministry is investing in research, development and sale of cow urine (cows being sacred animals) as a cure for every ailment from AIDS to TB (Nanda 2003).

> In the account of the ways Hinduism has adapted to life in modern India, find two similarities with the ways in which religion has been secularised in the USA.

Capitalism in East Asia

In recent decades, the so-called 'East Asian tiger economies' such as South Korea, Singapore and Taiwan, have successfully industrialised and become significant players in the global economy. Even more recently, China has become a major global industrial power.

The success of capitalism in East Asia has led some sociologists to argue that religion has played a role similar to the one Calvinism played in the development of capitalism in 16th and 17th century Europe.

For example, Gordon Redding (1990) describes the spirit of capitalism among Chinese entrepreneurs in the tiger economies. He sees their 'post-Confucian' values encouraging hard work, self-discipline, frugality and a commitment to education and self-improvement. (Confucianism is a traditional Chinese belief system.) The effect of this value system is similar to that of the Protestant ethic, in that it leads to economic productivity and the accumulation of capital.

Pentecostalism in Latin America

Similarly, Peter Berger (2003) argues that Pentecostalism in Latin America acts as a 'functional equivalent' to Weber's Protestant ethic. That is, it encourages the development of capitalism today in the same way as Calvinism did in 16th and 17th century Europe. Latin American Pentecostalists embrace a work ethic and lifestyle similar to that of the Calvinists. Like Calvinism, Pentecostalism demands an ascetic (self-denying) way of life that emphasises personal discipline, hard work and abstinence from alcohol. In this way, it encourages its members to prosper and become upwardly mobile. Berger concludes that Pentecostalism has a strong affinity with modern capitalism.

Berger agrees with Weber that something like Protestantism is necessary to promote economic development and raise a society out of poverty. This process can be led by an active minority with an ethic of this-worldly asceticism, such as the Pentecostalists. Thus in Chile and southern Brazil, there is now a growing and prosperous Pentecostalist middle class leading capitalist development.

However, Berger underlines Weber's point that religious ideas alone are not enough to produce economic development – natural resources are also needed. For example, while Pentecostalism has grown in northern Brazil, the region lacks resources and remains backward. By contrast, the south, which is developing rapidly, has both a work ethic derived from Pentecostalism and the necessary resources.

Pentecostalism: global and local

In the last five centuries, Christianity has globalised itself by expanding out of Europe, first into South America and then Africa. David Lehmann (2002) distinguishes between two phases in this expansion:

- In the first phase, Christianity accompanied colonisation and was imposed on the indigenous populations by conquest, often forcibly suppressing local religions.
- In the second phase, over the last century or so, it has spread because it gained a popular following from below. For example, by 2000 there were 80 million Pentecostalists in Brazil alone.

Lehmann attributes the success of Pentecostalism as a global religion in part to its ability to 'plug into' and incorporate local beliefs. Although it preaches a similar message worldwide, it uses imagery and symbolism drawn from local cultures and existing religious beliefs, especially from spirit possession cults. Pentecostalists attack such cults as the work of the devil, but their ministers will conduct exorcisms to rid people of evil spirits. By doing so, Pentecostalism accepts their existence and this validates local traditional beliefs, while at the same time claiming to give believers access to a greater power, that of the Christian Holy Spirit.

In this way, Pentecostalism creates new local religious forms, rather than simply replacing existing local beliefs with an imported one, as the first phase of Christianisation had done. In Africa, this has led to the 'Africanisation' of Christianity rather than the total disappearance of indigenous religions. As a result of this ability to adapt to local customs and establish a local identity for itself, Pentecostalism shows considerable local diversity in different parts of the world.

Pentecostalism has also been successful in developing countries because it is able to appeal particularly to the poor who make up the vast majority of the population, and because it uses global communications media to spread its message, along with 'road shows' and world tours by 'celebrity' preachers.

Religious fundamentalism

In a global context, the issue of religious fundamentalism has emerged as a major area of media and political concern in recent decades, notably in relation to international Islamist terrorism. However, the term 'fundamentalist' has also been applied to followers of other religions, including Protestant Christians. In this section, we examine explanations of fundamentalism and its relationship to globalisation.

Fundamentalism and cosmopolitanism

According to Anthony Giddens (1990; 1991; 1999), fundamentalists are traditionalists who seek to return to the basics or fundamentals of their faith. They believe unquestioningly in the literal and infallible truth of scripture and that it provides answers to all life's important questions, from politics to family life. Fundamentalists believe theirs is the only true view of the world. They are intolerant and refuse to engage in dialogue with others, and they justify their views by reference to dogma and sacred texts rather than rational argument. Fundamentalists tend to avoid contact with others who think differently. They rely upon guardians of tradition, such as the clergy or elders, to interpret the sacred text and lay down rules that determine their lifestyle.

Giddens notes that the term 'fundamentalism' is a relatively new one, and he sees its growth as a product of and reaction to globalisation, which undermines traditional social norms concerning the nuclear family, gender and sexuality (such as the prohibition of abortion, homosexuality and sex outside marriage). In today's 'late modern' society, individuals are constantly faced with choice, uncertainty and risk. The attraction of fundamentalism and its rigid, dogmatic beliefs is the certainty that it promises in an uncertain world. It is a retreat into faith-based answers and away from the globalising world that demands rational reasons.

Giddens contrasts fundamentalism with cosmopolitanism – a way of thinking that embraces modernity and is in keeping with today's globalising world. Cosmopolitanism is tolerant of the views of others and open to new ideas, constantly reflecting on and modifying beliefs in the light of new information (which Giddens calls 'reflexive' thinking). It requires people to justify their views by the use of rational arguments and evidence rather than by appealing to sacred texts or tradition. One's lifestyle is seen as a personal choice rather than something prescribed by an external religious or other authority. Cosmopolitan religion and spirituality emphasises the pursuit of personal meaning and self-improvement rather than submission to authority. Giddens sees fundamentalism as the enemy of cosmopolitan thought and modernity.

However, while fundamentalists detest modernity, they use modern methods to express and spread their beliefs – for example, the Internet and e-mail, televangelism and the 'electronic church'. Giddens identifies fundamentalist versions of several major religions, including Islam, Christianity and Hinduism.

Responses to postmodernity

In a similar argument to that of Giddens, Zygmunt Bauman (1992) sees fundamentalism as a response to living in postmodernity. Postmodern society brings freedom of choice, uncertainty and a heightened awareness of risk, undermining the old certainties about how to live that were grounded in tradition. In this situation, while some embrace the new freedom, others are attracted to fundamentalism by its claims of absolute truth and certainty.

Similarly, Manuel Castells (1998) distinguishes between two responses to postmodernity:

- **Resistant identity** – a defensive reaction of those who feel threatened and retreat into fundamentalist communities.
- **Project identity** – the response of those who are forward-looking and engage with social movements such as feminism and environmentalism.

Criticisms

Beckford (2003) criticises Giddens, Bauman and Castells on several grounds:

- They distinguish too sharply between cosmopolitanism and fundamentalism, ignoring 'hybrid' movements.
- They are 'fixated on fundamentalism', ignoring other important developments – including how globalisation is also affecting non-fundamentalist religions such as Catholicism.
- Giddens lumps all types of fundamentalism together, ignoring important differences between them.
- Giddens' description of fundamentalism as a defensive reaction to modernity ignores the fact that reinventing tradition is also a modern, 'reflexive' activity.

Jeff Haynes (1998) argues that we should not focus narrowly on the idea that Islamic fundamentalism is a reaction against globalisation. For example, in the Middle East, conflicts caused by the failure of local elites to deliver on their promises to improve the standard of living are often the fuel that drives fundamentalism.

Monotheism and fundamentalism

Like Giddens, Steve Bruce (2007) sees the main cause of fundamentalism as the perception of religious traditionalists that today's globalising world threatens their beliefs and lifestyle. When they feel threatened, traditionalists may develop rigid rules about what to believe and how to behave.

However, Bruce regards fundamentalism as being confined to monotheistic religions – that is, those believing in a single almighty God – such as Judaism, Islam and Christianity. Polytheistic religions that believe in the existence of many gods, such as Hinduism, are unlikely to produce fundamentalism.

In Bruce's view, this is because monotheistic religions are based on a notion of God's will as revealed through a single, authoritative sacred text such as the Qur'an or the Bible. This is believed to contain the actual word of God and it lays down

specific rules for believers to follow. By contrast, polytheistic religions lack a single all-powerful deity and a single authoritative text, so there is much more scope for different interpretations and none has an over-riding claim to legitimacy or absolute truth. For example, Hinduism has been described as being more like a collection of religions than just one.

Two fundamentalisms

In Bruce's view, while all fundamentalists share the same characteristics such as belief in the literal truth of the sacred text and detestation of modernity, different fundamentalist movements may have different origins. In particular, some are triggered by changes taking place within their own society, while others are a response to changes being thrust upon a society from the outside. Bruce illustrates this distinction with the examples of Protestant Christian and Islamic fundamentalisms:

- **In the West**, fundamentalism is most often a reaction to change taking place within a society, especially the trends towards diversity and choice typical of late modern or postmodern societies. For example, the New Christian Right in America has developed in opposition to family diversity, sexual 'permissiveness', gender equality and abortion rights, secular education and the privatisation of religion (its removal from public life). Its aim is to reassert 'true' religion and restore it to the public role where it can shape the laws and morals of wider society.
- **In the Third World**, fundamentalism is usually a reaction to changes being thrust upon a society from outside, as in the case of the Islamic revolution in Iran (see below). It is triggered by modernisation and globalisation, in which 'Western' values are imposed by foreign capitalism or by local elites supported by the West. Here, fundamentalism involves resistance to the state's attempts to sideline it and confine it to the private sphere.

Match up the following terms with their definitions: (i) Muslim; (ii) Islam; (iii) Islamic fundamentalism; (iv) Islamism. Definitions: (a) a religious ideology that advocates following the teachings of the Qur'an to the letter; (b) someone who adheres to the Islamic religion; (c) a political ideology advocating worldwide unity of believers and promotion of Islamic values; (d) a religion based on the Qur'an.

Cultural defence

As we saw in Topic 3, Steve Bruce (2002) sees one function of religion in today's world as that of cultural defence. This is where religion serves to unite a community against an external threat. In such situations, religion has special significance for its followers because it symbolises the group or society's collective identity. Defending the community

against a threat often gives religion a prominent role in politics.

Two examples of religion as cultural defence from the late 20th century are Poland and Iran. They illustrate how religion can be used in defence of national identity in the face of political domination by an external power. In Poland, the external power was Soviet communism, while in Iran it was Western culture and capitalism. In both cases, therefore, the role of religion has to be understood in a *transnational* context.

Poland

From 1945 to 1989, Poland was under communist rule, imposed from outside by the Soviet Union. During this time, the Catholic Church was suppressed, but for many Poles it continued to embody Polish national identity. Although the Church did not always challenge the communist regime openly, it served as a popular rallying point for opposition to the Soviet Union and the Polish communist party. In

▲ *The Catholic Church played an important role in the collapse of communism in Poland in the 1980s through its support of the free trade union Solidarity.*

particular, it lent its active support to the Solidarity free trade union movement in the 1980s that did much to bring about the fall of communism. Thereafter, the Church regained a public role and has had significant influence on Polish politics since the 1980s.

Activity

In small groups, do some research to find out about Solidarity. What part did the Catholic Church play in it? How significant was it that Pope John Paul II was Polish?

Iran

Western capitalist powers and oil companies had long had influence in Iran (formerly Persia), including involvement in the illegal overthrow of a democratic government in the 1950s to install a pro-Western regime headed by the Shah of Iran. During the 1960s and 70s, his successor embarked on a policy of modernisation and Westernisation. This included banning the veil and replacing the Muslim calendar with one based on the founding of the Persian Empire 2,500 years earlier. Meanwhile, modernisation was widening the gap between rich and poor, while protest was ruthlessly suppressed.

Change was imposed rapidly and from above, often causing great suffering. Under these conditions, Islam became the focus for resistance to the Shah's regime, led by clerics such as the Ayatollah Khomeini. The revolution of 1979 brought the creation of the Islamic Republic, in which clerics held state power and were able to impose Islamic Sharia law on the country.

However, Haynes argues that the Iranian revolution was not typical of politics in the Middle East, in that it was led by the mullahs – the religious leaders. In some other countries in the region, such as Saudi Arabia, the religious leadership is closely tied to the local elite, who in turn are tied to Western imperialism. As such, local religious leaders are opposed by local fundamentalists, who regard them as enemies of Islam.

Both Iran and Poland are examples of religion as cultural defence against a perceived external enemy and its local allies (the Shah and the Polish communist party) and the transnational dimension is an important element in understanding the role that religion played.

Synoptic link: core themes

The concept of cultural defence links religion to **culture** and **identity**. For example, in Poland during the 1980s the Catholic Church came to symbolise Polish national identity and the struggle of the Poles against Soviet communism.

Religion and the 'clash of civilisations'

In recent years, religion has been at the centre of a number of global conflicts. These include the '9/11' Islamist attacks in the United States on 11 September 2001 and subsequent bombings in Madrid, Bali and London. In the view of American neo-conservative thinkers such as Samuel Huntington (1993), such conflicts have intensified since the collapse of communism in 1989 and are symptoms of what Huntington sees as a wider 'clash of civilisations'.

Huntington identifies seven civilisations: Western, Latin American, Confucian (China), Japanese, Islamic, Hindu and Slavic-Orthodox (Russia and Eastern Europe). Most civilisations are larger than a single nation. Each has a common cultural background and history and is closely identified with one of the world's great religions. Shared religion creates social cohesion within civilisations, but can cause conflict between them. This is particularly true in today's globalised world, because religious differences have now become a major source of identity, for three reasons:

- With the fall of communism, political differences between nations have become less important as a source of identity.
- Globalisation has made nation-states less significant as a source of identity (see Chapter 4 Topic 6), creating a gap that religion has filled.
- Globalisation makes contact between civilisations easier and more frequent, increasing the likelihood of old conflicts re-emerging.

In Huntington's view, religious differences are creating a new set of hostile 'us and them' relationships, with increased competition between civilisations for economic and military power, for example in the Middle East. Conflict is also occurring on the boundaries between civilisations – as in the former Yugoslavia, with the war in the early 1990s between, as Huntington sees it, Western, Slavic-Orthodox and Islamic civilisations. He sees religious differences as harder than political ones to resolve because they are deeply rooted in culture and history.

Huntington sees history as a struggle of 'progress against barbarism'. He believes the West is under threat, especially from Islam, and predicts growing conflict between 'the West and the rest'. He fears the emergence of new anti-Western military alliances, for example between Confucian and Islamic civilisations, and urges the West to reassert its Christian identity.

Criticisms

Jackson (2006) sees Huntington's work as an example of *orientalism* – a western ideology that stereotypes Eastern nations and people (especially Muslims) as untrustworthy, inferior or fanatical 'Others' and serves to justify exploitation and human rights abuses by the West.

Casanova (2005) argues that Huntington ignores important religious divisions within the 'civilisations' he identifies – e.g. between Sunni and Shi'a Islam.

Horrie and Chippindale (2003) see 'the clash of civilisations' as a grossly misleading neo-conservative ideology that portrays the whole of Islam as an enemy. In reality, only a tiny minority of the world's 1.5 billion Muslims are remotely interested in a 'holy war' against the West.

Similarly, Karen Armstrong (2001) argues that hostility towards the West does not stem from fundamentalist Islam, but is a reaction to Western foreign policy in the Middle East. The West has propped up oppressive regimes and continues to support Israel despite its aggressive treatment of Palestinians.

The real clash of civilisations?

Using data from the *World Values Survey*, Inglehart and Norris (2003) conclude that the issue that divides the West from the Muslim world is not democracy but sexuality. They find that support for democracy is similarly high in both the West and the Muslim world, but there are great differences when it comes to attitudes to divorce, abortion, gender equality and gay rights. While Western attitudes have become more liberal, in the Muslim world they remain traditional (see Table 1C). Inglehart and Norris comment that in the last decade, democracy has become the political ideology to gain global appeal, but there is no global agreement about *self-expression values*, such as tolerance of diversity, gender equality and freedom of speech. In their view, 'these divergent values constitute the real clash of civilisations between Muslim societies and the West'.

Table 1C	Approval of political and social values in Western and Muslim societies (%)	
	Western societies	**Muslim societies**
Democratic ideals	86	87
Strong leaders	61	61
Gender equality	82	55
Divorce	60	35
Abortion	48	25
Homosexuality	53	25

Source: World Values Survey 1995–2001

For more activities on Religion in a global context...

Go to www.sociology.uk.net

Summary

Religion may contribute to development. In India, Hinduism legitimates middle-class prosperity and ultra-nationalism. In East Asia and Latin America, post-Confucian and Pentecostalist ideas perform a similar role to the Protestant ethic, encouraging hard work and self-discipline. Pentecostalism has achieved global success by incorporating local beliefs. Fundamentalism believes in the literal truth of scripture. It is seen as a reaction to globalisation or a quest for certainty in response to postmodernity. It may be a response to changes from within or from outside a society. Similarly, one function of religion today is cultural defence, as in the case of Poland and Iran. Huntington argues that globalisation is leading to a 'clash of civilisations' associated with the major religions and especially between the West and Islam.

QuickCheck Questions

1 What is meant by the term 'Hindu ultra-nationalism'?

2 Identify two characteristics of religious fundamentalism.

3 According to Lehmann, what were the two main stages in the globalisation of religion?

4 Identify two policies to which the New Christian Right are opposed.

5 According to Castells, what is the difference between a resistant identity and a project identity?

6 According to Huntington, why is a 'clash of civilisations' increasingly likely?

7 Suggest two criticisms of the view that there is a 'clash of civilisations'.

8 Over what type of values are Western and Muslim societies most likely to disagree?

Check your answers at www.sociology.uk.net

Examining religion in a global context

Assess sociological explanations of the relationship between globalisation and religion. (33 marks)

The examiner's advice

This question carries 15 AO1 marks (knowledge and understanding) and 18 AO2 marks (9 for interpretation and application, and 9 for analysis and evaluation). You need to look at a range of ways in which religion may be related to its global context and how sociologists explain them, making reference to different religions. Begin by examining how Hinduism legitimates the rising prosperity and success of India under the impact of globalisation. You can also consider religion's role as a new 'Protestant ethic' in Asia and Latin America (and evaluate by referring to the role of non-religious factors in development). Examine fundamentalism as a response to globalisation and related trends, e.g. as offering certainty in an uncertain world, and evaluate using Beckford. Link this to religion as cultural defence against the external changes that are a feature of globalisation, and to the 'clash of civilisations' that are brought into closer contact as a result of globalisation. Evaluate this view using Jackson, Armstrong or others.

Topic 6 Organisations, movements and members

At various points so far in the chapter, we have touched on different religious groups and organisations while we were examining other issues such as the role of religion or the secularisation debate.

In this Topic, we make these organisations and movements the focus of our attention. We examine the main types of religious organisation, such as churches, sects, denominations and cults, and how they develop.

In recent years, there has been a growth in the number of different religious organisations and spiritual movements such as the New Age, and we examine the reasons for this.

Membership and participation in different religious organisations and movements varies by social class, ethnicity, gender and age. In this Topic, we examine some of the explanations for these patterns.

Learning objectives

After studying this Topic, you should:

- Know the main types of religious organisation and their characteristics.

- Understand and be able to evaluate explanations of different types of religious/spiritual organisations and movements.

- Understand and be able to evaluate explanations of the reasons for the growth and development of different religious/spiritual organisations and movements.

- Know the main patterns of participation by class, ethnicity, gender and age and the reasons for these patterns.

Types of religious organisation

While some people hold religious beliefs without belonging to any organised group, many others express their faith through membership of a religious organisation such as a church. Sociologists are interested in the different types of religious organisation, how they develop and who joins them.

Church and sect

The first attempt to identify the features of different types of religious organisation was by Ernst Troeltsch (1912). He distinguished between two main types – the church and the sect. *Churches* are large organisations, often with millions of members such as the Catholic Church, run by a bureaucratic hierarchy of professional priests, and they claim a monopoly of the truth. They are universalistic, aiming to include the whole of society, although they tend to be more attractive to the higher classes because they are ideologically conservative and often closely linked to the state. For example, the British sovereign is head of both the state and the Church of England. They place few demands on their members.

By contrast, Troeltsch sees *sects* as small, exclusive groups. Unlike churches, sects are hostile to wider society and they expect a high level of commitment. They draw their members from the poor and oppressed. Many are led by a charismatic leader rather than a bureaucratic hierarchy. The only similarity with churches is that sects too believe they have a monopoly of religious truth.

Denomination and cult

In addition to the church and sect, sociologists have identified other types of religious organisation. Richard Niebuhr (1929) describes *denominations* such as Methodism as lying midway between churches and sects. Membership is less exclusive than a sect, but they don't appeal to the whole of society like a church. Like churches, they broadly accept society's values, but are not linked to the state. They impose some minor restrictions on members, such as forbidding alcohol, but are not as demanding as sects. Unlike both church and sect, they are tolerant of other religious organisations and do not claim a monopoly of the truth.

A fourth type of religious organisation – and the least organised of all – is the *cult*. This is a highly individualistic, loose-knit and usually small grouping around some shared themes and interests, but usually without a sharply defined and exclusive belief system. Cults are usually led by 'practitioners' or 'therapists' who claim special knowledge. Like denominations, cults are tolerant of other organisations and their beliefs. Cults do not demand strong commitment from followers, who are often more like customers or trainees than members. They may have little further involvement with the cult once they have acquired the beliefs or techniques it offers. Many cults are world-affirming, claiming to improve life in this world.

Similarities and differences

In summing up the similarities and differences between religious organisations, Roy Wallis (1974) highlights two characteristics:

- **How they see themselves** *Churches and sects* claim that their interpretation of the faith is the only legitimate or correct one. *Denominations and cults* accept that there can be many valid interpretations.
- **How they are seen by wider society** *Churches and denominations* are seen as respectable and legitimate, whereas *sects and cults* are seen as deviant.

From cathedrals to cults

Sociologists argue that some of the above descriptions of religious organisations do not fit today's reality. For example, Bruce (1996) argues that Troeltsch's idea of a church as having a religious monopoly only applies to the Catholic Church before the 16th century Protestant Reformation, when it had a religious monopoly over society, symbolised by its massive and imposing cathedrals. Since then, sects and cults have flourished and religious diversity has become the norm. In today's society, churches are no longer truly churches in Troeltsch's sense because they have lost their monopoly and been reduced to the status of denominations competing with all the rest.

What type of religious organisation is each of the following: the Jehovah's Witnesses; Roman Catholicism; Scientology; Methodism; Anglicanism; Baptists; Transcendental Meditation; the Mormons?

New religious movements

Since the 1960s, there has been an explosion in the number of new religions and organisations, such as the Unification Church or 'Moonies', the Children of God, Transcendental Meditation (TM), Krishna Consciousness and many more. This has led to new attempts to classify them. Roy Wallis (1984) categorises these new religious movements (NRMs) into three groups based on their relationship to the outside world – whether they reject the world, accommodate to it, or affirm it.

World-rejecting NRMs

These are similar to Troeltsch's sects. Examples include the Moonies, Krishna Consciousness, Children of God, the Manson Family, the Branch Davidian and the People's Temple. They vary greatly in size, from a handful of members to hundreds of thousands. They have several characteristics:

- They are clearly religious organisations with a clear notion of God.
- They are highly critical of the outside world and they expect or seek radical change.
- To achieve salvation, members must make a sharp break with their former life.
- Members live communally, with restricted contact with the outside world. The movement controls all aspects of their lives and is often accused of 'brainwashing' them.
- They often have conservative moral codes, for example about sex.

World-accommodating NRMs

These are often breakaways from existing mainstream churches or denominations, such as neo-Pentecostalists who split from Catholicism, or Subud, an offshoot of Islam. They neither accept nor reject the world, and they focus on religious rather than worldly matters, seeking to restore the spiritual purity of religion. For example, neo-Pentecostalists believe that other Christian religions have lost the Holy Spirit. Members tend to lead conventional lives.

World-affirming NRMs

These groups differ from all other religious groups and may lack some of the conventional features of religion, such as collective worship, and some are not highly organised. However, like religions, they offer their followers access to spiritual or supernatural powers. Examples include Scientology, Soka Gakkai, TM and Human Potential.

- They accept the world as it is. They are optimistic and promise followers success in terms of mainstream goals and values, such as careers and personal relationships.
- They are non-exclusive and tolerant of other religions, but claim to offer additional special knowledge or techniques that enable followers to unlock their own spiritual powers and achieve success or overcome problems such as unhappiness or illness. They have been described as *psychologising* religions offering this-worldly gratification.
- Most are cults, whose followers are often customers rather than members, and entry is through training. The movement places few demands on them and they carry on normal lives.

In general, world-affirming NRMs have been the most successful of the movements Wallis studied. For example, Scientology had about 165,000 members in the UK in 2005, as compared with only 1,200 Moonies.

Evaluation

Wallis offers a useful way of classifying the new religious movements that have developed in recent decades. However, some argue that it is not clear whether he is categorising them according to the movement's teachings, or individual members' beliefs. He also ignores the diversity of beliefs that may exist *within* an NRM.

Wallis himself recognises that real NRMs will rarely fit neatly into his typology (list of types) and some, such as 3HO (the Healthy Happy Holy Organisation), may have features of all three types. Nevertheless, many sociologists find such typologies useful as a way of analysing and comparing the significant features of NRMs.

However, Stark and Bainbridge (1985) reject the idea of constructing such typologies altogether. Instead, they argue that we should distinguish between religious organisations using just one criterion – the degree of conflict or tension between the religious group and wider society.

Sects and cults

Stark and Bainbridge identify two kinds of organisation that are in conflict with wider society – sects and cults:

- **Sects** result from *schisms* – splits in existing organisations. They break away from churches usually because of disagreements about doctrine.
- **Cults** are new religions, such as Scientology and Christian Science, or ones new to that particular society that have been imported, such as TM.

In general, Stark and Bainbridge see sects as promising *other-worldly* benefits (e.g. a place in heaven) to those suffering economic deprivation or ethical deprivation (where their values conflict with wider society). By contrast, cults tend to offer *this-worldly benefits* (e.g. good health) to more prosperous individuals who are suffering psychic deprivation (normlessness) and organismic deprivation (health problems).

> What similarities are there between Stark and Bainbridge's explanation of the attraction of sects for the deprived and the Marxist view of the role of religion in society?

Stark and Bainbridge subdivide cults according to how organised they are.

- **Audience cults** are the least organised and do not involve formal membership or much commitment. There is little interaction between members. Participation may be through the media. Examples include astrology and UFO cults.

- **Client cults** are based on the relationship between a consultant and a client, and provide services to their followers. In the past, they were often purveyors of medical miracles, contact with the dead etc, but the emphasis has shifted to 'therapies' promising personal fulfilment and self-discovery. Examples include homeopathy and Spiritualism.
- **Cultic movements** are the most organised and demand a higher level of commitment than other cults. The movement aims to meet all its members' religious needs and unlike followers of audience and client cults, they are rarely allowed to belong to other religious groups at the same time. An example of a cultic movement is the Moonies. Some client cults become cultic movements for their most enthusiastic followers, such as Scientology, which developed out of the client cult Dianetics. Some well publicised Doomsday cults that predict the end of the world and practise mass suicide may be best seen as cultic movements.

Stark and Bainbridge make some useful distinctions between organisations. However, their idea of using the degree of conflict with wider society to distinguish between them is similar to Troeltsch's distinction between church (which accepts society) and sect (which rejects society). In addition, some of the examples they use do not fit neatly into any one of their categories.

Explaining the growth of religious movements

Since the 1960s, there has been a rapid growth in the number of sects and cults, and in the number of people belonging to them. For example, there are estimated to be over 800 NRMs and over half a million individuals belonging to these and other non-mainstream Christian churches in the UK. Sociologists have offered three main explanations for this trend: marginality, relative deprivation, and social change.

Marginality

As Troeltsch noted, sects tend to draw their members from the poor and oppressed. Similarly, according to Max Weber (1922), sects tend to arise in groups who are marginal to society. Such groups may feel that they are disprivileged – that is, that they are not receiving their just economic rewards or social status.

In Weber's view, sects offer a solution to this problem by offering their members a *theodicy of disprivilege* – that is, a religious explanation and justification for their suffering and disadvantage. This may explain their misfortune as a test of faith, for example, while holding out the promise of rewards in the future for keeping the faith.

Historically, many sects, as well as millenarian movements, have recruited from the marginalised poor. For example, in the 20th century the Nation of Islam (the Black Muslims) recruited successfully among disadvantaged blacks in the USA. However, since the 1960s, the sect-like world-rejecting NRMs such as the Moonies have recruited mainly from more affluent groups of often well-educated young, middle-class whites. However, Wallis argues that this does not contradict Weber's view, because many of these individuals had become marginal to society. Despite their middle-class origins, most were hippies, dropouts and drug users.

Relative deprivation

Relative deprivation refers to the subjective sense of being deprived. This means that it is perfectly possible for someone who is in reality quite privileged nevertheless to *feel* that they are deprived or disadvantaged in some way compared with others. Thus, although middle-class people are materially well off, they may feel they are spiritually deprived, especially in today's materialistic, consumerist world, which they may perceive as impersonal and lacking in moral value, emotional warmth or authenticity. As a result, Wallis argues, they may turn to sects for a sense of community.

Similarly, Stark and Bainbridge argue that it is the relatively deprived who break away from churches to form sects. When middle-class members of a church seek to compromise its beliefs in order to fit into society, deprived members are likely to break away to form sects that safeguard the original message of the organisation.

For example, the deprived may stress Christ's claim that it is harder for a rich man to enter the Kingdom of Heaven than for a camel to pass through the eye of a needle – a message that the better off might want to play down. By contrast, the deprived may want to emphasise Christ's message that 'the meek shall inherit the earth'. Stark and Bainbridge argue that *world-rejecting sects* offer to the deprived the *compensators* that they need for the rewards they are denied in this world. By contrast, the privileged need no compensators or world-rejecting religion. They are attracted to *world-accepting churches* that express their status and bring them further success in achieving earthly rewards. This distinction is very similar to Wallis' two main types of NRMs. (For more on compensators, see Topic 4.)

Social change

A third explanation for the recent growth of religious movements is social change. Thus Wilson (1970) argues that periods of rapid change disrupt and undermine established norms and values, producing *anomie* or normlessness. In response to the uncertainty and insecurity that this creates, those who are most affected by the disruption may turn to sects as a solution. For example, the dislocation created by the industrial revolution in Britain in the late 18th and early 19th century led to the birth of Methodism, which offered a sense of community, warmth and fellowship, clear norms and values and the promise of salvation. Methodism succeeded in recruiting large numbers of the new industrial working class.

Similarly, Bruce (1995; 1996) sees the growth of sects and cults today as a response to the social changes involved in modernisation and secularisation. In Bruce's view, society is now secularised and therefore people are less attracted to the traditional churches and strict sects, because these demand too much commitment. Instead, people now prefer cults because they are less demanding and require fewer sacrifices.

The growth of NRMs

Explanations have been put forward for the growth of both world-rejecting and world-affirming NRMs.

World-rejecting NRMs Wallis points to social changes from the 1960s impacting on young people, including the increased time spent in education. This gave them freedom from adult responsibilities and enabled a counter-culture to develop. Also, the growth of radical political movements offered alternative ideas about the future. World-rejecting NRMs were attractive in this context because they offered young people a more idealistic way of life. Bruce (1995) argues that it was the failure of the counter-culture to change the world that led to disillusioned youth turning to religion instead.

World-affirming NRMs Bruce argues that their growth is a response to modernity, especially to the rationalisation of work. Work no longer provides meaning or a source of identity – unlike the past, when the Protestant ethic gave work a religious meaning for some people. Yet at the same time, we are expected to achieve – even though we may lack the opportunities to succeed. World-affirming NRMs provide both a sense of identity and techniques that promise success in this world.

Wallis also notes that some 'movements of the middle ground' such as the Jesus Freaks have grown since the mid-1970s. These have attracted disillusioned former members of world-rejecting NRMs (which have generally been less successful) because they provide a halfway house back to a more conventional lifestyle.

The dynamics of sects and NRMs

While churches such as the Catholic Church and the Church of England have a history stretching over many centuries, sects by contrast are often short-lived organisations, frequently lasting only a single generation or less. Sociologists have therefore been interested to understand the dynamics of sect development. There is also interest in how the NRMs described by Wallis will fare in the longer term.

Activity

In small groups, choose one of the following 'doomsday cults' and use the Internet to research it: the People's Temple; the Branch Davidian; the Solar Temple; Aum Shinrikyo; Heaven's Gate; the Manson Family. Find out when and where the group came from, and its beliefs, leader and members. What happened to the group? Are there any explanations for what they did? Present the story of the group to the rest of the class.

Denomination or death

Niebuhr (1929) argues that sects are world-rejecting organisations that come into existence because of *schism* – splitting from an established church because of a disagreement over religious doctrine. Niebuhr argues that sects are short-lived and that within a generation, they either die out, or they compromise with the world, abandon their extreme ideas and become a denomination. There are several reasons for this:

- **The second generation**, who are born into the sect, lack the commitment and fervour of their parents, who had consciously rejected the world and joined voluntarily.

- **The 'Protestant ethic' effect** Sects that practise asceticism (hard work and saving) tend to become prosperous and upwardly mobile, as was the case with the Methodists in the 19th century. Such members will be tempted to compromise with the world, so they will either leave or it will abandon its world-rejecting beliefs.
- **Death of the leader** Sects with a charismatic leader either collapse on the leader's death, or a more formal bureaucratic leadership takes over, transforming it into a denomination.

The sectarian cycle

Similarly, Stark and Bainbridge (1985) see religious organisations moving through a cycle. In the first stage, *schism*, there is tension between the needs of deprived and privileged members of a church. Deprived members break away to found a world-rejecting sect. The second stage is one of *initial fervour*, with a charismatic leadership and great tension between the sect's beliefs and those of wider society. In the third stage, *denominationalism*, the 'Protestant ethic' effect and the coolness of the second generation mean the fervour disappears. The fourth stage, *establishment*, sees the sect become more world-accepting and tension with wider society reduces. In the final stage, *further schism* results when more zealous or less privileged members break away to found a new sect true to the original message.

Established sects

However, Wilson (1966; 2003) argues that not all sects follow the patterns outlined above. Whether or not they do so, depends on how the sect answers the question, 'What shall we do to be saved?'

- **Conversionist** sects such as evangelicals, whose aim is to convert large numbers of people, are likely to grow rapidly into larger, more formal denominations.
- **Adventist** sects such as the Seventh Day Adventists or Jehovah's Witnesses await the Second Coming of Christ. To be saved, they believe they must hold themselves separate from the corrupt world around them. This separatism prevents them from compromising and becoming a denomination.

Wilson goes on to argue that some sects have survived over many generations, such as Adventists, Pentecostalists, the Amish, Mormons and Quakers for example. Instead of becoming denominations, these groups become *established sects*. Contrary to Niebuhr's predictions, many of them have succeeded in socialising their children into a high level of commitment, largely by keeping them apart from the wider world.

However, Wilson argues that globalisation will make it harder in future for sects to keep themselves separate from the outside world. On the other hand, globalisation

▲ *A Mormon service. The Mormons are an established sect with millions of members in the USA and worldwide.*

will make it easier to recruit in the Third World, where there are large numbers of deprived people for whom the message of sects is attractive, as the success of Pentecostalists has shown.

The growth of the New Age

The term 'New Age' covers a range of beliefs and activities that have been widespread since at least the 1980s – Heelas (2008) estimates that there are about 2,000 such activities and 146,000 practitioners in the UK. Many of them are very loosely organised audience or client cults. They are extremely diverse and eclectic (putting unconnected ideas together in new combinations). They include belief in UFOs and aliens, astrology, tarot, crystals, various forms of alternative medicine and psychotherapy, yoga, meditation, magic etc. However, according to Heelas (1996) there are two common themes that characterise the New Age:

- **Self-spirituality** New Agers seeking the spiritual have turned away from traditional 'external' religions such as the churches and instead look inside themselves to find it.
- **Detraditionalisation** The New Age rejects the spiritual authority of external traditional sources such as priests or sacred texts. Instead it values personal experience and believes that we can discover the truth for ourselves and within ourselves.

Beyond these common features, New Age beliefs vary. For example, they include world-affirming aspects that help people succeed in the everyday *outer world*, as well as world-rejecting elements that allow individuals to achieve enlightenment in their *inner world*. However, Heelas argues that most New Age beliefs and organisations offer both.

Postmodernity and the New Age

Several explanations for the popularity of the New Age have been offered. For example, John Drane (1999) argues that its appeal is part of a shift towards postmodern society. One of the features of postmodern society is a loss of faith in *meta-narratives* or claims to have 'the truth'. Science promised to bring progress to a better world but instead it has given us war, genocide, environmental destruction and global warming. As a result, people have lost faith in experts

and professionals such as scientists and doctors, and they are disillusioned with the churches' failure to meet their spiritual needs. As a result, they are turning to the New Age idea that each of us can find the truth for ourselves by looking within.

The New Age and modernity

By contrast, Bruce (1995) argues that the growth of the New Age is a feature of the latest phase of *modern* society, and not postmodernity. Modern society values individualism, which is also a key principle of New Age beliefs (e.g. the idea that each individual has the truth within themselves). It is also a particularly important value among those in the 'expressive professions' concerned with human potential, such as social workers or artists – the group to whom the New Age appeals most.

Bruce notes that New Age beliefs are often softer versions of much more demanding and self-disciplined traditional Eastern religions such as Buddhism that have been 'watered down' to make them palatable to self-centred Westerners. This explains why New Age activities are often audience or client cults, since these make few demands on their followers. Bruce sees the New Age eclecticism or 'pick and mix spiritual shopping' as typical of religion in late modern society, reflecting the consumerist ethos of capitalist society.

Similarly, Heelas (1996) sees the New Age and modernity as linked in four ways:

- **A source of identity** In modern society, the individual has many different roles (at work, in the family, with friends etc) but there is little overlap between them, resulting in a fragmented identity. New Age beliefs offer a source of 'authentic' identity.
- **Consumer culture** creates dissatisfaction because it never delivers the perfection that it promises (e.g. in advertising). The New Age offers an alternative way to achieve perfection.
- **Rapid social change** in modern society disrupts established norms and values, resulting in anomie. The New Age provides a sense of certainty and truth in the same way as sects.
- **Decline of organised religion** Modernity leads to secularisation, thereby removing the traditional alternatives to New Age beliefs. For example, in the USA, the New Age is strongest where churchgoing is at its lowest, in California.

Religiosity and social groups

There are important differences between social groups in their religious participation and in the types of belief they hold. As we have seen, different social classes are likely to be attracted by different organisations and ideas – lower

classes towards world-rejecting sects and higher classes towards world-accepting churches and cults. As this Topic so far has dealt mainly with class differences, we shall now focus on age, gender and ethnic differences in religiosity.

Gender and religiosity

There are clear gender differences in religious belief and participation. While the priesthoods of most religions are male, more women than men participate in religious activities and believe in God, sin, evil, the Devil and life after death (Table 1D). For example, in 2005, 1.8 million women in England were churchgoers, as against only 1.36 million men. This supports Miller and Hoffman's (1995) finding that women express greater interest in religion, have a stronger personal commitment to it and attend church more. This applies to all ages and all religious organisations and faiths. For example, Bruce (1996) estimates that there are twice as many women as men involved in sects. Similarly, Heelas and Woodhead (2005) found that 80% of the participants in the holistic milieu in Kendal were female. These differences may also be connected to differences in the way men and women see God – as the God of power and control, or as the God of love and forgiveness.

Table 1D	Religious beliefs, by gender				
	Percentage believing in:				
	God	Sin	Evil	The Devil	Life after death
Women	84	72	76	42	57
Men	75	66	58	32	39

Source: Davie (1994)

Reasons for gender differences

Sociologists have put forward several explanations for gender differences in religious belief and practice. These tend to focus on the reasons for women's relatively high levels of participation rather than men's lower levels.

Socialisation and gender role

According to Miller and Hoffman, women are more religious because they are socialised to be more passive, obedient and caring. These are qualities valued by most religions, so it follows that women are more likely than men to be attracted to religion. Interestingly, men who have these qualities are also more likely to be religious.

Miller and Hoffman note that women are more likely than men to work part-time or to be full-time carers, so they have more scope for organising their time to participate in religious activities. Women are also more likely to be attracted to the church as a source of gender identity, and Greeley (1992) argues that taking care of other family members increases women's religiosity because it involves responsibility for their 'ultimate' welfare as well as their everyday needs. Similarly, Davie (1994) argues that women's closer proximity to birth and death (through child-bearing and caring for elderly, sick and dying relatives) brings them closer to 'ultimate' questions about the meaning of life that religion is concerned with. This also fits with differences in the way men and women see God.

Women and the New Age

As women are more often associated with 'nature' (for example through childbirth) and a healing role, they may be more attracted than men to New Age movements in particular. For example, Heelas and Woodhead found that 80% of the participants in the holistic milieu in Kendal were female. This is because such movements often celebrate the 'natural' and involve cults of healing, which gives women a higher status and sense of self-worth. Bruce argues that women's experiences of child-rearing make them less aggressive and goal-oriented, and more cooperative and caring – where men wish to achieve, women wish to feel. In Bruce's view, this fits the expressive emphasis of the New Age.

Women may also be attracted to the New Age because it emphasises the importance of being 'authentic' rather than merely acting out roles – including gender roles. Women may be more attracted than men by this as they are more likely to perceive their ascribed roles as restrictive. For example, Callum Brown (2001) argues that New Age 'self' religions – those that emphasise subjective experience rather than external authority – appeal to women's wish for autonomy and attract women recruits. On the other hand, however, some women may be attracted to fundamentalism because of the certainties of a traditional gender role that it prescribes for them.

▲ *A female bishop: why are there so few?*

Compensation for deprivation

Glock and Stark (1969) and Stark and Bainbridge (1985) argue that people may participate in religion because of the compensators for social, organismic and ethical deprivation that it offers. Glock and Stark argue that these forms of deprivation are all more common among women and this explains their higher level of sect membership:

- **Organismic deprivation** This stems from physical and mental health problems. Women are more likely to suffer ill health and thus to seek healing through religion.
- **Ethical deprivation** Women tend to be more morally conservative. They are thus more likely to regard the world as being in moral decline and be attracted to sects, which often share this view.
- **Social deprivation** Women are more likely to be poor. This may explain why there are more women than men in sects, since these attract poorer groups.

Recent trends

Despite the traditional gender differences in participation, there is evidence that women are now leaving the church at a faster rate than men. For example, Brierley (2005) notes the 'drastic' decline in churchgoing among women aged 30–45, with a 16.4% fall in Sunday church attendance between 1990 and 2005. He suggests that this may be because pressures of home, family and work are very intense for these women. They are likely to have a young family, and Sunday working is particularly high (1 in 3) among women of this age, leaving little time for church.

Callum Brown (2001) offers a further explanation of the decline in women's churchgoing. He argues that since the 1960s, women have begun to reject traditional subordinate gender roles. Because Christianity was closely bound up with these traditional roles, women's rejection of subordination has led them to reject traditional religion at the same time.

▲ *Religious organisations may provide minority ethnic communities with a source of cultural identity and support.*

Ethnicity and religiosity

The UK today is a multi-ethnic, multi-religious society. Although the biggest religious group are those describing themselves as Christians (about 72% of the population), there are significant numbers of Muslims, Hindus and Sikhs, almost all of whom belong to ethnic minorities originating in the Indian subcontinent, while many Christians are of black African or Caribbean origin.

There are clear ethnic patterns in religious participation, with higher than average rates for most minority ethnic groups, as Table 1E shows. Muslims, Hindus and black Christians are considerably more likely than white Christians to see religion as important. Among Christians, blacks are more likely than whites to be found in the Pentecostal churches, where they make up 40% of the membership. However, while minorities have higher participation rates, Modood et al (1994) found some decline in the importance of religion for all ethnic groups and that fewer were observant, especially among the second generation.

Table 1E	Ethnic differences in religious affiliation	
	% rating religion very important in their lives	% likely to attend weekly worship
White Anglicans	11	9
White Catholics	32	29
Hindus	43	43
African Caribbean Protestants	81	57
Muslims	74	62
		Source: Policy Studies Institute (1997)

Reasons for ethnic differences

Several reasons have been suggested for ethnic differences in religiosity. One is the idea that most ethnic minorities originate from poorer countries with traditional cultures, both of which produce higher levels of religious belief and practice. On arrival in the UK, they and their children maintain the pattern they brought with them from their country of origin. However, this disregards the impact of their experiences as *immigrants* and as *minorities* in a new society, and how this may give religion a new role as cultural defence and cultural transition.

Cultural defence

As we saw in Topic 3, Bruce (2002) argues that religion in such situations offers support and a sense of cultural identity in an uncertain or hostile environment. As Bird (1999) notes, religion among minorities can be a basis for community solidarity, a means of preserving one's culture and language, and a way of coping with oppression in a racist society. In the case of black African and Caribbean Christians, many found that white churches in the UK did not actively welcome them and some turned to founding or joining black-led churches, especially Pentecostal churches.

Cultural transition

Religion can also be a means of easing the transition into a new culture by providing support and a sense of community for minority groups in their new environment. This is the explanation Will Herberg (1955) gives for high levels of religious participation among first-generation immigrants in the USA. Bruce sees a similar pattern in the history of immigration into the UK, where religion has provided a focal point for Irish, African Caribbean, Muslim, Hindu and other communities. However, once a group – such as Irish Catholics, for example – has made the transition into the wider society, religion may lose its role and decline in importance.

Ken Pryce's (1979) study of the African Caribbean community in Bristol shows both cultural defence and cultural transition have been important. He argues that Pentecostalism is a highly adaptive 'religion of the oppressed' that provided migrants with values appropriate to the new world in which they found themselves. Pentecostalism helped African Caribbeans to adapt to British society, playing a kind of 'Protestant ethic' role in helping its members succeed by encouraging self reliance and thrift. It gave people mutual support and hope of improving their situation. On the other hand, Rastafarianism represented a different response for some African Caribbeans radically rejecting the wider society as racist and exploitative.

Age and religious participation

The general pattern of religious participation is that the older a person is, the more likely they are to attend religious services. However, as Table 1F shows, there are two exceptions to this pattern – the under 15s and the over 65s:

- **The under 15s** are more likely to go to church than other age groups because they may be made to do so by their parents.
- **The over 65s** are more likely to be sick or disabled and thus unable to attend. Higher death rates also make this a smaller group, which also reduces the total number 'available' to attend.

Table 1F	Attendance at church services, England: by age (thousands)	
Age	1979	2005
Under 15	1,416	624
15–19	490	153
20–29	598	231
30–44	870	496
45–64	1,088	907
65 and over	979	755
	Source: English Church Census, Christian Research	

Reasons for age differences

According to Voas and Crockett (2005), there are two main sorts of explanation for age differences in religious participation:

- **The ageing effect** This is the view that people turn to religion as they get older. For example, using evidence from the Kendal Project, Heelas (2005) argues that people become more interested in spirituality as they get older. As we approach death, we 'naturally' become more concerned about spiritual matters and the afterlife, repentance of past misdeeds and so on. As a result, we are more likely to go to church.

- **The generational effect** This is the view that as society becomes more secular, each new generation is less religious than the one before. Thus, there are more old people than young people in church congregations today, not because they are more attracted to religion as they get older, but simply because they grew up at a time when religion was more popular.

Voas and Crockett argue that the generational effect is the more significant of the two explanations for age differences in religious participation. They claim that each generation is half as religious as their parents. If so, we can expect a continuing rise in the average age of churchgoers as the young become less and less willing to attend. As Table 1F shows, the number of 15–19 year olds in church has fallen very sharply since 1979, while two-fifths of churches have no-one under the age of 11 attending services.

Activity

In small groups, each of you should find one person over the age of 60 to interview. Use an unstructured interview. What was their experience of religion during childhood? Were their parents religious? Did they go to religious classes (e.g. Sunday school)? What did they do on Sundays or holy days? What sort of religious instruction did they have in school? What was considered normal religious behaviour? Has it changed? Do they attend services more or less often now they are older, or has it stayed the same? Why? Have they noticed declining attendance and, if so, how do they explain it?

Collate your findings as a group and discuss any differences you have found between your interviewees' experiences and your own.

Meanwhile, about 30% of churchgoers are now over 65. Bruce predicts that this trend will continue and that it won't be long before the over 65s become the majority. The only exception to this trend is the Pentecostal churches, which continue to attract younger members. As Gill (1998) notes, children are no longer receiving a religious socialisation, and those brought up without religious beliefs are less likely to

become churchgoers later in life. If so, it is likely that within two generations, Christian beliefs will only be held by a small minority.

Synoptic link: core themes

Some sociologists see a crisis of religious **socialisation** as the cause of declining church attendance among the young. For example, few parents read their children religious stories or teach them prayers. Very few children attend Sunday school.

For more activities on Organisations, movements and members...

 Go to www.sociology.uk.net

Summary

The main types of religious organisations are churches, sects, denominations and cults. The growth of sects can be seen as a response to marginality, relative deprivation and social change. Weber sees sects as providing a theodicy of disprivilege for the poor. Wallis identifies three types of new religious movement – world rejecting, world affirming and world accommodating. Niebuhr describes a sectarian cycle leading to denominationalism. Wilson identifies established sects as a separate type. Bruce sees sects and cults as resulting from secularisation where Stark and Bainbridge explain them as a response to different sorts of deprivation. New Age cults (audience and client cults) have grown since the 1970s, reflecting characteristics of modernity and postmodernity. Religious participation varies by class, gender, age and ethnicity. For example, it is higher among women and the old, as well as ethnic minorities for whom religion is a source of identity and community support.

QuickCheck Questions

1 Explain what is meant by a 'theodicy of disprivilege'.

2 Identify one similarity and one difference between churches and sects.

3 Suggest two examples of established sects.

4 Explain what is meant by an 'audience cult'.

5 Suggest two ways in which the New Age might be linked to modernity.

6 Suggest two reasons why women might be more religious than men.

7 How may religion be important for 'cultural transition'?

Check your answers at www.sociology.uk.net

Examining organisations, movements and members

Assess sociological explanations for the increasing number of religious and spiritual organisations and movements in society today.　　(33 marks)

The examiner's advice

This question carries 15 AO1 marks (knowledge and understanding) and 18 AO2 marks (9 for interpretation and application, and 9 for analysis and evaluation). You can begin by identifying the different types of religious and spiritual organisations and movements (e.g. church, sect, denomination and cult, different types of NRMs), identifying which types have increased. Then consider explanations for their growth in popularity, such as marginality, relative deprivation and social change, as well as factors such as immigration and globalisation. You should also consider views on how the increase is related to modernity and postmodernity, e.g. Drane, Bruce and Heelas, and on their development by referring to Niebuhr, Stark and Bainbridge and Wilson. Note that the question refers to spirituality as well as religion, so it's important to discuss reasons for the popularity of New Age movements. Use a range of examples of Christian and non-Christian groups.

Topic 7 Ideology and science

Although religions are major belief systems that make claims about what the world is like and how we ought to act in it, they are not the only belief systems to do this. For example, political ideologies make claims about how society ought to be organised. Similarly, although science doesn't tell us how we should behave, it does claim to tell us about how the world is. In other words, many different belief systems make *knowledge-claims* – they claim they are giving us the facts about how things are.

In this Topic, therefore, we focus on *science* as a belief system and in particular, whether and how it differs from other belief systems such as religion. We also examine the concept of *ideology* and how it has been used to understand belief systems.

Learning objectives

After studying this Topic, you should:

- Know the difference between open and closed belief systems.
- Understand and be able to evaluate different views of science as a belief system.
- Understand and be able to evaluate different views of the nature of ideology.

Science as a belief system

Many sociologists see modern science as a product of the process of rationalisation that began with the Protestant Reformation of the 16th century. Some sociologists, such as secularisation theorists, argue that it has undermined religion by changing the way we think and how we see the world.

The impact of science

Science has had an enormous impact on society over the last few centuries. Its achievements in medicine have eradicated many once fatal diseases. Many basic features of daily life today – transport, communications, work and leisure – would be unrecognisable to our recent ancestors due to scientific and technological development. Perhaps most strikingly, science and technology have revolutionised economic productivity and raised our standard of living to previously undreamt of heights. This success has led to a widespread 'faith in science' – a belief that it can 'deliver the goods'.

More recently, this faith has been somewhat dimmed by a recognition that science may cause problems as well as solve them. Pollution, global warming and weapons of mass destruction are as much a product of science and technology as are space flight, 'wonder drugs' and the internet. While science may have helped to protect us from natural dangers such as disease and famine, it has created its own 'manufactured risks' that increasingly threaten the planet.

Yet in fact, both the 'good' and the 'bad' effects of science demonstrate the key feature distinguishing it from other belief systems or knowledge-claims – that is, its *cognitive power*. In other words, it enables us to explain, predict and control the world in a way that non-scientific or pre-scientific belief systems cannot do.

Open belief systems

Why has science been successful in explaining and controlling the world? According to Sir Karl Popper (1959), science is an 'open' belief system where every scientist's theories are open to scrutiny, criticism and testing by others. Science is governed by the principle of *falsificationism*. That is, scientists set out to try and falsify existing theories, deliberately seeking evidence that would disprove them. If the evidence from an experiment or observation contradicts a theory and shows it to be false, the theory can be discarded and the search for a better explanation can begin. In science, knowledge-claims live or die by the evidence.

In Popper's view, discarding falsified knowledge-claims is what enables scientific understanding of the world to grow. Scientific knowledge is *cumulative* – it builds on the achievements of previous scientists to develop a greater and greater understanding of the world around us. As the discoverer of the law of gravity, Sir Isaac Newton, put it, 'If I have been able to see so far, it is because I have stood on the shoulders of giants' – that is, on the discoveries of his predecessors.

However, despite the achievements of great scientists such as Newton, no theory is ever to be taken as definitely true – there is always a possibility that someone will produce evidence to disprove it. For example, for centuries it was held to be true that the sun revolved around the earth, until Copernicus demonstrated that this knowledge-claim was false. In Popper's view, the key thing about scientific knowledge is that it is not sacred or absolute truth – it can always be questioned, criticised, tested and perhaps shown to be false. (For more on Popper, see Chapter 4, Topic 6.)

The CUDOS norms

If Popper is correct, this still leaves the question of why science has only grown so rapidly in the last few centuries. The functionalist Robert K. Merton (1973) argues that science can only thrive as a major social institution if it receives support from other institutions and values.

He argues that this first occurred in England as a result of the values and attitudes created by the Protestant Reformation, especially Puritanism (a form of Calvinism). The Puritans' this-worldly calling and industriousness, and their belief that the study of nature led to an appreciation of God's works, encouraged them to experiment. Puritanism also stressed social welfare and they were attracted by the fact that science could produce technological inventions to improve the conditions of life. The new institution of science also received support from economic and military institutions as the value of the practical applications of science became obvious in areas such as mining, navigation and weaponry.

Merton also argues, like Popper, that science as an institution or organised social activity needs an 'ethos' or set of norms that make scientists act in ways that serve the goal of increasing scientific knowledge. He identifies four such norms, known as 'CUDOS' for short from their initial letters:

Communism Scientific knowledge is not private property. Scientists must share it with the scientific community (by publishing their findings); otherwise, knowledge cannot grow.

Universalism The truth or falsity of scientific knowledge is judged by universal, objective criteria (such as testing), and not by the particular race, sex etc of the scientist who produces it.

Disinterestedness This means being committed to discovering knowledge for its own sake. Having to publish their findings makes it harder for scientists to practise fraud, since it enables others to check their claims.

Organised Scepticism No knowledge-claim is regarded as 'sacred'. Every idea is open to questioning, criticism and objective investigation.

What similarities are there between Merton's CUDOS norms and Popper's view of science as an open belief system?

Closed belief systems

In this respect, science appears to differ fundamentally from traditional religious belief systems. While scientific knowledge is provisional, open to challenge and potentially disprovable, religion claims to have special, perfect knowledge of the absolute truth. Its knowledge is literally sacred and religious organisations claim to hold it on God's divine authority. This means that it cannot be challenged – and those who do so may be punished for their heresy. It also means that religious knowledge does not change – how could it, if it already has the absolute truth? Unlike scientific knowledge, therefore, it is fixed and does not grow.

Robin Horton (1970) puts forward a similar argument. He distinguishes between open and closed belief systems. Like Popper, he sees science as an open belief system – one where knowledge-claims are open to criticism and can be disproved by testing. By contrast, religion, magic and many other belief systems are closed. That is, they make knowledge-claims that cannot be successfully overturned. Whenever its fundamental beliefs are threatened, a closed belief system has a number of devices or 'get-out clauses' that reinforce the system and prevent it from being disproved – at least in the eyes of its believers. These devices vary from one belief system to another. One example is witchcraft beliefs. Edward Evans-Pritchard's (1936) classic anthropological study of the Azande people of the Sudan illustrates Horton's idea of a self-reinforcing, closed belief system.

Witchcraft among the Azande

Like Westerners, the Azande believe that natural events have natural causes. For example, the snake bit me because I accidentally stepped on it as I was walking down the path. However, unlike most Westerners, the Azande do not believe in coincidence or chance. I have walked down the same path a thousand times and never been bitten before – so why me; why now? Thus, when misfortune befalls the Azande, they may explain it in terms of witchcraft. Someone – probably a jealous neighbour – is practising witchcraft against me.

In such cases, the injured party may make an accusation against the suspected witch and the matter may be resolved by consulting the prince's magic poison oracle. Here, the prince's diviner will administer a potion (called 'benge') to a chicken, at the same time asking the benge whether the accused is the source of the witchcraft and telling it to kill

the chicken if the answer is 'Yes'. If the chicken dies, the sufferer can go and publicly demand the witchcraft to stop.

This is usually enough to end the problem, because the Azande regard witchcraft as a psychic power coming from a substance located in the witch's intestines, and it is believed possible that the witch is doing harm unintentionally and unconsciously. This allows the accused to proclaim their surprise and horror, to apologise and promise that there will be no further bewitching.

Evans-Pritchard argues that this belief system performs useful social functions. It not only clears the air and prevents grudges from festering; it also encourages neighbours to behave considerately towards one another in order to reduce the risk of an accusation. In addition, since the Azande believe witchcraft to be hereditary (from father to son and mother to daughter), children have a vested interest in keeping their parents in line, since a successful accusation against the parent also damages the child's reputation. As such, the belief system is an important social control mechanism ensuring conformity and cooperation.

As Evans-Pritchard points out, this belief system is highly resistant to challenges – that is, it is a closed system that cannot be overturned by the evidence. For example, non-believers might argue that if the benge killed the chicken *without* the diviner first addressing the potion, this would be a decisive test showing that the oracle did not work. However, for the Azande, such an outcome would just prove that it was not good benge. As Evans-Pritchard says, 'The very fact of the fowl dying proves to them its badness'. Thus, the 'test' doesn't disprove the belief system in the eyes of the believers; instead, it actually reinforces it. The believers are trapped within their own 'idiom of belief' or way of thinking. Because they accept the system's basic assumptions (such as the existence of witchcraft), they cannot challenge it.

How does this description of witchcraft compare with the analysis of the functions of religion by Parsons and Durkheim?

Self-sustaining beliefs

Polanyi (1958) argues that belief systems have three devices to sustain themselves in the face of apparently contradictory evidence:

- **Circularity** Each idea in the system is explained in terms of another idea within the system and so on, round and round.
- **Subsidiary explanations** For example, if the oracle fails, it may be explained away as due to the incorrect use of the benge.
- **Denial of legitimacy to rivals** Belief systems reject alternative worldviews by refusing to grant any legitimacy to their basic assumptions. For example, creationism rejects outright the evolutionists' knowledge-claim that the earth is billions of years old, and therefore that species have gradually evolved over a long period rather than all having been created.

Science as a closed system

Despite Popper's view of science as open and critical, some other writers argue that science itself can be seen as a self-sustaining or closed system of belief. For example, Polanyi argues that *all* belief systems reject fundamental challenges to their knowledge-claims – science is no different, as the case of Dr Velikovsky indicates (see Box 1.5).

Box 1.5	The case of Dr Velikovsky

In 1950, Immanuel Velikovsky published *Worlds in Collision*, in which he put forward a new theory on the origins of the earth. Velikovsky's theory challenged some of the most fundamental assumptions of geology, astronomy and evolutionary biology. The response from the scientific community was far from the 'open' one advocated by Popper. Instead of putting the new theory to the test to see if it explained the observed facts, scientists rushed to reject it out of hand – without even having read the book. A boycott of Velikovsky's publisher was organised. Scientists who called for a fair hearing and for the theory to be put to the test were victimised and some even lost their jobs.

One explanation for scientists' refusal even to consider such challenges comes from a historian of science, Thomas S. Kuhn (1970). Kuhn argues that a mature science such as geology, biology or physics is based on a set of shared assumptions that he calls a *paradigm*. The paradigm tells scientists what reality is like, what problems to study and what methods and equipment to use, what will count as evidence, and even what answers they should find when they conduct research. For most of the time, scientists are engaged in normal science, which Kuhn likens to *puzzle solving* – the paradigm lays down the broad outlines and the scientists' job is to carefully fill in the details. Those who do so successfully are rewarded with bigger research grants, professorships, Nobel Prizes and so on.

Scientific education and training is a process of being socialised into faith in the truth of the paradigm, and a successful career depends on working within the paradigm. For these reasons, any scientist who challenges the fundamental assumptions of the paradigm, as Velikovsky did, is likely to be ridiculed and hounded out of the profession. Indeed, others in the scientific community will no longer regard him or her as a scientist at all. The only exceptions to this are during one of the rare periods that Kuhn describes as a *scientific revolution*, when faith in the truth of the paradigm has already been undermined by an accumulation of anomalies – results that the paradigm cannot account for. Only then do scientists become open to radically new ideas. (For more on Kuhn, see Chapter 4, Topic 6.)

The sociology of scientific knowledge

Interpretivist sociologists have developed Kuhn's ideas further. They argue that all knowledge – including scientific knowledge – is socially constructed. That is, rather than being objective truth, it is created by social groups using the resources available to them. In the case of science, scientific 'facts' – those things that scientists take to be true and real – are the product of shared theories or paradigms that tell them what they should expect to see, and of the particular instruments they use.

Thus, Karin Knorr-Cetina (1981; 1999) argues that the invention of new instruments, such as telescopes or microscopes, permits scientists to make new observations and construct or 'fabricate' new facts. Similarly, she points out that what scientists study in the laboratory is highly 'constructed' and far removed from the natural world that they are supposedly studying. For example, water is specially purified, animals specially bred and so on.

Little green men

According to the ethnomethodologist Steve Woolgar (1988), scientists are engaged in the same process of 'making sense' or interpreting the world as everyone else. When confronted by 'evidence' from their observations and experiments, they have to decide what it means. They do so by devising and applying theories or explanations, but they then have to persuade others to accept their interpretation.

For example, in the case of the discovery of 'pulsars' (pulsating neutron stars) by researchers at the Cambridge astronomy laboratory in 1967, the scientists initially annotated the patterns shown on their printouts from the radio telescope as 'LGM1', 'LGM2' and so on – standing for 'Little Green Men'. Recognising that this was an unacceptable interpretation from the viewpoint of the scientific community (and one that would have finished their careers had they published it), they eventually settled on the notion that the patterns represented the signals from a type of star hitherto unknown to science. However, more than a decade later, there was still disagreement among astronomers as to what the signals really meant. As Woolgar notes, a scientific fact is simply a social construction or belief that scientists are able to persuade their colleagues to share – not necessarily a real thing 'out there'.

Marxism, feminism and postmodernism

Other critical perspectives such as Marxism and feminism see scientific knowledge as far from pure truth. Instead, they regard it as serving the interests of dominant groups – the ruling class in the case of Marxists, and men in the case of feminists. Thus, many advances in supposedly 'pure' science have been driven by the need of capitalism for certain types of knowledge. For example, theoretical work on ballistics (the study of the path followed by objects under the influence of gravity) was driven by the need to develop new weaponry. Similarly, biological ideas have been used to justify both male domination and colonial expansion. In this respect, science can be seen as a form of *ideology* (see below).

> Suggest three ways in which science, technology or medicine can be seen as serving the interests of men rather than women.

In a different sense, postmodernists also reject the knowledge-claims of science to have 'the truth'. In the view of Jean-Francois Lyotard (1984), for example, science is one of a number of *meta-narratives* or 'big stories' that falsely claim to possess the truth. Other meta-narratives include religion, Marxism and psychoanalysis. In Lyotard's view, science falsely claims to offer the truth about how the world works as a means of progress to a better society, whereas, in reality, he argues, science is just one more 'discourse' or way of thinking that is used to dominate people. Similarly, rather like Marxists, some postmodernists argue that science has become *technoscience*, simply serving capitalist interests by producing commodities for profit. (For more on postmodernism, see Chapter 4, Topic 5.)

Ideology

A basic definition of ideology is that it is a worldview or a set of ideas and values – in other words, a belief system. However, the term is very widely used in sociology and has taken on a number of related meanings. These often include negative aspects such as the following:

- Distorted, false or mistaken ideas about the world, or a partial, one-sided or biased view of reality.
- Ideas that conceal the interests of a particular group, or that legitimate (justify) their privileges.
- Ideas that prevent change by misleading people about the reality of the situation they are in or about their own true interests or position.
- A self-sustaining belief system that is irrational and closed to criticism.

Therefore, very often when someone uses the term ideology to describe a belief system, it means they regard it as factually and/or morally wrong.

There are a number of theories of ideology. We focus here on three of them.

Marxism and ideology

Marxism sees society as divided into two opposed classes: a minority capitalist ruling class who own the means of production and control the state, and a majority working class who are propertyless and therefore forced to sell their labour to the capitalists. The capitalist class take advantage of this, exploiting the workers' labour to produce profit. It is therefore in the workers' interests to overthrow capitalism by means of a socialist revolution and replace it with a classless communist society in which the means of production are collectively, not privately, owned and used to benefit society as a whole.

For this revolution to occur, the working class must first become conscious of their true position as exploited 'wage slaves' – they

must develop *class consciousness*. However, the ruling class control not only the means of material production (factories, land etc); they also control the means of production of ideas, through institutions such as education, the mass media and religion. These produce *ruling-class ideology* – ideas that legitimate or justify the status quo (the existing social set-up).

Ruling-class ideology includes ideas and beliefs such as the following:

- That equality will never work because it goes against 'human nature'.
- Victim blaming ideas about poverty, such as what Bowles and Gintis (1976) call 'the poor are dumb' theory of meritocracy: everyone has an equal chance in life, so the poor must be poor because they are stupid or lazy – not because of capitalism.
- Racist ideas about the inferiority of ethnic minorities, which divide black and white workers and make them easier to rule.
- Nationalist ideas that workers and capitalists of one nation have more in common than do the workers of the world.

Thus the dominant ideas are the ideas of the ruling class and they function to prevent change by creating a *false consciousness* among the workers. However, despite these ideological barriers, Marx believes that ultimately the working class will develop a true class consciousness and unite to overthrow capitalism.

Hegemony and revolution

This idea is developed further by Antonio Gramsci (1971). Gramsci refers to the ruling class' ideological domination of society as hegemony. He argues that the working-class can develop ideas that challenge ruling-class hegemony. This is because in capitalist society, workers

▲ *Vladimir Lenin. Marxism-Leninism was the official ideology of the former Soviet Union from 1917 to 1991.*

Activity

Are Marxists correct about ruling-class hegemony in Britain today? Do we all adhere to ruling-class ideology?

In small groups, design six questions that aim to test this proposition. Then carry out a brief survey, using questionnaires or interviews, with four or five adults. Ask if your respondents believe people's position in society depends on their own efforts, or that ability is more important than social class in education. You could also use some of the ideas in the section on Marxism and ideology, on poverty, victim-blaming, or nationalism. Collate your results and report to the class.

have a *dual consciousness* – a mixture of ruling-class ideology and ideas they develop from their own direct experience of exploitation and their struggles against it. It is therefore possible for the working class to develop class consciousness and overthrow capitalism. In Gramsci's view, this requires a political party of 'organic intellectuals' – that is, workers who through their anti-capitalist struggles have developed a class consciousness and can spread it throughout the working class. (For more on Marx and Gramsci, see Chapter 4, Topic 2.)

However, some critics argue that it is not the existence of a dominant ideology that keeps the workers in line and prevents attempts to overthrow capitalism. For example, Abercrombie et al (1980) argue that it is economic factors such as the fear of unemployment that keep workers from rebelling.

Karl Mannheim: ideology and utopia

Much of Karl Mannheim's work on ideology was done between the two World Wars (1918-39) – a time of intense political and social conflict – and this undoubtedly influenced his views.

Mannheim (1929) sees all belief systems as a partial or one-sided worldview. Their one-sidedness results from being the viewpoint of one particular group or class and its interests. This leads him to distinguish between two broad types of belief system or worldview:

- **Ideological thought** justifies keeping things as they are. It reflects the position and interests of privileged groups such as the capitalist class. These benefit from maintaining the status quo, so their belief system tends to be conservative and favours hierarchy.
- **Utopian thought** justifies social change. It reflects the position and interests of the underprivileged and offers a vision of how society could be organised differently. For example, the working class are disadvantaged by the status quo and may favour radical change to a classless society. Mannheim sees Marxism as an example of utopian thought.

Mannheim sees these worldviews as creations of groups of intellectuals who attach themselves to particular classes or social groups. For example, the role of Gramsci's organic intellectuals is to create a working-class or socialist worldview.

However, because these intellectuals represent the interests of particular groups, and not society as a whole, they only produce partial views of reality. The belief system of each class or group only gives us a partial truth about the world.

For Mannheim, this is a source of conflict in society. Different intellectuals, linked to different groups and classes, produce opposed and antagonistic ideas that justify the interests and claims of their group as against the others.

The free-floating intelligentsia

In Mannheim's view, the solution is therefore to 'detach' the intellectuals from the social groups they represent and create a non-aligned or *free-floating intelligentsia* standing above the conflict. Freed from representing the interests of this or that group, they would be able to synthesise elements of the different partial ideologies and utopias so as to arrive at a 'total' worldview that represented the interests of society as a whole.

However, many of the elements of different political ideologies are diametrically opposed to one another and it is hard to imagine how these could be synthesised. For example, how could Marxist ideas about the need to create a classless society be synthesised with the conservative idea that hierarchy is essential and beneficial?

Feminism and ideology

Marxists see class division as the basis of ideologies justifying inequality. By contrast, feminists see gender inequality as the fundamental division and patriarchal ideology as playing a key role in legitimating it.

Because gender difference is a feature of all societies, there exist many different ideologies to justify it. For example, Pauline Marks (1979) describes how ideas from science have been used to justify excluding women from education. She quotes 19th century (male) doctors, scientists and educationalists expressing the view that educating females would lead to the creation of 'a new race of puny and unfeminine' females and 'disqualify women from their true vocation', namely the nurturing of the next generation. Higher education would, it was claimed, result in women being unable to suckle infants.

In addition to patriarchal ideologies in science, those embodied in religious beliefs and practices have also been used to define women as inferior. There are numerous examples from a wide range of religions of the idea that women are ritually impure or unclean, particularly because of childbirth or menstruation. This has given rise to purification rituals such as 'churching' after a woman has given birth. In some Christian churches, a new mother may not receive communion until after she has been churched.

However, not all elements of religious belief systems subordinate women. For example, there is evidence that in the early history of the Middle East, Europe and Asia, before the emergence of the monotheistic patriarchal religions (Judaism, Christianity and Islam), matriarchal religions with female deities were widespread, with female priests and the celebration of fertility cults. Similarly, in Hinduism, goddesses have often been portrayed as mothers or creators of the universe.

For more activities on Ideology and science....

 Go to www.sociology.uk.net

Summary

Science has transformed society but also causes 'manufactured risks'. Popper sees science as an open belief system based on criticism and testing, while religion and witchcraft are self-reinforcing closed systems.

Others argue that science is a closed system that does not permit challenges to its paradigm. Interpretivists argue that scientific knowledge is socially constructed. Marxists and feminists see it as serving dominant interests. Postmodernists regard it as a meta-narrative.

Ideology is a one-sided worldview, legitimating a group's interests or creating false consciousness. Marxists see institutions such as religion and education producing ruling-class ideology and maintaining capitalist hegemony.

Mannheim distinguishes between ideological and utopian thought. He sees the need to create a free-floating intelligentsia. Feminists see patriarchal ideology in science and religion as legitimating gender inequality.

QuickCheck Questions

1 What does Popper mean by 'falsificationism'?

2 What are the four CUDOS norms?

3 In what sense is witchcraft among the Azande a closed belief system?

4 Why does the case of Dr Velikovsky suggest that science may be a closed belief system?

5 Explain Mannheim's distinction between 'ideological thought' and 'utopian thought'.

6 What is false consciousness?

7 According to Mannheim, why is there a need for a 'free-floating intelligentsia'?

8 What does Gramsci see as the two sides of workers' dual consciousness?

 Check your answers at www.sociology.uk.net

Examining ideology and science

Assess sociological explanations of science and ideology as belief systems.

(33 marks)

The examiner's advice

This question carries 15 AO1 marks (knowledge and understanding) and 18 AO2 marks (9 for interpretation and application, and 9 for analysis and evaluation). Start by explaining what is meant by a belief system and giving one or two examples. In dealing with science, begin with Popper's views of it as an open belief system based on falsificationism, and with Merton's CUDOS norms. Contrast this with belief systems such as witchcraft and religion, explaining why they are regarded as 'closed'. You can evaluate Popper by using Kuhn and interpretivist views of science, and the case of Velikovsky, to suggest that science too is a closed system. You can use Marxism and feminism to link science to ideology, since they see it as a belief system serving the interests of powerful groups. Examine different theories of ideology, such as Marxism, Mannheim and feminism, using appropriate examples (e.g. ideas that justify class or gender inequality).

Exam question and student answer

Examining beliefs in society

Item A   Sociologists are interested in the reasons why particular groups and individuals are attracted to different religious organisations. Max Weber and Ernst Troeltsch were among the first to identify different patterns of membership for churches, denominations, sects and cults. Troeltsch observed that churches are large, establishment-oriented organisations attracting mainly middle-class members. By contrast, members of religious sects are frequently at odds with the world and unwilling to compromise with the beliefs of wider society. For example, Weber argued that religious sects often provide the poor with a theodicy of disprivilege.

Questions

1 (a) Identify and briefly explain **three** differences between churches and cults.   (9 marks)

   (b) Using material from **Item A** and elsewhere, assess the view that religious sects always compromise with wider society and become denominations.   (18 marks)

2 Assess the view that religion can either be a conservative force or it can contribute to social change.   (33 marks)

The examiner's advice

Q 1(b) carries 6 AO1 marks (knowledge and understanding) and 12 AO2 marks (interpretation, application, analysis and evaluation).

Start by explaining Niebuhr's model of sect development, and why he sees sects as inevitably either becoming denominations or dying out. Make sure you use material from the Item, for example about the nature of sects' beliefs and the theodicy of disprivilege that they offer the poor. You can assess the view in the question by using Stark and Bainbridge, Wilson and Wallis on sect development. Consider some specific examples of sects that have and those that have not become denominations.

Q2 carries 15 AO1 marks and 18 AO2 marks (9 for interpretation and application, and 9 for analysis and evaluation).

You need to examine religion's role both as an agent of change and as a conservative force. You should distinguish between religion as supporting traditional values and its functions in maintaining the status quo. Use functionalist, Marxist and feminist views of how it does the latter and whose interests this serves, plus examples, and evaluate by contrasting these theories. You must also examine religion's role in change. Use Weber on the Protestant ethic, and other examples e.g. millenarian movements, liberation theology etc. You can evaluate Weber from a Marxist perspective in terms of the role of ideas versus material factors. Consider whether religion can be both a conservative force and a force for change at the same time, e.g. by looking at Iran or the New Christian Right.

Answer by Joe

The view that religion can be either a conservative force or that it can contribute to change definitely has strong arguments and evidence to support it. Marxists and functionalists both see it as a conservative force, and functionalists such as Durkheim see it as positive for society. Durkheim believes that religion encourages a collective consciousness to create consensus and social solidarity. It also teaches people what is right and wrong and is the source of our norms and values.

> A focused start, but needs more detail on Durkheim.

Another functionalist, Malinowski, also sees religion as a positive force in society. He believes that religious rituals (funerals, baptisms, weddings, bar mitzvahs etc) help to reduce stress and anxiety and allow people to cope better, which reduces tensions and makes society function more smoothly. He gives the example of Trobriand Islanders who use magic before undertaking dangerous activities such as fishing expeditions. Parsons also sees religion teaching people right and wrong through religious commandments, which lay down rules of conduct for people. He also sees religion explaining why misfortunes, sickness etc occur to individuals.

> Some relevant functions but needs to explain why these are conservative.

Answer by Joe

Marxists also see religion as conservative, but they take a more negative view than the functionalists. Marx saw religion as 'the opium of the people', meaning that it acted like a drug to control the masses. It did so by making them think that there would be a reward in heaven to look forward to and this encouraged them to not rebel. It also justified the ruling class' position in society.

> Accurate but brief. Needs concepts like alienation and ideology.

On the other hand, neo-Marxists believe religion can be a force of change or revolution. For example, in Iran there was a revolution against the liberalisation that had occurred in the 1960s and 70s. When the Iranian Revolution occurred in 1979, it turned the country back to traditional Islamic ways and values.

> Suitable example. Could say it was a 'conservative change' that turned back the clock.

Religion also played a big part in changes such as the struggle for civil rights for black people in the USA with the role of Dr Martin Luther King in leading the campaign. Likewise, in South Africa, Archbishop Desmond Tutu played a major part in opposing apartheid. These are important examples of religion as a force of change and of religion changing society, rather than society changing religion.

> Needs to say *how* the churches helped the civil rights/anti-apartheid movements.

However, religion can also fail in its attempt to achieve change. For example, the New Christian Right (NCR) in the USA failed to 'return America to God'. Despite trying to influence policies in a conservative direction, they failed to do so.

> Useful point of evaluation, but needs to explain *why* the NCR failed.

Feminists tend to oppose religion. They believe it reinforces patriarchy and excludes women from key roles, even though women are the majority of churchgoers. However, El Saadawi sees religion as positive for women in some ways, for example, with Muslim women who wear the veil. El Saadawi sees it as positive because it allows women to be judged for who they were and what they could do rather than by their appearance, and it also meant that they avoided the 'male gaze'.

> Not really focused properly on either 'conservative' or 'change' aspects.

The view that religion is either a conservative force or that it contributes to social change is therefore true, but it varies. In some countries or situations it brings about change but in others it can prevent it occurring. Also it is possible that it is neither, because there might be some situations where changes in society cause changes in religion rather than vice versa.

> Interesting final point but not developed earlier.

The examiner's comments

Overall, Joe has produced a reasonable answer to the question that shows a fairly wide range of knowledge both of religion as a conservative force and as a force for social change. He includes material on functionalists (Durkheim, Malinowski and Parsons), as well as on Marxists, neo-Marxists and feminists. He also refers to a range of examples – the Iranian Revolution, the civil rights and anti-apartheid movements, the American New Christian Right and the veiling of Muslim women. However, quite often his material could provide more detail. For example, he fails to refer to key Marxist concepts such as alienation, exploitation or ideology, while on Durkheim he mentions the collective consciousness but doesn't explain what it is or how it relates to religion (e.g. he could refer to shared rituals, totemism, and the distinction between sacred and profane). Similarly, the examples need further development – e.g. he could look at Bruce's views on how the black churches assisted the civil rights movement. The paragraph on feminism needs to be more clearly focused – Joe should identify the specific aspects that promote or prevent change. There is some limited evaluation (e.g. on the New Christian Right) but it needs to be spelled out more.

(21/33)

Crime and Deviance

CHAPTER 2

Introduction

The sociology of crime and deviance is about rules and rule breaking. For example, sociologists are interested in who breaks rules and why they do so, why some groups of people are more likely to be rule breakers – or more likely to be seen as rule breakers – and who makes and enforces the rules.

Some sociologists look for the causes of crime and deviance in the offender's social background, upbringing or social position. For example, inadequate socialisation or poverty might be responsible for some people being unable or unwilling to conform.

Other sociologists are more interested in the way society reacts to rule breaking, for example by labelling certain people as offenders and treating them differently. For example, members of less powerful groups are more likely to be labelled 'criminal'.

Still others are interested in how and why some acts – but not others – come to be defined as crimes in the first place. For example, those with power to make and enforce the law may criminalise threats to their interests. At the same time, the powerful may be able to avoid punishment for the crimes they commit. They may even be able to avoid defining the harm that they cause as 'crime' in the first place.

In this chapter, we shall examine some major sociological theories. We shall also look at a range of issues in relation to crime and deviance, such as class, gender and ethnicity; the media; globalisation, the environment and human rights; crime prevention, control and victims, and suicide.

The AQA Specification

The specification is the syllabus produced by the exam board, telling you what you have to study. The AQA specification for Crime and Deviance requires you to examine the following:

- Different theories of crime, deviance, social order and social control.
- The social distribution of crime and deviance by age, ethnicity, gender, locality and social class, including recent patterns and trends in crime.
- Globalisation and crime in contemporary society; the mass media and crime; green crime; human rights and state crimes.
- Crime control, prevention and punishment, victims, and the role of the criminal justice system and other agencies.
- The sociological study of suicide and its theoretical and methodological implications.
- The connections between sociological theory and methods and the study of crime and deviance.

Methods Link: researching crime and deviance

In the exam, you have to answer a question that requires you to apply sociological research methods to a particular issue in crime and deviance.

Look out for Methods Links boxes like this one throughout this chapter. These deal with the way sociologists apply different research methods to particular issues in crime and deviance.

The Methods Links boxes also give you a link into the Research Methods chapter, where you will find special *Methods in Context* sections. These show you how each method can be applied to a range of different topics in crime and deviance.

Read more about researching crime and deviance in Chapter 3, Topic 1.

Vigil after the July 2005 terrorist attack on London – uniting society in reaction to the offence?

Topic 1 Functionalist, strain and subcultural theories

Functionalism was the first major sociological approach to crime and deviance, growing out of the work of Emile Durkheim (1858-1917). Functionalists see society as a stable system based on shared values and crime and deviance disrupt this stability. Nevertheless, functionalists recognise that deviance is both inevitable and even to some degree functional for society.

Functionalists such as Robert K. Merton (1910-2003) are interested in the conditions that foster crime and deviance. For example, if individuals are blocked from achieving success by lawful means, they may solve the problem by resorting to illegal ones instead.

Functionalism has also had a major influence on subcultural theories of crime and deviance. Delinquent subcultures are groups whose norms, values or goals are to some degree opposed to those of mainstream society.

Many subcultural theories see the delinquency of subcultural groups as a solution to a problem. For example, it may provide them with an alternative means of achieving status after they have failed to do so at school. In other words, even if their delinquency is not functional for society at large, it may be 'functional' for the subculture's members, despite the risks of punishment that it carries.

Learning objectives

After studying this Topic, you should:

- Understand the functionalist perspective on crime, including the functions of crime.
- Understand the concept of strain and its role in explaining deviance.
- Be able to explain the differences between different strain and subcultural theories.
- Be able to evaluate functionalist, strain and subcultural theories of crime and deviance.

Durkheim's functionalist theory

Functionalism sees society as based on value consensus. That is, it sees members of society as sharing a common culture. A culture is a set of shared norms (rules), values, beliefs and goals. Sharing the same culture produces social solidarity – it binds individuals together, telling them what to strive for and how to conduct themselves.

Functionalists argue that in order to achieve this solidarity, society has two key mechanisms:

- **Socialisation** instils the shared culture into its members. This helps to ensure that individuals internalise the same norms and values, and that they feel it right to act in the ways that society requires.
- **Social control** mechanisms include rewards (or positive sanctions) for conformity, and punishments (negative sanctions) for deviance. These help to ensure that individuals behave in the way society expects.

The inevitability of crime

From the above account, we might expect that functionalists would regard crime and deviance as wholly negative – a threat to social order and even the very existence of society. For example, if each of us chose to 'do our own thing' – whether it be refusing to work, helping ourselves to others' possessions, or deciding to commit suicide – it is hard to imagine how society could continue to exist.

However, while functionalists see too much crime as destabilising society, they also see crime as inevitable and universal. Every known society has some level of crime and deviance – a crime-free society is a contradiction in terms. For Durkheim (1893), 'crime is normal… an integral part of all healthy societies'.

There are at least two reasons why crime and deviance are found in all societies:

- Not everyone is equally effectively socialised into the shared norms and values, so some individuals will be prone to deviate.
- Particularly in complex modern societies, there is a diversity of lifestyles and values. Different groups develop their own subcultures with distinctive norms and values, and what the members of the subculture regard as normal, mainstream culture may see as deviant.

Furthermore, in Durkheim's view, in modern societies there is a tendency towards *anomie* or normlessness – the rules governing behaviour become weaker and less clear-cut. This is because modern societies have a complex, specialised division of labour, which leads to individuals becoming increasingly different from one another. This diversity means that the shared culture or *collective conscience* is weakened, and this results in higher levels of crime and deviance. For example, Durkheim sees anomie as a major cause of suicide in modern societies (see Topic 10).

The positive functions of crime

For Durkheim, not only is crime inevitable; it also fulfils two important positive functions: boundary maintenance and adaptation.

Boundary maintenance

Crime produces a reaction from society, uniting its members in condemnation of the wrongdoer and reinforcing their commitment to the shared norms and values.

For Durkheim, this explains the function of punishment. This is not to make the wrongdoer suffer or mend his ways, nor is it to remove crime from society. In Durkheim's view, the purpose of punishment is to reaffirm society's shared rules and reinforce social solidarity.

This may be done through the rituals of the courtroom, which dramatise wrongdoing and publicly stigmatise the offender. This reaffirms the values of the law-abiding majority and discourages others from rule breaking. Similarly, Stanley Cohen (1972) has examined the important role played by the media in this 'dramatisation of evil'. In his view, media coverage of crime and deviance often creates 'folk devils' (see Topic 7).

Adaptation and change

For Durkheim, all change starts with an act of deviance. Individuals with new ideas, values and ways of living must not be completely stifled by the weight of social control. There must be some scope for them to challenge and change existing norms and values, and in the first instance this will inevitably appear as deviance. For example, the authorities often persecute religious visionaries who espouse a new 'message' or value-system. However, in the long run their values may give rise to a new culture and morality. If those with new ideas are suppressed, society will stagnate and be unable to make necessary adaptive changes.

Thus, for Durkheim, neither a very high nor a very low level of crime is desirable. Each of these signals some malfunctioning of the social system:

- Too much crime threatens to tear the bonds of society apart.

- Too little means that society is repressing and controlling its members too much, stifling individual freedom and preventing change.

> How might the '9/11' terrorist attacks on New York and Washington DC on 11 September 2001, and the reactions of the media to them, illustrate the positive functions of crime that Durkheim identifies?

Other functions of crime

Others have developed Durkheim's idea that deviance can have positive functions. For example, Kingsley Davis (1937; 1961) argues that prostitution acts as a *safety valve* for the release of men's sexual frustrations without threatening the monogamous nuclear family. Similarly, Ned Polsky (1967) argues that pornography safely 'channels' a variety of sexual desires away from alternatives such as adultery, which would pose a much greater threat to the family.

Albert Cohen identifies another function of deviance: a *warning* that an institution is not functioning properly. For example, high rates of truancy may tell us that there are problems with the education system and that policy-makers need to make appropriate changes to it.

Functionalists have also developed Durkheim's idea of the normality or inevitability of crime and deviance. For example, Kai Erikson (1966) argues that if crime and deviance perform positive social functions, then perhaps it means society is actually organised so as to promote deviance. He suggests that the true function of agencies of social control such as the police may actually be to sustain a certain level of crime rather than to rid society of it. The idea that agencies of social control actually produce rather than prevent crime has been developed further by the labelling theory of deviance (see Topic 2).

Societies sometimes also manage and regulate deviance rather than seeking to eliminate it entirely. For example, demonstrations, carnivals, festivals and student rag weeks all license misbehaviour that in other contexts might be punished. Similarly, the young may be given leeway to 'sow their wild oats'. From a functionalist perspective, this may be to offer them a way of coping with the strains of the transition from childhood to adulthood.

Functionalism is useful in showing the ways in which deviance is integral to society. It provides an important and interesting analysis that directs attention to the ways in which deviance can have hidden or latent functions for society – i.e. not everything that is bad, is bad for society!

Criticisms

For Durkheim, society requires a certain amount of deviance to function successfully, but he offers no way of knowing how much is the right amount.

Functionalists explain the existence of crime in terms of its supposed function – for example, to strengthen solidarity. But this doesn't mean society actually creates crime in *advance* with the *intention* of strengthening solidarity. In other words, just because crime does these things is not necessarily why it exists in the first place.

Functionalism looks at what functions crime serves for society as a whole and ignores how it might affect different groups or individuals within society. For example, seeing a murderer punished for his crime might be functional in reinforcing the feeling of solidarity among the rest of society, but it obviously isn't 'functional' for the victim. Functionalism misses this because it fails to ask the question, 'functional *for whom*?'

Crime doesn't always promote solidarity. It may have the opposite effect, leading to people becoming more isolated, for example forcing women to stay indoors for fear of attack. On the other hand, some crimes do reinforce collective sentiments, for example uniting the community in condemnation of a brutal attack.

Merton's strain theory

Strain theories argue that people engage in deviant behaviour when they are unable to achieve socially approved goals by legitimate means. For example, they may become frustrated and resort to criminal means of getting what they want, or lash out at others in anger, or find comfort for their failure in drug use.

The first strain theory was that developed by the functionalist Robert K. Merton (1938), who adapted Durkheim's concept of anomie to explain deviance. Merton's explanation combines two elements:

- **Structural factors** – society's unequal opportunity structure.
- **Cultural factors** – the strong emphasis on success goals and the weaker emphasis on using legitimate means to achieve them.

For Merton, deviance is the result of a strain between two things:

- The goals that a culture *encourages* individuals to achieve.
- What the institutional structure of society *allows* them to achieve legitimately.

For example, American culture values 'money success' – individual material wealth and the high status that goes with it.

The American Dream

Americans are expected to pursue this goal by legitimate means: self-discipline, study, educational qualifications, and hard work in a career. The ideology of the 'American Dream' tells Americans that their society is a meritocratic one where anyone who makes the effort can get ahead – there are opportunities for all.

However, the reality is different: many disadvantaged groups are denied opportunities to achieve legitimately. For example, poverty, inadequate schools and discrimination in the job market may block opportunities for many ethnic minorities and the lower classes.

The resulting strain between the cultural goal of money success and the lack of legitimate opportunities to achieve it produces frustration, and this in turn creates a pressure to resort to illegitimate means such as crime and deviance. Merton calls this pressure to deviate, *the strain to anomie*.

According to Merton, the pressure to deviate is further increased by the fact that American culture puts more emphasis on achieving success at any price than upon doing so by legitimate means. Winning the game becomes more important than playing by the rules.

To summarise, the goal creates a desire to succeed, and lack of opportunity creates a pressure to adopt illegitimate means, while the norms are not strong enough to prevent some from succumbing to this temptation.

Deviant adaptations to strain

Merton uses strain theory to explain some of the patterns of deviance found in society. He argues that an individual's position in the social structure affects the way they adapt or respond to the strain to anomie. Logically, there are five different types of adaptation, depending on whether an individual accepts, rejects or replaces approved cultural goals and the legitimate means of achieving them. These are summarised below and in Table 2A.

Conformity Individuals accept the culturally approved goals and strive to achieve them legitimately. This is most likely among middle-class individuals who have good opportunities to achieve, but Merton sees it as the typical response of most Americans.

Innovation Individuals accept the goal of money success but use 'new', illegitimate means such as theft or fraud to achieve it. As we have seen, those at the lower end of the class structure are under greatest pressure to innovate.

Ritualism Individuals give up on trying to achieve the goals, but have internalised the legitimate means and so they

▲*The Wall Street Crash, New York 1929. The mismatch between aspiration and reality was central to the development of Merton's strain theory in depression-era America.*

follow the rules for their own sake. This is typical of lower-middle class office workers in dead-end, routine jobs.

Retreatism Individuals reject both the goals and the legitimate means and become dropouts. Merton includes 'psychotics, outcasts, vagrants, tramps, chronic drunkards and drug addicts' as examples.

Rebellion Individuals reject the existing society's goals and means, but they replace them with new ones in a desire to bring about revolutionary change and create a new kind of society. Rebels include political radicals and counter-cultures such as hippies.

Evaluation of Merton

Merton shows how both normal and deviant behaviour can arise from the same mainstream goals. Both conformists and innovators are pursuing money success – one legitimately, the other illegitimately.

He explains the patterns shown in official crime statistics:

- Most crime is property crime, because American society values material wealth so highly.
- Lower-class crime rates are higher, because they have least opportunity to obtain wealth legitimately.

However, the theory is criticised on several grounds:

- It takes official crime statistics at face value. These over-represent working-class crime, so Merton sees crime as a mainly working-class phenomenon. It is also too deterministic: the working class experience the most strain, yet they don't all deviate.

- Marxists argue that it ignores the power of the ruling class to make and enforce the laws in ways that criminalise the poor but not the rich.
- It assumes there is a value consensus – that everyone strives for 'money success' – and ignores the possibility that some may not share this goal.
- It only accounts for utilitarian crime for monetary gain, and not crimes of violence, vandalism etc. It is also hard to see how it could account for state crimes such as genocide or torture.

Table 2A	Types of adaptation to the strain to anomie	
Response	Goal	Means
Conformity	+	+
Innovation	+	−
Ritualism	−	+
Retreatism	−	−
Rebellion	−/+	−/+

Key: (+) acceptance (−) rejection (−/+) rejection of mainstream values and replacement with new ones

- It explains how deviance results from *individuals* adapting to the strain to anomie but ignores the role of *group* deviance, such as delinquent subcultures.

1 Which of Merton's types of adaptation do these illustrate?

(a) Someone who drops out of conventional society;

(b) the man who works to support his family and chases promotion so he can buy a bigger house;

(c) a woman in a low paid job who wants a good standard of living, so she turns to fraud.

2 Which two types are missing? Give an example of each.

Synoptic link: core themes

Merton's theory shows how the interplay between **stratification** and **culture** produces deviance. Stratification blocks opportunities to achieve the goals prescribed by society's shared culture, leading to deviant adaptations such as innovation.

Subcultural strain theories

Subcultural strain theories see deviance as the product of a delinquent subculture with different values from those of mainstream society. They see subcultures as providing an alternative opportunity structure for those who are denied the chance to achieve by legitimate means – mainly those in the working class. These theories both criticise Merton's theory and seek to build on it.

A.K. Cohen: status frustration

Albert K. Cohen (1955) agrees with Merton that deviance is largely a lower-class phenomenon. It results from the inability of those in the lower classes to achieve mainstream success goals by legitimate means such as educational achievement. However, Cohen criticises Merton's explanation of deviance on two grounds:

1 Merton sees deviance as an *individual* response to strain, ignoring the fact that much deviance is committed in or by groups, especially among the young.

2 Merton focuses on *utilitarian* crime committed for material gain, such as theft or fraud. He largely ignores crimes such as assault and vandalism, which may have no economic motive.

Cohen focuses on deviance among working-class boys. He argues that they face anomie in the middle-class dominated school system. They suffer from cultural deprivation and lack the skills to achieve. Their inability to succeed in this middle-class world leaves them at the bottom of the official status hierarchy.

As a result of being unable to achieve status by legitimate means (education), the boys suffer *status frustration*. They face a problem of adjustment to the low status they are given by mainstream society. In Cohen's view, they resolve their frustration by rejecting mainstream middle-class values and they turn instead to other boys in the same situation, forming or joining a delinquent subculture.

Alternative status hierarchy

According to Cohen, the subculture's values are characterised by spite, malice, hostility and contempt for those outside it. The delinquent subculture inverts the values of mainstream society – turns them upside down. What society condemns, the subculture praises and vice versa. For example, mainstream society upholds regular school attendance and respect for property, whereas in the subculture, boys gain status from vandalising property and truanting.

For Cohen, the subculture's function is that it offers the boys an alternative status hierarchy in which they can achieve. Having failed in the legitimate opportunity structure, the boys create their own illegitimate opportunity structure in which they can win status from their peers through their delinquent actions.

One strength of Cohen's theory is that it offers an explanation of non-utilitarian deviance among the working class. Unlike Merton, whose concept of innovation only accounts for crime with a profit motive, Cohen's ideas of status frustration, value inversion and alternative status hierarchy help to explain non-economic delinquency such as vandalism, fighting and truancy.

However, like Merton, Cohen assumes that working-class boys start off sharing middle-class success goals, only to reject these when they fail. He ignores the possibility that they didn't share these goals in the first place and so never saw themselves as failures.

Activity Car theft – the offender's perspective

Go to www.sociology.uk.net

Cloward and Ohlin: three subcultures

Like Cohen, Richard Cloward and Lloyd Ohlin (1960) take Merton's ideas as their starting point. They agree that working-class youths are denied legitimate opportunities to achieve 'money success', and that their deviance stems from the way they respond to this situation.

Cloward and Ohlin note that not everyone in this situation adapts to it by turning to 'innovation' – utilitarian crimes such as theft. Different subcultures respond in different ways to the lack of legitimate opportunities. For example, the subculture described by Cohen resorts to violence and vandalism, not economic crime, while other subcultures centre on illegal drug use.

Cloward and Ohlin attempt to explain why these different subcultural responses occur. In their view, the key reason is not only unequal access to the *legitimate* opportunity structure, as Merton and Cohen recognise – but unequal access to *illegitimate* opportunity structures. For example, not everyone who fails by legitimate means, such as schooling, then has an equal chance of becoming a successful safecracker. Just like the apprentice plumber, the would-be safecracker needs the opportunity to learn their trade and the chance to practise it.

Drawing on the ideas of the Chicago School (see Box 2.1), Cloward and Ohlin argue that different neighbourhoods provide different illegitimate opportunities for young people to learn criminal skills and develop criminal careers. They identify three types of deviant subcultures that result:

Criminal subcultures provide youths with an apprenticeship for a career in utilitarian crime. They arise only in those neighbourhoods where there is a longstanding and stable local criminal culture with an established hierarchy of professional adult crime. This allows the young to associate with adult criminals, who can select those with the right aptitudes and abilities and provide them with training and role models as well as opportunities for employment on the criminal career ladder.

Conflict subcultures arise in areas of high population turnover. This results in high levels of social disorganisation and prevents a stable professional criminal network developing. Its absence means that the only illegitimate opportunities available are within loosely organised gangs. In these, violence provides a release for young men's frustration at their blocked opportunities, as well as an alternative source of status that they can earn by winning 'turf' (territory) from rival gangs. This subculture is closest to that described by Cohen.

Retreatist subcultures In any neighbourhood, not everyone who aspires to be a professional criminal or a gang leader actually succeeds – just as in the legitimate opportunity structure, not everyone gets a well-paid job. What becomes of these 'double failures' – those who fail in both the legitimate and the illegitimate opportunity structures? According to Cloward and Ohlin, many turn to a retreatist subculture based on illegal drug use.

> What similarities and differences are there between Cloward and Ohlin's retreatist subculture and Merton's idea of a retreatist adaptation?

Box 2.1 The Chicago School

The University of Chicago sociology department was the first of its kind to be established in the United States, in 1892, and it remained extremely influential, notably in the study of crime and deviance. Among its contributions were:

Cultural transmission theory (Clifford Shaw and Henry McKay, 1942). They noted how some neighbourhoods develop a criminal tradition or culture that is transmitted from generation to generation, while other neighbourhoods remain relatively crime-free over the same period.

Differential association theory (Edwin Sutherland, 1939). Sutherland was interested in the processes by which people become deviant. He argued that deviance was behaviour learned through social interaction with others who are deviant. This includes learning both criminal values and criminal skills.

Social disorganisation theory (Robert Park and Ernest Burgess, 1925). They argued that deviance is the product of social disorganisation. Changes such as rapid population turnover and migration create instability, disrupting family and community structures. These become unable to exercise social control over individuals, resulting in deviance.

Evaluation of Cloward and Ohlin

They agree with Merton and Cohen that most crime is working-class, thus ignoring crimes of the wealthy. Similarly, their theory is too deterministic and over-predicts the extent of working-class crime. Like Merton and Cohen, they too ignore the wider power structure, including who makes and enforces the law.

While they agree with Cohen that delinquent subcultures are the source of much deviance, unlike Cohen they provide an explanation for different *types* of working-class deviance in terms of different subcultures.

However, they draw the boundaries too sharply between the different types. For example, Nigel South (1997) found that the drug trade is a mixture of both 'disorganised' crime, like the conflict subculture, and professional 'mafia' style criminal subcultures. Likewise, some supposedly 'retreatist' users are also professional dealers making a living from this utilitarian crime. In Cloward and Ohlin's theory, it would not be possible to belong to more than one of these subcultures simultaneously.

Strain theories such as Cloward and Ohlin's and Cohen's have been called *reactive* theories of subculture. This is because they explain deviant subcultures as forming in reaction to the failure to achieve mainstream goals. Such theories have been criticised for assuming that everyone starts off sharing the same mainstream success goal. By contrast, Walter B. Miller (1962) argues that the lower class has its own *independent* subculture separate from mainstream culture, with its own values. This subculture does not value success in the first place, so its members are not frustrated by failure.

Although Miller agrees deviance is widespread in the lower class, he argues that this arises out of an attempt to achieve their *own* goals, not mainstream ones. He calls these goals 'focal concerns'.

David Matza (1964) claims that most delinquents are not strongly committed to their subculture, as strain theories suggest, but merely drift in and out of delinquency.

Whatever its strengths and limitations, strain theory has had a major influence both on later theories of crime and on government policy. For example, Merton's ideas play an important part in left realist explanations of crime (see Topic 4). Similarly, in the 1960s, Cloward and Ohlin's work helped form the basis of President Johnson's 'war on poverty' policies, while Ohlin was appointed to help develop crime policy in the USA under President Kennedy.

Recent strain theories

Recent strain theorists have argued that young people may pursue a variety of goals other than money success. These include popularity with peers, autonomy from adults, or the desire of some young males to be treated like 'real men'. Like earlier strain theorists, they argue that failure to achieve these goals may result in delinquency. They also argue that middle-class juveniles too may have problems achieving such goals, thus offering an explanation for middle-class delinquency.

Institutional anomie theory

Like Merton's theory, Messner and Rosenfeld's (2001) institutional anomie theory focuses on the American Dream. They argue that its obsession with individual money success and its 'winner-takes-all' mentality, exert 'pressures towards crime by encouraging an anomic [normless] cultural environment in which people are encouraged to adopt an 'anything goes' mentality' in the pursuit of wealth.

In America (and arguably the UK), economic goals are valued above all others, and this undermines other institutions. For example, schools become ever more geared to preparing young people for the labour market at the expense of inculcating values such as respect for others, and this makes it harder for schools to exert social control over pupils. Messner and Rosenfeld conclude that in societies based on free-market capitalism and lacking adequate welfare provision, such as the USA, high rates of crime are inevitable.

Activity

Miller argues that the lower class have six distinctive focal concerns: (i) *excitement*; (ii) *smartness* – outsmarting others; (iii) *trouble*; (iv) *fatalism* – 'whatever will be, will be'; (v) *toughness*; (vi) *autonomy* – independence; not being pushed around.

In pairs, decide which focal concerns these illustrate: (a) cheeking authority; (b) gambling; (c) fighting; (d) drug-taking; (e) poor school achievement; (f) vandalism; (g) reckless driving; (h) macho attitudes; (j) joyriding; (k) 'conning' people.

Methods Link: using official statistics

If Merton is correct in claiming that blocked access to legitimate opportunities such as paid work leads to crime, then we might expect to find that unemployment and crime are linked. When Tarling (1982) analysed official statistics for England and Wales, he found that the crime rate and the unemployment rate rose steadily together from 1950 to 1980 – findings that are compatible with Merton's theory.

However, showing that the two are correlated does not prove that one causes the other. Also, we have no way of knowing if the individuals who are unemployed are the same people who are committing the crimes.

Read more about official statistics and researching crime and deviance in **Methods in Context**, Chapter 3, Topic 6.

Downes and Hansen (2006) offer evidence for this view. In a survey of crime rates and welfare spending in 18 countries, they found societies that spent more on welfare had lower rates of imprisonment. This backs up Messner and Rosenfeld's claim that societies that protect the poor from the worst excesses of the free market have less crime.

Similarly, Savelsberg (1995) applies strain theory to post-communist societies in Eastern Europe, which saw a rapid rise in crime after the fall of communism in 1989. He attributes this rise to communism's collective values being replaced by new western capitalist goals of individual 'money success'.

For more activities on Functionalist, strain and subcultural theories...

 Go to www.sociology.uk.net

Summary

For functionalists, society is based on value consensus, which deviance threatens, but it also performs positive functions such as reinforcing solidarity and adapting to change. Strain theories argue that deviance occurs when people cannot achieve society's goals by legitimate means. Merton argues that this produces a 'strain to anomie' that may result in innovation, ritualism, retreatism or rebellion. Subcultural theories see much deviance as a collective rather than individual response. A.K. Cohen argues that subcultural deviance results from status frustration and takes a non-utilitarian form. Cloward and Ohlin see three different deviant subcultures (criminal, conflict and retreatist) arising from differences in access to illegitimate opportunity structures. Recent strain theories argue that capitalist economies generate greater strain to crime.

QuickCheck Questions

1   Identify two ways in which crime and deviance may have positive functions.

2   What is meant by 'status frustration'?

3   Explain the difference between ritualism and retreatism.

4   In what sense is Merton's theory deterministic?

5   What is meant by non-utilitarian crime?

6   Why does Durkheim regard crime as inevitable in all societies?

7   Explain the difference between goals and means.

8   In Cloward and Ohlin's view, why are there different types of deviant subculture?

9   Identify two features of American society that Messner and Rosenfeld claim produce high crime rates.

 Check your answers at www.sociology.uk.net

Examining functionalist, strain and subcultural theories

Examine the role of access to opportunity structures in causing crime and deviance.

(12 marks)

The examiner's advice

This question carries 6 AO1 marks (knowledge and understanding) and 6 AO2 marks (interpretation, application, analysis and evaluation).

Start by outlining Merton's 'strain to anomie' theory and especially his idea that deviance results from unequal access to legitimate opportunities (education and career). Identify the different forms of deviance that result (innovation, ritualism, retreatism and rebellion).

Go on to examine subcultural theorists, using Cohen to evaluate Merton. Link Cohen's idea of status frustration to blocked opportunities and explain how subcultures provide an illegitimate opportunity structure. Use Cloward and Ohlin to show that access to illegitimate opportunity structures is also unequal, and how this gives rise to three different subcultures (criminal, conflict and retreatist). Include evaluation, for example of the functionalist assumptions of Merton and Cohen (do all deviants start out sharing mainstream goals?) or their failure to explain other types of crime (e.g. corporate).

SKATEBOARDING IS NOT A CRIME

Topic 2 Labelling theory

The theories we have looked at so far have all been described as 'problem takers'. That is, they take the official definitions of crime and criminals for granted. Crime is simply activity that breaks the criminal law, and criminals are the people who behave in this way. They also take it for granted that the official crime statistics are a reasonably accurate picture of the real patterns of crime and who commits it. The main aim of these theories is to discover the causes of crime (for example as a reaction to blocked opportunities or other external forces) and to provide solutions to the 'problem of crime'.

Labelling theorists take a very different approach. Instead of seeking the causes of criminal behaviour, they ask how and why some people and actions come to be labelled as criminal or deviant, and what effects this has on those who are so labelled.

Similarly, instead of accepting official statistics as a valid picture of crime, they regard them not as hard facts, but as social constructs. This reflects the origins of labelling theory in *social constructionist* perspectives such as interactionism and phenomenology. These take the view that individuals construct the social world through their face-to-face interactions.

For labelling theorists, this constructionist view applies also to crime and deviance. Crime is the product of interactions between suspects and police, for example, rather than the result of wider external social forces such as blocked opportunity structures.

Learning objectives

After studying this Topic, you should:

- Understand why labelling theorists regard crime and deviance as socially constructed.
- Understand the labelling process and its consequences for those who are labelled.
- Be able to evaluate the strengths and limitations of labelling theory in explaining crime and deviance.

The social construction of crime

Rather than simply taking the definition of crime for granted, labelling theorists are interested in how and why certain acts come to be defined or labelled as criminal in the first place. They argue that no act is inherently criminal or deviant *in itself*, in all situations and at all times. Instead, it only comes to be so when others label it as such. In other words, it is not the nature of the act that makes it deviant, but the nature of society's *reaction* to the act.

In this view, therefore, deviance is in the eye of the beholder. As Howard Becker (1963) puts it:

'Social groups create deviance by creating the rules whose infraction [breaking] constitutes deviance, and by applying those rules to particular people and labelling them as outsiders.'

For Becker, therefore, a deviant is simply someone to whom the label has been successfully applied, and deviant behaviour is simply behaviour that people so label.

This leads labelling theorists to look at how and why rules and laws get made. They are particularly interested in the role of what Becker calls *moral entrepreneurs*. These are people who lead a moral 'crusade' to change the law in the belief that it will benefit those to whom it is applied. However, Becker argues that this new law invariably has two effects:

- The creation of a new group of 'outsiders' – outlaws or deviants who break the new rule.
- The creation or expansion of a social control agency (such as the police) to enforce the rule and impose labels on offenders.

For example, Platt (1969) argues that the idea of 'juvenile delinquency' was originally created as a result of a campaign by upper-class Victorian moral entrepreneurs, aimed at protecting young people at risk. This established 'juveniles' as a separate category of offender with their own courts, and it enabled the state to extend its powers beyond criminal offences involving the young, into so-called 'status offences' such as truancy and sexual promiscuity.

Becker notes that social control agencies themselves may also campaign for a change in the law to increase their own power. For example, the US Federal Bureau of Narcotics successfully campaigned for the passing of the Marijuana Tax Act in 1937 to outlaw marijuana use. Supposedly, this was on the grounds of its ill effects on young people, but Becker argues it was really to extend the Bureau's sphere

of influence. Thus it is not the inherent harmfulness of a particular behaviour that leads to new laws being created, but rather the efforts of powerful individuals and groups to redefine that behaviour as unacceptable.

Who gets labelled?

Not everyone who commits an offence is punished for it. Whether a person is arrested, charged and convicted depends on factors such as:

- Their interactions with agencies of social control such as the police and courts.
- Their appearance, background and personal biography.
- The situation and circumstances of the offence.

This leads labelling theorists to look at how the laws are applied and enforced. Their studies show that agencies of social control are more likely to label certain groups of people as deviant or criminal.

For example, Piliavin and Briar (1964) found that police decisions to arrest a youth were mainly based on physical cues (such as manner and dress), from which they made judgments about the youth's character. Officers' decisions were also influenced by the suspect's gender, class and ethnicity, as well as by time and place. For example, those stopped late at night in high crime areas ran a greater risk of arrest. Similarly, a study of anti-social behaviour orders found they were disproportionately used against ethnic minorities.

Cicourel – the negotiation of justice

Officers' decisions to arrest are influenced by their stereotypes about offenders. For example, Aaron Cicourel (1968) found that officers' *typifications* – their commonsense theories or stereotypes of what the typical delinquent is like – led them to concentrate on certain 'types'. This resulted in law enforcement showing a class bias, in that working-class areas and people fitted the police typifications most closely. In turn, this led police to patrol working-class areas more intensively, resulting in more arrests and confirming their stereotypes.

Cicourel also found that other agents of social control within the criminal justice system reinforced this bias. For example, probation officers held the commonsense theory that juvenile delinquency was caused by broken homes, poverty and lax parenting. Therefore they tended to see youths from such backgrounds as likely to offend in future and were less likely to support non-custodial sentences for them.

Why do you think truancy and promiscuity among the young are called status offences? What aspects of their status might such behaviour offend against?

In Cicourel's view, justice is not fixed but negotiable. For example, when a middle-class youth was arrested, he was less likely to be charged. This was partly because his background did not fit the idea of the police's 'typical delinquent', and partly because his parents were more likely to be able to negotiate successfully on his behalf, convincing the control agencies that he was sorry, that they

▲ *Public labelling - convicted of burglary in Dougherty, Georgia, USA, this woman was sentenced to stand outside the courthouse wearing the sign.*

would monitor him and ensure he stayed out of trouble in future, etc. As a result, typically, he was 'counselled, warned and released' rather than prosecuted.

Topic versus resource

Cicourel's study has implications for the use we make of official crime statistics recorded by the police. He argues that these statistics do not give us a valid picture of the patterns of crime and cannot be used as a *resource* – that is, as facts about crime.

Instead, we should treat them as a *topic* for sociologists to investigate. That is, we must not take crime statistics at face value; instead, we should investigate the processes that created them. This will shed light on the activities of the control agencies and how they process and label certain types of people as criminal.

Methods Link: using observation

Cicourel used both participant and non-participant observation in his four-year study of juvenile justice. As an observer, he went out on patrol with the police and sat in on courtroom proceedings. As a participant, he took on the role of unpaid probation officer. He argues that first hand experience enabled him to uncover the taken-for-granted and often unconscious 'typifications' and assumptions of control agents in a way that other methods, such as interviews, would not.

Ultimately, however, we have no way of knowing for sure whether Cicourel's methods enabled him to produce valid interpretations of what he observed.

Read more about observation and researching crime and deviance in *Methods in Context*, Chapter 3, Topic 5.

The effects of labelling

Labelling theorists are interested in the effects of labelling upon those who are labelled. They claim that, by labelling certain people as criminal or deviant, society actually encourages them to become more so.

Primary and secondary deviance

Edwin Lemert (1951) distinguishes between primary and secondary deviance. Primary deviance refers to deviant acts that have not been publicly labelled. Lemert argues that it is pointless to seek the causes of primary deviance, since it is

so widespread that it is unlikely to have a single cause, and in any case it is often trivial, e.g. fare dodging, and mostly goes uncaught. These acts are not part of an organised deviant way of life, so offenders can easily rationalise them away, for example as a 'moment of madness'. They have little significance for the individual's status or self-concept. In short, primary deviants don't generally see themselves as deviant.

However, some deviance *is* labelled. Secondary deviance is the result of societal reaction – that is, of labelling. Being caught and publicly labelled as a criminal can involve being stigmatised, shamed, humiliated, shunned or excluded from normal society. Once an individual is labelled, others may come to see him only in terms of the label. This becomes his *master status* or controlling identity, overriding all others.

In the eyes of the world, he is no longer a colleague, father or neighbour; he is now a thief, junkie or paedophile – in short, an outsider.

This can provoke a crisis for the individual's *self-concept* or sense of identity. One way to resolve this crisis is for the individual to accept the deviant label and see themselves as the world sees them. In turn, this may lead to a *self-fulfilling prophecy*, in which the individual acts out or lives up to their deviant label, thereby becoming what the label says they are. Lemert refers to the further deviance that results from acting out the label as *secondary deviance*.

Synoptic links: theory & core themes

The labelling approach derives from interactionism, a **theory** that sees social reality as constructed through interactions, for example between police and suspect. Labelling theory sees deviant **identities** as partly created by such interactions with control agents.

Secondary deviance is likely to provoke further hostile reactions from society and reinforce the deviant's 'outsider' status. Again, this in turn may lead to more deviance and a *deviant career*. For example, the ex-convict finds it hard to go straight because no one will employ him, so he seeks out other outsiders for support. This may involve joining a *deviant subculture* that offers deviant career opportunities and role models, rewards deviant behaviour, and confirms his deviant identity.

Jock Young (1971) uses the concepts of secondary deviance and deviant career in his study of hippy marijuana users in Notting Hill. Initially, drugs were peripheral to the hippies' lifestyle – an example of primary deviance. However, persecution and labelling by the *control culture* (the police) led the hippies increasingly to see themselves as outsiders. They retreated into closed groups where they began to develop a deviant subculture, wearing longer hair and more 'way out' clothes. Drug use became a central activity, inviting further attention from the police and creating a self-fulfilling prophecy.

The work of Lemert and Young illustrates the idea that it is not the act itself, but the hostile societal reaction by the social audience, that creates serious deviance. Ironically, therefore, the social control processes that are meant to produce law-abiding behaviour may in fact produce the very opposite.

However, although a deviant career is a common outcome of labelling, labelling theorists are quick to point out that it is not inevitable. As Downes and Rock (2003) note, we cannot predict whether someone who has been labelled will follow a deviant career, because they are always free to choose not to deviate further.

Suggest two ways in which a person might try to resist a label.

Deviance amplification

The deviance amplification spiral is a term labelling theorists use to describe a process in which the attempt to control deviance leads to an increase in the level of deviance. This leads to greater attempts to control it and, in turn, this produces yet higher levels of deviance. More and more control produces more and more deviance, in an escalating spiral or snowballing feedback process, as in the case of the hippies described by Young.

Labelling theorists have applied the concept of the deviance amplification spiral to various forms of group behaviour. An example of this is Stanley Cohen's (1972) *Folk Devils and Moral Panics*, a study of the societal reaction to the 'mods and rockers' disturbances involving groups of youths at the seaside resort of Clacton at Easter in 1964.

Press exaggeration and distorted reporting of the events began a moral panic, with growing public concern and with moral entrepreneurs calling for a 'crackdown'. The police responded by arresting more youths, while the courts imposed harsher penalties. This seemed to confirm the truth of the original media reaction and provoked more public concern, in an upward spiral of deviance amplification. At the same time, the demonising of the mods and rockers as 'folk devils' caused their further marginalisation as 'outsiders', resulting in more deviant behaviour on their part. (See Topic 7 for more about the media's role in moral panics.)

We can see the deviance amplification spiral as similar to Lemert's idea of secondary deviance. In both cases, the societal reaction to an initial deviant act leads not to successful control of the deviance, but to further deviance, which in turn leads to a greater reaction and so on. It also illustrates an important difference between labelling theory and functionalist theories of deviance. As Lemert (1967) puts it, these theories:

'rest heavily on the idea that deviance leads to social control. I have come to believe that the reverse idea, i.e. social control leads to deviance, is equally tenable and the potentially richer premise for studying deviants in modern society'.

Labelling and criminal justice policy

Recent studies have shown how increases in the attempt to control and punish young offenders are having the opposite effect. For example, in the USA, Triplett (2000) notes an increasing tendency to see young offenders as evil and to be less tolerant of minor deviance. The criminal justice system has re-labelled status offences such as truancy as more serious offences, resulting in much harsher sentences. As predicted by Lemert's theory of secondary deviance, this has resulted in an increase rather than a decrease in offending, with levels of violence among the young rising. De Haan (2000) notes a similar outcome in Holland as a result of the increasing stigmatisation of young offenders.

These findings indicate that labelling theory has important policy implications. They add weight to the argument that negative labelling pushes offenders towards a deviant career. Therefore logically, to reduce deviance, we should make and enforce fewer rules for people to break.

For example, by decriminalising soft drugs, we might reduce the number of people with criminal convictions and hence the risk of secondary deviance. Similarly, labelling theory implies that we should avoid publicly 'naming and shaming' offenders, since this is likely to create a perception of them as evil outsiders and, by excluding them from mainstream society, push them into further deviance.

Reintegrative shaming

Most labelling theorists see labelling as having negative effects. However, John Braithwaite (1989) identifies a more positive role for the labelling process. He distinguishes between two types of shaming (negative labelling):

- **Disintegrative shaming**, where not only the crime, but also the criminal, is labelled as bad and the offender is excluded from society.
- **Reintegrative shaming**, by contrast labels the act but not the actor – as if to say, 'he has done a bad thing', rather than 'he is a bad person'.

The policy of reintegrative shaming avoids stigmatising the offender as evil while at the same time making them aware of the negative impact of their actions upon others,

and then encourages others to forgive them and accept them back into society. This makes it easier for both offender and community to separate the offender from the offence and re-admit the wrongdoer back into mainstream society. At the same time, this avoids pushing them into secondary deviance. Braithwaite argues that crime rates tend to be lower in societies where reintegrative rather than disintegrative shaming is the dominant way of dealing with offenders.

Evaluation of labelling theory

Labelling theory shows that the law is not a fixed set of rules to be taken for granted, but something whose construction we need to explain. It shows that the law is often enforced in discriminatory ways, and that crime statistics are more a record of the activities of control agents than of criminals. It also shows that society's attempts to control deviance can backfire and create more deviance, not less.

However, it is criticised on several grounds:

- It tends to be deterministic, implying that once someone is labelled, a deviant career is inevitable.
- Its emphasis on the negative effects of labelling gives the offender a kind of victim status. Realist sociologists argue that this ignores the real victims of crime.
- By assuming that offenders are passive victims of labelling, it ignores the fact that individuals may actively choose deviance.
- It fails to explain why people commit primary deviance in the first place, before they are labelled.
- It implies that without labelling, deviance would not exist. This leads to the strange conclusion that someone who commits a crime but is not labelled has not deviated. It also implies that deviants are unaware that they are deviant until labelled. Yet most are well aware that they are going against social norms.
- It was the first theory to recognise the role of power in creating deviance, but it fails to analyse the source of this power. For example, Marxists argue that it fails to examine the links between the labelling process and capitalism. As a result, it focuses on 'middle range officials' such as policemen who apply the labels, rather than on the capitalist class who make the rules in the first place. It also fails to explain the origin of the labels, or why they are applied to certain groups, such as the working class.

For more activities on Labelling theory...

 Go to www.sociology.uk.net

Summary

For labelling theory, an act only becomes deviant when labelled as such by others, through societal reaction. Not every offender is labelled, and labelling theory is interested in how the laws are selectively enforced against some groups by the agencies of social control. This means that official statistics are invalid: they only tell us about the types of people the control agencies have labelled, not the real patterns of crime.

Labelling theory is interested in the effects of labelling. It may cause the label to become the individual's master status. A deviance amplification spiral may result, in which increased control leads to increased deviance. Labelling theory has implications for criminal justice policies, suggesting we should avoid labelling individuals unnecessarily to avoid a self-fulfilling prophecy and deviant career. Labelling theory is criticised, for example for determinism and for failing to explain primary deviance and the origin of the labels.

QuickCheck Questions

1. Explain what is meant by the phrase, 'deviance is in the eye of the beholder'.

2. True or false? Secondary deviance is defined as less important acts of deviance.

3. Identify three agencies of social control.

4. Lemert argues that 'social control leads to deviance'. What does he mean?

5. What is a self-fulfilling prophecy?

6. According to Marxists, what does labelling theory fail to tell us about power?

7. What is determinism? Why do critics accuse labelling theory of being deterministic?

 Check your answers at www.sociology.uk.net

Examining labelling theory

Item A According to a study of anti-social behaviour orders (ASBOs) by the Youth Justice Board (2006), some parents and magistrates thought they were a 'diploma in deviance' and they believed that youths saw them as a 'badge of honour'. Many youths did not regard the threat of custody as a deterrent to breaching their order.

The study also found that the orders were disproportionately used against ethnic minorities: blacks and Asians were about two and a half times more likely than whites to be given an ASBO.

The study found that it was not uncommon for young people to openly flout the prohibitions placed on them by the order. Figures show that by 2008 two-thirds had breached their orders.

Essay Using material from **Item A** and elsewhere, assess the view that crime and deviance are the product of labelling processes.

(21 marks)

The examiner's advice

This question carries 9 AO1 marks (knowledge and understanding) and 12 AO2 marks (interpretation, application, analysis and evaluation).

Start with an account of labelling theory, identifying and explaining its key concepts, such as the social construction of deviance, selective enforcement, the role of control agencies' stereotyping or typifications, negotiation of justice, primary and secondary deviance, the self-fulfilling prophecy, master status, deviant career and the deviance amplification spiral.

Use studies to illustrate some of these concepts. Make sure that you also use the Item – e.g. you could link labelling to the 'badge of honour', the ethnic patterns to police stereotyping of ethnic minorities, and the high rate of breaching of orders to secondary deviance and the self-fulfilling prophecy. You should evaluate the view, e.g. by considering other causes of crime (e.g. strain, subcultures, poverty) and by examining some of the criticisms made of labelling theory.

Topic 3 Marxist theories

In the previous Topic, we saw that labelling theory develops two important points about crime and deviance:

- The law is enforced by control agents in ways that criminalise the powerless.
- Labelling can have negative effects on those who are labelled, resulting in deviance amplification.

Marxists agree that the law is enforced against powerless groups and that labelling often results in further deviance. However, they criticise labelling theory for failing to examine the wider social and economic structure in which law making, enforcement and offending take place.

Unlike functionalists, who hold the other main structural view of society, Marxists do not see the law as the reflection of a value consensus among society's members. Instead, they see law and crime as arising out of the structure of *capitalism*. In their view, the inequality of wealth and power that underpins capitalist society, and the conflicts to which this inequality gives rise, are the key to understanding the law, crime and deviance.

In this Topic, we first examine the traditional Marxist view of crime and the law. We then go on to consider the neo-Marxist approach, which seeks to integrate important features of labelling theory into a Marxist analysis of society.

Learning objectives

After studying this Topic, you should:

- Understand why Marxists see crime as inevitable in capitalist society.
- Understand traditional and neo-Marxist approaches to crime and deviance, and the similarities and differences between them.
- Be able to evaluate the strengths and limitations of Marxist and neo-Marxist approaches to crime and deviance.

Traditional Marxism

Traditional Marxism sees capitalist society as divided into two classes: the ruling capitalist class (or bourgeoisie) who own the means of production, and the working class (or proletariat), whose alienated labour the bourgeoisie exploit to produce profit.

Marxism is a structural theory. It sees society as a structure in which the economic base (the capitalist economy) determines the shape of the superstructure, which is made up of all the other social institutions, including the state, the law and the criminal justice system. Their function is to serve ruling-class interests and maintain the capitalist economy.

For traditional Marxists, the structure of capitalist society explains crime. Their view of crime has three main elements:

- **Criminogenic capitalism**
- **The state and law making**
- **Ideological functions of crime and law**

Criminogenic capitalism

For Marxists, crime is inevitable in capitalism because capitalism is *criminogenic* – by its very nature it causes crime.

Capitalism is based on the exploitation of the working class – that is, on using them as a means to an end (profit), whatever the human cost of doing so. It is therefore particularly damaging to the working class and this may give rise to crime:

- Poverty may mean that crime is the only way the working class can survive.
- Crime may be the only way they can obtain the consumer goods encouraged by capitalist advertising, resulting in utilitarian crimes such as theft.
- Alienation and lack of control over their lives may lead to frustration and aggression, resulting in non-utilitarian crimes such as violence and vandalism.

However, crime is not confined to the working class. Capitalism is a 'dog eat dog' system of ruthless competition among capitalists, while the profit motive encourages a mentality of greed and self-interest. The need to win at all costs or go out of business, along with the desire for self-enrichment, encourages capitalists to commit white-collar and corporate crimes such as tax evasion and breaches of health and safety laws.

Thus, as David Gordon (1976) argues, crime is a rational response to the capitalist system and hence it is found in all social classes – even though the official statistics make it appear to be a largely working-class phenomenon.

The state and law making

Unlike functionalists, who see the law as reflecting the value consensus and representing the interests of society as a whole, Marxists see law making and law enforcement as only serving the interests of the capitalist class. For example, William Chambliss (1975) argues that laws to protect private property are the cornerstone of the capitalist economy.

Chambliss illustrates this with the case of the introduction of English law into Britain's East African colonies. Britain's economic interests lay in the colonies' tea, coffee and other plantations, which needed a plentiful supply of local labour.

At the time, the local economy was not a money economy and so, to force the reluctant African population to work for them, the British introduced a tax payable in cash, non-payment of which was a punishable criminal offence. Since cash to pay the tax could only be earned by working on the plantations, the law served the economic interests of the capitalist plantation owners.

The ruling class also have the power to prevent the introduction of laws that would threaten their interests. Thus, for example, there are few laws that seriously challenge the unequal distribution of wealth. Laureen Snider (1993) argues that the capitalist state is reluctant to pass laws that regulate the activities of businesses or threaten their profitability.

▲ *Does capitalist consumerism encourage utilitarian crime?*

▲ *Bernard Madoff on his way to court. Madoff was convicted of the biggest investment fraud in history.*

Selective enforcement

Marxists argue that although all classes commit crime, when it comes to the application of the law by the criminal justice system, there is selective enforcement. While powerless groups such as the working class and ethnic minorities are criminalised, the police and courts tend to ignore the crimes of the powerful.

For example, Jeffrey Reiman's (2001) book *The Rich Get Richer and the Poor Get Prison* shows that the more likely a crime is to be committed by higher-class people, the less likely it is to be treated as a criminal offence. There is a disproportionately high rate of prosecutions for the kinds of 'street crimes' that poor people typically commit, such as burglary and assault. Yet with the kinds of crimes committed mostly by the higher classes, such as health and safety violations and serious tax evasion, the criminal justice system takes a more forgiving view.

1 Suggest two examples of 'dog eat dog' situations produced by capitalism.

2 Identify three more examples each of typical street crimes and typical higher-class crimes.

Ideological functions of crime and law

The law, crime and criminals also perform an ideological function for capitalism. Laws are occasionally passed that appear to be for the benefit of the working class rather than capitalism, such as workplace health and safety laws.

However, Frank Pearce (1976) argues that such laws often benefit the ruling class too – for example, by keeping workers fit for work. By giving capitalism a 'caring' face, such laws also create false consciousness among the workers.

In any case, such laws are not rigorously enforced. For example, W.G. Carson (1971), in a sample of 200 firms, found that they had all broken health and safety laws at least once, yet only a tiny proportion (1.5%) of these cases resulted in prosecution.

Furthermore, because the state enforces the law selectively, crime appears to be largely a working-class phenomenon. This divides the working class by encouraging workers to blame the criminals in their midst for their problems, rather than capitalism.

The media and some criminologists also contribute by portraying criminals as disturbed individuals, thereby concealing the fact that it is the nature of capitalism that makes people criminals.

Synoptic link: core themes

The concepts of **stratification** and **power** are central to the Marxist theory of crime. The ruling class's control of the state gives it the power to make and enforce the law to its own advantage, protecting its privileged position in the class structure by criminalising any threat to its property.

Evaluation of traditional Marxism

Traditional Marxism offers a useful explanation of the relationship between crime and capitalist society. It shows the link between law making and enforcement and the interests of the capitalist class. By doing so, it puts into a wider structural context the insights of labelling theory regarding the selective enforcement of the law.

The traditional Marxist view has also influenced recent approaches to the study of the crimes of the powerful. For example, Gary Slapper and Steve Tombs (1999) argue that corporate crime is under-policed and rarely prosecuted or punished severely. This encourages companies to use crime as a means of making profit, often at the expense of their workers or consumers.

However, the traditional Marxist approach is criticised on several grounds:

- It largely ignores the relationship between crime and important non-class inequalities such as ethnicity and gender.
- It is too deterministic and over-predicts the amount of crime in the working class: not all poor people commit crime, despite the pressures of poverty.
- Not all capitalist societies have high crime rates; for example, Japan and Switzerland have much less crime than the USA. The homicide rate in Japan is 1.0 per 100,000 and in Switzerland 1.2. By contrast, in the United States, the rate is about five times higher at 5.6 homicides per 100,000 of the population. However, Marxists point out that societies with little or no state welfare provision, such as the USA, tend to have higher crime rates.
- The criminal justice system does sometimes act against the interests of the capitalist class. For example, prosecutions for corporate crime do occur. (However, Marxists argue that such occasional prosecutions perform an ideological function in making the system seem impartial.)
- Left realists argue that Marxism focuses largely on the crimes of the powerful and ignores intra-class crimes (where both the criminals and victims are working class) such as burglary and 'mugging', which cause great harm to victims.

Activity

Use the Internet to research the story of the American company Enron, one of the world's leading energy corporations until it went bankrupt in 2001 amid financial scandal.

1 Find out what happened and who suffered harm as a result of the company's collapse.

2 Who was to blame and how, if at all, were they punished?

3 How might Marxists use this case as an example?

Neo-Marxism: critical criminology

Neo-Marxists are sociologists who have been influenced by many of the ideas put forward by traditional Marxism, but they combine these with ideas from other approaches such as labelling theory.

The most important neo-Marxist contribution to our understanding of crime and deviance has been *The New Criminology*, by Ian Taylor, Paul Walton and Jock Young (1973).

Taylor et al agree with traditional Marxists that:

- Capitalist society is based on exploitation and class conflict and characterised by extreme inequalities of wealth and power. Understanding this is the key to understanding crime.
- The state makes and enforces laws in the interests of the capitalist class and criminalises members of the working class.
- Capitalism should be replaced by a classless society. This would greatly reduce the extent of crime or even rid society of crime entirely.

However, the views of Taylor et al also differ significantly from those of traditional Marxists. Much of their book is a critique of existing theories of crime and deviance, including both Marxist and non-Marxist approaches, and they describe their approach as *critical criminology*.

Anti-determinism

Taylor et al argue that traditional Marxism is *deterministic*. For example, it sees workers as driven to commit crime out of economic necessity. They reject this explanation, along with theories that claim crime is caused by other external factors such as anomie, subcultures or labelling, or by biological and psychological factors.

Instead, Taylor et al take a more *voluntaristic* view (voluntarism is the idea that we have free will – the opposite of determinism). They see crime as meaningful action and a conscious choice by the actor. In particular, they argue that crime often has a political motive, for example to redistribute wealth from the rich to the poor. Criminals are not passive puppets whose behaviour is shaped by the nature of capitalism: they are deliberately striving to change society.

This emphasis on freedom is also evident in their view of what kind of society we should be aiming to create. Taylor et al share with traditional Marxism the goal of a classless socialist society and social equality, but they also emphasise the importance of individual *liberty and diversity*. They argue that individuals should not be labelled deviant just because they are different, as in capitalist society – instead, they should be free to live their lives as they wish.

Activity

1 What do sociologists mean by anomie?

2 Why might anomie be seen as a deterministic explanation of crime?

A fully social theory of deviance

Taylor et al aim to create what they call a 'fully social theory of deviance' – a comprehensive understanding of crime and deviance that would help to change society for the better. This theory would have two main sources:

- Traditional Marxist ideas about the unequal distribution of wealth and who has the power to make and enforce the law.
- Ideas from interactionism and labelling theory about the meaning of the deviant act for the actor, societal reactions to it, and the effects of the deviant label on the individual.

In their view, a complete theory of deviance needs to unite six aspects:

1 **The wider origins of the deviant act** in the unequal distribution of wealth and power in capitalist society.

2 **The immediate origins of the deviant act** – the particular context in which the individual decides to commit the act.

3 **The act itself** and its meaning for the actor – e.g. was it a form of rebellion against capitalism?

4 **The immediate origins of social reaction** – the reactions of those around the deviant, such as police, family and community, to discovering the deviance.

5 **The wider origins of social reaction** in the structure of capitalist society – especially the issue of who has the power to define actions as deviant and to label others, and why some acts are treated more harshly than others.

6 **The effects of labelling** on the deviant's future actions – e.g. why does labelling lead to deviance amplification in some cases but not in others?

> Taylor et al's sixth point comes from labelling theory. Which of the other five points owe most to labelling theory and which to Marxism?

For Taylor et al, these six aspects are interrelated and need to be understood together as part of a single unified theory.

Evaluation of critical criminology

Taylor et al's approach is criticised on several grounds:

Feminists criticise it for being 'gender blind', focusing excessively on male criminality and at the expense of female criminality.

Left realists make two related criticisms.

- Firstly, critical criminology romanticises working-class criminals as 'Robin Hoods' who are fighting capitalism by re-distributing wealth from the rich to the poor. However, in reality these criminals simply prey on the poor.
- Secondly, Taylor et al do not take such crime seriously and they ignore its effects on working-class victims.

Roger Hopkins Burke (2005) argues that critical criminology is both too general to *explain* crime and too idealistic to be useful in *tackling* crime. However, Stuart Hall et al (1978) have applied Taylor et al's approach to explain the moral panic over mugging in the 1970s (see Topic 6).

Taylor, Walton and Young have all changed their views since *The New Criminology* was published. However, Walton (1998) and Young (1998) defend some aspects of the book's approach. They argue that:

- In calling for greater tolerance of diversity in behaviour, the book combated the 'correctionalist bias' in most existing theories – the assumption that sociology's role is simply to find ways of correcting deviant behaviour.
- The book laid some of the foundations for later radical approaches that seek to establish a more just society, such as left realist and feminist theories.

> *For more activities on* Marxist theories...
>
> Go to www.sociology.uk.net

Summary

Traditional Marxists see crime as inevitable in capitalist society because it breeds poverty, competition and greed. All classes commit crime, but because the ruling class control the state, they make and enforce laws in their own interests, criminalising the working class while escaping punishment for their own corporate crimes.

The law also performs an ideological function by giving capitalism a caring face. Traditional Marxism is criticised for ignoring non-class inequalities that affect crime and for determinism (over-predicting working-class crime).

Neo-Marxism or critical criminology (CC) is less deterministic. It sees crime as a conscious meaningful choice often with a political motive – a rebellion against capitalism. CC combines elements of Marxism and labelling theory in a 'fully social theory' of deviance. It has been criticised by left realists as 'left idealism' that ignores the real harm crime does to working-class people.

QuickCheck Questions

1 Explain what is meant by 'criminogenic'.

2 Identify three ways in which capitalism can be said to be criminogenic.

3 How does the study of East Africa by Chambliss support the Marxist view of crime?

4 Identify two ways in which crime and the law perform an ideological function for capitalism.

5 Explain the difference between deterministic and voluntaristic views of behaviour.

6 Explain why critical criminology has been accused of being too idealistic to be useful in tackling crime.

7 What is meant by the 'correctionalist bias' in some theories of crime?

 Check your answers at www.sociology.uk.net

Examining Marxist theories

Examine some of the ways in which Marxists explain crime.

(12 marks)

The examiner's advice

This question carries 6 AO1 marks (knowledge and understanding) and 6 AO2 marks (interpretation, application, analysis and evaluation).

You should start with the idea that Marxists see capitalism as criminogenic because it creates the conditions for crime through exploitation and competition. You need to examine both traditional Marxist and neo-Marxist approaches. The key ideas of traditional Marxists include the power of the ruling class to make and selectively enforce the law, the ideological functions of the law, the way criminalisation is used to divide the working class, and the idea that capitalism creates crime in all classes but largely only convicts the working class.

You should evaluate this approach e.g. in terms of its determinism, and from this go on to consider neo-Marxism (critical criminology). Key ideas to cover include the idea of crime as a political choice or act of rebellion, and the incorporation of ideas from labelling theory. To evaluate it, you could use left realist criticisms that it ignores the reality of crime.

Street crime is up again.

Topic 4 Realist theories

Realist approaches to crime differ markedly from the theories examined in the last two Topics. Approaches such as labelling theory and critical criminology regard crime as socially constructed – the result of the way police and others label, stereotype and criminalise members of certain groups.

By contrast, realists see crime as a real problem to be tackled, and not just a social construction created by the control agencies. In addition, all realists:

- Argue that there has been a significant rise in the crime rate – especially in street crime, burglary and assault.
- Are concerned about the widespread fear of crime and about the impact of crime on its victims.
- Argue that other theories have failed to offer realistic solutions to the problem of crime and they propose what they regard as practical policies to reduce it.

Realist approaches emerged in the 1970s and 1980s in the political context of a shift to the right in politics. On both sides of the Atlantic, New Right conservative governments came to power, led by Margaret Thatcher in the UK and Ronald Reagan in the USA.

These governments favoured rolling back the welfare state together with a strong commitment to law and order. They favoured a 'get tough' stance on crime, with increased use of prison (and in the USA, the death penalty) and a 'short, sharp shock' approach to dealing with young offenders.

We can divide realist approaches along political lines:

- **Right realists** share the New Right or neo-conservative political outlook and support the policies described above.
- **Left realists** are socialists and favour quite different policies for reducing crime.

Learning objectives

After studying this Topic, you should:

- Understand the difference between realist and other approaches to crime.
- Know the main features of right and left realist approaches to crime and understand their political context and the similarities and differences between them.
- Be able to evaluate the strengths and limitations of right and left realist approaches to crime.

Right realism

Right realism sees crime, especially street crime, as a real and growing problem that destroys communities, undermines social cohesion and threatens society's work ethic. The right realist approach to crime has been very influential in the UK, the USA and elsewhere. For example, its main theorist, James Q. Wilson, was special adviser on crime to President Reagan, and it has provided the justification for widely adopted policies such as 'zero tolerance' of street crime and disorder.

Right realist views on crime correspond closely with those of neo-conservative governments during the 1970s and 1980s. For example, policy-makers argued that 'nothing works' – criminologists had produced many theories of crime, but no workable solutions to curb the rising crime rate.

This led to a shift in official thinking, away from the search for the causes of crime and towards a search for practical crime control measures. It also dovetailed with the US and UK governments' tough stance towards offenders and their view that the best way to reduce crime was through control and punishment, rather than rehabilitating offenders or tackling causes of crime such as poverty.

Right realism reflects this political climate. Right realists criticise other theories for failing to offer any practical solutions to the problem of rising crime. They also regard theories such as labelling and critical criminology as too sympathetic to the criminal and too hostile to the forces of law and order. Right realists are less concerned to understand the causes of crime and more concerned to provide what they see as realistic solutions. However, although their main emphasis is on practical crime reduction strategies, they do in fact offer an explanation of the causes of crime.

The causes of crime

Right realists reject the idea put forward by Marxists and others that structural or economic factors such as poverty and inequality are the cause of crime. For example, against the Marxist view, they point out that the old tend to be poor yet they have a very low crime rate. For right realists, crime is the product of three factors: individual biological differences, inadequate socialisation and the underclass, and rational choice to offend.

Biological differences

James Q. Wilson and Richard J. Herrnstein (1985) put forward a biosocial theory of criminal behaviour. In their view, crime is caused by a combination of biological and social factors.

Biological differences between individuals make some people innately more strongly predisposed to commit crime than others. For example, personality traits such as aggressiveness, extroversion, risk taking and low impulse control put some people at greater risk of offending. Similarly, Herrnstein and Murray (1994) argue that the main cause of crime is low intelligence, which they also see as biologically determined.

Socialisation and the underclass

However, while biology may increase the chance of an individual offending, effective socialisation decreases the risk, since it involves learning self-control and internalising moral values of right and wrong. For right realists, the best agency of socialisation is the nuclear family.

The right realist Charles Murray (1990) argues that the crime rate is increasing because of a growing underclass or 'new rabble' who are defined by their deviant behaviour and who fail to socialise their children properly. According to Murray, the underclass is growing in both the USA and the UK as a result of welfare dependency.

What Murray calls the welfare state's 'generous revolution' since the 1960s allows increasing numbers of people to become dependent on the state. It has led to the decline of marriage and the growth of lone parent families, because women and children can live off benefits. This also means that men no longer have to take responsibility for supporting their families, so they no longer need to work.

However, lone mothers are ineffective socialisation agents, especially for boys. Absent fathers mean that boys lack paternal discipline and appropriate male role models. As a result, young males turn to other, often delinquent, role models on the street and gain status through crime rather than supporting their families through a steady job. As Bennett, Dilulio and Walters (1996) argue, crime is the result of:

'growing up surrounded by deviant, delinquent, and criminal adults in a practically perfect criminogenic environment – that is, [one] that seems almost consciously designed to produce vicious, predatory unrepentant street criminals'.

For Murray, the underclass is not only a source of crime. Its very existence threatens society's cohesion by undermining the values of hard work and personal responsibility.

Rational choice theory

An important element in the right realist view of crime comes from rational choice theory, which assumes that individuals have free will and the power of reason. Rational choice theorists such as Ron Clarke (1980) argue that the decision to commit crime is a *choice* based on a rational calculation of the likely consequences. If the perceived rewards of crime outweigh the perceived costs of crime, or if the rewards of crime appear to be greater than those of non-criminal behaviour, then people will be more likely to offend.

Right realists argue that currently the perceived costs of crime are low and this is why the crime rate has increased. For example, in their view, there is often little risk of being caught and punishments are in any case lenient. As Wilson (1975) puts it:

'If the supply and value of legitimate opportunities (i.e. jobs) was declining at the very time that the cost of illegitimate opportunities (i.e. fines and jail terms) was also declining, a rational teenager might well conclude that it made more sense to steal cars than to wash them.'

A similar idea is contained in Marcus Felson's (1998) routine activity theory. Felson argues that for a crime to occur, there must be a motivated offender, a suitable target (a victim and/or property) and the absence of a 'capable guardian' (such as a policeman or neighbour). Offenders are assumed to act rationally, so that the presence of a guardian is likely to deter them from offending. Felson argues that informal guardians such as those provided by the community are more effective than formal ones such as police. For example, in the chaos immediately following Hurricane Andrew in Florida in 1982, patrols by local citizens to protect property during the absence of police prevented looting, and crime rates actually went down during this period (Cromwell et al 1995).

Tackling crime

Right realists do not believe it is fruitful to try to deal with the causes of crime (such as biological and socialisation differences) since these cannot easily be changed. Instead they seek to devise practical measures to make crime less attractive. Their main focus is on control, containment and punishment of offenders rather than eliminating the underlying causes of their offending or rehabilitating them. For example:

- Wilson and Kelling's (1982) article *Broken Windows* argues that it is essential to maintain the orderly character of neighbourhoods to prevent crime taking hold. Any sign of deterioration, such as graffiti or vandalism, must be dealt with immediately.
- They advocate a 'zero tolerance' policy towards

Methods Link: using field experiments

Crime prevention policies often take the form of field experiments. For example, Poyner and Webb (1997) discovered that there was a high rate of thefts of purses from women's shopping bags in the Bull Ring in Birmingham, a large retail area of over 1,000 stalls in four markets. Most of the thefts occurred in the two markets where stalls were most densely packed. When one of the markets was redesigned, the stalls were set further apart and lighting was improved. Thefts fell by nearly 70%.

Experiments seek to identify cause and effect relationships and the results suggest that the design changes caused a drop in crime. However, in field experiments it is not possible to control all the variables and it may be that something else caused the reduction. For example, there was also a decline in the amount of trade done in the market at the time.

Read more about experiments and researching crime and deviance in **Methods in Context**, Chapter 3, Topic 2.

undesirable behaviour such as prostitution, begging and drunkenness. The role of the police should be to focus on controlling the streets so that law-abiding citizens feel safe.

- Crime prevention policies should reduce the rewards and increase the costs of crime to the offender, for example by 'target hardening', greater use of prison and ensuring punishments follow soon after the offence to maximise their deterrent effect. For more on target hardening and zero tolerance, see Topic 9.

Criticisms of right realism

Right realism is criticised both for its explanation of crime and for its solutions.

- Right realism ignores wider structural causes such as poverty.
- It overstates offenders' rationality and how far they make cost-benefit calculations before committing a crime. While it may explain some utilitarian crime, it may not explain much violent crime.
- Its view that criminals are rational actors freely *choosing* crime conflicts with its view that their behaviour is *determined* by their biology and socialisation. It also over-emphasises biological factors. For example, according to Lilly et al (2002), IQ differences account for less than 3% of differences in offending.
- It is preoccupied with petty street crime and ignores corporate crime, which may be more costly and harmful to the public.
- Advocating a zero tolerance policy gives police free rein to discriminate against ethnic minority youth, the homeless etc. It also results in displacement of crime to

other areas. Jones (1998) notes that right realist policies in the USA failed to prevent the crime rate rising.

- It over-emphasises control of disorder, rather than tackling underlying causes of neighbourhood decline such as lack of investment.

1 What do right realist views of crime have in common with conservative political views?

2 Why might right realism be better at explaining utilitarian crime than violent crime?

3 What is meant by 'displacement'?

Left realism

Left realism has developed since the 1980s; its key figure is the former critical criminologist, Jock Young. It developed as a response to two main factors:

- The need to take the rising crime rate seriously and to produce practical solutions.
- The influence of right realism on government policy.

Like Marxists, left realists see society as an unequal capitalist one. However, unlike Marxists, left realists are reformist rather than revolutionary socialists: they believe in gradual social change rather than the violent overthrow of capitalism as the way to achieve greater equality. They believe we need to develop explanations of crime that will lead to practical strategies for reducing it in the here and now, rather than waiting for a revolution and a classless socialist utopia to abolish crime.

Taking crime seriously

The central idea behind left realism is that crime is a real problem, and one that particularly affects the disadvantaged groups who are its main victims. They accuse other sociologists of not taking crime seriously:

- **Traditional Marxists** have concentrated on crimes of the powerful, such as corporate crime. Left realists agree that this is important, but they argue that it neglects working-class crime and its effects.
- **Neo-Marxists** romanticise working-class criminals as latter-day Robin Hoods, stealing from the rich as an act of political resistance to capitalism. Left realists point out that in fact working-class criminals mostly victimise other working-class people, not the rich.
- **Labelling theorists** see working-class criminals as the victims of discriminatory labelling by social control agents. Left realists argue that this approach neglects the real victims – working-class people who suffer at the hands of criminals.

Part of the left realists' project of taking crime seriously is to recognise that there has been a real increase in crime rates since the 1950s, especially working-class crime. Young (1997) argues that this has led to an *aetiological crisis* – a crisis in explanation – for theories of crime. For

example, critical criminology and labelling theory tend to deny that the increase is real. Instead, they argue that it is just the result of an increase in the reporting of crime, or an increased tendency to label the poor. In other words, the increase in the crime statistics is just a social construction, not a reality.

However, left realists argue that the increase is too great to be explained in this way and is a real one: more people are reporting crime because more people are actually falling victim to crime. As evidence, they cite the findings of victim surveys such as the nationwide British Crime Survey and many local surveys.

▲ *Realists argue that vulnerable groups such as the old are at greater risk of being victims.*

Taking crime seriously also involves recognising who is most affected by crime. Local victim surveys show that the scale of the problem is even greater than that shown by official statistics. They also show that disadvantaged groups have a greater risk of becoming victims, especially of burglary, street crime and violence. For example, unskilled workers are twice as likely to be burgled as other people.

Understandably, therefore, disadvantaged groups have a greater fear of crime and it has a greater effect on their lives. For example, fear of attack prevents women from going out at night. At the same time, these groups are less likely to report crimes against them and the police are often reluctant to deal with crimes such as domestic violence, rape or racist attacks.

The causes of crime

The second part of the left realist project to take crime seriously involves explaining the rise in crime. Lea and Young (1984) identify three related causes of crime: relative deprivation, subculture and marginalisation.

Relative deprivation

For Lea and Young, crime has its roots in deprivation. However, deprivation in itself is not directly responsible for crime. For example, poverty was rife in the 1930s, yet crime rates were low. By contrast, since the 1950s living standards have risen, but so too has the crime rate.

Left realists draw on W.G. Runciman's (1966) concept of relative deprivation to explain crime. This refers to how deprived someone feels in relation to others, or compared with their own expectations. This can lead to crime when people feel resentment that others unfairly have more than them and resort to crime to obtain what they feel they are entitled to.

Lea and Young explain the paradox that today's society is both more prosperous and more crime-ridden. Although people are better off, they are now more aware of relative deprivation due to the media and advertising, which raise everyone's expectations for material possessions. Those who cannot afford them may resort to crime instead.

However, relative deprivation does not necessarily lead to crime. For Young (1999), 'the lethal combination is relative deprivation and individualism'. Individualism is a concern with the self and one's own individual rights, rather than those of the group. It causes crime by encouraging the pursuit of self-interest at the expense of others.

For left realists, increasing individualism is causing the disintegration of families and communities by undermining the values of mutual support and selflessness on which they are based. This weakens the informal controls that such groups exercise over individuals, creating a spiral of increasing anti-social behaviour, aggression and crime.

Subculture

The left realist view of criminal subcultures owes much to Merton, A.K. Cohen and Cloward and Ohlin discussed in Topic 1, especially their concepts of blocked opportunity and subcultures as a group's reaction to the failure to achieve mainstream goals. Thus for left realists, a subculture is a group's collective solution to the problem of relative deprivation.

However, different groups may produce different subcultural solutions to this problem. For example, some may turn to crime to close the 'deprivation gap', while others may find that religion offers them spiritual comfort and what Weber calls a 'theodicy of disprivilege' – an explanation for their situation. Such religious subcultures may encourage respectability and conformity. Within the African Caribbean community in Bristol, Ken Pryce (1979) identified a variety of subcultures or lifestyles, including hustlers (pleasure-seeking and criminal), Rastafarians, 'saints' (members of Pentecostal churches) and working-class 'respectables'.

For left realists, criminal subcultures still subscribe to the values and goals of mainstream society, such as materialism and consumerism. For example, as Young (2002) notes, there are ghettos in the USA where there is 'full immersion in the American Dream: a culture hooked on Gucci, BMW, Nikes'. However, opportunities to achieve these goals legitimately are blocked, so they resort to street crime instead.

Marginalisation

Marginalised groups lack both clear goals and organisations to represent their interests. Groups such as workers have clear goals (such as better pay and conditions) and organisations (such as trade unions) to put pressure on employers and politicians. As such, they have no need to resort to violence to achieve their goals.

By contrast, unemployed youth are marginalised. They have no organisation to represent them and no clear goals, just a sense of resentment and frustration. Being powerless to use political means to improve their position, they express their frustration through criminal means such as violence and rioting.

Synoptic links: theory & core themes

Right realism has links with New Right **theory**, for example through Murray's view of a criminal underclass created through welfare dependency. Left realism has links with conflict theories, especially the idea that class and gender **stratification** means that the poor and women are the main victims of crime.

Late modernity, exclusion and crime

Young (2002) argues that we are now living in the stage of late modern society, where instability, insecurity and exclusion make the problem of crime worse. He contrasts today's society (since the 1970s) with the period preceding it, arguing that the 1950s and 1960s represented the 'Golden Age' of modern capitalist society. This was a period of stability, security and social inclusion, with full employment, a fairly comprehensive welfare state, low divorce rates and relatively strong communities. There was general consensus about right and wrong, and lower crime rates.

Since the 1970s, instability, insecurity and exclusion have increased. De-industrialisation and the loss of unskilled manual jobs have increased unemployment and poverty, especially for young people and ethnic minorities, while many jobs are now insecure, short term or low paid. These changes have destabilised family and community life and contributed to rising divorce rates, as have New Right government policies designed to hold back welfare spending on the poor. All this has contributed to increased marginalisation and exclusion of those at the bottom.

Meanwhile, greater inequality between rich and poor and the spread of free market values encouraging individualism have increased the sense of relative deprivation. Young also notes the growing contrast between *cultural inclusion* and *economic exclusion* as a source of relative deprivation:

- Media-saturated late modern society promotes cultural inclusion: even the poor have access to the media's materialistic, consumerist cultural messages.
- Similarly, there is a greater emphasis on leisure, which stresses personal consumption and immediate gratification and leads to higher expectations for the 'good life'.
- At the same time, despite the ideology of meritocracy, the poor are systematically excluded from opportunities to gain the 'glittering prizes of a wealthy society'.

Young's contrast between cultural inclusion and economic exclusion is very similar to Merton's notion of anomie – that society creates crime by setting cultural goals (such as material wealth), while denying people the opportunity to achieve them by legitimate means (such as decent jobs).

A further trend in late modernity is for relative deprivation to become generalised throughout society rather than being confined to those at the bottom. There is widespread resentment at the undeservedly high rewards that some receive, whether top-flight footballers or fat-cat bankers. There is also 'relative deprivation downwards', where the middle class, who have to be hardworking and disciplined to succeed in an increasingly competitive work environment, resent the stereotypical underclass as idle, irresponsible and hedonistic, living off undeserved state handouts.

The result of the trend towards exclusion is that the amount and types of crime are changing in late modern society. Firstly, crime is more widespread and is found increasingly throughout the social structure, not just at the bottom. It is also nastier, with an increase in 'hate crimes' – often the result of relative deprivation downwards, as in the case of racist attacks against asylum seekers, for example.

Reactions to crime by the public and the state are also changing. With late modernity, society becomes more diverse and there is less public consensus on right and wrong, so that the boundary between acceptable and unacceptable behaviour becomes blurred. At the same time, informal controls become less effective as families and communities disintegrate. This, along with rising crime rates, makes the public more intolerant and leads to demands for harsher formal controls by the state and increased criminalisation of unacceptable behaviour. Late modern society is thus a high-crime society with a low tolerance for crime.

Activity

Left realists incorporate ideas from other perspectives into their approach. Using the section on left realism, identify which perspective – functionalist, labelling, Marxist or postmodernist – would be most likely to support each of the following left realist ideas: (1) relative deprivation; (2) economic change and de-industrialisation; (3) the importance of societal values and goals; (4) lack of consensus on right and wrong; (5) stereotyping of the underclass; (6) lack of a political voice; (7) some groups feeling marginalised; (8) increased individualism; (9) expression of frustration through criminal behaviour; (10) exclusion from economic opportunity; (11) government policies increase marginalisation and poverty; (12) crime is a real problem affecting many people.

Tackling crime

The final part of the left realists' project is to devise solutions to the problem of crime. They argue that we must both improve policing and control, and deal with the deeper structural causes of crime.

Policing and control

Kinsey, Lea and Young (1986) argue that police clear-up rates are too low to act as a deterrent to crime and that police spend too little time actually investigating crime. They argue that the public must become more involved in determining the police's priorities and style of policing.

The police depend on the public to provide them with information about crimes (90% of crimes known to the police are reported to them by the public). However, the police are losing public support, especially in the inner cities and among ethnic minorities and the young. As a result, the flow of information dries up and police come to rely instead on *military policing*, such as 'swamping' an area and using random stop and search tactics. This alienates communities, who see the police as victimising local youth, and results in a vicious circle: locals no longer trust the police and don't provide them with information, so the police resort to military policing, and so on.

Left realists argue that policing must therefore be made more accountable to local communities and must deal with local concerns. Routine beat patrols are ineffective in detecting or preventing crime, and stop and search tactics cause conflict. The police need to improve their relationship with local communities by spending more time investigating crime, changing their priorities (they over-police minor drug crime, but under-police racist attacks and domestic violence) and involving the public in making policing policy.

Left realists also argue that crime control cannot be left to the police alone – *a multi-agency approach* is needed. This would involve agencies such as local councils' social services, housing departments, schools and leisure services, as well as voluntary organisations and victim support, as well as the public.

> Suggest possible roles for agencies such as social services, housing and leisure departments, and schools in reducing crime.

Tackling the structural causes

However, left realists do not see improved policing and control as the main solution. In their view, the causes of crime lie in the unequal structure of society and major structural changes are needed if we want to reduce levels of offending. For example, Young argues that we must deal with inequality of opportunity and the unfairness of rewards, tackle discrimination, provide decent jobs for everyone, and improve housing and community facilities. We must also become more tolerant of diversity and cease stereotyping whole groups of people as criminal.

Left realism and government policy

Left realists have had more influence on government policy than most theorists of crime. In particular, their views have strong similarities with the New Labour government's stance of being 'tough on crime, tough on the causes of crime'.

For example, New Labour's firmer approach to the policing of hate crimes, sexual assaults and domestic violence, along with the introduction of anti-social behaviour orders (ASBOs), echoes left realist concerns to protect vulnerable groups from crime and low-level disorder. Similarly, New Labour's New Deal for unemployed youth and their anti-truanting policies attempt to reverse the exclusion of those young people who are at greatest risk of offending.

However, Young regards many of these policies as nostalgic and doomed attempts to recreate the conditions of the 'Golden Age' of the 1950s. For example, the New Deal does not lead to secure, permanent jobs, while ASBOs will not recreate good neighbourliness and a sense of community. Young also criticises the record of governments, including New Labour. He argues that they have largely only addressed the symptoms, such as anti-social behaviour – they have been tougher on crime than on tackling its underlying causes, such as the insecurity, inequality and discrimination that produce relative deprivation and exclusion.

Evaluation of left realism

Left realism has succeeded in drawing attention to the reality of street crime and its effects, especially on victims from deprived groups. However, it is criticised on several grounds.

- Henry and Milovanovic (1996) argue that it accepts the authorities' definition of crime as being street crime committed by the poor, instead of defining the problem as being one of how powerful groups do harm to the poor. Marxists argue that it fails to explain corporate crime, which is much more harmful even if less conspicuous.
- Interactionists argue that, because left realists rely on quantitative data from victim surveys, they cannot explain offenders' motives. Instead, we need qualitative data to reveal their meanings.
- Their use of subcultural theory means left realists assume that value consensus exists and that crime only occurs when this breaks down.
- Relative deprivation cannot fully explain crime because not all those who experience it commit crime. The theory over-predicts the amount of crime.
- Its focus on high-crime inner-city areas gives an unrepresentative view and makes crime appear a greater problem than it is.

Comparing right and left realism

There are both similarities and differences between the two types of realism. For example, both left and right realists see crime as a real problem and fear of crime as rational. On the other hand, they come from different ends of the political spectrum: right realists are neo-conservative, while left realists are reformist socialists. This is reflected in how they explain crime – right realists blame individual lack of self-control, while left realists blame structural inequalities and relative deprivation. Likewise, political differences are reflected in their aims and solutions to the problem of crime: the right prioritise social order, achieved through a tough stance against offenders, while the left prioritise justice, achieved through democratic policing and reforms to create greater equality.

Summary

Realists see crime as a real problem, especially for the poor. Right realists are conservatives. They see the cause of crime as partly biological (some are innately predisposed to offend) and partly social (e.g. inadequate socialisation). They see crime as a rational choice based on calculating the risks and rewards. Because causes cannot easily be changed, they focus on deterring offenders through prevention and punishment. They are criticised e.g. for ignoring structural causes of crime.

Left realists are reformist socialists. They argue that Marxists and labelling theorists have not taken crime seriously. They identify three causes of crime: relative deprivation, subculture and marginalisation. In late modern society, economic insecurity together with the media's materialistic messages is increasing relative deprivation. The solution lies in accountable policing and tackling structural causes of crime. They are criticised e.g. for focusing on street crime and ignoring corporate crime.

For more activities on Realist theories...

Go to www.sociology.uk.net

QuickCheck Questions

1　What is the main focus of right realism in crime prevention?

2　Explain what is meant by 'zero tolerance policing'.

3　Identify two biological factors that right realists see as important in causing criminal behaviour.

4　Why might a prosperous society be more likely to have high crime rates?

5　Explain what is meant by 'marginalisation'.

6　Explain what is meant by 'relative deprivation'.

7　Identify three policy changes suggested by left realists to reduce crime.

8　Identify two similarities between left and right realism.

Check your answers at www.sociology.uk.net

Examining realist theories

Item A　Right realists such as James Q. Wilson argue that crime is partly the result of biological factors. Some individuals are more biologically predisposed to crime, for example because they are less able to control their impulses or because they are of low intelligence and do not understand the likely rewards or punishments attached to different actions.

Right realists also see social factors such as the role of the welfare state as playing a part in crime. Its generosity encourages the growth of an underclass in which crime can thrive. For example, an estimated 70% of young offenders come from lone parent families.

The solution favoured by right realism is to increase the costs of crime and reduce its rewards, for example by tougher sentences for offenders.

Essay　Using material from **Item A** and elsewhere, assess the value of the right realist approach to crime and deviance.　(21 marks)

The examiner's advice

This question carries 9 AO1 (knowledge and understanding) marks and 12 AO2 (interpretation, application, analysis and evaluation) marks.

You need to give a clear account of the right realist approach. Start by putting it into context as a conservative view, and link it to New Right politics. Make sure you use the Item, for example to begin examining the right realist view of the causes of crime. Here you should explain Murray's view that welfare dependency produces an underclass and link this to lone parenting and inadequate socialisation. You should also use the Item to launch a discussion of right realist solutions to crime in terms of prevention and punishment. You should link this to rational choice theory.

You must also evaluate the right realist approach, for example in terms of its neglect of structural causes (such as poverty) and of corporate crime, its failure to explain non-utilitarian crime etc.

In what ways does the bouncer's image signify his masculinity?

Topic 5 Gender, crime and justice

There are striking gender differences in the patterns of recorded crime. Girls and women appear to commit fewer crimes than boys and men and, when they do offend, females tend to commit different kinds of crimes from males.

Traditionally, male-dominated criminology neglected female criminality, both because females were seen as committing less crime, and because their behaviour was seen as less in need of controlling. However, more recently, feminists have focused attention on the patterns and causes of female criminality.

Sociologists have also turned their attention to the causes of *male* criminality. In particular, there has been considerable interest in the relationship between masculinity and crime, and some sociologists have argued that crime is a way for some males to achieve and express their masculinity.

Learning objectives

After studying this Topic, you should:

- Know the main gender differences in recorded patterns of offending.
- Understand and be able to evaluate the debates about the treatment of men and women in the criminal justice system.
- Be able to evaluate explanations of the relationship between women and crime, and between men and crime.

Gender patterns in crime

Most crime appears to be committed by males. As Frances Heidensohn (1996) observes, gender differences are perhaps 'the most significant feature of recorded crime'. For example, official statistics show that:

- Four out of five convicted offenders in England and Wales are male.
- By the age of 40, 9% of females had a criminal conviction, as against 32% of males.

Among offenders, there are some significant gender differences. For example, official statistics show that:

- A higher proportion of female than male offenders are convicted of property offences (except burglary). A higher proportion of male than female offenders are convicted of violence or sexual offences.
- Males are more likely to be repeat offenders, to have longer criminal careers and to commit more serious crimes. For example, men are about 15 times more likely to be convicted of homicide.

Such statistics raise three important questions:

1 Do women really commit fewer crimes, or are the figures an invalid picture of the gender patterns of crime?

2 How can we explain why those women who do offend commit crimes?

3 Why do males commit more crimes than females?

> One of the most common crimes committed by women is shoplifting. Suggest three reasons for this.

Do women commit more crime?

Do the official statistics on offending give us a true picture of the extent of gender differences in crime? Some sociologists and criminologists argue that they underestimate the amount of female as against male offending. Two arguments have been put forward in support of this view.

- Typically female crimes such as shoplifting are less likely to be reported. For example, property crime is less likely to be noticed or reported than the violent or sexual crimes more often committed by men. Similarly, prostitution – which females are much more likely than males to engage in – is unlikely to be reported by either party.
- Even when women's crimes are detected or reported, they are less likely to be prosecuted or, if prosecuted, more likely to be let off relatively lightly.

The chivalry thesis

This second argument is known as the leniency or 'chivalry thesis'. The thesis argues that most criminal justice agents – such as police officers, magistrates and judges – are men, and men are socialised to act in a 'chivalrous' way towards women.

For example, Otto Pollak (1950) argues that men have a protective attitude towards women and that

> 'Men hate to accuse women and thus send them to their punishment, police officers dislike to arrest them, district attorneys to prosecute them, judges and juries to find them guilty, and so on.'

The criminal justice system is thus more lenient with women and so their crimes are less likely to end up in the official statistics. This in turn gives an invalid picture that exaggerates the extent of gender differences in rates of offending.

The chivalry thesis has been hotly debated. Evidence from some self-report studies – where individuals are asked about what crimes they have committed – does suggest that female offenders are treated more leniently.

For example, John Graham and Ben Bowling's (1995) research on a sample of 1,721 14-25-year-olds found that although males were more likely to offend, the difference was smaller than that recorded in the official statistics.

They found that males were 2.33 times more likely to admit to having committed an offence in the previous twelve months – whereas the official statistics show males as four times more likely to offend.

Similarly, Flood-Page et al (2000) found that, while only one in 11 female self-reported offenders had been cautioned or prosecuted, the figure for males was over one in seven self-reported offenders.

Women are also more likely than men to be cautioned rather than prosecuted. For example, according to the Ministry of Justice (2009), 49% of females recorded as offending received a caution in 2007, whereas for males the figure was only 30%.

Similarly, Roger Hood's (1992) study of over 3,000 defendants found that women were about one-third less likely to be jailed in similar cases.

Evidence against the chivalry thesis

There is considerable evidence against the chivalry thesis. For example, David Farrington and Alison Morris' (1983) study of sentencing of 408 offences of theft in a magistrates' court found that women were not sentenced more leniently for comparable offences.

Similarly, Abigail Buckle and David Farrington's (1984) observational study of shoplifting in a department store witnessed twice as many males shoplifting as females – despite the fact that the numbers of male and female offenders in the official statistics are more or less equal. This small-scale study thus suggests that women shoplifters may be more likely to be prosecuted than their male counterparts.

If women appear to be treated more leniently, it may simply be because their offences are less serious. For example, Steven Box's (1981) review of British and American self-report studies concludes that women who commit serious offences are not treated more favourably than men. Similarly, the lower rate of prosecutions of females as compared with their self-reported offending may be because the crimes they admit to are less serious and less likely to go to trial. Women offenders also seem more likely to show remorse, and this may help to explain why they are more likely to receive a caution instead of going to court.

Bias against women

Many feminists argue that, far from the criminal justice system being biased in favour of women, as the chivalry thesis claims, it is biased *against* them. As Heidensohn (1996) argues, the courts treat females more harshly than males when they deviate from gender norms. For example:

- Double standards – courts punish girls but not boys for premature or promiscuous sexual activity. 'Wayward' girls can end up in care without ever having committed an offence.
- Women who do not conform to accepted standards of monogamous heterosexuality and motherhood are punished more harshly. As Stewart (2006) found, magistrates' perceptions of female defendants' characters were based on stereotypical gender roles.

Pat Carlen (1997) puts forward a similar view in relation to custodial sentences. She argues that when women are jailed, it is less for 'the seriousness of their crimes and more according to the court's assessment of them as wives, mothers and daughters'. Girls whose parents believe them to be beyond control are more likely to receive custodial sentences than females who live more 'conventional' lives.

▲ *A typical female crime?*

Carlen found that Scottish judges were much more likely to jail women whose children were in care than women who they saw as good mothers.

Feminists argue that these double standards exist because the criminal justice system is patriarchal. Nowhere is this more evident than in the way the system deals with rape cases. There have been numerous cases of male judges making sexist, victim-blaming remarks. For example, Carol Smart (1989) quotes Judge Wild as saying that

> 'Women who say no do not always mean no. It is not just a question of how she says it, how she shows and makes it clear. If she doesn't want it she only has to keep her legs shut.'

Similarly, as Sandra Walklate (1998) argues, in rape cases it is not the defendant who is on trial but the victim, since she has to prove her respectability in order to have her evidence accepted. According to Adler (1987), women who are deemed to lack respectability, such as single parents, punks and peace protestors, find it difficult to have their testimony believed by the court.

How might the concept of patriarchy be used to explain
(a) bias in *favour* of women (the chivalry thesis);
(b) bias *against* women?

Activity   Women demonised by the media

Go to www.sociology.uk.net

Explaining female crime

Whether or not the criminal justice system is more lenient towards women, as the chivalry thesis claims, women in general do seem to have a lower rate of offending than men. How then can we explain the behaviour of those women who do commit crimes?

The first explanations of female crime were biological rather than sociological. For example, Lombroso and Ferrero (1893) argued that criminality is innate, but that there were very few 'born female criminals'. Some more recent psychological explanations have also argued that biological factors such as higher levels of testosterone in males can account for gender differences in violent offending.

However, sociologists take the view that social rather than biological factors are the cause of gender differences in offending. Sociologists have put forward three main explanations of gender differences in crime: sex role theory, control theory and the liberation thesis.

Functionalist sex role theory

Early sociological explanations of gender differences in crime focused on differences in the socialisation of males and females. For example, boys are encouraged to be tough, aggressive and risk taking, and this can mean they are more disposed to commit acts of violence or take advantage of criminal opportunities when they present themselves.

The functionalist Talcott Parsons (1955) traces differences in crime and deviance to the gender roles in the conventional nuclear family. While men take the instrumental, breadwinner role, performed largely outside the home, women perform the expressive role in the home, where they take the main responsibility for socialising the children.

While this gives girls access to an adult role model, it tends to mean that boys reject feminine models of behaviour that express tenderness, gentleness and emotion. Instead, boys seek to distance themselves from such models by engaging in 'compensatory compulsory masculinity' through aggression and anti-social behaviour, which can slip over into acts of delinquency.

Because men have much less of a socialising role than women in the conventional nuclear family, socialisation can be more difficult for boys than for girls. According to Albert K. Cohen (1955), this relative lack of an adult male role model means boys are more likely to turn to all-male street gangs as a source of masculine identity. As we saw in Topic 1, in these subcultural groups, status is earned by acts of toughness, risk-taking and delinquency.

Similarly, New Right theorists argue that the absence of a male role model in matrifocal lone parent families leads to boys turning to criminal street gangs as a source of status and identity.

Sandra Walklate (2003) criticises sex role theory for its biological assumptions. According to Walklate, Parsons assumes that because women have the biological capacity to bear children, they are best suited to the expressive role.

Thus, although the theory tries to explain gender differences in crime in terms of behaviour learned through socialisation, it is ultimately based on biological assumptions about sex differences.

More recently, feminists have put forward alternative explanations for women's lower rates of crime and deviance. Feminists locate their explanations in the patriarchal (male-dominated) nature of society and women's subordinate position in it.

We can distinguish between two main feminist approaches: control theory and the liberation thesis.

Heidensohn: patriarchal control

Frances Heidensohn (1985) argues that the most striking thing about women's behaviour is how *conformist* it is – they commit fewer crimes than men. In her view, this is because patriarchal society imposes greater control over women and this reduces their opportunities to offend. This patriarchal control operates at home, in public spaces and at work.

Control at home Women's domestic role, with its constant round of housework and childcare, imposes severe restrictions on their time and movement and confines them to the house for long periods, reducing their opportunities to offend. Women who try to reject their domestic role may find that their partners seek to impose it by force, through domestic violence.

As Dobash and Dobash (1979) show, many violent attacks result from men's dissatisfaction with their wives' performance of domestic duties. Men also exercise control through their financial power, for example by denying women sufficient funds for leisure activities, thereby restricting their time outside the home.

Methods Link: using interviews

Russell and Rebecca Dobash (1979) investigated domestic violence using relatively unstructured interviews with women in refuges. This enabled them to gain the trust of the women and establish a rapport, resulting in more detailed and valid data that suggested domestic violence was much more widespread than indicated by police statistics.

However, even with this method, many victims may not wish to talk to strangers about their abuse and it may be difficult to obtain a representative sample to study. In some cases there may also be problems in finding a safe setting for the interview.

Read more about interviews and researching crime and deviance in *Methods in Context*, Chapter 3, Topic 4.

Daughters too are subject to patriarchal control. Girls are less likely to be allowed to come and go as they please or to stay out late. As a result, they develop a 'bedroom culture', socialising at home with friends rather than in public spaces. Girls are also required to do more housework than boys. As a result, they have less opportunity to engage in deviant behaviour on the streets.

Control in public Women are controlled in public places by the threat or fear of male violence against them, especially sexual violence. For example, the Islington Crime Survey found that 54% of women avoided going out after dark for fear of being victims of crime, as against only 14% of men.

Heidensohn notes that sensationalist media reporting of rapes adds to women's fear. Distorted media portrayals of the typical rapist as a stranger who carries out random attacks frightens women into staying indoors.

Females are also controlled in public by their fear of being defined as not respectable. Dress, make-up, demeanour and ways of speaking and acting that are defined as inappropriate can gain a girl or woman a 'reputation'. For example, women on their own may avoid going into pubs – which are sites of criminal behaviour – for fear of being regarded as sexually 'loose' or even as prostitutes.

Similarly, Sue Lees (1993) notes that in school, boys maintain control through sexualised verbal abuse, for example labelling girls as 'slags' if they fail to conform to gender role expectations.

Control at work Women's behaviour at work is controlled by male supervisors and managers. Sexual harassment is widespread and helps keep women 'in their place'. Furthermore, women's subordinate position reduces their opportunities to engage in major criminal activity at work. For example, the 'glass ceiling' prevents many women from rising to senior positions where there is greater opportunity to commit fraud.

In general, these patriarchal restrictions on women's lives mean they have fewer opportunities for crime. However, Heidensohn also recognises that patriarchy can also push women into crime. For example, women are more likely to be poor and may turn to theft or prostitution to gain a decent standard of living.

Activity

In small groups, using the information in the section on patriarchal control, design a questionnaire and use it to survey male and female students. Your aim is to uncover any gender differences or similarities in control.

You could investigate restrictions on time away from home, chores at home, fears of going out alone, etc. Try using a scale of responses to measure patterns – e.g. *Question*: How happy are you about going out at night alone? *Answer*: Very happy; fairly happy; fairly unhappy; very unhappy. Report your findings to the class. What differences or similarities did you find? How would you interpret your findings?

Carlen: class and gender deals

Using unstructured tape-recorded interviews, Pat Carlen (1988) conducted a study of thirty-nine 15-46 year old working-class women who had been convicted of a range of crimes including theft, fraud, handling stolen goods, burglary, drugs, prostitution, violence and arson. Twenty were in prison or youth custody at the time of the interviews. Although Carlen recognises that there are some middle-class female offenders, she argues that most convicted serious female criminals are working-class.

Carlen uses a version of Travis Hirschi's (1969) control theory to explain female crime. Hirschi argues that humans act rationally and are controlled by being offered a 'deal': rewards in return for conforming to social norms. People will turn to crime if they do not believe the rewards will be forthcoming, and if the rewards of crime appear greater than the risks.

Carlen argues that working-class women are generally led to conform through the promise of two types of rewards or 'deals':

- **The class deal:** women who work will be offered material rewards, with a decent standard of living and leisure opportunities.
- **The gender deal:** patriarchal ideology promises women material and emotional rewards from family life by conforming to the norms of a conventional domestic gender role.

If these rewards are not available or worth the effort, crime becomes more likely. Carlen argues that this was the case with the women in her study.

In terms of the *class deal*, the women had failed to find a legitimate way of earning a decent living and this left them feeling powerless, oppressed and the victims of injustice.

- Thirty-two of them had always been in poverty.
- Some found that qualifications gained in jail had been no help in gaining work upon release, while others had been on YTS courses but still could not get a job.
- Many had experienced problems and humiliations in trying to claim benefits.

As they had gained no rewards from the class deal, they felt they had nothing to lose by using crime to escape from poverty.

In terms of the *gender deal* for conforming to patriarchal family norms, most of the women had either not had the opportunity to make the deal, or saw few rewards and many disadvantages in family life.

- Some had been abused physically or sexually by their fathers, or subjected to domestic violence by partners.
- Over half had spent time in care, which broke the bonds with family and friends.
- Those leaving or running away from care often found themselves homeless, unemployed and poor.

Many of the women reached the conclusion that 'crime was the only route to a decent standard of living. They had nothing to lose and everything to gain.'

Carlen concludes that, for these women, poverty and being brought up in care or an oppressive family life were the two main causes of their criminality. Drug and alcohol addiction, and the desire for excitement, were contributory factors, but these often stemmed from poverty or being brought up in care. Being criminalised and jailed made the class deal even less available to them and made crime even more attractive.

▲ *Binge drinking among young women is rising rapidly. Is such deviance a product of women's liberation?*

Evaluation

Heidensohn and Carlen's approaches to female crime are based on a combination of feminism and control theory:

- Heidensohn shows the many patriarchal controls that help prevent women from deviating.
- Carlen shows how the failure of patriarchal society to deliver the promised 'deals' to some women removes the controls that prevent them from offending.

However, both control theory and feminism can be accused of seeing women's behaviour as determined by external forces such as patriarchal controls or class and gender deals. Critics argue that this underplays the importance of free will and choice in offending.

Furthermore, Carlen's sample was small and may be unrepresentative, consisting as it did largely of working-class and serious offenders.

The liberation thesis

If patriarchal society exercises control over women to prevent them from deviating, then it would seem logical to assume that, if society becomes less patriarchal and more equal, women's crime rates will become similar to men's.

This is the 'liberation thesis' put forward by Freda Adler (1975). Adler argues that, as women become liberated from patriarchy, their crimes will become as frequent and as serious as men's. Women's liberation has led to a new type of female criminal and a rise in the female crime rate.

Adler argues that changes in the structure of society have led to changes in women's offending behaviour. As patriarchal controls and discrimination have lessened, and opportunities in education and work have become more equal, women have begun to adopt traditionally 'male' roles in both legitimate activity (work) and illegitimate activity (crime).

As a result, women no longer just commit traditional 'female' crimes such as shoplifting and prostitution. They now also commit typically 'male' offences such as crimes of violence and white-collar crimes.

This is because of women's greater self-confidence and assertiveness, and the fact that they now have greater opportunities in the legitimate structure. For example, there are more women in senior positions at work and this gives them the opportunity to commit serious white-collar crimes such as fraud.

There is some evidence to support this view. For example:

- Both the overall rate of female offending and the female share of offences have gone up. For example, between the 1950s and 1990s, the female share of offences rose from one in 7 to one in 6.
- Adler argues that the pattern of female crime has shifted. She cites studies showing rising levels of female participation in crimes previously regarded as 'male', such as embezzlement and armed robbery.
- More recently, there has been media talk of the growth of 'girl gangs', while a study by Martin Denscombe (2001) of Midlands teenagers' self-images found that females were as likely as males to engage in risk-taking behaviour and that girls were adopting more 'male' stances, such as the desire to be in control and look 'hard'.

Criticisms of the liberation thesis

Critics reject Adler's thesis on several grounds:

- The female crime rate began rising in the 1950s – long before the women's liberation movement, which emerged in the late 1960s.

- Most female criminals are working-class – the group least likely to be influenced by women's liberation, which has benefited middle-class women much more. According to Chesney-Lind (1997), in the USA poor and marginalised women are more likely than liberated women to be criminals.
- Chesney-Lind did find evidence of women branching out into more typically male offences such as drugs. However, this is usually because of their link with prostitution – a very 'unliberated' female offence.
- There is little evidence that the illegitimate opportunity structure of professional crime has opened up to women. Laidler and Hunt (2001) found that female gang members in the USA were expected to conform to conventional gender roles in the same way as non-deviant girls.

However, Adler's thesis does draw our attention to the importance of investigating the relationship between changes in women's position and changes in patterns of female offending.

However, it can be argued that she overestimates both the extent to which women have become liberated and the extent to which they are now able to engage in serious crime.

Activity Gender and risk factors for offending

Go to www.sociology.uk.net

▲ *The judiciary remains male-dominated. What effect does this have on cases involving women?*

Why do men commit crime?

Feminists argue that, although 'malestream', non-feminist theories of crime have in reality focused only on males, these theories have assumed that they were explaining *all* crime, rather than solely *male* crime. For example, as Maureen Cain (1989) puts it:

'Men as males have not been the subject of the criminological gaze. Yet the most consistent and dramatic finding [of criminology] is not that most criminals are working-class – a fact which has received continuous theoretical attention – but that most criminals are, and always have been, men.'

In other words, although criminologists have focused mainly on male criminality, until recently they have not generally asked what it is about *being male* that leads men to offend.

Masculinity and crime

However, influenced by recent feminist and postmodernist ideas, sociologists have begun to take an interest in why men are more likely to commit crime. Their attention has focused on the concept of masculinity as a way of explaining men's higher rate of offending.

For example, James Messerschmidt (1993) argues that masculinity is a social construct or 'accomplishment' and men have to constantly work at constructing and presenting it to others. In doing so, some men have more resources than others to draw upon.

Messerschmidt argues that different masculinities co-exist within society, but that one of these, *hegemonic masculinity*, is the dominant, prestigious form that most men wish to accomplish. Hegemonic masculinity is defined through:

'work in the paid-labour market, the subordination of women, heterosexism [i.e. difference from and desire for women] and the driven and uncontrollable sexuality of men'.

However, some men have *subordinated masculinities*. These include gay men, who have no desire to accomplish hegemonic masculinity, as well as lower-class and some ethnic minority men, who lack the resources to do so.

Messerschmidt sees crime and deviance as resources that different men may use for accomplishing masculinity. For example, class and ethnic differences among youths lead to different forms of rule breaking to demonstrate masculinity:

- **White middle-class youths** have to subordinate themselves to teachers in order to achieve middle-class status, leading to an *accommodating masculinity* in school. Outside school, their masculinity takes an oppositional form, for example through drinking, pranks and vandalism.
- **White working-class youths** have less chance of educational success, so their masculinity is oppositional both in and out of school. It is constructed around sexist attitudes, being tough and opposing teachers' authority. The 'lads' in Willis' (1977) study are a good example of this kind of masculinity.
- **Black lower working-class youths** may have few expectations of a reasonable job and may use gang membership and violence to express their masculinity, or turn to serious property crime to achieve material success.

Messerschmidt acknowledges that middle-class men too may use crime. The difference lies in the type of crime – while middle-class males commit white-collar and corporate crime to accomplish hegemonic masculinity, poorer groups may use street robbery to achieve a subordinated masculinity.

Criticisms of Messerschmidt

Several criticisms have been made of Messerschmidt:

- Is masculinity an *explanation* of male crime, or just a *description* of male offenders (e.g. tough, controlling etc)? Messerschmidt is in danger of a circular argument, that masculinity explains male crimes (e.g. violence) because they are crimes committed by males (who have violent characteristics).
- Messerschmidt doesn't explain why not all men use crime to accomplish masculinity.
- He over-works the concept of masculinity to explain virtually all male crimes, from joy riding to embezzlement.

Synoptic links: theory & core themes

Functionalist and feminist **theory** can both be linked to gender and crime. For example, radical feminists see male violence against women as a key feature of patriarchal **power** and gender **stratification**. Functionalism sees **socialisation** differences as responsible for gender patterns in offending. Postmodernist theory sees crime as a resource some men use for constructing a masculine **identity**.

Winlow: postmodernity, masculinity and crime

In recent decades, globalisation has led to a shift from a modern industrial society to a late modern or postmodern de-industrialised society. This has led to the loss of many of the traditional manual jobs through which working-class men were able to express their masculinity by hard physical labour and by providing for their families.

At the same time as job opportunities in industry have declined, there has been an expansion of the service sector, including the night-time leisure economy of clubs, pubs and bars. For some young working-class men, this has provided a combination of legal employment, lucrative criminal opportunities and a means of expressing their masculinity.

One example of this is Simon Winlow's (2001) study of bouncers in Sunderland in the north east of England, an area of de-industrialisation and unemployment. Working as bouncers in the pubs and clubs provided young men with both paid work and the opportunity for illegal business ventures in drugs, duty-free tobacco and alcohol and protection rackets, as well as the opportunity to demonstrate their masculinity through the use of violence.

Winlow draws on Cloward and Ohlin's distinction between conflict and criminal subcultures (see Topic 1). He notes that in *modern* society, there had always been a violent, conflict subculture in Sunderland, in which 'hard men' earned status through their ability to use violence. However, the absence of a professional criminal subculture meant there was little opportunity for a career in organised crime.

Bodily capital

Under *postmodern* conditions, by contrast, an organised professional criminal subculture has emerged as a result of the new illicit business opportunities to be found in the night-time economy. In this subculture, the ability to use violence becomes not just a way of displaying masculinity, but a commodity with which to earn a living.

To maintain their reputation and employability, the men must use their *bodily capital*. For example, many of the bouncers seek to develop their physical assets by bodybuilding. Winlow notes that this is not just a matter of being able to use violence and win fights, but of maintaining the sign value of their bodies, 'looking the part' so as to discourage competitors from challenging them. In other words, the signs of masculinity become an important commodity in their own right. This reflects the idea that in postmodern society, *signs* take on a reality of their own independent of the thing they supposedly represent.

Winlow's study is important because it shows how the expression of masculinity changes with the move from a modern industrial society to a postmodern, de-industrialised one. At the same time, this change opens up new criminal opportunities for men who are able to use violence to express masculinity, by creating the conditions for the growth of an organised criminal subculture.

For more activities on Gender, crime and justice...

Go to www.sociology.uk.net

Summary

Official statistics show males commit more crime than females, but the chivalry thesis argues that they underestimate female offending because the criminal justice system treats women more leniently. However, this may be because their offences are less serious. Some feminists argue that the system is biased *against* women, especially when they deviate from gender norms.

In explaining gender differences in offending, sex role theory focuses on socialisation. Feminist theories emphasise patriarchal control that reduces females' opportunity to offend. Carlen argues that when the reward system for female conformity fails, females are likely to offend. The liberationist thesis argues that as women become more liberated, they adopt 'male' patterns of offending.

Messerschmidt argues that crime is a resource some subordinated men use to accomplish masculinity. Winlow argues that globalisation and de-industrialisation mean that some men now achieve masculinity through participation in a combination of paid work and crime in the night-time economy.

QuickCheck Questions

1 What proportion of convicted offenders are male?

2 Suggest two ways in which 'chivalry' might operate in the treatment of females by the law.

3 Suggest two ways in which females may be treated more harshly than males by the criminal justice system.

4 How does sex role theory account for gender differences in offending?

5 According to Carlen, in what ways may lower-class women miss out on both gender and class deals?

6 Suggest two criticisms of the liberation thesis.

7 According to Messerschmidt, what type of masculinity do white middle-class youths typically adopt?

8 Messerschmidt is said to 'overwork the concept of masculinity'. Explain what this means.

 Check your answers at www.sociology.uk.net

Examining gender, crime and justice

Item A   The so-called 'chivalry thesis' argues that women are treated more leniently than men by the criminal justice system. As a result, criminal statistics underestimate the true extent of female offending.

For example, Otto Pollak (1961) argued that men – including police officers, for example – are socialised to be protective towards women and thus are less likely to charge them or prosecute them. Similarly, when they appear in court, female defendants are treated more sympathetically by male judges and jurors. Pollak also argues that women are accustomed to deceiving men, for example in faking orgasm during sex. This skill in deceit means that their crimes, such as poisoning and infanticide, are less easily uncovered.

Essay   Using material from **Item A** and elsewhere, assess the value of the 'chivalry thesis' in understanding gender differences in crime.

(21 marks)

The examiner's advice

This question carries 9 AO1 (knowledge and understanding) marks and 12 AO2 (interpretation, application, analysis and evaluation) marks.

Start by using the Item to help you outline the chivalry thesis, adding your own examples (e.g. what sorts of offences might policemen let off women but not men for?). You should examine relevant evidence in support of the thesis – e.g. Graham and Bowling's and Flood-Page et al's self-report data, or studies showing a higher rate of cautions or lower rate of imprisonment for women in similar cases.

You also need to evaluate the thesis. Start by presenting evidence arguing that women are not treated more leniently, such as Buckle and Farrington, Farrington and Morris or Box. You can put this material into theoretical context by introducing a feminist perspective to argue that women are often treated more harshly, especially if they deviate from gender norms, whether as defendants or as victims (as in many rape cases).

Los Angeles police beat black motorist Rodney King, 3 March 1991. Four officers were tried but acquitted, touching off riots throughout the city.

Topic 6 Ethnicity, crime and justice

Official statistics on the criminal justice process show some striking differences between ethnic groups. For example, black people are more likely to be imprisoned than other groups. How are we to explain these ethnic differences in criminalisation?

- Is it because some ethnic groups are more likely to offend in the first place – and if so, how do we explain such differences?
- Or is it because the criminal justice system is racist and discriminates against ethnic minorities (for example, by police targeting and harassment)?

Not only are there ethnic differences in criminalisation, but some ethnic groups are also more at risk of being victims of a crime. For example, there is considerable evidence of the scale of racially motivated offences against minority groups. In addition, minorities are more likely to be victims of 'ordinary' crimes such as burglary.

In this Topic, we examine these different aspects of the relationship between ethnicity, crime and justice.

Learning objectives

After studying this Topic, you should:

- Know the patterns of ethnicity and criminalisation as shown by different sources of data.
- Understand the relationship between the criminal justice process and ethnicity.
- Be able to evaluate sociological explanations of the relationship between ethnicity, offending and criminalisation.
- Understand the relationship between ethnicity, racism and victimisation.

Ethnicity and criminalisation

According to official statistics, there are some significant ethnic differences in the likelihood of being involved in the criminal justice system. Black people, and to a lesser extent Asians, are over-represented in the system. For example:

- Black people make up just 2.8% of the population, but 11% of the prison population.
- Asians make up 4.7% of the population, but 6% of the prison population.

By contrast, white people are under-represented at all stages of the criminal justice process. As the Ministry of Justice (2008) notes:

'Members of our Black communities are seven times more likely than their White counterparts to be stopped and searched, three and a half times more likely to be arrested, and five times more likely to be in prison.'

However, such statistics do not tell us whether members of one ethnic group are more likely than members of another group to commit an offence in the first place – they simply tell us about involvement with the criminal justice system. For example, differences in stop and search or arrest rates may simply be due to policing strategies or to discrimination by individual officers, while differences in rates of imprisonment may be the result of courts handing down harsher sentences to minorities.

Alternative sources of statistics

In addition to statistics on the ethnicity of those individuals who are involved with the criminal justice system, we can call on two other important sources of statistics that can throw a more direct light on ethnicity and offending. These are victim surveys and self-report studies.

Victim surveys

Victim surveys ask individuals to say what crimes they have been victims of (usually during the past 12 months). We can gain information about ethnicity and offending from such surveys when they ask victims to identify the ethnicity of the person who committed the crime against them. For example, in the case of 'mugging' (a term that has no legal definition but is used to cover robberies and some thefts from the person), black people are significantly over-represented among those identified by victims as offenders.

Victim surveys also show that a great deal of crime is intra-ethnic – that is, it takes place *within* rather than between ethnic groups. For example, according to the British Crime Survey (2007), in 90% of crimes where the victim was white, at least one of the offenders was also white.

However, while victim surveys are useful in helping us to identify ethnic patterns of offending, they have several limitations:

- They rely on victims' memory of events. According to Ben Bowling and Coretta Phillips (2002), evidence suggests that white victims may 'over-identify' blacks – saying the offender was black even when they are not sure.
- They only cover personal crimes, which make up only about a fifth of all crimes. Muggings are an even smaller fraction – about 1.7% of recorded crimes.
- They exclude the under 16s: minority ethnic groups contain a higher proportion of young people.
- They exclude crimes by and against organisations (such as businesses), so they tell us nothing about the ethnicity of white-collar and corporate criminals.

As a result, victim surveys can only tell us about the ethnicity of a small proportion of offenders, which may not be representative of offenders in general.

Self-report studies

Self-report studies ask individuals to disclose their own dishonest and violent behaviour. Based on a sample of 2,500 people, Graham and Bowling (1995) found that blacks (43%) and whites (44%) had very similar rates of offending, while Indians (30%), Pakistanis (28%) and Bangladeshis (13%) had much lower rates.

Similarly, Sharp and Budd (2005) note that the 2003 Offending, Crime and Justice survey of 12,000 people found that whites and those of 'mixed' ethnic origins were most likely to say they had committed an offence (around 40%), followed by blacks (28%) and Asians (21%).

The Home Office has conducted nine self-report studies on drug use since the early 1990s, all with remarkably similar findings. For example, Sharp and Budd (2005) found that 27% of males of 'mixed' ethnicity said they had used drugs (mostly cannabis) in the last year, compared with 16% of both black and white males and 5% of Asian males. Use of Class A drugs such as heroin and cocaine was much higher among whites (6%) than blacks (2%) or Asians (1%).

The findings of self-report studies challenge the stereotype of black people as being more likely than whites to offend, though they support the widely held view that Asians are less likely to offend. However, self-report studies have their limitations in relation to ethnicity and offending.

Overall, the evidence on ethnicity and offending is somewhat inconsistent. For example, while official statistics and victim surveys point to the likelihood of higher rates of offending by blacks, this is generally not borne out by the results of self-report studies.

Methods Link: using questionnaires

Self-report studies using self-completion questionnaires are a popular method of researching crime and they have been used to study ethnic differences in offending among young people. Respondents are usually given a list of offences and asked to tick those they have committed and indicate how frequently.

Self-report questionnaires provide a useful check on official statistics – typically they reveal smaller gaps between offending rates of different ethnic groups. However, Hindelang et al (1981) found that black males with criminal records were less likely to report offences already known to the police. Such studies also tend not to ask about more serious offences (e.g. homicide), where there is evidence of a higher rate of offending by blacks, and they exclude prisoners, which means they under-represent non-white offenders.

Read more about questionnaires and researching crime and deviance in **Methods in Context**, Chapter 3, Topic 3.

Ethnicity, racism and the criminal justice system

There are ethnic differences at each stage of the criminal justice process. How can we explain them? How far are they the result of racism within the criminal justice system? We need to look at the main stages of the process that an individual may go through, possibly culminating in a custodial sentence.

Policing

As Phillips and Bowling (2007) note, since the 1970s there have been many allegations of oppressive policing of minority ethnic communities, including:

'mass stop and search operations, paramilitary tactics, excessive surveillance, armed raids, police violence and deaths in custody, and a failure to respond effectively to racist violence.'

Stop and search

Members of minority ethnic groups are more likely to be stopped and searched by the police. Police can use this power if they have 'reasonable suspicion' of wrongdoing. Compared with white people, black people are seven times more likely to be stopped and searched and Asian people over twice as likely. Data from the BCS indicate similar patterns. It should be noted that only a small proportion of stop and searches result in arrest.

In addition, under the Terrorism Act 2000, police can stop and search persons or vehicles whether or not they have reasonable suspicion. Statistics for 2006/7 show that Asians were over three times more likely to be stopped and searched than other people under the Terrorism Act.

It is therefore unsurprising that members of minority ethnic communities are less likely to think the police acted politely when stopping them, or to think they were stopped fairly. As Phillips and Bowling (2007) note, members of these communities are more likely to think they are 'over-policed and under-protected' and to have limited faith in the police.

Explaining stop and search patterns

There are three possible reasons for the disproportionate use of stop and search against members of minority ethnic groups:

Police racism The Macpherson Report (1999) on the police investigation of the racist murder of the black teenager Stephen Lawrence concluded that there was institutional racism within the Metropolitan Police. Others have found deeply ingrained racist attitudes among individual officers.

For example, Phillips and Bowling (2007) point out that many officers hold negative stereotypes about ethnic minorities as criminals, leading to deliberate targeting for stop and search. Such stereotypes are endorsed and upheld by the 'canteen culture' of rank and file officers.

Ethnic differences in offending An alternative explanation is that disproportionality in stop and searches simply reflects ethnic differences in levels of offending. However, it is useful to distinguish between low discretion and high discretion stops.

- In low discretion stops, police act on relevant information about a specific offence, for example a victim's description of the offender.
- In high discretion stops, police act without specific intelligence. It is in these stops, where officers can use their stereotypes, that disproportionality and discrimination are most likely.

Demographic factors Ethnic minorities are over-represented in the population groups who are most likely to be stopped, such as the young, the unemployed, manual workers and urban dwellers. These groups are all more likely to be stopped, regardless of their ethnicity, but they are also groups who have a higher proportion of ethnic minorities in them, and so minorities get stopped more.

Arrests and cautions

Figures for England and Wales show that in 2006/7 the arrest rate for blacks was 3.6 times the rate for whites. By contrast, once arrested, blacks and Asians were less likely than whites to receive a caution.

One reason for this may be that members of minority ethnic groups are more likely to deny the offence and to exercise their right to legal advice (possibly out of mistrust of the police). However, not admitting the offence means they cannot be let off with a caution and are more likely to be charged instead.

Prosecution

The Crown Prosecution Service (CPS) is the body responsible for deciding whether a case brought by the police should be prosecuted in court. In doing so, the CPS must decide whether there is a realistic prospect of conviction and whether prosecution is in the public interest.

Studies suggest that the CPS is more likely to drop cases against ethnic minorities. Bowling and Phillips (2002) argue that this may be because the evidence presented to the CPS by the police is often weaker and based on stereotyping of ethnic minorities as criminals.

Trial

When cases do go ahead, members of minority ethnic groups are more likely to elect for trial before a jury in the Crown Court, rather than in a magistrates' court, perhaps due to mistrust of magistrates' impartiality. However, Crown Courts can impose more severe sentences if convicted.

Convictions

It is therefore interesting to note that black and Asian defendants are less likely to be found guilty: in 2006/7, 60% of white defendants were found guilty as against only 52% of blacks and 44% of Asians.

This suggests discrimination, in that the police and CPS may be bringing weaker or less serious cases against ethnic minorities that are thrown out by the courts.

Sentencing

In 2006/7, custodial sentences were given to a greater proportion of black offenders (68%) than white (55%) or Asian offenders (59%), whereas whites and Asians were more likely than blacks to receive community sentences. This may be due to differences in the seriousness of the offences, or in defendants' previous convictions.

However, a study of five Crown Courts by Roger Hood (1992) found that, even when such factors were taken into account, black men were 5% more likely to receive a custodial sentence, and were given sentences on average three months (and Asian men nine months) longer than white men.

Pre-sentence reports

One possible reason for harsher sentences is the pre-sentence reports (PSRs) written by probation officers. A PSR is intended as a risk assessment to assist magistrates in deciding on the appropriate sentence for a given offender.

However, Hudson and Bramhall (2005) argue that PSRs allow for unwitting discrimination. They found that reports on Asian offenders were less comprehensive and suggested that they were less remorseful than white offenders. They place this bias in the context of the 'demonising' of Muslims in the wake of the events of 11 September 2001.

Prison

In 2007, just over a quarter of the male prison population were from minority ethnic groups, including 15% Black and 7% Asian. Among British nationals, 7.4 per 1,000 black people were in jail compared with 1.7 per 1,000 Asians and 1.4 per 1,000 white people.

As such, blacks were five times more likely to be in prison than whites. Black and Asian offenders are more likely than whites to be serving longer sentences (of four years or more).

Within the total prison population, all minority groups have a higher than average proportion of prisoners on remand (awaiting trial rather than actually convicted and serving a sentence). This is because ethnic minorities are less likely to be granted bail while awaiting trial.

Finally, we can note the existence of similar patterns in other countries. For example, in the United States, two out of five prisoners held in local jails (both convicted and those awaiting trial) are black, while one in five is Hispanic.

Explaining the differences in offending

Large-scale migration from the Caribbean and the Indian subcontinent began in the 1950s. Until the 1970s, there was general agreement that the minority ethnic communities had a lower rate of offending than the white population. However, from the mid-1970s, increased conflict between the police and the African Caribbean community and higher arrest rates for street crime meant that 'black criminality' increasingly came to be seen as a problem.

By contrast, it was not until the 1990s that Asian crime also began to be viewed as a problem, with media concerns about the growth of 'Asian gangs'. The events of 2001 – widespread clashes between police and Asian youths in towns in northern England and 9/11 (the Islamist terrorist attacks in the United States on 11 September) – helped to crystallise the idea that Asians, and especially Muslims, were an 'enemy within' that threatened public order and safety.

As we have seen, official statistics on the criminal justice process show differences between ethnic groups. The question is therefore how we explain these patterns. There are two main explanations for ethnic differences in the statistics:

- **Left realism:** the statistics represent real differences in rates of offending.
- **Neo-Marxism:** the statistics are a social construct resulting from racist labelling and discrimination in the criminal justice system.

Left realism

Left realists such as Lea and Young (1993) argue that ethnic differences in the statistics reflect real differences in the levels of offending by different ethnic groups. As we saw in Topic 4, left realists see crime as the product of relative deprivation, subculture and marginalisation. They argue that racism has led to the marginalisation and economic exclusion of ethnic minorities, who face higher levels of unemployment, poverty and poor housing. At the same time, the media's emphasis on consumerism promotes a sense of relative deprivation by setting materialistic goals that many members of minority groups are unable to reach by legitimate means.

One response is the formation of delinquent subcultures, especially by young unemployed black males. This produces higher levels of *utilitarian* crime, such as theft and robbery, as a means of coping with relative deprivation. Furthermore, because these groups are marginalised and have no organisations to represent their interests, their frustration is liable to produce *non-utilitarian* crime such as violence and rioting.

> How could you use Merton's concept of anomie and A.K. Cohen's concept of status frustration to explain these two patterns of crime?

Lea and Young acknowledge that the police often act in racist ways and that this results in the unjustified criminalisation of some members of minority groups. However, they do not believe that discriminatory policing fully explains the differences in the statistics. For example, they note that over 90% of crimes known to the police are reported by members of the public rather than discovered by the police themselves. Under these circumstances, even if the police do act in discriminatory ways, it is unlikely that this can adequately account for the ethnic differences in the statistics.

Similarly, Lea and Young argue that we cannot explain the differences between minorities in terms of police racism. For example, blacks have a considerably higher rate of criminalisation than Asians. The police would have to be very selective in their racism – against blacks but not against Asians – for their racism to be the cause of these differences.

Lea and Young thus conclude that the statistics represent real differences in levels of offending between ethnic groups, and that these are caused by real differences in levels of relative deprivation and marginalisation.

However, Lea and Young can be criticised for their views on the role of police racism. For example, arrest rates for Asians may be lower than for blacks not because they are less likely to offend, but because police stereotype the two groups differently, seeing blacks as dangerous, Asians as passive. Furthermore, these stereotypes may have changed since 9/11, because police now regard Asians too as dangerous – thus explaining the rising criminalisation rates for this group.

Neo-Marxism

While left realists see the official statistics as reflecting real differences in offending between ethnic groups, albeit in a somewhat distorted way, other sociologists argue that the differences in the statistics do not reflect reality. On the contrary, these differences are the outcome of a process of social construction that stereotypes ethnic minorities as inherently more criminal than the majority population. The work of the neo-Marxists Paul Gilroy (1982) and Stuart Hall et al (1979) illustrates this view.

Gilroy: the myth of black criminality

Gilroy argues that the idea of black criminality is a myth created by racist stereotypes of African Caribbeans and Asians. In reality, these groups are no more criminal than any other. However, as a result of the police and criminal justice system acting on these racist stereotypes, ethnic minorities come to be criminalised and therefore to appear in greater numbers in the official statistics.

In Gilroy's view, ethnic minority crime can be seen as a form of political resistance against a racist society, and this resistance has its roots in earlier struggles against British imperialism. Gilroy holds a similar view to that of critical criminology, which argues that working-class crime is a political act of resistance to capitalism.

Most blacks and Asians in the UK originated in the former British colonies, where their anti-imperialist struggles taught them how to resist oppression, for example through riots and demonstrations. When they found themselves facing racism in Britain, they adopted the same forms of struggle to defend themselves, but their political struggle was criminalised by the British state.

However, Lea and Young criticise Gilroy on several grounds:

- First-generation immigrants in the 1950s and 60s were very law-abiding, so it is unlikely that they passed down a tradition of anti-colonial struggle to their children.
- Most crime is intra-ethnic (criminals and their victims usually have the same ethnic background), so it can't be seen as an anti-colonial struggle against racism. Lea and Young argue that, like the critical criminologists, Gilroy romanticises street crime as somehow revolutionary, when it is nothing of the sort.
- Asian crime rates are similar to or lower than whites. If Gilroy were right, then the police are only racist towards blacks and not Asians, which seems unlikely.

Hall et al: policing the crisis

Stuart Hall et al adopt a neo-Marxist perspective. They argue that the 1970s saw a moral panic over black 'muggers' that served the interests of capitalism.

Hall et al argue that the ruling class are normally able to rule the subordinate classes through consent. However, in times of crisis, this becomes more difficult. In the early 1970s, British capitalism faced a crisis. High inflation and rising unemployment were provoking widespread industrial unrest and strikes, conflict in Northern Ireland was intensifying and student protests were spreading. At such times, when opposition to capitalism begins to grow, the ruling class may need to use force to maintain control. However, the use of force needs to be seen as legitimate or it may provoke even more widespread resistance.

The 1970s also saw the emergence of a media-driven moral panic about the supposed growth of a 'new' crime – mugging. In reality, mugging was just a new name for the old crime of street robbery with violence, and Hall et al note that there was no evidence of a significant increase in this crime at the time. Mugging was soon to be associated by the media, police and politicians with black youth.

Hall et al argue that the emergence of the moral panic about mugging as a specifically 'black' crime at the same time as the crisis of capitalism was no coincidence – in their view, the moral panic and the crisis were linked. The myth of the black mugger served as a scapegoat to distract attention from the true cause of problems such as unemployment – namely the capitalist crisis.

The black mugger came to symbolise the disintegration of the social order – the feeling that the British way of life was 'coming apart at the seams'. By presenting black youth as a threat to the fabric of society, the moral panic served to divide the working class on racial grounds and weaken opposition to capitalism, as well as winning popular consent for more authoritarian forms of rule that could be used to suppress opposition.

However, Hall et al do not argue that black crime was solely a product of media and police labelling. The crisis of capitalism was increasingly marginalising black youth through unemployment, and this drove some into a lifestyle of hustling and petty crime as a means of survival.

Hall et al have been criticised on several grounds:

- Downes and Rock (2003) argue that Hall et al are inconsistent in claiming that black street crime was not rising, but also that it *was* rising because of unemployment.
- They do not show *how* the capitalist crisis led to a moral panic, nor do they provide evidence that the public were in fact panicking or blaming crime on blacks.
- Left realists argue that inner-city residents' fears about mugging are not panicky, but realistic.

Activity

How far do the media report details of the ethnicity of victims and offenders? How far do they use ethnic stereotypes when reporting crime? In groups, collect and analyse crime stories from a range of local and national newspapers by visiting their websites. If possible, also record and analyse some local TV news broadcasts and programmes such as *Crimewatch*.

Synoptic links: theory & core themes

Left realist and neo-Marxist **theories** offer alternative views of whether black criminality is a fact or a social construct. However, both link ethnic differences in recorded crime to the relative lack of **power** and marginal position of ethnic minorities in the **stratification** system.

Ethnicity and victimisation

Until recently, the focus of the 'ethnicity and crime' debate has been largely on the over-representation of black people in the criminal justice system. However, more recently, sociologists have taken an interest in other issues such as the racist victimisation of ethnic minorities.

Racist victimisation occurs when an individual is selected as a target because of their race, ethnicity or religion. Racist victimisation is nothing new, but was brought into greater public focus with the racist murder of the black teenager Stephen Lawrence in 1993 and the subsequent inquiry into the handling of the police investigation (Macpherson 1999).

Our information on racist victimisation comes from two main sources: victim surveys such as the British Crime Survey, and police-recorded statistics. These generally cover:

- *Racist incidents* any incident that is perceived to be racist by the victim or another person.
- *Racially or religiously aggravated offences* (assault, wounding, criminal damage and harassment) where the offender is motivated by hostility towards members of a racial or religious group.

Extent and risk of victimisation

- The police recorded 61,000 *racist incidents* in England and Wales in 2006/7 – mostly damage to property or verbal harassment.
- However, most incidents go unreported. The British Crime Survey estimates there were around 184,000 racially motivated incidents in 2006/7.
- The police also recorded 42,600 *racially or religiously aggravated offences* in 2006/7, mostly harassment. 10,600 people were prosecuted or cautioned for racially aggravated offences in 2006.

Methods Link: using interviews

The British Crime Survey (BCS) is an annual survey using structured interviews. It asks people what crimes they have been victims of in the past 12 months and includes questions on racist incidents and racially or religiously aggravated offences.

The BCS uses a very large representative sample and has a high response rate. Together with the use of trained interviewers and similar questions from year to year, this means that reliable estimates of the extent of racial victimisation nationally can be made and trends identified.

However, like all interviews, it relies on the memory of respondents. It also tends to produce a 'snapshot' of separate incidents and cannot convey the experience of living every day in a climate of racist hostility.

Read more about interviews and researching crime and deviance in *Methods in Context*, Chapter 3, Topic 4.

The risk of being a victim of any sort of crime – not just racist crime – varies by ethnic group. The 2006/7 British Crime Survey shows that people from mixed ethnic backgrounds had a higher risk (36%) of becoming a victim of crime than did blacks (27%), Asians (25%) or whites (24%).

The differences may be partly the result of factors other than ethnicity. For example for violent crime, factors such as being young, male and unemployed are strongly linked with victimisation. Ethnic groups with a high proportion of young males are thus likely to have higher rates of victimisation. However, some of these factors (such as unemployment) are themselves partly the result of discrimination.

While the statistics record the instances of victimisation, they do not necessarily capture the victims' experience of it. As Sampson and Phillips (1992) note, racist victimisation tends to be ongoing over time, with repeated 'minor' instances of abuse and harassment interwoven with periodic incidents of physical violence.

The resulting long-term psychological impact needs to be added to the physical injury and damage to property caused by the offenders.

Responses to victimisation

Members of minority ethnic communities have often been active in responding to victimisation. Responses have ranged from situational crime prevention measures such as fireproof doors and letterboxes, to organised self-defence campaigns aimed at physically defending neighbourhoods from racist attacks.

Such responses need to be understood in the context of accusations of under-protection by the police, who have often ignored the racist dimensions of victimisation and failed to record or investigate reported incidents properly.

For example, the Macpherson Enquiry (1999) concluded that the police investigation into the death of the black teenager Stephen Lawrence was 'marred by a combination of professional incompetence, institutional racism and a failure of leadership by senior officers'. Others have found deeply ingrained racist attitudes and beliefs among individual officers.

For more activities on Ethnicity, crime and justice...

Go to www.sociology.uk.net

Summary

Official statistics show that blacks and other ethnic minorities are more likely to be stopped, arrested and imprisoned. This may be because they are more likely to offend, or because of racism in the criminal justice system, or because they are more likely to fall into the demographic groups who are stopped. Self-report studies show lower offending rates among minorities than among whites. Black defendants are more likely to be acquitted but if convicted are more likely to be jailed.

Left realists argue that blacks do have a higher crime rate because of their greater relative deprivation and social exclusion, whereas Neo-Marxists argue that black criminality is a social construction serving to distract attention from the crisis of capitalism.

Minorities are more likely to be victims of crime, while being both over-policed and under-protected.

QuickCheck Questions

1 How much more likely are black people to be stopped and searched than whites: (a) 5 (b) 7 (c) 10 times?

2 Identify two problems in using self-report studies to study ethnic differences in offending.

3 How do Lea and Young account for (a) utilitarian and (b) non-utilitarian crime among blacks?

4 In what way does Gilroy see ethnic minority crime as political?

5 Suggest two criticisms of Gilroy's views.

6 According to Hall et al, how did the moral panic over mugging help capitalism?

7 What is meant by the term 'institutional racism'?

8 Identify two social characteristics of ethnic minority groups that make them more likely to be victims.

 Check your answers at www.sociology.uk.net

Examining ethnicity, crime and justice

Examine some of the reasons for ethnic differences in experiences of the criminal justice system.　　　　(12 marks)

The examiner's advice

This question carries 6 AO1 marks (knowledge and understanding) and 6 AO2 marks (interpretation, application, analysis and evaluation).

For this question, you need to identify a range of reasons. You should distinguish between the experiences of different ethnic minorities where relevant (e.g. Asians and blacks have different rates of imprisonment), not just between whites and non-whites.

You should describe some of the patterns in areas such as stop and search, arrest, caution, prosecution, conviction and sentencing. You could also refer to the experience of being 'over-policed and under-protected'.

Reasons include institutional racism and individual discrimination, e.g. by police and judges, demographic factors, concerns about terrorism, likelihood of denying the offence (so caution is not an option) or of opting for jury trial (where sentences are higher), ethnic differences in offending, witness bias etc.

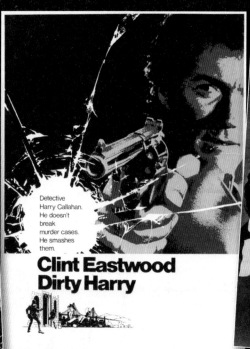

Topic 7 Crime and the media

We live today in a media-saturated society. The media are all around us – and the media are obsessed with crime. Crime is the central theme of media output, both fiction and non-fiction. In a world where we often have very little contact with people whose lifestyles and values differ from our own, the media have become our main source of knowledge about crime. What we know – or *think* we know – about crime is heavily influenced by the media's representation of it.

Sociologists are interested in several aspects of the media in relation to crime and deviance. In this Topic, we shall examine:

- How the media represent crime, both in fiction and in non-fiction such as news broadcasts – how far does this portray an accurate picture of crime?
- Do the media cause crime and fear of crime – for example, do the young imitate the deviance they see in the media? Do the media make us more afraid of becoming victims of crime?
- Moral panics – what role do the media play in defining some groups as 'folk devils' and in amplifying deviance?
- Cybercrime – how far do the Internet and other information and communication technology create new opportunities for crime, and for the surveillance and control of the population?

Learning objectives

After studying this Topic, you should:

- Know the patterns of media representations of crime and how these differ from the picture of crime in official statistics.
- Understand and be able to evaluate different views about the media as a cause of crime and fear of crime.
- Know and be able to evaluate views of the media's role in the creation of moral panics.
- Understand the relationships between the new information media and crime and social control.

Media representations of crime

Crime and deviance make up a large proportion of news coverage. For example, Richard Ericson et al's (1991) study of Toronto found that 45-71% of quality press and radio news was about various forms of deviance and its control, while Williams and Dickinson (1993) found British newspapers devote up to 30% of their news space to crime.

However, while the news media show a keen interest in crime, they give a distorted image of crime, criminals and policing. For example, as compared with the picture of crime we gain from official statistics:

- **The media over-represent violent and sexual crime**. For example, Ditton and Duffy (1983) found that 46% of media reports were about violent or sexual crimes, yet these made up only 3% of all crimes recorded by the police. One review by Marsh (1991) of studies of news reporting in America found that a violent crime was 36 times more likely to be reported than a property crime.
- **The media portray criminals and victims as older and more middle-class** than those typically found in the criminal justice system. Felson (1998) calls this the 'age fallacy'.
- **Media coverage exaggerates police success** in clearing up cases. This is partly because the police are a major source of crime stories and want to present themselves in a good light, and partly because the media over-represents violent crime, which has a higher clear-up rate than property crime.
- **The media exaggerate the risk of victimisation**, especially to women, white people and higher status individuals.
- **Crime is reported as a series of separate events** without structure and without examining underlying causes.
- **The media overplay extraordinary crimes** and underplay ordinary crimes – Felson calls this the 'dramatic fallacy'. Similarly, media images lead us to believe that to commit crime (and to solve it) one needs to be daring and clever – the 'ingenuity fallacy'.

There is some evidence of changes in the type of coverage of crime by the news media. For example, Schlesinger and Tumber (1994) found that in the 1960s the focus had been on murders and petty crime, but by the 1990s murder and petty crime were of less interest to the media. The change came about partly because of the abolition of the death penalty for murder and partly because rising crime rates meant that a crime had to be 'special' to attract coverage. By the 1990s, reporting had also widened to include drugs, child abuse, terrorism, football hooliganism and mugging.

There is also evidence of increasing preoccupation with sex crimes. For example, Keith Soothill and Sylvia Walby (1991) found that newspaper reporting of rape cases increased from under a quarter of all cases in 1951 to over a third in 1985. They also note that coverage consistently focuses on identifying a 'sex fiend' or 'beast', often by use of labels (such as 'the balaclava rapist'). The resulting distorted picture of rape is one of serial attacks carried out by psychopathic strangers. While these do occur, they are the exception rather than the rule – in most cases the perpetrator is known to the victim.

News values and crime coverage

The distorted picture of crime painted by the news media reflects the fact that news is a social construction. That is, news does not simply exist 'out there' waiting to be gathered in and written up by the journalist. Rather, it is the outcome of a social process in which some potential stories are selected while others are rejected. As Stan Cohen and Jock Young (1973) note, news is not discovered but *manufactured*.

A central aspect of the manufacture of news is the notion of 'news values'. News values are the criteria by which journalists and editors decide whether a story is newsworthy enough to make it into the newspaper or news bulletin. If a crime story can be told in terms of some of these criteria, it has a better chance of making the news. Key news values influencing the selection of crime stories include:

- **Immediacy**
- **Dramatisation** – action and excitement
- **Personalisation** – human interest stories about individuals
- **Higher-status** persons and 'celebrities'
- **Simplification** – eliminating shades of grey
- **Novelty or unexpectedness** – a new angle
- **Risk** – victim-centred stories about vulnerability and fear
- **Violence** – especially visible and spectacular acts.

One reason why the news media give so much coverage to crime is that news focuses on the unusual and extraordinary, and this makes deviance newsworthy almost by definition, since it is abnormal behaviour.

Activity

Working in pairs, use newspapers or TV news to find examples of each of the above forms of media distortion of crime, criminals and policing.

Activity

Find some crime stories in the national and local press. Which news values do the stories reflect? Can you identify any other news values that make the stories newsworthy?

Fictional representations of crime

We don't just get our images of crime from the news media. Fictional representations from TV, cinema and novels are also important sources of our knowledge of crime, because so much of their output is crime-related. For example, Ernest Mandel (1984) estimates that from 1945 to 1984, over 10 billion crime thrillers were sold worldwide, while about 25% of prime time TV and 20% of films are crime shows or movies.

Fictional representations of crime, criminals and victims follow what Surette (1998) calls 'the law of opposites': they are the opposite of the official statistics – and strikingly similar to news coverage.

- Property crime is under-represented, while violence, drugs and sex crimes are over-represented.
- While real-life homicides mainly result from brawls and domestic disputes, fictional ones are the product of greed and calculation.
- Fictional sex crimes are committed by psychopathic strangers, not acquaintances. Fictional villains tend to be higher status, middle-aged white males.
- Fictional cops usually get their man.

However, three recent trends are worth noting. Firstly, the new genre of 'reality' infotainment shows tends to feature young, non-white 'underclass' offenders. Secondly, there is an increasing tendency to show police as corrupt and brutal (and as less successful). Thirdly, victims have become more central, with law enforcers portrayed as their avengers and audiences invited to identify with their suffering.

The media as a cause of crime

There has long been concern that the media have a negative effect on attitudes, values and behaviour – especially of those groups thought to be most susceptible to influence, such as the young, the lower classes and the uneducated. In the 1920s and '30s, cinema was blamed for corrupting youth; in the 1950s, horror comics were held responsible for moral decline, while in the 1980s it was 'video nasties'. More recently, rap lyrics and computer games such as *Grand Theft Auto* have been criticised for encouraging violence and criminality.

There are numerous ways in which the media might possibly cause crime and deviance. These include:

- Imitation – by providing deviant role models, resulting in 'copycat' behaviour.
- Arousal, e.g. through viewing violent or sexual imagery.
- Desensitisation, e.g. through repeated viewing of violence.
- By transmitting knowledge of criminal techniques.
- As a target for crime, e.g. theft of plasma TVs.
- By stimulating desires for unaffordable goods, e.g. through advertising.
- By portraying the police as incompetent.
- By glamourising offending.

As a result of fears about the possible negative effects of the media on their audiences, literally thousands of studies have been conducted. Overall, however, most studies have tended to find that exposure to media violence has at most a small and limited negative effect on audiences.

Methods Link: using laboratory experiments

Much research into media effects uses laboratory experiments and focuses on whether viewing violence leads to violent behaviour. Albert Bandura et al (1977) measured the effect on children of watching filmed images of aggression. Dividing them into an experimental group who saw the aggression and a control group who did not, they found those who had seen it displayed more aggression afterwards.

Laboratory experiments allow the researcher to control the variables and measure their effect. However, the artificiality of the setting reduces the validity of the findings and may produce the Hawthorne effect, and it is difficult to measure long-term effects.

Read more about experiments and researching crime and deviance in **Methods in Context**, Chapter 3, Topic 2.

As Schramm et al (1961) say in relation to the effects of TV viewing on children:

'For some children, under some conditions, some television is harmful. For some children under the same conditions, it may be beneficial. For most children, under most conditions, most television is probably neither particularly harmful nor particularly beneficial.'

However, as Sonia Livingstone (1996) notes, despite such conclusions, people continue to be preoccupied with the effects of the media on children because of our desire as a society to regard childhood as a time of uncontaminated innocence in the private sphere.

Fear of crime

As we have seen, the media exaggerate the amount of violent and unusual crime, and they exaggerate the risks of certain groups of people becoming its victims, such as young women and old people. There is therefore concern that the media may be distorting the public's impression of crime and causing an unrealistic fear of crime.

Research evidence to some extent supports the view that there is a link between media use and fear of crime. For example, in the USA, Gerbner et al found that heavy users of television (over four hours a day) had higher levels of fear of crime. Similarly, Schlesinger and Tumber (1992) found a correlation between media consumption and fear of crime, with tabloid readers and heavy users of TV expressing greater fear of becoming a victim, especially of physical attack and mugging.

However, the existence of such correlations doesn't prove that media viewing causes fear. For example, it may be that those who are already afraid of going out at night watch more TV just because they stay in more.

Finally, as Richard Sparks (1992) notes, much 'media effects' research – whether on the media as a cause of crime or as a cause of fear of crime – ignores the meanings that viewers give to media violence. For example, they may give very different meanings to violence in cartoons, horror films and news bulletins. This criticism reflects the interpretivist view that if we want to understand the possible effects of the media, we must look at the meanings people give to what they see and read.

The media, relative deprivation and crime

Laboratory based research has focused on whether media portrayals of crime and deviant lifestyles lead viewers to commit crime themselves. An alternative approach is to consider how far media portrayals of 'normal' rather than criminal lifestyles might also encourage people to commit crime.

For example, left realists argue that the mass media help to increase the sense of relative deprivation – the feeling of being deprived relative to others – among poor and marginalised social groups. As Lea and Young (1996) put it:

'The mass media have disseminated a standardized image of lifestyle, particularly in the areas of popular culture and recreation, which, for those unemployed and surviving through the dole queue or only able to obtain employment at very low wages, has accentuated the sense of relative deprivation.'

In today's society, where even the poorest groups have media access, the media present everyone with images of a materialistic 'good life' of leisure, fun and consumer goods as the norm to which they should conform. The result is to stimulate the sense of relative deprivation and social exclusion felt by marginalised groups who cannot afford these goods. As Merton argues, pressure to conform to the norm can cause deviant behaviour when the opportunity to achieve by legitimate means is blocked. In this instance, the media are instrumental in setting the norm and thus in promoting crime.

Activity

In groups of four, design a set of interview questions to investigate the relationship between media consumption and fear of crime. Include questions about how much and what TV people watch (e.g. crime drama, news etc), what newspapers they read; how fearful they are of being victims of different types of crime.

Do a couple of pilot interviews to iron out any problems. Each person should then carry out at least four interviews. Try to interview a range of ages and both sexes.

Collate all your results and look for any patterns. Are there any factors that stand out, or age or gender differences? Can you see any relationship between media consumption and fear of crime?

Moral panics

One further way in which the media may cause crime and deviance is through labelling. As we saw in Topic 2, moral entrepreneurs who disapprove of some particular behaviour – drug taking, for instance – may use the media to put pressure on the authorities to 'do something' about the alleged problem. If successful, their campaigning will result in the negative labelling of the behaviour and perhaps a change in the law, such as the introduction of the Marijuana Tax Act in the USA. By helping to label marijuana smoking, which previously had been legal, as criminal, the media helped to cause crime.

An important element in this process is the creation of a moral panic. A moral panic is an exaggerated over-reaction by society to a perceived problem – usually driven or inspired by the media – where the reaction enlarges the problem out of all proportion to its real seriousness. In a moral panic:

■ The media identify a group as a *folk devil* or threat to societal values.
■ The media present the group in a negative, stereotypical fashion and exaggerate the scale of the problem.
■ Moral entrepreneurs, editors, politicians, police chiefs, bishops and other 'respectable' people condemn the group and its behaviour.

▲ *Margate 1964: Mods armed with sticks, broken deckchairs and bottles race across the beach.*

This usually leads to calls for a 'crackdown' on the group. However, this may create a self-fulfilling prophecy that amplifies the very problem that caused the panic in the first place. For example, in the case of drugs, setting up special drug squads led the police to discover more drug taking. As the crackdown identifies more deviants, there are calls for even tougher action, creating a deviance amplification spiral.

Mods and rockers

The most influential study of moral panics and the role of the media is Stanley Cohen's (1972) book, *Folk Devils and Moral Panics*. Cohen examines the media's response to disturbances between two groups of largely working-class teenagers, the mods and the rockers, at English seaside resorts from 1964 to 1966, and the way in which this created a moral panic.

Mods wore smart dress and rode scooters; rockers wore leather jackets and rode motorbikes – though in the early stages, distinctions were not so clear-cut, and not many young people identified themselves as belonging to either 'group'. The initial confrontations started on a cold, wet Easter weekend in 1964 at Clacton, with a few scuffles, some stone throwing, some windows being broken and some beach huts wrecked.

However, although the disorder was relatively minor, the media over-reacted. In his analysis, Cohen uses the analogy of a disaster, where the media produce an inventory or stocktaking of what happened. Cohen says this inventory contained three elements:

Exaggeration and distortion The media exaggerated the numbers involved and the extent of the violence and damage, and distorted the picture through dramatic reporting and sensational headlines such as 'Day of Terror by Scooter Gangs' and 'Youngsters Beat Up Town – 97 Leather Jacket Arrests'. Even non-events were news – towns 'held their breath' for invasions that didn't materialise.

Prediction The media regularly assumed and predicted further conflict and violence would result.

Symbolisation The symbols of the mods and rockers – their clothes, bikes and scooters, hairstyles, music etc – were all negatively labelled and associated with deviance. The media's use of these symbols allowed them to link unconnected events. For example, bikers in different parts of the country who misbehaved could be seen as part of a more general underlying problem of disorderly youth.

Cohen argues that the media's portrayal of events produced a deviance amplification spiral by making it seem as if the problem was spreading and getting out of hand. This led to calls for an increased control response from the police and courts. This produced further marginalisation and stigmatisation of the mods and rockers as deviants, and less and less tolerance of them, and so on in an upward spiral.

The media further amplified the deviance by defining the two groups and their subcultural styles. This led to more youths adopting these styles and drew in more participants for future clashes. By emphasising their supposed differences, the media crystallised two distinct identities and transformed loose-knit groupings into two tight-knit gangs. This encouraged polarisation and helped to create a self-fulfilling prophecy of escalating conflict as youths acted out the roles the media had assigned to them.

Cohen notes that media definitions of the situation are crucial in creating a moral panic, because in large-scale modern societies, most people have no direct experience of the events themselves and thus have to rely on the media for information about them. In the case of the mods and rockers, this allowed the media to portray them as folk devils – major threats to public order and social values.

Methods Link: using documents

In his research on the mods and rockers, Cohen used a range of documentary sources. These included national and local press articles, a collection of 724 press cuttings compiled for Margate Council by an agency, recordings of radio and TV broadcasts, parish newsletters, minutes of council meetings and records of parliamentary debates.

These gave Cohen insight into how the moral panic developed and the responses of moral entrepreneurs, politicians, police and judiciary. However, such sources might be less likely to represent the views of the youths and the general public, and Cohen also used a range of primary methods. For example, he conducted on the spot observations of events at the seaside, interviewed onlookers watching the events, and worked as a volunteer for action groups working with young people in Brighton.

Read more about documents and researching crime and deviance in *Methods in Context*, Chapter 3, Topic 6.

The wider context

Cohen puts the moral panic about the mods and rockers into the wider context of change in post-war British society. This was a period in which the newfound affluence, consumerism and hedonism of the young appeared to challenge the values of an older generation who had lived through the hardships of the 1930s and 1940s.

Cohen argues that moral panics often occur at times of social change, reflecting the anxieties many people feel when accepted values seem to be undermined. He argues that the moral panic was a result of a *boundary crisis*, where there was uncertainty about the where the boundary lay between acceptable and unacceptable behaviour in a time of change. The folk devil created by the media symbolises and gives a focus to popular anxieties about social disorder.

From a functionalist perspective, moral panics can be seen as ways of responding to the sense of anomie or normlessness created by change. By dramatising the threat to society in the form of a folk devil, the media raises the collective consciousness and reasserts social controls when central values are threatened.

Other sociologists have also used the concept of moral panics. For example, Stuart Hall et al (1979) adopt a neo-Marxist approach that locates the role of moral panics in the context of capitalism. They argue that the moral panic over 'mugging' in the British media in the 1970s served to distract attention from the crisis of capitalism, divide the working class on racial grounds and legitimate a more authoritarian style of rule.

In addition to concerns about mods and rockers and about mugging, commentators have claimed to identify numerous other examples of folk devils and moral panics in recent decades. These include dangerous dogs, New Age travellers, bogus asylum seekers, child sexual abuse, Aids, binge drinking, 'mad cow' disease and single parents.

Criticisms of the idea of moral panics

There are several criticisms of the concept of moral panics:

It assumes that the societal reaction is a disproportionate over-reaction – but who is to decide what is a proportionate reaction, and what is a panicky one? This relates to the left realist view that people's fear of crime is in fact rational.

What turns the 'amplifier' on and off: why are the media able to amplify some problems into a panic, but not others? Why do panics not go on increasing indefinitely once they have started?

Do today's media audiences, who are accustomed to 'shock, horror' stories, really react with panic to media exaggerations? McRobbie and Thornton (1995) argue that moral panics are now routine and have less impact. Also, in late modern society, there is little consensus about what is deviant. Lifestyle choices that were condemned forty years ago, such as single motherhood, are no longer universally regarded as deviant and so it is harder for the media to create panics about them.

Activity

In small groups, identify a current or recent example of a folk devil covered in the media. Using newspapers or other media sources, look for examples of the three elements Cohen describes: exaggeration and distortion, prediction, and symbolisation. Is there any evidence to suggest that members of the public do actually panic about the folk devil you have investigated?

Synoptic links: theory & core themes

In addition to links with functionalist and neo-Marxist **theories**, moral panics can be seen from an interactionist perspective. Interactionism examines how the media construct a deviant **identity** for folk devils, which may be internalised to produce further deviance and heightened control. The media also act as a **socialisation** agent, creating popular understandings and fears of crime, and making crime central to the **culture**.

Global cyber-crime

The arrival of new types of media is often met with a moral panic. For example, horror comics, cinema, television, videos and computer games have all been accused of undermining public morality and corrupting the young. The same is true of the Internet – both because of the speed with which it has developed and its scale: almost half the world's population are now online. The arrival of the Internet has led to fears of cyber-crime, which Douglas Thomas and Brian Loader (2000) define as computer-mediated activities that are either illegal or considered illicit by some, and that are conducted through global electronic networks.

As Yvonne Jewkes (2003) notes, the Internet creates opportunities to commit both 'conventional crimes', such as fraud, and 'new crimes using new tools', such as software piracy. Wall (2001) identifies four categories of cybercrime:

Cyber-trespass – crossing boundaries into others' cyber-property. It includes hacking and sabotage, such as spreading viruses.

For more activities on Crime and the media...

Go to www.sociology.uk.net

Summary

The media give a distorted image of crime. For example, they over-represent violent crime and exaggerate the risk of victimisation. The fact that news is a social construction based on news values such as dramatisation and violence helps to explain the media's interest in crime.

Some see the media as causing crime, for example through imitation. However, studies generally show only small and limited effects. Left realists argue that the media increase relative deprivation among the poor, who then turn to crime to achieve the lifestyle portrayed by the media.

The media also cause moral panics, identifying a group as folk devils and exaggerating the threat they pose, leading to a crackdown and creating a deviance amplification spiral. New media such as the Internet have created new opportunities both for cyber-crime and for surveillance and control of the population.

Cyber-deception and theft – including identity theft, 'phishing' (obtaining identity or bank account details by deception) and violation of intellectual property rights (e.g. software piracy, illegal downloading and file-sharing). An estimated 95% of music available online is downloaded illegally (Swash, 2009).

Cyber-pornography – including porn involving minors, and opportunities for children to access porn on the Net.

▲ *Cyber-crime, USA: hackers interfere with electronic road sign.*

Cyber-violence – doing psychological harm or inciting physical harm. Cyber-violence includes cyber-stalking (e.g. sending unwanted, threatening or offensive emails) and hate crimes against minority groups, as well as bullying by text.

Policing cyber-crime is difficult partly because of the sheer scale of the Internet and the limited resources of the police, and also because of its globalised nature, which poses problems of jurisdiction (e.g. in which country should someone be prosecuted for an Internet offence?). Police culture also gives cyber-crime a low priority because it is seen as lacking the excitement of more conventional policing.

However, the new information and communication technology (ICT) also provides the police and state with greater opportunities for surveillance and control of the population. As Jewkes (2003) argues, ICT permits routine surveillance through the use of CCTV cameras, electronic databases, digital fingerprinting and 'smart' identity cards, as well as the installation of listening devices called 'carnivores' at Internet service providers to monitor email traffic.

QuickCheck Questions

1 Identify three news values that the media use to select crime stories.

2 Identify three ways in which the media's fictional portrayal of crime and policing differs from that of the official statistics.

3 In what way may the media and fear of crime be linked?

4 Suggest three ways in which the media may encourage or cause crime and deviance.

5 Explain what is meant by the term 'deviance amplification'.

6 Identify three ways in which the media amplified the deviance of the mods and rockers.

7 Identify two criticisms of the concept of moral panic.

8 Suggest three examples of cyber-crimes.

Check your answers at www.sociology.uk.net

Examining crime and the media

Examine the ways in which the media stimulate moral panics and create folk devils.

(12 marks)

The examiner's advice

This question carries 6 AO1 marks (knowledge and understanding) and 6 AO2 marks (interpretation, application, analysis and evaluation).

You should start by defining the terms 'moral panic' and 'folk devils' and then explain the relationship between the two. You need to use examples of moral panics from studies such as Cohen on mods and rockers, Hall et al on mugging, or Young on drug takers. You should use concepts such as exaggeration or distortion, prediction and symbolisation to describe the reporting. Examine the stages in a deviance amplification spiral using concepts such as self-fulfilling prophecy and deviant career. To evaluate, you can consider the reasons for moral panics, such as preserving ruling-class hegemony, reaffirming solidarity, etc, or you could consider whether moral panics really do have an effect on media audiences.

Globalised terror: suicide attack on the Twin Towers, 11 September 2001.

Topic 8 Globalisation, green crime, human rights and state crimes

Running through this Topic are three themes: power, harm, and the interconnectedness of the world today.

Crimes of the powerful Nation-states and large corporations have the power to inflict serious damage on the environment. The state also has great power to cause harm to its own citizens and those of other countries. Yet in both cases, this power also means that such harm may be concealed, go unpunished or even be defined as something other than crime.

Zemiology The above seems to take us beyond the boundaries of traditional criminology. If an act is not a crime – however 'bad' it may be – then perhaps it is not a suitable subject for criminologists? Some reject this view and argue that we should broaden our investigations so as to include the study of *harms*: the many acts which may injure humans or the environment, but which very often are not against any law. This field of study is sometimes called *zemiology*, from the Greek word for harm. It raises the issue of why some harms get defined as crimes, while others are not.

Crimes without frontiers Some of the harms done to the environment do not respect national boundaries – they inflict damage on a global scale. Many other crimes too are not confined to a single nation-state, such as cybercrime, for example. As the world becomes ever more interconnected, the scope for globalised crime increases. We begin this Topic by examining this issue.

Learning objectives

After studying this Topic, you should:

- Understand the ways in which globalisation and crime are related and be able to evaluate explanations of this relationship.
- Understand the different types of green crime and be able to evaluate sociological explanations of environmental harm.
- Understand the relationship between state crimes and human rights and be able to evaluate explanations of such crimes.

Crime and globalisation

Globalisation refers to the increasing interconnectedness of societies, so that what happens in one locality is shaped by distant events and vice versa. For example, David Held et al (1999) define globalisation as:

'the widening, deepening and speeding up of world wide interconnectedness in all aspects of life, from the cultural to the criminal, the financial to the spiritual'.

Globalisation has many causes. These include the spread of new information and communication technologies (ICT) and the influence of global mass media, cheap air travel, the deregulation of financial and other markets and their opening up to competition, and easier movement so that businesses can easily relocate to countries where profits will be greater.

The global criminal economy

As Held et al suggest, there has also been a *globalisation of crime* – an increasing interconnectedness of crime across national borders. The same processes that have brought about the globalisation of legitimate activities have also brought about the spread of *transnational organised crime*. Globalisation creates new opportunities for crime, new means of committing crime and new offences, such as the various cyber-crimes.

As a result of globalisation, Manuel Castells (1998) argues, there is now a global criminal economy worth over £1 trillion per annum. This takes a number of forms:

- **Arms trafficking** to illegal regimes, guerrilla groups and terrorists.
- **Trafficking in nuclear materials**, especially from the former communist countries.
- **Smuggling of illegal immigrants**, for example, the Chinese Triads make an estimated $2.5 billion annually.
- **Trafficking in women and children**, often linked to prostitution or slavery. Up to half a million people are trafficked to Western Europe annually.
- **Sex tourism**, where Westerners travel to Third World countries for sex, sometimes involving minors.
- **Trafficking in body parts** for organ transplants in rich countries. An estimated 2,000 organs annually are taken from condemned or executed criminals in China.
- **Cyber-crimes** such as identity theft and child pornography.
- **Green crimes** that damage the environment, such as illegal dumping of toxic waste in Third World countries.
- **International terrorism** Much terrorism is now based on ideological links made via the Internet and other ICT, rather than on local territorial links as in the past.
- **Smuggling of legal goods**, such as alcohol and tobacco, to evade taxes, and of stolen goods, such as cars, to sell in foreign markets.
- **Trafficking in cultural artefacts** and works of art, sometimes having first been stolen to order.
- **Trafficking in endangered species** or their body parts, for example to produce traditional remedies.
- **The drugs trade** worth an estimated $300-400 billion annually at street prices.
- **Money laundering** of the profits from organised crime, estimated at up to $1.5 trillion per year.

The global criminal economy has both a demand side and a supply side. Part of the reason for the scale of transnational organised crime is the demand for its products and services in the rich West. However, the global criminal economy could not function without a supply side that provides the source of the drugs, sex workers and other goods and services demanded in the West.

This supply is linked to the globalisation process. For example, Third World drugs-producing countries such as Colombia, Peru and Afghanistan have large populations of impoverished peasants. For these groups, drug cultivation is an attractive option that requires little investment in technology and commands high prices compared with traditional crops. In Colombia, for instance, an estimated 20% of the population depends on cocaine production for their livelihood, and cocaine outsells all Colombia's other exports combined. To understand drug crime, we cannot confine our attention merely to the countries where the drugs are consumed.

Activity Investigating global crime

Go to www.sociology.uk.net

Global risk consciousness

Globalisation creates new insecurities and produces a new mentality of 'risk consciousness' in which risk is seen as global rather than tied to particular places. For example, the increased movement of people, as economic migrants seeking work or as asylum seekers fleeing persecution, has given rise to anxieties among populations in Western countries about the risks of crime and disorder and the need to protect their borders.

Whether such fears are rational or not is a different matter. Much of our knowledge about risks comes from the media, which often give an exaggerated view of the dangers we face. In the case of immigration, the media create moral panics about the supposed 'threat', often fuelled by politicians. Negative coverage of immigrants – portrayed as terrorists or as scroungers 'flooding' the country – has led to hate crimes against minorities in several European countries including the UK.

One result is the intensification of social control at the national level. The UK has toughened its border control regulations, for example fining airlines if they bring in undocumented passengers. Similarly, the UK now has no legal limits on how long a person may be held in immigration detention. Other European states with land borders have introduced fences, CCTV and thermal imaging devices to prevent illegal crossings. Another result of globalised risk is the increased attempts at international cooperation and control in the various 'wars' on terror, drugs and crime – particularly since the terrorist attacks of 11 September 2001.

Globalisation, capitalism and crime

Writing from a socialist perspective, Ian Taylor (1997) argues that globalisation has led to changes in the pattern and extent of crime. By giving free rein to market forces, globalisation has created greater inequality and rising crime.

Globalisation has created crime at both ends of the social spectrum. It has allowed transnational corporations to switch manufacturing to low-wage countries, producing job insecurity, unemployment and poverty. Deregulation means that governments have little control over their own economies, for example to create jobs or raise taxes, while state spending on welfare has declined. Marketisation has encouraged people to see themselves as individual consumers, calculating the personal costs and benefits of each action, undermining social cohesion. As left realists note, the increasingly materialistic culture promoted by the global media portrays success in terms of a lifestyle of consumption.

All these factors create insecurity and widening inequalities that encourage people, especially the poor, to turn to crime. The lack of legitimate job opportunities destroys self-respect and drives the unemployed to look for illegitimate ones, for instance in the lucrative drugs trade. For example, in Los Angeles, de-industrialisation has led to the growth of drugs gangs numbering 10,000 members.

At the same time, globalisation also creates criminal opportunities on a grand scale for elite groups. For example, the deregulation of financial markets has created opportunities for insider trading and the movement of funds around the globe to avoid taxation. Similarly, the creation of transnational bodies such as the European Union has offered opportunities for fraudulent claims for subsidies, estimated at over $7 billion per annum in the EU.

Globalisation has also led to new patterns of employment, which have created new opportunities for crime. It has led to the increased use of subcontracting to recruit 'flexible' workers, often working illegally or employed for less than the minimum wage or working in breach of health and safety or other labour laws.

Taylor's theory is useful in linking global trends in the capitalist economy to changes in the pattern of crime. However, it does not adequately explain how the changes make people behave in criminal ways. For example, not all poor people turn to crime.

> What advantages might there be for large companies in switching their production to a less developed country?

Patterns of criminal organisation

As we saw with Winlow's study of bouncers in Sunderland, globalisation and de-industrialisation have created new criminal opportunities and patterns at a local level. Another local study of a post-industrial town, by Dick Hobbs and Colin Dunningham, shows similar results.

Hobbs and Dunningham found that the way crime is organised is linked to the economic changes brought by globalisation. Increasingly, it involves individuals with contacts acting as a 'hub' around which a loose-knit network forms, composed of other individuals seeking opportunities, and often linking legitimate and illegitimate activities. Hobbs and Dunningham argue that this contrasts with the large-scale, hierarchical 'Mafia'-style criminal organisations of the past, such as that headed by the Kray brothers in the East End of London.

'Glocal' organisation

These new forms of organisation sometimes have international links, especially with the drugs trade, but crime is still rooted in its local context. For example, individuals still need local contacts and networks to find opportunities and to sell their drugs. Hobbs and Dunningham therefore conclude that crime works as a 'glocal' system. That is, it is still locally based, but with global connections. This means that the form it takes will vary from place to place, according to local conditions, even if it is influenced by global factors such as the availability of drugs from abroad.

Hobbs and Dunningham argue that changes associated with globalisation have led to changes in patterns of crime – for example, the shift from the old rigidly hierarchical gang structure to loose networks of flexible, opportunistic, entrepreneurial criminals. However, it is not clear that such patterns are new, nor that the older structures have disappeared. It may be that the two have always co-existed. Equally, their conclusions may not be generalisable to other criminal activities elsewhere.

McMafia

Another example of the relationship between criminal organisation and globalisation is what Misha Glenny (2008) calls 'McMafia'. This refers to the organisations that emerged in Russia and Eastern Europe following the fall of communism – itself a major factor in the process of globalisation.

Glenny traces the origins of transnational organised crime to the break-up of the Soviet Union after 1989, which coincided with the deregulation of global markets.

Under communism, the Soviet state had regulated the prices of everything. However, following the fall of communism, the Russian government deregulated most sectors of the economy except for natural resources such as oil. These commodities remained at their old Soviet prices – often only a fortieth of the world market price. Thus anyone with access to funds – such as former communist officials and KGB (secret service) generals – could buy up oil, gas, diamonds or metals for next to nothing. Selling them abroad at an astronomical profit, these individuals became Russia's new capitalist class – often popularly referred to as 'oligarchs'.

Meanwhile, the collapse of the communist state heralded a period of increasing disorder. To protect their wealth capitalists therefore turned to the 'mafias' that had begun to spring up. These were often alliances between former KGB men and ex-convicts. Among the most ruthless were the Chechen mafia.

However, these mafias were unlike the old Italian and American mafias, which were based on ethnic and family ties, with a clear-cut hierarchy. The new Russian mafias were purely economic organisations formed to pursue self-interest. For example, the Chechen mafia originated in Chechnya, but soon began to 'franchise' its operations to non-Chechen groups. 'Chechen mafia' became a brand name that they sold to protection rackets in other towns, so long as they always carried out their word – otherwise the brand would be damaged.

With the assistance of these fluid and violent organisations, the billionaires were able to find protection for their wealth and a means of moving it out of the country. Criminal organisations were vital to the entry of the new Russian capitalist class in the world economy. At the same time, the Russian mafias were able to build links with criminal organisations in other parts of the world.

Green crime

Green or environmental crime can be defined as crime against the environment. Much green crime can be linked to globalisation and the increasing interconnectedness of societies. Regardless of the division of the world into separate nation-states, the planet is a single eco-system, and threats to the eco-system are increasingly global rather than merely local in nature. For example, atmospheric pollution from industry in one country can turn into acid rain that falls in another, poisoning its watercourses and destroying its forests. Similarly, an accident in the nuclear industry – such as the one at Chernobyl in Ukraine in 1986 – can spread radioactive material over thousands of miles, showing how a problem caused in one locality can have worldwide effects.

'Global risk society' and the environment

The above examples also show that most of the threats to human well being and the eco-system are now human-made rather than natural. Unlike the natural dangers of the past, such as drought and famine, the major risks we face today are of our own making.

Ulrich Beck (1992) argues that in today's late modern society we can now provide adequate resources for all (at least in the developed countries). However, the massive increase in productivity and the technology that sustains it have created new, 'manufactured risks' – dangers that we have never faced before. Many of these risks involve harm to the environment and its consequences for humanity, such as global warming caused by greenhouse gas emissions from industry. Like climate change, many of these risks are global rather than local in nature, leading Beck to describe late modern society as 'global risk society'.

Green criminology

But what if the pollution that causes global warming or acid rain is perfectly legal and no crime has been committed – is this a matter for criminologists? We can identify two opposed answers to this question.

Traditional criminology has not been concerned with such behaviour, since its subject matter is defined by the criminal law, and no law has been broken. The starting point for this approach is the national and international laws and regulations concerning the environment. For example,

Situ and Emmons (2000) define environmental crime as 'an unauthorised act or omission that violates the law'. Like other traditional approaches in criminology, it investigates the patterns and causes of law breaking.

The advantage of this approach is that it has a clearly defined subject matter. However, it is criticised for accepting official definitions of environmental problems and crimes, which are often shaped by powerful groups such as big business to serve their own interests.

Green criminology takes a more radical approach. It starts from the notion of *harm* rather than criminal law. For example, Rob White (2008) argues that the proper subject of criminology is any action that harms the physical environment and/or the human and non-human animals within it, even if no law has been broken. In fact, many of the worst environmental harms are not illegal, and so the subject matter of green criminology is much wider than that of traditional criminology. For this reason, green criminology is a form of *transgressive criminology* – it oversteps (transgresses) the boundaries of traditional criminology to include new issues.

Furthermore, different countries have different laws, so that the same harmful action may be a crime in one country but not in another. Thus, legal definitions cannot provide a consistent standard of harm, since they are the product of individual nation-states and their political processes. By moving away from a legal definition, therefore,

---

| Box 2.2 | The Bhopal disaster |

On the night of 2 December 1984, the US majority-owned Union Carbide pesticide plant at Bhopal, India, started leaking cyanide gas. The plant was no longer in active production and had fallen into disrepair. All six safety-systems failed to operate and 30 tons of gas spread through the city. Half a million people were exposed and some estimate that over 20,000 died. (Union Carbide acknowledges only 3,800 deaths and claims the explosion was caused by sabotage.) 120,000 continue to suffer effects such as cancers, blindness, breathing difficulties, gynaecological disorders and birth defects. As one survivor has said, 'the lucky ones are the ones who died on that night'. Heavy metals have been found in the breast milk of women living nearby. Fifteen years after the accident, local groundwater was found to contain up to 6 million times more mercury than normal. Campaigners say the site has never been cleaned up. No one has ever faced a criminal court.

The approach of traditional criminology to Bhopal focuses on the breaches of safety legislation and failure to follow proper maintenance procedures. The approach of green criminology takes a wider view, noting the advantages for the company in locating their plant in a country with weak health and safety and environmental protection legislation.

For more on Bhopal, visit www.bhopal.org/whathappened.html

---

green criminology can develop a *global* perspective on environmental harm.

This approach is like the Marxist view of 'crimes of the powerful'. Marxists argue that the capitalist class are able to shape the law and define crime so that their own exploitative activities are not criminalised or, where they are, to ensure that enforcement is weak. Similarly, green criminologists argue that powerful interests, especially nation-states and transnational corporations, are able to define in their own interests what counts as unacceptable environmental harm.

Synoptic links: theory & core themes

There are links between globalisation and **theories** of postmodernity and late modernity. For example, postmodernism points to the fluid networks typical of today's globalised crime rather than the rigid criminal hierarchies of modern societies, while theories of late modernity focus on environmental risk. State **power** is such that it can inflict massive violations of human rights, far exceeding those caused by typically working-class crime.

Two views of harm

In general, nation-states and transnational corporations adopt what White (2008) calls an *anthropocentric* or human-centred view of environmental harm. This view assumes that humans have a right to dominate nature for their own ends, and puts economic growth before the environment.

White contrasts this with an *ecocentric* view that sees humans and their environment as interdependent, so that environmental harm hurts humans also. This view sees both humans and the environment as liable to exploitation, particularly by global capitalism. In general, green criminology adopts the ecocentric view as the basis for judging environmental harm.

1 What rights if any do (a) animals and (b) the physical environment have?

2 Do humans have more rights than animals and the environment? If so, what are they?

Types of green crimes

From a green criminology perspective, Nigel South (Carrabine et al 2008) classifies green crimes into two types: primary and secondary.

Primary crimes

Primary green crimes are 'crimes that result directly from the destruction and degradation of the earth's resources'. South identifies four main types of primary crime:

▲ *Cleaning up oil-covered beaches after the Exxon Valdez tanker disaster, Alaska, 1989.*

Crimes of air pollution Burning fossil fuels from industry and transport adds 3 billion tons of carbon to the atmosphere every year and carbon emissions are growing at around 2% per annum, contributing to global warming. The potential criminals are governments, business and consumers.

Crimes of deforestation Between 1960 and 1990, one-fifth of the world's tropical rainforest was destroyed, for example through illegal logging. In the Amazon, forest has been cleared to rear beef cattle for export. In the Andes, the 'war on drugs' has led to pesticide spraying to kill coca and marijuana plants, but this has created a new green crime, destroying food crops, contaminating drinking water and causing illness. The criminals include the state and those who profit from forest destruction, such as logging companies and cattle ranchers.

Crimes of species decline and animal rights 50 species a day are becoming extinct, and 46% of mammal and 11% of bird species are at risk. 70-95% of earth's species live in the rainforests, which are under severe threat. There is trafficking in animals and animal parts. Meanwhile, old crimes such as dog-fights and badger-baiting are on the increase.

Crimes of water pollution Half a billion people lack access to clean drinking water and 25 million die annually from drinking contaminated water. Marine pollution threatens 58% of the world's ocean reefs and 34% of its fish. Criminals include businesses that dump toxic waste and governments that discharge untreated sewage into rivers and seas.

Secondary crimes

Secondary green crime is crime that grows out of the flouting of rules aimed at preventing or regulating environmental disasters. For example, governments often break their own regulations and cause environmental harms. South suggests two examples of secondary crimes.

State violence against oppositional groups States condemn terrorism, but they have been prepared to resort to similar illegal methods themselves. For example, in 1985 the French secret service blew up the Greenpeace ship *Rainbow Warrior* in Auckland harbour, New Zealand, killing one crew member. The vessel was there in an attempt to prevent a green crime, namely French nuclear weapons testing in the south Pacific. As Day (1991) says, 'in every case where a government has committed itself to nuclear weapons or nuclear power, all those who oppose this policy are treated in some degree as enemies of the state'.

Hazardous waste and organised crime Disposal of toxic waste from the chemical, nuclear and other industries is highly profitable. Because of the high costs of safe and legal disposal, businesses may seek to dispose of such waste illegally. For example, in Italy, *eco-mafias* profit from illegal dumping of toxic waste. Much is dumped illegally at sea. As Reece Walters (2007) notes, 'the ocean floor has been a radioactive rubbish dump for decades'. For example, 28,500 rusting barrels of radioactive waste lie on the seabed off the Channel Islands, reportedly dumped by UK authorities and corporations in the 1950s.

Illegal waste dumping often has a *globalised* character. For example, Fred Bridgland (2006) describes how, after the tsunami of 2004, hundreds of barrels of radioactive waste, illegally dumped by European companies, washed up on the shores of Somalia. In other cases, Western businesses ship their waste to be processed in Third World countries where costs are lower and safety standards often non-existent. For example, as Rosoff et al (1998) note, the cost of legitimately disposing of toxic waste in the USA is about $2,500 a ton, but some Third World countries will dispose of it for $3 a ton. Similarly, transnational corporations may offload products (such as pharmaceuticals) onto Third World markets after they have been banned on safety grounds in the West.

Illegal waste disposal illustrates the problems of law enforcement in a globalised world. The very existence of laws to regulate waste disposal in developed countries pushes up the costs to business and creates an incentive to dump illegally in Third World countries. In some cases, it is not even illegal, since less developed countries may lack the necessary legislation outlawing it.

Evaluation of green criminology

Both the strengths and the weaknesses of green criminology arise from its focus on global environmental concerns. It recognises the growing importance of environmental issues and the need to address the harms and risks of environmental damage, both to humans and non-human animals.

However, by focusing on the much broader concept of harms rather than simply on legally defined crimes, it is hard to define the boundaries of its field of study clearly. Defining these boundaries involves making moral or political statements about which actions ought to be regarded as wrong. Critics argue that this is a matter of values and cannot be established objectively.

State crimes

As we saw in Topic 3, Marxist and critical criminologists argue that traditional criminology focused on the 'crimes of the streets' and ignored the 'crimes of the suites' committed by big business. Like corporate crime, state crime is another example of the crimes of the powerful, and Marxists such as William Chambliss (1989) argue that sociologists should investigate 'state-organized crime' as well as the crimes of capitalism.

Penny Green and Tony Ward (2005) define state crime as 'illegal or deviant activities perpetrated by, or with the complicity of, state agencies.' It includes all forms of crime committed by or on behalf of states and governments in order to further their policies. State crimes can include genocide, war crimes, torture, imprisonment without trial and assassination. State crimes do not include acts that merely benefit individuals who work for the state, such as a police officer who accepts a bribe.

Eugene McLaughlin (2001) identifies four categories of state crime:

1 Political crimes, for example corruption and censorship.

2 Crimes by security and police forces, such as genocide, torture and disappearances of dissidents.

3 Economic crimes, for example official violations of health and safety laws.

4 Social and cultural crimes, such as institutional racism.

▲ *Skulls of victims of the Cambodian genocide*

State crime is one of the most serious forms of crime for two reasons:

1 The scale of state crime

The power of the state enables it to commit extremely large-scale crimes with widespread victimisation. For example, in Cambodia between 1975 and 1978, the Khmer Rouge government of Pol Pot is believed to have killed up to two million people – a fifth of the country's entire population. As Michalowski and Kramer (2006) note, 'Great power and great crimes are inseparable.' They argue that we need to study:

> 'the ways that economic and political elites can bring death, disease, and loss to tens of thousands with a single decision, and can affect entire human groups through the creation of criminal systems of oppression and exploitation'.

The state's monopoly of violence gives it the potential to inflict massive harm, while its power means it is well placed to conceal its crimes or evade punishment for them. Although media attention is often on state crimes committed by Third World dictatorships such as Pol Pot's, democratic states such as Britain and the United States have also been guilty of crimes such as the military use of torture in Iraq, Northern Ireland and elsewhere.

However, the principle of national sovereignty – that states are the supreme authority within their own borders – makes it very difficult for external authorities (such as the United Nations) to intervene. This is despite the existence of international conventions and laws against acts such as genocide, war crimes and racial discrimination.

2 The state is the source of law

It is the state's role to define what is criminal, and to manage the criminal justice system and prosecute offenders. State crime undermines the system of justice. Its power to make the law also means that it can avoid defining its own harmful actions as criminal. For example, in Nazi Germany, the state created laws permitting it to sterilise disabled people against their will. State control of the criminal justice system also means that it can persecute its enemies.

Human rights and state crime

One approach to the study of state crime is through the notion of human rights. There is no single agreed list of what constitutes human rights. However, most definitions include the following:

- **Natural rights** that people are regarded as having simply by virtue of existing, such as rights to life, liberty and free speech.
- **Civil rights**, such as the right to vote, to privacy, to a fair trial, or to education.

A right is an entitlement to something; as such, it acts as a protection against the power of the state over an individual. For example, the right to a fair trial means that the state may not imprison a person without due process of law.

Crime as the violation of human rights

Critical criminologists such as Herman and Julia Schwendinger (1970) argue that we should define crime in terms of the violation of basic human rights, rather than the breaking of legal rules. This means that states that deny individuals' human rights must be regarded as criminal. For example, states that practise imperialism, racism or sexism, or that inflict economic exploitation on their citizens, are committing crimes, because they are denying individuals and groups their basic rights. The Schwendingers object to the idea that:

> 'a man who steals a paltry sum can be called a criminal, while agents of the State can legally reward men who destroy food so that price levels can be maintained whilst a sizable portion of the population suffers from malnutrition.'

From a human rights perspective, the state can be seen as a perpetrator of crime and not simply as the authority that defines and punishes crime.

In this view, the definition of crime is inevitably political. For example, in the 1930s, the Nazi state attacked the human rights of Jews and other German citizens, perfectly legally, simply by passing laws that persecuted them. If we accept a *legal* definition (that crimes are simply whatever the state says they are), we risk becoming subservient to the state that makes the law. The Schwendingers argue that the sociologist's role should be to defend human rights, if necessary against the state and its laws. In this respect, their view is an example of *transgressive* criminology, since it oversteps the traditional boundaries of criminology that are defined by the criminal law.

However, Stanley Cohen (1996; 2001) criticises the Schwendingers' view. For example, while 'gross' violations of human rights, such as genocide, torture and disappearances of dissidents are clearly crimes (of murder, assault and kidnapping respectively), other acts, such as economic exploitation, are not self-evidently criminal, even if we find them morally unacceptable. Other critics argue that there is only limited agreement on what counts as a human right. For example, while there would be little disagreement that life and liberty are human rights, some would argue that freedom from poverty is not.

State crime and the culture of denial

Although Cohen criticises the Schwendingers, he nevertheless sees the issue of human rights and state crime as increasingly central both to political debate and criminology, as a result of two factors:

- The growing impact of the international human rights movement, for example through the work of organisations such as Amnesty International.
- The increased focus within criminology upon victims.

The spiral of denial

Cohen is particularly interested in the ways in which states conceal and legitimate their human rights crimes. He argues that while dictatorships generally simply deny committing human rights abuses, democratic states have to legitimate their actions in more complex ways. In doing so, their justifications follow a three-stage 'spiral of state denial':

Stage 1 'It didn't happen'. For example, the state claims there was no massacre. But then human rights organisations, victims and the media show it did happen: 'here are the graves; we have the photos; look at the autopsy reports'.

Stage 2 'If it did happen, "it" is something else'. The state says it is not what it looks like – it's 'collateral damage' or 'self-defence'.

Stage 3 'Even if it is what you say it is, it's justified' – for example, 'to protect national security' or 'fight the war on terror'.

Neutralisation theory

Cohen examines the ways in which states and their officials deny or justify their crimes. He draws on the work of Sykes and Matza (1957), who identify five *neutralisation techniques* that delinquents use to justify their deviant behaviour.

Cohen shows how states use the same techniques when they are attempting to justify human rights violations such as torture, massacres etc:

- **Denial of victim** They exaggerate; they are terrorists; they are used to violence; look what they do to each other.
- **Denial of injury** They started it; we are the real victims, not them.

- **Denial of responsibility** I was only obeying orders, doing my duty. (This justification is often used by individual policemen, death camp guards etc.)
- **Condemning the condemners** The whole world is picking on us; it's worse elsewhere; they are condemning us only because of their anti-Semitism (the Israeli version), their hostility to Islam (the Arab version), their racism.
- **Appeal to higher loyalty** Self-righteous justification – the appeal to the higher cause, whether the nation, the revolution, Zionism, Islam, the defence of the 'free world', state security etc.

These techniques do not seek to deny that the event has occurred. Rather, as Cohen says, 'they seek to negotiate or impose a different construction of the event from what might appear to be the case'.

Activity   Neutralisation techniques and the conflict in Gaza

Go to www.sociology.uk.net

The social conditions of state crime

It is often thought that those who carry out crimes such as torture and massacres must be psychopaths. However, research suggests that there is little psychological difference between them and 'normal' people.

Instead, sociologists argue that such actions are part of a role into which individuals are socialised. They focus on the social conditions in which such behaviour becomes acceptable or even required. For example, Kelman and Hamilton (1989) studied 'crimes of obedience' such as the one at My Lai in Vietnam, where a platoon of American soldiers massacred 400 civilians.

Kelman and Hamilton identify three features that produce crimes of obedience:

- **Authorisation** When acts are ordered or approved by those in authority, normal moral principles are replaced by the duty to obey.
- **Routinisation** Once the crime has been committed, there is strong pressure to turn the act into routine which individuals can perform in a detached manner.
- **Dehumanisation** When the enemy is portrayed as sub-human rather than human and described as animals, monsters etc, the usual principles of morality do not apply.

Some argue that modern society creates the conditions for such crime on a vast scale. For example, Zygmunt Bauman (1989) argues that the Holocaust – in which the Nazis murdered six million Jews and millions of Gypsies, Slavs, political opponents, disabled people, homosexuals and

others – was a product of modernity, and not a return to some pre-modern barbarism.

Bauman argues that for the Nazis to be able to commit mass murder, many of the features of modernity were essential. These included science, technology and the division of labour. He claims that the key to understanding the Holocaust is the ability of modern society to dehumanise the victims and turn mass murder into a routine administrative task.

For *more activities on* Globalisation, green crime, human rights and state crime...

Go to www.sociology.uk.net

Summary

Globalisation has brought with it the spread of transnational organised crime, for example trafficking drugs and people. Globalisation also brings de-industrialisation and insecurity, which lead to increased crime. It has also led to new forms of 'glocal' criminal organisation, with fluid networks and 'franchises' rather than the old mafia-style fixed hierarchies.

We now live in 'global risk society', where human-made threats include massive environmental damage. Green criminology adopts an ecocentric view and starts from the notion of *harm* rather than criminal law. It identifies both primary and secondary green crimes.

State crimes include genocide, war crimes and torture. The state has the power to commit massive human rights abuses and to legitimate its crimes using neutralisation techniques such as denial of responsibility. Human rights abuses are more likely to occur e.g. when the enemy is portrayed as sub-human.

QuickCheck Questions

1 Identify four types of globalised crime.

2 What is meant by 'global risk society'?

3 Explain what is meant by 'glocal' criminal organisation.

4 What advantage is there in defining green crime as breaking of the criminal law?

5 What is the disadvantage of defining green crime simply as breaking of the criminal law?

6 Suggest two examples of transgressive criminology.

7 Explain the difference between an anthropocentric and an ecocentric view of environmental harm.

8 Explain the difference between primary and secondary green crimes.

9 Explain what is meant by 'state crime'.

10 Explain what is meant by 'neutralisation techniques' and give one example of such a technique.

 Check your answers at www.sociology.uk.net

Examining globalisation, green crime, human rights and state crimes

Examine the relationship between crimes against the environment and the process of globalisation. (12 marks)

The examiner's advice

This question carries 6 AO1 marks (knowledge and understanding) and 6 AO2 marks (interpretation, application, analysis and evaluation).

You could begin your answer by defining globalisation as growing interconnectedness across national frontiers. You should then go on to consider the different ways in which globalisation may increase the risk of environmental damage, e.g. through global warming, acid rain, illegal dumping of toxic waste etc. The distinction between primary and secondary green crimes could be used here. You also could note that globalisation may give rise to coordinated international responses to such problems, including laws, treaties and policing.

You can evaluate the relationship between globalisation and environmental crime by raising questions about how we define such crime. For example, traditional criminology has a narrower, legal definition, while green criminology starts from the wider notion of environmental harm.

Topic 9 Control, punishment and victims

Most of this chapter has focused on criminals and criminalisation. By contrast, in this Topic, we turn our attention first to what can be done to prevent crime, ranging from changing the immediate situation where crime occurs, to community programmes designed to tackle the root causes of offending.

One view increasingly popular with politicians is that tougher punishments, especially prison, are the best way to prevent crime. In this Topic, we look at the nature and functions of punishment from a number of perspectives, and we consider reasons for the rapid growth in the prison population.

In previous Topics, we have seen how certain groups are likely to be victims of crime. We conclude this Topic with a closer look at victims and 'victimology', including which groups are at greatest risk of victimisation.

Learning objectives

After studying this Topic, you should:

- Understand and be able to evaluate a range of crime prevention and control strategies.
- Understand and be able to evaluate different perspectives on punishment.
- Know the main trends in sentencing and understand their significance.
- Know the main patterns of victimisation and be able to evaluate sociological perspectives on victimisation.

Crime prevention and control

What makes people conform? And when they are tempted not to do so, what can be done to prevent them deviating? These questions raise the issue of social control – the capacity of societies to regulate their members' behaviour – and crime prevention. This section examines different approaches to these questions.

> What prevention measures (i) do you take personally to avoid being a victim of crime in different situations; (ii) are taken in the family home; (iii) have you seen elsewhere (e.g. school/college, shops, transport) in the last few days?

Situational crime prevention

Ron Clarke (1992) describes situational crime prevention as 'a pre-emptive approach that relies, not on improving society or its institutions, but simply on reducing opportunities for crime'. He identifies three features of measures aimed at situational crime prevention:

- They are directed at specific crimes.
- They involve managing or altering the immediate environment of the crime.
- They aim at increasing the effort and risks of committing crime and reducing the rewards.

For example, 'target hardening' measures such as locking doors and windows increase the effort a burglar needs to make, while increased surveillance in shops via CCTV or security guards increase the likelihood of shoplifters being caught. Similarly, replacing coin-operated gas meters with pre-payment cards reduces the burglar's rewards.

Underlying situational crime prevention approaches is an 'opportunity' or rational choice theory of crime. This is the view that criminals act rationally, weighing up the costs and benefits of a crime opportunity before deciding whether to commit it. (For more on rational choice theory, see Topic 4.)

This contrasts with theories of crime that stress 'root causes' such as the criminal's early socialisation or capitalist exploitation. To deal with crime, we would have to transform the socialisation of large numbers of children or carry out a revolution. Clarke argues that most theories offer no realistic solutions to crime. The most obvious thing to do, he argues, is to focus on the immediate crime situation, since this is where scope for prevention is greatest. Most crime is opportunistic, so we need to reduce the opportunities.

Marcus Felson (1998) gives an example of a situational crime prevention strategy. The Port Authority Bus Terminal in New York City was poorly designed and provided opportunities for deviant conduct. For example, the toilets were a setting for luggage thefts, rough sleeping, drug dealing and homosexual liaisons. Re-shaping the physical environment to 'design crime out' greatly reduced such activity. For example, large sinks, in which homeless people were bathing, were replaced by small hand basins.

Displacement

One criticism of situational crime prevention measures is that they do not reduce crime; they simply displace it. After all, if criminals are acting rationally, presumably they will respond to target hardening simply by moving to where targets are softer. For example, Chaiken et al (1974) found that a crackdown on subway robberies in New York merely displaced them to the streets above.

Displacement can take several forms:

- **Spatial** – moving elsewhere to commit the crime.
- **Temporal** – committing it at a different time.
- **Target** – choosing a different victim.
- **Tactical** – using a different method.
- **Functional** – committing a different type of crime.

Perhaps the most striking example of the success of situational measures is not about crime, but about suicide. In the early 1960s, half of all suicides in Britain were the result of gassing. At that time, Britain's gas supply came from highly toxic coal gas. From the 1960s, coal gas was gradually replaced by less toxic natural gas, and by 1997 suicides from gassing had fallen to near zero. What is striking, however, is that the *overall* suicide rate declined, not just deaths from gassing. Those who might otherwise have killed themselves by gassing seem not to have switched to another method. In other words, there was no displacement.

Evaluation

- Situational crime prevention works to some extent in reducing certain kinds of crime. However, with most measures there is likely to be some displacement.
- It tends to focus on opportunistic petty street crime. It ignores white-collar, corporate and state crime, which are more costly and harmful.
- It assumes criminals make rational calculations. This seems unlikely in many crimes of violence, and crimes committed under the influence of drugs or alcohol.
- It ignores the root causes of crime, such as poverty or poor socialisation. This makes it difficult to develop long-term strategies for crime reduction.

- CCTV surveillance has been criticised. Norris and Armstrong (1999) found that camera operators focus disproportionately on young males. For feminists, CCTV is an extension of the 'male gaze' and is part of the problem, not the solution.

Activity **Devising an anti-burglary strategy**

Go to www.sociology.uk.net

Environmental crime prevention

This approach is based on James Q. Wilson and George Kelling's (1982) article, *Broken Windows*, which has been described as 'perhaps the most influential single article on crime prevention ever written' (Downes 1999).

Wilson and Kelling use the phrase 'broken windows' to stand for all the various signs of disorder and lack of concern for others that are found in some neighbourhoods. This includes undue noise, graffiti, begging, dog fouling, littering, vandalism and so on. They argue that leaving broken windows unrepaired, tolerating aggressive begging etc, sends out a signal that no one cares.

In such neighbourhoods, there is an absence of both formal social control (the police) and informal control (the community). The police are only concerned with serious crime and turn a blind eye to petty nuisance behaviour, while respectable members of the community feel intimidated and powerless. Without remedial action, the situation deteriorates, tipping the neighbourhood into a spiral of decline. Respectable people move out (if they can) and the area becomes a magnet for deviants.

Zero tolerance policing

Wilson and Kelling's key idea is that disorder and the absence of controls leads to crime. Their solution is to crack down on any disorder, using a twofold strategy. First, an *environmental improvement strategy*: any broken window must be repaired immediately, abandoned cars towed without delay etc, otherwise more will follow and the neighbourhood will be on the slide.

Secondly, the police must adopt a *zero tolerance policing strategy*. Instead of merely reacting to crime, they must proactively tackle even the slightest sign of disorder, even if it is not criminal. This will halt neighbourhood decline and prevent serious crime taking root.

The evidence

Great successes have been claimed for zero tolerance policing, especially in New York (where Kelling was an adviser to the police). For example, a 'Clean Car Program' was instituted on the subway, in which cars were taken out of service immediately if they had any graffiti on them, only returning once clean. As a result, graffiti was largely removed from the subway. Other successful programs to tackle fare dodging, drug dealing and begging followed.

Later, the same approach was extended to the city's police precincts. For example, a crackdown on 'squeegee merchants' discovered that many had outstanding warrants for violent and property crimes. Between 1993 and 1996, there was a significant fall in crime in the city, including a 50% drop in the homicide rate – from 1,927 to 986.

However, it is not clear how far zero tolerance was the cause of the improvements.

- The NYPD benefited from 7,000 extra officers.
- There was a general decline in the crime rate in major US cities at the time – including ones where police did *not* adopt a zero tolerance policy.
- The early 1990s had seen a major recession and high unemployment, but from 1994 many new jobs were being created.
- There was a decline in the availability of crack cocaine.
- While deaths from homicides fell sharply, attempted homicides remained high. It has been suggested that the fall in the murder rate owed more to improved medical emergency services than policing.

Nonetheless, zero tolerance has been very influential globally, including the UK, where it has influenced New Labour's anti-social behaviour policies.

What problems might arise if a zero tolerance policy is introduced into a neighbourhood?

Social and community crime prevention

While Wilson and Kelling show some recognition of the role of the community and informal controls in preventing crime, the main emphasis of policies based on their ideas has been in terms of policing.

By contrast, social and community prevention strategies place the emphasis firmly on the potential offender and their social context. The aim of these strategies is to remove the conditions that predispose individuals to crime in the first place. These are longer-term strategies, since they attempt to tackle the root causes of offending, rather than simply removing opportunities for crime.

Because the causes of crime are often rooted in social conditions such as poverty, unemployment and poor housing, more general social reform programmes addressing these issues may have a crime prevention role, even if this is not their main focus. For example, policies to promote full employment are likely to reduce crime as a 'side effect'.

The Perry pre-school project

One of the best-known community programmes aimed at reducing criminality is the experimental Perry pre-school project for disadvantaged black children in Ypsilanti, Michigan. An experimental group of 3-4 year olds was offered a two-year intellectual enrichment programme, during which time the children also received weekly home visits.

A longitudinal study followed the children's subsequent progress. It showed striking differences with a control group who had not undergone the programme. By age 40, they had significantly fewer lifetime arrests for violent crime, property crime and drugs, while more had graduated from high school and were in employment. It was calculated that for every dollar spent on the programme, $17 were saved on welfare, prison and other costs.

Activity The Perry pre-school project and crime prevention

Go to www.sociology.uk.net

What is missing?

The approaches that we have discussed above take for granted the nature and definition of crime. They generally focus on fairly low-level and/or interpersonal crimes of violence. This disregards the crimes of the powerful and environmental crimes.

This definition of the 'crime problem' reflects the priorities of politicians and agencies tasked with crime prevention. For example, Whyte conducted a survey of 26 crime and disorder area partnerships in the North West of England to discover what crimes their strategies were targeting. The results are in Table 2B.

Table 2B	Targets of crime reduction strategies in the North West of England
Vehicle crime	26
Burglary	24
Drug related crime	15
Violent crime	15
Anti social behaviour	12
Youth offending/causing a nuisance	12
Road safety/speeding	11
Domestic violence	8
Robbery	8
Fear of crime	7

Source: Walklate (2005)

At the same time, the Environment Agency instituted 98 prosecutions in 2001-02 in the North West, including 62 for waste offences, 32 for water quality offences, and two for radioactive substance offences. The North West also has one of the most heavily concentrated sites of chemical production in Europe, where just two plants between them release into the air about 40% of all the factory-produced cancer-causing chemicals in the UK every year.

Whyte points out that there is no logical reason why such activities should not be included in the crime and disorder partnership agendas – yet despite their potential and actual effect on the health of local communities, they are not.

Punishment

One measure that many believe to be effective in crime prevention is of course punishment. Given that punishment involves deliberately inflicting harm, two main justifications have been offered for it: reduction and retribution. These justifications link to different penal policies.

Reduction

One justification for punishing offenders is that it prevents future crime. This can be done through:

- **Deterrence** Punishing the individual discourages them from future offending. 'Making an example' of them may also serve as a deterrent to the public at large. Deterrence policies include Mrs Thatcher's Conservative government's 'short, sharp shock' regime in young offenders' institutions in the 1980s.

- **Rehabilitation** is the idea that punishment can be used to reform or change offenders so they no longer offend. Rehabilitation policies include providing education and training for prisoners so that they are able to 'earn an honest living' on release, and anger management courses for violent offenders.

- **Incapacitation** is the use of punishment to remove the offender's capacity to offend again. Policies in different societies have included imprisonment, execution, the cutting off of hands, and chemical castration. Incapacitation has proved increasingly popular with politicians, with the American 'three strikes and you're out' policy (where committing even a minor third offence can lead to lengthy prison time) and the view that 'prison works' because it removes offenders from society.

This justification is an *instrumental* one – punishment is a means to an end, namely crime reduction.

Retribution

Retribution means 'paying back'. It is a justification for punishing crimes that have already been committed, rather than preventing future crimes. It is based on the idea that offenders deserve to be punished, and that society is entitled to take its revenge on the offender for having breached its moral code. This is an *expressive* rather than instrumental view of punishment – it expresses society's outrage.

Sociological perspectives on punishment

Sociologists are interested in the relationship between punishment and society. They ask questions about its function, why its form varies over time, and how it relates to the society in which it is found.

Durkheim: a functionalist perspective

Functionalists such as Durkheim (1893) argue that the function of punishment is to uphold social solidarity and reinforce shared values. Punishment is primarily expressive – it expresses society's emotions of moral outrage at the offence. Through rituals of order, such as public trial and punishment, society's shared values are reaffirmed and its members come to feel a sense of moral unity.

Two types of justice

While punishment functions to uphold social solidarity, it does so differently in different types of society. Durkheim identifies two types of justice, corresponding to two types of society.

Retributive justice In traditional society, there is little specialisation, and solidarity between individuals is based on their similarity to one another. This produces a strong collective conscience, which, when offended, responds with vengeful passion to repress the wrongdoer. Punishment is severe and cruel, and its motivation is purely expressive.

Restitutive justice In modern society, there is extensive specialisation, and solidarity is based on the resulting interdependence between individuals. Crime damages this interdependence, so it is necessary to repair the damage, for example through compensation. Durkheim calls this restitutive justice, because it aims to make restitution – to restore things to how they were before the offence. Its motivation is instrumental, to restore society's equilibrium. Nevertheless, even in modern society, punishment still has an expressive element, because it still expresses collective emotions.

In reality, however, traditional societies often have restitutive rather than retributive justice as Durkheim thought. For example, blood feuds (where a member of one clan is killed by a member of another) are often settled by payment of compensation rather than execution.

Marxism: capitalism and punishment

Marxists see society as divided into two classes, in which the ruling class exploits the labour of the subordinate class. They are interested in how punishment is related to the nature of class society and how it serves ruling-class interests.

For Marxists, the *function of punishment* is to maintain the existing social order. As part of the 'repressive state apparatus', it is a means of defending ruling-class property against the lower classes. For example, E.P. Thompson (1977) describes how in the 18th century punishments such as hanging and transportation to the colonies for theft and poaching were part of a 'rule of terror' by the landed aristocracy over the poor.

The *form of punishment* reflects the economic base of society. As Georg Rusche and Otto Kirchheimer (1939) argue, each type of economy has its own corresponding penal system. For example, money fines are impossible without a money economy. They argue that under capitalism, imprisonment becomes the dominant form of punishment because the capitalist economy is based on the exploitation of wage labour.

Similarly, Melossi and Pavarini (1981) see imprisonment as reflecting capitalist relations of production. For example:

- Capitalism puts a price on the worker's time; so too prisoners 'do time' to 'pay' for their crime (or 'repay a debt to society').
- The prison and the capitalist factory both have a similar strict disciplinary style, involving subordination and loss of liberty.

Foucault: birth of the prison

Michel Foucault's (1977) *Discipline and Punish* opens with a striking contrast between two different forms of punishment, which he sees as examples of *sovereign power* and *disciplinary power* (see Box 2.3).

Sovereign power was typical of the period before the 19th century, when the monarch had power over people and their bodies. Inflicting punishment on the body was the means of asserting control. Punishment was a *spectacle*, such as public execution.

Disciplinary power becomes dominant from the 19th century. In this form of control, a new system of discipline seeks to govern not just the body, but the mind or 'soul'. It does so through *surveillance*.

Foucault illustrates disciplinary power with the panopticon. The panopticon was a design for a prison in which all prisoners' cells are visible to the guards from a central watchtower, but the guards are not visible to the prisoners. Thus the prisoners don't know if they *are* being watched, but they do know that they *might* be being watched. As a result, they have to behave at all times as if they were being watched, so the surveillance turns into *self*-surveillance and discipline becomes *self*-discipline. Instead of being a public spectacle, control takes place 'inside' the prisoner.

Foucault argues that the prison is one of a range of institutions that, from the 19th century, increasingly began to subject individuals to disciplinary power to induce conformity through self-surveillance. These include mental asylums, barracks, factories, workhouses and schools. In Foucault's view, disciplinary power has now infiltrated every part of society, bringing its effects 'to the most minute and distant elements' – to the human 'soul', in fact. Thus he argues that the change in the form of punishment from sovereign to disciplinary power in the penal system also tells us about how power operates in society as a whole.

Foucault's work has stimulated considerable research into surveillance and the exercise of disciplinary power but has also been criticised on several grounds:

- The shift from corporal punishment to imprisonment is less clear than he suggests.

Box 2.3   Sovereign power and disciplinary power

Foucault illustrates the difference between the two types of power as follows:

Sovereign power: a description of an execution in 1757

On a scaffold that will be erected, the flesh will be torn from his breasts, arms, thighs and calves with red hot pincer, his right hand burnt with sulphur, and, on those places where the flesh will be torn away, poured molten lead, boiling oil, burning resin, wax and sulphur melted together and then his body drawn and quartered by four horses and his limbs and body consumed by fire, reduced to ashes and thrown to the winds.

Disciplinary power: from a prison timetable in the 1830s

Article 17 The prisoners' day will begin at six in the morning… and they will work for nine hours a day.

Article 18 Rising. At the first drum-roll, the prisoners must rise and dress in silence. At the second drum-roll, they must be dressed and make their beds. At the third, they must line up and proceed to the chapel for morning prayers.

Article 19 The prayers are conducted by the chaplain and followed by a moral or religious reading. This exercise must not last more than half an hour.

- Unlike Durkheim, he neglects the expressive (emotional) aspects of punishment.
- He exaggerates the extent of control. For example, Goffman (1962) shows how inmates are able to resist controls in institutions such as prisons and mental hospitals.

The changing role of prisons

Pre-industrial Europe had a wide range of punishments, including warnings, banishment, transportation, corporal punishment and execution. Until the 18th century, prison was used mainly for holding offenders *prior* to their punishment (such as flogging). It was only following the Enlightenment that imprisonment began to be seen as a form of punishment in itself, where offenders would be 'reformed' through hard labour, religious instruction and surveillance.

Imprisonment today

In liberal democracies that do not have the death penalty, imprisonment is regarded as the most severe form of punishment. However, it has not proved an effective method of rehabilitation – about two-thirds of prisoners commit further crimes on release. Many critics regard prisons as simply an expensive way of making bad people worse.

Nevertheless, since the 1980s there has been a move towards 'populist punitiveness', where politicians have sought electoral popularity by calling for tougher sentences. For example, New Labour governments after 1997 took the view that prison should be used not just for serious offenders, but also as a deterrent for persistent petty offenders.

As a result, the prison population has swollen to record size: between 1993 and 2005, the number of prisoners in England and Wales grew by about 70% to reach a total of 77,000. One consequence has been overcrowding, added to existing problems of poor sanitation, barely edible food, clothing shortages, lack of educational and work opportunities, and inadequate family visits (Carrabine et al 2008).

This country imprisons a higher proportion of people than almost any other in Western Europe. For example, in England and Wales, 139 out of every 100,000 people are in prison. Corresponding figures for some other countries are France 99, Germany 91, Ireland 86, Sweden 64 and Iceland 37. However, the world leaders are Russia (607) and the USA (730).

The prison population is largely male (only about 5% are female), young and poorly educated. Black and ethnic minorities are over-represented.

The era of mass incarceration?

According to David Garland (2001), the USA, and to a lesser extent the UK, is moving into an era of mass incarceration. For most of the last century, the American prison population was stable, at around 100-120 per 100,000. In 1972, there were about 200,000 inmates in state and federal prisons.

However, from the 1970s, the numbers began to rise rapidly, and there are now 1.5 million state and federal prisoners, plus 700,000 in local jails. A further 5 million are under the supervision of the criminal justice system (on parole, probation etc) – in total, over 3% of the adult population.

Once figures reach these proportions, Garland argues,

> 'It ceases to be the incarceration of individual offenders and becomes the systematic imprisonment of whole groups of the population. In the case of the USA, the group concerned is, of course, young black males'.

For example, in 2001, for every 100,000 black males, 3,535 were in prison, as against 462 for white males.

This may have an ideological function. As David Downes (2001) argues, the US prison system soaks up about 30-40% of the unemployed, thereby making capitalism look more successful.

Garland argues that the reason for mass incarceration is the growing politicisation of crime control. For most of the last century there was a consensus, which Garland calls 'penal welfarism' – the idea that punishment should reintegrate offenders into society.

However, since the 1970s, there has been a move towards a new consensus based on more punitive and exclusionary 'tough on crime' policies, and this has led to rising numbers in prison.

Another reason is the use of prison to wage America's 'war on drugs'. As Simon (2001) argues, because drug use is so widespread, this has produced 'an almost limitless supply of arrestable and imprisonable offenders'.

Transcarceration

As well as mass incarceration, there is a trend towards transcarceration – the idea that individuals become locked into a cycle of control, shifting between different carceral agencies during their lives.

For example, someone might be brought up in care, then sent to a young offenders' institution, then adult prison, with bouts in mental hospital in between.

Some sociologists see transcarceration as a product of the blurring of boundaries between criminal justice and welfare agencies. For example, health, housing and social services are increasingly being given a crime control role, and they often engage in multi-agency working with the police, sharing data on the same individuals.

Alternatives to prison

In the past, a major goal in dealing with young offenders was 'diversion' – diverting them away from contact with the criminal justice system to avoid the risk of a self-fulfilling prophecy turning them into serious criminals. The focus was on welfare and treatment, using non-custodial, community-based controls such as probation.

In recent years there has been a growth in the range of community-based controls, such as curfews, community service orders, treatment orders and electronic tagging. However, at the same time, the numbers in custody have been rising steadily, especially among the young.

This has led Stanley Cohen to argue that the growth of community controls has simply cast the *net of control* over more people (Innes 2003). Following Foucault's ideas, Cohen argues that the increased range of sanctions available simply enables control to penetrate ever deeper into society.

Far from diverting young people from the criminal justice system, community controls may divert them into it. For example, some argue that the police use ASBOs as a way of fast-tracking young offenders into custodial sentences.

Synoptic links: theory & core themes

Zero tolerance policing strategies reflect New Right **theories** of the threat to social stability posed by the underclass, while social and community prevention strategies such as the Perry project stress the importance of early **socialisation**.

Patterns of imprisonment show the influence of **stratification**, with black people and the poor greatly over-represented in jail.

Poststructuralist theory sees surveillance and discipline as a form of '**power**/knowledge' exercising control over the population.

The victims of crime

The United Nations defines victims as those who have suffered harm (including mental, physical or emotional suffering, economic loss and impairment of their basic rights) through acts or omissions that violate the laws of the state.

Nils Christie (1986) takes a different approach, highlighting the notion that 'victim' is socially constructed. The stereotype of the 'ideal victim' favoured by the media, public and criminal justice system is a weak, innocent and blameless individual – such as a small child or old woman – who is the target of a stranger's attack.

It is important to study victims not least because they play an essential role in the criminal justice process. For example, they provide much of the evidence used in the detection of offenders and they act as witnesses at trials. The study of victims is sometimes known as 'victimology'. We can identify two broad perspectives: positivist victimology, and critical victimology.

Positivist victimology

Miers (1989) defines positivist victimology as having *three* features:

- It aims to identify the factors that produce *patterns in victimisation* – especially those that make some individuals or groups more likely to be victims.
- It focuses on *interpersonal crimes of violence*.
- It aims to identify victims who have *contributed to their own victimisation*.

The earliest positivist studies focused on the idea of *victim proneness*. They sought to identify the social and psychological characteristics of victims that make them different from, and more vulnerable than, non-victims. For example, Hans Von Hentig (1948) identified 13 characteristics of victims, such as that they are likely to be females, elderly or 'mentally subnormal'. The implication is that the victims in some sense 'invite' victimisation by being the kind of person that they are. This can also include lifestyle factors such as victims who ostentatiously display their wealth.

An example of positivist victimology is Marvin Wolfgang's (1958) study of 588 homicides in Philadelphia. Wolfgang found that 26% involved *victim precipitation* – the victim triggered the events leading to the homicide, for instance by being the first to use violence. For example, this was often the case where the victim was male and the perpetrator female.

Evaluation

- As Fiona Brookman (2005) notes, Wolfgang shows the importance of the victim-offender relationship and the fact that in many homicides, it is a matter of chance which party becomes the victim.
- This approach identifies certain patterns of interpersonal victimisation, but ignores wider structural factors influencing victimisation, such as poverty and patriarchy.
- It can easily tip over into victim blaming. For example, Amir's (1971) claim that one in five rapes are victim precipitated is not very different from saying that the victims 'asked for it'.
- It ignores situations where victims are unaware of their victimisation, as with some crimes against the environment, and where harm is done but no law broken.

Critical victimology

Critical victimology is based on conflict theories such as Marxism and feminism, and shares the same approach as critical criminology. It focuses on two elements:

- **Structural factors**, such as patriarchy and poverty, which place powerless groups such as women and the poor at greater risk of victimisation. As Mawby and Walklate (1994) argue, victimisation is a form of *structural powerlessness*.
- **The state's power to apply or deny the label of victim** 'Victim' is a social construct in the same way as 'crime' and 'criminal'. Through the criminal justice process, the state applies the label of victim to some but withholds it from others – for example when police decide not to press charges against a man for assaulting his wife, thereby denying her victim status.

Similarly, Tombs and Whyte (2007) show that 'safety crimes', where employers' violations of the law lead to death or injury to workers, are often explained away as the fault of 'accident prone' workers. As with many rape cases, this both denies the victim official 'victim status' and blames them for their fate.

Tombs and Whyte note the ideological function of this 'failure to label'. By concealing the true extent of victimisation and its real causes, it hides the crimes of the powerful and denies the powerless victims any redress. In the *hierarchy of victimisation*, therefore, the powerless are most likely to be victimised, yet least likely to have this acknowledged by the state.

Evaluation

- Critical victimology disregards the role victims may play in bringing victimisation on themselves through their own choices (e.g. not making their home secure) or their own offending.
- It is valuable in drawing attention to the way that 'victim' status is constructed by power and how this benefits the powerful at the expense of the powerless.

Patterns of victimisation

The average chance of an individual being the victim of a crime in any one year is about one in four. However, the risk is very unevenly distributed between social groups.

Class The poorest groups are more likely to be victimised. For example, crime rates are typically highest in areas of high unemployment and deprivation.

The fact that marginalised groups are most likely to become victims is borne out by a survey of 300 homeless people (Newburn and Rock 2006). This found that they were 12 times more likely to have experienced violence than the general population. One in ten had been urinated on while sleeping rough.

> Suggest three reasons why the poorest social groups are most likely to be victims of crime.

Age Younger people are at more risk of victimisation. Those most at risk of being murdered are infants under one, while teenagers are more vulnerable than adults to offences including assault, sexual harassment, theft, and abuse at home. The old are also at risk of abuse, for example in nursing homes, where victimisation is less visible.

Ethnicity Minority ethnic groups are at greater risk than whites of being victims of crime in general, as well as of racially motivated crimes. In relation to the police, ethnic minorities, the young and the homeless, are more likely to report feeling under-protected yet over-controlled.

Gender Males are at greater risk than females of becoming victims of violent attacks, especially by strangers. About 70% of homicide victims are male. However, women are more likely to be victims of domestic violence, sexual violence, stalking and harassment, people trafficking and – in times of armed conflict – mass rape as a weapon of war.

Repeat victimisation refers to the fact that, if you have been a victim once, you are very likely to be one again. According to the British Crime Survey, about 60% of the population have not been victims of any kind of crime in a given year, whereas a mere 4% of the population are victims of 44% of all crimes in that period.

Methods Link: using interviews

Ditton et al (2000) used qualitative interviews with open-ended questions to explore people's feelings about crime. They argue that previous attempts to measure 'fear of crime' using quantitative methods were imposing the researchers' own concerns on the respondents. The results of the interviews suggested that anger rather than fear was the main concern people had about crime.

Qualitative or unstructured interviews can produce valid data through exploring people's feelings and meanings, but they generally involve small samples and are less likely to be representative. For this reason, Ditton et al constructed a questionnaire that they distributed to 1600 Scottish households to test their findings.

Read more about interviews and researching crime and deviance in *Methods in Context*, Chapter 3, Topic 4.

The impact of victimisation

Crime may have serious physical and emotional impacts on its victims. For example, research has found a variety of effects (depending on the crime), including disrupted sleep, feelings of helplessness, increased security-consciousness, and difficulties in social functioning.

Crime may also create 'indirect' victims, such as friends, relatives and witnesses to the crime. For example, Pynoos et al (1987) found that child witnesses of a sniper attack continued to have grief-related dreams and altered behaviour a year after the event.

Similarly, hate crimes against minorities may create 'waves of harm' that radiate out to affect others. These are 'message' crimes aimed at intimidating whole communities, not just the primary victim. Even more widely, such crimes also challenge the value system of the whole society.

Secondary victimisation is the idea that in addition to the impact of the crime itself, individuals may suffer further victimisation at the hands of the criminal justice system. feminists argue that rape victims are often so poorly treated by the police and the courts, it amounts to a double violation.

Fear of victimisation Crime may create fear of becoming a victim. Some sociologists argue that surveys show this fear to be often irrational. For example, women are more afraid of going out for fear of attack, yet it is young men who are the main victims of violence from strangers. However, Feminists have attacked the emphasis on 'fear of crime'. They argue that it focuses on women's passivity and their psychological state, when we should be focusing on their *safety* – i.e. on the structural threat of patriarchal violence that they face.

Summary

Situational crime prevention focuses on reducing opportunities for crime, e.g. through target hardening. One problem is displacement, where criminals respond by seeking softer targets. Environmental crime prevention focuses on mending 'broken windows' and zero tolerance policing. Social and community prevention strategies attempt to tackle the root causes of offending. However, most prevention strategies ignore crimes of the powerful.

For functionalists, punishment functions to promote solidarity. For Marxists, it preserves the status quo and is shaped by the economic base. Foucault argues that disciplinary power now governs individuals through surveillance and self-surveillance. Prisons have become the key institution of punishment and there is a trend towards mass incarceration. Community punishments may simply cast the net of control more widely.

Positivist victimology focuses on victim proneness or precipitation. Critical victimology emphasises structural factors such as poverty, and the state's power to apply or deny the label of victim. The poor, the young and ethnic minorities are at greater risk of victimisation.

For more activities on Control, punishment and victims...

 **Go to www.sociology.uk.net**

QuickCheck Questions

1 Explain the difference between target hardening and displacement.

2 Suggest two criticisms of situational crime prevention strategies apart from displacement.

3 What is meant by 'zero tolerance policing'?

4 Explain the difference between retributive and restitutive justice.

5 According to Marxists, why has imprisonment become the dominant form of punishment?

6 Explain what Foucault means by 'disciplinary power'.

7 What is meant by 'transcarceration'?

8 Suggest two criticisms of positivist victimology.

 Check your answers at www.sociology.uk.net

Examining control, punishment and victims

Item A In 1982, Wilson and Kelling wrote: 'A piece of property is abandoned, weeds grow up, a window is smashed. Adults stop scolding rowdy children; the children, emboldened, become more rowdy. Families move out; unmarried adults move in. Teenagers gather in front of the corner store. The merchant asks them to move; they refuse. Fights occur. Litter accumulates.'

Wilson and Kelling argue that the police have a key role to play in warding off neighbourhood decline by policing this kind of disorder, for example moving the rowdy elements out of the area. In their view, this will prevent crime developing.

However, critics such as Jock Young argue that this is a 'quick fix' to complex problems.

Essay Using material from **Item A** and elsewhere, assess sociological views of crime reduction strategies. (21 marks)

The examiner's advice

This question carries 9 AO1 (knowledge and understanding) marks and 12 AO2 (interpretation, application, analysis and evaluation) marks.

You could begin by identifying the approach in the Item as an environmental crime prevention or 'zero tolerance policing' strategy, linking it to right realism. You should outline this strategy and evaluate its effectiveness – e.g. does dealing with *disorder* actually prevent *crime*? What evidence is there to support this strategy? Use the Item to discuss the problem of displacement, and to consider the 'complex problems' Young refers to, such as social exclusion or relative deprivation. You should also consider both situational and social and community crime reduction strategies. Link these to other theories such as right and left realism. How far do all the strategies take the definition of the crime problem to mean simply street crime?

Jodhpur, India. The handprints of widows made just before they threw themselves on their husbands' funeral pyres. The last recorded case of sati was in the mid 19th century.

Topic 10 Suicide

Learning objectives

After studying this Topic, you should:

- Know the main features of the main sociological explanations of suicide.
- Understand the similarities and differences between positivist, interactionist, ethnomethodological and realist approaches to suicide.
- Be able to evaluate the strengths and limitations of different sociological explanations of suicide.

Only a tiny minority of deaths are the result of suicide. Yet suicide is of interest to sociologists for at least two reasons:

- Suicide is a disturbing and fascinating topic in its own right – how can we explain why an individual should choose to end his or her own life?
- The study of suicide has a unique place in sociology, because it was the subject that Emile Durkheim chose to use in order to demonstrate that sociology had its own distinctive contribution to understanding human behaviour.

Since Durkheim, some sociologists have sought to develop and refine his work. By contrast, others have rejected Durkheim's approach as fundamentally misplaced and proposed quite different ways of studying suicide.

In this Topic, we examine the main sociological theories of suicide.

Durkheim, positivism and suicide

The first major sociological contribution to our understanding of suicide came from the French positivist sociologist, Emile Durkheim, writing in the late 19th century. Positivism is the belief that society can and should be studied scientifically and that sociology should model itself on the logic and methods of the natural sciences such as chemistry and physics. These disciplines observe patterns in the natural world and develop laws of cause and effect to explain them. The goal of sociology should be to produce laws to explain observed patterns in human behaviour.

Durkheim was writing at a time when sociology was struggling to establish itself as an academic discipline in its own right, and his study of suicide was part of his project to demonstrate the validity of sociology as a subject.

At first sight, his choice of suicide seems an odd one, given that we tend to think of it as an intensely personal act and often as the product of mental illness. As such, it might be thought a better subject for psychologists than sociologists. Nevertheless, Durkheim believed he could show that suicide had social causes and that this would prove that sociology was a distinct and genuinely scientific discipline.

For Durkheim, sociology can discover real scientific laws. There are observable patterns or regularities in human behaviour, and we can discover causal explanations (laws) for them. If Durkheim could show that there were social patterns in suicide and discover their social causes, he would in his view have shown sociology to be a science.

Before presenting his own sociological explanation of suicide, however, Durkheim examines and rejects a number of other theories. As well as demonstrating that factors such as climate have no effect on the suicide rate (a popular view at the time), he argues that psychological theories of suicide are also inadequate. While Durkheim accepts that some individuals may be psychologically more predisposed to suicide than others – for example as a result of depression – he rejects the view that psychological factors can explain the differences in the suicide rates of whole groups or societies. For instance, he shows that while Jews had higher rates of mental illness than Protestants, they nonetheless had lower suicide rates.

Suicide rates as social facts

In Durkheim's view, our behaviour is caused by *social facts* – social forces found in the structure of society. According to Steven Lukes (1992), social facts have three features:

- They are external to individuals
- They constrain individuals, shaping their behaviour
- They are greater than individuals - they exist on a different 'level' from the individual.

For Durkheim, the suicide rate is a social fact.

Using quantitative data from official statistics, Durkheim analysed the suicide rates for various European countries over a period of several decades in the 19th century. He noted four regular patterns:

1 Suicide rates for any given society remained more or less constant over time.

2 When the rates did change, this coincided with other changes. For example, the rates fell during wartime, while they rose at times of economic depression and – perhaps surprisingly – times of rising prosperity.

3 Different societies have different rates.

4 Within a society, the rates varied considerably between different social groups. For example, Catholics had lower rates than Protestants, married people with children had lower rates than the single, widowed or childless, and rural dwellers had lower rates than city dwellers.

For Durkheim, these patterns were evidence that suicide rates could not simply be the result of the motives of individuals. For example, the population of the city of Paris is constantly changing, and the French army, too, is made up of different individuals as the years go by. Yet in both cases, Durkheim notes, the suicide rate remains more or less constant over time.

Instead of giving a psychological explanation, therefore, Durkheim explains the suicide rate as the effect of social facts or forces acting upon individuals. In different groups and societies, these forces act with different degrees of intensity, resulting in different suicide rates.

Durkheim's four types of suicide

What are the social facts that act on individuals to cause different rates of suicide? Durkheim identifies two social facts that determine the rate of suicide:

- **Social integration** refers to the extent to which individuals experience a sense of belonging to a group and obligation to its members. In highly integrated groups and societies, individuals feel a strong bond with and sense of duty towards others.
- **Moral regulation** refers to the extent to which individuals' actions and desires are kept in check by norms and values. In Durkheim's view, without regulation by socially defined goals and rules, individuals' desires are infinite and incapable of satisfaction.

Durkheim argues that suicide results from either too much or too little integration or regulation. This gives a fourfold typology (classification system) of suicide:

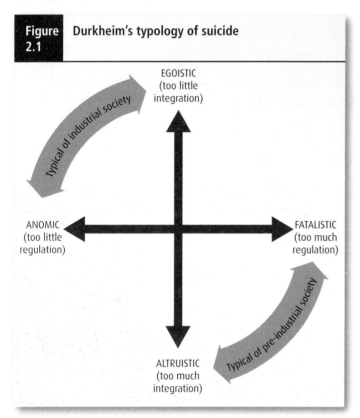

Figure 2.1	Durkheim's typology of suicide

1 Egoistic suicide is caused by too little social integration. Durkheim argues that this is the most common type of suicide in modern society, caused by excessive individualism and lack of social ties and obligations to others.

This explains the lower rate among Catholics than among Protestants. Both religions condemn suicide, but Protestants have more individual freedom in what to believe and how to express their faith, whereas Catholics are more tightly integrated by shared beliefs and collective ritual. Egoistic suicide is also less common in times of war and political upheaval, since these create a stronger sense of belonging and common purpose.

2 Altruistic suicide is the opposite of egoistic suicide and is caused by too much social integration. Altruism is the opposite of selfishness or egoism, and involves putting others before oneself. Altruistic suicide occurs where the individual has little value and where the group's interests override those of the individual. Suicide here is an obligatory self-sacrifice for the good of the group, rather than something freely chosen, since the individual feels it as their *duty* to die.

For example, during World War Two, Japanese kamikaze pilots were expected to crash their planes into American warships, while in the past, Hindu widows were expected to perform *sati*, throwing themselves on their husband's burning funeral pyre so as not to be a burden on the family. Among some Inuit peoples, the old were expected to walk out into the cold to die for similar reasons.

3 Anomic suicide is caused by too little moral regulation. Anomie means 'normlessness' or deregulation, and anomic suicide occurs where society's norms become unclear or are made obsolete by rapid social change, creating uncertainty in individuals as to what society expects of them.

For example, sudden economic slumps, such as the Wall Street stock exchange crash of 1929 that led to the great depression of the 1930s, produce an increase in anomic suicides. So too do economic booms and rapid increases in prosperity. Durkheim attributes this to the fact that booms lead to expectations and desires rising more quickly than the means of fulfilling them.

4 Fatalistic suicide is the opposite of anomic suicide and is caused by too much moral regulation. Fatalism means a belief on the part of the individual that they can do nothing to affect their situation or destiny. Fatalistic suicide occurs where society regulates or controls the individual completely – where individuals find their 'futures pitilessly blocked and passions violently checked by oppressive discipline', crushing all hope. Slaves and prisoners are the most commonly cited examples of groups likely to commit fatalistic suicide.

Suicide and type of society

For Durkheim, modern societies and traditional societies differ from one another in their levels of integration and regulation, and this means that we tend to find different types of suicide in each type of society:

Modern industrial societies have lower levels of integration. Individuals' rights and freedoms become more important than obligations towards the group. This weakens social bonds and gives rise to *egoistic suicides*. Similarly, modern societies are less effective in regulating individuals because they undergo rapid social change, which undermines accepted norms and produces *anomic suicides*.

Traditional pre-industrial societies have higher levels of integration. The group is more important than the individual and this gives rise to *altruistic suicides*. Similarly, these societies strictly regulate their members' lives and impose rigidly ascribed statuses that limit individuals' opportunities, and this produces *fatalistic suicides*.

Later positivist approaches

Other positivists since Durkheim have sought to build on his work. For example, Maurice Halbwachs (1930), a student of Durkheim's, accepted his positivist approach but sought to modify and add to his theory. Halbwachs had access to more recent and probably more reliable statistics than Durkheim, as well as more sophisticated statistical techniques.

Although largely confirming Durkheim's findings, Halbwachs argued that differences between urban and rural residence were the main reason for variations in suicide rates. Higher rates among Protestants, people living alone and so on were more a function of their urban location – these groups were more likely to be found in towns, where people lead more isolated lives. Similarly, Sainsbury (1955) found that suicide rates in London boroughs were highest where the levels of social disorganisation (such as divorce and illegitimacy) were highest.

Gibbs and Martin

Jack Gibbs and Walter Martin (1964) regard Durkheim's as 'the foremost sociological theory of variability in suicide rates'. Like Durkheim, they wish to make law-like, cause-and-effect generalisations and predictions. However, they argue that Durkheim does not operationalise his concept of integration (define it in such a way that it can be measured).

Gibbs and Martin go on to define integration as a situation where there are stable and lasting relationships. They argue that these tend to occur when an individual has *status integration* – compatible statuses that do not conflict with one another, for example, when their educational and occupational statuses are similar. They predict that in societies where there is little status integration (for instance, where many well educated people are forced to take low

status jobs), the suicide rate will be higher.

Other aspects of Durkheim's study have also been criticised. For example, it is argued that the statistics he used were unreliable and incomplete – in the 19th century, medical knowledge of the causes of death was limited and autopsies rarely performed. Similarly, many countries lacked the sophisticated modern administrative system needed to collect and compile reliable statistics on a national basis. However, these criticisms do not challenge the basic aim of Durkheim's study, to achieve a scientific explanation of suicide. By contrast, other sociologists, adopting an interpretivist perspective, offer a more fundamental critique of his positivist approach.

▲ *The Hollywood Museum: pill bottle found by Marilyn Monroe's bedside the night she died. Controversy continues as to whether her overdose was deliberate.*

Interpretivism and suicide

While positivists have sought to build on Durkheim's theory, interpretivists have sought to demolish it. Interpretivists focus on the meanings of suicide for those involved.

Douglas: the social meanings of suicide

Jack D. Douglas (1967) takes a largely interactionist approach to suicide. He is interested in the meaning that suicide has for the deceased, and in the way that coroners label deaths as suicides. He criticises Durkheim's study of suicide on two main grounds.

1 The use of suicide statistics

The decision to classify a death as suicide is taken by a coroner and influenced by other social actors, and this may produce bias in the verdicts reached. Douglas argues that this may explain the patterns that Durkheim found. For example, the finding that a high level of integration leads to low suicide rates can be explained by the fact that well integrated individuals may have friends and relatives who might deny that the death was suicide out of their own feelings of guilt, or even cover it up by destroying a suicide note.

By contrast, socially isolated individuals will have no one to oppose a suicide verdict on their behalf. Thus, although it might seem as if integration prevents suicide, in fact integration merely affects the likelihood of a death being *labelled and recorded* as suicide, rather than of it actually *being* a suicide.

For Douglas, suicide verdicts and the statistics based on them are the product of interactions and negotiations between those involved – relatives, friends, doctors, police, the coroner and so on, and factors such as integration influence these negotiations.

2 Actors' meanings and qualitative data

Douglas criticises Durkheim for ignoring the meanings of the act for those who kill themselves and for assuming that suicide has a fixed or constant meaning. In particular, Douglas notes that the meanings of suicide can vary between cultures. For example, the dishonoured Japanese samurai warrior and the western businessman facing financial ruin may attach very different meanings to their deaths. These motives and meanings must be understood within their own social and cultural context, and this means that Durkheim's attempt to compare rates across cultures is faced with problems.

Douglas also rejects Durkheim's aim to categorise suicides in terms of their social causes. Instead we must classify each death according to its actual meaning for the deceased. To do this, we must use qualitative methods and sources to produce case studies based on the analysis of suicide notes and diaries, and in-depth interviews with the suicide's friends and relatives. From these, we can build up a typology of suicidal meanings.

Although Douglas did not carry out any case studies himself, he suggests that in Western societies the social meanings of suicide include escape, repentance, a search for help or sympathy, self-punishment, revenge and seriousness. However, he points out that suicide may have different

Methods Link: using documents

Jerry Jacobs (1967) analysed 112 suicide notes to gain an understanding of the social meanings of suicide. By putting himself into the actor's place and using verstehen, he was able to classify 102 of the notes into a typology of six categories based on the actor's intentions. For example, one category was people who were ill and felt they could not go on. Jacobs argues that the notes are coherent and rational, and reflect the deceased's conscious deliberation.

Interpretivists see suicide notes as a direct and meaningful form of communication from the deceased. Because they are not written for the researcher, they are likely to be a valid account of motives and meanings.

However, Jacobs' relatively small sample may not be representative of suicides in general. For example, those with less coherent motives or who act on impulse may not leave notes. There is also no guarantee that Jacobs' interpretation of their meaning is correct.

Read more about documents and researching crime and deviance in **Methods in Context**, Chapter 3, Topic 6.

meanings in other cultures, for example religious ones such as transformation of the soul (getting to heaven).

For Douglas, using qualitative data also overcomes the problems caused by relying on official statistics. Analysis of suicide notes and so on would allow us to 'get behind' the labels that coroners attach to cases and discover the real meaning of the death for the person involved. From this, we could get a better idea of the real rate of suicide than the socially constructed one that appears in the statistics.

Activity   Suicide risk to service personnel

Go to www.sociology.uk.net

Criticisms of Douglas

Douglas produces a classification of suicide based on the supposed meanings for the actors. However, there is no reason to believe that sociologists are any better than coroners at interpreting a dead person's meanings.

Sainsbury and Barraclough (1968) found that the rank order of suicides for immigrant groups to the USA correlated closely with that of the suicide rates for their countries of origin, despite the fact that a different set of labellers were involved – American coroners rather than those of their home countries. This suggests that statistics reflect real differences between groups, rather than coroners' labelling.

Douglas is inconsistent, sometimes suggesting that official statistics are merely the product of coroners' opinions. At other times, he claims we really can discover the causes of suicide – yet how can we, if we can never know whether a death was a suicide and all we have is coroners' opinions?

Atkinson: ethnomethodology and suicide

J. Maxwell Atkinson (1978) takes a different interpretivist approach from Douglas, that of ethnomethodology. Ethnomethodology argues that social reality is simply a construct of its members. We create reality using a stock of taken-for-granted, commonsense knowledge. The sociologist's job is to uncover what this knowledge is and how we use it to make sense of the world. (For more on ethnomethodology, see Chapter 4, Topic 3.)

Starting from this perspective, Atkinson reviews Douglas' contribution. As we have seen, Douglas argues that:

- Official statistics are merely the constructs or labels coroners give to deaths.
- Using qualitative data allows us to get behind these labels to find the deceased's real meanings. From this we can discover the real rate of suicide.

Atkinson accepts Douglas' first point but rejects his second. For Atkinson, we can never know the real rate of suicide, since we would have to know for sure what meanings the dead gave to their deaths, which is impossible. Therefore it is pointless trying to discover the 'real rate'. All we can study is how people make sense of their world. With suicide, this means studying how the living come to classify a death as a suicide, accident etc. The statistics are neither right nor wrong – they too are merely interpretations made by certain officials, and so all we can study is how they were constructed. As Atkinson puts it, the only task for sociologists is to discover 'How do deaths get categorised as suicide?'

Atkinson therefore focuses on how coroners categorise deaths (though others, such as police, doctors and relatives, also play a part in the process). To do so, he uses a range of qualitative methods, including conversations with coroners, observations of inquests and examination of court records. From this research, he concludes that coroners have a commonsense theory about the typical suicide. This includes what kind of person commits suicide, for what reasons, what is a typical mode or place of death and so on. If a particular case fits their *commonsense theory*, coroners are more likely to categorise the death as a suicide.

> How might police, doctors, friends and relatives affect the way coroners categorise deaths? Suggest an example for each.

Atkinson argues that coroners' commonsense theories lead them to see the following types of evidence as relevant:

- **A suicide note** or suicide threats prior to death.
- **Mode of death** For example, hanging is seen as 'typically suicidal', whereas road deaths are 'typically accidental'. Deaths from drug overdoses or drowning are generally less clear-cut.
- **Location and circumstances** Death by shooting is more likely to be recorded as suicide if it occurs in a deserted lay-by than when out with a hunting party.
- **Life history** A disturbed childhood, a history of mental illness, or a difficult social or personal situation, such as problems at work, social isolation, bereavement, divorce, bankruptcy or redundancy are seen as likely causes of suicide.

Coroners regard information such as this as clues to whether the deceased intended to take their own life. For example, Atkinson (1971) quotes one coroner as saying that in the case of drownings, he looked for whether the clothes had been left 'neatly folded on the beach. If so, it usually points to a suicide.' Another said:

'My real problem is when someone has taken less than ten barbiturates. That's when I have to be on the lookout for special evidence. If he takes more than ten, I can be almost sure it was a suicide.'

Atkinson concludes that coroners are engaged in analysing cases using taken-for-granted assumptions about what constitutes a 'typical suicide', a 'typical suicide life history' and so on. A verdict of suicide is simply an interpretation of a death based on these taken-for-granted assumptions.

If correct, this poses serious problems for theories such as Durkheim's that treat statistics as facts – because all they are doing is spelling out the coroners' theories about suicide. For example, if coroners believe that typical suicides are socially isolated people, then more of these people will end up in the statistics. The sociologist who then takes the statistics at face value and produces a theory saying that lack of integration causes suicide is merely echoing the coroners' commonsense theory – not discovering the cause of suicide.

Evaluation of Atkinson

Structuralists such as Barry Hindess (1973) criticise ethnomethodologists' approach as self-defeating. Atkinson's view that the only thing we can study about suicide is coroners' interpretations can be turned back on him. If all we can have is interpretations of the social world, rather than objective truth about it (such as the real suicide rate), then ethnomethodologists' own accounts are themselves no more than interpretations. If so, there is no good reason why we should accept them.

However, most ethnomethodologists accept that their accounts are merely interpretations. Unlike positivists, who claim to produce objective, scientific accounts, they do not claim that their interpretations are superior to those of the people (such as coroners) they study.

> ## Synoptic link: theory
>
> The debate about how best to understand suicide is closely linked to the theoretical debate about sociology as a science. Positivists see the study of suicide as a test case demonstrating that sociology is the scientific study of objective facts, while interpretivists argue that it shows sociology's subject matter to be actors' meanings and social constructs.

Taylor: realism and suicide

Steve Taylor (1982; 1989) takes a different approach to both positivists and interpretivists. Like the interpretivists, he argues that suicide statistics cannot be taken as valid. For example, in a study of 32 people who had died after being hit by London tube trains, just over half the cases resulted in a verdict of suicide, even though there was no conclusive evidence of suicidal intent. Taylor found that coroners saw factors such as a history of mental illness as indicators of suicidal intent and this increased the likelihood of a suicide verdict.

However, like the positivists, Taylor still believes we can explain suicide. He believes we can discover real patterns and causes, although unlike positivists, he does not base his explanation on suicide statistics. Instead, he adopts a *realist* approach. This aims to reveal underlying structures and causes, which though not directly observable, can explain the observable evidence. He uses case studies to discover the underlying structures of meaning that cause suicide.

Defining suicide

Many theories of suicide focus on acts where the individual was intent on dying and that resulted in death. For example, Durkheim's study is about 'cases of death resulting directly or indirectly from a positive or negative act by the victim himself, which he knows will produce this result'.

However, Taylor notes that in many cases, those who attempt suicide are not certain that their actions will kill them. Nor are all who attempt suicide simply aiming to die – some are communicating with others. Therefore we should look at both successful and unsuccessful attempts and adopt a broader definition of suicide as:

'any deliberate act of self-damage or potential self-damage where the individual cannot be sure of survival'.

Types of suicide

Taylor suggests that the situations where a person is most likely to attempt suicide are those where there is complete certainty or complete uncertainty, either about themselves or about others. This gives him the four possible types of suicide shown in Figure 2.2.

The first two types are inner- or *self-directed* suicides (which Taylor calls 'ectopic'), where the individual is psychologically detached from others. Because of this, the suicide attempt is a private, self-contained act. There are two types of ectopic suicide:

1 **Submissive suicides**, where the person is *certain about themselves*. For example, they may know they have no future or reason to go on (e.g. terminal illness). Their suicide attempt is deadly serious, because they know they want to die.

2 **Thanatation suicides**, where they are *uncertain about themselves*. For example they may be uncertain about what others think of them. Their suicide attempt involves risk taking – they may or may not survive it, chance will decide – for example, playing Russian roulette.

The other two types are *other-directed* (or symphysic) suicides, where the individual has an overwhelming attachment to some other person(s). For example, they feel that the other gives them a reason for living.

These suicides are not self-contained, but a way of communicating with others. Again, there are two types:

3 **Sacrifice suicides**, where they are *certain about others* and know they have to kill themselves. Like submissive suicides, their attempt is deadly serious. Usually, either they or the other person has done something that makes it impossible for the individual to go on living, for example betrayal through an affair. This suicide is a form of communication in which they may seek to blame the other for their death, usually so they will suffer guilt.

4 **Appeal suicides**, where the person is *uncertain about others*. They have doubts about their importance to the other and attempt suicide to resolve the uncertainty. The attempt is a form of communication that seeks to change the other's behaviour. Like thanatation suicides, they involve risk taking and uncertainty about the outcome. They are 'acts of despair and of hope', combining the wish to die and the wish to change things for the better.

Figure 2.2	Taylor's four types of suicide

Self-directed (ectopic)	Other-directed (symphysic)
1. Submissive suicides – certainty about self	3. Sacrifice suicides – certainty about others
2. Thanatation suicides – uncertainty about self	4. Appeal suicides – uncertainty about others

Evaluation

Taylor's theory is based on his interpretations of the actors' meanings and there is no way of knowing if these are correct, especially in the case of those whose attempts succeeded. Also, individual cases may involve a combination of motives and be difficult to categorise.

Taylor's small sample of case studies, while useful in giving insight into motives, is unlikely to be representative of suicides in general.

Unlike Durkheim, Taylor has not connected the four types to wider social structures. However, there are similarities between the two:

- Taylor's ideas of certainty and uncertainty parallel Durkheim's notions of fatalism and anomie respectively.
- Taylor's self-directed and other-directed suicides parallel Durkheim's egoistic and altruistic suicides respectively.

Nevertheless, his theory is original and useful in explaining some of the observed patterns of suicide, such as why attempts differ in seriousness and why only some leave notes. It also deals with both failed and successful attempts.

For more activities on Suicide...

Go to www.sociology.uk.net

Summary

Durkheim used suicide to demonstrate that a scientific sociology was possible. Using official statistics, it would study social facts that shape behaviour. Two social facts, integration and regulation, determine the type and level of suicide.

Douglas criticises Durkheim for using statistics, since these are merely the product of coroners' labels, and for ignoring actors' meanings. He recommends qualitative case studies to discover these and the real rate of suicide.

Atkinson disagrees that it is possible to discover the real rate. Instead we should seek to uncover the commonsense theories and assumptions that coroners use in reaching a verdict, such as ideas about the mode of death.

Taylor's realist approach aims to reveal the underlying structures of meaning that cause suicide. He classifies suicides according to degree of certainty and whether they are self or other-directed.

QuickCheck Questions

1 Why did Durkheim choose to study such a personal act as suicide?

2 What are the three characteristics of a social fact?

3 Which of Durkheim's types of suicide results from too little regulation in a rapidly changing society?

4 Why do modern industrial societies have low levels of integration?

5 Suggest three common social meanings given to suicide in the UK today.

6 Identify three types of evidence coroners might look for to determine whether or not a death is suicide.

7 What does Taylor mean by 'other-directed' suicides?

8 Taylor's sacrifice suicide is similar to which of Durkheim's types?

Check your answers at www.sociology.uk.net

Examining suicide

Item A In a comparative study of decision making about suicide conducted by Atkinson, Kessel and Dalgaard, four English coroners and five Danish coroners were given 40 cases and asked to give their verdict on each of them.

The Danish coroners were much more likely to give a verdict of suicide compared with the English coroners. For example, out of the 40 cases, the Danes gave on average 29 suicide verdicts, whereas the English averaged only 19.25.

The study concludes that the difference is due to the fact that in Denmark, a suicide verdict can be given when suicide seems likely 'on the balance of probability', whereas in England coroners must find evidence of 'definite suicidal intention'.

Essay Using material from **Item A** and elsewhere, assess the usefulness of different sociological approaches to suicide. (21 marks)

The examiner's advice

This question carries 9 AO1 (knowledge and understanding) marks and 12 AO2 (interpretation, application, analysis and evaluation) marks.

You need to examine a number of theories of suicide, but you should avoid lengthy descriptions of the various suicide typologies and focus on the differences in perspective. Start with Durkheim's positivist approach, covering key concepts such as social facts, integration and regulation. You could evaluate this by using Douglas's ideas on the social meanings of suicide.

Make use of the Item to illustrate the idea that suicide verdicts are labels socially constructed by coroners, and that the law is one factor affecting how labels are constructed. You could use this to introduce Atkinson's ethnomethodological approach focusing on coroners' commonsense knowledge and the issue of the 'real rate'. Also include reference to Taylor's realist approach; for example, you can use it to evaluate both positivist and interpretivist approaches.

Exam question and student answer

Examining crime and deviance

Item A   Most offenders are young, working-class urban dwellers. However, perhaps the most striking finding is not that most criminals are working-class, but – as Maureen Cain (1989) points out – that 'most criminals are, and always have been, men'.

For example, four out of five convicted offenders are male. Male offenders have longer criminal careers and typically commit more serious crimes, including violent and sexual offences, as well as over 90 per cent of all homicides.

(a) Examine some of the reasons for the existence of deviant subcultures.   (12 marks)

(b) Using material from **Item A** and elsewhere, assess the view that gender is the best predictor of criminality.   (21 marks)

The examiner's advice

Part (a) carries 6 AO1 marks (knowledge and understanding) and 6 AO2 marks (interpretation, application, analysis and evaluation), so you need to show a balance of knowledge and skills.

You need to examine a range of reasons and you should draw them from more than one study. You could begin with the idea of blocked access to legitimate opportunities as a reason for subcultures in general and then look at A.K. Cohen's status frustration theory, showing how the subculture provides an alternative status hierarchy for those who fail in the mainstream.

You should also distinguish between different types of subcultural deviance, e.g. by comparing Cohen with Cloward and Ohlin's three types of subculture, using the concept of illegitimate opportunity structures. You can also contrast Walter Miller's idea of an independent lower-class culture with its own focal concerns with the other theories, which all see subcultures as a *reaction* to failure in the mainstream.

Part (b) carries 9 AO1 marks and 12 AO2 marks, so in addition to a good knowledge, you must show well-developed AO2 skills.

You need to put forward arguments and evidence both for and against the view in the question. You could begin by drawing upon the Item to note that according to official statistics, gender is a good predictor of criminality in that men commit the vast majority of crimes, especially the more serious ones. You should go on to consider some possible explanations for this pattern, for example, social control and socialisation differences between genders.

You could evaluate this view with the claim that women's offending is under-recorded, explaining why by reference to the chivalry thesis. You should also put the counter-argument that other sources such as self-report studies still show a gender gap in offending. Finally, you could note that other variables, such as age, class or urban dwelling, might make equally good or better predictors of criminality than gender.

Answer by Hana

Many sociologists argue that there are differences in offending between males and females. As Item A says, four-fifths of those convicted are male, and they commit more serious crimes, such as assault, rape and murder. This leads some writers such as Maureen Cain to conclude that most criminals are and always have been men.

> Summarises the Item but it would be a good idea to explain the question as well.

Feminist sociologists such as Frances Heidensohn have tried to explain this pattern by arguing that women and girls are subjected to more social control than males. At work, women are usually in more junior positions and so they get less chance to commit major crimes such as defrauding the company on a large scale. They may also be subjected to sexual harassment by their male supervisors and colleagues.

> Shows good knowledge of Heidensohn.

Heidensohn also argues that at home females are under patriarchal control and have less opportunity to commit crimes because they are obliged to spend much of their time indoors doing housework and childcare. Also, because they earn less than men, they may have less money to go out. Girls too are more closely supervised than boys and more likely to have curfews that keep them from getting into trouble on the streets. If they do go out, there is social pressure to behave in 'respectable' ways or risk getting a 'reputation' – although nowadays, there is more binge drinking and 'laddish' behaviour among young women, so it could be that social control is weakening.

> Further relevant knowledge and good, brief analysis point at the end.

However, even where females do commit offences, supporters of the chivalry thesis such as Otto Pollak argue that they do not necessarily get charged or prosecuted for it. He argues that this is because the police, judges, juries etc are mainly male and are socialised to be protective towards women. For example, police might let a woman motorist off with a warning but prosecute a man.

> Some relevant evaluation, but could be developed further.

Self-report studies back this up by showing that women have a higher rate of offending than appears to be the case from the official crime statistics. Women also have a better chance of getting let off with a caution rather than getting taken to court, so this masks the extent of female crime.

> Yes, but still not as high as men – and less serious crimes.

Women are also often the victims of male crime rather than the offenders, but this is also under-reported. For example, according to Stephanie Yearnshire, on average a woman suffers 35 domestic violence assaults before reporting it. Successful prosecutions for rape are also at a low rate. One reason for this is the sexist attitudes of the police and judges, who often treat women as if they were the ones on trial, not the rapist. The victims find they have to prove their respectability in order to be taken seriously.

> Should focus on women and men as offenders, not victims.

Overall I would conclude that gender is the best predictor of criminality, although not perfect because some crimes by women may not be counted by the official statistics because of chivalry factors.

The examiner's comments

Hana shows a reasonably good knowledge of some sociological material on gender and crime, and she makes some use of the material in the Item at the start. There is a good account of Heidensohn and she also has knowledge of relevant material on the chivalry thesis and on self-report studies.

Most of Hana's answer is relevant except towards the end, where she includes material on women as victims of domestic violence and rape. This needs to be tied in to the set question, which is about offending rather than victimisation. To make it relevant, she could talk about how men rather than women are more likely to commit domestic violence or sexual offences.

There is some relevant evaluation, using material on the chivalry thesis and self-report studies. However, the point could be made more explicitly that this challenges the idea of a gender gap in offending. Also it could be subjected to some evaluation – e.g. perhaps women are let off with cautions more because their offences are less serious and they are more likely to show remorse. A better answer would need to develop the evaluation further, for example by returning to the Item and the idea that most offenders are also young and working-class as well as male. This could be used to argue that class and age make equally good predictors of criminality. 14/21

Research Methods
with special application to crime and deviance

CHAPTER 3

Introduction

Sociologists seek to answer questions and develop theories about the social world. Theories are sets of abstract general ideas. Sociological theories usually take the form of explanations of how or why social life follows the patterns that it does.

A good theory is one that successfully explains all the available evidence that can be found about the topic in question. The test of a theory is whether it stands up to the evidence. If a theory fails to explain the evidence fully, then we need either to modify it or abandon it and replace it with one that does.

But where and how do we obtain the evidence? Sociologists engage in empirical research – that is, research to obtain facts about the real world – using a variety of research methods to gather information. The findings of this research are used to test sociological theories.

This chapter focuses on the different research methods sociologists use to gather their evidence. It begins with an overview of the different types of data and the practical, ethical and theoretical issues associated with the choice of research methods.

We then go on to look at the strengths and limitations of the major research methods used by sociologists.

We also examine the usefulness of each method in relation to the study of crime and deviance.

The AQA Specification

The specification is the syllabus produced by the exam board, telling you what you have to study. The AQA specification for Sociological Methods requires you to examine the following:

- Quantitative and qualitative methods of research; their strengths and limitations; research design.
- Sources of data, including questionnaires, interviews, observation (participant and non-participant), experiments, documents and official statistics; the strengths and limitations of these sources.
- The distinction between primary and secondary data, and between quantitative and qualitative data.
- The relationship between positivism, interpretivism and sociological methods; the nature of 'social facts'.
- The theoretical, practical and ethical considerations influencing choice of topic, choice of method(s) and the conduct of research.

You will have studied these topics at AS level, but at A2 you must show a broader and deeper knowledge and understanding, and more highly developed skills of interpretation, application, analysis and evaluation.

An overview of research methods

This section summarises the main features of research methods that you will be familiar with from your studies at AS level.

Types of data

In their research, sociologists make use of data from two types of source:

- **Primary data**, collected by sociologists themselves for their own research purposes. To gather it, they use methods such as questionnaires, interviews, observation and experiments.
- **Secondary data**, collected or created by someone else for their own purposes, but which the sociologist can then use. Sources include official statistics produced by government, and personal and public documents.

Data may be either quantitative or qualitative:

- **Quantitative data** are in numerical form. Examples include official statistics and most data from questionnaires, structured interviews and experiments.
- **Qualitative data** give a 'feel' for what something is like. Examples include data from participant observation, unstructured interviews and personal documents.

When selecting which research method(s) to use, sociologists need to take practical, ethical and theoretical considerations into account.

Practical issues

- **Time and money** Some methods are more costly or time consuming than others, and some researchers have access to more resources than others.
- **Requirements of funding bodies** Those funding the research may need a particular kind of data. For example, government may require quantitative data to assess whether a school had met its targets for exam passes.
- **Personal skills and characteristics** of the researcher may affect choice of methods. For example, unstructured interviews may require the ability to establish rapport. Some researchers may find this difficult and thus opt for a different method.
- **Subject matter** It may be harder to study a particular group or subject using one method rather than another. For example, written questionnaires may be useless for studying those who cannot read.
- **Research opportunity** If the opportunity to carry out research occurs unexpectedly, it may not be possible to use structured methods such as questionnaires, which take longer to prepare.

Ethical issues

- **Informed consent** Research participants should be offered the right to refuse to participate. The research must be explained clearly so that they can make an informed decision.
- **Confidentiality and privacy** Researchers should keep secret the identity of research participants, respect their privacy and keep personal information confidential.
- **Effects on research participants** Researchers need to be aware of any possible harmful effects of their work on those they study and should try to prevent them.
- **Vulnerable groups** Special care should be taken where research participants are particularly vulnerable because of age, disability, or physical or mental health.
- **Covert research** This may involve deceiving people and makes it impossible to gain informed consent. However, some sociologists argue that covert methods may be justified in order to gain access to secretive, deviant or powerful groups.

Theoretical issues

- **Validity** A valid method is one that produces a true picture of what something is really like.
- **Reliability** A reliable method is one that, when repeated by another researcher, gives the same results.
- **Representativeness** If the sample that we study is a typical cross-section of the wider population from which it is taken, we can use our findings to make generalisations about the wider population.
- **Methodological perspective** Positivists prefer methods that produce quantitative data, while interpretivists favour ones that yield qualitative data. This reflects their differing views as to whether sociology should be scientific or not.
- **Theoretical perspective** Action theories such as interactionism are micro perspectives – they see reality as socially constructed by individuals and their interactions. They prefer qualitative methods, since they see these as giving a valid account of individuals' meanings. Structural theories such as functionalism and Marxism are macro theories – they see the wider social structure shaping individuals' behaviour. They often prefer large-scale quantitative methods, since they see these as giving a picture of the social structure as a whole.

Quantitative or qualitative data?

In general, a sociologist's *preferred* method is likely to be one that fits with their methodological and theoretical perspective. For example, interpretivists might prefer to use participant observation for its valid, qualitative data, while positivists might favour questionnaires for their reliable, representative, quantitative data.

However, *practical and ethical considerations* may impose restrictions on our choice of method. Covert participant observation might give more valid data, but it is unethical to study a group without their knowledge. Instead, we may have to opt for unstructured interviews, for example. Similarly, a large, nationwide questionnaire may be too costly; we may have to settle for structured interviews with a smaller sample of people.

Reliability, representativeness and validity

Most sociologists would probably like a method that produced data that is reliable, *and* representative, *and* valid. Unfortunately, no single method is likely to deliver all three. Whichever method we choose, there is likely to be a trade-off. In practice, we often have to choose between *either* reliability and representativeness, *or* validity.

Generally, the quantitative methods favoured by positivists, such as questionnaires, are more structured and standardised, giving us more *reliable* (repeatable) results. These methods also allow us to study larger numbers, giving us results that are more *representative* of the wider population. On the other hand, they do not allow the researcher to be personally involved with the respondents and so they produce a more superficial understanding.

By contrast, the qualitative methods favoured by interpretivists, such as participant observation, require the researcher to become closely involved with the group they are studying. This brings a deeper understanding and a more *valid* picture of their lives. On the other hand, qualitative methods only permit the sociologist to study fairly small numbers of people, who may not be representative of the wider population. They are also less likely to produce reliable data, because they are hard to replicate.

Triangulation

For these reasons, sociologists sometimes use triangulation – combining different methods to obtain a more rounded picture.

For example, we might combine participant observation with questionnaires. This would allow us to see whether the valid insights we gained from observing a small group were applicable to a wider population.

Box 3.1	Some examples of types of data	
	Quantitative data	**Qualitative data**
Primary sources	Questionnaires Structured interviews Laboratory experiments	Participant observation Unstructured interviews
Secondary sources	Official statistics	Diaries, media content

Summary

Sociologists use primary and secondary sources of quantitative and qualitative data. In selecting a research method, sociologists take account of practical, ethical and theoretical factors.

Methodological and theoretical perspectives are important influences on choice of method, as are the quest for reliability, representativeness and validity.

QuickCheck Questions

1 Explain the difference between reliability and validity.
2 Why might questionnaires be expected to produce representative data?
3 Suggest three ethical considerations sociologists may need to take into account when conducting research.
4 Identify two practical issues affecting sociologists' choice of research method.

 Check your answers at www.sociology.uk.net

Why might police officers be a difficult group for sociologists to study?

Topic 1 Crime and deviance – the research context

As we saw in Chapter 2, sociologists have studied many different issues in crime and deviance, such as the media and crime, victims, gender differences in offending and so on.

In studying these and other issues, sociologists need to take account of the particular characteristics of crime and deviance, since these will affect their choice of research method.

For example, in studying prisoners there might be practical problems using participant observation, because it would prove difficult for a researcher to adopt a suitable role. Similarly, there would be both practical and ethical problems in using experiments to discover victims' experiences of crime.

In this Topic, we examine some of the key characteristics of crime and deviance as an area of research for sociologists, and we look at the opportunities and problems these characteristics can present to the researcher. From this, you will be able to see the kinds of things that you need to take account of when using different methods to research particular issues in crime and deviance.

This will help you to prepare for the compulsory **Methods in Context** question in the A2 Unit 4 exam. In this exam, you are required to apply a given research method to a particular issue in crime and deviance, such as crime prevention, ethnicity and crime, green crime and so on.

Throughout the rest of this chapter, we will be applying each of the different research methods we look at to the study of crime and deviance. You will find this in the special **Methods in Context** sections at the end of each Topic.

Learning objectives

After studying this Topic, you should:

- Know the main characteristics of crime and deviance as a context for sociological research.
- Understand some of the problems and opportunities that researching issues in crime and deviance presents for sociologists.
- Be aware of some of the research strategies sociologists use to investigate crime and deviance.

Researching crime and deviance

We can identify a number of characteristics of crime and deviance as important areas for research. These include the following:

- Domestic and other crimes of violence
- White-collar and corporate crime
- Young offenders
- Victims of crime
- The criminal justice system
- Societal reaction to crime and deviance
- Suicide

Each of these presents particular problems and opportunities for the sociologist in choosing a suitable method to use. We shall examine each of these characteristics in turn.

Researching domestic violence

Domestic violence takes place mainly in private, with few if any adult witnesses, and this makes it particularly difficult to study. For example, there are few opportunities for observation and interview data is difficult to validate.

Domestic violence is under-represented in official statistics, partly because the police are often not called. Similarly, it is under-reported in victimisation studies. The extent of under-reporting is difficult to estimate, but Dobash and Dobash found that the 109 semi-structured interviews they carried out with female victims exposed 32,000 assaults, of which only 517 were reported to the police.

There are few sampling frames for studying domestic violence. Official records are incomplete and information about victims is confidential and not readily available to researchers. Dobash and Dobash used a domestic violence refuge in Edinburgh for their sample. However, this raises doubts about the representativeness of their findings.

The traumatic nature of domestic violence also means that victims may go into unexpected and very personal areas in their responses, so the researcher needs to use methods that are flexible enough to accommodate this.

There is a greater need for confidentiality because of the danger of repeat violence to research subjects. It is also difficult to find a venue that offers the victim a safe setting for an interview.

> 1 How might women in a refuge differ from those still in their homes? Why does this make them potentially unrepresentative?
> 2 Suggest three reasons why female victims of domestic violence might not wish to involve the police.

Researching violent crimes

Violent crime is difficult to study in the context where it occurs. By their nature, violent acts are often swift and unexpected. There are few observational opportunities – a researcher may have to wait around for a long time before observing a violent act.

An alternative is to investigate a high-crime area or to participate in a subcultural group whose activities involve violence. Both approaches involve greater danger than the study of most social activities. Researchers working in high-crime areas may find themselves being 'asked' to leave, as were one Home Office-sponsored team investigating victim intimidation (Maynard 1994). In order not to draw attention to themselves, Sandra Walklate's researchers were told to carry their questionnaires around in plastic carrier bags rather than in more official-looking briefcases.

Some violent acts, for example domestic violence, take place in private and cannot be observed, so research has to be retrospective (conducted after the event), for example using interviews. However, victims of violent crime are less likely to agree to be interviewed than victims of other crimes – especially if the violence was recent, as Crawford et al (1990) discovered. In most participant observation studies of violent groups, observers record some instances of being involved in or threatened with violence. This raises both ethical issues and safety concerns.

Investigating the perpetrators of violent crime after the event also raises problems of cooperation, memory and ethics. For example, the researcher may be given information about violent crime that the police could use to prevent future acts.

Researching corporate crime

Some white-collar and corporate crimes have a low visibility. For example, they are less likely than most crimes to be reported by the media unless they fit some aspect of news values. Lower level white-collar crime may also be more socially acceptable than other forms of crime. As a result, it is likely to be under-reported to the police and under-estimated in crime statistics.

Corporate crime is often more complex than other forms of crime, so it is more difficult for sociologists (and police) to investigate. Some is international and studying it may be beyond the sociologist's resources. Corporate crime also often involves a *diffusion of responsibility* among many individuals, and tracking the role of each is difficult. There is also a *diffusion of impact*, making it difficult to identify and find victims who can answer questions.

Unlike most 'street' criminals, those committing corporate crime are likely to be powerful, organised groups who may enjoy political protection. The way crime is defined tends to exclude corporate crime. For example, 'crimes against the person' logically could, but in fact do not, extend to corporate decisions that lead to injury. As a result, official statistics on corporate crime under-estimate the extent and scale of such activities.

Suggest two reasons why it might be difficult to access a situation to study corporate crime as an observer.

Researching young offenders

The age of young offenders creates particular problems. Their language, literacy and cognitive skills are likely to be less developed, especially as many under-achieve at school. This may give rise to problems devising questions, while their under-achievement may also encourage a hostility to authority that they transfer onto the researcher. Members of youth subcultures may also make greater use of street slang and intra-group language that researchers need to learn.

The age of young offenders may generate some sympathy for them on the part of researchers and this may affect the direction and output of the study. For example, Howard Parker (1974) withheld some information about the boys he studied, publication of which might have caused them difficulties.

Young people are more vulnerable than adults and have less power. However, this relationship may be inverted when studying young offenders who are prepared to use violence.

Creating samples of young offenders is not straightforward. For example, the electoral register cannot be used as a sampling frame because many are too young to vote. Most samples use court records, school lists or snowball sampling.

Both overt and covert observation of delinquent youth subcultures may be difficult because the researcher may not easily fit in, due to class, age or gender differences. The group may also fear that the researcher is an informer. This can prevent the researcher working with local criminal justice agencies, since this risks alienating the group, who may see the researcher as a 'police officer in disguise'. There may also be personal danger, although this depends on the seriousness of the criminal activity and degree of organisation behind it.

There is a need to put young respondents at ease. Mike Maguire (2007) decided never to use tape recorders when interviewing because it was too formal and made interviewees guarded in their responses. He notes the suspicion young offenders had but also found it surprising just how many offenders volunteered information on recently committed offences once an interview was under way.

Researching victims of crime

There are particular issues to consider when researching victims of crime:

- With crimes such as drug deals there may be no easily identifiable victim.
- It is not always self-evident who is a victim. For example, some may be partially responsible for the offence (starting a fight, for example), while others reject the label of 'victim' because it implies weakness.
- Not everyone who is a victim of crime knows they are. This is especially true with corporate crime.
- Some victimisation is hidden from view – for example, domestic violence and child abuse.

Being a victim of crime is often traumatic and this has an important impact on the research process. Victims are more vulnerable and this requires greater sensitivity on the part of researchers. Researcher and victim may have different aims – to the researcher an interview is research, but to the victim it may be therapy.

Most research with victims has to be retrospective and so is dependent on their memory. It might be assumed that being a victim is memorable and easily recalled, but researchers find that even recent experiences are quickly forgotten or suppressed. In addition, studies typically ask victims to recall events from the last 12 months; unsurprisingly, people tend to recall more recent events better. Concealing or fabricating experiences of victimisation can also occur. All these problems may undermine the validity of retrospective investigations of victims' experiences.

Researching criminal justice

The criminal justice system includes among others, the police, courts and court officials, judges, solicitors and barristers, jurors, probation officers, prisons and prison officers. Here we examine the issues involved in studying some of these groups.

The police

The definition of 'policing' is problematic. It is carried out not only by regular police officers, but also by police community support officers and private security companies of various kinds.

The police are relatively isolated from wider society and often feel under public scrutiny. Lower ranking officers especially have a strong sense of group solidarity and a 'canteen culture' that is a barrier to research. Simon Holdaway (1983) claims that the lower ranks 'shield questionable practices' from the view of outsiders. This strong sense of group identity makes it difficult for an individual officer to 'break ranks', and means confidentiality during the research is particularly important.

▲ *What is the best method for measuring the effectiveness of crime prevention campaigns?*

Although there is pressure on the police to accept public scrutiny, some aspects of policing are off-limits to most researchers. For example, Robert Reiner was not allowed to ask police officers about their political opinions (Reiner and Newburn 2007).

A lot of police work takes place on the streets, outside immediate managerial control. The scattered nature of ground-level police work creates access issues for researchers. Some aspects of policing also take place within closed settings, off-limits to researchers.

Getting 'backstage' with police officers is more difficult than with many other groups. Officers often regard researchers as outsiders and see them as critical of the police. Unlike their research subjects, researchers usually have no official status. Even when they are carrying out official research for a government department, researchers may be treated with suspicion. The officers Reiner studied thought of him as a 'Home Office spy'.

Through their training and role within the criminal justice system (for example, making court appearances), police officers have a lot of experience in the presentation of professional self. Researchers thus need to use methods that enable them to get behind the impression management strategies of police officers.

Access to senior police officers is often very difficult. For example, it took Reiner ten years to get permission to research chief constables. This is one reason why there have been so few studies of this important group.

Researchers have the advantage of knowing where to locate the police because they are necessarily a high profile public body. Also, once permission for the research has been obtained, the hierarchical nature of the police service means that officers may be required by their superiors to cooperate. As it is an official organisation, ready-made local and regional sampling frames exist. Officers are also used to form filling, record keeping and being monitored, so they will have some familiarity with the research process. However, they are more used to asking than to being asked questions.

The courts and legal profession

Although much court activity is open to the public, some aspects take place in closed settings. For example, the law prohibits anyone from questioning jurors about cases. Many decisions are reached out of public view, in judges' chambers or in pre-trial discussions between lawyers.

The public nature of some aspects of justice offers useful observational opportunities to researchers, but only of the non-participant kind. Trials are often tedious affairs, with lengthy wrangles between lawyers and complex points of law being argued over, so an observer's time is easily wasted. Researchers not trained in the law may find court procedure hard to follow.

The power and status of the legal profession can make lawyers unwilling to be researched. However, the publicity surrounding miscarriages of justice and a growing demand for more transparency in their activities may have reduced their power to resist investigation.

The public nature of justice means that a good deal of official data about court decisions is in the public domain. Documents relating to legislation and information about legal processes are also publicly available.

Prisons

Prisons are generally among the most closed and controlled of social settings. However, prison regimes and their closure to the outside world vary greatly. Those who commit serious offences are held in higher security prisons or prison wings, while non-violent offenders not thought likely to abscond are often held in open prisons. Researchers generally have greater access to all aspects of life in open prisons. More than in most other areas of social life, the lack of roles for the researcher to occupy in prisons means that research has to be overt.

There are separate establishments for males and females, and for young offenders. This means that a single prison will not be representative of all institutions or prisoners. The vast majority of prisoners are young, male and working-class. This has to be taken into account in research. For example, literacy levels are lower than in the general population.

Prisons are very hierarchical settings and several layers of permission may be required before research can begin, including the Prison Service, the prison governor and the individual prisoners or officers.

Even once the research is under way, there may still be resistance from staff. For example, Davies (2000) felt the prison managers hoped she would get fed up with their blocking tactics and go away. Any disruption caused by the research is unlikely to be tolerated by the prison authorities, so researchers have to maintain good relations with staff.

The researcher's safety is a major consideration, especially when dealing with violent offenders. The risk of being taken hostage means the researcher needs to inform others of their whereabouts and intended time of return. However, there is usually a prison officer or 'panic button' nearby, and assaults on non-uniformed people in prison are rare. There is a further need not to jeopardise prison security.

Offenders who are in prison are easier to locate than those who are not. Once access for research has been negotiated, the refusal rate of the 'captive audience' is low, mainly because prison is often excruciatingly boring and participation in the research offers a diversion. Inmates may also cooperate as a way of winning favour with the authorities or in hopes of getting the researcher to do something for them, such as helping with their appeal.

However, the degree of institutional control over prisoners means they may not be available for research purposes. For example they may be in solitary confinement or appearing in court.

Researchers have to be aware of how they are viewed by prisoners. Boredom means prisoners spend a lot of their time analysing the minutiae of day-to-day interaction. Consequently, every minor action by the researcher may be subject to intense scrutiny.

Carol Martin (2000) identifies the ethical dilemmas faced by researchers who receive 'guilty knowledge' from inmates or staff. This includes being warned that a prisoner is at risk of attack, as well as staff or prisoners revealing that they are seriously depressed, or admitting to an assault for which they have not been charged.

Other ethical problems may arise when prisoners disclose disturbing information about their crimes, or when the researcher becomes too sympathetic to individuals living in a closed institution.

Researching societal reaction

The mass media play a major part in societal reactions to crime (see Chapter 2, Topic 7.) They report extensively on crime and deviance and this material is readily accessible. However, its sheer volume poses a problem for researchers in selecting a representative sample, while content analysis of large quantities of media output also takes time.

The structure of media ownership and control makes the process of news creation difficult to investigate. Although the media's output is publicly available, evidence of the backstage processes that create it is harder to obtain.

The media may trigger moral panics, but there are problems studying the process:

- People may not know where their knowledge of events comes from, so it is hard to track the development of a panic. Measuring public responses to media messages is also difficult.
- It is hard to know how much deviance is 'real' and pre-dates the panic, and how much is 'amplified'.
- It is impossible to re-create the process in laboratory environments.
- Different researchers interpret media messages differently, thus posing problems of validity.

Activity

In pairs, write a short questionnaire to assess people's attitudes towards street crime and white-collar crime.

How would you operationalise your measure of the social acceptability or unacceptability of these crimes?

Researching suicide

The absence of the main actor makes suicide an exceptionally difficult issue to investigate. However, survivors of failed suicide attempts may be interviewed. All research has to be retrospective.

There are many pressures on those involved not to identify a death as a suicide. For example, families may wish to cover up the real nature of the death, as might police or prison authorities faced with a suicide in their custody. Such pressure to redefine the act as something other than suicide is a major barrier to research.

Suicide is a highly sensitive issue to investigate. People close to the deceased may experience grief, guilt and depression and be unwilling or unable to cooperate with researchers.

Because a coroner's court has to investigate such deaths, there is a documentary trail researchers can follow. This may tell them more about how coroners determine whether a death is a suicide than about the reasons behind the death. As such, this is an important area of study in itself.

The existence of documentary evidence allows researchers to test the theories held by coroners in different areas. For example, Atkinson et al (1975) gave Danish and English coroners the case notes on forty deaths. They found that Danish coroners were much more likely than the English coroners to classify deaths as suicide. Official suicide statistics may thus be regarded as a summary of coroners' opinions rather than a picture of the real rate of suicide.

Activity

We can identify themes running through the Topic you have just read. These include:

1 issues of legality and danger

2 access to respondents

3 availability of sampling frames

4 ethical issues

5 rapport and gaining trust

6 confidentiality

7 concealment and distortion

In small groups, draw up a chart using these seven themes. Now go through the Topic and find as many examples of each theme as you can, including the study of criminals, victims and the agencies of social control.

Add any other examples you may think of. Report back to the rest of the class.

Summary

Crime and deviance include a number of distinctive research areas, e.g. different forms of crime such as domestic violence, street and corporate crime etc.

The institutions of the criminal justice system are also important areas of study. Both the institutions and the individuals and groups involved – e.g. offenders, victims, prisoners, police officers etc – may be difficult to access. For example, prisons are closed institutions; offenders may not welcome the attentions of researchers.

Research methods have different strengths and limitations in studying crime and deviance. For example, covert participant observation can give insight into offending, but raises practical and ethical issues.

QuickCheck Questions

1 Identify one problem of using (a) official statistics and (b) unstructured interviews to study domestic violence.

2 Identify two problems of using written questionnaires to study offending.

3 Suggest two ways in which sociologists might use documents to gain an understanding of crime and deviance.

4 Identify three problems of researching prisoners.

5 Suggest three reasons why it might prove difficult to research police officers.

 Check your answers at www.sociology.uk.net

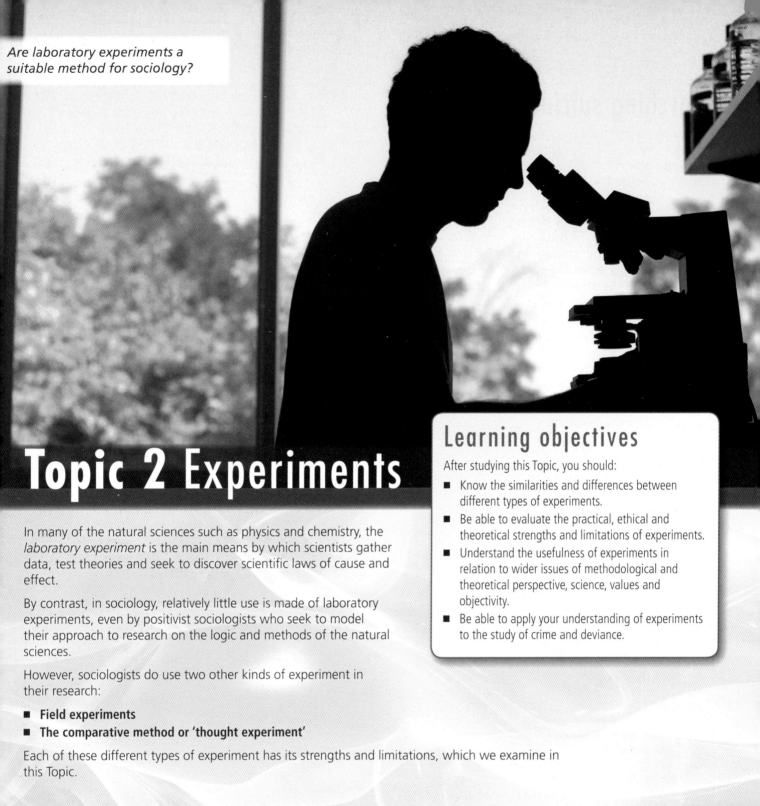

Are laboratory experiments a suitable method for sociology?

Topic 2 Experiments

In many of the natural sciences such as physics and chemistry, the *laboratory experiment* is the main means by which scientists gather data, test theories and seek to discover scientific laws of cause and effect.

By contrast, in sociology, relatively little use is made of laboratory experiments, even by positivist sociologists who seek to model their approach to research on the logic and methods of the natural sciences.

However, sociologists do use two other kinds of experiment in their research:

- **Field experiments**
- **The comparative method or 'thought experiment'**

Each of these different types of experiment has its strengths and limitations, which we examine in this Topic.

Learning objectives

After studying this Topic, you should:

- Know the similarities and differences between different types of experiments.
- Be able to evaluate the practical, ethical and theoretical strengths and limitations of experiments.
- Understand the usefulness of experiments in relation to wider issues of methodological and theoretical perspective, science, values and objectivity.
- Be able to apply your understanding of experiments to the study of crime and deviance.

Laboratory experiments

A laboratory experiment is a *controlled* experiment. The laboratory is an artificial environment in which the scientist can control different variables in order to discover what effect they have. In this way, the scientist can test hypotheses about the cause of a phenomenon, with the aim of discovering a causal law.

In a laboratory experiment, the researcher first takes a set of subjects (things or people on whom the experiment will be conducted). These must be identical in all relevant respects. They are then divided at random into two groups – an experimental group and a control group. The researcher then treats the two groups differently:

- **The experimental group** are exposed to a variable (called the independent variable) that the researcher believes may have a particular effect.
- **The control group** are not exposed to the independent variable – their conditions are kept constant.

The condition of both groups is measured before the experiment starts and again at the end. If we discover a change in the experimental group but none in the control group, we may conclude that this was caused by the different treatments the two groups received. In other words, by following the logic of the experimental method, we can discover cause-and-effect relationships. This allows us to *predict* what will happen under the same conditions in the future.

While laboratory experiments are the basic research method in most natural sciences, they are rarely used in sociology. There are a number of practical, ethical and theoretical reasons for this.

Practical issues

Open systems Sociologists such as Keat and Urry (1982) argue that laboratory experiments are only suitable for studying *closed systems* where the researcher can control and measure all the relevant variables and make precise predictions, as in physics or chemistry. However, society is an *open system* where countless factors are at work in any given situation, interacting with each other in complex ways. This makes it impossible for the researcher even to identify, let alone control, all the relevant variables. This makes laboratory experiments unsuitable for studying social phenomena.

Individuals are complex and therefore it is not really possible to 'match' the members of the control and experimental groups exactly. While we can find identical samples of chemicals, no two human beings are exactly alike.

Studying the past Laboratory experiments cannot be used to study an event in the past, since we cannot control variables that were acting in the past rather than the present. Nor can we keep people in laboratory conditions for long time periods so we can study them.

Small samples Laboratory experiments can usually only study small samples. This makes it very difficult to investigate large-scale social phenomena. For example, we cannot study all or even a large sample of the members of a major religion. Small samples also bring the risk that a result that appears to show one variable causing another, may in fact just be a chance correlation between the two.

The Hawthorne effect A laboratory experiment is an artificial environment and any behaviour that occurs in it may also be artificial. In particular, if the subjects know they are being experimented on, this may make them act differently. For example, they may feel self-important, anxious or resentful about being in the experiment and act differently as a result.

This is known as the *experimental effect* or *Hawthorne effect*, after the experiments in the 1920s at the Hawthorne factory in the United States where it was first observed. This 'subject reactivity' will of course ruin the experiment, since it depends on the subjects responding to the variables that the researcher introduces into the situation, and not reacting to the fact that they are being studied.

The expectancy effect is a form of experimenter bias. It refers to the fact that what a researcher *expects* to happen in the experiment can affect its actual outcome. This can occur by the experimenter consciously or unconsciously treating the subjects in such a way that it influences how they respond and produces the result the experimenter expected. Box 3.2 illustrates this.

Identify and explain three reasons why it may be difficult to apply the results of laboratory experiments to the real world.

Ethical issues

The main ethical issues in relation to conducting experiments on human beings are informed consent and harmful effects on subjects.

Informed consent The researcher needs the informed consent of the subjects of the experiment. This means gaining their agreement to take part, having first explained to them in terms they can understand, the nature and purpose of the experiment, what risks and effects there may be, and the uses to which the findings will be put.

Box 3.2	Students, rats and the expectancy effect

In an interesting experiment, Rosenthal and Fode (1963) showed how the expectancy effect works. They told two groups of psychology students that they were to train laboratory rats to learn their way through a maze. One group was told they had 'bright' rats, while the other was told they had 'dull' rats. In fact, there was no difference between them.

We should note that it was the students who were the real subjects of this experiment, not the rats. Rosenthal and Fode predicted that the students would act according to the experimenters' expectancy and ensure that the bright rats did better than the dull ones, and this is in fact what happened – the bright rats seemed to learn faster.

One reason for this was that the students with bright rats tended to disregard their rats' errors as 'false starts' and not record them, so they appeared to learn more quickly, while those with dull rats tended to record all their failures. Thus, Rosenthal and Fode influenced the subjects (the students) by telling them the two sets of rats were different, and the subjects duly behaved in accordance with the expectation.

However, sometimes explaining the aim of the experiment beforehand will be self-defeating. In these cases, for the experiment to work, the subjects must be deceived because, if they know its true purpose, they may very well act differently.

Harm to subjects Research should not normally harm the participants. However, some argue that minor or temporary harm may be justified ethically if the results yield significant social benefits.

Research should also seek to do good. Where an experiment is seen to be benefiting the experimental group (who gain from the treatment to which they are subjected), there is an ethical case for halting the experiment and making the same treatment available to the control group. This is often done in medical experiments. It can also be done in sociological experiments, for example where two groups of pupils are subjected to different teaching methods: if one method is shown to be more effective, it can be offered to both groups.

Theoretical issues

For positivists, laboratory experiments have a major theoretical strength – their reliability. However, in other respects they suffer from important limitations even from a positivist perspective. Interpretivists go even further, criticising laboratory experiments as lacking validity and as unsuitable for studying actors' meanings.

Reliability and hypothesis testing

A reliable method is one that can be replicated – repeated exactly in every detail by other researchers to obtain the same results. Positivists see reliability as important because it enables us to check the work of other researchers by repeating it. If we can repeat the research and arrive at the same results, we can have more confidence that the original findings are true.

Positivists regard the laboratory experiment as highly reliable for three reasons:

- The original experimenter can control the conditions and specify the precise steps that were followed in the original experiment, so others can easily repeat these steps to re-run it.
- It produces quantitative data, so the results of the re-run experiments can be easily compared to the original.
- It is a very detached and objective method: the researcher merely manipulates the variables and records the results. Their subjective feelings and values have no effect on the conduct or outcome of the experiment.

Because laboratory experiments can isolate and control any variable that is of interest to the researcher, they are also an effective way to test hypotheses and predictions. If we believe a particular variable is the cause of a phenomenon, we simply set up an experiment where an experimental group is exposed to that variable and a control group is not, and then compare the outcomes.

Representativeness

For positivists, representativeness is important because they aim to make generalisations about how the wider social structure shapes individuals' behaviour. However, with laboratory experiments there is a danger that their findings lack *external validity*. That is, we cannot be confident they are true for the wider population. There are two reasons for this.

Firstly, because experiments can only study small samples, there is a greater risk that they are not a representative cross-section of the population the researcher is interested in. If so, the findings cannot be generalised beyond the experiment itself.

Secondly, lack of external validity arises out of the high level of control the experimenter has. Control over the conditions in the experiment is valuable, because it enables us to establish that a particular variable causes a particular effect. On the other hand, however, the higher the level of control we have over the experiment, the more unnatural

Activity Milgram's experiments on obedience

www.sociology.uk.net

the circumstances this creates – which may not be at all true of the world outside the laboratory.

Internal validity

Laboratory experiments may also lack *internal* validity. That is, their findings may not even be true for the subjects of the experiment itself, let alone the wider world.

One reason for this is the artificiality of the laboratory environment. As we saw earlier, this may encourage the Hawthorne effect, where the subjects react simply to being studied, and do so in ways that produce invalid results.

Interpretivism and free will

Interpretivists argue that human beings are fundamentally different from the plants, rocks and other natural phenomena that natural scientists study. Unlike these objects, we have free will and choice. Our behaviour is not 'caused' by external forces, so it cannot be explained in terms of cause-and-effect statements, as positivists believe.

Instead, our actions can only be understood in terms of the choices we freely make on the basis of the meanings we give to events. For interpretivists, therefore, the laboratory experiment, with its search for causes, is a fundamentally inappropriate method for studying human beings.

Field experiments

Given the limitations of laboratory experiments, sociologists have developed two alternative methods. These follow the same logic in seeking to identify causes, but they aim to overcome the unnaturalness and lack of validity of laboratory experiments. These methods are field experiments and the comparative method.

A field experiment differs from a laboratory experiment in two ways:

- **It takes place in the subject's natural surroundings** rather than in an artificial laboratory environment.
- **Those involved do not know they are the subjects** of an experiment, thereby avoiding the Hawthorne effect.

The researcher isolates and manipulates one or more of the variables in the situation to see what effect it has on the unwitting subjects of the experiment. For example, Rosenthal and Jacobson (1968) manipulated teachers' expectations about pupils by giving them misleading information about the pupils' abilities in order to discover what effects this had on the children's achievement.

Actor tests and correspondence tests are also types of field experiment. For example, to test the hypothesis that there is racial discrimination in employment, Colin Brown and Pat Gay (1985) sent a white actor and a black actor for interviews for the same posts, to see which one would be offered the job. The actors were of different ethnicity, but matched for age, gender, qualifications, etc. Similarly, in a correspondence test, Mike Noon (1993) sent matched letters enquiring about jobs at the top hundred UK companies, apparently from two applicants of different ethnicity (Noon gave them the names Evans and Patel).

Such studies show the value of field experiments. They are more natural and valid for real life, and they avoid the artificiality of laboratory experiments. However, there is a trade-off between naturalism and control: the more natural and realistic we make the situation, the less control we

have over the variables that might be operating. If so, we cannot be certain that we have identified the true cause. For example, while it may have been racism that resulted in the white actor getting more job offers, we cannot be certain, because Brown and Gay could not control (or even know about) all the other variables in the situation.

Critics also argue that field experiments are unethical, since they involve carrying out an experiment on subjects without their knowledge or consent. However, it can be argued that in the case of Brown and Gay's and Noon's experiments, although the researchers did deceive their subjects (the employers), no harm was done, and something of value to society was learnt as a result.

Activity

Sissons (1970) reports a field experiment on perceptions of social class in which an actor, working for the researcher, stood outside Paddington station in London dressed first as a businessman and later as a labourer, and asked passers-by for directions. It was found that people were more helpful when asked by the 'businessman', rather than the 'labourer'.

1   What was the independent variable in this experiment?

2   Can you suggest any other variables that might be controlled for this experiment?

3   Suggest two reasons for the public responses to the actor.

The comparative method

Unlike both field experiments and laboratory experiments, the comparative method is carried out only in the mind of the sociologist. It is a 'thought experiment' – sometimes called a 'natural experiment'. That is, it does not involve the researcher actually experimenting on real people at all.

Instead, it usually relies on re-analysing secondary data that have already been collected. However, like the laboratory experiment, it too is designed to discover cause-and-effect relationships. It works as follows:

- Identify two groups that are alike in all major respects except for the one variable we are interested in.
- Then compare the two groups to see if this one difference between them has any effect.

The most famous example of the comparative method is Emile Durkheim's (1897) classic study of suicide, which relied on analysing official statistics.

In seeking to discover cause-and-effect relationships, the comparative method has three advantages over laboratory experiments:

- It avoids artificiality.
- It can be used to study past events.
- It avoids the ethical problems of harming or deceiving subjects.

However, it gives the researcher even less control over variables than do field experiments, so we can be even less certain whether a thought experiment really has discovered the cause of something.

For more activities on Experiments...

Go to www.sociology.uk.net

Summary

Natural scientists use laboratory experiments to discover causal laws. Despite their reliability, they are rare in sociology, because of practical problems (e.g. being unsuited to studying open systems like societies), ethical problems of experimenting on humans, and theoretical problems such as the Hawthorne effect. Sociologists use field experiments and the comparative method as alternatives. However, although more naturalistic, these methods give the sociologist less control over variables.

QuickCheck Questions

1 Why is control so important in a laboratory experiment?
2 What is the 'expectancy effect'?
3 Suggest two ethical problems of conducting laboratory experiments in sociology.
4 Identify two reasons why experiments are seen as high in reliability.
5 Identify two reasons why experiments are seen as low in validity.
6 What is the difference between internal and external validity?
7 What are the similarities and differences between a laboratory experiment and a field experiment?
8 Suggest one advantage and one disadvantage of using the comparative method.

Check your answers at www.sociology.uk.net

Examining experiments

Outline and critically assess the arguments for and against using experiments in sociology. (33 marks)

The examiner's advice

This question carries 15 AO1 marks (knowledge and understanding) and 18 AO2 marks (interpretation, application, analysis and evaluation).

You should note at the start of your answer that there are different types of experiment – laboratory, field, and comparative method or 'thought experiment'. It's probably best to start with laboratory experiments. Describe their features, including control, artificiality, and the aim of discovering cause-and-effect relationships. Evaluate their usefulness in terms of practical, ethical and theoretical issues. The latter should include reliability, representativeness and validity, and positivist and interpretivist views of experiments. You can also evaluate by comparing laboratory experiments with field and thought experiments, explaining how they overcome some of the problems of the former such as artificiality, but at the expense of loss of control. Where possible, illustrate points with reference to studies that have used experiments.

METHODS IN CONTEXT
using experiments to investigate crime and deviance

Sociologists sometimes use experiments to study issues such as:

- The nature of aggression
- Prisoners and prison guards
- The effectiveness of crime prevention policies

Before reading this section, re-visit Topic 1 to refresh your understanding of what is different about researching crime and deviance.

Laboratory experiments

The *laboratory experiment* does not lend itself to the study of most aspects of crime and deviance. The complexity of 'real world' deviant situations means it is very difficult to recreate them in a controlled laboratory setting.

Where experiments have been used, they tend to examine rather general issues such as the nature of aggression or responses to authority. For example, Philip Zimbardo and colleagues used a laboratory experiment to investigate the effect of prison on the behaviour of both guards and prisoners (Haney et al 1973).

The researchers created a simulated prison and randomly allocated the roles of 'prisoner' and 'guard' to their volunteer sample of 21 college students. They collected data through observation of the interactions between prisoners and guards, as well as questionnaires and interviews. The researchers found that the guards acted aggressively towards the prisoners, who responded by becoming submissive. This study produced some important insights into the dehumanising effects of prisons on both inmates and staff.

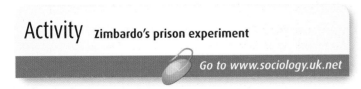

Activity   **Zimbardo's prison experiment**

Go to www.sociology.uk.net

Ethics

Many crime-related research issues are sensitive, involving danger, victimisation, and the exercise of power over others. Re-creating these in a laboratory experiment may have harmful effects. For example, in Zimbardo's study, subjects acted in extreme ways outside their normal

behavioural range and some suffered distress as a result. One prisoner had to be released after three days because of uncontrolled crying and severe depression, and the experiment had to be stopped entirely after six days instead of the 14 intended.

Some groups are particularly vulnerable, such as young children. Bandura et al (1977) investigated imitative aggression using samples of nursery-age children. Some children watched an adult being aggressive towards an inflatable Bobo doll and were then subjected to a frustrating experience of not being allowed to play with some toys they were shown. Placed in a room with only a Bobo doll and a hammer, those children who had seen the adult attack the Bobo doll were more likely to imitate the adult and act aggressively. Although this experiment may offer some insight into the roots of aggression, it did so by risking psychological harm to the children involved.

Validity

Most aspects of crime and deviance do not lend themselves to study using laboratory experiments. The few issues investigated using laboratory experiments tend to be rather generalised, such as aggression. The complexity of the factors involved means that the manipulation of single variables tells us little about the real world. For example, unlike real people, Bobo dolls are specifically designed to invite violent actions. Similarly, the simple sequence of a violent event, a frustrating event and an opportunity to imitate the behaviour seen immediately before, bears little relation to everyday reality. The differences between real life and the laboratory undermine the validity of such experiments. Furthermore, such issues might be investigated more effectively using other techniques such as observation.

Field experiments

Field experiments are used more often than laboratory experiments to research crime. The political importance of crime and crime control means governments may fund research into the effectiveness of their crime prevention policies. Consequently, they use field experiments to test these policies, by comparing situations where a policy is being implemented with situations where it is not. Because the method is designed to evaluate the effectiveness of policies, it is sometimes called *evaluation research*.

Field experiments usually monitor two groups exposed to different conditions – for example, two different rehabilitation programmes for prisoners. Alternatively, the experiment may use an experimental group and a control group. The former is exposed to the particular crime prevention policy, while the latter is not.

The 'tougher regimes' project

In the early 1980s, the Conservative government announced a 'short, sharp shock' approach to dealing with young offenders. This would involve tougher regimes being introduced in young offenders' institutions, partly modelled on army routines.

To test whether tougher regimes were more effective in deterring young offenders from re-offending, two institutions were selected as the experimental group: one for convicted youths aged 14-17, the other for 17-21 year olds. A tough regime based on physical training, reduced education time, formal drill sessions and more inspections was introduced in these institutions.

Four other young offenders' institutions that operated the existing regime were used as a control group. Data was collected at two points in time through observation, interviews, questionnaires, and from official records. From a comparison of the outcomes of the control and experimental groups, it was evident that the 'short, sharp shock' approach did not have any significant effect on the youths' re-conviction rates after release.

Experiments like these require a 'captive' population, and several aspects of the criminal justice system provide possible research settings. Such populations include not just prisoners and those who are electronically tagged, but also other fairly fixed populations such as neighbourhoods and those employed in the criminal justice system.

The fact that such evaluation research is often government-sponsored also means that access is much easier for the researcher. For example, in the 'tougher regimes' project:

> 'no part of the regime was closed to researchers, who were given their own set of keys…they were able to attend all staff meetings, the night watch, the reception and discharge as well as the more ordinary points of the working day' (Home Office 1984).

Field experiments used as evaluation research can be costly and take a long time. However, being government funded often means that cost is not a problem. For example, New Labour's £250 million Crime Reduction Programme included £25 million just for evaluating the programme.

Ethics

Those involved in such field experiments are not usually aware that they are part of a research programme, and they are not usually given a choice. Yet an individual's chances of being rehabilitated could be affected by which research group they are in. This is particularly likely when using young offenders as research subjects. Young offenders are both more vulnerable and more capable of changing their ways, and therefore their imprisonment should not be treated as an experiment.

Researchers conducting government-sponsored field experiments often have no control over the use of their findings. In the case of the 'tougher regimes' project, Mrs Thatcher's Conservative government still introduced the 'short, sharp shock' approach as part of inmates' induction into young offenders' institutions, even though the research had shown it had no deterrent effect.

Reliability

For the government, the purpose of evaluation research is to discover what policy works best (for example in reducing crime), so that it can be applied elsewhere in the country. This gives researchers the opportunity to check the reliability of the initial research.

For example, Nick Tilley (2007) worked on the government's *Safer Cities* strategy in the 1980s and 1990s. A pilot scheme, the Kirkholt project, had led to a dramatic fall in the number of burglaries in the Rochdale housing estate it focused on. As a result, the government encouraged *Safer Cities* co-ordinators throughout the country to replicate this project in their areas. Tilley examined three other places where it was introduced and found marked differences in its impact on burglary rates. When he examined the characteristics of the original project, Tilley identified ten key elements. None of the three 'replications' had all ten elements. He concluded that it was impossible to replicate a real-life project exactly in other locations.

Validity

Even though those involved in a field experiment may not have been informed that it is taking place, in many settings word gets around. In a controlled social environment such as a prison, any change to the routine is quickly noticed and speculated about on the prison grapevine. Similarly, among other groups with a close-knit network, such as the police or a local neighbourhood, changes are also soon noticed. The danger is the Hawthorne effect – once the subjects know they are being studied, they may change their behaviour as a result, thereby undermining validity.

Activity

Field experiments are sometimes used to assess the effectiveness of policies. Pitts and Phillips (1991) studied what happened when some police forces changed their drugs policy by turning a blind eye to the selling of needles and syringes. They investigated patterns of needle sharing, crucial in the spread of HIV. They found that the new approach had led to the development of 'safe houses' where drug taking was less dangerous because clean equipment was available and this made sharing less likely.

1   How sure can the authors be that the changed behaviour was due to the police action?

2   What other policies might be measured for effectiveness in this way?

Examining experiments in context

Item A   Researching power and authority in prisons

Prisons are very closed and controlled social settings. Several layers of permission are needed from the Prison Service, the prison governor, the prisoners and so on. Any perceived disruption caused by the research is unlikely to be tolerated by the prison authorities, so researchers have to maintain constant care with their work.

There are many particular ethical issues when studying prisons. Safety is a major issue for researchers in prison, especially when dealing with those who have committed serious offences. Prisoners may reveal that they are seriously depressed or that they have committed a further crime for which they have not been charged. In both cases, researchers face the ethical dilemma of whether they should reveal this information – probably given in confidence – to the prison authorities.

Experiments in a simulated environment are useful because they allow the researcher to investigate an issue like prisons without facing these and other ethical problems in real prisons. However, re-creating power and authority relationships in an artificial laboratory situation can cause other ethical problems.

Question

Using material from **Item A** and elsewhere, assess the strengths and weaknesses of using experiments to investigate power and authority in prisons.
(15 marks)

The examiner's advice

This question carries 6 AO1 marks (knowledge and understanding) and 9 AO2 marks (interpretation, application, analysis and evaluation). It requires you to **apply** your knowledge and understanding of experiments to the study of the **particular** issue of power and authority in prisons. It is not enough simply to discuss experiments in general.

You need to attach one or more of the strengths and limitations of experiments to the research characteristics of power and authority in prisons. A good place to start is Item A. For example, it states that one research characteristic of power and authority in prisons is that a researcher has to work through many layers of permission in order to gain access. One strength of experiments is that such permission is not required if the experiment is going to create a simulated prison environment. However, as Item A also points out, there are many ethical concerns associated with researching prisons and these also apply to simulated 'experimental' prisons.

Other research characteristics not mentioned in Item A include the fact that most prisoners are from disadvantaged backgrounds and that there are few roles in prison for the researcher to occupy without drawing attention to themselves.

Try to keep a reasonable balance between the strengths and limitations of experiments. You can also refer to studies that have used this method (e.g. Zimbardo) and to any relevant research you have been involved in.

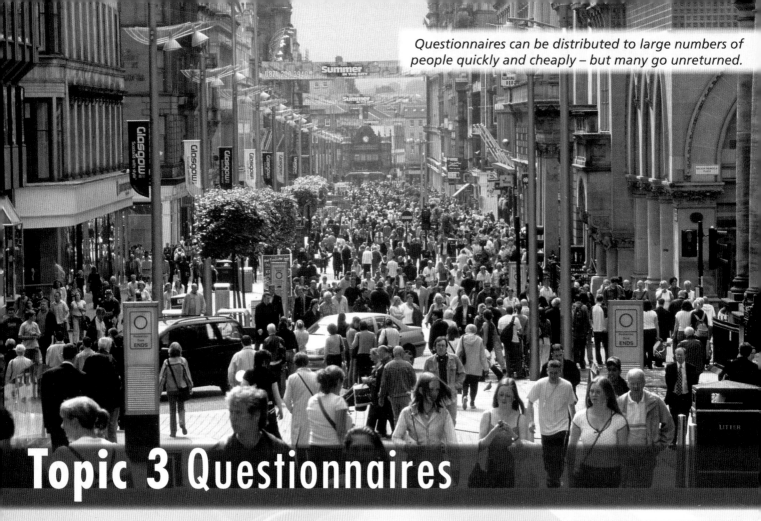

Questionnaires can be distributed to large numbers of people quickly and cheaply – but many go unreturned.

Topic 3 Questionnaires

Written or self-completed questionnaires are the most commonly used form of social survey. The ten-yearly Census of the whole population is a written questionnaire. Questionnaires can be distributed to people at home and returned by post or in person, e-mailed, or completed and collected on the spot.

Questionnaires ask respondents to provide answers to pre-set questions. These may be:

- **Closed-ended** (also called 'forced choice') Respondents must choose from a limited range of possible answers that the researcher has selected in advance, such as yes/no/don't know. Questions are often pre-coded for ease of analysis.
- **Open-ended** Respondents are free to answer however they wish, in their own words, without any pre-selected choices being offered by the researcher.

Questions tend to be closed-ended, but open-ended questions can also be used.

As we shall see in this Topic, the usefulness of questionnaires can be evaluated in terms of a number of practical, ethical and theoretical considerations.

Learning objectives

After studying this Topic, you should:

- Know and be able to evaluate the practical, ethical and theoretical strengths and limitations of questionnaires.
- Know the main types of sampling procedures used in surveys.
- Understand the usefulness of questionnaires in relation to wider issues of methodological perspective, science, values and objectivity.
- Be able to apply your understanding of questionnaires to the study of crime and deviance.

Practical issues in using questionnaires

Questionnaires are probably the most widely used research method in sociology. This is due in part to their practical strengths:

- They are a quick and cheap way to gather large amounts of quantitative data from large numbers of people, widely spread geographically.
- There is no need to recruit and train interviewers – respondents complete the questionnaires themselves.
- Data is usually easy to quantify, particularly where pre-coded questions are used, and can be computer-processed to reveal relationships between variables.

Limitations

However, questionnaires face certain practical limitations:

- Data is often limited and superficial. This is because questionnaires need to be fairly brief – most people are unlikely to complete a long, time-consuming questionnaire.
- It may be necessary to offer incentives (such as entry into a prize draw) to persuade respondents to complete the questionnaire. This adds to the cost.
- With *postal* questionnaires, we cannot be sure whether an unreturned questionnaire was ever actually received by the respondent. Also, we cannot be sure that the intended recipient completed the questionnaire and not someone else.

- Very low response rates are a major problem. A higher response rate can be obtained by sending follow-up questionnaires or by collecting them by hand, but this adds to the cost and time. Non-response may be caused by faulty questionnaire design. For example, a questionnaire that uses complex language may only be completed by the well educated.
- Questionnaires are *inflexible*. Once it is finalised, the researcher is stuck with the questions they have decided to ask and cannot explore any new areas of interest should they come up during the course of the research.
- Because the questionnaire is drawn up in advance, the researcher must already have some knowledge of the subject and a clear hypothesis to test. This makes it less suitable for investigating unfamiliar topics where the researcher has little idea as to the important issues.
- Questionnaires are only snapshots – pictures of reality at one moment in time, when the respondent answers the questions. They fail to capture the way people's attitudes and behaviour change.

Suggest two advantages and two disadvantages of postal questionnaires as compared with those given out and collected in person. (Hint: there are several to find in this Topic.)

Theoretical issues in using questionnaires

A major factor in the decision whether to use questionnaires is the sociologist's methodological perspective. While positivists favour questionnaires, interpretivists and others are more critical of their use.

Positivism

Positivists take a scientific approach and they believe questionnaire-based research achieves the main goals of scientific sociology. For positivists, questionnaires produce representative findings that can be generalised to the wider population. They are a reliable, objective and detached method for producing quantitative data, testing hypotheses and developing causal laws of social behaviour.

Hypothesis testing

Positivists model their approach on the natural sciences and seek to discover laws of cause and effect. Questionnaires are attractive to positivists because they enable us to test hypotheses and identify possible cause-and-effect relationships between different factors or variables.

For scientists to test the hypothesis that variable A causes variable B, they must first establish whether there is a correlation between the two. (A correlation is a pattern of relationship between variables – for example, between social class and educational achievement.)

Questionnaires can establish correlations because they yield quantitative data about the links between different variables. For example, by correlating respondents' answers to a question about their occupation and one about their level of education, we might be able to make the generalisation that working-class people are less likely to go to university.

Once the correlation has been established, we can construct a hypothesis about its possible cause – for example, working-class people are less likely to go to university, because of material deprivation. In turn, this can be tested with a further questionnaire. In this way, laws of cause and effect can be discovered, just as in the natural sciences.

Reliability

Reliability involves replicability: if another researcher repeats the research using the same method, they should gain the same results (a replica) as the first researcher. For positivists, reliability is important because it allows a scientist's findings to be checked and confirmed or falsified by others. If others can repeat the research and obtain the same results, we can have more confidence that its findings are true.

Questionnaires are regarded as a reliable method of collecting data. This is because, when we repeat someone's research, we can use a questionnaire identical to the original one, so new respondents are asked exactly the same questions as the original ones. In other words, the questionnaire is a *standardised measuring instrument* – a fixed yardstick that can be used by any researcher, just like a thermometer or pressure gauge in the natural sciences. This means one researcher's study can easily be replicated and checked by another.

It also means that, if we do find differences in the answers that respondents give, we can assume that these are the result of real differences between the respondents, and not simply the result of different questions – since the questions were the same for all respondents.

A related advantage is that questionnaires allow us to make comparisons. By asking the same questions in different times or societies, we can compare the results obtained. If the results differ, we can assume this is because there is a real difference between the societies or times we are comparing.

Box 3.3	Sampling

Sociologists often aim to produce generalisations that apply to all cases of a topic. However, we may not have the resources to study every case, so we must choose a *sample* or smaller sub-group drawn from the wider research population we are interested in.

The aim of sampling is usually to ensure that the people we have chosen to study are *representative* or typical of the research population. If they are, we can *generalise* our findings to the whole research population. This is particularly attractive to positivists, who wish to make law-like statements.

The sampling frame is a list of members of the research population. From this, we select a representative sample of the research population, using a technique such as:

- **Random sampling**, where the sample is selected purely by chance, e.g. names drawn out of a hat.
- **Quasi-random sampling** is similar, e.g. selecting every tenth name on a list.
- **Stratified random sampling** We subdivide ('stratify') the population into the relevant categories (e.g. working-class males, working-class females), and then randomly select a sample of each, ensuring that the proportions of the total sample in each category are the same as in the overall population.
- **Quota sampling** is similar, but instead of choosing the samples randomly, researchers go looking for the right number (quota) of each sort of person required in each category.

Non-representative sampling may be used where there is no sampling frame for the population, e.g. there is no complete list of all criminals. Techniques include:

- **Snowball** sampling collects a sample by contacting key individuals, who are asked to suggest others to be interviewed, and so on, adding to the sample 'snowball' fashion. This is a way to contact a sample who might otherwise be difficult to find, e.g. criminals.
- **Opportunity** (or convenience) sampling chooses from those individuals who are easiest to access, e.g. a captive audience such as prisoners.

Interpretivists have less need for representative samples. They believe it is more important to gain a valid understanding of actors' meanings than to discover laws of behaviour, so they are less concerned to make generalisations.

Representativeness

If a method produces representative data, then the findings can be generalised from the sample studied to the wider population from which the sample is drawn. Representativeness is important to positivists because they are macro or structural theorists – they aim to make generalisations about how the wider social structure shapes our behaviour. Positivists favour questionnaires because they are more likely to yield representative data. There are two main reasons for this:

- **They are large-scale** Because questionnaires can be distributed quickly and cheaply by post or e-mail over wide geographical areas, they can collect information from a large sample of people. As a result, their findings stand a better chance of being truly representative of the wider population.

- **They use representative samples** Researchers who use questionnaires tend to use more sophisticated sampling techniques designed to obtain a representative sample.

However, representativeness can be undermined by low response rate, especially if those who do return their questionnaires are different in some way from those who don't (for example, better educated). If so, this will produce distorted and unrepresentative results, from which no accurate generalisations can be made.

A trendy British magazine includes a questionnaire on loneliness and asks its readers to complete it online. In what ways are the respondents to this questionnaire unlikely to be representative of the population of the UK?

Detachment and objectivity

For positivists, scientific research is objective (unbiased) and detached. The scientist's own subjective opinions and values must be kept separate from the research and not be allowed to 'contaminate' or affect the subject matter or the research findings in any way.

Positivists favour questionnaires because they see them as a detached and scientific form of research, where the sociologist's personal involvement with their respondents is kept to a minimum. For example, postal questionnaires are completed at a distance and involve little or no personal contact between researchers and respondents. Unlike in an interview, no researcher is present to influence the answers.

Interpretivism

Interpretivists seek to discover the meanings that underlie our actions and from which we construct social reality. Their main concern is with validity – obtaining an authentic or truthful picture of how actors construct and experience social reality.

For this reason, interpretivists tend to reject the use of

Box 3.4	Ethics and questionnaires

Questionnaires pose relatively few ethical problems. Questions are often about less sensitive, routine factual topics. Even where questions are about more sensitive or personal issues, respondents are not obliged to answer them. Nevertheless, researchers should still take care to avoid causing psychological harm through their questions.

Researchers should gain respondents' informed consent and make it clear that they have a right not to answer any of the questions that they do not wish to. Parental consent may be required before administering questionnaires to children. Guaranteeing confidentiality is generally straightforward, since most questionnaires are completed anonymously.

---

questionnaires. They argue that questionnaires cannot yield valid data about the meanings of social actors. In their view, there are several reasons for this.

Detachment

Interpretivists reject the positivist preference for detachment and objectivity because they believe it fails to produce a valid picture of actors' meanings. To obtain valid data, they argue, we must use methods that involve us closely with the people we research, so that we can gain a subjective understanding of their meanings – ideally, by enabling us to see the world through their eyes.

For interpretivists, questionnaires fail to do this because they are the most detached of all primary methods. The lack of contact between researcher and respondent makes it almost impossible to clarify what the questions mean for the respondent or to check that the researcher has correctly understood the answers given. This can be a serious problem, especially where there are cultural or language differences between researcher and respondent. Interpretivists argue that the price of this detachment is invalid data that fails to give a true picture of the respondent's meanings.

Activity

In pairs, draw a table showing the advantages and disadvantages of questionnaires:

	Advantages	Disadvantages
Practical	A	B
Theoretical & ethical	C	D

1 In A and B, put all the practical advantages and disadvantages.

2 In C, put all the reasons a positivist would choose to use questionnaires. In D, put the reasons an interpretivist would choose not to. Also include in these boxes any ethical issues.

Note: You will find this activity useful when revising for *any* method.

Lying, forgetting and trying to impress

The validity of questionnaire data depends on the willingness and ability of respondents to provide full and accurate answers. Problems of validity are created when respondents lie, forget, do not know or do not understand (and do not admit that they don't understand). For example, in Michael Schofield's (1965) research on the sexual behaviour of teenagers, in reply to the question, 'Are you a virgin?' one girl answered, 'No, not yet'. Whether she did not understand, or was simply being mischievous, the resulting data lacked validity.

Similarly, respondents may try to please or second-guess the researcher, or impress them by giving 'respectable' answers they feel they ought to give, rather than tell the truth. For example, among groups where churchgoing is thought socially desirable, respondents to questionnaires on church attendance exaggerate how often they attend.

It is often impossible to confirm whether respondents are telling the truth or not. For this reason, interpretivists often favour observation instead of questionnaires, since this allows us to see for ourselves what people actually do, rather than what they say they do.

Imposing the researcher's meanings

For interpretivists, it is important that our research methods reveal the meanings of the social actors we are studying. In their view, however, questionnaires are more likely to impose the researcher's framework of ideas on the respondent than to reveal the respondent's meanings. For example, by choosing in advance which questions to ask, the researcher has already decided what is important and what isn't.

Furthermore, whatever type of questions we use, we risk distorting the reality and undermining validity:

- **Closed-ended questions** are a kind of straitjacket where respondents have to try and fit their views into the answers on offer. If they feel some other answer to be important, they have no opportunity to express it.
- **Open-ended questions** allow respondents to give whatever answer they wish, but when the researcher codes them to produce quantitative data, non-identical answers may get lumped together. As Marten Shipman (1997) says, when the researcher's categories are not the respondent's categories, 'pruning and bending' of the data is inevitable.

Feminism and questionnaires Some feminists are critical of the use of survey methods such as questionnaires and structured interviews. We deal with these criticisms, and with the use of unstructured interviews as an alternative feminist approach, in Topic 4.

For more activities on Questionnaires...

 Go to www.sociology.uk.net

Summary

Questionnaires are lists of written questions, usually closed-ended. They can gather easily analysable data cheaply, quickly and on a large scale, but there are practical problems such as non-response and inflexibility. However, they pose few ethical problems compared with most methods.

In the positivist view, questionnaires are detached and objective, and can produce reliable, representative data that can be used for hypothesis testing and developing causal laws. However, interpretivists regard them as lacking validity: their detachment means they produce superficial data and fail to yield an understanding of the actor's meanings, instead imposing those of the researcher.

QuickCheck Questions

1 What is a pre-coded question? Identify two advantages of pre-coded questions.
2 'Questionnaires are only snapshots.' Why might this be a disadvantage?
3 Suggest two reasons why questionnaires usually have few ethical problems.
4 Explain why questionnaires are high in reliability.
5 Explain the difference between random and quasi-random sampling.
6 What is a snowball sample?
7 Explain why (a) positivists see 'detachment' as an advantage and (b) interpretivists see it as a disadvantage.

 Check your answers at www.sociology.uk.net

Examining questionnaires

Evaluate the advantages and disadvantages of using questionnaires in sociological research. (33 marks)

The examiner's advice

This question carries 15 AO1 marks (knowledge and understanding) and 18 AO2 marks (interpretation, application, analysis and evaluation).

Consider the advantages and disadvantages in terms of practical, theoretical and ethical issues. Practical benefits include the large scale and low cost of questionnaires, ease of analysis etc. Problems include non-response, superficiality and inflexibility.

Theoretical disadvantages centre on validity, so make sure you explain what this is, as well as the ways in which questionnaires fail to produce valid data. Theoretical advantages could focus on objectivity, reliability and representativeness. Explain what these are and why questionnaires might deliver them. Put your discussion of theoretical issues into the context of positivist versus interpretivist views of sociology. Try to link theoretical and practical issues (e.g. response rate and representativeness). There are few ethical issues, but make sure you mention them. Also refer to different types of questionnaires (e.g. postal, e-mail, by hand etc) and their strengths and limitations (e.g. cost, response rate).

METHODS IN CONTEXT
using questionnaires to investigate crime and deviance

Sociologists sometimes use questionnaires to study issues such as:

- Attitudes to crime and policing
- Experiences of being a victim
- Self-reported offending

Before reading this section, re-visit Topic 1 to refresh your understanding of what is different about researching crime and deviance.

Practical issues

Questionnaires are a quick and cheap way to gather large amounts of quantitative data about some aspects of crime. For example, Sandra Walklate and her colleagues needed six months of intensive work to carry out 596 interviews in their victimisation survey, yet in just a few weeks they were able to send and receive back questionnaires from over 300 community groups and local businesses.

The degree of cooperation of different groups varies greatly. Potential victims may be keen to cooperate because it is in their interests to see crime reduced. For example, surveys of commercial crime usually find no problem obtaining lists of businesses from local Chambers of Commerce, because they want to help reduce crime that affects their members' business interests. On the other hand, criminals are unlikely to volunteer their identity or location to the researcher.

Question order can affect the responses given. For example, when asked about police effectiveness early on in a questionnaire, respondents usually indicate more positive attitudes towards the police. However, if asked near the end of the questionnaire – after they have answered lots of questions about crime – attitudes are often less positive.

Some groups involved in crime have low literacy levels. The researcher should therefore avoid complex language and limit the number of questions, or use an alternative method such as interviewing.

Groups involved in crime and criminal justice, such as police officers and criminal gangs, are often close-knit. Therefore, instead of being completed by the intended respondent on their own, questionnaires may be completed in a group setting. Consequently, responses may reflect group values or peer group pressure rather than the individual's own views.

Funding bodies often impose time constraints on research. Government departments are under media and political pressure to deal with crime-related issues and therefore want quick results. This, along with an official preference for quantitative data, means that questionnaires are widely used in government-sponsored research.

The formal nature of a questionnaire tends to identify it with authority. This can be a major problem when investigating anti-authority groups. Venkatesh (2008) initially turned up with his questionnaire at the Robert Taylor Homes housing project (28 drab high-rise blocks in one of the worst projects in Chicago) and started asking residents about how it felt to be poor and living with violence. He was held at gunpoint overnight by the local drug gang, the Black Kings, only surviving because he managed to convince JT, the gang leader, that he had no association with the police.

Formulating questions is difficult. For example, one study asked, 'In your everyday life, are you afraid of someone breaking into your home?' Later in the survey, the question was asked differently, as 'Could you tell me how worried you are about having your home broken into and something stolen?' Nearly a third of the sample who were not worried in the first question were worried in the second –

presumably as a result of having answered lots of questions about fear of crime. Because of the emotive nature of crime, questionnaires about it have more potential for *response inconsistency* than questionnaires about other areas of social life.

Many self-report studies concentrate on the reporting of less serious offences. Due to fear of the possible consequences, few people will admit to a serious crime, even in an anonymous questionnaire, but most will acknowledge minor law breaking. However, the inclusion of large numbers of trivial offences can lead to distorted results.

Overlap between the types of crimes listed in self-report studies can lead to respondents reporting the same crime twice.

> Identify three problems you might face when designing a questionnaire intended for members of several youth subcultures. How would you determine the precise language and wording to use?

Ethical issues

There are few ethical problems with questionnaires, especially if delivered through the post or by email, because returning them indicates that respondents have given their consent. However, under-16s require parental consent to complete and return a questionnaire about crime. As a result, this age group – an important one in terms of both crime and victimisation – tends to be excluded from questionnaire research.

Because of the distress it may cause, it may be inappropriate to ask young people about certain issues, such as being the victim of sexual crimes. Questionnaires on these issues therefore seek to overcome this ethical problem by asking older respondents about their experiences when they were younger. However, retrospective data relies on the respondent's memory and poses problems of validity.

Reliability and representativeness

Although a self-report study is replicable because it is a fixed questionnaire, disagreements between sociologists about what crimes should be included in the list, their order and so on, means that different surveys are not always directly comparable.

Obtaining a sampling frame is the first step towards obtaining a representative sample. Lists of many of the groups we might want to study (such as school age children, police officers and potential victims such as shopkeepers) either exist or can easily be compiled.

However, for other groups – such as unconvicted criminals – there is no list of members.

Questionnaires about youth crime are often distributed to pupils in school. However, this means that truants – who are also more likely to be delinquents – are more likely to be left out of the sample.

Low or varying response rates can be a problem, often leading to unrepresentative data. Junger-Tas (1989) reports a sliding scale of responses to self-report questionnaires depending on how much contact respondents have had with the criminal justice system. Response rates from individuals with a criminal record were lower than from those without.

Response rates depend partly on who is behind the questionnaire and who is the target group. For example, a postal questionnaire assessing the satisfaction of the courts with the probation service had a response rate of 80%. This was because it was sent by a government department to other official organisations. However, a questionnaire from someone in authority might have the opposite effect on the response rate if it were sent to people involved in law-breaking activities.

Detachment and objectivity

Most large-scale crime research is developed through consultation between criminologists, government, funding bodies and user groups. Official interests therefore dominate the selection of the topic, operationalisation of concepts and the questions asked. Typically, a government department puts out a project to tender and research teams bid for the work. The tender document specifies the main issues and the type of data required. Although the successful research team would have some input, the questionnaire's contents will be driven primarily by government concerns.

> Questionnaires about crime and policing have considerable potential for 'response inconsistency' because of the 'emotive nature' of the subject. Explain the phrases in inverted commas and then explain why this might lead to (a) problems of reliability; (b) problems of validity; (c) ethical problems.

Validity

Studying crime and deviance using questionnaires does not always produce valid data. For example, self-report studies are retrospective and depend on respondents being able to remember what crimes they have committed in the previous twelve months. Others may exaggerate their offences to create an impression of being 'tough', or alternatively conceal their crimes for fear of the police being informed.

One danger with questionnaires is that they impose the researcher's meanings through the choice and wording of the questions. For example, Jason Ditton et al (2000) argue that victim surveys on 'fear of crime' reflect government and media agendas rather than uncovering the public's real concerns. To avoid this problem, they first conducted qualitative interviews to establish what people's feelings about crime really were. They then presented the findings to focus groups for discussion, before finally condensing the results into a questionnaire sent to 1600 people. This revealed that for most people, the issue was not fear of crime but anger at it. Ditton et al conclude that because of the meanings imposed on victim surveys by political and media pressure, such surveys were asking the wrong questions.

Examining questionnaires in context

Item A   Researching violent crime

Violent acts tend to be swift and unexpected. It is very difficult, if not impossible, for a researcher to know when and where violent crime is likely to be committed. Of course, it is possible to identify the sort of subcultural group whose activities involve violence. However, research with such groups or in high-crime areas has a higher level of physical danger for the researcher if they become too closely involved with the group. It might therefore be useful for the researcher to keep a distance between themselves and the group they are researching.

Investigating both perpetrators and victims of violent crime after the event raises problems of cooperation, memory and ethics. Victims may exaggerate aspects of the crime or may have suppressed unpleasant memories.

Questionnaires help to maintain a distance from the research group. However, the highly structured nature of questionnaires may limit the responses that perpetrators and victims can give.

Question

Using material from **Item A** and elsewhere, assess the strengths and weaknesses of using questionnaires to investigate violent crime.

(15 marks)

The examiner's advice

This question carries 6 AO1 marks (knowledge and understanding) and 9 AO2 marks (interpretation, application, analysis and evaluation). It requires you to **apply** your knowledge and understanding of questionnaires to the study of the **particular** issue of violent crime. It is not enough simply to discuss questionnaires in general.

You need to attach one or more of the strengths and limitations of questionnaires to the research characteristics of violent crime. A good place to start is Item A. For example, it states that one research characteristic of violent crime is that there is a higher degree of physical danger to researchers than when studying other aspects of social life. Questionnaires have the advantage of keeping a distance between the researcher and those involved in violent crime, thus reducing risk of harm.

However, Item A also points out that there are particular problems with the memories victims have of violent events. Questionnaires, as fixed lists of questions, tend to assume that respondents know and can recall the information the researcher is seeking.

Other research characteristics not mentioned in Item A include the fact that many violent acts take place in private with few or no witnesses, and that not every violent episode involves a clear-cut 'victim' and 'perpetrator'.

Try to keep a reasonable balance between the strengths and limitations of questionnaires. You can also refer to studies that have used this method and to any relevant research you have been involved in.

What advantages might there be in using group interviews rather than one-to-one interviews?

Topic 4 Interviews

While social surveys can be conducted by means of written questionnaires, a widely used alternative is interviews. These can be carried out either face to face or by telephone.

Sociologists use different types of interview. The main difference is in how free the interviewer is to vary the questions:

- **Structured** or formal interviews are like questionnaires. Each interview is conducted in the same standardised way, with precisely the same questions, wording, order, tone of voice etc.
- **Unstructured**, informal or discovery interviews are like a guided conversation. The interviewer is free to vary the questions, wording, order etc, pursuing whatever line of questioning seems appropriate, asking follow-up questions etc.
- **Semi-structured** interviews have the same set of questions in common, but the interviewer can also probe for more information and ask additional questions.
- **Group** interviews are usually relatively unstructured. They include focus groups, where the researcher asks the group to discuss certain topics and records their views.

Methodological perspective is an important influence on which type of interview a sociologist prefers. As with questionnaires, positivists favour structured interviews. By contrast, interpretivists prefer unstructured interviews. Many feminists also prefer to use unstructured interviews.

Learning objectives

After studying this Topic, you should:

- Understand the differences between structured and unstructured interviews.
- Be able to evaluate the practical, ethical and theoretical strengths and limitations of different types of interview.
- Understand the usefulness of interviews in relation to wider issues of methodological perspective, science, values and objectivity.
- Be able to apply your understanding of interviews to the study of crime and deviance.

Structured interviews

Structured interviews are like questionnaires: both involve asking people a fixed set of prepared questions. In both cases, the questions are usually closed-ended with pre-coded answers. Both produce mainly quantitative data.

The main difference is that in a structured interview, the questions are read out and the answers filled in by a trained interviewer, rather than by the interviewee. Interviews thus involve a *social interaction* between interviewer and interviewee, whereas with written questionnaires the respondent usually answers the questions without the researcher's involvement.

The basic similarity between the two methods means they share many of the same strengths and limitations. Where there are differences, these often come from the fact that structured interviews involve interaction between researcher and interviewee.

Practical issues

- Structured interviews can cover quite large numbers of people because they are quick and fairly cheap to administer. For example, Young and Willmott (1962) interviewed 933 people in this way in their research on families in east London.
- They are suitable for gathering straightforward factual information such as a person's age, job, religion, daily routine etc.
- Results are easily quantified because they use closed-ended questions with pre-coded answers. This makes them suitable for hypothesis testing.
- Training interviewers is relatively straightforward and inexpensive, since all they are really required to do is follow a set of instructions. However, this is more costly than simply posting questionnaires to people.
- Response rates are usually higher than for questionnaires – perhaps because people find it harder to turn down a face-to-face request, and some may welcome the opportunity to talk. Young and Willmott had only 54 refusals out of 987 people they approached. Higher response rates can be obtained by making additional call backs, but this adds to the cost and time.
- Like questionnaires, structured interviews are *inflexible*, because the interview schedule is drawn up in advance and the interviewer must stick to it rigidly. This makes it impossible to pursue any interesting leads that may emerge in the course of the interview.

- Because the interview schedule is drawn up in advance, researchers must already have some knowledge of the subject and a clear hypothesis to test. This makes structured interviews unsuitable for investigating unfamiliar topics where the researcher has little idea what the important issues are.
- Structured interviews are only *snapshots* taken at one moment in time, so they fail to capture the dynamic nature of social life.

Box 3.5	Ethics and interviewing

Most sociologists argue that there are relatively few ethical problems in using structured interviews. Questions are more likely to be of a routine factual nature about less sensitive topics. Even where questions are intrusive, interviewees are under no obligation to answer them.

Nevertheless, because the interview is a social interaction, the interviewee may feel under some pressure to answer questions. Some feminists also regard structured interviews as at least potentially oppressive to women interviewees.

Where unstructured interviews deal with sensitive or painful issues, care needs to be exercised to avoid causing psychological harm.

Researchers should gain interviewees' informed consent, make it clear they have a right not to answer any questions that they do not wish to, and guarantee anonymity and confidentiality.

However, there may sometimes be difficulties. For example, Fiona Brookman (1999) notes that it can be difficult to keep confidential the identity of murderers who have been interviewed. If their case has received much publicity, even minimal details may make them identifiable.

There are also special considerations in interviewing vulnerable people, such as children or those with mental health problems. For example, such interviews may need to be kept brief and special care needs to be taken not to put pressure on the interviewee. Parental consent may be required when interviewing children.

Activity Researching research

Go to www.sociology.uk.net

Theoretical issues and structured interviews

The sociologist's methodological perspective plays an important part in deciding whether to use structured interviews. While positivists favour structured interviews, interpretivists, feminists and others are more critical of them.

Positivism

Positivists adopt a scientific approach to the study of society. In their view, research using structured interviews can achieve the main goals of scientific sociology. For positivists, structured interviews produce representative and generalisable findings. They are a reliable, objective and detached method for producing quantitative data, testing hypotheses and developing causal laws of social behaviour.

Hypothesis testing

Positivists model their approach on the natural sciences and seek to discover laws of cause and effect. Structured interviews are attractive to positivists because they enable them to test hypotheses and identify possible cause-and-effect relationships.

Just like questionnaires, structured interviews can establish correlations between variables (between gender and crime, say) by analysing interviewees' answers. This allows us to make generalisations about behaviour patterns – for example, that women are less likely than men to commit crime.

Once a correlation has been established, we can construct a hypothesis about its possible cause – for example, women commit less crime because of their socialisation. In turn, this hypothesis can be tested with a further set of interviews. In this way, causal laws can be discovered, just as in the natural sciences.

Reliability

If a method is reliable, then any other sociologist can repeat the research and obtain the same results. Positivists see structured interviews, like questionnaires, as a fixed yardstick or *standardised measuring instrument* – they are reliable because they are easy to standardise and control.

For example, interviewers can be trained to conduct each interview in precisely the same way, with the same questions, wording, order, tone of voice and so on.

These procedures are easy for other researchers to replicate, since they do not depend on the interviewer's personal characteristics – all interviewers conduct each interview in identical fashion. Similarly, pre-coded answers to questions mean that a later researcher will categorise answers in the same way as the original researcher. The structured interview thus provides a 'recipe' for repeating the research: as in cookery, anyone who follows it should get the same result.

The fact that all interviewees are asked exactly the same questions also means we can compare their answers easily to identify similarities and differences.

> Is it possible for, say, twenty trained interviewers all to ask a set of questions in exactly the same way? Give your reasons.

Representativeness

Structured interviews are relatively quick and cheap to conduct, so large numbers can be surveyed. This increases the chances of obtaining a representative sample. Relatively high response rates and the sophisticated sampling techniques that are often used also help to improve representativeness.

These features make structured interviews attractive to positivists because they can use the representative data as a basis for making generalisations and cause-and-effect statements about the wider population.

On the other hand, as with questionnaires, those with the time or willingness to be interviewed may be untypical (for example, they may be lonely). This makes for unrepresentative findings and undermines the validity of any generalisations made.

Interpretivism

Interpretivists are concerned to uncover the meanings that actors use to construct social reality. They argue that to do this, we need a method high in validity – one that gives a true picture of the subject being researched. In their view, this can only be achieved through the use of qualitative methods. Quantitative methods such as structured interviews tend to produce a false picture. There are several reasons for this:

- Structured interviews usually use closed-ended questions. This forces interviewees to choose from a limited number of pre-set answers. If none of these fits what the interviewee really wishes to say, the data produced will be invalid.
- Structured interviews give interviewers little freedom to explain questions or clarify misunderstandings.
- People may lie or exaggerate and this will produce invalid data.
- The sociologist has to draw up the interview schedule in advance, perhaps with little prior knowledge of the topic. In effect, the researcher has to decide in advance what is important – yet this may not coincide with what the *interviewee* thinks is important. Structured interviews thus risk imposing the researcher's framework of ideas on interviewees. Their findings may lack validity because they do not reflect the interviewee's concerns and priorities.

All interviews – whether structured or unstructured – are interaction situations. The interaction between interviewer and interviewee may undermine the validity of the interview, as Box 3.6 shows.

Box 3.6	Interviews as social interactions

All interviews involve social interaction between interviewer and interviewee, and this may undermine the validity of the data in several ways.

Status differences between interviewer and interviewee may affect the latter's honesty or willingness to cooperate. In general, the bigger the status difference, the less valid the data.

Cultural differences may lead to misunderstandings when different meanings are given to words. Interviewers may also not realise when they are being lied to.

Social desirability Interviewees may give answers that make them appear more interesting, normal etc. They may wish not to appear ignorant and so may offer any answer at all rather than admit they don't know.

Interviewer bias The interviewer may ask 'leading' questions, or influence answers by their tone of voice. Interviewer bias can also occur where the interviewer identifies too closely with the interviewees.

While all interviews risk distorting the data, structured interviews may be less susceptible because there are more controls over the interaction. For example, following a standard list of pre-set questions restricts the interviewer's ability to ask leading questions.

Feminism

Many feminists reject survey methods such as structured interviews and questionnaires. They argue that the relationship between researcher and researched reflects the exploitative nature of gender relationships in patriarchal society. Shulamit Reinharz (1983) goes so far as to call this approach to data collection 'research as rape':

▲ *How do the interviewer effect and the social desirability effect undermine validity?*

'The researchers take, hit and run. They intrude into their subjects' privacy… manipulate the relationships, and give little or nothing in return. When the needs of the researchers are satisfied, they break off contact with the subjects.'

Ann Oakley (1981) argues that this positivistic 'masculine' approach to research places a high value on objectivity, detachment and hierarchy, and regards 'science' as more important than furthering the interests of the people it researches.

Thus, interviewers must remain detached and in control and avoid any personal involvement with interviewees. In structured interviews, there is a strict division of labour:

- **The researcher takes the active role** in asking the questions.
- **Interviewees have a passive role** as mere objects of study, to be milked of information by answering the questions. They have no role in deciding the subject or direction of the interview.

This mirrors the gender divisions and hierarchies of patriarchal society.

Hilary Graham (1983) takes a similar view. She claims that questionnaires and structured interviews give a distorted and invalid picture of women's experience. They impose the researcher's categories on women, making it difficult for them to express their experiences, and concealing the unequal power relationships between the sexes.

This 'masculine' approach to interviewing is very similar to the positivist view of how research should be conducted. Similarly, the feminist criticisms of structured interviews and questionnaires recall those made by interpretivists.

Like the interpretivists, Oakley and Graham argue that sociologists should use methods that allow the researcher to understand women's experiences and viewpoint. For example, Graham advocates the use of direct observation, while Oakley argues for unstructured interviews (see page 188).

Unstructured interviews

Whereas structured interviews follow a standardised format, unstructured interviews give the interviewer freedom to vary the interview.

Practical issues

Probably the main attraction of unstructured interviews is that they can produce rich, detailed qualitative data that give an insight into the meanings and life-world of the interviewee.

- Their informality allows the interviewer to develop a rapport (relationship of trust and understanding). This helps to put the interviewee at ease and encourage them to open up, and is particularly useful when researching sensitive topics. Empathy can enable interviewees to discuss difficult subjects such as abuse.
- Training needs to be more thorough than for structured interviews. Interviewers need to have a background in sociology so they can recognise when the interviewee has made a sociologically important point and can probe further with appropriate questioning. All this adds to the cost. Interviewers also need good interpersonal skills to establish rapport with interviewees.
- They take a long time – often several hours each. This limits the number that can be carried out and means the researcher will have a relatively small sample.

- They produce large amounts of data, which can take time to transcribe (e.g. from recordings of the interviews). There are no pre-coded answers, making analysis and categorisation of data time-consuming and difficult.
- Unstructured interviews make it much easier for interviewer and interviewee to check they have understood each other's meanings. If the interviewee doesn't understand a question, it can be explained. If the interviewer doesn't understand an answer, they can ask follow-up questions to clarify matters.
- They are very flexible. The interviewer is not restricted to a fixed set of questions, but can explore whatever seems interesting. The researcher can formulate new hypotheses and put them to the test as they arise during the interview.
- They are useful where the subject is one we know little about, because they are open-ended and exploratory – they allow us to learn as we go along. Some sociologists use unstructured interviews as a starting point to develop their initial ideas before using more structured methods.
- Because there are no pre-set questions, unstructured interviews allow the interviewee more opportunity to speak about those things they think are important.

Theoretical issues: interpretivism

A major factor in deciding whether to use unstructured interviews is the sociologist's methodological and theoretical perspective. While positivists reject their use, interpretivists favour unstructured interviews. The key criterion by which interpretivists judge the usefulness of a method is how far it produces valid (true and authentic) data.

Interpretivists are concerned with understanding actors' meanings. They prefer to use qualitative methods such as unstructured interviews, because they regard these as producing a more valid picture of how actors give meaning to their actions. They argue that there are several reasons for this, as follows.

Validity through involvement

For interpretivists, valid data can only be obtained by getting close to people's experiences and meanings – understanding only comes through involvement. They argue that unstructured interviews allow us to do this. By becoming involved and developing a rapport with the interviewee, the researcher can see the world through their eyes and appreciate what is important to them and why they act as they do.

Grounded theory

Interpretivists such as Glaser and Strauss (1968) reject the positivist idea that research involves beginning with a fixed hypothesis that we then test by collecting data, for example through a set of predetermined questions. They argue that it is important to approach the research with an open mind; otherwise we are unlikely to discover the truth about the situation or the actors' meanings.

In their view, we should develop *grounded theory*. That is, we build up and modify our hypothesis during the actual course of the research itself, based on the facts we discover as we learn more about the subject.

In this view, unstructured interviews are an ideal research tool, particularly when investigating unfamiliar subjects. They allow us to ask whatever questions we like, and to pursue lines of enquiry that appear important as and when they arise – unlike a structured interview, with its fixed set of questions.

Unstructured interviews thus fit well with the interpretivist view of research as a flexible, open-ended and open-minded process of exploration.

The interviewee's view

The absence of a pre-set structure of fixed questions gives interviewees freedom to raise issues and discuss what is important to them. This may bring fresh insights that had not previously occurred to the sociologist. Conversely, the interviewer's probing and encouragement can help the interviewee to formulate their thoughts more clearly.

The open-ended questions used also permit interviewees to express themselves as they choose, in their own words, rather than having to select one from a limited range of forced choice answers, none of which may fully match their real opinions. Thus an unstructured interview is more likely to reveal the interviewee's true meanings.

Theoretical issues: positivism

Positivists reject the use of unstructured interviews as unscientific. In their view, this method lacks objectivity and reliability and fails to produce representative data that can be generalised to the wider population.

Reliability

Positivists argue that the unstructured interview is not reliable, because it is not a standardised measuring instrument. This is because each interview is unique. For example, interviewers are free to omit or add questions, ask different ones or change their wording each time if they feel it is relevant to do so.

As a result, it is virtually impossible for another researcher to replicate the interviews and check the findings or compare them with their own. For positivists, this is a major shortcoming: if the original study cannot be checked by others by replicating its methods, we cannot be confident that its findings are in fact true.

Quantification

Because unstructured interviews use open-ended questions, answers cannot easily be categorised and quantified. In turn, this makes unstructured interviews less useful for correlating variables, testing hypotheses and establishing cause-and-effect relationships.

Representativeness

Positivists dislike unstructured interviews because they are less likely to produce representative data from which generalisations can be made and causal laws discovered.

Because they take longer, sample sizes are often much smaller than with structured interviews. This means there is a greater likelihood that the sample interviewed will not be representative. Therefore it will be harder to make valid generalisations about the wider population based on the findings of the interviews.

However, interpretivists see this as less of a problem because they do not place as much emphasis on representativeness and generalisation. This is because they are not seeking to discover causal laws about the workings of the social structure, but to understand the meanings of actors in specific contexts.

Lack of validity

Interpretivists see unstructured interviews as producing valid data. However, positivists argue that the interaction between interviewer and interviewee inevitably undermines their validity. Because the success of unstructured interviews often relies on establishing rapport, there is a danger of this distorting the information obtained.

For example, interviewees may be more concerned to please their 'friend' the interviewer by providing what they believe are the expected answers.

However, not all unstructured interviews rely on rapport. For example, Becker (1971) used aggression, disbelief and 'playing dumb' to get teachers to reveal how they classified pupils in stereotypical ways.

Unstructured interviews yield qualitative data, and positivists argue that this too can undermine validity. Because the answers are not pre-coded, the sociologist has to analyse and categorise the data as they see fit. Positivists argue that this inevitably involves the researcher making value judgments about the meanings of answers.

Therefore, rather than giving us a valid picture of social life, unstructured interviews merely give us a picture as seen through the eyes of the sociologist.

Thus, positivists turn the standard interpretivist criticism of *structured* interviews – that they inevitably involve imposing the researcher's categories on the data – into a criticism of *unstructured* interviews.

> Suggest two reasons why the data from unstructured interviews 'merely gives us a picture as seen through the eyes of the sociologist'.

Feminism

As we saw above, many feminists reject the use of structured interviews, which they regard as 'masculine' and positivistic. Some feminists, such as Oakley, argue that there is a superior and distinctively feminist approach to research.

This kind of research:

- Is *value-committed*: it takes women's side and aims to give a voice to their experience and to free them from patriarchal oppression.
- Requires the researcher's *involvement* with, rather than detachment from, the lives of the women she studies.
- Aims for *equality and collaboration* between the researcher and researched, rather than hierarchy and control by the researcher.

To illustrate this approach, Oakley draws on her own experience of conducting 178 unstructured interviews with women about becoming mothers. On average, she spent over nine hours interviewing each woman and even attended some of the births. Unlike in the 'masculine' approach, Oakley wished to involve the women as active collaborators and friends. She willingly answered their questions about herself and her research and met their requests for advice about childbirth. She also helped them with housework and childcare, and many of the women showed an interest in the research and assisted by phoning her up with more information.

Oakley argues that developing a more equal and intimate relationship improved the quality of her research by allowing her to get closer to the women's experiences and point of view. As a feminist, it was also important to her that the research helped to improve the women's lives. For example, many of them found that being interviewed helped reduce their anxieties about childbirth.

Evaluation of Oakley

However, Ray Pawson (1992) argues that there is nothing distinctively feminist or original about Oakley's approach. Her view of interviewing is basically the same as that of interpretivism, with its 'time-honoured tradition of positivism-bashing in general, and structured-interviewing bashing in particular'.

However, feminists argue that Oakley goes beyond the interpretivist approach. For example, she had direct involvement in the women's lives outside the interview situation, offering them help and advice. This reflects the value-committed nature of feminist research, which explicitly takes women's side and seeks to improve their lives.

For more activities on Interviews…

Go to www.sociology.uk.net

Summary

Structured interviews have similar strengths and limitations to questionnaires. They can gather basic information quickly and cheaply, but they are inflexible. Positivists favour them because they are standardised measuring instruments, offering reliability. Sample sizes are large, permitting representativeness and generalisation of findings. Interpretivists criticise them for lacking validity and imposing the researcher's meanings. They favour unstructured interviews as a way of accessing interviewees' meanings. However, these are more costly, time-consuming and harder to analyse, while small samples mean that they are less likely to yield representative data. Feminists tend to prefer unstructured rather than structured interviews, since the latter reflect patriarchal approaches to research and knowledge.

QuickCheck Questions

1   Explain why structured interviews are described as standardised measuring instruments.
2   Suggest two advantages of structured interviews over postal questionnaires.
3   Suggest two reasons why structured interviews may lack validity.
4   Suggest two reasons why unstructured interviews may lack reliability.
5   Why are unstructured interviews particularly useful when investigating unfamiliar subjects?
6   What is 'rapport'? Why is it important?
7   Suggest two advantages and two disadvantages of using group interviews in research.
8   True or false? Unstructured interviews produce more representative results than structured interviews.

Check your answers at www.sociology.uk.net

Examining interviews

Assess the value of interviews in sociological research.   (33 marks)

The examiner's advice

This question caries 15 AO1 marks (knowledge and understanding) and 18 AO2 marks (interpretation, application, analysis and evaluation).

You need to consider different types of interviews and your main focus should be on structured and unstructured interviews. You must examine both the strengths and the limitations of interviews, in terms of practical, ethical and theoretical issues.

Practical issues include cost, time, numbers covered, response rate, type of data required, flexibility/inflexibility etc. There are relatively few ethical issues, though some feminists criticise structured interviews, while unstructured interviews may cause distress when dealing with sensitive issues. Theoretical aspects include reliability, representativeness, validity, objectivity, grounded theory etc, and you should put these into a broader context of positivism and interpretivism (you could also include feminism). Try to link practical and theoretical issues where possible. You can also make comparisons and contrasts, both between structured and unstructured interviews, and with other methods (e.g. questionnaires, experiments or observation).

METHODS IN CONTEXT
using interviews to investigate crime and deviance

Sociologists sometimes use interviews to study issues such as:

- Victims of crime
- Fear of crime
- Crime networks
- Perpetrators and victims of domestic violence
- Police attitudes

Before reading this section, re-visit Topic 1 to refresh your understanding of what is different about researching crime and deviance.

Practical issues

There are a number of practical issues in using interviews to study crime and deviance, including language, recording of interviews, safety and access to interviewees.

Language

Literacy is an issue for some groups. For example, convicted criminals have on average much lower literacy levels than the general population. For groups like this, interviews are likely to be a more effective research method than written questionnaires.

Recording interviews

In the interests of ensuring validity, it is important to make an accurate record of interviewees' responses. However, writing notes during an interview may put some interviewees off. To a suspect, offender or police officer, this may look too much like writing a report on them and may inhibit their responses.

Recording responses on a digital recorder also has problems. Given the sensitivity of the topic, few involved in crime and its policing might feel comfortable if their statements were taken down in a way that could later be used against them in legal or disciplinary contexts.

Recording is also likely to make interviewees suspicious of the researcher's intentions. Maguire (2007), studying street criminal networks:

'decided early on never to use a tape-recorder, even in prison interviews, as it could damage the crucial trust I had to build up with those I spoke to'.

Safety

Research involving direct contact with certain offenders raises safety issues. For example, Davies (2000) was aware of the risk of being taken hostage when interviewing women prisoners. Some sociologists suggest that a researcher should always tell colleagues where and when they are going to meet interviewees. Ironically, given the high level of security around them, interviewers are probably safer interviewing in prison and police contexts. For example, Hoyle (2007) was accompanied by off-duty police officers when she went to interview victims of domestic violence.

Access

There are particular access issues for interviewing most groups involved in crime. Some are in protected environments and others are hidden. For example, there are problems interviewing victims of domestic violence because access to refuges is very difficult. However, access to those victims who choose to stay in the family home may also be difficult. On the other hand, some groups – police, court officials and prisoners – are easily located.

However, there are still issues of finding a time and place for interviews. For example, because unstructured interviews take longer, it is hard to fit them into a workplace or prison timetable. Finding an appropriate venue can also be problematic. In the case of prisoners, this can normally only be in prison. However, the researcher must still find a suitable unthreatening location within the prison. Other groups involved in the criminal justice system can be interviewed at work, home or elsewhere. However, when interviewing criminals, the need for anonymity and confidentiality means that home or workplace may be unsuitable. Davies became desperate to find an interview venue and often ended up using a local café.

Reliability

The nature of some groups makes it very difficult to replicate an interview. For example, in Maguire's (2007) study of street criminals some interviews lasted a few minutes, while others developed into lengthy informal focus groups in a pub or at people's homes. This amount of variation in length and content makes it impossible to standardise and replicate such unstructured interviews.

On the other hand, structured interviews offer greater opportunity for reliable data. For example, the British Crime Survey's standardised questions and responses, piloting in

▲ *What difficulties might you find in conducting interviews with prisoners?*

advance and training of interviewers all contribute to its reliability (see Box 3.7).

Validity

Some groups involved in the criminal justice system have their own language codes. Pamela Davies (2000) argues that the slang expressions that offenders use are the only ones that can fully express their meanings. Open-ended, unstructured interviews allow this slang to be quickly absorbed, meanings clarified and validity enhanced.

Few researchers have much personal experience of committing crime, being a victim or being involved with the criminal justice system. It is important that they avoid imposing their personal assumptions on the research process. Unstructured interviews allow interviewees' worldviews to emerge in ways that reduce this risk.

Those involved in the criminal justice system are often likely to be defensive. The higher level of trust and rapport that unstructured interviews can create helps the researcher to overcome this barrier.

Carolyn Hoyle's (2007) research on police attitudes to domestic incidents shows the usefulness of unstructured interviews in revealing the truth beneath the surface. Initial questions to police about their attitude towards dealing with domestic incidents usually resulted in 'canteen culture' comments such as 'domestics are so much trouble'. However, when asked open-ended questions about specific incidents, officers said they had taken the time to be sympathetic when investigating them. Such claims were usually substantiated by Hoyle's observations of their actions in similar incidents.

Interviewees' perceptions of the interviewer may affect the validity of their responses. For example, Davies was known as 'the Miss' to the women prisoners she studied, while one victim of domestic violence called Hoyle 'a nosy bloody cow' after spotting her with the police, as this meant she had been identified as an authority figure. Carol Adams (2000) was conscious that her appearance might affect the responses of the police officers and suspects she interviewed. Consequently, when interviewing police, she dressed to look like a 'normal, law abiding citizen', but she 'dressed down' when interviewing suspects to avoid looking like an official person intruding into their lives.

Not being able to 'fit in' when seeking to interview offenders may prevent any data at all being collected. For example, when Walklate and her colleagues studied two high-crime areas in Salford, the interviewers they used were all mature students with northern connections. Previously, a government study using a professional survey company had tried to research the same area and had been told to leave by local street criminals.

There is a power and status hierarchy within the police, courts and similar organisations. Differences in power and status can affect an individual's preparedness to participate in an interview and how forthcoming they are in answering questions. For example, it may be harder to obtain an interview with a high court judge than with the clerk of a magistrates' court.

Activity

Walklate points out how important it is to 'fit in' with interviewees. Imagine you are selecting people to carry out interviews in a men's prison. Discuss in a group the following decisions:

1   Would you choose males or females?

2   Would you ask them to dress (a) formally; (b) casually; (c) scruffily?

3   What age range would you choose: (a) 20-34; (b) 35-49; (c) 50-65?

4   What sort of accent would you want them to have?

Explain the reasons for your decisions and explain what you think would be the effect if you made a different choice.

Ethics

Investigating law breaking using interviews can raise ethical issues. Because unstructured interviews encourage trust and openness, an offender may provide the researcher with 'guilty knowledge', for example about crimes they had got away with or were planning to commit. This faces the researcher with the dilemma of whether to breach confidentiality and inform the police. Maguire (2007) made it a rule never to record particularly sensitive information, such as that relating to recent offences the interviewee had committed. However, this approach could still be considered unethical because he had not passed this information on to the police.

The interviewer may dig too deep and the interviewee may reveal distressing experiences, for example, of abuse as a child. This may cause psychological harm to the interviewee.

There is also the issue of payment to criminals for taking part in interviews. Some researchers see passing a few cigarettes to interviewees in prison contexts as part of the 'research bargain' and this minimal level of payment is unlikely to create any ethical problems.

A further ethical concern is the possibility of the research placing victims of crime at further risk. Hoyle was accompanied by police officers for her safety when visiting domestic violence victims in their homes. Although this increased the interviewer's safety, it increased the risk of further violence against the victim.

Representativeness

Unstructured interviews are usually time consuming, especially because of the sensitive nature of issues of deviant behaviour. They are therefore unlikely to be carried out with large enough samples to produce representative findings.

Many aspects of criminal activity have no ready-made sampling frames. For example, there are no lists of whistleblowers or of unconvicted criminals. In these cases, the researcher has to rely on snowball samples and these are unlikely to be representative.

Box 3.7   The British Crime Survey (BCS)

The BCS is a Home Office victimisation survey that measures the amount of crime in England and Wales by asking people about crimes they have experienced in the last year. It collects data on the victims of crime, the circumstances of incidents and the behaviour of those committing crimes. Carried out at intervals since 1982, the BCS is now an annual survey.

The BCS formerly used a random sample of adults aged 16 and over, but from 2009 this was extended to include 10-15 year olds. The sample used is very large, 47,000 in 2005/6, and has a response rate of around 75% (although this is lower in inner-city areas). Both the large sample size and high response rate are products of the official nature of the BCS.

The survey is a structured interview carried out by 22 trained interviewers who record responses on a laptop. The vast majority of the questions asked are pre-coded, although the category 'other' allows interviewees to answer in their own words. Contact is made in advance by letter and interviews are carried out in private unless the interviewee requests that someone is present. The interview takes about 48 minutes to complete. Some crimes are omitted from the survey such as murder, fraud and 'victimless' crimes.

Some other Home Office funded surveys use Audio CASI – a self-completion method where respondents listen to the questions whilst completing a questionnaire on a laptop. This approach may be used in future for the BCS.

Activity   The British Crime Survey

Go to www.sociology.uk.net

Examining interviews in context

Item A   **Researching the real rate of street crime**

Street crime includes acts such as demanding money or mobile phones with the threat of violence, bag snatching, and damage to vehicles. Unlike with some other crimes, people are usually aware that they are the victims of such crimes. Indeed, street crime can be an intense emotional experience for the victim and not something they can easily forget about.

However, many street crimes are not reported to the police. Victims may feel that the amount of time involved in going to a police station, giving statements and so on is simply not worth the cost of whatever loss had resulted from the crime. Other victims may feel that crimes such as these are one of the normal risks of everyday life. On the other hand, if the damage is substantial or an insurance claim could be made, victims are more likely to report the crime.

Structured interviews are useful for investigating the real rate of street crime because they can be carried out with a large sample of people, thus gaining a representative picture of the amount of such crime. However, they rely on the accuracy of people's memories of street crime experiences.

Question

Using material from **Item A** and elsewhere, assess the strengths and weaknesses of using structured interviews to investigate the real rate of street crime.

(15 marks)

The examiner's advice

This question carries 6 AO1 marks (knowledge and understanding) and 9 AO2 marks (interpretation, application, analysis and evaluation). It requires you to **apply** your knowledge and understanding of structured interviews to the study of the **particular** issue of the real rate of street crime. It is not enough simply to discuss structured interviews in general.

You need to attach one or more of the strengths and limitations of structured interviews to the research characteristics of the real rate of street crime. A good place to start is Item A. For example, it states that one research characteristic is that many street crimes are not reported to the police, so the real rate of crime is not apparent from official statistics of reported crime. One strength of structured interviews is that their standardised nature means they can be replicated on a large scale, allowing the real rate of crime to be identified.

However, structured interviews are retrospective research and rely on the accuracy of interviewees' memory. Relatively minor episodes may be forgotten; equally, being the victim of a major street crime may have traumatised the individual and this may not be something they want to re-visit in an interview.

Other research characteristics not mentioned in Item A include defining street crime. For example, does the researcher include drug deals in which both sides consent to the act so there may be no immediately identifiable 'victim'? Most street crime, however defined, is unpredictable and swift, so a victim's awareness and subsequent recollection of events may not be accurate.

Try to keep a reasonable balance between the strengths and limitations of structured interviews. You can also refer to studies that have used this method (e.g. the British Crime Survey) and to any relevant research you have been involved in.

Druids celebrating the summer solstice at Stonehenge. What are the advantages of using participant observation to study groups such as this?

Topic 5 Observation

Learning objectives

After studying this Topic, you should:

■ Know the different observational methods and the main stages in conducting a participant observation study.

■ Understand and be able to evaluate the practical, ethical and theoretical strengths and limitations of overt and covert participant observation.

■ Be able to apply your understanding of observational methods to the study of crime and deviance.

One problem of using interviews or questionnaires is that what people say they do and what they actually do are often two quite different things. One way round this might be simply to see what people really do by observing them in their natural environment.

We can distinguish between participant and non-participant observation:

■ **Non-participant observation** The researcher simply observes the group without taking part.

■ **Participant observation** The researcher takes part in the life of the group while observing it.

Whether participant or non-participant, observation can be either overt or covert:

■ **Overt observation** The researcher reveals their true identity and purpose to those being studied and asks their permission to observe.

■ **Covert observation** The researcher conceals their true identity and purpose, usually posing as a genuine member of the group.

In sociology, most observation is *unstructured participant observation*. The main reason for using this method is the insight it offers into a group's way of life. For this reason, it is often used by interpretivists.

However, positivists sometimes use *structured non-participant observation*. This involves using a structured observational schedule. This is a pre-determined list of the types of behaviour the sociologist is interested in. Each time the behaviour occurs, the observer records it on the schedule. The number of times each event occurs is added up to produce quantitative data, from which patterns and correlations can be established.

Participant observation

Whether sociologists use overt or covert participant observation, they face problems of getting into, staying in and finally getting out of the group that they are studying.

Getting in

Some groups that we may wish to study are easier to enter than others. For example, joining a football crowd is likely to be easier than joining a criminal gang. Making initial contact with the group may depend on factors such as personal skills, having the right connections, or even pure chance.

Once contact is made, the researcher may have to overcome the group's suspicions and win their trust. In doing so, it may help to make friends with a key informant. However, the researcher's age, gender, class or ethnicity may prove an obstacle if it differs from the group's.

On entering the group, the researcher may need to adopt a particular role. If so, then ideally the role should offer a good vantage point from which to make observations.

At the same time, it should not disrupt the group's normal behaviour. Unfortunately, it is not always possible to take a role that is both non-disruptive and a good vantage point.

Some roles may also involve taking sides in conflicts, with the result that the researcher may become estranged from one faction or the other, making observation more difficult.

> How might the researcher 'going native' threaten the validity of the study?

Staying in

Once accepted, the researcher is faced with a dilemma:

- They must be *involved* in the group and its activities to understand it fully.
- Yet they must also be *detached* from the group so as to remain objective and unbiased.

If they are too detached, they risk not understanding what they observe. Yet if they become too involved, they risk *going native* – over-identifying with the group. They have ceased to be an objective researcher and are simply a member of the group. Striking a balance between these two extremes can be very difficult.

A further problem is that the longer the researcher spends with the group, the less strange its ways will appear. The researcher gradually ceases to notice things that would earlier have struck them as noteworthy: the observer becomes less observant. As William F. Whyte (1955) put it, 'I started as a non-participating observer and ended as a non-observing participator.'

Getting out

Getting out of the group at the end of the research is generally less of a problem: if the worst comes to the worst, the researcher can usually just leave. Nevertheless, leaving a group with whom one has become close can be difficult – as can re-entering one's normal world. These problems can be worse if the research is conducted on and off over a period of time, with multiple 'crossings' between the two worlds. Researchers may also find that loyalty to the group prevents them from fully disclosing everything they have learnt, for fear that this might harm group members.

Practical issues in participant observation

In addition to getting in, staying in and getting out, there are other practical issues for the researcher who chooses to use participant observation.

Insight

For supporters of participant observation, the best way to truly understand what something is like is to experience it for oneself. The key strength of the method is that it gives us insight into other people's lives by allowing us to put ourselves in their place – a process known as *verstehen*, a German word meaning empathy or subjective understanding.

Participant observation allows the sociologist to gain verstehen through first hand experience. By living as a member of a group, in their natural environment, we can develop a rapport with its members and gain insight into their way of life, their meanings, values and problems. We can come to understand their life-world as they themselves understand it. In the process, participant observation produces large amounts of rich, detailed qualitative data that give us a 'feel' for what it is like to be a member of the group.

Access

Sometimes participant observation may be the *only* suitable method for accessing and studying certain groups. For example:

- Groups who engage in deviant activities may be suspicious of outsiders who come asking questions, but more willing to cooperate with someone who seeks to share their way of life.
- Where a group are unaware of the unconscious assumptions or stereotypes behind their actions, observation may be the only means of uncovering them – since it would be pointless asking questions about them.

Flexibility

By comparison with survey methods (questionnaires and structured interviews), participant observation is very *flexible*. With survey methods, we have to begin with a fixed hypothesis and pre-set questions. One problem with this is that, if the questions we think are important turn out not to be important to the subjects of our research, we are still stuck with them.

With participant observation, this is not a problem. We can enter the research with a relatively open mind and formulate new hypotheses and research questions as and when we encounter new situations. This allows the researcher to discover things that other methods miss. As Whyte noted, simply by observing, 'I learned answers to questions that I would not have had the sense to ask if I had been using interviews.' Similarly, Ned Polsky (1971) offers some sound,

if blunt, advice: 'initially, keep your eyes and ears open but keep your mouth shut'.

Limitations

There are several practical disadvantages in using participant observation:

- The fieldwork is very time-consuming and may take years to complete. It also produces large amounts of qualitative data, which can be hard to analyse and categorise.
- The researcher needs to be sociologically trained so they recognise the aspects of a situation that are significant and worth investigating.
- It can be personally stressful and demanding, and sometimes dangerous.
- It requires observational and interpersonal skills that not everyone possesses.
- Powerful groups may be able to prevent sociologists participating in them. This is one reason why participant observation often focuses on relatively powerless groups – they are less able to resist being studied.

While these practical strengths and limitations are largely true of both overt and covert participant observation, others are more typical of one than of the other, as Box 3.8 shows.

Activity   Participant and non-participant observation

Go to www.sociology.uk.net

Box 3.8	Overt versus covert observation – practical issues

Overt	Covert
The researcher can behave normally and does not have to put on an act.	The researcher must keep up an act. This can be stressful, especially if it involves staying in role for long periods.
Because the researcher is known to be an outsider, they do not need any special knowledge or personal characteristics to join.	The researcher may need detailed knowledge of the group's way of life before joining, and characteristics (e.g. gender) that allow them to fit in.
The group may refuse to let an outsider join them, or may prevent them witnessing certain activities.	It may be the only way to obtain information. The researcher may have more chance of being accepted and seeing things outsiders could not.
As an outsider, the researcher can ask naïve but important questions.	The researcher cannot ask naïve questions, as this could blow their cover.
The researcher can take notes openly and does not have to rely on memory.	The researcher usually has to rely on memory and write notes in secret.
The researcher can use interviews or other methods to check insights derived from observations.	The researcher cannot combine observation with any 'overt' methods such as interviews.
The researcher can opt out of any dangerous or illegal activities.	To maintain cover, the researcher may have to engage in dangerous activities.
It risks creating the Hawthorne effect, where those who know they are being observed behave differently as a result.	There is less risk of altering the group's behaviour, because they don't know they are being observed.

Theoretical issues in participant observation

A major factor in the decision whether to use participant observation is the sociologist's methodological perspective. While interpretivists favour participant observation, positivists are critical of its use in research. When using observational methods, positivists are more likely to employ structured non-participant observation (see Box 3.9).

Interpretivism

The main concern of interpretivists is to understand actors' meanings. The key criterion by which they judge the usefulness of a method is how far it is able to produce valid data – that is, a true account of the phenomena it studies. Interpretivists thus prefer to use a qualitative method such as participant observation, because they regard it as producing a richly detailed and authentic picture of actors' meanings and life-worlds. Interpretivists argue that there are several reasons for this, as follows.

Validity through involvement

Participant observation requires the sociologist to have a higher level of involvement with the group being studied than any other method. Interpretivists argue that by experiencing the life of the group at first hand, the sociologist is able to get close to people's lived reality and gain a deep subjective understanding of their meanings. This produces uniquely valid, insightful, qualitative data.

This compares favourably with methods such as questionnaires and interviews. While people may lie when answering questions about themselves, direct observation can give us a truer picture of how they really live.

Flexibility and grounded theory

The flexibility of participant observation also helps to produce valid data and is particularly useful when studying unfamiliar situations, groups or cultures about which we know little before we start the research. As Glaser and Strauss (1968) argue, by being able to enter the research without a pre-formed hypothesis or questions, the researcher can develop and modify their ideas in the course of the research to produce *grounded theory*. That is, concepts, categories and hypotheses are grounded in the observed realities, rather than imposed on the data by the researcher.

Similarly, by spending lengthy periods of time with a group, we are able to see actors' meanings as they develop. For this reason, participant observation gives us a more valid picture than the 'snapshots' taken at a single moment in time by interviews or questionnaires.

Positivism

Positivists reject the use of participant observation as an unscientific research method. In their view, it lacks objectivity and reliability and does not yield representative data that can be generalised to the wider population. They also reject the interpretivists' claim that it produces uniquely valid data.

Representativeness

Quantitative methods such as questionnaires usually study large, carefully selected representative samples that provide a sound basis for making generalisations. By contrast, with participant observation:

- The group studied is usually very small.
- The 'sample' is often selected haphazardly, for example through a chance encounter with someone who turns out to be a key informant.

This means that the group studied may be unrepresentative of the wider population and therefore not a suitable basis for making generalisations. As Downes and Rock (2003) note, although participant observation may provide valid insights into the particular group being studied, it is doubtful how far these 'internally valid' insights are 'externally valid' – that is, generalisable to the wider population.

Reliability

Reliability means that if another researcher repeats the method, they will obtain the same results. To achieve reliability, research procedures must be standardised so that other researchers can reproduce them. For example, in structured interviews all interviewers ask the same questions, and so other sociologists can easily repeat the research later.

Positivists criticise participant observation as unsystematic and lacking in reliability. Unlike structured methods, it is not a standardised, scientific measuring instrument. Instead, the success of the research depends heavily on the personal skills and characteristics of the lone researcher. For example, as Whyte recognised, his method was to some extent unique to him alone. This means it is almost impossible for any other investigator to check the original study by replicating it, and so we cannot be as confident that its findings are true.

The fact that participant observation usually produces qualitative data also makes comparisons with other studies difficult. This is a further reason why the method is unlikely to produce reliable data.

Go to www.sociology.uk.net

Box 3.9   Positivism and structured observation

When positivists use observational methods, they generally favour *structured non-participant observation*:

- It is quicker, so a larger, more representative sample can be studied, from which firmer generalisations can be made.
- The observer remains detached. By avoiding involvement, they do not influence the group's behaviour, and they do not 'go native' and lose objectivity.
- Like the standardised questions in a questionnaire, standardised observational categories produce reliable data because other researchers can replicate the observation.
- Pre-coded observational categories allow the sociologist to produce quantitative data, identify and measure behaviour patterns, and establish cause-and-effect relationships.

However, interpretivists reject structured observation because it imposes the researcher's view of reality and risks producing invalid data.

Activity Observing children

Bias and lack of objectivity

Positivists argue that the researcher's close involvement with the group results in a lack of objectivity.

- Involvement means the sociologist risks 'going native', over-identifying with the group and producing a biased or over-sympathetic view of them.

- Involvement breeds loyalty to the group and may lead the sociologist to conceal sensitive information. This denies those who read the published study a full and objective account of the research.
- Participant observation appeals to sociologists whose sympathies often lie with the underdog, such as interactionists. Because it is seen as an effective method for 'telling it like it is' from the actor's point of view, some of those who use it may be biased in favour of their subjects' viewpoint.

Lack of validity

For interpretivists, participant observation's great strength lies in its validity. They claim that it avoids imposing the sociologist's own categories and ideas on the facts. Instead, as a form of verstehen, it gives an authentic account of the actor's world, from the actor's viewpoint.

Positivists reject this claim. They argue that findings of such studies are merely the biased subjective impressions of the observer. In reality, rather than being the actor's view of their world, it is merely the *observer's* view of things. The observer selects only those facts they think are worth recording, and these are likely to fit in with their own values and prejudices.

In any case, participant observation studies generally collect masses of qualitative data, only a small portion of which is likely to be published. The sociologist therefore has to make judgments about what to omit from the final account, and this too will reflect their values.

Can engaging in illegal or immoral actions in the course of a covert study ever be justifiable? If so, on what grounds?

Box 3.10   Ethics and observation

Covert participant observation (PO) raises serious ethical issues. These often conflict with the practical advantage it offers of avoiding the Hawthorne effect and enabling us to observe people's natural behaviour.

- It is unethical to deceive people in order to obtain information by pretending to be their friend or 'in the same boat' as them. Researchers should obtain their informed consent, revealing the purpose of the study and the use to which its findings will be put. With covert observation, this cannot normally be done. However, some argue that the ends may justify the means if the results of the research are of benefit to society.
- Covert observers may have to lie about why they are leaving the group at the end of their research. Others simply abandon the group without explanation. Critics argue that this is unethical.
- They may have to participate in immoral or illegal activities as part of their 'cover' role.

Overt PO avoids these problems, but is not free of other ethical problems. As witnesses to immoral or illegal activities, both overt and covert researchers may have a moral or legal duty to intervene or to report them to the police. Yet this could undermine their relationship with the group and, for covert PO, blow the researcher's cover.

Because PO is open-ended, researchers may not know where it will lead – so they cannot easily explain the research to subjects to obtain their informed consent. Also, as many people float in and out of view during the course of the research; it would be impractical to ask them all for their consent.

PO leads to close personal attachments with the group, so the researcher risks 'going native'. This may result in condoning ethically unacceptable behaviour, or withholding information from the police etc about the group's activities.

Non-participant observation (NPO) avoids most of these ethical problems, but covert NPO involves 'spying' on people without their knowledge and consent.

The Hawthorne effect

The Hawthorne effect can also undermine the validity of participant observation studies, because the observer's presence may make the subjects act differently. This defeats a central aim of participant observation, namely to produce a 'naturalistic' account of behaviour. This is more of a problem in overt observation, but even in covert studies, the presence of an extra member (the researcher) may change the group's behaviour.

However, interpretivists argue that, over time, the group generally gets used to the observer's presence and behaves normally. The researcher can also try to adopt a less obtrusive role to minimise the threat to validity.

Structure versus action perspectives

Participant observation is normally associated with 'action' perspectives, especially symbolic interactionism. This is because interactionists see society as constructed from the 'bottom up', through the small-scale, face-to-face interactions of individual actors and their meanings. In the interactionists' view, participant observation is a valuable tool for examining these micro-level interactions and meanings at first hand because it allows us to see them through the actor's eyes.

However, structural sociologists such as Marxists and functionalists see this as inadequate. They argue that, because participant observation focuses on the micro level of actors' meanings, it tends to ignore the macro (large-scale) structural forces that shape our behaviour, such as class inequality or the shared value system into which we are socialised.

In the structuralist view, therefore, seeing things only through the individual actors' eyes will never give us an adequate picture. For example, Marxists argue that the actors may suffer from false consciousness and misunderstand their true position or class interests.

If so, then their own account of their lives, revealed through participant observation, will give us only a distorted or partial view. Similarly, functionalists distinguish between an action's manifest function – what the actors *think* its purpose is – and its latent or 'true' function for society, which may be very different.

However, theoretical perspective is not the only factor affecting the choice of method. For example, functionalists have employed participant observation as the only practical way of studying small-scale, non-literate societies and cultures. Similarly, neo-Marxists such as Willis (1977) have used qualitative data from participant observation to support their Marxist analysis.

For more activities on Observation...

Go to www.sociology.uk.net

Summary

Participant observation (PO) involves joining in with the activities and life of the group being studied to gain first hand insight. There may be difficulties both joining and leaving the group; while in the group, there is the danger of 'going native'. PO can be time-consuming and stressful.

Covert PO may produce more valid data, but is ethically questionable and poses practical problems such as maintaining cover. Overt observation avoids some of these difficulties but may mean the group act differently.

Interpretivists favour PO for its flexibility, validity and the opportunity to develop grounded theory. However, positivists argue that PO studies are unreliable and the small scale makes findings unrepresentative; they prefer to use structured non-participant observation.

Structural approaches argue that the focus on micro-level interaction means PO cannot study macro-level structural factors.

QuickCheck Questions

1 What is a structured observation schedule?
2 Suggest two reasons why participant observation might not produce representative data.
3 Identify two ethical problems of covert participant observation.
4 Explain why participant observation is attractive to 'action' approaches in sociology.
5 Explain what is meant by 'going native'.
6 Suggest two reasons why participant observation may produce unreliable results.
7 Explain how the Hawthorne effect might undermine the validity of a participant observation study.
8 Identify three advantages of using overt rather than covert observation.

Check your answers at www.sociology.uk.net

Examining observation

Assess the usefulness of observation in sociological research.

(33 marks)

The examiner's advice

This question carries 15 AO1 marks (knowledge and understanding) and 18 AO2 marks (interpretation, application, analysis and evaluation).

Begin by noting the different types of observation that sociologists may use and then focus most of your answer on participant observation (PO). Identify gaining insight into a group as a major reason for using PO and link this to interpretivism.

Examine the practical, ethical and theoretical issues involved in using different types of observation, using examples from studies (many could come from deviance). Practical issues include time, cost, access, what role to adopt, danger, personal characteristics etc. Theoretical issues centre on validity, reliability and representativeness. Explain these terms and link them to PO and to the positivism-interpretivism debate. Many ethical issues, and some practical and theoretical ones, are linked to whether one uses overt or covert PO, so make this distinction a major focus of your answer. Although your main focus should be PO, mention structured non-PO as an alternative method favoured by positivists.

METHODS IN CONTEXT
using observation to investigate crime and deviance

Sociologists sometimes use observation to study issues such as:

- Delinquent youth subcultures
- Police and policing
- 'Outsider' groups
- Court processes
- Minor crime such as shoplifting

Before reading this section, re-visit Topic 1 to refresh your understanding of what is different about researching crime and deviance.

Practical issues

There are a number of practical advantages and practical disadvantages to using observation as a means of researching crime and deviance.

Advantages

Crime involves activities that society sees as disreputable and for which there are penalties. As a result, criminals are likely to be secretive, anti-authority and suspicious of any formal research. To the offender, sociological investigations may seem very similar to those carried out by the police. As

Lewis Yablonsky (1973) points out, a teenage gang is likely to see researchers who come armed with questionnaires as the unwelcome representatives of authority.

As a result, participant observation may be the *only* method for studying deviant groups. Because it enables the sociologist to build a rapport with the group and gain its trust, it has proved a successful method of studying delinquent gangs, football hooligans, thieves, drug users, religious sects and other 'outsider' groups.

Participant observation can also be used in situations where questioning would be ineffective. This is shown in Aaron Cicourel's (1968) study of how police categorise juveniles by making unconscious assumptions about whether they are criminal 'types'. Precisely because they are unaware of their assumptions, it would be pointless to ask them questions about them. For Cicourel, therefore, the only way to get at these assumptions is to observe the police directly.

Disadvantages

Many groups involved in crime and its control may not wish to be studied in this way and often have the power to make access difficult. This is one reason why participant observation often focuses on relatively powerless groups who are less able to resist being studied, such as petty criminals.

Gaining access to observe those working in the criminal justice system, such as the police, is problematic. In the case of Simon Holdaway (1983), being a serving police officer made this easier. Even so, he found that the power of the lower ranks and their resistance to external control of their work made observation difficult at times. Any research strategy would have to pierce what Holdaway calls the 'protective shield' that police officers erect.

Many areas of the criminal justice system, such as police stations, prisons and courts, are formally closed or strictly controlled by the power of the law. This may severely restrict access opportunities for observers. Other groups, for example those involved in corporate crime, also have the power to deny the observer access.

Many deviant acts do not happen in a predictable way. As a result, an observer can end up hanging around waiting for an event that may never occur. On the other hand, some events are predictable, for example court cases. However, because their timetabling is out of the observer's control, they may still take a long time to study.

Observation can also take a long *time* for other reasons. Settings such as courts and prisons are complex places and it can take the observer a long time to familiarise themselves with the rules and roles. Similarly, it may require considerable time to become accepted into some criminal groups. For example, Adler (1985) describes the drug dealers and smugglers she studied as having a 'secretive, deceitful, mistrustful, and paranoid' culture. As a result, it took her six years of fieldwork to complete her study. Similarly, Bourgois spent three years living in 'El Barrio' observing crack dealing.

The researcher's *personal characteristics* such as age, gender or ethnicity may restrict what groups they can study. As Downes and Rock put it, 'not everyone would pass uneventfully into the world of punk rockers or Hell's Angels'. In the observation of groups with a culture of violence, the danger can be acute. Ken Pryce was murdered when he tried to research organised crime, while Venkatesh was only spared a beating by the intervention of the gang's leader.

Activity

There are clearly opportunities for any student to carry out participant observation in school or college. However, your age and gender restrict where you can go, what you can do and what you can observe. Discuss as a group how age and gender could restrict your observational study of deviance in school/college.

Going native

The strength of the police's work culture is such that it can draw researchers into their worldview. For example, Maurice Punch (1979) found himself over-identifying with the police he was observing so much that at times he acted as a 'policeman' himself – chasing and holding suspects, searching houses, cars and people, and shouting at those who abused his police 'colleagues'.

This can also occur with deviant or criminal subcultures. Whyte (1955) famously declared that he began to identify so much with the Italian-American street gang he studied that he 'started as a non-participating observer and ended as a non-observing participator'.

As the subtitle of Venkatesh's book – 'crossing the line' – suggests, he recognised that he was forming personal relationships with members of a very violent subculture and that this might invalidate his data as a result of becoming too sympathetic to them. Critics argue that he romanticises the gang culture.

Overt observation

Deviants and control agents may be particularly defensive towards overt observers. They may refuse the researcher permission to observe them – or, as two of the Amsterdam police officers that Punch had done his research with later told him, 'When you were with us, we only let you see what we wanted you to see'.

However, acceptance by the group allows the overt observer to ask the kind of naïve but important questions that only an outsider could ask. For example, the researcher could ask a gang member, 'Why do you rob and steal?'

▲ *Crime or politics? Greenpeace protestors scale the fence at Sellafield nuclear plant. Participant observation can be risky.*

Covert observation

The main advantage of covert observation is that it reduces the risk of altering people's behaviour, and is sometimes the only way to obtain valid information. This is particularly true where people are engaged in activities they would rather keep secret. As Laud Humphreys (1970), who studied gay men's casual sexual encounters in public toilets, notes:

'There is only one way to watch highly discreditable behaviour and that is to pretend to be in the same boat with those engaging in it.'

Finding and maintaining a role that permits the researcher to observe covertly but safely is particularly difficult with deviants and control agents. Thus for example, Humphreys took on the role of 'watch queen' or lookout. Dick Hobbs (1988) befriended a detective whose son played in the football team Hobbs coached. He was able to go drinking with the detective and his police friends as they discussed their work in more relaxed circumstances.

There is always a risk of one's cover being 'blown' by even a trivial mistake. Patrick was almost found out by the gang he had joined, when he bought his suit with cash instead of credit and when he fastened the middle button of his jacket rather than the top one – things the gang would never have done. This is likely to bring the research to an abrupt end and may even lead to physical harm. As Polsky advises, therefore:

'You damned well better not pretend to be "one of them" because they will test this claim out and you will either find yourself involved in illegal activities, or your cover will be blown.'

This was something Patrick also discovered when he was handed an axe to use in an anticipated gang fight.

The sociologist cannot usually take notes openly and must rely on memory and the chance to write them in secret. Both Leon Festinger et al (1956), studying a religious sect that had predicted the imminent end of the world, and Jason Ditton (1977), studying theft among bread deliverymen, had to use the toilet as a place to record their observations. In Ditton's case, this eventually aroused suspicion.

Validity

Validity involves gaining a true or authentic picture of something. Interpretivists argue that participant observation can provide valid accounts of deviance and social control. For example, few sociologists have much personal experience of crime. This makes open and non-directive methods like participant observation particularly useful in exploring an unfamiliar world and uncovering worldviews of which they have little personal knowledge.

Participant observation is useful for penetrating outward appearance to obtain a true picture of crime and control. For example, there may be a difference between the official police view of the world and what police officers 'on the ground' believe. Officers may have their own view of 'criminal types' that is at odds with the official view. However, if questioned, they may simply 'parrot' the official view, whereas participant observation is more likely to uncover what they really think.

However, the nature of deviant activity means that a researcher may not fully disclose everything they have learnt for fear that this might harm members of the group. For example, exposure of their crimes might lead to their prosecution, or to reprisals against the researcher. Clearly, such concealment of data will reduce the validity of the study.

Ethics

Of all research methods, covert observation probably has the greatest ethical problems. Lack of informed consent, the difficulty of de-briefing those involved and, particularly in the study of deviance, what to do in situations of law-breaking all pose ethical problems for the observer.

The usual justification is that covert observation is the only way to study the behaviour of suspicious and defensive groups. Humphreys calls this 'situational ethics' – meaning that the ethics of research are driven by the nature of the group and issues being studied.

A further moral dilemma for the observer is what to do with their 'guilty knowledge' of criminal acts. For example, Venkatesh refers to 'shades of grey' to describe his legal and ethical position, in two respects:

- He knew about the gang's law breaking but did not inform on them.
- He himself participated to some extent. For example, when the gang made him 'leader for a day', he was responsible for deciding on internal disciplinary matters that included punishing members.

He also questions who gained from his research. He himself benefited by gaining a career out of it, but the gang gained little.

Covert observers may have to lie about why they are leaving the group at the end of their research. Others, such as Patrick (who feared for his safety), have simply abandoned the group without explanation. Critics argue that this is unethical.

Examining observation in context

Item A Researching the judicial process

Justice is required to be transparent. Therefore courts are public places and, with certain restrictions, anyone can access the process of justice. However, some aspects of the judicial process occur in closed settings. For example, pre-trial discussions between judges and lawyers take place in private in judges' chambers, as do decisions about sentencing.

Minor criminal cases are dealt with relatively swiftly in court, but for major crimes, the public process of justice is often very long. Court processes are often complex, with arguments over points of law taking up hours of court time.

Observation is useful because it allows the researcher to see and record the process of justice as it unfolds. However, the researcher is limited to a passive observer role. For example, the law limits who they can ask questions of and where they can observe in court.

Question

Using material from **Item A** and elsewhere, assess the strengths and weaknesses of using observation to investigate the judicial process.

(15 marks)

The examiner's advice

This question carries 6 AO1 marks (knowledge and understanding) and 9 AO2 marks (interpretation, application, analysis and evaluation). It requires you to **apply** your knowledge and understanding of observation to the study of the **particular** issue of the judicial process. It is not enough simply to discuss observation in general.

You need to attach one or more of the strengths and limitations of observation to the research characteristics of the judicial process. A good place to start is Item A. For example, it states that one research characteristic of the judicial process is that it is largely carried out in public. You could connect this to observation by pointing out the importance of gaining access to whatever is being observed.

However, Item A also points out that an observer would have no control at all over the time taken by the justice process. This means that their time may well be wasted sitting through extensive discussions that have little relevance to their research.

Other research characteristics not mentioned in Item A include the unwillingness of some of those involved in the administration of justice to be involved in research. Similarly, the legal restrictions on access to juries and others involved in the judicial process limits the observer's access.

Try to keep a reasonable balance between the strengths and limitations of observation. You can also refer to studies that have used this method and to any relevant research you have been involved in.

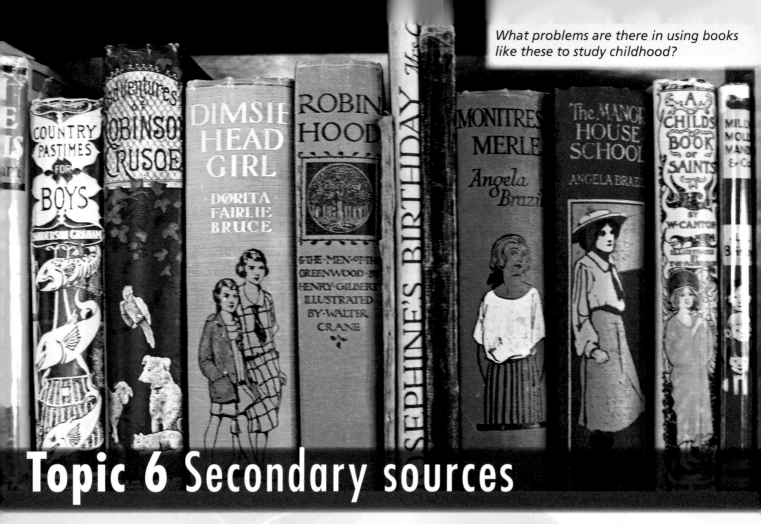

What problems are there in using books like these to study childhood?

Topic 6 Secondary sources

As well as collecting their own primary data through surveys or observation, sociologists also use pre-existing or secondary data – that is, data that has been created or gathered by other people for their own particular purposes, but which sociologists then make use of in their research.

There are two main sources of secondary data:

- **Official statistics**
- **Documents**

For example, governments produce statistics on births, marriages and deaths, crime, education, health and so on. Similarly, individuals often keep diaries or write letters and e-mails that record their experiences. Sociologists may use these sources to gather facts, test hypotheses or gain insight.

Positivists make much use of official statistics as a source of quantitative data that in their view provides objective facts about society. By contrast, interpretivists are more likely to make use of documents. As qualitative sources of data, they can give valuable insight into actors' meanings.

Secondary data is often cheap or free, and may be readily accessible. Sometimes, it may be the only material available on a given topic, for example when studying the past.

Learning objectives

After studying this Topic, you should:

- Know the different types of secondary data.
- Be able to evaluate the practical, ethical and theoretical strengths and limitations of official statistics and documents.
- Understand the usefulness of different types of secondary data in relation to wider issues of methodological and theoretical perspective, science, values and objectivity.
- Be able to apply your understanding of secondary data to the study of crime and deviance.

Official statistics

Official statistics are quantitative data created by the government or other official bodies. Examples include statistics on births, deaths, marriages and divorces, exam results, school exclusions, crime, suicide, unemployment and health. The ten-yearly Census of the entire UK population is a major source of official statistics. Examples of many other official statistics can be found in the annual publication, *Social Trends*.

Governments use official statistics in policy-making. For example, statistics on the age structure of the population help the government to plan future pension provision.

There are several types of source for the information that is used to create official statistics:

- **Registration** – for example, the law requires parents to register births.
- **Official surveys**, such as the Census or the General Household Survey.
- **Administrative records** of state agencies such as hospitals, courts and schools. These include records of illnesses, convictions, truancy etc.

As well as official statistics produced by government, various non-state organisations also produce 'non-official' statistics. For example, churches produce membership and attendance statistics, while the charity Shelter produces statistics on homelessness.

Both the advantages and the disadvantages of official statistics stem largely from the fact that they are secondary data. That is, they are collected not by sociologists, but by official agencies for their own particular purposes – which may differ from those of the sociologist.

Practical advantages

They are a free source of huge amounts of quantitative data. Only the state has the resources to conduct large-scale surveys costing millions of pounds, such as the ten-yearly Census of every household in the UK. The results of these are usually published and can be accessed by sociologists to use in their research.

Similarly, only the state has the power to compel individuals to supply certain data. For example, parents are required by law to register births, while heads of household must complete the Census form. This reduces the problem of non-response – for example, in the last Census the refusal rate was only 5%.

Official statistics allow us to make comparisons between groups. For example, the Census covers the whole UK population at the same time and asks everyone the same core questions. This makes it easy to compare different social groups, regions and so on.

Because official statistics are collected at regular intervals, they show trends and patterns over time. This means sociologists can use them for 'before and after' studies to identify correlations between variables and suggest possible cause-and-effect relationships.

Practical disadvantages

The government creates statistics for its own purposes, and not for the benefit of sociologists, so there may be none available on the topic we are interested in. For example, the French state does not collect data on the race, religion or ethnicity of its citizens. This means it produces no official statistics on issues such as the religion of people who commit suicide or of prisoners in its jails.

There may be mismatches between sets of statistics. For example, if we want to compare statistics on ill health with statistics on unemployment for the people of a particular town, we may find that the two sets of data cover slightly different areas and therefore different populations. This makes it impossible to establish the degree of correlation between ill health and unemployment precisely.

The definitions that the state uses in collecting the data may be different from those that sociologists would use. For example, they may define 'homelessness' or 'truancy' differently. In turn, this may lead to different views of how large the problem is. It may be in the state's interests to make a problem appear smaller by redefining it.

The state may change the definitions it uses over time, and different states may define the same term differently. This makes comparisons over time or between countries difficult. Some statistics are collected infrequently, such as the ten-yearly Census, and therefore do not always give an up-to-date picture of social trends.

Theoretical issues and official statistics

A major factor in the decision whether to use official statistics is the sociologist's methodological and theoretical perspective. While positivists favour official statistics as objective facts about society, others are more critical. Interpretivists see them as social constructs, and Marxists and feminists regard them as performing an ideological function.

Positivism and statistics

Positivists take it for granted that official statistics are reliable, objective social facts. As such, they are a very important resource in the scientific study of society. They are a major source of representative, quantitative data that allows the sociologist to identify and measure behaviour patterns, test hypotheses and develop causal laws to explain the patterns of behaviour that the statistics reveal.

For example, by using official statistics to identify patterns in mental illness, positivists can establish correlations. Statistics might reveal, say, gender differences in rates of depression.

From this knowledge, a testable hypothesis can be put forward to explain a possible causal link between the variables. For instance, if the statistics show a correlation between being a full-time housewife and a high risk of depression, we might hypothesise that this is due to social isolation.

Representativeness

Representativeness is important to positivists because they wish to make general statements about society as a whole and how it shapes our behaviour. It is therefore important that the samples they study are typical or representative, so that the findings can be generalised to the wider population and used to test hypotheses.

Official statistics often provide a more representative sample than surveys conducted with the limited budget available to the sociologist. This is because they are very large-scale, often covering the entire population. For example, statistics gathered by compulsory registration, such as birth and death statistics, are likely to cover virtually all cases and therefore be extremely 'representative'.

Statistics from official surveys may be somewhat less representative because they are only based on a *sample* of the relevant population. Nonetheless, these surveys are still much bigger than most sociologists could afford to carry out. For example, the General Household Survey in 2006 interviewed almost 23,000 people.

Furthermore, great care is taken with sampling procedures when conducting official surveys. For these reasons, official statistics may provide a sound basis for making generalisations and testing hypotheses.

Activity **Investigating social trends**

Go to www.sociology.uk.net

Reliability

Positivists regard official statistics as a reliable source of data. In other words, if a different person collected the statistics, it is argued that they would produce the same set of figures. This is because they are compiled by trained staff who use standardised categories and collection techniques, and follow set procedures that can be easily replicated by others.

This is particularly true of statistics created from *official surveys* such as the Census. In these cases, the survey is carried out using a *standardised measuring instrument* such as a written questionnaire or an interview schedule, which is then administered in the same way to all respondents. The official statistics created from the survey results are therefore reliable, because any other researcher could repeat the survey and get the same results.

Similarly, when producing statistics from *registration data* such as births, marriages and deaths, government statisticians follow a standard procedure. For example, in compiling death rates for different social classes, they use the occupation recorded on each person's death certificate to identify their class. The statistics are therefore reliable because, in principle, any properly trained person will allocate a given case to the same category.

However, official statistics are not always wholly reliable. For example, Census coders may make errors or omit information when recording data from Census forms, or members of the public may fill in the form incorrectly.

Interpretivism and statistics

Interpretivists such as Cicourel (1968) reject the positivist claim that official statistics are real, objective social *facts* that exist out there in the world. In their view, statistics are merely social *constructs* that represent the labels officials attach to people. Therefore, rather than taking statistics at face value as a useful resource – as positivists do – we should treat them as a topic in themselves and investigate how they are socially constructed.

For example, official statistics on mental illness are largely a record of the number of people who consult a doctor about their problem, and whom the doctor then deems to be suffering from a mental illness. Thus to end up as a statistic, the individual has to go through a series of social interactions. These may include pressure from relatives to see a doctor, consultations with the GP and perhaps also a psychiatrist. At the end of this process, the individual may or may not have achieved the label 'officially mentally ill' and become a statistic.

Interpretivists therefore reject the positivist view that such statistics are a true and valid measure of the 'real rate' of mental illness. Instead, they are merely the total number of decisions made by doctors to *label* people as mentally ill. The statistics are therefore more a measure of the way doctors go about labelling patients than of the actual level of mental illness in society. For this reason, interpretivists are interested in studying the social processes, such as labelling and stereotyping, by which official statistics are constructed. The same can be said about suicide statistics, as we saw in Chapter 2, Topic 10.

Hard and soft statistics

For interpretivists, then, official statistics such as those for mental illness are invalid – they do not measure what they claim to measure. However, this doesn't mean that all official statistics are equally invalid. We can distinguish between 'hard' and 'soft' statistics.

Soft statistics tend to give a much less valid picture of reality. They are often compiled from the administrative records created by state agencies such as the health service, police, courts, schools and so on. What they represent is a record of the decisions made by these agencies, rather than a picture of the world 'out there'. For example, truancy statistics represent the number of pupils that schools have *defined* as truanting – not necessarily the same thing as the number who *actually* truanted.

Soft statistics also often neglect an unknown or 'dark figure' of unrecorded cases. For example, schools may keep a record of racist incidents, but pupils don't report every incident, and teachers don't record all those that are reported. The problem is that there may be no way of discovering what proportion of actual cases goes unrecorded.

Hard statistics by contrast provide a much more valid picture. For example, they include statistics on births, deaths, marriages and divorces. While a small number of births and deaths go unrecorded, we can place a high level of trust in the validity of hard statistics. This is because:

■ There is little dispute as to how to define the categories used to collect the data (e.g. death, divorce).

■ They are often created from registration data – for example, there is a legal requirement to register births and deaths.

> Suggest three other examples of (a) hard and (b) soft statistics. In each case, explain your answer.

Marxism and statistics

Like interpretivists, Marxists reject the positivist claim that official statistics are objective facts. However, unlike interpretivists, Marxists do not see them as merely the outcome of the labels applied by officials. Instead they regard official statistics as serving the interests of capitalism.

Marxists see capitalist society as composed of two social classes in conflict with each other: the capitalist ruling class and the working class. In this conflict, the state is not neutral, but serves the interests of the capitalist class. The statistics that the state creates are part of what Althusser terms the *ideological state apparatus* – a set of institutions that produce ruling-class ideology. As ideology, the function of official statistics is to conceal or distort reality and maintain the capitalist class in power.

Ideological functions

Marxists see official statistics as performing this function in several ways. For example, politically sensitive data that would reveal the unequal, exploitative nature of capitalism may not be published. For example, since the 1980s, data derived from analysis of Census returns no longer includes class differences in death rates.

The *definitions* used in creating official statistics also conceal the true reality of capitalism. For example, the state has frequently changed its definition of unemployment, and this has reduced the numbers officially defined as unemployed. Similarly, social class categories used in official statistics are based on occupation. This gives the impression of a gradual hierarchy of several classes, rather than a conflict between two opposed classes. It also conceals the existence of a ruling class whose position is based on ownership of vast wealth, not on occupation.

However, critics argue that not all official statistics reflect the interests of capitalism. For example, statistics on differences in illness and life expectancy show clear evidence of class inequality.

Feminism and statistics

Feminists criticise official statistics for several reasons. Firstly, as we saw in Topic 4, feminists such as Oakley and Graham reject the use of quantitative survey methods such as structured interviews and questionnaires because they regard this as a 'masculine' or patriarchal model of research. Since official statistics are often created using these methods, this is also a criticism of the statistics they produce.

Secondly, official statistics are created by the *state*, which feminists regard as maintaining patriarchal oppression. In this view, official statistics are a form of patriarchal ideology – they conceal or legitimate gender inequality and maintain women's subordination. For example, while there is a wealth of official data on paid employment outside the home, few statistics are collected on women's unpaid domestic labour, thereby maintaining its invisibility and giving the impression that it is of little importance. In fact, full-time housewives are defined for statistical purposes as 'economically inactive'.

Thus official statistics underestimate women's economic contribution and they reflect the patriarchal nature of the state. However, not all official statistics can be seen as reflecting patriarchy. Some statistics, such as those on earnings from paid work, show clear evidence of gender inequality.

There have also been changes in the definitions used in official statistics that may reveal women's position more clearly. For example, a family's class used to be determined by the occupation of the male head of household. This changed in 2001 so that the person who owns or rents the home is now the 'household reference person' (HRP) and their occupation is used to define the family's class. Where the home is jointly owned, the person with the highest income becomes the HRP. These changes increase the chance that a woman's occupation will determine her family's class.

However, as men are still more likely both to be the homeowner and to earn more, official statistics continue to give a distorted picture of gender and social class. For this reason, many feminists argue that official statistics should allocate women and men to a social class as individuals, not as households.

> Suggest one other type of statistic that (a) conceals or legitimates gender inequality; (b) reveals gender inequality.

Documents

Documents include the following kinds of information sources:

- **Written texts:** diaries, letters, e-mails, SMS texts, Internet pages, novels, newspapers, school reports, government reports, medical records, parish registers, train timetables, shopping lists, financial records, graffiti etc.
- **Other texts:** paintings, drawings, photographs, maps, and recorded or broadcast sounds and images from film, TV, music, radio, home video etc.

Sociologists make use of the following types of documents:

- **Public documents** produced by organisations such as government departments, schools, welfare agencies, businesses and charities. Public documents include Ofsted reports, council meeting minutes, media output, published company accounts, records of parliamentary debates and the reports of public inquiries such as the Macpherson Inquiry into the death of the black teenager Stephen Lawrence.
- **Personal documents** include items such as letters, diaries, photo albums and autobiographies. These are first-person accounts of social events and personal experiences and often include the writer's feelings and attitudes.
- **Historical documents** are simply personal or public documents created in the past.

Practical issues and documents

Documents have several advantages for the researcher:

- They may be the only available source of information, for example in studying the past.
- They are a free or cheap source of large amounts of data, because someone else has already gathered the information.
- For the same reason, using existing documents saves the sociologist time.

However, there may be practical difficulties in using documents. For example:

- It is not always possible to gain access to them.
- Individuals and organisations create documents for their own purposes, not the sociologist's. Therefore they may not contain answers to the kinds of questions the sociologist wishes to ask.

Theoretical issues and documents

The choice of whether and how to use documents in sociological research depends in part on the sociologist's methodological perspective. While interpretivists often favour the use of documents, positivists tend to reject them other than as material for content analysis (see below). Positivists regard them as unreliable and unrepresentative sources. However, they do sometimes carry out content analysis on documents as a way of producing quantitative data.

Validity

Interpretivists' preference for documents comes from the fact that they believe documents can give the researcher a valid picture of actors' meanings. For example, the rich qualitative data of diaries and letters give us an insight into the writer's worldview and meanings by enabling us to get close to their reality.

For example, *The Polish Peasant in Europe and America*, William Thomas and Florian Znaniecki's (1919) interactionist study of migration and social change, used

▲ *Certificates of birth, marriage, death and right of burial. What use can sociologists make of such documents?*

a variety of documents. These included 764 letters bought after placing an advertisement in a Polish newspaper in Chicago, several autobiographies, and public documents such as newspaper articles and court and social work records. They used the documents to reveal the meanings individuals gave to their experience of migration.

Also, because documents are not written with the sociologist in mind, they are more likely to be an authentic statement of their author's views – unlike interviews or questionnaires, where the respondent knows that their answers are to be used for research purposes.

However, documents may lack validity as a source of data. John Scott (1990) identifies three reasons for this. Firstly, a document can only yield valid data if it is *authentic* – if it is genuinely what it claims to be. Researchers may not be certain whether it really was written by its supposed author, for example, or whether it is a forgery.

Secondly, there is the issue of *credibility*. Is what the document says believable? For example, politicians may write diaries or autobiographies intended for publication that produce a self-serving account of events, for example by glossing over their mistakes. A document may also lack credibility if it was written long after the events it describes, when key details might have been forgotten, rather than at the time they actually happened.

Thirdly, while interpretivists value documents because they give us access to their authors' meanings, there is always a danger of the sociologist *misinterpreting* what the document actually meant to the writer and the intended audience, imposing instead their own meaning on the data. There may also be added difficulties if the document is in a foreign language, or if words have changed their meaning since it was written. Furthermore, different sociologists may interpret the same document differently.

Reliability

Positivists regard documents as unreliable sources of data. Unlike official statistics on a topic, which are compiled in a standard format according to fixed criteria that allow us to compare them, documents are not standardised in this way. For example, every person's diary is unique, compiled in its own way according to the writer's own meanings and concerns. This is true even when each diarist is recording the same events, such as their experiences of a war. Their uniqueness also undermines their representativeness and makes it difficult to draw generalisations from them.

Representativeness

Documents may also be unrepresentative for other reasons. As Scott notes, some groups may not be represented in documents. For example, the illiterate and those with limited leisure time are unlikely to keep diaries.

In addition, the evidence in the documents that we have access to may not be typical of the evidence in other documents that we don't have access to. For example:

- Not all documents survive: are the surviving ones typical of the ones that get destroyed or lost?
- Not all documents are available. The 30-year rule prevents access to many official documents for 30 years. If classified as official secrets, they will not be available at all. Private documents such as diaries may never become available.

If we cannot be sure that the information we extract from the documents is representative, we cannot safely generalise from it.

Content analysis

Content analysis is a method for dealing with the contents of documents, especially those produced by the mass media. It has been used to analyse news broadcasts, advertisements, children's reading schemes, newspaper articles and so on. There are two main types of content analysis:

- Formal content analysis
- Thematic analysis

Formal content analysis

Although documents are normally regarded as a source of qualitative data, formal content analysis allows us to produce quantitative data from them. Ros Gill (1988) describes how formal content analysis works as follows. Imagine we want to measure particular aspects of a media message – for example, how many female characters are portrayed as being in paid employment in women's magazine stories.

- First we select a representative sample of women's magazine stories – for example, all the stories appearing in the five most popular magazines during the last six months.
- Then we decide what categories we are going to use, such as employee, full-time housewife etc.
- Next, we study the stories and place the characters in them into the categories we have decided upon. This is called coding.
- We can then quantify how women are characterised in the stories simply by counting up the number in each category.

Formal content analysis is attractive to positivists because they regard it as producing objective, representative, quantitative data from which generalisations can be made. It is also a reliable method because it is easy for others to repeat and check the findings. Repeating studies also allows us to identify trends over time, for example to see if media images of a group have changed.

Formal content analysis has also proved attractive to feminists in analysing media representations of gender. For example, Lesly Best (1993) analysed gender roles in children's reading schemes, while Gaye Tuchman (1978) analysed television's portrayal of women. Both found that females were portrayed in a limited range of stereotyped roles.

However, interpretivists criticise formal content analysis for its lack of validity. They argue that simply counting up how many times something appears in a document tells us nothing about its meaning, either to its author or its audience.

The method is also not as objective as positivists claim. For example, the processes of drawing up the categories and deciding in which one to place each case are subjective processes involving value judgments by the sociologist.

Thematic analysis

This is a qualitative analysis of the content of media texts and has been used by interpretivists and feminists. It usually involves selecting a small number of cases for in-depth analysis. The aim is to reveal the underlying meanings that have been 'encoded' in the documents, as a way of uncovering the author's ideological bias. For example, working from a feminist perspective, Keith Soothill and Sylvia Walby (1991) made a thematic analysis of the ways newspapers reported rape cases.

However, thematic analysis can be criticised on several grounds:

- It does not attempt to obtain a representative sample, so its findings cannot be safely generalised to a wider range of documents.
- There is often a tendency to select evidence that supports the sociologist's hypothesis rather than seeking to falsify it, which Karl Popper argues is unscientific.
- There is no proof that the meaning the sociologist gives to the document is the true one. For example, postmodernists would argue that there is no fixed or 'correct' meaning to a text and that the sociologist's reading of it is just one among many.

Content analysis, whether formal or thematic, has practical advantages: it is cheap, and it is easy to find sources of material in the form of newspapers, television broadcasts and so on. However, in both formal and thematic analysis, coding or analysing the data can be very time-consuming.

Activity Content analysis

Go to www.sociology.uk.net

For more activities on Secondary sources...

Go to www.sociology.uk.net

Summary

Secondary sources are those created by someone other than the sociologist who is using them. They include official statistics and documents. They save the sociologist time and money, and they provide useful data that sociologists may not be able to gather themselves. Positivists regard official statistics as providing reliable and representative data from which causal statements can be derived. However, statistics – especially 'soft' ones – may lack validity. Interpretivists see official statistics as social constructs, and Marxists and feminists regard them as ideological.

Sociologists use both personal and public documents, such as diaries, letters, media output and government reports. Documents may give insight into the meanings of those who created them, but they may not be authentic or representative. Sociologists may apply formal or thematic content analysis to documents.

QuickCheck Questions

1 Identify three advantages of official statistics.
2 What are the three main sources of information from which official statistics are collected?
3 What is the difference between 'hard' and 'soft' statistics?
4 True or false? Marxists see official statistics as a reliable and valid picture of modern life.
5 Why do secondary sources usually present fewer ethical problems to the sociologist than other methods of research?
6 Explain what is meant by 'content analysis'.
7 Which of the following are documents that could be used by sociologists: (a) the Census; (b) photographs; (c) comics; (d) club rules?
8 What does Scott mean by the 'credibility' of a document?

Check your answers at www.sociology.uk.net

Examining secondary sources

Outline the sources of secondary data that sociologists use and assess their advantages and disadvantages. (33 marks)

The examiner's advice

This question carries 15 AO1 marks (knowledge and understanding) and 18 AO2 marks (interpretation, application, analysis and evaluation).

The question clearly asks for sources *plural*, so make sure you deal with a range. Your answer must include both official statistics and documents, and you should distinguish between different kinds of document (e.g. personal versus public), and between 'hard' and 'soft' statistics. You should give examples of each type of secondary source you refer to.

You should consider the practical, ethical and theoretical advantages and disadvantages of the different sources. These include time, cost, scale, access, anonymity and confidentiality, representativeness and generalisation, hypothesis testing, reliability and validity. A useful way to organise your evaluation is by relating some of these to positivist and interpretivist perspectives (though you can also mention Marxist and feminist views of statistics), and to quantitative versus qualitative data.

METHODS IN CONTEXT
using secondary sources to investigate crime and deviance

Sociologists use secondary sources to study a variety of issues in crime and deviance. The main secondary sources that they use are official statistics and a variety of documents, both personal and official.

Before reading this section, re-visit Topic 1 to refresh your understanding of what is different about researching crime and deviance.

Using official statistics

Official statistics on crime and deviance are used to study issues such as:

- The level of crime in society
- Patterns of offending
- The effectiveness of the police
- The work of the courts and probation service
- Patterns of suicide

Practical issues

The government collects a huge amount of statistical data on crime. Annual publications for England and Wales include crime, judicial, prison and probation statistics, with similar data produced for the rest of the UK. In addition, there is the British Crime Survey and bulletins with statistics on drugs seizures, motoring offences etc. The Home Office also sponsors a wide range of research projects that produce quantitative data, for example on crime reduction strategies. The huge volume and range of official statistics on crime and justice reflects the high political profile of these issues.

Official crime statistics in the UK are heavily biased towards 'notifiable offences' or more serious, indictable crimes. 'Summary offences' such as many motoring offences and parking tickets were not recorded before1998.

There may be differences between official and sociological views of a particular crime. For example, Steve Tombs (2000) points out that instances of employer breaches of safety laws leading to injury or death are largely missing from official categories of violent crime (murder, manslaughter, violence against the person), yet could reasonably be categorised as such. For Marxists, this reflects the ideological nature of crime statistics.

Representativeness

Official crime statistics appear at first sight to be highly representative. Agencies of social control such as the police and the courts are required by law to keep certain data about crime.

One of the main purposes of official crime statistics is to monitor police activities and patterns of crime in order to inform policy. Because the state has a need to know the social characteristics of those involved in crime, their gender, occupation, ethnicity, age, etc are recorded by the police and courts.

However, concerns about the whole process of reporting, recording and clearing up crime indicates that, as well as having problems of validity, crime statistics may not be representative of all crimes committed. Similarly, changes in legislation and especially the creation of new laws, for example against discrimination, mean that crime statistics are not always directly comparable over time.

Reliability

Counting criminal offences is problematic and can lead to inconsistencies that undermine the reliability of crime statistics. Take for example a case where a man repeatedly assaults his wife over a period of time – how many crimes have been committed? The police operate the rule of thumb that if there is a social relationship between offender and victim, a series of acts counts as one offence. Similarly, where several offences occur in the same incident, only the most serious is counted.

Validity

About 90% of crimes are discovered and reported by the public, rather than by the police. Whether or not members of the public report a crime depends on factors such as their relationship to the offender, the type of crime, attitudes to the police, the likely consequences of reporting (e.g. reprisals from the offender), and insurance issues.

For example, victims report nearly all vehicle thefts, but only a minority of sexual and domestic abuse cases. Private security operatives such as caretakers and bouncers may or may not report crimes they discover depending on company policy.

Activity

The public are much more likely to report some crimes than others.

In groups, decide which of the following crimes you think have high or low reporting rates. Rank them from 1 (highest rate) to 11 (lowest): (a) theft from the person; (b) robbery; (c) burglary with loss; (d) theft from vehicle; (e) vandalism; (f) bicycle theft; (g) wounding; (h) vehicle theft; (i) common assault (no injury); (j) attempted vehicle theft; (k) burglary with no loss (including attempts). Why are these differences in reporting important for understanding levels of crime?

Find the correct rankings by searching online for the British Crime Survey 2005-06, pages 52 and 59.

The police do not record all the crimes reported to them. The British Crime Survey estimates that they only record about 60% of reported offences. Reasons for non-recording include officers not accepting the victim's story, seeing the act as too trivial, or believing the issue had been resolved in some other way.

Police recording practices may also reflect political and media agendas on crime. As a result, the likelihood of a particular type of crime being recorded may vary according to the political climate of the day. Furthermore, some offences known to the authorities are not recorded as crimes. For example, some are dealt with through administrative procedures such as HM Revenue and Customs settling with tax evaders out of court.

Once recorded, a crime may eventually be categorised as 'cleared up'. Most offences are so categorised because the crime has resulted in a charge or summons. However, some other cases are also designated 'cleared up'. These include those where the offender is below the age of criminal responsibility, the victim is unwilling or unable to give evidence, or someone currently in jail admits to the crime. This is not everyone's definition of 'cleared up' crimes.

Using documents

A variety of personal and official documents can be used to study issues in crime and deviance, including:

- Offenders' motives and experiences
- The work of probation, police and other services
- The process of law making
- The motives of suicides
- The history of crime and law

Practical issues

The criminal justice system is a bureaucratic organisation and creates a huge quantity of official documents relating to crime, criminals, victims, police forces, courts, legal processes, prisons, the probation service and so on. Because crime has a high political profile, the Home Office also commissions a great deal of research into the operation of the criminal justice system.

However, the coverage is not comprehensive: for some crimes, such as those of the powerful, there may be limited information. By contrast, for others there may be too much information for a researcher to work through. Much of this official documentary material is in the public domain, so it is easily accessible, but some of it is confidential and not available to researchers.

Official documents can be very useful for developing a historical perspective on crime-related issues. Robb (1992) examined white-collar crime in England between 1845 and 1929. He used reports of parliamentary committees and special commissions, company records, bankruptcy and Inland Revenue reports, laws passed and the records of parliamentary debates – a huge range of accessible, relevant official documentation. Robb also supplemented material from official archives with biographies, plays, novels and poetry.

Some crimes and deviant acts leave documentary evidence – literally, a paper trail for researchers to follow. For example, suicide notes can be taken to be the final thoughts of the individual committing suicide. Graffiti is an instance of the crime itself being a document, while crime prevention posters and leaflets come from within the criminal justice system.

Some crimes, such as credit card, tax and financial fraud, leave a substantial documentary trail. However, at times the documentary evidence is extremely complex and the existence of a crime is often buried deep in the paperwork. This requires a great deal of time, skill and effort to sift through. In other cases, there is only a limited amount of usable data because the offenders have destroyed the documents.

Documents may also come from unexpected sources. Venkatesh established such a good relationship with T-Bone, the bookkeeper to the Black Kings gang, that he was handed the gang's accounts. As a result, Venkatesh was able to examine their income and expenses in full, giving him a more complete picture of their activities.

Ethical issues

Official documents relating to crime that are in the public domain have few ethical problems. However, there are ethical issues when accessing some official material, such as individuals' criminal records, when there may be some dispute as to whose property such documents are.

Given the sensitive nature of crime and its effects, researchers need to be particularly aware of issues of anonymity and potential consequences attached to the use of personal documents.

Representativeness and reliability

The nature of criminal activity means that few of those involved leave personal records that may incriminate them and leave them open to prosecution. As a result, personal documents relating to crime tend to be more self-selecting than for other aspects of social life, which means that the ones that do exist may be quite unrepresentative.

By its nature, much documentary evidence on crime and deviance is created and collected in a less standardised way than statistical data and this makes it less reliable. For example, *personal documents* such as suicide notes are not written to a standard format. However, many *official documents* are created in a relatively structured way. For example, individual criminal records, company accounts and Inland Revenue data are all compiled in standardised ways.

Validity

Many historical studies of crime have relied on literary sources. Sharpe (1999) argues that material taken from such sources reflects public and government fears of crime. As such, they are not perfect guides to criminality, and they tell us more about the perspective of ruling elites controlling the criminal justice system than they do about criminals and victims.

There is a danger in relying on official documents, because they may tilt a study towards the perspective of law enforcement agencies. However, in some cases it may be possible to triangulate material to correct this bias. For example, Braithwaite (1984) investigated corporate crime using trial transcripts, reports from regulatory agencies and government investigations, but he also interviewed some of those involved in the particular criminal events to hear their views, providing a counter-balance to the official picture.

The biographies of criminals may be nostalgic and sentimental but nevertheless, they can still offer insights into for example, the role of masculinity, violence and maintaining a 'reputation' among serious criminals.

▲ *From the film,* The Godfather. *What use can we make of such sources when studying crime?*

Media documents

The prominence of crime in the mass media means that the problems of using media material in crime research are considerable. The main issue is that of validity. Media representations of crime, its nature, perpetrators and victims, are very different from the picture offered by official crime statistics. The way news values affect the representation of crime, and issues of media bias and exaggeration of crime are covered in Chapter 2, Topic 7.

The cumulative effect of these processes is that media representation of crime lacks validity and distorts reality. As a result, sociologists have become interested in how and why the media do this. Research into media coverage uses content and thematic analysis to establish the patterns and reasons for bias and selectivity in media documents.

Many sociologists also comment on the way the media cover their research. News values are applied not just to crime and deviance, but also to sociological research into crime and deviance. For example, Robert Hollands' (2000) investigation of youth leisure and cultural activity was reduced by the media to highlighting the more quirky aspects of the research, presenting images of his research subjects as deviants and law-breakers. Hollands himself did not escape. For example, the Daily Star headlined coverage of his study with 'Boozy Bob's Going on a £16,000 Pub Crawl'.

Examining documents in context

Item A **Researching corporate crime**

Crimes carried out by large corporations often have low visibility. Corporate crime, especially financial fraud, is often complex and international in scope. It is also difficult to pin the responsibility for the crime on individuals - sometimes it just seems that the corporation's own system takes a course of its own.

Similarly, it is sometimes difficult to see who has been injured through corporate crime. Sometimes corporate crime has no apparent 'victim' and where there is an identifiable victim, they may be unwilling to answer questions. Few people want to represent themselves as the gullible victims of a fraud. All these factors make the study of corporate crime more difficult.

Public documents such as parliamentary select committee reports, legislation, bankruptcy reports, court documents, company records and so on are the only substantial source of information about this form of crime. However, few corporate criminals leave incriminating personal documents, because of the likely legal repercussions.

Question

Using material from **Item A** and elsewhere, assess the strengths and weaknesses of using public and personal documents to investigate corporate crime.

(15 marks)

The examiner's advice

This question carries 6 AO1 marks (knowledge and understanding) and 9 AO2 marks (interpretation, application, analysis and evaluation). It requires you to **apply** your knowledge and understanding of public and personal documents to the study of the **particular** issue of corporate crime. It is not enough simply to discuss public and personal documents in general.

You need to attach one or more of the strengths and limitations of public and personal documents to the research characteristics of corporate crime. A good place to start is Item A. For example, it states that one research characteristic of corporate crime is that such crimes often have low visibility, leaving few traces of the crime process behind. One strength of public documents is that they can give some clues as to how a particular corporate crime was carried out.

However, Item A also points out that few corporate criminals leave incriminating personal information, so there would be few accessible personal documents relevant to researching a particular case of corporate crime.

Other research characteristics not mentioned in Item A include the diffused responsibility involved in many such crimes and that those involved in corporate crime may have a degree of political protection.

Try to keep a reasonable balance between the strengths and limitations of public and personal documents. You can also refer to studies that have used this method and to any relevant research you have been involved in.

Exam questions and student answer

Examining research methods

Item A   Researching street crime

Street crime includes acts such as demanding money or mobile phones with the threat of violence, bag snatching and damage to vehicles. Many of these criminal acts are difficult to study in the context in which they occur. For example, by their nature, violent acts are swift, often unexpected and transient.

It is possible to attempt to study groups that are involved in street crime – although there are particular problems of gaining access to such groups. Furthermore, as many offenders are fairly young, there are particular ethical and practical issues with researching such groups.

Questions

1 Using material from **Item A** and elsewhere, assess the strengths and weaknesses of using participant observation to investigate street crime.   (15 marks)

2 Assess the value of quantitative sources of data in sociological research.   (33 marks)

The examiner's advice

Q1 This carries 6 AO1 marks and 9 AO2 marks. You must apply your knowledge and understanding of participant observation to the study of the **particular** issue of street crime. It is not enough simply to discuss PO in general. Attach one or more of PO's strengths to the research characteristics of street crime. A good place to start is Item A – e.g. it states that one research characteristic of street crime is that it is swift and unexpected. You could link this to observation by pointing out the waste of the observer's time hanging around waiting. Item A also points out the problems in accessing groups involved in street crime. Being accepted into the group is difficult unless the observer has a friendly contact. Also, some crime is committed by 'loners', so there is no group to participate with. Other research characteristics of street crime include danger and the ethical dilemmas of having 'guilty knowledge' of those involved. Try to keep a reasonable balance between the strengths and limitations of PO. You can also refer to studies that have used this method and to any relevant research you have been involved in.

Q2 This essay carries 15 AO1 marks and 18 AO2 marks. First explain what quantitative data is and the reasons why positivists in particular prefer it. Then identify the wide range of quantitative sources: questionnaires, structured interviews, experiments, official statistics and content analysis. You don't have time to cover all these in detail, so organise your answer instead around practical, ethical and theoretical strengths and weaknesses of quantitative data, e.g. in terms of time, cost, numbers covered, access, confidentiality, reliability, representativeness and validity. As you deal with each of these, use examples from the different sources, making some comparisons – e.g. structured interviews are like questionnaires, but cover smaller numbers and have higher response rates. Make contrasts with qualitative methods, but don't go into lengthy descriptions of them – keep focused on quantitative sources. Use examples from studies.

Answer by Rosie

Q1 The first problem is to find examples of the target group or activity to study. With street crime, Item A suggests, most is sudden and quickly over. How can an observer predict when and where it will take place? They may spend a lot of time waiting for something that never happens. Many other social activities - religious rituals, leisure pursuits - are far more predictable.

An alternative approach is to participate with a group whose activities involve street crime. There are probably more problems gaining access to such groups than any other group except prisoners or the very powerful. Direct research opportunities may be limited by their deviant nature. The observer has to gain legitimate entry, which often depends on a lucky break. However, accessing groups involved in street crime is difficult whatever method is used.

Depending on how serious and organised it is, there is greater personal danger participating in street crime. The observer also has to make difficult ethical choices about how far to become involved. This depends on whether they are observing covertly or overtly. If they have to maintain their 'insider' identity, they have little choice but to become involved in some way in law breaking.

The young age of street criminals creates particular problems for observers. For example, they may use lots of 'street' language. It will also be hard for adult researchers to find an appropriate role for covert observation because of differences in age and appearance. The youthfulness of some offenders may win the researcher's sympathy, which may affect the direction of the study.

However, PO has many strengths. It is probably the only way to really find out what happens and why. Interpretivists are interested in exploring the meanings people attach to their actions and PO is an important way to uncover these. This is particularly true for street crime. Most sociologists have no experience of it (except perhaps as a victim), so they don't have the same mind-set as those involved. Participating in such activities enables them to access a way of thinking far from their own.

Most research into crime has to be retrospective. By being present through PO, there are no problems of relying on people's memory. PO offers the chance of direct experience with all the insights that brings.

Develops an element in the Item and also suggests why street crime is particularly difficult to study.

Explains another problem, links it to PO and compares it to other methods – good evaluation.

Several relevant points about PO and a major characteristic of those involved in street crime.

A well developed strength of PO.

A brief but sound way to round off the answer.

The examiner's comments

Q1 Rosie highlights several research characteristics of the issue by contrasting it with others we might investigate. When linked to PO, this is an effective way to gain marks. Rosie takes a good general approach. Rather than just listing strengths and weaknesses without discussing them, she identifies fewer but develops each in depth, thus accessing AO2 marks. Overall, this is a very good answer, although somewhat unbalanced, with more on the problems than the strengths.

13/15

Sociological Theory

CHAPTER 4

The AQA Specification

The specification is the syllabus produced by the exam board, telling you what you have to study. The AQA specification for Theory requires you to examine the following:

- Consensus, conflict, structural and social action theories.
- The concepts of modernity and postmodernity in relation to sociological theory.
- The nature of science and the extent to which sociology can be regarded as scientific.
- The relationship between theory and methods.
- Debates about subjectivity, objectivity and value freedom.
- The relationship between sociology and social policy.

Introduction

The simplest definition of a theory is that it is an idea – usually one that tries to *explain* something – for example, the causes of crime or divorce. And usually, sociological theories are concerned with making generalisations about social life rather than one-off statements. In other words, they try to explain the *patterns* we see in the world around us.

We can add some other important characteristics to our definition. A theory should be logically consistent and avoid contradicting itself. And, because it is trying to explain the real world, it should fit the facts that we observe. Lastly, it must be open to testing by other sociologists, as this allows others to discover its weaknesses and build on its strengths.

Sociology and the Enlightenment project

Many of the assumptions underlying modern sociological theory can be traced back to the 18th century Enlightenment, an extremely influential philosophical movement. It had two key features:

- **The power of human reason**, especially science, would enable us to understand the world by providing us with true knowledge – correct theories – about how it works.
- **Human progress** Knowledge gained through reason and science would enable us to create a better world. Technology would cure disease, while social science would solve problems such as poverty and conflict.

These two features have been described as the 'Enlightenment project' – the goal of changing the world for the better by the application of human reason.

Sociology first emerged in the 19th century in the rapidly developing modern industrial societies of Europe. In keeping with the Enlightenment project, sociologists sought to develop theories that they could use to improve society, or perhaps even to create the perfect society. These theories are often called *modernist* theories.

However, sociologists have never agreed about what kind of society is desirable, or how to create it. As a result, rather than one theory of modern society, there are a number. Topics 1 to 4, on *functionalism*, *Marxism*, *feminist theories* and *action theories*, examine what they have to say.

More recently, society has begun to undergo changes that many people see as being just as profound as the industrial revolution of the 19th century, especially in relation to the process of globalisation and the impact of new information technology and the media.

In this context, postmodernist writers rejected the Enlightenment project, arguing that it is not possible to gain true knowledge of how the world works. Topic 5 examines the changes brought by globalisation and the debates surrounding the postmodernists' claims.

If modernist theories are correct in believing that we can gain true knowledge about society, how is this to be achieved? Positivist sociologists argue sociology should model itself on the natural sciences. After all, the sciences have had spectacular success in understanding the natural world, so perhaps sociology can achieve similar success in understanding society by borrowing the logic, methods and procedures of science. Whether this is possible or desirable is the subject of Topic 6, *Sociology and science*.

Topic 7 deals with the related issue of *values and objectivity in sociology*. Given that sociologists are humans who study other humans, is it possible or desirable for them to keep their personal values out of their research? Can and should we seek to be detached and objective, as the natural sciences are said to be, or do values inevitably intrude into sociology?

Finally, Topic 8 deals with the relationships between *sociology and social policy*. This picks up the theme of the Enlightenment project, which was to provide true knowledge so that we could use it to improve society – in this case, through appropriate social policies.

However, sociology is not the only influence at work on government social policies, and sociologists of different perspectives hold different views about what relationship sociology ought to have to policy.

Are we just puppets, pulled by the strings of society?

Topic 1 Functionalism

Learning objectives

After studying this Topic, you should:

- Know the main features of the functionalist view of the social system.
- Understand Merton's contribution to the development of functionalism.
- Be able to evaluate the strengths and limitations of the functionalist perspective on society.

The first major sociological perspective we deal with in this chapter is functionalism. Many of the key ideas of functionalism can be traced back to Emile Durkheim (1858-1917) in the 19th century. However, it was the American sociologist Talcott Parsons (1902-79) who developed functionalism as a systematic theory of society in the mid 20th century. Parsons' theory became the basis of the dominant school of thought in sociology during the 1950s and 1960s, especially in the United States.

Functionalism is a macro, structural theory. It focuses on the needs of the social system as a whole and how these needs shape all the main features of society – from the form that social institutions such as the family take, right down to the behaviour patterns of individuals and the roles they perform.

Functionalism is a consensus theory. It sees society as based on a basic consensus or agreement among its members about values, goals and rules.

Functionalism is very much a modernist theory of society and shares the goals of the Enlightenment project. Functionalists believe that we can obtain true knowledge of the functioning of society and that this knowledge can be used to improve society.

Society as a system

In describing society, functionalists often use an *organic analogy* – in other words, they say that society is like a biological organism. Parsons (1970) identifies three similarities between society and a biological organism.

1 **System** Organisms, such as the human body, and societies are both self-regulating systems of inter-related, interdependent parts that fit together in fixed ways. In the body, these parts are organs, cells and so on. In society, the parts are institutions (the education system, the family), individual roles (such as teacher, mother) and so on.

2 **System needs** Organisms have needs, such as nutrition for example. If these are not met, the organism will die. Functionalists see the social system as having certain basic needs that must be met if it is to survive. For example, its members must be socialised if society is to continue.

3 **Functions** For functionalists, the function of any part of a system is the contribution it makes to meeting the system's needs and thus ensuring its survival. For example, the circulatory system of the body carries nutrients and oxygen to the tissues. Similarly, the economy helps maintain the social system by meeting the need for food and shelter.

What other features do organisms have? Do societies have these features too?

Value consensus and social order

For Parsons, the central question that sociology tries to answer is 'how is social order possible?' How are individuals able to cooperate harmoniously?

Parsons argues that social order is achieved through the existence of a shared culture or, in his words, a central value system. A culture is a set of norms, values, beliefs and goals shared by members of a society. It provides a framework that allows individuals to cooperate by laying down rules about how they should behave and what others may expect of them, defining the goals they should pursue, and so on. Social order is only possible so long as members of society agree on these norms and values. Parsons calls this agreement *value consensus*. Value consensus is the glue that holds society together.

Integration of individuals

The basic function of the value consensus is therefore to make social order possible. It does this by integrating individuals into the social system, thereby directing them towards meeting the system's needs. For example, the system has to ensure that people's material needs are met, and so the consensus may include a general value about the need for people to work. To achieve this goal, there also needs to be a set of specific rules of conduct or norms – for example about punctuality, how to obtain jobs etc.

For Parsons, the system has two mechanisms for ensuring that individuals conform to shared norms and meet the system's needs:

■ **Socialisation** The social system can ensure that its needs are met by teaching individuals to want to do what it requires them to do. Through the socialisation process, individuals internalise the system's norms and values so that society becomes part of their personality structure. Different agencies of socialisation, such as the family, education system, media and religion, all contribute to this process.

Box 4.1	Durkheim and functionalism

Emile Durkheim (1858–1917) was the most important forerunner of functionalism. He was concerned by rapid social change and the transition to modern industrial society. He saw this as a change from a simple social structure to one with a complex, specialised division of labour.

Traditional society was based on 'mechanical solidarity' with little division of labour, where all its members were fairly alike. A strong *collective conscience* bound them so tightly together that individuals in the modern sense did not really exist. However, in modern society, the division of labour promotes differences between groups and weakens social solidarity. It brings greater freedom for the individual, but this must be regulated to prevent extreme egoism destroying all social bonds. Similarly, rapid change undermines old norms without creating clear new ones, throwing people into a state of anomie or normlessness that threatens social cohesion. These ideas are echoed in the functionalists' concern with social order and value consensus.

Another contribution of Durkheim's is the idea that society exists as a separate entity over and above its members – a system of external 'social facts' shaping their behaviour to serve society's needs. This is similar to Parsons' idea of a social system with its own needs. Similarly, Durkheim's belief that social facts can be explained in terms of their function is the basic principle of functionalist analysis.

- **Social control** Positive sanctions reward conformity, while negative ones punish deviance. For example, if the value system stresses individual achievement through educational success, those who conform may be rewarded with college diplomas, while those who deviate by dropping out may be stigmatised as layabouts.

Because individuals are integrated, through socialisation and social control, into a shared value system, their behaviour is oriented towards pursuing society's shared goals and meeting its needs. The behaviour of each individual will be relatively predictable and stable, allowing cooperation between them. This integration into the shared normative order makes orderly social life possible. From these basic ideas, Parsons builds up a more detailed model of the social system.

The parts of the social system

We can take a 'building block' approach to describing Parsons' model of the social system. At the bottom, so to speak, we have individual *actions*. Each action we perform is governed by specific *norms* or rules. These norms come in 'clusters' called *status-roles*. Statuses are the positions that exist in a given social system; for example, 'teacher'. Roles are sets of norms that tell us how the occupant of a status must carry out their duties – for example, teachers must not show favouritism, must be knowledgeable and so on.

Status-roles also come in clusters, known as institutions. For example, the family is an institution made up of the related roles of father, mother, child, etc. In turn, related institutions are grouped together into *sub-systems*. For example, shops, farms, factories, banks and so on all form part of the economic sub-system, whose function is to meet society's material needs. Finally, these sub-systems together make up the *social system* as a whole.

The system's needs

As we have seen, for Parsons society is a system with its own needs. The shared value system coordinates the different parts of society to ensure that the system's needs are met. But what exactly are the system's needs?

Parsons identifies four basic needs, sometimes known as the 'AGIL schema' (from their initial letters). Each need is met by a separate sub-system of institutions:

1 **Adaptation** The social system meets its members' material needs. These needs are met by the economic sub-system.
2 **Goal attainment** Society needs to set goals and allocate resources to achieve them. This is the function of the political sub-system, through institutions such as parliament.
3 **Integration** The different parts of the system must be integrated together in order to pursue shared goals. This

is performed by the sub-system of religion, education and the media.
4 **Latency** refers to processes that maintain society over time. The kinship sub-system provides *pattern maintenance* (socialising individuals to go on performing the roles society requires) and *tension management* (a place to 'let off steam' after the stresses of work).

Parsons describes adaptation and goal attainment as *instrumental* needs – instrumental refers to the means to an end, such as producing food to sustain the population. He describes integration and latency as *expressive* needs, since they involve the expression or channelling of emotions. By carrying out their respective functions, the four sub-systems ensure that society's needs are met and social stability is maintained.

Types of society

Parsons identifies two types of society – traditional and modern. Each type has its own typical pattern of norms (which he calls pattern variables A and B). As Table 4A shows, Parsons identifies five basic sets of norms for each type of society.

Within each type, the variables 'fit' together. For example, in modern society (pattern variables B), students are expected to pursue their own *individual* self-interest, *achieving* their status through their efforts in education, attained through *deferred gratification*. They are all judged by the same *universal* standards of the exams. By contrast, in traditional society (pattern variables A), an individual's status is *ascribed*

Table 4A	Differences between the norms of traditional and modern societies	

Traditional societies (Pattern variables A)	Modern societies (Pattern variables B)
Ascription Status is based on fixed characteristics such as gender – i.e. who you are, not what you have achieved.	**Achievement** Status is based on performance such as effort in education – i.e. what you do, not who you are or who you know.
Diffuseness Relationships are broad with a range of purposes (e.g. on the family farm, relatives are also workmates).	**Specificity** Relationships are narrow and limited to specific purposes (e.g. lawyer and client).
Particularism Norms emphasise treating different people differently (e.g. employing someone just because they are a relative).	**Universalism** Norms emphasise everyone being treated the same (e.g. giving the job to the best qualified person).
Affectivity Immediate gratification of desires (e.g. leaving school early to start earning).	**Affective neutrality** Deferred gratification (e.g. staying on at school).
Collective orientation Putting the group's interests first.	**Self orientation** Individualism, pursuing one's own self-interest.

at birth and they are expected to put the kinship group's interests before their own (*collective orientation*).

Social change

If there are two types of society, how do societies change from one to the other? For Parsons, change is a gradual, evolutionary process of increasing complexity and structural differentiation. The organic analogy is relevant here. Organisms have evolved from simple structures such as the amoeba, where a single cell performs all the essential functions, to highly complex organisms like humans with many different cells and organs, each performing its own specialised function.

Similarly, societies move from simple to complex structures. For example, in traditional society, a single institution – the kinship system – performs many functions. It organises

production and consumption (adaptation), often provides political leadership (goal attainment), socialises its members (latency) and performs religious functions, for example in ancestor-worship (integration).

However, as societies develop, the kinship system loses these functions – to factories, political parties, schools, churches and so on. Parsons calls this *structural differentiation* – a gradual process in which separate, functionally specialised institutions develop, each meeting a different need.

In addition to the process of structural differentiation, Parsons also sees gradual change occurring through what he calls *moving (or dynamic) equilibrium*. As a change occurs in one part of the system, it produces compensatory changes in other parts. For example, the rise of industry brings about a change in the family from extended to nuclear. In this way society gradually changes from one type to another.

Merton's internal critique of functionalism

Criticisms of Parsons' systems theory have come from both outside and inside functionalism. Within functionalism, the most significant criticisms come from Robert K. Merton (1968). Merton criticises three key assumptions of Parsons.

1 **Indispensability** Parsons assumes that everything in society – the family, religion and so on – is functionally indispensable *in its existing form*. Merton argues that this is just an untested assumption and he points to the possibility of 'functional alternatives'. For example, Parsons assumes that primary socialisation is best performed by the nuclear family, but it may be that one-parent families or communes do it just as well or better.

2 **Functional unity** Parsons assumes that all parts of society are tightly integrated into a single whole or 'unity' and that each part is functional for all the rest. Similarly, he assumes that change in one part will have a 'knock-on' effect on all other parts. However, neither of these assumptions is necessarily true. Complex modern societies have many parts, some of which may be only distantly 'related' to one another. Instead of functional unity, some parts may have 'functional autonomy' (independence) from others. It is hard to see the connections between, say, the structure of banking and the rules of netball.

3 **Universal functionalism** Parsons assumes that everything in society performs a positive function for society as a whole. Yet some things may be functional for some groups and dysfunctional for others. The idea of dysfunction (negative function) introduces a neglected note into functionalism, by suggesting that there may be conflicts of interest and that some groups may have the power to keep arrangements in place that benefit them

at the expense of others. Critics writing from a conflict perspective have developed this idea further.

The central point behind Merton's criticisms is that we cannot simply assume, as Parsons does, that society is always and necessarily a smooth-running, well-integrated system.

Does unemployment have a positive function for (a) society as a whole; (b) the unemployed; (c) other groups? If so, what is it?

Manifest and latent functions

In addition to his criticisms of Parsons, Merton also contributes a useful distinction between 'manifest' and 'latent' functions. He cites the example of the Hopi Indians who, in times of drought, perform a rain-dance with the deliberate aim of magically producing rain. This is its *manifest* or intended function. From a scientific viewpoint, of course, this is unlikely to achieve its intended goal.

However, the ritual may also have an unintended or *latent* function – such as promoting a sense of solidarity in times of hardship, when individuals might be tempted to look after themselves at the expense of others. Merton's distinction is therefore useful in helping to reveal the hidden connections between social phenomena, which the actors themselves may not be aware of.

Activity

Working in pairs, suggest at least one latent function for each of the following: homework; holidays; criminal trials; saying your prayers; playing in an amateur football team.

External critiques of functionalism

While Merton's criticisms came from within functionalism, many far less sympathetic writers have attacked it from the outside. We can divide these criticisms into four kinds.

1 Logical criticisms

Teleology is the idea that things exist because of their effect or function. For example, the functionalist claim that the family exists because children need to be socialised is teleological – it explains the existence of the family in terms of its effect.

However, critics argue that a real explanation of something is one that identifies its cause – and logically, a cause must come *before* its effect. By contrast, functionalism explains the existence of one thing (the family) in terms of something else that can only be its *effect* (socialisation), since socialisation can only come *after* we have families.

Functionalism is also criticised for being unscientific. For many, a theory is only scientific if in principle it is falsifiable by testing. Yet this is not true of functionalism. For example, functionalists see deviance as both dysfunctional (since society's needs can only be met if individuals conform) *and* functional (for example by reinforcing social solidarity). If deviance is both functional and dysfunctional, then the theory cannot be disproved and is unscientific.

2 Conflict perspective criticisms

Conflict theorists such as Marxists criticise functionalism for its inability to explain conflict and change. This inability arises partly out of the organic analogy: organisms are relatively stable and harmonious systems in which all the parts work together for the common good.

Marxists argue that society is not a harmonious whole. Rather, it is based on exploitation and divided into classes with conflicting interests and unequal power. Stability is simply the result of the dominant class being able to prevent change by using coercion (force) or ideological manipulation. In this view, 'shared' values are merely a cloak concealing the interests of the dominant class.

Conflict theorists see functionalism as a *conservative ideology* legitimating the status quo. Its focus on harmony and stability rather than conflict and change, along with its assumptions of 'universal functionalism' and 'indispensability', all help to justify the existing social order as inevitable and desirable. Critics argue that this approach legitimates the privileged position of powerful groups who would have most to lose from any fundamental changes in society. (See Topic 2 on Marxist approaches.)

3 Action perspective criticisms

From an action perspective, Dennis Wrong (1961) criticises functionalism's 'over-socialised' or *deterministic* view of the individual. He describes the functionalist view as follows: the social system uses socialisation to shape people's behaviour so that they will meet the system's needs by performing their prescribed roles. Individuals have no free will or choice – they are mere puppets whose strings are pulled by the social system. From an action perspective, this is fundamentally mistaken. While functionalism sees human beings as shaped by society, the action approach takes the opposite view – that individuals create society by their interactions.

A related criticism is that functionalism *reifies* society – that is, treats it as a distinct 'thing' over and above individuals, with its own needs. By contrast, action approaches argue that society is not a thing 'out there' with its own independent existence. For them, the only social reality is the one that individuals construct by giving meaning to their worlds. (See Topic 4 on action approaches.)

4 Postmodernist criticisms

Postmodernists argue that functionalism assumes that society is stable and orderly. As such, it cannot account for the diversity and instability that exist in today's postmodern society.

In the postmodernist view, functionalism is an example of a meta-narrative or 'big story' that attempts to create a model of the workings of society as a whole. However, according to postmodernists, such an overall theory is no longer possible because today's society is increasingly fragmented. (See Topic 5 on postmodernism.)

Conclusion

Functionalism seeks to answer the fundamental question of how social order is possible – even if its answer neglects conflict and is too deterministic. It can also be said that Merton's move away from Parsons' 'grand theory', his notion of dysfunctions, and his distinction between manifest and latent functions, all provide useful starting points for research. It is also true that many of functionalism's critics – especially conflict theorists – end up 'borrowing' its basic notion that society is a system of interdependent parts.

Finally as Ian Craib (1992) notes, Parsons' theory 'has its faults, but at least it is a theory of society as a whole'.

For more activities on Functionalism…

Go to www.sociology.uk.net

Summary

Functionalism is a structural perspective that sees social order as based on value consensus. Parsons sees society as a system of interdependent parts (the organic analogy), such as sub-systems, institutions and status-roles. The function of each part is to help meet the needs of the system. Individuals are integrated into the system through socialisation into the shared culture and social control, ensuring that they perform the roles expected of them. Merton introduces ideas of dysfunction, and manifest and latent functions. Critics argue that functionalism is a conservative ideology that neglects conflict, exploitation and change, and has an over-socialised view of individuals as puppets of the social system.

QuickCheck Questions

1 What is the difference between a manifest and a latent function?

2 What does Wrong mean by 'over-socialised'?

3 Is functionalism a conservative or a radical ideology?

4 According to Parsons, how do societies change?

5 What is the organic analogy?

6 Identify Parsons' four system needs.

7 Identify two agencies of a) socialisation and b) social control.

Check your answers at www.sociology.uk.net

Examining functionalism

Assess the strengths and weaknesses of the functionalist approach to society.   (33 marks)

The examiner's advice

This question carries 15 AO1 marks (knowledge and understanding) and 18 AO2 marks (interpretation, application, analysis and evaluation). Start with Parsons' ideas, analysing functionalism's key concepts and showing how they fit together. Focus on the organic analogy, concepts of function and system needs, value consensus, social integration, socialisation and social control. Outline the different parts of the social system (roles, institutions etc) and the 'AGIL' schema.

You should evaluate Parsons' model from a variety of perspectives. Begin with Merton's internal criticisms (indispensability, functional unity and universal functionalism) and his ideas of functional autonomy, dysfunction and manifest and latent functions. You should also evaluate functionalism from other perspectives, e.g. Marxist views that it is a conservative ideology ignoring conflict and change, 'action' criticisms that it sees individuals as 'puppets', and the postmodernist view that it cannot account for diversity. On the other hand, it does attempt to understand society as a whole and the idea that the different parts of society are interlinked is useful.

Russia 1917: crowds run for cover during the revolution.

Topic 2 Marxism

Marxism has at least one thing in common with functionalism. It tends to share the view that society is a structure or system that shapes individuals' behaviour and ideas.

However, Marxism differs sharply from functionalism in two ways:

- **Conflict of interests** Marxists reject the functionalist view that the social structure is a harmonious one based on value consensus. Instead, they see it as based on a conflict of interests – especially economic interests – between social classes of unequal power and wealth.
- **Instability and change** Marxists also reject functionalism's view of society as stable, and stress the possibility of sudden, profound and revolutionary change. Stability is merely the result of the dominant class being able to impose their will on society.

However, there are differences among Marxists, especially over the way in which social change comes about. For example, humanistic Marxists give a greater role to the conscious decisions and actions of human beings than do structural Marxists, for whom social change comes as the product of changes within the structures of society.

Learning objectives

After studying this Topic, you should:

- Know and understand Marx's main ideas and concepts.
- Understand the differences between humanistic and structural Marxism.
- Be able to evaluate the strengths and limitations of Marxist approaches to the study of society.

Marx's ideas

Marxism is a perspective based on the ideas of Karl Marx (1818–83). Like Durkheim, Marx saw both the harm caused by the modern industrial society that was taking shape in 19th century Europe, and the promise of progress to a better world that it held. Also like Durkheim, Marx believed that it was possible to understand society scientifically and that this knowledge would point the way to a better society – indeed, he described his theory as 'scientific socialism'. In these ways, Marxism is a continuation of the Enlightenment project described earlier.

Unlike functionalists, however, Marx did not see progress as a smooth and gradual evolution. Instead, he saw historical change as a contradictory process in which capitalism would increase human misery before giving way to a classless communist society in which human beings would be free to fulfil their potential.

Marx was not just a theorist; he was also a revolutionary socialist. As he himself wrote, 'Philosophers have merely interpreted the world; the point, however, is to change it'. In other words, the classless society would need to be brought into being by the conscious actions of human beings.

After his death, Marx's ideas came to form the basis of communism, a political movement that was enormously influential in shaping the modern world, and Marxism became the official doctrine of the former Soviet Union and other communist states. Here we shall examine his key ideas about human history, and about capitalism and its replacement by a future communist society.

1 Historical materialism

Materialism is the view that humans are beings with material needs, such as food, clothing and shelter, and must therefore work to meet them. In doing so, they use the *forces of production* (sometimes called means of production).

In the earliest stage of human history, these forces are just unaided human labour, but over time people develop tools, machines and so on to assist in production. In working to meet their needs, humans also cooperate with one another: they enter into *social relations of production* – ways of organising production.

Over time, as the forces of production grow and develop, so too the social relations of production also change. In particular, a division of labour develops, and this eventually gives rise to a division between *two classes*:

- A class that owns the means of production
- A class of labourers.

From then on, production is directed by the class of owners to meet their own needs.

Marx refers to the forces and relations of production together as the *mode of production*. For example, currently we live in a society with a capitalist mode of production. The mode of production forms the *economic base* of society. This economic base shapes or determines all other features of society – the *superstructure* of institutions, ideas, beliefs and behaviour that arise from this base. For example, it shapes the nature of religion, law, education, the state and so on.

2 Class society and exploitation

In the earliest stage of human history, there are no classes, no private ownership and no exploitation – everyone works, and everything is shared. Marx describes this early classless society as 'primitive communism'. But as the forces of production grow, different types of class society come and go.

In class societies, one class owns the means of production. This enables them to exploit the labour of others for their own benefit. In particular, they can control society's *surplus product*. This is the difference between what the labourers actually produce and what is needed simply to keep them alive and working.

Marx identifies three successive class societies, each with its own form of exploitation:

- **Ancient society**, based on the exploitation of slaves legally tied to their owners
- **Feudal society**, based on the exploitation of serfs legally tied to the land
- **Capitalist society**, based on the exploitation of free wage labourers.

3 Capitalism

Like previous class societies, capitalism is based on a division between a class of owners, the *bourgeoisie* or capitalist class, and a class of labourers, the *proletariat* or working class. However, capitalism has three distinctive features.

Firstly, unlike slaves or serfs, the proletariat are legally free and separated from the means of production. Because they do not own any means of production, they have to sell their labour power to the bourgeoisie in return for wages in order to survive.

However, this is not an equal exchange. The proletariat do not receive the value of the goods that their labour produces, but only the cost of subsistence – of keeping them alive. The difference between the two is the *surplus value* – the profit that the capitalist makes by selling the commodities that the proletariat have produced.

Secondly, through competition between capitalists, ownership of the means of production becomes *concentrated* in fewer and fewer hands (culminating in today's giant transnational corporations). This competition drives small independent producers into the ranks of the proletariat, until ultimately the vast majority are proletarianised. Competition also forces capitalists to pay the lowest wages possible, causing the *immiseration* (impoverishment) of the proletariat.

Thirdly, capitalism continually expands the forces of production in its pursuit of profit. Production becomes concentrated in ever-larger units. Meanwhile, technological advances de-skill the workforce.

Concentration of ownership and the deskilling of the proletariat together produce class *polarisation*. That is, society divides into a minority capitalist class and a majority working class that in Marx's words, 'face each other as two warring camps'.

4 Class consciousness

According to Marx, capitalism sows the seeds of its own destruction. For example, by polarising the classes, bringing the proletariat together in ever-larger numbers, and driving down their wages, capitalism creates the conditions under which the working class can develop a consciousness of its own economic and political interests in opposition to those of its exploiters.

As a result, the proletariat moves from being merely a *class in itself* (one whose members occupy the same economic position), to becoming a *class for itself*, whose members are class conscious – aware of the need to overthrow capitalism.

5 Ideology

For Marx, the class that owns the means of production also owns and controls the means of *mental* production – the production of ideas. The dominant ideas in society are therefore the ideas of the economically dominant class. The institutions that produce and spread ideas, such as religion, education and the media, all serve the dominant class by producing ideologies – sets of ideas and beliefs that legitimise (justify) the existing social order as desirable or inevitable.

Ideology fosters a *false consciousness* in the subordinate classes and helps to sustain class inequality. However, as capitalism impoverishes the workers, so they develop class consciousness. They see through capitalist ideology and become conscious of their true position as 'wage slaves'.

6 Alienation

Marx believes that our true nature is based on our capacity to create things to meet our needs. Alienation is the result of our loss of control over our labour and its products and therefore our separation from our true nature.

Alienation exists in all class societies, because the owners control the production process for their own needs. However, under capitalism alienation reaches its peak, for two reasons:

- Workers are completely separated from and have no control over the forces of production.
- The division of labour is at its most intense and detailed: the worker is reduced to an unskilled labourer mindlessly repeating a meaningless task.

Marx also sees religion as originating in the alienation of human labour (see Chapter 1, Topic 1).

7 The state, revolution and communism

Marx defines the state as 'armed bodies of men' – the army, police, prisons, courts and so on. The state exists to protect the interests of the class of owners who control it. As such, they form the *ruling class*. They use the state as a weapon in the class struggle, to protect their property, suppress opposition and prevent revolution. Any class that wishes to lead a revolution and become the economically dominant class must overthrow the existing ruling class.

Previous revolutions had always been one minority class overthrowing another, but in Marx's view, the proletarian revolution that overthrows capitalism will be the first revolution by the majority against the minority. It will:

- Abolish the state and create a classless communist society.
- Abolish exploitation, replace private ownership with social ownership, and replace production for profit with production to satisfy human needs.
- End alienation as humans regain control of their labour and its products.

▼ *Armed bodies of men*

Marx predicted the ultimate victory of the proletarian revolution and the establishment of communist society on a world scale. He expected the revolution to occur first of all in the most advanced capitalist societies. However, he wrote relatively little about exactly how the revolution would come about. This has led to debate among Marxists ever since.

Criticisms of Marx

Several criticisms have been made of Marx's theory of society.

1 Class

- Marx has a simplistic, one-dimensional view of inequality – he sees class as the only important division. Weber argues that status and power differences can also be important sources of inequality, independently of class. For example, a 'power elite' can rule without actually owning the means of production, as it did in the former Soviet Union. Similarly, feminists argue that gender is a more fundamental source of inequality than class.
- Marx's two-class model is also simplistic. For example, Weber sub-divides the proletariat into skilled and unskilled classes, and includes a white-collar middle class of office workers and a petty bourgeoisie (small capitalists).
- Class polarisation has not occurred. Instead of the middle class being swallowed up by an expanding proletariat, it has grown, while the industrial working class has shrunk, at least in Western societies. On the other hand, the proletariat in countries such as China and India is growing as a result of globalisation.

2 Economic determinism

Marx's base-superstructure model is criticised for economic determinism – the view that economic factors are the sole cause of everything in society, including social change. Critics argue that this fails to recognise that humans have free will and can bring about change through their conscious actions.

Similarly, the base-superstructure model neglects the role of *ideas*. For example, Weber argues that it was the emergence of a new set of ideas, those of Calvinistic Protestantism, which helped to bring modern capitalism into being.

A related criticism is that Marx's predictions of revolution have not come true. Marx predicted that revolution would occur in the most advanced capitalist countries, such as Western Europe and North America. However, it is only economically backward countries such as Russia in 1917 that have seen Marxist-led revolutions.

However, in defence of Marx, while there are examples of economic determinism in his work, there are also instances where he argues that 'men make their own history' and that the working class would free themselves by their own conscious efforts – indicating that he gave a role to human action as well as economic forces.

Activity

In pairs, consider the examples below of conflict in modern society and discuss how critics of Marxism might use them as evidence that conflict is not always caused by economic factors. How might Marxists answer such criticisms?

1 Anti-war demonstrations
2 Violent crime

The 'two Marxisms'

Since Marx's death in 1883, the absence of revolutions in the West has led many Marxists to reject the economic determinism of the base-superstructure model. Instead, they have tried to explain why capitalism has persisted and how it might be overthrown. We can identify two broad approaches to these questions, which Alvin Gouldner (1973) describes as:

- **Humanistic or critical Marxism** This has some similarities with action theories and interpretive sociology.
- **Scientific or structuralist Marxism** As its name indicates, this is a structural approach and has similarities with positivist sociology.

Table 4B outlines the key differences between the two approaches.

Table 4B	The two Marxisms	

Humanistic or critical Marxism	Scientific or structuralist Marxism
Example: Antonio Gramsci	Example: Louis Althusser
Draws on Marx's early writings, where he focuses on *alienation* and people's subjective experience of the world.	Draws on Marx's later work, where he writes about the *laws* of capitalist development working with 'iron necessity' towards inevitable results.
Marxism is a *political critique* of capitalism as alienating and inhuman, and a call to overthrow it.	Marxism is a *science*. It discovers the laws that govern the workings of capitalism.
Voluntarism: humans have free will. They are active agents who make their own history. Their consciousness and ideas are central in changing the world.	*Determinism*: structural factors determine the course of history. Individuals are passive puppets – victims of ideology manipulated by forces beyond their control.
Socialism will come about when people become *conscious* of the need to overthrow capitalism. *Encourages* political action, believing the time is always ripe for revolution.	Socialism will come about only when the *contradictions* of capitalism ultimately bring about the system's inevitable collapse. Tends to *discourage* political action.

Gramsci and hegemony

The most important example of humanistic Marxism is Antonio Gramsci (1891-1937). Gramsci introduces the concept of *hegemony*, or ideological and moral leadership of society, to explain how the ruling class maintains its position. He argues that the proletariat must develop its own 'counter-hegemony' to win the leadership of society from the bourgeoisie.

Gramsci was the first leader of the Italian Communist Party during the 1920s. He rejects economic determinism as an explanation of change: the transition from capitalism to communism will never come about simply as a result of economic forces. Even though factors such as mass unemployment and falling wages may create the preconditions for revolution, ideas play a central role in determining whether or not change will actually occur.

This can be seen in Gramsci's concept of hegemony. Gramsci sees the ruling class maintaining its dominance over society in two ways:

- **Coercion**: it uses the army, police, prisons and courts of the capitalist state to force other classes to accept its rule.
- **Consent (hegemony)**: it uses ideas and values to persuade the subordinate classes that its rule is legitimate.

Hegemony and revolution

In advanced capitalist societies, the ruling class rely heavily on consent to maintain their rule. Gramsci agrees with Marx that they are able to do so because they control the institutions that produce and spread ideas, such as the media, the education system and religion. So long as the rest of society accepts ruling-class hegemony, there will not be a revolution, even when the economic conditions might seem favourable.

However, the hegemony of the ruling class is never complete, for two reasons:

- **The ruling class are a minority**. To rule, they need to create a *power bloc* by making alliances with other groups, such as the middle classes. They must therefore make ideological compromises to take account of the interests of their allies.
- **The proletariat have a *dual consciousness***. Their ideas are influenced not only by bourgeois ideology, but also by their material conditions of life – the poverty and exploitation they experience. This means they can 'see through' the dominant ideology to some degree.

Therefore there is always the possibility of ruling-class hegemony being undermined, particularly at times of economic crisis, when the worsening material conditions of the proletariat cause them to question the status quo.

However, this will only lead to revolution if the proletariat are able to construct a *counter-hegemonic bloc*. In other words, they must be able to offer moral and ideological leadership to society.

In Gramsci's view, the working class can only win this battle for ideas by producing their own 'organic intellectuals'. By this he means a body of workers, organised into a revolutionary political party, who are able to formulate an alternative vision of how society could be run.

This counter-hegemony would win ideological leadership from the ruling class by offering a new vision of how society should be organised, based on socialist rather than capitalist values.

Evaluation of Gramsci

Gramsci is accused of over-emphasising the role of ideas and under-emphasising the role of both state coercion and economic factors.

For example, workers may wish to overthrow capitalism, but be reluctant to try because they fear state repression or unemployment. They may tolerate capitalism simply because they feel they have no choice, not because they accept the moral leadership of the ruling class.

Sociologists working within a Marxist framework have adopted a similar approach to Gramsci. They stress the role of ideas and consciousness as the basis for resisting domination and changing society.

For example, Paul Willis (1977) describes the working-class lads he studied as 'partially penetrating' bourgeois ideology – seeing through the school's ideology to recognise that meritocracy is a myth.

These writers often draw on perspectives such as interactionism (Topic 4) that emphasise the role of ideas and meanings as the basis for action. Because they combine Marxism with other approaches, they are sometimes called neo-Marxists – 'new Marxists'.

Althusser's structuralist Marxism

While humanistic Marxists see humans as creative beings, able to make history through their conscious actions, for structuralist Marxists, it is not people's actions but social structures that really shape history and these are the proper subject of scientific enquiry. The task of the sociologist is to reveal how these structures work.

The most important structuralist Marxist thinker is Louis Althusser (1918-90), a leading intellectual of the French Communist Party. Althusser's version of Marxism rejects both economic determinism and humanism.

Criticisms of the base-superstructure model

In Marx's original base-superstructure model, society's economic base determines its superstructure of institutions, ideologies and actions. Contradictions in the base cause changes in the superstructure and ultimately bring about the downfall of capitalism.

Althusser rejects this model in favour of a more complex one, which Craib calls 'structural determinism'. In this model, capitalist society has three structures or levels:

- **The economic level**, comprising all those activities that involve producing something in order to satisfy a need.
- **The political level**, comprising all forms of organisation.
- **The ideological level**, involving the ways that people see themselves and their world.

In the base-superstructure model, there is a one-way causality: the economic level determines everything about the other two levels. By contrast, in Althusser's model, the political and ideological levels have *relative autonomy* or partial independence from the economic level. The political and ideological levels are not a mere reflection of the economic level, and they can even affect what happens to the economy. Instead of a one-way causality, we have *two-way causality* (see Box 4.2).

Ideological and repressive state apparatuses

Although the economic level dominates in capitalism, the political and ideological levels perform indispensable functions. For example, if capitalism is to continue, future workers must be socialised, workers who rebel must be punished, and so on.

In Althusser's model, the *state* performs political and ideological functions that ensure the reproduction of capitalism. He divides the state into two 'apparatuses':

- **The repressive state apparatuses (RSAs)** These are the 'armed bodies of men' – the army, police, prisons and so on – that coerce the working class into complying with the will of the bourgeoisie. This is how Marxists have traditionally seen the state.
- **The ideological state apparatuses (ISAs)** These include the media, the education system, the family, reformist political parties, trade unions and other institutions. ISAs ideologically manipulate the working class into accepting capitalism as legitimate. This is a much wider definition of the state than the traditional Marxist view.

This is similar to Gramsci's distinction between coercion (the RSAs) and consent (the ISAs) as different ways of securing the dominance of the bourgeoisie.

Box 4.2	Althusser's structures: an analogy

Ian Craib (1992) uses an analogy to picture the ideas of relative autonomy and two-way causality. He compares the three levels in Althusser's model of society to a three-storey building housing a family business.

On the ground floor is a shop, while the first floor houses the office and the top floor is the family's living quarters. What goes on in the office is obviously partly affected by the nature of the activity in the shop, but there are different ways the office work might be organised, and some features of it might be the same whatever the kind of business. Similarly, the standard of living and lifestyle enjoyed by the owners on the top floor is affected by the business they run (for example, they may be well off but cannot take long holidays away from it), but family life has its own dynamics and may be shaped by quite separate factors. And not only are the goings-on upstairs at least partly independent of what happens down below, they may also have an effect on it. For example, a divorce settlement may lead to the business being split up or sold off.

Which parts of the analogy illustrate (a) relative autonomy; (b) two-way causality between structures?

▲ *The capitalist news machine: does it report events from a ruling-class viewpoint?*

Althusser's criticisms of humanism

For structuralist Marxists, our sense of free will, choice and creativity is an illusion. The truth is that everything about us is the product of underlying social structures. As Ian Craib (1992) puts it, society is a puppet theatre, we are merely puppets, and these unseen structures are the hidden puppet master, determining all our thoughts and actions.

Althusser is therefore dismissive of humanism, including humanistic Marxists such as Gramsci. Humanists believe that people can use their creativity, reason and free will to change society. For example, humanistic Marxists believe that a socialist revolution will come about as a result of the working class actively developing class consciousness and consciously choosing to overthrow capitalism.

Althusser argues that we are not the free agents that humanists think we are – our belief that we possess free will and choice is simply false consciousness produced by the ideological state apparatuses. For example, we may believe that education gives us the chance to achieve what we are capable of, but this is an illusion – the 'myth of meritocracy'.

In reality, we are merely products of social structures that determine everything about us, preparing us to fit into pre-existing positions in the structure of capitalism. This is similar to Parsons' idea of status-roles, where society socialises individuals to slot into pre-existing roles that will meet society's needs.

Therefore, in Althusser's view, socialism will not come about because of a change in consciousness – as humanistic Marxists argue – but will come about because of a crisis of capitalism resulting from what Althusser calls *over-determination*: the contradictions in the three structures that occur relatively independently of each other, resulting in the collapse of the system as a whole.

Evaluation of Althusser

Althusser claims to oppose both humanism and determinism, but he is harsher on humanism. Although he rejects *economic* determinism, he simply replaces it with a more complex 'structural determinism' in which everything is determined by the three structures and their interrelationships.

For humanistic Marxists such as Gouldner, this 'scientific' approach discourages political activism because it stresses the role of structural factors that individuals can do little to affect. Similarly, the Marxist historian, E.P. Thompson (1978), criticises Althusser for ignoring the fact that it is the active struggles of the working class that can change society. He accuses Althusser of elitism – the belief that the Communist Party knows what is best for the workers, who should therefore blindly follow the Party's lead.

In Craib's view, Althusser 'offers the most sophisticated conception of social structure available in the social sciences'. Ironically, however, while Althusser believed he was developing a scientific analysis of society to help bring about progress to a better society, his structuralist Marxism has been a major influence on theories such as postmodernism that reject the very idea that scientific knowledge can be used to improve society.

For more activities on Marxism…

Go to www.sociology.uk.net

Summary

Marxism is a structural perspective that sees society as based on class conflict. In capitalism, the bourgeoisie exploit the labour of the proletariat. They maintain their position through control of the repressive state apparatus and through ideology or hegemony. However, Marx believed that ultimately, revolution leading to a classless, communist society was inevitable.

Critics argue that Marxism is too deterministic. However, there are differences between Marxists. For example, Gramsci takes a more voluntaristic view that sees a greater role for human consciousness and action in bringing about change, whereas Althusser sees change as the outcome of 'structural determinism'. Other critics argue that Marx's two-class model is simplistic, and that Marxism neglects non-class forms of inequality such as gender and ethnicity.

QuickCheck Questions

1 What is the difference between a 'class in itself' and a 'class for itself'?

2 Suggest two similarities between Marxism and functionalism.

3 Which part of society did Marx see as dominating all other parts?

4 What is meant by 'alienation'?

5 Identify two aspects of Marxist theory that may no longer apply to modern society.

6 What is the difference between 'determinism' and 'voluntarism'?

7 According to Marxists, how may ruling-class hegemony be maintained?

8 What is meant by the term 'repressive state apparatus'?

9 Identify three classes of labourers from different historical periods.

10 According to Marx, what are the features of communist society?

Check your answers at www.sociology.uk.net

Examining Marxism

Critically examine Marxist perspectives on today's society.

(33 marks)

The examiner's advice

This question carries 15 AO1 marks (knowledge and understanding) and 18 AO2 marks (interpretation, application, analysis and evaluation). Begin your answer with an account of Marx's key ideas. Make sure you include materialism, class conflict, alienation, exploitation, false consciousness, ideology, the state and revolution. A good focus would be Marx's theory of change, so explain how Marx sees capitalism being replaced by communism.

The question asks about Marxist perspectives *plural*, so look at developments since Marx. A good approach is to examine the 'two Marxisms' – humanistic and structuralist – using Gramsci and Althusser. Outline their key concepts, such as hegemony, RSAs and ISAs. You can contrast them in terms of their view of how change occurs. You should also evaluate by assessing the strength of some of the criticisms of Marxism such as economic determinism, neglect of non-class inequality and of the middle classes, and that Marx's predictions of revolution have not come true.

Kurdish women celebrating International Women's Day, Istanbul, Turkey.

Topic 3 Feminist theories

Feminism sees society as male dominated and it seeks to describe, explain and change the position of women in society. It is therefore both a theory of women's subordination and a political movement.

The roots of feminism, like those of other modernist theories, can be traced back to the late 18th century Enlightenment. This proclaimed universal principles of liberty and equality, along with the idea that human reason can liberate us from ignorance and create a better society.

Feminists argued that, since both sexes had the same power of reason, these principles should apply to women as much as to men and that women's emancipation must be included as part of the Enlightenment project.

A 'first wave' of feminism appeared in the late 19th century, with the suffragettes' campaign for the right to vote. The 1960s saw a 'second wave' emerge on a global scale.

Since then, feminism has had a major influence on sociology. Feminists criticise mainstream sociology for being 'malestream' – seeing society only from a male perspective. By contrast, feminists examine society from the viewpoint of women. Feminist sociologists see their work as part of the struggle against women's subordination.

However, although all feminists oppose women's subordination, there are disagreements among feminists about its causes and how to overcome it. In this Topic, we concentrate on those feminist theories that have had most impact on sociology:

- Liberal or reformist feminism
- Radical feminism
- Marxist feminism
- Dual systems feminism
- Difference feminism and poststructuralism

Learning objectives

After studying this Topic, you should:

- Know the main types of feminist theories.
- Understand the similarities and differences between feminist theories.
- Be able to evaluate the strengths and limitations of feminist theories.

Liberal or reformist feminism

Liberals are concerned with the human and civil rights and freedoms of the individual. In keeping with the Enlightenment tradition, they believe that all human beings should have equal rights. Since both men and women are human beings, so both should have the same inalienable rights and freedoms. Reformism is the idea that progress towards equal rights can be achieved by gradual reforms or piecemeal changes in society, without the need for revolution.

Liberal feminists (sometimes called reformist or 'equal rights' feminists) believe women can achieve gender equality in this way. For example, they argue that laws and policies against sex discrimination in employment and education can secure equal opportunities for women.

As well as campaigning for changes in the law, liberal feminists call for cultural change. In their view, traditional prejudices and stereotypes about gender differences are a barrier to equality. For example, beliefs that women are less rational and more dominated by emotion and instinct are used to legitimate their exclusion from decision-making roles and their confinement to childrearing and housework. Liberal feminists reject the idea that biological differences make women less competent or rational than men, or that men are biologically less emotional or nurturing than women.

Sex and gender

Like Ann Oakley (1972), liberal feminists distinguish between sex and gender:

- **Sex** refers to biological differences between males and females, such as their reproductive role, hormonal and physical differences.
- **Gender** refers to culturally constructed differences between the 'masculine' and 'feminine' roles and identities assigned to males and females. It includes the ideas that cultures hold about the abilities of males and females, such as whether they are capable of rationality. These ideas are transmitted to each generation through socialisation.

While sex differences are seen as fixed, gender differences vary between cultures and over time. Thus, what is considered a proper role for women in one society or at one time may be disapproved of or forbidden in another. For example, until fairly recently it was rare to see women bus drivers in Britain, but this is now quite common, while in Saudi Arabia women are forbidden to drive any vehicle whatsoever.

For liberal feminists, then, sexist attitudes and stereotypical beliefs about gender are culturally constructed and transmitted through socialisation. Therefore, to achieve gender equality, we must change society's socialisation patterns. Hence, liberal feminists seek to promote appropriate role models in education and the family – for example, female teachers in traditional male subjects, or fathers taking responsibility for domestic tasks. Similarly, they challenge gender stereotyping in the media. Over time, they believe, such actions will produce cultural change and gender equality will become the norm.

Liberal feminism is an optimistic theory, very much in keeping with the Enlightenment project and its faith in progress. Liberal feminists believe that:

- Changes in socialisation and culture are gradually leading to more rational attitudes to gender and overcoming ignorance and prejudice.
- Political action to introduce anti-discriminatory laws and policies is steadily bringing about progress to a fairer society in which a person's gender is no longer important.

Activity Anti-discrimination laws

Go to www.sociology.uk.net

Liberal feminism can be seen as a critique of the functionalist view of gender roles. Functionalists such as Parsons distinguish between instrumental and expressive roles:

- **Instrumental roles** are performed in the *public sphere* of paid work, politics, and decision-making. This sphere involves rationality, detachment and objectivity.
- **Expressive roles** are performed in the *private sphere* of unpaid domestic labour, childrearing and caring for family members. This sphere involves emotion, attachment and subjectivity.

In Parsons' view, instrumental roles are the domain of men, while expressive roles are the domain of women.

Liberal feminism challenges this division. It argues that men and women are equally capable of performing roles in both spheres, and that traditional gender roles prevent both men and women from leading fulfilling lives. Liberal feminism aims to break down the barrier between the two spheres.

However, despite its critique of the functionalist view of gender divisions, liberal feminism is the feminist theory closest to a consensus view of society. Although it recognises conflicts between men and women, these are not seen as inevitable but merely a product of outdated attitudes. Moreover, women's emancipation is a 'win-win' situation from which men too will gain. For example, ending the gender division of labour would allow men to express their 'feminine' nurturing side, which current gender stereotypes force them to suppress.

Evaluation of liberal feminism

In sociology, studies conducted by liberal feminists have produced evidence documenting the extent of gender inequality and discrimination, and legitimising the demand for reform in areas such as equal pay and employment practices, media representations of gender, and so on. Their work has also helped to demonstrate that gender differences are not inborn but the result of different treatment and socialisation patterns.

However, liberal feminists are criticised for over-optimism. They see the obstacles to emancipation as simply the prejudices of individuals or irrational laws that can be gradually reformed away by the onward 'march of progress'. They ignore the possibility that there are deep-seated structures causing women's oppression, such as capitalism or patriarchy. As Sylvia Walby (1997) argues, they offer no explanation for the overall structure of gender inequality.

Marxist feminists and radical feminists argue that liberal feminism fails to recognise the underlying causes of women's subordination and that it is naïve to believe that changes in the law or attitudes will be enough to bring equality. Instead, they believe that far-reaching, revolutionary changes are needed.

Radical feminism

Radical feminism emerged in the early 1970s. Its key concept is patriarchy. Literally, this means 'rule by fathers', but it has come to mean a society in which men dominate women. Radical feminists make the following claims:

- Patriarchy is universal: male domination of women exists in all known societies. According to Shulamith Firestone (1974), the origins of patriarchy lie in women's biological capacity to bear and care for infants, since performing this role means they become dependent on males.
- Patriarchy is the primary and most fundamental form of social inequality and conflict. The key division in society is between men and women. Men are women's main enemy.
- All men oppress all women. All men benefit from patriarchy – especially from women's unpaid domestic labour and from their sexual services.

The personal is political

For radical feminists, patriarchal oppression is direct and personal. It occurs not only in the public sphere of work and politics, but also in the private sphere of the family, domestic labour and sexual relationships. Radical feminists see the personal as political. All relationships involve power and they are political when one individual tries to dominate another. Personal relationships between the sexes are therefore political because men dominate women through them. Radical feminists refer to these power relationships as *sexual politics*.

Radical feminists therefore focus on the ways in which patriarchal power is exercised through personal relationships, often through sexual or physical violence or the threat of it. This has the effect of controlling all women, not just those against whom it is exercised. For example, as Susan Brownmiller (1976) notes, fear of rape is a powerful deterrent against women going out alone at night.

> Suggest three ways in which patriarchal power may be exercised within the family.

Radical feminism also sheds new light on the nature of sexuality. In general, malestream sociology regards sexuality as a natural biological urge – and therefore outside the scope of sociology. By contrast, radical feminists argue that patriarchy constructs sexuality so as to satisfy men's desires. For example, women are portrayed in pornography as passive sex objects and penetration as the main source of sexual pleasure. Similarly, Adrienne Rich (1981) argues that men force women into a narrow and unsatisfying 'compulsory heterosexuality', which becomes the only socially acceptable form of sexuality.

Change

Given that patriarchy and women's oppression are reproduced through personal and sexual relationships, these must be transformed if women are to be free. Radical feminists have proposed a number of solutions or strategies to achieve this. These include:

Separatism Given that men's oppression of women is exercised through intimate domestic and sexual relationships, some radical feminists advocate separatism – that is, living apart from men and thereby creating a new culture of female independence, free from patriarchy. For example, Germaine Greer (2000) argues for the creation of all-female or 'matrilocal' households as an alternative to the heterosexual family.

Consciousness-raising Through sharing their experiences in women-only consciousness-raising groups, women come to see that other women face the same problems. This may lead to collective action, such as 'reclaim the night' marches.

Political lesbianism Many radical feminists argue that heterosexual relationships are inevitably oppressive because they involve 'sleeping with the enemy' and that lesbianism is the only non-oppressive form of sexuality.

Evaluation of radical feminism

Radical feminists' idea that the personal is political reveals how intimate relationships can involve domination. They draw attention to the political dimension of areas such as marriage, domestic labour, domestic violence, rape and pornography. However, radical feminism is criticised on several grounds.

Marxists assert that class, not patriarchy, is the primary form of inequality. They also argue that capitalism is the main cause and beneficiary of women's oppression, and not men, as radical feminism claims.

Radical feminism offers no explanation of why female subordination takes different forms in different societies. Similarly, it assumes all women are in the same position and ignores class, ethnic etc differences between women. A middle-class woman may have more in common with a middle-class man than with a working-class woman, for example.

Anna Pollert (1996) argues that the concept of patriarchy is of little value in explaining women's position because it involves a circular argument. For example, male violence is explained as patriarchy, while patriarchy is seen as being maintained by male violence – so patriarchy is maintaining itself!

Radical feminism has an inadequate theory of how patriarchy will be abolished. Critics argue that vague utopian notions of separatism are unlikely to be achievable. Jenny Somerville (2000) argues that heterosexual attraction makes it unlikely that the nuclear family will be replaced by single-sex households.

Patriarchy may already be in decline. Liberal feminists argue that women's position has improved greatly in recent years as a result of social reforms and changing attitudes. Better education, job opportunities etc mean that gender equality is beginning to become a reality.

While drawing attention to male violence against women, radical feminism neglects women's violence against men and violence within lesbian relationships.

▼ *Chiswick, West London, 1976: the first refuge for victims of domestic violence.*

Marxist feminism

Marxist feminists dismiss the liberal feminist view that women's subordination is merely the product of stereotyping or outdated attitudes. They also reject the radical feminist view that it is the result of patriarchal oppression by men. Instead, as Marxists, they see women's subordination as rooted in capitalism. Although individual men may benefit from women's subordination, the main beneficiary is capitalism.

For Marxist feminists, women's subordination in capitalist society results from their primary role as unpaid homemaker, which places them in a dependent economic position in the family. Their subordination performs a number of important functions for capitalism:

- **Women are a source of cheap, exploitable labour** for employers. They can be paid less because it is assumed they will be partially dependent on their husbands' earnings.
- **Women are a reserve army of labour** that can be moved into the labour force during economic booms and out again at times of recession. They can be treated as marginal workers in this way because it is assumed their primary role is in the home.
- **Women reproduce the labour force** through their unpaid domestic labour, both by nurturing and socialising children to become the next generation of workers and by maintaining and servicing the current generation of workers – their husbands. They do this at no cost to capitalism.
- **Women absorb anger** that would otherwise be directed at capitalism. Fran Ansley (1972) describes wives as 'takers of shit' who soak up the frustration their husbands feel because of the alienation and exploitation they suffer at work. For Marxist feminists, this explains male domestic violence against women.

Because of these links between women's subordination and capitalism, Marxist feminists argue that women's interests lie in the overthrow of capitalism.

> What do nurturing and socialising the next generation of workers and maintaining and servicing the current generation actually involve?
>
> How might women's domestic role enable capitalists to pay male workers less?

Barrett: the ideology of familism

All Marxist feminists agree that women's subordination within the family performs important *economic* functions for capitalism. However, some argue that non-economic factors must also be taken into account if we are to understand and change women's position. For example, Michèle Barrett (1980) argues that we must give more emphasis to women's consciousness and motivations, and to the role of *ideology* in maintaining their oppression.

For example, why do women marry and live in the conventional nuclear family when this is precisely what oppresses them? According to Barrett, the answer lies in the ideology of 'familism'. This ideology presents the nuclear family and its sexual division of labour (where women perform unpaid domestic work) as natural and normal. The family is portrayed as the only place where women can attain fulfilment, through motherhood, intimacy and sexual satisfaction. This ideology helps to keep women subordinated.

Therefore, while Barrett believes that the overthrow of capitalism is necessary to secure women's liberation, she argues that it is not sufficient. We must also overthrow the ideology of familism that underpins the conventional family and its unequal division of labour. This would free the sexes from restrictive stereotypes and ensure domestic labour was shared equally.

Some feminists take the analysis of ideology further to explain why women seem to freely accept oppressive family and marital relationships. These writers often draw on non-Marxist and even non-sociological ideas. For example, Juliet Mitchell (1975) uses Freud's psychoanalytic theory to argue that ideas about femininity are so deeply implanted in women's unconscious minds that they are very difficult to dislodge. The implication is that even after the overthrow of capitalism, it would still be hard to overcome patriarchal ideology because it is so deeply rooted.

Evaluation of Marxist feminism

Given the importance of economic production to most other areas of social life, Marxist feminists are correct to give weight to the relationship between capitalism and women's subordination. They show a greater understanding of the importance of structural factors than liberal feminism. However, Marxist feminism is criticised on several grounds.

It fails to explain women's subordination in non-capitalist societies. As women's subordination is also found in non-capitalist societies, it cannot be explained solely in terms of the needs of capitalism. However, in their defence, Marxist feminists are only seeking to explain the position of women in contemporary capitalist society.

Unpaid domestic labour may benefit capitalism, as Marxist feminists claim, but this doesn't explain why it is women and not men who perform it. Heidi Hartmann (1981) argues that this is because Marxism is 'sex-blind'.

Marxist feminism places insufficient emphasis on the ways in which men (including working-class men) – and not just capitalism – oppress women and benefit from their unpaid labour.

It is not proven that unpaid domestic labour is in fact the cheapest way of reproducing labour power. For example, it might be done more cheaply through the market or through state provision such as publicly funded nurseries.

Dual systems feminism

Dual systems feminists have sought to combine the key features of Marxist and radical feminism in a single theory. The two systems referred to are:

- **An economic system** – capitalism
- **A sex-gender system** – patriarchy

As we have seen, radical feminism regards patriarchy as the cause of women's oppression, while Marxist feminism sees capitalism as responsible. Dual systems theorists such as Heidi Hartmann (1979) see capitalism and patriarchy as two intertwined systems that form a single entity, 'patriarchal capitalism'. Like radical feminism, these theorists accept that patriarchy is universal, but they argue that patriarchy takes a specific form in capitalist societies.

From this viewpoint, to understand women's subordination, we must look at the relationship between their position both in the domestic division of labour (patriarchy) and

in paid work (capitalism). For example, domestic work limits women's availability for paid work – but the lack of work opportunities drives many women into marriage and economic dependence on a man. Thus, the two systems reinforce each other.

Similarly, Sylvia Walby (1988) argues that capitalism and patriarchy are inter-related. However, she argues that the interests of the two are not always the same. In particular, they collide over the exploitation of female labour. While capitalism demands cheap female labour for its workforce, patriarchy resists this, wanting to keep women subordinated to men within the private, domestic sphere. However, in the long run, capitalism is usually more powerful and so patriarchy adopts a strategy of segregation instead: women are allowed into the capitalist sphere of paid work, but only in low status 'women's' jobs, subordinated to men.

Walby's approach is useful because it shows how the two systems interact and structure one another, without assuming that their interests always coincide. However, Anna Pollert (1996) argues that patriarchy is not actually a system in the same sense as capitalism, which is driven by its own internal dynamic of profit making. By contrast, 'patriarchy' is merely a descriptive term for a range of practices such as male violence and control of women's labour.

Activity

Feminists hold different views about the nature of women's oppression and these have different strengths and weaknesses. Working in pairs, compile a table entitled 'Types of feminism' to cover all the theories you have looked at so far.

You will need four columns, headed liberal, radical, Marxist and dual systems feminism.

Down the left hand side, you will need the following rows:
1. What is the main cause of oppression? 2. How is oppression maintained? 3. How will oppression be ended? 4. Major strengths 5. Major weaknesses 6. Significant authors.

Difference feminism and poststructuralism

All the feminist perspectives we have examined so far assume that all women share a similar situation and similar experience of oppression. By contrast, 'difference feminists' do not see women as a single homogeneous group. They argue that middle-class and working-class women, white and black women, lesbian and heterosexual women have very different experiences of patriarchy, capitalism, racism, homophobia and so on.

Difference feminism argues that feminist theory has claimed a 'false universality' for itself – it claimed to be about all

women, but in reality was only about the experiences of white, Western, heterosexual, middle-class women. For example, by seeing the family only as a source of oppression, white feminists have neglected black women's experience of racial oppression. By contrast, many black feminists view the black family positively as a source of resistance against racism.

This criticism raises two important issues – the problem of essentialism, and the relationship of feminism to the Enlightenment project.

The problem of essentialism

As applied to gender, essentialism is the idea that all women share the same fundamental 'essence' – all women are essentially the same and all share the same experiences of oppression.

Difference feminists argue that liberal, Marxist and radical feminists are essentialist – they see all women as the same. As a result, they fail to reflect the diversity of women's experiences and they exclude other women and their problems. For example, some argue that the preoccupation of Western feminism with sexuality is irrelevant to women in poorer countries, where access to clean water and primary healthcare are far more pressing problems.

Poststructuralist feminism

Poststructuralist feminists such as Judith Butler (Butler and Scott, 1992) offer an alternative approach. Poststructuralism is concerned with *discourses* and *power/knowledge*. Discourses are ways of seeing, thinking or speaking about something. The world is made up of many, often competing, discourses – for example, religious, scientific, medical and artistic.

By enabling its users to define others in certain ways, a discourse gives power over those it defines. For example, by defining childbirth as a medical condition and healthy women as patients, medical discourse empowers doctors and disempowers women. Knowledge is power – the power to define or 'constitute' the identities of others. (For more on poststructuralism, see Topic 5.)

Poststructuralists argue that the Enlightenment project, with its talk of reason, humanity and progress, is one such discourse – a form of power/knowledge. Butler uses this idea in her critique of existing feminist theories.

Butler argues that the Enlightenment ideals were simply a form of power/knowledge that legitimated the domination of Western, white, middle-class males over other groups. These supposedly universal ideals that claimed to apply to all humanity in reality excluded women, black people and other oppressed groups.

Similarly, Butler argues that the white, Western, middle-class women who dominate the feminist movement have falsely claimed to represent 'universal womanhood'. She concludes that feminists are wrong to believe they can adapt the Enlightenment project so that it somehow includes all women – because women are not a single entity who all share the same 'essence'.

For poststructuralism, there *is* no fixed essence of what it is to be a woman. Because our identities are constituted through discourses, and because there are many different discourses in different times and cultures, there can be no fixed entity called 'womanhood' that is the same everywhere. For example, womanhood in Saudi Arabia is constituted partly by Islamic discourse. By contrast, womanhood in the West is constituted to a greater extent by the discourses of advertising and the media.

Butler argues that poststructuralism offers advantages for feminism. It enables feminists to 'de-construct' (analyse) different discourses to reveal how they subordinate women – as in the medicalisation of childbirth, for example. Thus, we can examine the discourses of medicine, sexuality, advertising, art, religion, science, pornography etc to uncover the power/knowledge by which they define and oppress women. Different discourses give rise to different forms of oppression, and thus to different identities and experiences for women. Likewise, each discourse provokes its own distinct form of resistance and struggle, with its own aims and demands.

In Butler's view, therefore, by rejecting essentialism and by stressing the diversity of discourses, poststructuralism recognises and legitimates the diversity of women's lives and struggles, rather than prioritising some and excluding others.

Activity

In groups of four, obtain two women's and two men's magazines. Study one magazine each and then collate your results. Look for examples of how 'womanhood' is perceived in Western society – for example, what sorts of images are used? How are women defined? What aspects of their lives are shown as important? How much stress is put on appearance? Finally, what differences do you notice between men's and women's magazines? Discuss your findings together.

Evaluation of poststructuralist feminism

While poststructuralist feminism seems to offer a theoretical basis for recognising the diversity of women's experiences and struggles against oppression, critics argue that it has some weaknesses.

For example, Sylvia Walby (1992) agrees that there are differences among women, but she argues that there are also important similarities – they are all faced with patriarchy. For example, compared with men, women face a greater risk of low pay, domestic violence and sexual assault.

Similarly, celebrating difference may have the effect of dividing women into an infinite number of sub-groups, thereby weakening feminism as a movement for change.

Lynne Segal (1999) criticises poststructuralist feminism for abandoning any notion of real, objective social structures. Oppression is not just the result of discourses – how we think and speak about women – it is about real inequality. Feminists should therefore continue to focus on the struggle for equality of wealth and income.

For more activities on Feminist theories…

Go to www.sociology.uk.net

Summary

Feminists study society from the viewpoint of women. They see society as divided by gender and women as subordinated by men, and seek to liberate women from oppression. However, there are different strands within feminism. Liberal feminists seek legal reforms and changes in attitudes and socialisation to bring gender equality. Radical feminists see patriarchy as the fundamental conflict in society – men are women's oppressors and separatism is the only solution. Marxist feminists see capitalism rather than men as the main beneficiary of women's oppression, for example through women reproducing the labour force at no cost to capitalism. Dual systems feminists regard patriarchy and capitalism as intertwined, though sometimes in conflict. Difference and poststructuralist feminists argue that other feminist theories are essentialist and disregard differences between women.

QuickCheck Questions

1 Explain the difference between the terms 'female' and 'feminine'.

2 How might capitalism and patriarchy reinforce each other?

3 Why do difference feminists criticise white Western feminists?

4 Suggest three sources of patriarchal power.

5 Which type of feminist is most likely to believe equality can be gained through reforming legislation and changing attitudes?

6 True or false? Marxist feminists believe gender inequalities only benefit capitalism.

7 In what way was sociology before the 1960s 'malestream'?

8 What is meant by 'essentialism'?

9 Suggest two criticisms of poststructuralist feminism.

Check your answers at www.sociology.uk.net

Examining feminist theories

Assess the usefulness of feminist contributions to our understanding of society today.

(33 marks)

The examiner's advice

This question carries 15 AO1 marks (knowledge and understanding) and 18 AO2 marks (interpretation, application, analysis and evaluation). You should start your answer by identifying the common feature of all feminist approaches, namely the opposition to female oppression.

However, the question refers to contributions in the plural, so you need to consider a range of different feminist views and approaches. You should at least cover liberal, radical and Marxist feminism. In each case, identify their key concerns and concepts, such as (for liberals) gender socialisation, stereotyping and anti-discrimination legislation; (for radicals) patriarchy, sexual politics and separatism; (for Marxists) reserve army of labour, reproduction of the labour force and socialist revolution. You can analyse and evaluate by making comparisons and contrasts between these approaches, e.g. in terms of their solutions to women's oppression, and by examining attempts to synthesise them, e.g. dual systems theory. Difference feminism and poststructuralist feminism can also be used as critiques of modernist (i.e. liberal, radical and Marxist) feminist theories.

The looking glass self: do we learn to see ourselves as others see us?

Topic 4 Action theories

As we saw in the Introduction to this chapter, we can divide sociological theories into two broad types: structural theories and action theories. Structural theories such as functionalism and Marxism are macro (large scale), top-down and deterministic: they see society as a real thing existing over and above us, shaping our ideas and behaviour – individuals are like puppets, manipulated by society. To understand people's behaviour, we must first understand the social structure that shapes it.

Action theories start from the opposite position. They are 'micro' level, bottom-up approaches that focus on the actions and interactions of individuals. Action theories are more voluntaristic – they see individuals as having free will and choice. Our actions and ideas are not determined by society. Rather, we possess agency – the ability to act as free agents, creating and shaping society through our choices, meanings and actions.

In this Topic we shall look at the four most important action theories in sociology:

- Weber's social action theory
- Symbolic interactionism
- Phenomenology
- Ethnomethodology

Although all four emphasise action or interaction, they differ in how far they see a role for structural explanations of behaviour. Weber and symbolic interactionism assume that the social structure can influence how we act. By contrast, phenomenology and ethnomethodology reject the very idea that there is a social structure 'out there' influencing our behaviour. For them, what we call 'society' is a construct, not a real thing.

Learning objectives

After studying this Topic, you should:

- Understand the difference between structural and action theories.
- Know the main types of action theory and understand the differences between them.
- Be able to evaluate the strengths and limitations of action theories.

Max Weber: social action theory

Max Weber (1864-1920) was one of the 'founding fathers' of sociology. Weber saw both structural and action approaches as necessary for a full understanding of human behaviour. He argued that an adequate sociological explanation involves two levels:

- **The level of cause** – explaining the objective structural factors that shape people's behaviour.
- **The level of meaning** – understanding the subjective meanings that individuals attach to their actions.

Unless we account for both of these levels, our explanation will be incomplete or false.

We can illustrate Weber's point by referring to his study *The Protestant Ethic and the Spirit of Capitalism*, originally published in 1905. At the level of structural *cause*, the Protestant Reformation introduced a new belief system, Calvinism. This changed people's worldview, which led to changes in their behaviour. For example, Calvinism promoted a work ethic that brought about the rise of capitalism.

At the level of subjective *meaning*, work took on a religious meaning for the Calvinists, as a calling by God to glorify his name through their labours. This motivated them to work systematically. As a result they accumulated wealth and became the first modern capitalists.

1 How would you apply Weber's concepts of objective structural factors and subjective meanings to explain a) hooliganism; b) unemployment?

2 Suggest four possible meanings that unemployment might have for a person.

Types of action

However, there are an infinite number of subjective meanings that actors may give to their actions. Weber attempts to classify actions into four types, based on their meaning for the actor:

Instrumentally rational action is where the actor calculates the most efficient means of achieving a given goal. For example, a capitalist may calculate that the most efficient way of maximising profit is to pay low wages. This action is not about the whether the goal itself is desirable – for example, it could be distributing charity or committing genocide. It is simply about the most efficient way of reaching that goal, whatever it may be.

Value-rational action involves action towards a goal that the actor regards as desirable for its own sake – for example, a believer worshipping their god in order to get to heaven. Unlike instrumental rationality, there is no way of calculating whether the means of achieving the goal are effective. For example, the believer has no way of knowing whether performing a particular ritual will gain him salvation.

Traditional action involves customary, routine or habitual actions. Weber does not see this type of action as rational, because no conscious thought or choice has gone into it. Rather, the actor does it because 'we have always done it'.

Affectual action is action that expresses emotion – for example, weeping out of grief, or violence sparked by anger. Weber sees affectual action as important in religious and political movements with charismatic leaders who attract a following based on their emotional appeal.

Evaluation of Weber

Weber's ideas are a valuable corrective to the over-emphasis on structural factors that we see in functionalism and many forms of Marxism, and an affirmation that we must also understand actors' subjective meanings if we want to explain their actions adequately.

However, Weber has been criticised on several grounds.

- Alfred Schutz (1972) argues that Weber's view of action is too individualistic and cannot explain the *shared* nature of meanings. For example, when a person at an auction raises their arm, *they* mean that they are making a bid – but Weber doesn't explain how everyone else present also comes to give this gesture the same meaning.
- Weber's typology of action is difficult to apply. For example, among the Trobriand Islanders, individuals exchange ritual gifts called 'kula' with others on neighbouring islands. This could either be seen as traditional action (it has been practised in the same way for generations) – or it could be seen as instrumentally rational action (because it is a good way of cementing trading links between kula partners).
- Weber advocated the use of *verstehen* or empathetic understanding of the actor's subjective meaning – where we put ourselves in the actor's place to understand their motives and meanings. However, as we cannot actually *be* that other person, we can never be sure we have truly understood their motives.

Symbolic interactionism

Symbolic interactionism first developed at the University of Chicago in the first half of the 20th century. Like other action theories, it focuses on our ability to create the social world through our actions and interactions, and it sees these interactions as based on the *meanings* we give to situations. We convey these meanings through symbols, especially language.

G.H. Mead

The work of George Herbert Mead (1863-1931) forms the basis for that of many later interactionists.

Symbols versus instincts

Mead observed that, unlike animals, our behaviour is not shaped by fixed, pre-programmed instincts. Instead, we respond to the world by giving meanings to the things that are significant to us. In effect, we create and inhabit a world of meanings. We do this by attaching symbols to the world. A symbol is something that stands for or represents something else.

Unlike animals, therefore, we do not simply respond to a stimulus in an automatic, pre-determined way. Instead, an *interpretive phase* comes between the stimulus and our response to it – before we know how to respond to the stimulus, we have to interpret its meaning. Once we have done this, we can then choose an appropriate response.

Mead illustrates this with an example. When one dog snarls at another, the snarl acts as a direct stimulus, to which the second dog responds instinctively, automatically adopting a defensive posture. There is no conscious interpretation by the dog of the other's actions.

By contrast, if I shake my fist at you, I am using a *symbol* – one that has a variety of possible meanings. To understand what is going on, you must interpret the meaning of this symbol. For instance, am I angry, or just joking? You may decide I am angry with you. Only then will you be able to choose how to respond.

Taking the role of the other

But how do we manage to interpret other people's meanings? In Mead's view, we do so by *taking the role of the other* – putting ourselves in the place of the other person and seeing ourselves as they see us.

Our ability to take the role of the other develops through social interaction. We first do this as young children: through imitative play when we take on the role of

significant others such as parents, and learn to see ourselves as they see us. Later, we come to see ourselves from the point of view of the wider community – the *generalised other.*

For Mead, to function as members of society, we need the ability to see ourselves as others see us. Through shared symbols, especially language, we become conscious of the ways of acting that others require of us.

Herbert Blumer

After Mead's death, Herbert Blumer (1900-87) did much to systematise his ideas. Blumer identified three key principles:

1 Our actions are based on the meanings we give to situations, events, people etc. Unlike animals, our actions are not based on automatic responses to stimuli.

2 These meanings arise from the interaction process. They are not fixed at the outset of the interaction, but are negotiable and changeable to some extent.

3 The meanings we give to situations are the result of the interpretive procedures we use – especially taking the role of the other.

Blumer's view of human conduct contrasts strongly with structural theories such as functionalism. Functionalists see the individual as a puppet, passively responding to the system's needs. Socialisation and social control ensure that individuals conform to society's norms and perform their roles in fixed and predictable ways.

By contrast, Blumer argues that although our action is *partly* predictable because we internalise the expectations of others, it is not completely fixed. There is always some room for negotiation and choice in how we perform our roles – even where very strict rules prevail, as in 'total institutions' such as prisons.

Activity

Humans are able to have internal conversations with themselves to consider possible actions or interpretations. Identify a situation where you needed to prepare in advance what to say.

1 How did you prepare? Did you consider the likely reaction of the other person?

2 How did you interpret and negotiate while the conversation was ongoing?

3 Afterwards, did you assess how the encounter went or think, 'I wish I had said *that*'?

Labelling theory

The best-known application of interactionist ideas is that of labelling theory. Labelling theorists use interactionist concepts in the study of many areas, including education, health, and crime and deviance. Here, we examine three key interactionist concepts that underpin labelling theory – the definition of the situation, the looking glass self, and career.

The definition of the situation A definition of something is of course a *label* for that thing. W.I. Thomas (1966) argued that if people define a situation as real, then it will have real consequences. That is, if we believe something to be true, then this belief will affect how we act, and this in turn may have consequences for those involved. For example, if a teacher labels a boy as 'troublesome' (whether or not he really is), the teacher will be likely to act differently towards him – for example, punishing him more harshly.

The looking glass self Charles Cooley (1922) uses this idea to describe how we develop our *self-concept* – our idea of who we are. He argues that our self-concept arises out of our ability to take the role of the other. In interactions, by taking the role of the other, we come to see ourselves as they see us. In other words, others act as a looking glass to us – we see our self mirrored in the way they respond to us. Through this process, a *self-fulfilling prophecy* occurs – we become what others see us as.

Labelling theorists use the definition of the situation and the looking glass self to understand the effects of labelling. For example, an individual may find that relatives or psychiatrists define him as mentally ill and respond to him differently, reflecting their view of him as sick or abnormal.

Through the looking glass self, the label becomes part of the individual's self-concept. He takes on the role of 'mental patient' and a self-fulfilling prophecy is created when he acts it out. Even if the initial definition of him was false, it has become true and may have real consequences. For example, he may find himself detained in a psychiatric hospital.

Career In normal usage, a career is the stages through which an individual progresses in their occupation, each with its own status, job title, problems etc. However, labelling theorists such as Howard S. Becker (1961; 1963) and Edwin Lemert (1962) have extended the concept to apply it to groups such as medical students, marijuana smokers and those suffering from paranoia.

For example, in relation to mental illness, we can see the individual as having a career running from 'pre-patient' with certain symptoms, through *labelling* by a psychiatrist, to hospital in-patient, to discharge. Each stage has its own status and problems. For example, on discharge the ex-patient may find it hard to reintegrate into society. And just as a 'normal' career may give us our status, so 'mental patient' may become our *master status* in the eyes of society.

Interactionism is generally regarded as a voluntaristic theory that emphasises free will and choice in how we act. However, labelling theory has been accused of determinism – of seeing our actions and identities as shaped by the way others label them.

Goffman's dramaturgical model

Labelling theory describes how the self is shaped through interaction. It often sees the individual as the passive victim of other people's labels. By contrast, the work of another interactionist, Erving Goffman (1963; 1967; 1968; 1969), describes how we actively construct our 'self' by manipulating other people's impressions of us.

Goffman's approach is often described as *dramaturgical* because he uses analogies with drama as a framework for analysing social interaction. We are all 'actors', acting out 'scripts', using 'props', resting 'backstage' between 'performances' we present to our 'audiences' and so on. Our aim is to carry off a convincing performance of the role we have adopted – just as the actor aims to persuade the audience that he is really Hamlet.

▲ Shakespeare's Hamlet: *how useful is the dramaturgical model for understanding interaction?*

Impression management

Two key dramaturgical concepts are *the presentation of self and impression management*. For Goffman, we seek to present a particular image of ourselves to our audiences. To do so, we must control the impression our performance gives. This involves constantly studying our audience to see how they are responding, and monitoring and adjusting our performance to present a convincing image.

As social actors, we have many techniques for impression management. We may use language, tone of voice, gestures and facial expressions, as well as props and settings such as dress, make-up, equipment, furniture, décor and premises. By using these techniques skilfully, we can 'pass' for the kind of person we want our audience to believe we are.

Goffman uses the dramaturgical analogy to describe the different settings of interactions. As in the theatre, there is a 'front' or stage where we act out our roles, while backstage, we can step out of our role and 'be ourselves'. For example, the classroom is a front region where students must put on a convincing role-performance for the teacher, while the common room is a back region where they can 'drop the act'. However, the common room may become another front region where students may have to carry off a different performance in front of their friends.

> How might you behave differently at home or with intimate friends compared with when you are in the student common room?

Roles

Goffman's view of roles differs sharply from that of functionalism. Functionalists see roles as tightly 'scripted' by society and they see us as fully internalising our scripts through socialisation. As a result, they become part of our identity and society determines exactly how we will perform them.

Goffman rejects this view. Instead, he argues, there is a 'gap' or *role distance* between our real self and our roles. Like the stage actor who is not really Hamlet, we are not really the roles we play. In Goffman's view, roles are only loosely scripted by society and we have a good deal of freedom in how we play them – for example, some teachers are strict, others easy-going.

The idea of role distance also suggests that we do not always believe in the roles we play and that our role performance may be cynical or calculating. In Goffman's studies, the actor sometimes resembles a confidence trickster, manipulating his audience into accepting an impression that conceals his true self and real motives. In the dramaturgical model, appearances are everything and actors seek to present themselves to their best advantage.

Activity

Consider the following people: a doctor; a nightclub bouncer; a partygoer who doesn't know anyone at the party; a job interviewee; a waiter or waitress; a beggar:

1 Who is their audience? (It may be more than one group of people.)

2 What impression are they likely to try to give to their audiences?

3 What props do they use to manage this impression more effectively?

If you have the opportunity, discreetly observe one or more of the above.

Evaluation of symbolic interactionism

Interactionism largely avoids the determinism of structural theories such as functionalism. It recognises that people create society through their choices and meanings. However, interactionism is criticised on several counts.

Some argue that it is more a loose collection of descriptive concepts (such as labelling, and Goffman's dramaturgical concepts) than an explanatory theory.

It focuses on face-to-face interactions and ignores wider social structures such as class inequality, and it fails to explain the origin of labels. Similarly, it cannot explain the consistent patterns we observe in people's behaviour. Functionalists argue that these patterns are the result of norms dictating behaviour.

Larry Reynolds (1975) offers some interesting evidence to show that interactionism lacks an idea of structure. Reynolds sent a questionnaire to 124 interactionists, of whom 84 responded. When asked to identify the concepts they felt were essential, the most popular were 'role' (chosen by 38), 'self' (37) and 'interaction' (37). Only two chose 'power' or 'class' – concepts that structural sociologists see as crucial.

Not all action is meaningful – like Weber's category of traditional action, much is performed unconsciously or routinely and may have little meaning for actors. If so, interactionism lacks the means to explain it.

Goffman's dramaturgical analogy is useful but has its limitations. For example, in interactions everyone plays the part of both actor and audience, and interactions are often improvised and unrehearsed.

Ethnomethodologists argue that interactionism is correct in focusing on actors' meanings, but that it fails to explain *how* actors create meanings (see page 248).

Phenomenology

In philosophy, the term 'phenomenon' is used to describe things as they appear to our senses. Some philosophers argue that we can never have definite knowledge of what the world outside our minds is really like 'in itself' – all we can know is what our senses tell us about it. This is the starting point for the philosophy known as phenomenology, developed by Edmund Husserl (1859-1938).

Husserl's philosophy

Husserl argues that the world only makes sense because we impose meaning and order on it by constructing mental categories that we use to classify and 'file' information coming from our senses. For example, a category such as 'four-legged furniture for eating off' enables us to identify a particular set of sensory data as 'table'.

In this view, we can only obtain knowledge about the world through our mental acts of categorising and giving meaning to our experiences. The world *as we know it* is, and can only be, a product of our mind.

Schutz's phenomenological sociology

Alfred Schutz (1899-1959) applies this idea to the social world. He argues that the categories and concepts we use are not unique to ourselves – rather, we share them with other members of society.

Typifications

Schutz calls these shared categories *typifications*. Typifications enable us to organise our experiences into a shared world of meaning.

In Schutz's view, the meaning of any given experience varies according to its social context. For example, raising your arm means one thing in class and quite another at an auction. The meaning is not given by the action in itself, but by its context. For this reason, meanings are potentially unclear and unstable – especially if others classify the action in a different way from oneself. Imagine what would happen if, at an auction, you behaved as if you were in class and raised your hand to ask a question.

Fortunately, however, typifications stabilise and clarify meanings by ensuring that we are all 'speaking the same language' – all agreeing on the meaning of things. This makes it possible for us to communicate and cooperate with one another and thus to achieve our goals. Without shared typifications, social order would become impossible.

For example, if you see a certain object as a desk (for writing at), while I take it for an altar (for worshipping at), considerable problems might result.

However, in Schutz's view, members of society to a large extent do have a shared 'life world' – a stock of shared typifications or commonsense knowledge that we use to make sense of our experience. It includes shared assumptions about the way things are, what certain situations mean, what other people's motivations are and so on. Schutz calls this 'recipe knowledge': like a recipe, we can follow it without thinking too much, and still get the desired results in everyday life. For example, we all 'know' that a red light means stop or danger and this knowledge enables us to drive safely.

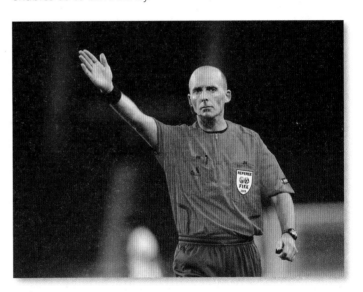

▲ *The meaning of any action depends on its context.*

This commonsense knowledge is not simply knowledge *about* the world – it *is* the world. As we saw, for Husserl the world as we know it can only be a product of our mind. Similarly, for Schutz the social world is a shared, inter-subjective world that can only exist when we share the same meanings. For example, a red traffic light only 'means' stop because we all agree that it does.

The natural attitude

However, society *appears* to us as a real, objective thing existing outside of us. To illustrate this, Schutz gives the example of posting a letter to a bookshop to order a book. In doing so, he says, we assume that some unknown and unseen individuals (postal workers, a bookshop owner) will perform a whole series of operations in a particular sequence – and that all this will result in our receiving the book.

The fact that we *do* get the book encourages us to adopt what he calls 'the natural attitude' – that is, it leads us to assume that the social world is a solid, natural thing out there. However, for Schutz, it simply shows that all those involved (the book buyer and seller, the postal workers) share the same meanings, and this allows us to cooperate and achieve goals.

However, Peter Berger and Thomas Luckmann (1971) argue that while Schutz is right to focus on shared commonsense knowledge, they reject his view that society is merely an inter-subjective reality. Although reality is socially constructed, as Schutz believes, once it has been constructed, it takes on a life of its own and becomes an external reality that reacts back on us. For example, religious ideas may start off in our consciousness, but they become embodied in powerful structures such as churches, which then constrain us – for example, by influencing laws about our sexual relationships.

Ethnomethodology

Ethnomethodology (EM for short) emerged in America in the 1960s, mainly from the work of Harold Garfinkel (1967). Garfinkel's ideas stem from phenomenology. Like Schutz, Garfinkel rejects the very idea of society as a real objective structure 'out there'.

Like functionalists such as Parsons, Garfinkel is interested in how social order is achieved. However, he gives a very different answer from Parsons. Parsons argues that social order is made possible by a shared value system into which we are socialised. Parsons' explanation is in keeping with his top-down, structural approach: shared norms ensure that we perform our roles in an orderly, predictable way that meets the expectations of others.

Garfinkel takes the opposite view – social order is created from the bottom up. Order and meaning are not achieved because people are 'puppets' whose strings are pulled by the social system, as functionalists believe. Instead, social order is an *accomplishment* – something that members of society actively construct in everyday life using their commonsense knowledge. EM attempts to discover *how* we do this by studying people's methods of making sense of the world.

This is also where EM differs from interactionism. While interactionists are interested in the effects of meanings (for example, the effects of labelling), EM is interested in the methods or rules that we use to produce the meanings in the first place.

Indexicality and reflexivity

Like Schutz, EM sees meanings as always potentially unclear – a characteristic Garfinkel calls *indexicality*. Nothing has a fixed meaning: everything depends on the context. For example as we saw earlier, raising one's arm means different things in different situations. Now, indexicality is clearly a threat to social order because if meanings are inherently unclear or unstable, communication and cooperation become difficult and social relationships may begin to break down.

Activity

Work in pairs. One of you should try to define an everyday object, such as a table. The other's role is to ask awkward questions so as to make your task more difficult. For example: Does it always have four legs? Can it have two legs? Can it be alive? Now swap roles and try defining another object.

Finally, try defining something more difficult, such as social class. How difficult did you find each of these? In what way does this activity illustrate indexicality?

However, there is a paradox here. Indexicality suggests that we cannot take any meaning for granted as fixed or clear – yet in everyday life, this is exactly what we do most of the time. For Garfinkel, what enables us to behave *as if* meanings are clear and obvious is *reflexivity*. Reflexivity refers to the fact that we use commonsense knowledge in everyday interactions to construct a sense of meaning and order and stop indexicality from occurring. This is similar to Schutz's idea of typifications.

Language is of vital importance in achieving reflexivity. For EM, when we describe something, we are simultaneously *creating* it. Our description gives it reality, removing uncertainty about what is going on, and making it seem clear, solid and meaningful. But although language gives us a sense of reality existing 'out there', in fact all we have done is to construct a set of shared meanings.

Experiments in disrupting social order

Garfinkel and his students sought to demonstrate the nature of social order by a series of so-called 'breaching experiments'. For example, they acted as lodgers in their own families – being polite, avoiding getting personal etc.

The aim was to disrupt people's sense of order and challenge their reflexivity by undermining their assumptions about the situation. For example, parents of students who behaved as lodgers became bewildered, anxious, embarrassed or angry. They accused the students of being nasty, or assumed they were ill.

Garfinkel concludes that by challenging people's taken-for-granted assumptions, the experiments show how the orderliness of everyday situations is not inevitable but is actually an *accomplishment* of those who take part in them. In his view, social order is 'participant produced' by members themselves.

Suicide and reflexivity

Garfinkel is interested in the methods we use to achieve reflexivity – to make sense of the world as orderly. In the case of suicide, coroners make sense of deaths by selecting particular features from the infinite number of possible 'facts' about the deceased – such as their mental health, employment status etc. They then treat these features as a real pattern. For example, they may use this information to conclude that 'typical suicides' are mentally ill, unemployed etc.

For Garfinkel, humans constantly strive to impose order by seeking patterns, even though these patterns are really just social constructs. For example, the seeming pattern that suicides are mentally ill becomes part of the coroner's taken-for-granted knowledge about what suicides are like. Thus, when faced with future cases with similar features (mentally ill people who have died), the coroner interprets them as examples of the assumed pattern: 'the deceased was mentally ill, therefore he probably committed suicide'. Finally, cases fitting the pattern will be classified as suicides and will seem to prove the existence of the pattern the coroner had originally constructed. The assumed pattern becomes self-reinforcing – but it tells us nothing about any external reality.

Garfinkel is critical of conventional sociology. He accuses it of merely using the same methods as ordinary members of society to create order and meaning. If so, then conventional sociology is little more than commonsense,

rather than true and objective knowledge. For example, positivists such as Durkheim take it for granted that official suicide statistics are social facts that tell us the real rate of suicide. In fact, they are merely the decisions made by coroners, using their commonsense understandings of what types of people kill themselves. Therefore the supposed 'laws' positivists produce about suicide are no more than an elaborate version of the coroners' commonsense understandings. Sociologists' claims to know about suicide are thus no truer than those of other members of society, such as coroners.

Evaluation of ethnomethodology

EM draws attention to how we actively construct order and meaning, rather than seeing us as simply puppets of the social system, as functionalism does. However, it has come in for considerable criticism.

Craib argues that its findings are trivial. Ethnomethodologists seem to spend a lot of time 'uncovering' taken-for-granted rules that turn out to be no surprise to anyone. For example, one study found that in phone conversations, generally only one person speaks at a time!

EM argues that everyone creates order and meaning by identifying patterns and producing explanations that are essentially fictions. If so, this must also apply to EM itself, and so we have no particular reason to accept its views.

EM denies the existence of wider society, seeing it as merely a shared fiction. Yet, by analysing how members apply general rules or norms to specific contexts, it assumes that a structure of norms really exists beyond these contexts. From a functionalist perspective, such norms are social facts, not fictions.

EM ignores how wider structures of power and inequality affect the meanings that individuals construct. For example, Marxists argue that 'commonsense knowledge' is really just ruling-class ideology, and the order it creates serves to maintain capitalism.

Structure and action

So far in this chapter, we have examined a range of sociological theories and grouped them into 'structural' and 'action' theories. As we have seen, structural theories tend to be deterministic, seeing society as something objective, existing outside individuals and constraining them. By contrast, action theories tend to be voluntaristic, seeing society as the creation of its members through their subjective actions and meanings.

Both types of theory appear to hold some truth. It is easy to see society as a real, external structure constraining us.

For example, society's laws regulate our behaviour, and its economic structure affects the jobs we can obtain.

Similarly, it is easy to feel that we freely choose our actions. For example, the existence of a law doesn't stop us from choosing to break it. Likewise, although only certain jobs may be available, we may still have a choice of which (if any) to take.

Given that there is much to be said for both types of approach, some sociologists have sought to combine them into a single unified theory of structure *and* action. The best known of these is Anthony Giddens' (1984) structuration theory.

Giddens' structuration theory

According to Giddens, there is a *duality of structure*. By this Giddens means that structure and action – or agency as he calls it – are two sides of the same coin; neither can exist without the other. Through our actions we produce and reproduce structures over time and space, while these structures are what make our actions possible in the first place. Giddens calls this relationship *structuration*.

Giddens illustrates this with language. A language is a structure – it is made up of a set of rules of grammar that govern how we can use it to express meanings. This structure seems to exist independently of any individual, and it constrains our behaviour, like one of Durkheim's 'social facts'. For example, if we wish to use a language to communicate, we must obey its rules, otherwise, we will not be understood. This shows how our action (communication) depends on the existence of structure (our knowledge of language rules).

But structure also depends on action. For example, a language would not exist if no one used it. It is produced and reproduced over time through the actions of individuals speaking and writing it. Furthermore, these actions can also *change* the structure. People give words new meanings and create new rules.

> Suggest two examples, apart from language, that illustrate the duality of structure and action.

Reproduction of structures through agency

For Giddens, structure has two elements:

- *Rules* – the norms, customs and laws that govern or affect action.
- *Resources* – both economic (raw materials, technology etc) and power over others.

Rules and resources can be either reproduced or changed through human action. For example, obeying the law reproduces the existing structure, while inventing new technology may change it. However, in Giddens' view, although our action can change existing structures, it generally tends to reproduce them. He identifies two reasons for this.

First, society's *rules* contain a stock of knowledge about how to live our lives. Earning a living, shopping and so on largely involve applying this knowledge to everyday

situations. Similarly, when shopping, for example, we use *resources* in the form of money. Thus as we go about our routine activities, we tend to reproduce the existing structure of society.

Second, we reproduce existing structures through our action because we have a deep-seated need for *ontological security* – a need to feel that the world, both physical and social, really is as it appears to be, and especially that it is orderly, stable and predictable. This need tends to encourage action that maintains existing structures, rather than changing them.

Change of structures through agency

However, despite this tendency to maintain the structure of society, action or agency can also change it. This can occur in two ways.

First, we 'reflexively monitor' our own action. That is, we constantly reflect on our actions and their results, and we can deliberately choose a new course of action. Giddens notes that this is more likely in late or high modern society, where tradition no longer dictates action and where individuals become more reflexive, thus increasing both the likelihood and the pace of change.

Second, our actions may change the world, but not always as we intended. They may have unintended consequences, producing changes that were not part of our goal. For example, according to Weber, the Calvinists who adopted the Protestant work ethic did so with the intention of glorifying God, but the consequence was the creation of modern capitalism.

Evaluation of Giddens

Although Giddens makes an important attempt to overcome the division between structure and action in sociological theory, his approach has been criticised.

Giddens implies that actors can change structures simply by deciding to do so. Margaret Archer (1995) argues that he underestimates the capacity of structures to resist change. For example, slaves may wish to abolish slavery but lack the power to do so.

According to Craib, structuration theory isn't really a theory at all, because it doesn't explain what actually happens in society. Instead, it just describes the kinds of things we will find when we study society, such as actions, rules, resources etc.

Craib argues that Giddens fails to unite structure and action. He regards Giddens' work as 'a thoroughgoing action theory' that reduces the idea of structure to the rules governing routine everyday actions. Giddens fails to explain how his theory applies to large-scale structures such as the economy and the state.

For more activities on Action theories...

Go to www.sociology.uk.net

Summary

Unlike structural theories, action theories are micro level, bottom up approaches that see society as constructed by members' interactions and meanings. Weber's social action theory identifies four main types of action. Symbolic interactionists see us as creating meanings through interactions in which we take the role of the other. Meanings are not fixed but negotiable. Labelling theory and Goffman's dramaturgical analogy are two major interactionist approaches. While Weber and interactionism have a notion of external social structure, phenomenology and ethnomethodology do not. They see society as an inter-subjective reality created out of members' typifications or commonsense understandings. Giddens' structuration theory attempts to unite structure and action. We reproduce structures through our everyday actions, but can also change them by choosing to act differently. However, critics argue that Giddens fails to account for the ability of structures to resist change.

QuickCheck Questions

1 What are 'micro' level theories?

2 Suggest two examples of techniques someone might use for impression management.

3 What are the main differences between structural and action theories?

4 Identify the four types of action classified by Weber.

5 Explain what is meant by a 'dramaturgical model'.

6 What is 'empathy'?

7 Why is Mead's interactionism *symbolic*?

8 According to Giddens, why does human 'agency' tend to reproduce rather than change existing structures?

9 Explain the difference between indexicality and reflexivity.

10 Explain what is meant by 'ontological security'.

Check your answers at www.sociology.uk.net

Examining action theories

Assess the usefulness of interactionist approaches to the study of society. (33 marks)

The examiner's advice

This question carries 15 AO1 marks (knowledge and understanding) and 18 AO2 marks (interpretation, application, analysis and evaluation). You should begin your answer by identifying interactionism as an 'action' approach that focuses on the study of people's meanings. You could develop this through an account of G.H. Mead's ideas about symbols versus instincts and taking the role of the other, and Herbert Blumer's three principles of interactionism.

The question asks about approaches plural, so you need to examine the different ideas that interactionists have developed. Focus on labelling theory and its key concepts, such as the definition of the situation, the looking glass self, self-fulfilling prophecy and career. Give examples from areas such as education or crime and deviance to illustrate some of these. Use Goffman's dramaturgical model as an alternative interactionist approach. You can evaluate by discussing issues such as interactionism's neglect of structure, its descriptive rather than explanatory approach, its failure to explain *how* meanings are created, labelling theory as deterministic etc.

Time-space compression

Topic 5 Globalisation, modernity and postmodernity

Learning objectives

After studying this Topic, you should:

- Know some of the reasons for the trend towards globalisation.
- Understand the difference between modernity, postmodernity and late modernity.
- Be able to evaluate the strengths and limitations of postmodernist and other theories of recent changes in society.

In this Topic, we examine two main issues:

- Some of the major changes that have occurred in society in recent decades.
- Theories that have been put forward to explain these changes.

Society has been undergoing important changes in recent times. For example, there is the growing impact of new technology and the media, as well as new social and political movements based on gender, environmental concerns and so on. This has led to debate about the nature, extent and causes of these changes.

Some sociologists argue that these changes are so profound that they represent a fundamental shift, from the modern society of the past two centuries, to a new, postmodern society – from the era of modernity to the era of postmodernity.

Others disagree. They argue that, although recent changes have been very significant, these are actually part of modernity itself – just an intensification of the existing features of modern society, and *not* a move to postmodern society.

In addition to whether we have moved to a new type of society, there is the related question of what *theory* we need to understand these changes. Again, opinions are divided: some have adopted the perspective known as postmodernism to describe society today, while others have adapted existing modernist theories, such as Marxism.

To summarise, then, there are two views as to what kind of *society* we are now living in – modern or postmodern society. There are also disagreements about what kind of *theory* can explain what is going on – postmodernism, or some version of the modernist theories we have encountered so far in this chapter.

Modernity and globalisation

Most of the theories we have examined so far in this chapter can be placed under the general heading of 'modernism'. Modernist theories are part of the Enlightenment project – the idea that society can progress through the use of human reason. Rationality and science will enable us to discover true knowledge about society and the natural world. With this knowledge, we can progress to a better future of freedom and prosperity.

Modernist theories therefore set out to explain the workings of modern society and to identify the direction it should take if it is to progress.

Modern society

Modern society first emerged in Western Europe from about the late 18th century. It has a number of characteristics that distinguish it from previous traditional societies.

The nation-state is the key political unit in modern society – a bounded territory ruled by a powerful centralised state, whose population usually shares the same language and culture. We tend to think of the modern world as made up of a series of separate societies, each with its own state.

The state is the focal point of modern society, organising social life on a national basis. Modern states have created large administrative bureaucracies and educational, welfare and legal institutions to regulate their citizens' lives. The nation-state is also an important source of identity for citizens, who identify with its symbols such as the flag.

Capitalism The economy of modern societies is capitalist – based on private ownership of the means of production and the use of wage labourers. Capitalism brought about the industrialisation of modern society, with huge increases in wealth. However, wealth distribution is unequal, resulting in class conflict. The nation-state becomes important in regulating capitalism and maintaining the conditions under which it operates. Scott Lash and John Urry (1987; 1994) describe this as 'organised capitalism'.

In modern industry, production is organised on Fordist principles (after the Ford Motor Company's system): the mass production of standardised products in large factories, using low skilled labour. Cheap, mass produced consumer goods lead to a rising standard of living.

Rationality, science and technology Rational, secular, scientific ways of thinking dominate and the influence of magico-religious explanations of the world declines. Technically efficient forms of organisation, such as bureaucracies and factories, dominate social and economic life. Science becomes increasingly important in industry, medicine and communications.

Individualism Tradition, custom and ascribed status become less important as the basis for our actions. We experience greater personal freedom and can increasingly choose our own course in life and define our own identity. However, structural inequalities such as class remain important in shaping people's identity and restricting their choices.

Globalisation

Until recently, the nation-state provided the basic framework for most people's lives. However, many sociologists argue that we are now increasingly affected by *globalisation* – the increasing interconnectedness of people across national boundaries. We live in one interdependent 'global village' and our lives are shaped by a global framework. Four related changes have helped bring this about.

1 Technological changes

We can now cross entire continents in a matter of hours, or exchange information across the globe with the click of a mouse. Satellite communications, the internet and global television networks have helped to create *time-space compression*, closing the distances between people.

Technology also brings risks on a global scale. For example, greenhouse gases produced in one place contribute to global climate change that leads to a rise in sea levels and flooding in low-lying countries. Ulrich Beck (1992) argues that we are now living in 'risk society', where increasingly the threats to our well being come from human-made technology rather than natural disasters.

2 Economic changes

Economic factors play a huge part in globalisation. Economic activity now takes place within a set of global networks that are creating ever-greater interconnectedness.

The global economy is increasingly a 'weightless' or *electronic economy*. Instead of producing physical goods, much activity now involves the production of information, such as music, TV programmes and data processing. These commodities are produced, distributed and consumed through global electronic networks.

In the electronic economy, money never sleeps. Global 24-hour financial transactions permit the instantaneous transfer of funds around the world in pursuit of profit. This too contributes to the 'risk society'. For example, the world financial crisis in 2008 brought the economy of Iceland, which was heavily dependent on banking, to the brink of ruin.

Another major economic force pushing globalisation forward is *trans-national companies* (TNCs). These companies operate across frontiers, organising production on a global scale.

Most TNCs are Western-based. Some, such as Coca-Cola, are colossal enterprises, and the largest 500 together account for half the total value of the commodities produced in the whole world. So powerful are the small elite who control these companies, that Leslie Sklair (2003) argues they now form a separate *global capitalist class*.

3 Political changes

Some sociologists claim that globalisation has undermined the power of the nation-state. For example, Kenichi Ohmae (1994) argues that we now live in a 'borderless world' in which TNCs and consumers have more economic power than national governments. States are now less able to regulate the activities of large capitalist enterprises, a situation Lash and Urry describe as 'disorganised capitalism'.

4 Changes in culture and identity

Globalisation makes it much harder for cultures to exist in isolation from one another. A major reason for this is the role of information and communications technology (ICT), especially the mass media.

Today we find ourselves living in a *global culture* in which Western-owned media companies spread Western culture to the rest of the world. Economic integration also encourages a global culture. For example, TNCs such as Nike, selling the same consumer goods in many countries,

help to promote similar tastes across national borders. In addition, the increased movement of people as tourists, economic migrants, refugees and asylum seekers helps to create globalised culture.

Globalisation also undermines traditional sources of *identity* such as class. For example, the shift of manufacturing from the West to developing countries has led to the fragmentation and decline of working-class communities that previously gave people their class identity.

Explaining the changes

The changes that we have just examined raise some important questions:

■ Do they mean we are no longer living in modernity – are we now in a new, postmodern society?
■ Do we need new theories to understand society as we now find it, or can we use our existing modernist theories to explain it?
■ Is the Enlightenment project still viable – can we still hope to achieve objective knowledge and use it to improve society? Or have the rapid changes associated with globalisation made society too chaotic for us to understand and control?

We can identify three theories that offer answers to these questions:

1 **Postmodernism**
2 **Theories of late modernity**
3 **Marxist theories of postmodernity**

Postmodernism

Postmodernism is a major intellectual movement that has emerged since the 1970s. It has been influential in many areas, including sociology. Postmodernists argue that we are now living in a new era of postmodernity. Postmodernity is an unstable, fragmented, media-saturated global village, where image and reality are indistinguishable. In postmodern society, we define ourselves by what we consume. It is not a continuation of modernity, but a fundamental break with it. For postmodernists, this new kind of society requires a new kind of theory – modernist theories no longer apply.

Knowledge

Drawing on the ideas of Michel Foucault (see Box 4.3), postmodernists argue that there are no sure foundations to knowledge – no objective criteria we can use to prove whether a theory is true or false. This view – known as anti-foundationalism – has two consequences:

1 The Enlightenment project of achieving progress through true, scientific knowledge is dead. If we cannot guarantee our knowledge is correct, we cannot use it to improve society.
2 Any all-embracing theory that claims to have the absolute truth about how to create a better society, such as Marxism, is a mere *meta-narrative* or 'big story' – just someone's *version* of reality, not the truth. Therefore there is no reason to accept the claims that the theory makes.

Postmodernists also reject meta-narratives such as Marxism on the grounds that they have helped to create oppressive totalitarian states that impose their version of the truth on people. For example, in the former Soviet Union, the state's attempt to re-mould society on Marxist principles led to political repression and slave labour camps.

Rejecting meta-narratives that claim absolute truth, postmodernists take a *relativist* position instead. That is, they argue that all views are true for those who hold them. No one has special access to the truth – including sociologists. All accounts of reality are equally valid. We should therefore recognise and celebrate the diversity of views rather than seek to impose one version of the truth on everyone.

But if knowledge is not about the truth, what is it about? According to Jean-Francois Lyotard (1992), in postmodern society, knowledge is just a series of different 'language games' or ways of seeing the world. However, in his view, postmodern society, with its many competing views of the truth, is preferable to modern society, where meta-narratives claimed a monopoly of truth and sometimes sought to impose it by force, as in the Soviet Union. Postmodernity allows groups who had been marginalised by modern society, such as ethnic minorities and women, to be heard.

Baudrillard: simulacra

Like Lyotard, Jean Baudrillard (1983) argues that knowledge is central to postmodern society. He argues that society is no longer based on the production of material goods, but rather on buying and selling knowledge in the form of images and signs. However, unlike signs in past societies, those today bear no relation to physical reality.

Instead, signs stand for nothing other than themselves – they are not symbols of some other real thing. Baudrillard calls such signs *simulacra* (singular: simulacrum). For example, tabloid newspaper articles about fictitious soap opera characters are 'signs about signs' rather than about an underlying reality.

▲ *Baudrillard describes the Gulf War as having only happened on TV. What do you think he meant by this?*

Baudrillard describes this situation as *hyper-reality*: where the signs appear more real than reality itself and substitute themselves for reality. However, because the signs do not represent anything real, they are literally meaningless. In this respect, Baudrillard is particularly critical of television, which he sees as the main source of simulacra and of our inability to distinguish between image and reality.

> 1 Suggest two other examples that would fit the category of 'simulacra'.
>
> 2 Discuss with two fellow students how reality TV fits into Baudrillard's analysis.

Culture, identity and politics

Postmodernists argue that culture and identity in postmodern society differ fundamentally from modern society, especially because of the role of the media in creating hyper-reality. The media are all pervading and they produce an endless stream of ever changing images, values and versions of the truth. As a result, culture becomes fragmented and unstable, so that there is no longer a coherent or fixed set of values shared by members of society.

This bewildering array of different messages and ideas also undermines people's faith in meta-narratives. Confronted by so many different versions of the truth, people cease to believe wholeheartedly in any one version. Furthermore, given the failure of meta-narratives such as Marxism to deliver a better society, people lose faith in the possibility of rational progress.

In postmodernity, *identity* also becomes destabilised. For example, instead of a fixed identity ascribed by our class, we can now construct our own identity from the wide range of images and lifestyles on offer in the media. We can easily change our identity simply by changing our consumption patterns – picking and mixing cultural goods and media-produced images to define ourselves.

Baudrillard is pessimistic about the postmodern condition. Media-created hyper-reality leaves us unable to distinguish image from reality. This means that we have lost the power to improve society: if we cannot even grasp reality, then we have no power to change it. Political activity to improve the world is impossible, and so the central goal of the Enlightenment project is unachievable. It seems that, while we can change our identity by going shopping, we cannot change society.

Evaluation of postmodernism

Postmodernists make some important points about today's society, such as the significance of the media for culture and identity. Some also argue that its rejection of all-embracing meta-narratives is valuable. However, postmodernism is widely criticised.

Box 4.3	Poststructuralism: power, truth and discourse

Michel Foucault (1979) sees a discourse as a set of ideas that have become established as knowledge or a way of thinking and speaking about the world. When we use a discourse, it makes us see things in a particular way, and so it is not only a form of knowledge, but also a form of domination – Foucault describes discourse as *power/ knowledge*.

For example, today our view of madness is formed by the discourse of psychiatry, which describes it using terms such as 'schizophrenia'. By contrast, in the past, when religious discourse was dominant, madness was seen as 'possession by spirits'. Accepting psychiatric discourse constrains us to think of madness as an absence of rationality, while in the past it was often seen as a divine 'gift'.

Although psychiatric discourse has now largely displaced religious discourse, this does not make it truer. Discourses are simply different and we cannot judge between them: truth is relative – each discourse is true for those who believe it and false for those who don't. There is no objective way of judging between opposed claims to knowledge.

This kills off the Enlightenment project, which depends on the idea that we can achieve progress by discovering true knowledge and using it to improve the world. For Foucault, there can be no progress, since our knowledge is no truer than anyone else's. New knowledge is not progress, just a new form of domination.

From a Marxist perspective, Philo and Miller (2001) make several criticisms of postmodernism:

- It ignores power and inequality. For example, the idea that media images are unconnected with reality ignores the ruling class' use of the media as a tool of domination.
- Similarly, the claim that we freely construct our identities through consumption overlooks the effect of poverty in restricting such opportunities.
- Postmodernists are simply wrong to claim that people cannot distinguish between reality and media image.
- By assuming all views are equally true, it becomes just as valid to deny that the Nazis murdered millions as it does to affirm it. This is a morally indefensible position.

Postmodernism can be criticised on logical grounds. For example, Lyotard's theory is self-defeating: why should we believe a theory that claims that no theory has the truth? Moreover, Best and Kellner (1991) point out that postmodernism is a particularly weak theory: while it identifies some important features of today's society (such as the importance of the media and consumption), it fails to explain how they came about.

Postmodernists are criticised for their pessimism about the Enlightenment project – their view that objective knowledge is impossible and that nothing can be done to improve society. David Harvey (1989) rejects this pessimistic view. He argues that political decisions do make a real difference to people's lives and that knowledge *can* be used to solve human problems. Even if our theories cannot guarantee absolute truth, many sociologists argue that they are at least an approximation to it. As such, they are the best guide we have to improving the world.

While postmodernism has identified some important features of today's society, it is poorly equipped to explain them. By contrast, recent sociological theories have offered more satisfactory explanations of the changes society is undergoing. The remainder of this Topic looks at some of these sociological theories.

> Is Harvey correct in claiming that political decisions do make a real difference to people's lives? Identify three recent government decisions that could be said to have made a difference.

Theories of late modernity

Unlike postmodernism, theories of late modernity argue that the rapid changes we are witnessing are not the dawn of a new, postmodern era. On the contrary, these changes are actually a continuation of modernity itself.

However, theories of late modernity do recognise that something important is happening. In their view, key features of modernity that were always present have now become intensified. For example, social change has always been a feature of modern society, but now the pace of change has gone into overdrive. In other words, we are still within modernity, but we have entered its 'late' phase.

In this view, if we are still in the modern era, then the theories of modernist sociology are still useful. Unlike postmodernism, theories of late modernity do subscribe to the Enlightenment project – they still believe we can discover objective knowledge and use it to improve society.

Giddens: reflexivity

According to Giddens, we are now at the stage of late or *high modernity*. A defining characteristic of modern society is that it experiences rapid change – often on a global scale. This is because of two key features of modernity: disembedding and reflexivity.

Giddens defines *disembedding* as 'the lifting out of social relations from local contexts of interaction'. In other words, today we no longer need face-to-face contact in order to interact – disembedding breaks down geographical barriers and makes interaction more impersonal.

Giddens argues that in high modern society, tradition and custom become much less important and no longer serve as a guide to how we should act, and we become more individualistic. For example, sons are no longer expected to follow the same occupation as their fathers but are free to pursue their own individual goals instead.

Because tradition no longer tells us how to act, we are forced to become *reflexive*. That is, we have to constantly monitor, reflect on and modify our actions in the light of information about the possible risks and opportunities that they might involve.

Consequently, reflexivity means that we are all continually re-evaluating our ideas and theories – nothing is fixed or permanent, everything is up for challenge. Under these conditions, culture in late modern society becomes increasingly unstable and subject to change.

Together, disembedding and reflexivity account for the rapid and widespread nature of social change in high modernity. In particular, by enabling social interaction to spread rapidly across the globe, they help to drive the process of globalisation.

Modernity and risk

According to Giddens, in late modernity we face a number of *high consequence* risks – major threats to human society. These include military risks such as nuclear war, economic risks such as the instability of the capitalist economy, environmental risks such as global warming, and threats to our freedom from increased state surveillance. All of these are 'manufactured' or human-made rather than natural risks.

However, Giddens rejects the postmodernist view that we cannot intervene to improve things. He believes we can make rational plans to reduce these risks and achieve progress to a better society.

Beck: risk society

Like Giddens, Ulrich Beck (1992) is in the Enlightenment tradition. That is, he believes in the power of reason to create a better world. However, he believes that today's late modern society – which he calls 'risk society' – faces new kinds of dangers:

- In the past, society faced dangers as a result of its inability to control nature, such as drought, famine and disease.
- Today, the dangers we face are *manufactured risks* resulting from human activities, such as global warming and pollution.

Also like Giddens, Beck sees late modernity as a period of growing *individualisation*, in which we become increasingly reflexive. Tradition no longer governs how we act. As a result, we have to think for ourselves and reflect on the possible consequences of our choice of action. This means we must constantly take account of the risks attached to the different courses of action open to us. Beck calls this *reflexive modernisation*.

As a result, 'risk consciousness' becomes increasingly central to our culture – we become more aware of perceived risks and seek to avoid or minimise them. For example, we read of the dangers or benefits of this or that food and change our eating habits accordingly. However, a great deal of our knowledge about risks comes from the mass media, which often give a distorted view of the dangers we face.

Activity

In a period of growing individualism, there is less certainty in terms of expectations about personal relationships and family life. In small groups, collect some examples of problem pages from different magazines and newspapers. What aspects of 'risk society' do the letters reveal?

Risk, politics and progress

Postmodernists such as Baudrillard reject the Enlightenment project, with its belief in the possibility of progress through action based on rational knowledge. Beck disagrees with this position. Although he is sceptical about scientific progress because of the risks it has brought, he still believes in our ability to use rationality to overcome them. Because we are capable of reflexivity, we can evaluate risks rationally and take political action to reduce them. For example, Beck looks to new political movements such as environmentalism to challenge the direction of technological and industrial development.

Evaluation of theories of late modernity

The concept of reflexivity suggests that we reflect on our actions and then are free to re-shape our lives accordingly to reduce our exposure to risks. However, not everyone has this option. For example, the poor are generally exposed to more environmental risks because they are more likely to live in heavily polluted areas, but may be unable to afford to move to a healthier one.

Criticising Beck, Mike Rustin (1994) argues that it is capitalism, with its pursuit of profit at all costs, that is the source of risk, not technology as such.

Paul Hirst (1993) rejects Beck's view that movements such as environmentalism will bring about significant change, because they are too fragmented to challenge capitalism.

However, theories of late modernity do provide a sociological alternative to postmodernism. They show that rational analysis of society remains possible. They also recognise that, while our knowledge may never be perfect, we can still use it to improve society and reduce the risks we face.

Marxist theories of postmodernity

Like Beck and Giddens, Marxists believe in the Enlightenment project of achieving objective knowledge and using it to improve society. For example, Marx claimed that his theory showed how a working-class revolution could overthrow capitalism and bring an end to exploitation.

However, unlike Beck and Giddens, some Marxists such as Fredric Jameson (1984) and David Harvey (1989) believe that today's society has indeed moved from modernity to postmodernity. They agree with postmodernists that there have been major changes in society, and they describe postmodern culture in similar terms, emphasising the importance of media images, diversity and instability.

However, Marxists offer a very different analysis of postmodernity to Lyotard or Baudrillard. Rather than seeing postmodernity as a fundamental break with the past, Marxists regard it as merely the product of the most recent stage of capitalism. To understand postmodernity, therefore, we must examine its relationship to capitalism.

For Harvey, capitalism is a dynamic system, constantly developing new technologies and ways of organising production to make profits. However, capitalism is prone to periodic crises of profitability, and these produce major changes. Postmodernity arose out of the capitalist crisis of the 1970s, which saw the end of the long economic boom that had lasted since 1945.

Flexible accumulation

This crisis gave rise to a new *regime of accumulation* – a new way of achieving profitability, which Harvey describes as 'flexible accumulation' or post-Fordism. This replaced the more rigid pre-1970s Fordist mass production system.

Flexible accumulation involves the use of ICT, an expanded service and finance sector, job insecurity and the requirement for workers to be 'flexible' to fit their employers' needs. It permits the production of customised products for small, 'niche' markets instead of standardised products for mass markets, and easy switching from producing one product to producing another.

These changes brought many of the cultural characteristics of postmodernity, such as diversity, choice and instability. For example:

- Production of customised products for niche markets promotes cultural diversity.
- Easy switching of production from one product to another encourages constant shifts in fashion.

Flexible accumulation also brought changes in consumption. It turned leisure, culture and identity into commodities. Cultural products such as fashion, music, sports and computer games have become an important source of profit. As Jameson argues, postmodernity represents a more developed form of capitalism because it commodifies virtually all aspects of life, including our identities.

Harvey argues that this more developed form of capitalism also leads to another feature of postmodernity – the *compression of time and space*. The commodification of culture (for example, foreign holidays), the creation of worldwide financial markets, and new information and communications technologies, all serve to shrink the globe.

Politics and progress

Harvey and Jameson argue that flexible accumulation has also brought *political changes* characteristic of postmodernity. In particular, it has weakened the working-class and socialist movements. In their place, a variety of oppositional movements have emerged, such as environmentalism, women's liberation, anti-racism and so on. However, Harvey and Jameson are hopeful that these new social movements can form a 'rainbow alliance' to bring about change.

Thus, Marxist theorists of postmodernity agree with postmodernists that we have moved from modernity to postmodernity. However, as Best and Kellner note, they differ from postmodernists in two ways:

- They retain a faith in Marxist theory as a means of explaining these changes.
- They argue that the goal of the Enlightenment project – to change society for the better – can still be achieved.

Evaluation

Marx 's original view of the Enlightenment project was that it would be achieved by the working class leading a revolution to overthrow capitalism and create a better society. By contrast, by accepting that political opposition to capitalism has fragmented into many different social movements such as feminism and environmentalism, Marxist theories of postmodernity appear to abandon this possibility.

However, the strength of these theories is that by relating the recent changes in society to the nature of capitalism, they are able to offer a sociological explanation of them – something that postmodernists fail to do.

For more activities on Globalisation, modernity and postmodernity…

Go to www.sociology.uk.net

Summary

The nation-state is the focal point of modern society, but with globalisation this is undermined. Technological, economic, political and cultural changes are creating a 'global village'. Postmodernists argue that these changes indicate the arrival of postmodern society. This society is unstable, fragmented and media-saturated. Postmodernists reject the possibility of progress and meta-narratives such as Marxism that claim to have the truth about how to achieve it. By contrast, Giddens and Beck argue that rapid change is a characteristic of late modern rather than postmodern society. Although this is increasingly a 'risk society', they believe progress to a better society is still possible. Marxist theories of modernity argue that postmodernity is simply the latest phase of capitalism and a new means of achieving profits.

QuickCheck Questions

1 Identify three features of modern society.

2 Suggest two factors that may be giving rise to a global culture.

3 What does Foucault mean by the term 'discourse'?

4 What do postmodernists mean by the term 'meta-narrative'?

5 What criticisms do postmodernists make of meta-narratives?

6 What are 'simulacra'?

7 What does Giddens mean by 'reflexivity'?

8 What does Beck mean by 'risk society'?

9 Suggest two criticisms of postmodernism.

10 Suggest two ways in which Marxists see flexible accumulation as promting a postmodern culture.

Check your answers at www.sociology.uk.net

Examining globalisation, modernity and postmodernity

'Society has now entered a new, postmodern age and we need new theories to understand it.' Assess this view.　　(33 marks)

The examiner's advice

This question carries 15 AO1 marks (knowledge and understanding) and 18 AO2 marks (interpretation, application, analysis and evaluation). You need to deal with both aspects of this question – first, the claim that we are living in postmodernity, and second, that this calls for new (postmodernist or late modernist) theories. Begin by outlining what has changed about society, focusing on globalisation and its social, economic, technological etc causes, and on changes such as the increased importance of the media.

You need to assess theories that try to understand these changes. Begin with postmodernist criticisms of modernist theories and concepts such as diversity, instability, relativism, simulacra, hyper-reality etc. You should also examine late modernist theories (e.g. Giddens and Beck) and Marxist theories of postmodernity. Focus on the idea that they see today's society as a development of modern capitalist society, not a break with it, and that we can use our knowledge to change it for the better.

We can use scientific methods to study rocks, plants and animals – but can we use the same methods to study people?

Topic 6 Sociology and science

Science is a central feature of today's society. Science and technology have revolutionised practically every aspect of life, from living standards and healthcare to communications and warfare.

As we saw in the Introduction to this chapter, science was central to the 18th century Enlightenment project. Enlightenment thinkers were deeply impressed by the success of science in explaining and controlling nature. They believed that the natural sciences – such as physics, chemistry and biology – would produce true, objective knowledge of the world around us, and that this would be used for progress and human betterment, for example by eradicating disease and hunger. Science would be the cornerstone of modern society.

The success of science also made a powerful impression on the 19th century modernist sociologists such as Comte, Durkheim and Marx. They sought to copy its success by producing a science of society. Just as the natural sciences enabled us to control nature, sociology would bring true knowledge of society that could be used to eradicate problems such as poverty, injustice and conflict. It seemed that sociologists simply needed to borrow the methods of the natural sciences, and success would be sure to follow.

Since then, however, others have argued that it is not possible or desirable for sociology to model itself on the natural sciences. In this Topic, we examine two related debates:

- Can and should sociology be a science?
- What is science, and what implications does this have for sociology?

Learning objectives

After studying this Topic, you should:

- Know the difference between positivist and interpretivist views of whether sociology can be a science and be able to apply this to the issue of suicide.
- Know a range of views on natural science and their implications for sociology as a science.
- Be able to evaluate the arguments for and against the view that sociology can or should be a science.

Positivism

The 'founding fathers' of sociology in the 19th century were very impressed by the success of science in explaining the natural world and providing the knowledge with which humans could extend their control over nature. Many of these sociologists, such as Auguste Comte (1798-1857) who coined the term 'sociology', described themselves as 'positivists'.

Positivists believe that it is possible and desirable to apply the logic and methods of the natural sciences to the study of society. Doing so will bring us true, objective knowledge of the same type as that found in the natural sciences. This will provide the basis for solving social problems and achieving progress.

A key feature of the positivist approach is the belief that reality exists outside and independently of the human mind:

- Nature is made up of objective, observable, physical facts, such as rocks, cells, stars etc, which are external to our minds and which exist whether we like it or not.
- Similarly, society is an objective factual reality – it is a real 'thing' made up of social facts that exists 'out there', independently of individuals, just like the physical world.

Patterns, laws and inductive reasoning

For positivists, reality is not random or chaotic but patterned, and we can observe these empirical (factual) patterns or regularities – for example, that water boils at 100 degrees Celsius. It is the job of science to observe, identify, measure and record these patterns systematically – preferably through laboratory experiments – and then to explain them.

Positivists believe, in Durkheim's words, that 'real laws are discoverable' that will explain these patterns. Just as physicists have discovered laws that govern the workings of nature, such as the law of gravity, sociologists can discover laws that determine how society works. The method for doing so is known as *induction*, or inductive reasoning.

Induction involves accumulating data about the world through careful observation and measurement. As our knowledge grows, we begin to see general patterns. For example, we may observe that objects, when dropped, always fall towards the earth at the same rate of acceleration.

Verificationism

From this, we can develop a *theory* that explains all our observations so far. After many more observations have confirmed or verified the theory, we can claim to have discovered the truth in the form of a general *law*. In our example above, we can confirm the existence of a universal law of gravity. Because inductive reasoning claims to verify a theory – that is, prove it true – this approach is also known as *verificationism*.

For positivists, the patterns we observe, whether in nature or in society, can all be explained in the same way – by finding the facts that cause them. For example, physics explains an apple falling to the ground (one fact) in terms of gravity (another fact). Similarly, in sociology we might explain the social fact of educational failure in terms of another social fact such as material deprivation.

Positivist sociologists thus seek to discover the causes of the patterns they observe. Like natural scientists, they aim to produce general statements or scientific laws about how society works. These can then be used to predict future events and to guide social policies. For example, if we know that material deprivation causes educational failure, we can use this knowledge to develop policies to tackle it.

Positivists favour 'macro' or structural explanations of social phenomena, such as functionalism and Marxism. This is because macro theories see society and its structures as social facts that exist outside of us and shape our behaviour patterns.

Objective quantitative research

Positivists believe that as far as possible sociology should take the experimental method used in the natural sciences as the model for research, since this allows the investigator to test a hypothesis in the most systematic and controlled way. (A hypothesis is a statement such as 'A causes B'.) Basically, experiments involve examining each possible causal factor to observe its effect, while simultaneously excluding all other factors.

Like natural scientists, positivists use quantitative data to uncover and measure patterns of behaviour. This allows them to produce mathematically precise statements about the relationship between the facts they are investigating. By analysing quantitative data, positivists seek to discover the laws of cause and effect that determine behaviour.

Positivists believe that researchers should be detached and objective. They should not let their own subjective feelings, values or prejudices influence how they conduct their research or analyse their findings. In the natural sciences, it is claimed that the scientist's values and opinions make no difference to the outcome of their research. For example, water boils at 100 degrees Celsius whether the scientist likes that fact or not.

However, in sociology we are dealing with people, and there is a danger that the researcher may 'contaminate' the research – for example, by influencing interviewees to answer in ways that reflect the researcher's opinions rather than their own. Positivists therefore employ methods that allow for maximum objectivity and detachment, and so they use quantitative methods such as experiments, questionnaires, structured interviews, structured non-participant observation and official statistics. These methods also produce reliable data that can be checked by other researchers repeating the research.

1 How might scientists test for the effect of light on plants? What variables (factors) would they need to control?

2 Compare this with the task of measuring the effect of material deprivation on educational achievement. What variables would be difficult to control?

An example: positivism and suicide

Emile Durkheim (1897) chose to study suicide to demonstrate that sociology was a science with its own distinct subject matter. He believed that if he could show that even such a highly individual act had social causes, this would establish sociology's status as a distinct and genuinely scientific discipline.

Using quantitative data from official statistics, Durkheim observed that there were patterns in the suicide rate. For example, rates for Protestants were higher than for Catholics. He concluded that these patterns could not be the product of the motives of individuals, but were social facts. As such, they must be caused by other social facts – forces acting upon members of society to determine their behaviour.

According to Durkheim, the social facts responsible for determining the suicide rate were the levels of integration and regulation. Thus, for example, Catholics were less likely than Protestants to commit suicide because Catholicism was more successful in integrating individuals.

Thus Durkheim claimed to have discovered a 'real law': that different levels of integration and regulation produce different rates of suicide. He claimed to have demonstrated that sociology had its own unique subject matter – social facts – and that these could be explained scientifically. (For more about Durkheim's views on suicide, see Chapter 2, Topic 10).

▲ Japanese kamikaze suicide pilots, 1945. Their 'sacred mission' was to crash their planes into American warships.

Interpretivism

Interpretivist sociologists do not believe that sociology should model itself on the natural sciences. Interpretivism includes the action theories we examined in Topic 4, such as interactionism and ethnomethodology. Interpretivists criticise positivism's 'scientific' approach as inadequate or even as completely unsuited to the study of human beings.

The subject matter of sociology

Interpretivists argue that the subject matter of sociology is meaningful social action, and that we can only understand it by successfully interpreting the meanings and motives of the actors involved. Interpretivists say sociology is about internal meanings, not external causes. In their view, sociology is not a science, because science only deals with laws of cause and effect, and not human meanings.

Because of this, many interpretivists completely reject the use of natural science methods and explanations as a model for sociology. They argue that there is a fundamental difference between the subject matter of the natural sciences and that of sociology.

- **Natural science** studies matter, which has no consciousness. As such, its behaviour can be explained as a straightforward reaction to an external stimulus. For example, an apple falls to the ground because of the force of gravity. It has no consciousness, and no choice about its behaviour.
- **Sociology** studies people, who do have consciousness. People make sense of and construct their world by attaching meanings to it. Their actions can only be understood in terms of these meanings, and meanings are internal to people's consciousness, not external stimuli – they are ideas or constructs, not things.

Unlike matter, people have free will and can exercise choice. As G.H. Mead argued, rather than responding automatically to external stimuli, human beings interpret the meaning of a stimulus and then choose how to respond to it.

For example, on seeing a red light, a motorist must first interpret it as meaning 'stop'. Even then, this does not determine their behaviour, since they could still choose either to obey the signal or jump the light. How they act will depend on the meaning they give to the situation – for example, escaping a pursuing police car, avoiding a collision etc.

Thus, when motorists stop at a red light, it is not because there is some force outside them determining their behaviour. It is because they understand and interpret the social rule concerning the meaning of red traffic lights,

and because they then choose to act in accordance with the rule.

For interpretivists, then, individuals are not puppets on a string, manipulated by supposed external 'social facts', as positivists believe, but autonomous (independent) beings who construct their social world through the meanings they give to it. The job of the sociologist therefore is to uncover these meanings.

Verstehen and qualitative research

Interpretivists therefore reject the logic and methods of the natural sciences. They argue that to discover the meanings people give to their actions, we need to see the world from their viewpoint. For interpretivists, this involves abandoning the detachment and objectivity favoured by positivists. Instead, we must put ourselves in the place of the actor, using what Weber calls *verstehen* or empathetic understanding to grasp their meanings.

For this reason, interpretivists favour the use of qualitative methods and data such as participant observation, unstructured interviews and personal documents. These methods produce richer, more personal data high in validity and give the sociologist a subjective understanding of the actor's meanings and life-world.

Types of interpretivism

All interpretivists seek to understand actors' meanings. However, they are divided about whether or not we can combine this understanding with positivist-style causal explanation of human behaviour.

Interactionists believe that we can have causal explanations. However, they reject the positivist view that we should have a definite hypothesis before we start our research. For example, Barney Glaser and Anselm Strauss (1968) argue that this risks imposing our own view of what is important, rather than the actors', so we end up distorting the reality we are seeking to capture.

Instead, Glaser and Strauss favour a 'bottom-up' approach, or *grounded theory*. Rather than entering the research with a fixed hypothesis from the start (when we know little about the topic we are researching), our ideas emerge gradually from the observations we make during the course of the research itself. These ideas can then be used at a later stage to produce testable hypotheses of the sort favoured by positivists.

Phenomenologists and ethnomethodologists such as Garfinkel completely reject the possibility of causal explanations of human behaviour. They take a radically

Activity

1. In pairs, consider again the 'traffic lights' example and the following situations where actions may seem 'automatic'. Explain what is happening in terms of meanings and how our interpretation may affect our actions.

   (a) The doorbell rings. How does our interpretation of the situation affect whether and how we answer?

   (b) As people enter a place of worship, how and why do they change the way they talk to each other?

2. Suggest two situations relating to crime and deviance where different interpretations by the actors involved may lead to different outcomes.

3. In light of your answers, why do some sociologists argue that meanings are always potentially unstable and ambiguous?

anti-structuralist view, arguing that society is not a real thing 'out there' determining our actions. In this view, social reality is simply the shared meanings or knowledge of its members. As such, society is not an external force – it exists only in people's consciousness.

Therefore, in this view, the subject matter of sociology can only consist of the interpretive procedures by which people make sense of the world. Because people's actions are not governed by external causes, there is no possibility of cause-and-effect explanations of the kind sought by positivists.

An example: interpretivism and suicide

The interactionist Jack Douglas (1967) rejects the positivist idea of external social facts determining our behaviour. Individuals have free will and they choose how to act on the basis of meanings. To understand suicide, therefore, we must uncover its meanings for those involved, instead of imposing our own meanings – such as Durkheim's four 'types' of suicide – onto the situation.

Douglas also rejects Durkheim's use of quantitative data from official statistics. These are not objective facts, but simply social constructions resulting from the way coroners label certain deaths as suicides. Instead, Douglas proposes we use qualitative data from case studies of suicides, since he believes these can reveal the actors' meanings and give us a better idea of the real rate of suicide than the official statistics.

Like Douglas, the ethnomethodologist J. Maxwell Atkinson (1978) rejects the idea that external social facts determine behaviour, and agrees that statistics are socially constructed.

Unlike Douglas, however, Atkinson argues that we can never know the 'real rate' of suicide, even using qualitative methods, since we can never know for sure what meanings the deceased held.

For Atkinson, the only thing we can study about suicide is the way that the living make sense of deaths – the interpretive procedures coroners use to classify deaths. For ethnomethodologists, members of society have a stock of taken-for-granted assumptions with which they make sense of situations – including deaths. The sociologist's role is to uncover what this knowledge is and how coroners use it to arrive at a verdict. (For more about interpretivist views of suicide, see Chapter 2, Topic 10.)

Postmodernism, feminism and scientific sociology

Postmodernists also argue against the idea of a scientific sociology. This is because they regard natural science as simply a *meta-narrative*. Despite its claim to have special access to the truth, science is just one more 'big story'; its account of the world is no more valid than any other. If this is so, there is no particular reason why we should adopt science as a model for sociology.

In fact, given the postmodernist view that there are as many different truths as there are points of view, a scientific approach is dangerous because it claims a monopoly of the truth and therefore excludes other points of view. Hence a scientific sociology not only makes false claims about having the truth; it is also a form of domination. For example, in the former Soviet Union, Marxism – a theory claiming to have discovered scientifically the truth about the ideal society – was used to justify coercion and oppression.

Some feminists, notably poststructuralist feminists, share this view of scientific sociology. They argue that the quest for a single, scientific feminist theory is a form of domination, since it covertly excludes many groups of women. Some other feminists argue that the quantitative scientific methods favoured by positivists are also oppressive and cannot capture the reality of women's experiences.

Some writers also argue that science is an undesirable model for sociology to follow because, in practice, science has not always led to the progress that positivists believed it would. For example, the emergence of 'risk society', with scientifically created dangers such as nuclear weapons and global warming, has undermined the idea that science inevitably brings benefits to humankind. If science produces such negative consequences, it is argued, it would be inappropriate for sociology to adopt it as a model.

What is science?

Although interpretivists reject the positivist view that sociology is a science, they tend to agree with positivists that the natural sciences are actually as the positivists describe them. As we have seen above, positivists see natural science as inductive reasoning or verificationism applied to the study of observable patterns.

However, not everyone accepts the positivists' portrayal of the natural sciences. A number of sociologists, philosophers and historians have put forward quite different pictures of science. We now examine three of these views, and we consider what implications each one has for whether sociology can or should be a science.

Karl Popper: how science grows

Sir Karl Popper (1902-94) was probably the most influential philosopher of science of the 20th century. His ideas about science have important implications for sociology.

Popper notes that many systems of thought claim to have true knowledge about the world, such as religions, political ideologies, tradition, intuition and common sense, as well as science. Given this, Popper sets out to answer two related questions about science:

1 What is it that distinguishes scientific knowledge from other forms of knowledge – what makes scientific knowledge unique?
2 Why has scientific knowledge been able to grow so spectacularly in just a few centuries?

The fallacy of induction

Popper differs from the positivists in that he rejects their view that the distinctive feature of science lies in inductive reasoning and verificationism. In Popper's view, the main reason why we should reject verificationism is what he calls 'the fallacy [error] of induction'. As we have seen, induction is the process of moving from the observation of particular instances of something to arrive at a general statement or law.

To illustrate the fallacy of induction, Popper uses the example of swans. Having observed a large number of swans, all of which were white, we might make the generalisation, 'All swans are white'. It will be relatively easy for us to make further observations that seem to verify this – there are plenty more white swans out there. But however many swans we observe, we cannot *prove* that all swans are white – a single observation of a black swan will destroy the theory. Thus, we can never prove a theory is true simply by producing more observations that support or 'verify' it.

Falsificationism

In Popper's view, what makes science a unique form of knowledge is the very opposite of verificationism – a principle he calls falsificationism. A scientific statement is one that in principle is capable of being falsified – proved wrong – by the evidence. That is, we must be able to say what evidence would count as falsifying the statement when we come to put it to the test. For example, a test would disprove the law of gravity if, when we let go of an object, it did not fall.

For Popper, a good theory has two features:

■ It is in principle falsifiable but when tested, stands up to all attempts to disprove it.

■ It is bold – that is, it claims to explain a great deal. It makes big generalisations that precisely predict a large number of cases or events, and so is at greater risk of being falsified than a more timid theory that only tries to explain a small number of events.

1 Explain what Popper means by the 'fallacy of induction'.
2 In Popper's view, what are the features of a good theory?

Truth

For Popper (1965), 'all knowledge is provisional, temporary, capable of refutation at any moment' – there can never be absolute proof that any knowledge is true. This is because, as the renowned physicist Stephen Hawking (1988) puts it:

'No matter how many times the results of experiments agree with some theory, you can never be sure that the next time the result will not contradict the theory.'

A good theory isn't necessarily a true theory, therefore – it is simply one that has withstood attempts to falsify it *so far*.

Criticism and the open society

For a theory to be falsifiable, it must be open to criticism from other scientists. In Popper's view, therefore, science is essentially a *public* activity. He sees the scientific community as a hothouse environment in which everything is open to criticism, so that the flaws in a theory can be readily exposed and better theories developed. Popper believes that this explains why scientific knowledge grows so rapidly.

Popper argues that science thrives in 'open' or liberal societies – ones that believe in free expression and the right to challenge accepted ideas. By contrast, 'closed' societies are dominated by an official belief system that claims to have the absolute truth – whether a religion, or a political ideology such as Marxism or Nazism. Such belief systems stifle the growth of science because they conflict with the provisional, falsifiable nature of scientific knowledge. For example, the 17th century astronomer Galileo was punished as a heretic by the church authorities in Rome for claiming that the earth revolved around the sun and not vice versa, as the church taught. We can see Rome at this time as a closed society, dominated by the church's doctrines.

Implications for sociology

Popper believes that much sociology is unscientific because it consists of theories that cannot be put to the test with the possibility that they might be falsified. For example, Marxism predicts that there will be a revolution leading to a classless society, but that it has not yet happened because of the false consciousness of the proletariat. Hence the prediction cannot be falsified. If there is a revolution, Marxism is correct – and if there isn't a revolution, Marxism is *still* correct.

However, Popper believes that sociology can be scientific, because it is capable of producing hypotheses that can in principle be falsified. For example, Julienne Ford (1969) hypothesised that comprehensive schooling would produce social mixing of pupils from different social classes. She was able to test and falsify this hypothesis through her empirical research.

Although Popper rejects Marxism as unscientific because it is untestable, he does not believe that untestable ideas are necessarily worthless. Such ideas may be of value, firstly because they may become testable at some later date, and secondly because we can still examine them for clarity and logical consistency. For example, debates between different sociological perspectives can clarify woolly thinking, question taken-for-granted assumptions and help to formulate testable hypotheses. While sociology may have a larger quantity of untestable ideas than the natural sciences, this may simply be because it has not been in existence as long as they have.

Thomas Kuhn: scientific paradigms

Thomas S. Kuhn (1970) is a historian of science who presents a radically different view of what makes science unique. Like Popper's ideas, those of Kuhn also have important implications for sociology.

The paradigm

Kuhn's central idea is the paradigm. A paradigm is shared by members of a given scientific community (such as physicists) and defines what their science is. It provides a basic framework of assumptions, principles, methods and techniques within which members of that community work. It is a worldview that tells scientists what nature is like, which aspects of it are worth studying, what methods should be used, what kinds of questions they should ask and even the sort of answers they should expect to find.

The paradigm is thus a set of norms, or a kind of culture, because it tells scientists how they ought to think and behave. Scientists come to accept the paradigm uncritically as a result of their socialisation. For example, unlike sociology students, those in the natural sciences are not invited to consider rival perspectives. Scientists' conformity to the paradigm is rewarded with publication of their research and career success, while non-conformity may mean their work goes unpublished, or may even lead to dismissal (see Chapter 1, Topic 7 on the Velikovsky affair).

In Kuhn's view, a science cannot exist without a shared paradigm. Until there is general consensus on a single paradigm, there will only be rival schools of thought, not a science as such.

Normal science

For most of the time, the paradigm goes unquestioned and scientists do what Kuhn calls *normal science*. In normal science, scientists engage in puzzle solving. That is, the paradigm defines the questions and in broad terms, the answers. Scientists are left to fill in the detail or work out the 'neatest' solution.

This is rather like completing a jigsaw puzzle: we know from the picture on the box what the solution should be – our job is simply to figure out how to put the pieces together to get the right result. We are not discovering or creating anything new. As Kuhn says:

> *'Everything but the detail is known in advance. The challenge is not to uncover the unknown, but to obtain the known.'*

For Kuhn, the great advantage of the paradigm is that it allows scientists to agree on the basics of their subject and get on with productive 'puzzle-solving' work, steadily fleshing out the bare bones of the paradigm with more and more detail, thereby enlarging their picture of nature. This contrasts sharply with Popper's view of science. As John Watkins (1970) says, while Popper sees falsification as the unique feature of science, for Kuhn it is puzzle solving within a paradigm that makes science special.

Scientific revolutions

However, not all puzzle solving is successful. From time to time, scientists obtain findings contrary to those the paradigm led them to expect – pieces that don't fit the jigsaw puzzle. As these *anomalies* gradually mount up, confidence in the paradigm begins to decline, and this leads to arguments about basic assumptions and to efforts to reformulate the paradigm so as to account for the anomalies.

The science has now entered a period of *crisis*. Its previously taken-for-granted foundations are now in question; scientists become demoralised and begin to lose their sense of purpose. As Albert Einstein wrote about the crisis in physics in the early 20th century:

> *'It was as if the ground had been pulled out from under one, with no firm foundation to be seen anywhere upon which one could have built.'*

Scientists begin to formulate rival paradigms and this marks the start of a *scientific revolution*. For Kuhn, rival paradigms are *incommensurable* – two competing paradigms cannot be judged or measured by the same set of standards to decide which one is 'best'. What supporters of one paradigm regard as a decisive refutation of the other, supporters of the rival paradigm will not even recognise as a valid test, because each paradigm is a totally different way of seeing the world. To move from one to the other requires a massive shift of mind-set.

▲ *There are two faces here. Can you see both at once? Can you switch between them? Similarly, two paradigms look at the same universe, but they are so incommensurable they seem to be looking at two different ones. Many scientists find it impossible to switch from an old paradigm to a new one.*

Eventually, one paradigm does win out and becomes accepted by the scientific community, allowing normal science to resume, but with a new set of basic assumptions, puzzles and so on. However, the process is not a rational one – in fact, Kuhn compares it with a religious conversion. Generally, the new paradigm gains support first of all from

1 What do you understand by the term 'revolution'?
2 What similarities can you see between a scientific revolution and a political revolution?

younger scientists, partly because they have less to lose than senior colleagues whose reputations have been built on the old one. In fact, as the physicist Max Planck said, the new theory triumphs 'because its opponents eventually die'.

Kuhn's view of the scientific community contrasts sharply with that of Popper. For Popper the scientific community is open, critical and rational, constantly seeking to falsify existing theories by producing evidence against them. Progress occurs by *challenging* accepted ideas.

For Kuhn, by contrast, the scientific community is not normally characterised by its openness, originality or critical spirit. For most of the time, during periods of normal science, scientists are conformists who unquestioningly *accept* the key ideas of the paradigm as a basis for making progress. Only during a scientific revolution does this change. Even then, scientists have no *rational* means of choosing one paradigm rather than another.

Implications for sociology

Currently sociology is pre-paradigmatic and therefore pre-scientific, divided into competing perspectives or schools of thought. There is no shared paradigm – no agreement on the fundamentals of what to study, how to study it, what we should expect to find and so on. For example, functionalists disagree with Marxists about basic questions such as whether society is based on consensus or on conflict.

On Kuhn's definition, sociology could only become a science if such basic disagreements were resolved. Whether this is even *possible* is open to doubt. For example, so long as there are political differences between conservative and radical sociologists, rival perspectives will probably continue to exist in sociology. Even *within* perspectives, there are often disagreements about key concepts, issues and methods. It is hard to imagine such differences being overcome to create a unified paradigm.

Postmodernists might argue that a paradigm would also not be *desirable* in sociology. The paradigm sounds suspiciously like a meta-narrative – a dominant and dominating view of what reality is like. As we saw in Topic 5, postmodernists object to this both on the grounds that it silences minority views, and that it falsely claims to have special access to the truth.

Realism, science and sociology

A third view of science comes from the approach known as realism. Realists such as Russell Keat and John Urry (1982) stress the similarities between sociology and certain kinds of natural science in terms of the degree of control the researcher has over the variables being researched. They distinguish between *open systems* and *closed systems*.

Closed systems are those where the researcher can control and measure all the relevant variables, and therefore can make precise predictions of the sort Popper advocates. The typical research method is the laboratory experiment, as used in sciences such as physics or chemistry.

Open systems are those where the researcher cannot control and measure all the relevant variables and so cannot make precise predictions. For example, a meteorologist cannot normally predict the weather with 100% accuracy. This is because the processes involved are too complex to measure or too large-scale to be studied in a laboratory.

Realists argue that sociologists study open systems where the processes are too complex to make exact predictions. For example, we cannot predict the crime rate precisely, because there are too many variables involved, most of which cannot be controlled, measured or identified.

▲ The 'butterfly effect' refers to the idea that even a variable as small as the flapping of a butterfly's wing in say, Brazil, could create minute atmospheric changes that might ultimately contribute to a tornado in Texas. The atmosphere is an open system where countless uncontrollable variables interact in complex ways to affect weather patterns.

Activity

In groups of two or three, make a list of all the possible variables that might affect (a) the crime rate and (b) the divorce rate. Which of these variables would be easy to measure and which would be difficult?

Underlying structures

Realists reject the positivist view that science is only concerned with observable phenomena. Keat and Urry argue that science often assumes the existence of unobservable structures – e.g. physicists cannot directly observe the interior of a black hole in space.

In the realist view, this also means that interpretivists are wrong in assuming that sociology cannot be scientific. Interpretivists believe that because actors' meanings are in their minds and not directly observable, they cannot be studied scientifically. However, if realists are correct and science can study unobservable phenomena, then this is no barrier to studying meanings scientifically.

For realists, then, both natural and social science attempt to explain the causes of events in terms of underlying structures and processes. Although these structures are often unobservable, we can work out that they exist by observing their effects. For example, we cannot directly see a thing called 'social class', but we can observe its effects on people's life chances.

In this view, much sociology is scientific. For example, unlike Popper, realists regard Marxism as scientific because it sees underlying structures such as capitalism producing effects such as poverty. Similarly, sociologists can also be scientific when they interpret behaviour in terms of actors' internal meanings – even though they are unobservable.

Unlike interpretivists, therefore, realists see little difference between natural science and sociology, except that some natural scientists are able to study closed systems under laboratory conditions.

Conclusion

Sociologists are divided as to whether sociology can be a science. While positivists favour adopting the natural sciences as a model, interpretivists reject the view that sociology can be scientific. This division derives largely from disagreement about the nature of sociology and its subject matter:

- **Positivists** see sociology as the study of causes: the social facts or structures external to individuals that cause them to behave as they do. In the positivists' view, this is the same approach as the natural sciences – to discover the cause of the patterns they observe, whether in nature or society.

- **Interpretivists** see sociology as the study of meaningful social action: the internal meanings that lead actors to choose their course of action. Human actions are not governed by external causes, unlike events in nature, so they cannot be studied in the same way as natural phenomena.

However, while positivists and interpretivists disagree about whether sociology can be a science, they both accept the positivist model of the natural sciences as described above. Basically, the positivist view sees natural science as inductive reasoning or verificationism applied to the study of observable patterns.

Yet as we have seen, since the positivist view of science was formulated in the 19th century, quite different pictures of science have emerged, and these have very different implications for the question of whether sociology can or should be scientific. For example:

- **Popper** rejects verificationism in favour of falsificationism as the defining feature of science and argues that on this definition much sociology is unscientific, but that a scientific sociology is possible in principle.
- **Kuhn** argues that sociology can only become a science once all sociologists adopt a single shared paradigm.

Summary

Positivists argue that sociology can be a science by modelling itself on the natural sciences, using quantitative methods and induction or verificationism to establish observable patterns in behaviour and develop causal laws. Interpretivists argue that sociology cannot be scientific, because human conduct is not governed by external causes but by internal meanings. The task of sociology is to use qualitative methods to uncover these meanings through verstehen. Others argue that natural science differs from what positivists and interpretivists imagine it to be. Popper argues that science is based on falsificationism, not verificationism. Kuhn argues that a shared paradigm is the hallmark of a science, while realists argue that science studies unobservable structures as well as observable facts. Each of these views has implications for whether or not we regard sociology as a science.

- **Realists** argue that science does not only deal in observable phenomena, as positivists argue, but in underlying unobservable structures. On this basis, both Marxism and interpretivism may be seen as scientific.

For more activities on Sociology and science…

Go to www.sociology.uk.net

QuickCheck Questions

1   What does Durkheim mean by 'social facts'?

2   Why do positivists favour 'macro' or structural explanations of behaviour?

3   According to interpretivists, what is the subject matter of sociology?

4   What is meant by verstehen and why do interpretivists favour its use?

5   Explain the difference between verificationism and falsificationism.

6   What does Kuhn mean by a 'paradigm'?

7   Explain what Kuhn means when he says that in normal science, scientists engage in puzzle solving.

8   According to realists, what is the difference between open and closed systems?

Check your answers at www.sociology.uk.net

Examining sociology and science

Assess the view that sociology can and should model itself on the natural sciences.   (33 marks)

The examiner's advice

This question carries 15 AO1 marks (knowledge and understanding) and 18 AO2 marks (interpretation, application, analysis and evaluation). Start with the positivist view that sociology can adopt the logic and methods of the natural sciences as the best way to gain true knowledge of society. Use Durkheim's study of suicide as an example, but avoid describing his findings and focus on quantitative data, social facts, objectivity and detachment. Evaluate the positivist view from an interpretivist perspective. Focus here on ideas such as sociology as the study of meaningful social action, verstehen and choice.

Much of the answer to the question depends on how we see the natural sciences. You should therefore examine different views of science, including Popper, Kuhn and the realists. In each case, you need to use their key concepts (e.g. falsificationism, paradigms, open and closed systems) and then explain what implications their view has for whether sociology can be regarded as scientific.

Should scientists be morally responsible for how their research is used?

Topic 7 Objectivity and values in sociology

As we saw in Topic 6, one view of science is that it produces true knowledge. According to this view, scientists take a detached and objective approach to their research. They don't allow their subjective values to get in the way of discovering the facts.

Every member of society has values – beliefs, opinions and prejudices about right or wrong, good and bad. Our values are influenced by many factors, including our class, gender, ethnicity, upbringing and experiences.

Given that sociologists are also members of society, can they study it objectively and without bias, unaffected by their own personal values? Can sociologists' research be 'value free' – free from contamination or distortion by their values? This question has divided sociologists for well over a century:

- Some argue that it is both *possible and desirable* to keep subjective values out of research in the same way as natural scientists are said to do. Only in this way can we produce true, scientific knowledge about society.
- Others argue that, because sociologists are humans (with values) studying other humans (with values), it is *impossible* to keep personal values out of one's research.
- Some go further, arguing that it is actually *desirable* for sociologists to use their values to improve society through their work. This is sometimes called 'committed sociology'.

In this Topic, we explore the answers different sociologists have given to the question of whether sociology can or should be objective and value-free.

Learning objectives

After studying this Topic, you should:

- Understand the meaning of objectivity, subjectivity and value freedom.
- Know the main views put forward of the relationship between sociology and values.
- Be able to evaluate the strengths and limitations of different views as to whether sociology can and should be value-free.

The classical sociologists and values

The classical thinkers who shaped sociology in its early years, such as Comte, Durkheim, Marx and Weber, all had important views on the question of objectivity and value freedom.

The early positivists

For the early positivists Auguste Comte (1798-1857) and Emile Durkheim (1858-1917), the creation of a better society was not a matter of subjective values or personal opinions about what was 'best'. They shared the Enlightenment or modernist view of the role of sociology. As the science of society, sociology's job was to discover the truth about how society works, uncovering the laws that govern its proper functioning. Equipped with this knowledge, social problems could be solved and human life improved.

In their view, scientific sociology would reveal the one correct society. This gave sociologists a crucial role. By discovering the truth about how society worked, sociologists would be able to say objectively and with scientific certainty what was really best for society – they would be able to prescribe how things ought to be. In fact, Comte regarded sociology as the 'queen of the sciences' and saw sociologists as latter-day priests of a new scientific religion of truth.

Karl Marx

There is debate about whether or not Karl Marx (1818-83) was a positivist. However, it is certainly true that he saw himself as a scientist and that he believed his method of historical analysis, historical materialism, could reveal the line of development of human society. This development involved an evolution through a series of different types of class-based society, leading ultimately to a future classless communist society, in which exploitation, alienation and poverty would be ended, and each individual would be free to achieve their true potential.

The role of Marx's sociology, therefore, was to reveal the truth of this development, especially to the proletariat, since they would be the class to overthrow capitalism and herald the birth of communist society. Marx thus takes for granted the value of the ideal communist society and argues that his scientific approach will show us how to reach it. In this he is similar to Comte and Durkheim, in that he sees science as helping to 'deliver' the good society.

Max Weber

Marx, Durkheim and Comte tended not to see a distinction between the facts as revealed by science and the values that we should hold – since they believed that science could tell us what these should be. By contrast, Max Weber (1864-1920) makes a sharp distinction between value judgments and facts and he argues that we cannot derive the one from the other.

For example, research might establish the fact that divorcees are more likely to commit suicide. However, this does not logically demonstrate the truth of the value judgment that we should make divorce harder to obtain. There is nothing about the fact that logically compels us to accept the value. For example, we might argue that we should instead make it harder to get *married* (another value), or that people have every right to commit suicide if they wish (a third value). None of these three value judgments are 'proven' by the established fact. Indeed, in Weber's view, a value can be neither proved nor disproved by the facts: they belong to different realms.

However, despite making a sharp distinction between facts and values, Weber still saw an essential role for values in sociological research. We can divide his views into four stages of the research process.

1 Values as a guide to research

Weber took the idea from phenomenology that social reality is made up of a 'meaningless infinity' of facts that make it impossible to study it in its totality. Therefore the best the researcher can do is to select certain facts and study these.

But how do we choose which facts to study? In Weber's view, we can only select them in terms of what we regard as important based on our own values – in other words, their *value relevance* to us. Values are thus essential in enabling us to select which aspects of reality to study and in developing concepts with which to understand these aspects. For example, feminists value gender equality and this leads them to study women's oppression and to develop concepts such as patriarchy with which to understand it.

2 Data collection and hypothesis testing

While values are essential in selecting what to study, in Weber's view we must be as objective and unbiased as possible when we are actually collecting the facts, and this means keeping our values and prejudices out of the process. For example, we should not ask leading questions designed to give the answers that we *want* to hear: our questions should aim to get respondents to give us their view, not our own.

Once we have gathered the facts, we can use them to test a hypothesis. Again, we must keep our values out of the process – the hypothesis must stand or fall solely on whether or not it fits the observed facts.

3 Values in the interpretation of data

Values become important again when we come to interpret the data we have collected. The facts need to be set in a theoretical framework so that we can understand their significance and draw conclusions from them. In Weber's view, our choice of theoretical framework or perspective is influenced by our values. Therefore, we must be explicit about them, spelling out our values so that others can see if unconscious bias is present in our interpretation of our data.

4 Values and the sociologist as a citizen

Research findings often have very real effects on people's lives, but sociologists and scientists sometimes choose to ignore the uses to which their work is put. They argue that their job is merely to conduct objective research and discover the facts; it is for the politicians or public to decide what use to make of their findings.

Weber rejects this view. He argues that scientists and sociologists are also human beings and citizens and they must not dodge the moral and political issues their work raises by hiding behind words such as 'objectivity' or 'value freedom'. They must take moral responsibility for the harm their research may do. For example, Albert Einstein's theories in physics helped make the atomic bomb possible; yet subsequently, Einstein voiced his opposition to nuclear weapons. In the social sciences, Box 4.4 illustrates this issue well.

To summarise, Weber sees values as relevant to the sociologist in choosing what to research, in interpreting the data collected, and as a citizen and member of society in deciding the use to which the findings should be put. By contrast, the sociologist's values must be kept out of the actual process of gathering the facts.

Value freedom and commitment

The issue of commitment that Weber raised has remained at the centre of debates about the place of the sociologist's values in research. For example, some modern positivists have shied away from any value commitments. By contrast, Marxists, interactionists and feminists have argued for a 'committed sociology' in which the sociologist spells out the importance of their personal values to their research.

Modern positivists

Unlike Durkheim and Comte, who were openly committed to re-shaping society in certain ways, by the mid 20th century positivists tended to argue that their own values were irrelevant to their research. There were two reasons for this:

1 The desire to appear scientific

Science is concerned with matters of fact, not value – with 'is' questions, not 'ought' questions. Therefore, sociologists should remain morally neutral – their job is simply to establish the truth about people's behaviour, not to praise or condemn it.

Critics argue that this reflected a desire to make sociology respectable. Science has high prestige in modern society, so mimicking its ways would raise the subject's status and earn it respectability. This was particularly important in the early 20th century, when sociology was just becoming established as an academic discipline.

2 The social position of sociology

Alvin Gouldner (1975) argues that by the 1950s, American sociologists in particular had become mere 'spiritless technicians'. Earlier in the century, sociology had been a critical discipline, often challenging accepted authority. However, by the 1950s, sociologists were no longer 'problem makers' who defined their own research problems. Instead they had become 'problem takers' who hired themselves out to other organisations such as government, business and the military, to take on and solve *their* problems for them.

Gouldner argues that, by leaving their own values behind them, sociologists were making a 'gentleman's promise' that they would not rock the boat by criticising or questioning their paymasters. Because sociologists were simply hired hands, they saw their own values as irrelevant to their work. This is exactly the attitude that Weber was criticising when he said that sociologists must take moral responsibility for the effects of their work.

Activity

Search the web for information on Project Camelot, a US Army programme from 1964. What similarities are there between Camelot and HTS (in Box 4.4)? How far do you think social scientists should become involved in such projects as these? Give your reasons.

Committed sociology

By contrast with the positivists, some sociologists argue for a committed sociology. For example, Gunnar Myrdal (1969) argues that sociologists should not only spell out their values – as Weber recommends – they should also openly 'take sides' by espousing the values and interests of particular individuals or groups.

Committed sociologists who advocate this approach, such as Myrdal and Gouldner, argue that it is neither possible nor desirable to keep values out of research. In Gouldner's view, value-free sociology is:

- **Impossible**, because either the sociologist's own values, or those of their paymasters, are bound to be reflected in their work.
- **Undesirable**, since without values to guide research, sociologists are merely putting their services at the disposal of the highest bidder. For example, Gouldner argues that:

'From such a standpoint, there is no reason why one cannot sell his knowledge to spread a disease just as freely as he can to fight it. Indeed, some sociologists have had no hesitation about doing market research designed to sell more cigarettes, although well aware of the implications of recent cancer research.'

Whose side are we on?

If all sociology is influenced by values, this means the sociologist must inevitably take sides. By not choosing a side, the sociologist is in fact taking the side of the more powerful against the less powerful.

The interactionist Howard Becker (1970) poses the question, 'Whose side are we on?' He argues that values are always present in sociology. Traditionally, however, sociologists (especially positivists and functionalists) have tended to take the viewpoint of the powerful – police, psychiatrists and so on.

Becker argues that instead of seeing things from the perspective of these 'overdogs', sociologists should adopt a compassionate stance and take the side of the underdogs – the criminals, mental patients and other powerless groups. This is partly because less is known about these groups and their story needs to be told in order to redress the balance. By identifying with the underdog and giving them a voice, we can reveal a previously hidden side of social reality.

For example, by empathising with the mental patient, we can show the hidden rationality of their behaviour – behaviour that the psychiatrist thinks of as irrational. In fact, as the interactionist Erving Goffman (1968) argues, to describe the situation of the mental patient faithfully, we have to take their side. We have to be biased in favour of the patient and against the psychiatrist.

This emphasis on identifying and empathising with the powerless has clear links to the kinds of research methods favoured by interactionists. They have a strong preference for qualitative methods such as participant observation, which they see as revealing the meanings of these 'outsiders'.

However, Gouldner criticises Becker for taking a romantic and sentimental approach to disadvantaged groups. He accuses Becker of being concerned only with those who are 'on their backs' – the misunderstood, negatively labelled, exotic specimens of deviant behaviour that interactionists tend to focus on.

Box 4.4 Social science and the military

The US military has developed a programme known as the Human Terrain System (HTS) to study social groups in Iraq and Afghanistan. HTS depends heavily on anthropologists, with their expertise in the study of non-western societies. In the words of Steve Fondacaro, the colonel overseeing HTS, 'You have social scientists to understand the deep complexity of the problems on the ground and the military personnel who then take that information and apply it to the military decision-making process'. According to the recruitment advert, winning the trust of the population 'is at the heart of the struggle between coalition forces and the insurgents'. The anthropologist David Kilcullen, an architect of the strategy, calls it 'armed social work'.

In 2007 the US government authorised a $40 million expansion of HTS to assign teams of social scientists to each of the 26 US combat brigades in Iraq and Afghanistan. The cost is about $400,000 annually for each social scientist, including the cost of kidnap insurance.

HTS has met with opposition. Some anthropologists say it exploits social science for political gain. One, Roberto González, accuses the military of trying to 'weaponise' anthropology, and believes that HTS units are likely to operate 'as full-blown counterinsurgency teams akin to what the British employed in the colonies over a half-century ago'. The work also has echoes of Project Camelot, another military programme involving social scientists.

Meanwhile, the Network of Concerned Anthropologists has organised an online pledge calling for a boycott of HTS. It says that HTS contributes to a brutal war of occupation and breaches the relationship of trust between anthropologists and the people they study, especially since much of the programme's work is covert. You can find the pledge at http://concerned.anthropologists.googlepages.com/

Adapted from The New York Times, 5 October 2007; BBC News, 16 October 2007

Instead, Gouldner adopts a Marxist perspective. He argues that sociologists should take the side of those who are 'fighting back' – the political radicals struggling to change society. Sociology should not confine itself to describing the viewpoint of the underdog and the oppressed, as Becker and Goffman do. It should be committed to ending their oppression by unmasking the ways in which the powerful maintain their position.

Funding and careers

Most sociological research is funded by someone other than sociologists themselves. Sources of funding include government departments, businesses and voluntary organisations. Often, the body that pays for the research controls the direction it takes and the kinds of questions that it asks – and fails to ask. Thus the sociologist's work is likely to embody the values and interests of their paymasters.

In some cases, funding organisations may prevent publication of the research if its findings prove unacceptable. In the case of the Black Report (1980) into class inequalities in health, the Conservative government arranged for its release over a bank holiday weekend, allegedly in the hope of reducing the publicity it would receive – because the report's findings ran counter to government views.

In addition to the influence of those who fund the research, we should also consider the sociologist's own personal values deriving from their background, upbringing and so on. Sociologists may also wish to further their careers and reputations, and this may influence their choice of topic (for example, choosing something that is in fashion), their research questions and methods and how they interpret their findings. Some may censor themselves for fear that being too outspoken will harm their career prospects or even cost them their job. Sociologists in university departments are also likely to be under pressure to publish research, perhaps regardless of its quality or usefulness.

Perspectives and methods

For Gouldner, all research is inevitably influenced by values – whether it is the values of the sociologist, or those of the funding body that pays for the research.

Different sociological perspectives can be seen as embodying different assumptions and values about how society is or should be. For example:

- **Feminism** sees society as based on gender inequality and promotes the rights of women.
- **Functionalism** sees society as harmonious and espouses conservative values that favour the status quo.
- **Marxism** sees society as conflict-ridden and strives for a classless society.

These assumptions and values influence the topics that sociologists of different perspectives choose to research, the concepts they develop and the conclusions they reach. For example, functionalists have concluded that inequality is beneficial for society, whereas Marxists conclude that it produces exploitation of the poor by the rich.

Similarly, there is a link between the kinds of methods sociologists prefer and their value-stance. For example, interactionists' preference for qualitative methods fits with their desire to empathise with the underdog, since such methods give them access to the actor's meanings and worldview. Likewise, the functionalist and positivist tendency to take the side of the 'establishment' and see things from the viewpoint of those in authority fits well with their uncritical acceptance of official statistics produced by government departments. Both interactionists and functionalists can be accused of selecting methods that produce facts that reflect their values and outlook.

Objectivity and relativism

If all sociological perspectives involve values, are their findings just a reflection of their values, rather than a true picture of society? If so, there would be no way of deciding which of these different versions of reality – if any – was true.

One version of this idea is known as relativism. Relativism argues that:

- Different groups, cultures and individuals – including sociologists – have different views as to what is true. Each one sees the world in their own distinctive way, through their own perspectives, concepts, values and interests.
- There is no independent way of judging whether any view is truer than any other.

All sociologists would agree with the first statement. For example, as we saw in Chapter 1, different cultures hold often widely different religious beliefs that affect what they believe to be true.

However, relativism goes much further. It argues that there is no absolute or objective truth – just truths plural. What you believe is true, *is* true – for you. What I believe is true, *is* true – but only for me. So if you believe the earth is round, while I think it is flat, there is no way of saying who is right or wrong.

Relativism and postmodernism

In sociology, postmodernists take a relativist view of knowledge. They reject the idea that any one account of the social world is superior to any other – there are no 'privileged accounts' that have special access to the truth. Any perspective that claims to have the truth, such as Marxism, is just a meta-narrative or 'big story'. All knowledge, from whatever perspective, is based on values and assumptions and thus no perspective has any special claim to be true.

Of course, if this is correct, then it must apply to postmodernism too – which leads to the paradoxical conclusion that we shouldn't believe what postmodernism says either! In other words, relativism is logically self-defeating, since it claims to be telling us something true, while simultaneously telling us that no one can tell us what is true.

In practice, sociologists rarely go this far. After all, there is a real factual world 'out there', in which women generally do more housework than men, in which some children go hungry, in which ethnic background may affect a person's life chances and so on. Regardless of the sociologist's values or perspective, we can observe and record these facts. And once we have established the existence of such facts, they can be used to judge the value of competing theories and perspectives. In the end, it matters less whether a theory contains certain values, than whether it can explain the world that we observe.

For more activities on Objectivity and values in sociology…

 **Go to www.sociology.uk.net**

Summary

The early positivists and Marx believed that we could discover objective scientific knowledge and use it to improve society. Weber argued that values are essential in deciding what to research, in interpreting findings and in determining how they should be used, but must be kept out of the data-collection process. However, 20th century positivists claimed to be 'value-free', leading Gouldner to accuse them of being subservient to their paymasters. Becker argues that sociologists should take the side of the underdog. The values of those funding the research play a part in determining what gets researched and published. Sociologists' own values influence the kinds of research questions they ask, their methods and findings.

QuickCheck Questions

1 According to Weber, which is the stage of research into which values must not be allowed to enter?

2 True or false? Relativism argues that everyone's view of the world is equally valid.

3 What is Gouldner's main criticism of modern positivist sociologists?

4 Why do interactionists argue we should see things from the point of view of the underdog?

5 Why might the military see anthropologists as useful to them in Iraq and Afghanistan?

6 Explain what is meant by 'objectivity'.

7 Why do many sociologists wish to be seen as scientific?

 Check your answers at www.sociology.uk.net

Examining objectivity and values in sociology

Assess the view that values can and should be kept out of sociological research.

(33 marks)

The examiner's advice

This question carries 15 AO1 marks (knowledge and understanding) and 18 AO2 marks (interpretation, application, analysis and evaluation). Start your answer with the views of classical sociologists that scientific sociology would discover objectively which values were best and how society should be organised. Contrast this with Weber's view that values and facts are distinct, and describe his view that values must be involved in selecting research topics, interpreting data and deciding the use to which findings are put, but should be kept out of data collection.

You can also contrast Weber with 20th century positivists' 'value neutral' view that we can keep values out of research. Examine criticisms of this view, including the idea that the values of those who provide the funds, or the sociologist's own career interests, inevitably determine research topics and findings. You can discuss whether values should be kept out by examining the view of 'committed sociologists' that researchers must actively take the side of the underdog, as Gouldner, Becker and Myrdal argue.

POVERTY HISTORY

Topic 8 Sociology and social policy

Social policy is generally thought of as tackling 'social problems', especially the welfare of the population. For example, T.H. Marshall (1975) defines social policy as the actions of governments that have 'a direct impact on the welfare of the citizens, by providing them with services or income'. This view focuses on areas such as education, social security and health. However, we should note that social policy is not just about welfare. For example, it may be concerned with social control.

Many sociologists are also interested in social problems and in finding ways to solve them, and much sociological research is aimed at producing social policy proposals for government to act upon.

In this Topic, we examine the relationship between sociology and social policy. For example:

- Should it be the job of sociologists to influence social policies?
- What kinds of policies do different perspectives favour?
- How far does sociological research actually influence government policies? What other factors affect social policies?

Learning objectives

After studying this Topic, you should:

- Understand the difference between social problems and sociological problems.
- Know the factors that may affect the extent to which sociology can influence social policy.
- Know the main sociological perspectives on the relationship between sociology and social policy, and be able to evaluate their strengths and limitations.

Social problems and sociological problems

In order to understand the role of sociology in relation to social policy, it is useful to distinguish first between social problems and sociological problems.

Social problems

According to Peter Worsley (1977), 'a "social problem" is some piece of social behaviour that causes public friction and/or private misery and calls for collective action to solve it'. For example, poverty, educational under-achievement, juvenile delinquency and divorce may all be seen as social problems by members of society, and governments may be called upon to produce policies to tackle them.

Sociological problems

According to Worsley, a sociological problem is 'any pattern of relationships that calls for explanation'. In other words, it is any piece of behaviour that we wish to make sense of.

This might be something that society regards as a social problem, for example why some people are poor, commit crime, or fail in school. But it can also include behaviour that society doesn't normally regard as a problem – for example, why people are prosperous or law-abiding, or succeed at school or remain happily married. As Worsley puts it:

'From the point of view of the State or the neighbours, quiet families are not problem families. Sociologically speaking, they are.'

In other words, 'normal' behaviour is just as interesting to sociologists as behaviour that people see as a social problem. In fact, many sociologists show little or no interest in studying or solving practical social problems. These sociologists would regard their goal as simply being to discover knowledge for its own sake.

For example, Georg Simmel (1950) was interested in revealing the universal characteristics present in all social relationships, whether in an office, a family or a bus queue. Similarly, historical studies of, say, the social structure of the Roman Empire may have little relevance to today's social problems.

On the other hand, of course, many sociologists *are* interested in solving social problems through their research. For example, sociologists who feel strongly about poverty or about inequalities in educational achievement have conducted research aimed at discovering solutions to these social problems. Similarly, many sociologists are employed directly by government departments such as the Home Office or the Department for Children, Schools and Families. These sociologists often have a direct input into making policies and evaluating their effectiveness, for example in reducing crime or raising pupils' achievements.

> Suggest three other features of behaviour that are usually regarded as normal rather than as problems. Why might sociologists be interested in them?

The influence of sociology on policy

However, even when sociologists do conduct research into social problems, there is no guarantee that policy-makers will study their findings, or that any solutions they propose will find their way into social policies. Many factors may affect whether or not sociological research succeeds in influencing policy:

- **Electoral popularity** Research findings and recommendations might point to a policy that would be unpopular with voters.
- **Ideological and policy preferences of governments** If the researcher's value-stance or perspective is similar to the political ideology of the government, they may stand more chance of influencing its policies.
- **Interest groups** These are pressure groups that seek to influence government policies in their own interests. For example, business groups may succeed in persuading government not to raise the minimum wage, even

though this might be an effective measure to reduce poverty.
- **Globalisation** Social policy isn't just made by nation states in isolation. International organisations such as the European Union and the International Monetary Fund (IMF) may influence the social policies of individual governments. For example, the IMF's 'structural adjustment programmes' have required less developed countries to introduce fees for education and health care as a condition for receiving aid, despite evidence from some social scientists that this makes development less likely.
- **Critical sociology** Sociologists who are critical of the state and powerful groups, such as Marxists, may be regarded as too extreme, hostile or impractical and therefore unlikely to influence policy.
- **Cost** Even if the government is sympathetic to the

sociologist's findings, it may not have sufficient funds to implement an appropriate policy based on them, or it may have other spending priorities and commitments.

- **Funding sources** In some cases, sociologists may tone down their findings and policy recommendations so as to fit in with their paymasters' wishes – a case of 'he who pays the piper calls the tune'. Similarly, policy-makers may recruit sociologists who share their assumptions and political values. The research findings may then be used to justify what the policy-makers intended to do in the first place. Similarly, 'think tanks' or research institutes often have particular political sympathies – for example, some are generally seen as left leaning, while others tend to have right-wing sympathies. Politicians seeking a particular result to justify their favoured policies can be selective in which think tanks they turn to for research.

Activity

Visit the websites of some of the following research institutes or use online encyclopaedias: the Institute for Public Policy Research; the Adam Smith Institute; the Policy Studies Institute; the Joseph Rowntree Foundation; the Centre for Policy Studies; the Fabian Society; the Bow Group. What topics have they researched? Try to categorise them according to their political sympathies.

In addition to any direct influence on policy-makers, social scientists' ideas sometimes become part of mainstream culture and influence the way people see social problems. This in turn can affect the policies that governments produce. For example, John Bowlby's (1965) idea that young children's relationships with their mother are crucial for normal development became widely accepted by many people in society. When this happens, it can influence the climate of opinion in favour of policies that reflect these social science-derived ideas. In the example above, it may have influenced policies on day care, juvenile delinquency and so on.

The power to define the problem

Sociological research is thus only one possible element in shaping social policy. Ultimately, any policy is the result of a political decision by those in power. As Tom Burden (1998) says, social policies:

> 'cannot be very well understood if they are simply treated as "neutral" attempts to deal with "problems". Indeed, what is to count as a problem is itself generally a matter of political debate.'

Often, those with power are the ones who are able to define what is and what is not a problem, and what if anything should be done about it.

Perspectives on social policy and sociology

Different sociological perspectives hold different views of the nature of the state and the social policy it produces. As a result, each perspective tends to take a different view of the role of sociology in relation to social policy. We shall now examine the major perspectives on policy and its relationship to sociology.

Positivism and functionalism

Early positivists such as Comte and Durkheim took the view that sociology was a science and would discover both the cause of social problems and scientifically based solutions to them. As such, their approach was part of the Enlightenment project to use science and reason to improve society. For example, Durkheim's analysis led him to propose a meritocratic education system and the abolition of inherited wealth as ways to foster a sense that society was fair, which would promote social cohesion.

Functionalists see society as based on value consensus and free from fundamental conflicts. Like the positivists, they see the state as serving the interests of society as a whole, producing and implementing rational social policies for the

good of all. These policies help society run more smoothly and efficiently. For example, educational policies are seen as promoting equal opportunity and social integration, while health and housing policies assist the family in performing its functions more effectively.

For both functionalists and positivists, the sociologist's role is to provide the state with objective, scientific information. By investigating social problems and discovering their causes, sociologists provide the necessary information on which the state can base its policies.

In this view, the sociologist is rather like the medical researcher. Just as medical research discovers the causes of disease as a basis for prevention or cure, so the sociologist's role is to investigate social problems scientifically. This provides the state with objective information about their extent and explanations of their causes as well as possible 'cures' in the shape of policy recommendations.

Functionalists favour social policies that are sometimes referred to as 'piecemeal social engineering'. In other words, they favour a cautious approach, tackling one specific issue at a time.

However, the piecemeal approach has been criticised. For example, Marxists argue that educational policies aimed at equalising opportunity for children of different classes are often defeated by the influence of poverty in wider society. In other words, social problems such as under-achievement are simply aspects of a wider structure of class inequality, and so we need to change the basic structure of society in order to solve these specific problems.

The social democratic perspective

The social democratic perspective on social policy shares this view. It favours a major redistribution of wealth and income from the rich to the poor. Sociologists adopting this perspective, such as Peter Townsend (1979), argue that they should be involved in researching social problems and making policy recommendations to eradicate them. For example, Townsend conducted extensive research on poverty. On the basis of his findings, he made recommendations for policies such as fairer, higher benefit levels, and more public spending on health, education and welfare services.

Similarly, the Black Report (1980) on class inequalities in health made no fewer than 37 far-reaching policy recommendations for reducing these deep-rooted inequalities. These included free school meals for all children, improved working conditions, better benefits for the disabled and more spending to improve housing. The Labour government had originally commissioned the report in 1977 but it was only completed in 1980, the year after Mrs Thatcher's Conservative government came to power. The new government refused to implement the report's recommendations on grounds of cost, and even tried to restrict its publication.

Criticisms

Marxists criticise the social democratic perspective. While they agree that social problems such as class inequalities in health are deep-rooted, they reject the idea that even policies as far-reaching as those proposed by the Black Report are enough to solve the problem. In their view, it is capitalism that is ultimately responsible for these inequalities and so the problem cannot be solved without abolishing capitalism. They also argue that in any event, as the government response to the Black Report showed, the capitalist state is unlikely to introduce costly public spending policies to benefit the working class. Thus, rational social policies proposed by sociologists such as Townsend will fall on deaf ears as far as policy-makers are concerned.

From a different perspective, postmodernists criticise attempts by sociologists to influence policy. For

postmodernists, it is impossible to discover objective truth. All knowledge produced by research is uncertain, and so sociological findings cannot provide a satisfactory basis for policy-making. In this view, sociologists can only take the role of 'interpreters', offering one view of reality among many, and not the role of 'legislators' (law-makers), as modernist sociologists such as functionalists and social democrats have tried to do.

Marxism

Marxists see society as divided by a fundamental conflict of interest in which the ruling capitalist class exploit the labour of the working class. Unlike functionalists, they do not see the state and its policies as benefiting all members of society. In the Marxist view, the state represents the ruling class, and its social policies serve the interests of capitalism, not those of society as a whole:

- **They provide ideological legitimation** to mask capitalist exploitation. For example, the welfare state gives capitalism a 'human face', making it appear that the system cares about the poor, sick and old.
- **They maintain the labour force for further exploitation** For example, the NHS serves capitalism by keeping workers fit enough to work.
- **They are a means of preventing revolution** when class conflict intensifies and threatens the stability of capitalism. For example, Marxists see the policies that created the welfare state after the Second World War (1939-45) as a way of buying off working-class opposition to capitalism.

Marxists recognise that social policies do sometimes provide real, if limited, benefits to the working class. However, such gains are constantly threatened with reversal by capitalism's tendency to go into periodic crises of profitability, leading to cuts in state spending on welfare.

Therefore, research that reveals the unpleasant truth about the social problems capitalism creates will not be used to formulate policies to solve these problems – as the fate of the Black Report shows. In fact, for Marxists, such problems cannot be solved by the capitalist state in any case, since capitalism is based on putting profits before human needs. The only solution to social problems is a revolution to overthrow capitalism and create a classless society.

For Marxists, therefore, the sociologist's main role should be to criticise capitalist social policy, not to serve the capitalist state. The sociologist must reveal the exploitation that underpins capitalism, and the way in which the ruling class use social policies to mask this exploitation and buy off revolt with minor concessions.

However, critics argue that Marxist views on social policy and the role of sociologists are impractical and unrealistic. Social democrats criticise them for rejecting the idea that sociological research can help bring about progressive policies within the existing capitalist system. For example, poverty researchers have at times had some positive impact on policy.

What functions might the following policies perform for capitalism: benefits for the unemployed; compulsory schooling; winter fuel payments for pensioners?

Feminism

Like Marxists, feminists see society as based on conflict, but in their view the fundamental conflict is between genders, not classes. Society is patriarchal (male dominated), benefiting men at women's expense, and the state perpetuates women's subordination through its social policies.

For example, family policies may be based on the assumption that the 'normal' family is a conventional nuclear family with a heterosexual married couple and their children. Thus, if the state assumes this and offers benefits to married couples but not to cohabiting ones, these policies may produce a self-fulfilling prophecy, encouraging the kind of family that the state assumed to be the norm in the first place and making it more difficult for people to live in other kinds of family.

Feminist research has had an impact in a number of policy areas. For example, in education, it has influenced policies such as:

- **Learning materials** that promote more positive images of females.
- **Teacher training** to sensitise teachers to the need to avoid gender bias and promote inclusiveness for both sexes.

Many of these policies reflect the liberal feminist view that anti-discrimination reforms will ultimately bring about gender equality.

On the other hand, radical feminist ideas have also had some influence on social policy. Radical feminists regard men as the direct oppressors of women, especially through the family, where women are kept subordinate through the use or threat of physical and sexual violence. They therefore favour *separatism* – the idea that women need to separate themselves from men to be free from patriarchy. One area of social policy that reflects this view is the establishment of women's refuges for women escaping domestic violence. For example, the Women's Aid Federation supports a national network of over 500 such services, often with funding from local and central government.

Overall, it is clear that feminist sociological research has had some impact on social policies in areas that affect women, in part due to the success of the broader feminist movement in gaining greater political influence since the 1970s.

However, many feminists reject the view that reformist social policies can liberate women. For example, both Marxist and radical feminists call for more far-reaching changes that the existing state cannot deliver.

The New Right

The New Right believe that the state should have only minimal involvement in society. In particular, they are opposed to using state provision of welfare to deal with social problems. In their view, state intervention in areas such as family life, income support, education and health care robs people of their freedom to make their own choices and undermines their sense of responsibility. This in turn leads to greater social problems, such as crime and delinquency.

For example, Charles Murray (1984) argues that generous welfare benefits and council housing for lone parents act as 'perverse incentives' that weaken the family's self-reliance. They encourage the growth of a dependency culture and an underclass of lone mothers, undisciplined children, and irresponsible fathers who abandon their families in the knowledge that the welfare state will provide for them. For this reason, Murray favours a reduction in state spending on welfare.

The New Right are therefore highly critical of many existing social policies. However, they are not opposed to social policy as such, and they see the role of sociologists as being to propose alternative policies to the present ones. These policies should aim to restore individuals' responsibility for their own and their families' welfare, rather than leaving this to the state.

For example, *Breakdown Britain*, a report by Conservative think tank, the Social Justice Policy Group (2007), proposes a range of new social policies aimed at the family. These include marriage preparation and parenting classes, and support from the tax and benefit system for mothers who stay at home. The report's main thrust is that governments have stripped citizens of responsibility for their own welfare and neglected the support networks that give people their quality of life. The role of social policy should be to enable people to help themselves, rather than the welfare state attempting, and failing, to do it for them.

Influence of New Right thinking

Because of its ideological opposition to the state having a major role in welfare, New Right thinking has tended to be particularly attractive to the Conservative Party. However, some New Labour policies have shown the influence of New Right views. For example, New Labour regards a married couple as normally the best place to bring up children.

While not favouring a major role for the state in welfare provision, the New Right support a strong 'law and order' policy and research by right realist criminologists, such as

Wilson and Kelling's article *Broken Windows*, has been influential in the widespread introduction of zero tolerance policies (see Chapter 2, Topic 9).

However, the quality and the objectivity of the social research used by the New Right have been questioned. For example, the validity of the data on which Murray bases his claims about a link between absent fathers and delinquency has been widely challenged. Similarly, New Right policy proposals seldom draw on sociologists' research findings, using instead the findings of politically sympathetic think tanks. For example, the study *Breakdown Britain* was produced by a think tank set up by former Conservative Party leader Iain Duncan Smith.

Summary

Social problems are issues causing public concern. Sociological problems are issues of theoretical interest to sociologists and include 'normal' behaviour. Sociologists often research social problems, but many other factors influence policies, such as the government's ideological preferences. There are different perspectives on the relationship between sociology and social policy. Positivists and functionalists see sociology as providing objective knowledge to guide policy for the good of society. Social democrats see sociology as proposing policies to make major structural changes, such as the abolition of poverty. Marxists argue that sociology must remain critical of the policies of the capitalist state. Feminists see policy as reflecting patriarchy and use research to influence policy in favour of women. The New Right propose policies to tackle the culture of dependency and have had some influence with governments.

For more activities on Sociology and social policy...

Go to www.sociology.uk.net

QuickCheck Questions

1 Explain the difference between a social problem and a sociological problem.

2 Identify three factors affecting social policy apart from sociologists' research findings.

3 Which early sociologists argued that sociology should act as a guide to social policy?

4 Identify three ways in which Marxists see social policies as helping to maintain capitalism.

5 How might social research be affected by sources of funding?

6 Suggest three policies that feminist research may have influenced.

Check your answers at www.sociology.uk.net

Examining sociology and social policy

Assess the relationship between sociology and social policy.
(33 marks)

The examiner's advice

This question carries 15 AO1 marks (knowledge and understanding) and 18 AO2 marks (interpretation, application, analysis and evaluation). You could start by noting that some 'pure' sociology is not interested at all in policy or social problems. However, the main part of your answer should focus on a range of views of the relationship between sociology and policy. You could note that many sociologists seek to research social problems so that their findings can guide social policy, but that other factors may have more influence, e.g. the government's ideology, resources to implement policies, electoral popularity etc.

Consider the views of different perspectives on whether sociology can or should be involved in providing information and advice for policy-makers – e.g. you could look at the Marxist view that most policies prop up capitalism and that sociologists should take a critical stance, or the extent to which New Right, feminist or social democratic research has had an influence on policy (e.g. in areas such as welfare, gender and education, poverty etc).

Exam question and student answer

Activity

Here are two things you can do to practise your exam skills:

1 Attempt the question below. If you do it under timed conditions, you should allow yourself about 10 minutes to study the examiner's advice first of all, and then give yourself a total of 45 minutes to write your answer. This also includes time to make your plan and check your answer through when you have finished it.

2 Read the student answer (below) to the question. Study the examiner's advice and comments. Then write an improved version of it that takes on board the advice and comments, plus any extra points of your own. (You can copy any bits of the original that you want to keep.) You don't need to do this under timed conditions.

In both cases, try swapping your answer with a friend and marking each other's work, using the examiner's advice to help you.

For further exam practice, see Chapter 5, where you will find mock exam papers for both A2 units.

Examining sociological theory

Critically examine the usefulness of the concepts of modern society and postmodern society to sociological understanding of today's society.

(33 marks)

The examiner's advice

This question carries 15 AO1 marks (knowledge and understanding) and 18 AO2 marks (interpretation, application, analysis and evaluation). You could begin your answer by distinguishing between modern and traditional society, with an account of the features of modern society such as industrial capitalism, the nation-state, the importance of science etc, linking this to the Enlightenment project. Then you could go on to examine ways in which some sociologists see modern society as changing, e.g. as a result of globalisation, the impact of the media etc.

To evaluate the usefulness of the concepts, examine different theories that have attempted to understand these changes, such as postmodernism (e.g. Lyotard and Baudrillard), theories of late modernity (e.g. Giddens and Beck) and Marxist theories of postmodernity (e.g. Harvey). Focus on whether or not they see society as still basically 'modern' and on whether they believe it is possible to have rational scientific knowledge of society that can be used as a basis for improving it.

Answer by Steve

Some sociologists argue that today's society has become postmodern, literally meaning 'after modern', so to understand this idea we need to look first at the idea of modern society. Most sociologists agree that modern society came into existence with the industrial revolution, which changed the economy of countries like Britain from agricultural and rural to industrial capitalism. People left the land to move to the towns and factories. This created a much wealthier society, but a more unequal one, as Marxists note. However, functionalists argue that it was also more meritocratic, because people could now achieve their own status in life.

> Quite a good opening. Some knowledge of origins of modern society and a bit of theory.

Modern society is seen as having a clear structure. For example, the nuclear family becomes the dominant type, replacing the pre-industrial extended family. An important feature is the political structure, which takes the form of the nation-state. The state provides for the welfare and control of the population. The state also regulates the economy, which Lash and Urry call 'organised capitalism' or Fordism, based on mass production and mass consumption. Culture is also national, partly due to a state education system that imposes a common curriculum on everybody.

> Good knowledge of a range of features of modern society.

With modern society, religion declines, society becomes more secular, and science becomes more important in the economy and in shaping people's outlook. The 18th century Enlightenment took a rational view, arguing that reason and science would solve humanity's problems such as disease and hunger. This greatly influenced the early sociologists such as Comte, Durkheim and Marx, who believed that scientific sociology would solve social problems and lead to peace, harmony and prosperity.

> Good points about importance of science and early sociologists.

However, some sociologists now argue that we have moved beyond the stage of modern society. They argue that all the features of modern society have begun to break up, so much so that we are in a new type of society called postmodernity. For example, everyone used to believe in science, thinking that it would deliver 'miracles' and solve all our problems, but now people have 'lost faith' in science, because it has created many problems, such as global warming, pollution, weapons of mass destruction etc.

> It would help to identify these sociologists as postmodernists – but relevant analysis of loss of faith in science. Could link this to Beck's risk society.

In postmodern society, all the fixed things that were found in modern society become unstable and start to fragment. For example, instead of the nuclear family as the only (or main) family type, we now find increasing family diversity, with lone parents, reconstituted families, same sex families etc.

> Relevant description of features of 'postmodern society' – could link this to postmodernist theory.

A major cause of the change to postmodern society is globalisation. This is the process where national boundaries begin to break down and the different parts of the world become more and more linked together so that what happens in one place has effects on other places in other countries. For example, the crisis in the financial system in America that started in 2008 had effects all over the world, leading to a global economic recession.

> Useful account of globalisation of the economy but needs theoretical context.

Another major factor leading to postmodernism is the media. We now live in a global village dominated by the media, who bombard us with images to such an extent that they take over from reality and become hyper-reality. We can pick and mix from media products to shape our own identity, so instead of it being fixed as in modern society (e.g. by our class background), it becomes fluid. Because we are all free to choose our identities in this way, the culture begins to fragment and we have less and less binding us to other people.

> Good knowledge again, but could link it to Baudrillard's views.

Overall, therefore, the concepts of modern and postmodern society are very useful in describing what has happened to society in the last couple of centuries and especially the changes that have occurred in the last few decades.

> Sums up the answer but doesn't add anything – and still no theory.

The examiner's comments

Overall, this is a good answer in terms of the knowledge and understanding it shows. Steve gives a detailed account of many features of 'modern society', such as the nation-state, 'organised capitalism', the importance of science, and the kinds of social structures (e.g. family and education) typically found in this type of society. Similarly, Steve gives a good account of 'postmodern society', including loss of faith in science, family diversity, globalisation, the role of the media etc.

In terms of AO2 skills, Steve's material is relevant and accurately interpreted, and there is some analysis (e.g. of the role of science). However, because of the lack of specific theories, there is no real debate about the terms. For example, instead of taking it for granted that we have moved from modern to postmodern society, Steve could use postmodernism, theories of late modernity and Marxist theories of postmodernity to debate the nature of the change and whether or not we really have moved to a new type of society.

23/33

Preparing for the Exam

CHAPTER 5

Tackling the A2 sociology exam

This chapter focuses on the examination itself. It deals with:

- The knowledge and skills you have to show in your exams
- The format of the exam papers
- The different types of question and how to tackle them.

This chapter also includes mock exam papers for each of the two A2 Sociology units, along with the examiner's advice on how to tackle the essay questions on these papers.

The Assessment Objectives

In A2 sociology exams, your answers are assessed in terms of two aims or 'assessment objectives'. These are:

- **Assessment Objective 1** (AO1): Knowledge and Understanding
- **Assessment Objective 2** (AO2): the skills of Interpretation, Application, Analysis and Evaluation.

More of the marks are for AO2 than for AO1 so, while you need to show evidence of both, it's particularly important that you show strong AO2 skills. Let's take a closer look at the knowledge, understanding and skills you need to show in your answers.

Knowledge and Understanding

You need to know about and understand some of the main theories, methods and concepts (ideas) that sociologists use in their work.

You also need to be familiar with some of the studies they have carried out and what these studies have found.

Interpretation

The skill of interpretation is about being able to select only the material that is relevant to the particular question you are answering, and avoiding writing an 'everything I know about this whole topic' answer. Interpretation includes:

- Explaining what an essay question involves.
- Using material from an Item when the question tells you to, linking it to your own knowledge and to the question.
- Using relevant examples, e.g. from studies, news and current events, personal experience, other topics you have studied in sociology etc.

Application

The skill of application includes:

- Linking ideas, concepts, theories, studies, methods etc to each other and to the question.
- Showing how the material you have selected is relevant to the question.
- In questions on 'methods in context', connecting the strengths and limitations of a method to the characteristics of a particular research issue.

Analysis

The skill of analysis includes:

- Breaking down an argument or explanation into the ideas that make it up and showing how they fit together.
- Comparing and contrasting ideas to show their similarities and differences.
- Organising your essays with a well-focused introduction and a clear, logical line of reasoning from paragraph to paragraph, leading to an appropriate conclusion.

Evaluation

Evaluation is about weighing things up, giving informed opinions or making balanced judgements about something. The 'something' could be different evidence, ideas, views, theories or methods. In exams, evaluation is often signalled by the word 'assess'.

The skill of evaluation includes:

- Looking at the arguments and evidence for and against a particular view.
- Examining a theory's assumptions or linking it to a particular perspective.
- Putting forward alternative views and perspectives.
- Discussing the strengths (or advantages) and limitations (or disadvantages) of a theory, perspective or research method.

In practice, the two assessment objectives often overlap. For example, in order to select and apply the right information (AO2), you first need to know some sociology and understand the set question (AO1).

The exam papers

For A2 Sociology, you will take two written exam papers. These take the format described below.

Unit 3

- This is a one-and-a-half hour exam worth 40% of the A2 (20% of the A level).
- There are **four** sections on this paper, each covering a different topic: *Beliefs in Society; Global Development; Mass Media* and *Power and Politics*.
- You must choose **one** of these sections, e.g. Section A – *Beliefs in Society*.
- Each section consists of one Item of stimulus material, plus three questions.
- **Question 1** is compulsory. It is sub-divided into parts (a) and (b). Part (b) will normally be linked to the Item.
- **Questions 2 and 3** are essays. You must choose **one** of these.

Before reading on, look at the mock exam paper at the end of this chapter. Focus on its overall structure rather than trying to figure out the answers to the questions, and check the paper against the list above.

Unit 4

- This is a two-hour exam worth 60% of the A2 (30% of the A level).
- There are **two** sections on this paper: Section A – *Crime and Deviance plus Theory and Methods*, and Section B – *Stratification and Differentiation plus Theory and Methods*. There are three questions in each section.
- You must choose **one** of these sections. Let us assume you have chosen Section A.
- **Question 1** is on Crime and Deviance. It has one Item and two parts, (a) and (b).
- **Question 2** is on Research Methods in the context of Crime and Deviance. It has one Item and two parts, (a) and (b).
- **Question 3** is an essay on Theory and Methods. There is no Item for this question.

Now look at the mock exam at the end of this chapter. Focus again on its overall structure and check it against the list above.

Further details of the different types of question are given below, along with advice on how to tackle them.

How long to spend on each question

Unit 3

You should divide your time roughly as follows:

- **Question 1:** spend about 10 minutes answering (a) and 30 minutes answering (b) (including reading the Item).
- **Essay question:** spend about 50 minutes on this.

Unit 4

You should divide your time roughly as follows:

- **Question 1:** spend 45 minutes on this: about 15 minutes on part (a) and about 30 minutes on part (b) (including reading the Item).
- **Question 2:** spend 30 minutes on this: about 10 minutes on part (a) and about 20 minutes on part (b) (including reading the Item).
- **Question 3:** spend 45 minutes on this.

For both Units, remember that these time allocations also include planning time. Spend a couple of minutes making a brief plan for the longer questions (ones worth more than

9 marks). You should also read through each answer as you finish it and make any necessary alterations.

Across the two Units, questions range from short questions worth 9 marks to long essays worth 33 marks. The following sections give you guidance on how to tackle the different types of question you will be asked.

The 9-mark questions

Both Units have a 9-mark question. It will ask you to *identify and briefly explain three* things. These might be three reasons, problems, criticisms, examples, policies and so on. For example:

Identify and briefly explain three reasons for gender differences in participation in religion.

You gain one mark for each of the three points you identify (so three marks for the identifications), plus a further two marks for each of these points that you go on to explain or describe (so six marks for the explanations).

The best way to set out your answer is as follows. On the first line, briefly state the identification point. In the above example, you could simply say:

Women are likely to be alone as they get older and turn to religion.

Now add another sentence (or two at most) to explain the point you have identified. For example, you might add:

As women tend to have a longer life expectancy than men, they are likely to be alone and widowed in their old age and so they turn to religion as a source of comfort.

Once you have done this, leave a line in your answer book and repeat the process for your second point.

Points to remember

- Set your answer out clearly, as described above.
- Your answer should be quite short: '*briefly* explain' means you only need a couple of sentences per point.
- Don't write a mini-essay: this wastes your valuable time, and it usually makes it harder for the examiner to find your identification points and therefore harder to give you marks.
- Make sure your three identified points are clearly different from each other and that you're not just repeating the same point in different terms.
- If you're *really* not sure whether all your points are right but you can think of an extra one, you can put this down too – you won't be penalised. If you're asked for three reasons but give four, any three that are right will get the marks, even if the other one is wrong. But remember, the more points you give, the more time you use up.

The Unit 3 longer questions

There are two longer questions in this Unit: question (b) and the long essay question.

Question (b)

Question (b) is worth 18 marks (6 marks for AO1 and 12 for AO2). It takes the following form: *Using material from Item A and elsewhere, assess....* For example:

Using material from Item A and elsewhere, assess the reasons why older generations appear to participate in religion much more than the young.

'Assess' means the same as 'evaluate'. You need to show good AO2 skills on this question, so try to analyse and evaluate the material you use, rather than just describing it.

The Item

The other key feature of question (b) is that it tells you to use material from the Item.

The Item is a very important source of help, so read it through very carefully at least twice, and check back to the question in between readings. Highlight or underline any words or phrases that seem important. Sometimes, line references are given in the questions. Use these to find key terms in the Item.

You will be rewarded for selecting and using material from the Item – so it's a good idea to draw the examiner's attention to the fact that you have done so by using a phrase like, 'as Item A says'.

You can quote from the Item or put it in your own words, but always try to build on it by linking it to the question and to your own knowledge, rather than merely quoting it.

Remember, too, that if you don't use the Item when told to, you won't be able to gain the higher marks. Box 5.2 gives an example of how you might use an Item.

You will also see that 'Assess' questions ask you to use 'material from elsewhere'. This is a signal that you must apply your own knowledge as well. In other words, you won't find everything in the Item that you need to answer the question.

The long essay question

The long essay is worth 33 marks. There is more emphasis on AO2 (18 marks) than AO1 (15 marks) so, as well as knowing your material, you need to be able to use it appropriately to answer the question in order to score high marks.

These questions usually begin with 'assess', 'critically examine' or 'discuss'. For example:

Critically examine the view that cults and sects are inevitably short-lived organisations with little influence on society.

- These words signal that you are expected to do more than just describe the issue or view in the question – you must *analyse and evaluate* it (9 marks are available for these two skills).
- You must also avoid simply writing all you know about the topic in general, regardless of its relevance. Instead, you must *interpret and apply* your material carefully so that it is relevant to the set question (9 marks are available for these two skills).
- For these reasons, and because this is a very long answer (about 50 minutes), it is vital that you *think and plan* before you start it.

The Unit 4 longer questions

Unit 4 contains several longer questions, ranging from 12 to 33 marks.

Question 1(a)

This is worth 12 marks. It asks you to *examine* something. For example:

Examine the role of access to opportunity structures in causing crime and deviance.

This is the only question at A2 where there are as many AO1 marks as AO2 marks. There are six for each, so you need to show both a reasonable range of knowledge and an ability to use it appropriately. This is best done by making a number of points and writing a solid paragraph developing each one in a way that links it clearly to the question.

Question 1(b)

This is worth 21 marks. Here is an example:

Using material from Item A and elsewhere, assess the value of the right realist approach to crime and deviance.

This is very similar to the 18-mark question (b) on Unit 3 (see above) – 'assess' signals that you must analyse and evaluate, and you must also use material from the Item to score high marks. The only difference is that there are three more marks for AO1, so you need to show good knowledge as well as AO2 skills.

Question 2(b)

This is worth 15 marks. It takes the same form as question 1(b), but it has a specific focus on Methods in Context. For example:

Using material from Item A and elsewhere, assess the strengths and weaknesses of using experiments to investigate power and authority in prisons.

Six of the marks are for AO1 and 9 for AO2. The same advice applies as for question 1(b), but in addition you must focus on the particular issue that the Item deals with. For this reason, it is vital to make maximum use of the Item.

Question 3

This is worth 33 marks. It is very similar to the 33-mark question on Unit 3, and all the information and advice above on that question applies to this one too – except that you have about 45 minutes to answer it rather than 50.

Box 5.1	AO1 and AO2 marks at a glance		
Question type	**AO1**	**AO2**	**Total**
Unit 3			
1(a) Identify and briefly explain	3	6	9
1(b) Using Item… assess	6	12	18
2 *or* 3 Essay: Assess	15	18	33
Total	*24*	*36*	*60*
Unit 4			
1(a) Examine	6	6	12
1(b) Using Item…assess	9	12	21
2(a) Identify and briefly explain	3	6	9
2(b) Using Item… assess	6	9	15
3 Essay: Assess	15	18	33
Total	*39*	*51*	*90*

Points to remember for essay questions

- Read the question carefully until you understand it; then make a brief plan.
- Write a short introduction linking to key aspects of the question.
- Stick to the question. Don't write 'Everything I know about crime and deviance (or beliefs in society, or theory and methods)' answers.
- Discuss a range of concepts, explanations, theories/perspectives and/or methods. Use evidence from sociological studies.
- Use the Items when instructed to, and use examples.
- Write a brief conclusion following logically from the main points in your essay.
- For all questions apart from the 'Examine' question on Unit 4, there are more marks for AO2 than for AO1. You will show these skills best by focusing throughout on the actual question and how your material helps to answer it.

Box 5.2   Using an Item

The Item and question below are from 'Examining labelling theory' in chapter 2. We have highlighted some of the key words and phrases you could use as a starting point when answering the question. We have suggested how you could connect these ideas to other material on the topic and to the question.

When using an Item, always try to find ways to link it to what you already know and to the question you have been asked.

Item A   According to a study of anti-social behaviour orders (ASBOs) by the Youth Justice Board (2006), some parents and magistrates thought they were a 'diploma in deviance' and they believed that youths saw them as a 'badge of honour'. Many youths did not regard the threat of custody as a deterrent to breaching their order.

The study also found that the orders were disproportionately used against ethnic minorities: blacks and Asians were about two and a half times more likely than whites to be given an ASBO.

The study found that it was not uncommon for young people to openly flout the prohibitions placed on them by the order. Figures show that by 2008 two-thirds had breached their orders.

Question   Using material from **Item A** and elsewhere, assess the view that crime and deviance are the product of labelling processes.

(21 marks)

Here are some examples of how you could use the highlights to stimulate your thinking and make links to other material and to the question:

- ASBOs are an example of a non-custodial sentence. You could link them to the idea that the net of social control is becoming wider.
- Why a 'diploma' in deviance? Can you link this to the notion of a deviant *career*?
- A 'badge of honour' is a label. You could use this to introduce a range of related concepts such as secondary deviance, self-fulfilling prophecy, master status etc.
- You could link the idea that youths did not regard the threat of custody as a deterrent to ideas about the nature and role of punishment.
- You could link the fact that ASBOs are disproportionately used against ethnic minorities and that blacks and Asians were about two and a half times more likely than whites to be given one, to police stereotyping or 'typifications' of ethnic minority youth. What stereotypes do the police hold and why?
- You could link the fact that many openly flout the prohibitions placed on them, to the concept of deviance amplification and to Lemert's idea that social control simply produces more deviance.
- On the other hand, two-thirds had breached their orders, which means that one-third of the youths had *not* breached their ASBOs – so you could use this as a way to criticise labelling theory (namely, the idea that control *does* sometimes prevent further deviance).

Unit 3 mock exam

Answer both questions.   **Time allowed: 1 hour 30 minutes**

1. Read **Item A** and answer parts (a) and (b) that follow.

Item A

Karl Marx, writing with Friedrich Engels, provided what has become a famous view of religion and its role. In their view:

'Religious distress is both the expression of real distress and the protest against real distress. Religion is the sigh of the oppressed creature, the heart of a heartless world, just as it is the spirit of a spiritless situation. It is the opium of the people. The abolition of religion as the illusory happiness of the people is required for their real happiness.'

Marx defines religion as an ideology that provides people with compensation for the fact that they are exploited. This exploitation is based on the division of society into a capitalist ruling class who own the means of production and who control the labour of others, and a working class who are forced to sell their labour power to survive.

                                                            Adapted from Bird (1999)

(a) Identify and briefly explain **three** reasons why some individuals might choose to join religious sects or cults.

                                                            (9 marks)

(b) Using material from **Item A** and elsewhere, assess the view that the main function of religion is ideological control of the working class.   (18 marks)

2. Assess the arguments for and against the view that contemporary societies are becoming more secular.

                                                            (33 marks)

Unit 4 mock exam

Answer all the questions.   **Time allowed: 2 hours**

You are advised to spend approximately 45 minutes on Question 1, 30 minutes on Question 2 and 45 minutes on Question 3.

1 Read **Item A** and answer parts (a) and (b) that follow.

Item A

For Marxists such as William Chambliss, the fundamental cause of crime is the state and the capitalist economic system that it serves. The ruling class use the state both to make the laws and to enforce them in their own class interests and against those of the working class. At the same time, the very nature of capitalism itself encourages criminal behaviour.

Neo-Marxist critical criminologists such as Taylor, Walton and Young share the view that capitalism causes crime. However, they argue that working-class crime can be seen as an act of political resistance against the ruling class, for example by redistributing wealth from the rich to the poor.

However, critics argue that this ignores the reality of crime and offers no practical solution to it.

(a) Examine the influences on the distribution of suicide in society.   (12 marks)

(b) Using material from **Item A** and elsewhere, assess the strengths and limitations of Marxist theories in explaining crime and deviance.   (21 marks)

2 This question requires you to **apply** your knowledge and understanding of sociological research methods to the study of this **particular** issue in crime and deviance.

Read **Item B** below and answer parts (a) and (b) that follow.

Item B

Researching young people and crime

Young people have less access to personal spaces, so most youth crime occurs in public places. There is also greater control and surveillance of young people, not only by the criminal justice system but also by family and school. More so than others, young people tend to carry out their activities in groups and the evidence suggests that group crime is generally more easily identified and apprehended. These factors increase the chances of youth crime being detected.

There are particular ethical issues when studying young people and crime. They are more vulnerable than adults and tend to have less status and power. Therefore researchers have to be particularly careful not to cause emotional or psychological damage to young people and to guarantee their anonymity.

Official statistics are useful because they allow the researcher to investigate young people and crime without facing these, and other, ethical problems. However, given the way crime statistics are socially constructed, a researcher should not rely too heavily on official crime statistics.

(a) Identify and briefly explain:
  (i) **two** problems of using victim surveys to study the victims of crime;   (6 marks)
  (ii) **one** problem of studying crime by interviewing prisoners.   (3 marks)
(b) Assess the strengths and weaknesses of using official statistics to investigate the relationship between young people and crime.   (15 marks)
3 Assess the usefulness of structural theories for an understanding of society.   (33 marks)

The examiner's advice: Unit 3

Q1(b) carries 6 AO1 and 12 AO2 marks. Start by explaining the Marxist view of religion as a means of ideological control of the working class, but consider other functions too. Make sure you use the Item – e.g. to examine how Marx saw religion as both consolation and protest. Evaluate by comparing Marxism with alternatives – e.g. the feminist view that religion functions to maintain patriarchy and the functionalist view that it performs beneficial functions for individuals and society as a whole.

Q2 carries 15 AO1 and 18 AO2 marks. You need to explain the arguments for and against secularisation and evaluate both viewpoints. Start with statistical evidence for secularisation (e.g. falling church attendance), then examine possible explanations, e.g. rationalisation, structural differentiation, social diversity and religious pluralism. Evaluate these by considering counter-trends, e.g. cultural defence/transition and growth of the New Age.

You should go on to examine arguments against secularisation, such as believing without belonging, religious market theory and postmodernist views of religion. You can evaluate anti-secularisation views e.g. by using Bruce or existential security theory. Consider whether all societies are becoming secular by looking at cross-cultural differences (e.g. Europe versus America) and how different viewpoints explain them.

The examiner's advice: Unit 4

Q1(a) carries 6 AO1 and 6 AO2 marks. The distribution of suicide refers to which groups commit or are recorded as suicides. Start with Durkheim's idea that moral regulation and social integration shape the suicide rate. Outline his typology and illustrate with examples, e.g. Protestants and egoistic suicide. Make reference to other positivists and the factors they see as influencing suicide. Use Douglas to consider the influence of coroners, relatives etc in shaping verdicts and the distribution of recorded suicides. Atkinson can also be used to evaluate Durkheim.

Q1(b) carries 9 AO1 and 12 AO2 marks. Begin by outlining the traditional Marxist view of crime and the law, using the Item to illustrate some of your points. You should include an explanation of why Marxists see capitalism as criminogenic, e.g. because of its competitive, exploitative nature. You should also explain the functions of the law for capitalism, e.g. in protecting ruling-class property, legitimising capitalism, criminalising the working class through selective enforcement etc.

You also need to deal with the neo-Marxist view, including its criticism of traditional Marxism as deterministic and how it introduces elements of labelling theory. You can evaluate from the standpoint of other perspectives, including the left realist view that neo-Marxism romanticises street crime and ignores the fact that its victims are the working class, not capitalism.

Q2(b) carries 6 AO1 and 9 AO2 marks. You must apply your knowledge of official statistics to the study of the particular issue of young people and crime. It is not enough simply to discuss statistics in general. Attach one or more strengths and limitations of official statistics to the research characteristics of young people and crime. Start with Item A – e.g. it states that there are particular ethical problems associated with investigating young people. You could link this to official statistics by noting that they enable the researcher to keep a distance from their research subjects and avoid most ethical concerns.

A characteristic not mentioned in Item A is how the age of young offenders may generate sympathy for them among researchers and affect the direction of the study. Try to balance strengths and limitations. You can also refer to studies using this method and any relevant research you have been involved in.

Q3 carries 15 AO1 and 18 AO2 marks. First you should explain that 'structural' theories are ones that see the social structure shaping the behaviour of individuals. These include functionalist, Marxist and many feminist theories. You can contrast how these theories see the social structure, e.g. as based on consensus (functionalist) or conflict (Marxism and feminism). Explain how they see the individual as shaped by socialisation, the class structure, patriarchy etc. You can evaluate them from an 'action' perspective – e.g. that structural theories have an 'over-socialised' view of individuals as puppets of the social system, and neglect actors' meanings and how they construct social reality. Also consider attempts to synthesise structure and action by neo-Marxists, e.g. Gramsci or Willis, or Giddens' structuration theory.

Key Concepts

The following is an alphabetical list of some of the key concepts you need to know for A2 Sociology. You can use the list as:

- **a handy reference** to find a quick definition of a term you're not sure of
- **a revision aid** to ensure you know and understand important sociological ideas.

When you look up a concept in the list, you may find that a lot of entries give you a 'see also' reference. Following these up will show you some of the links between concepts and broaden your understanding of them.

action theories see individuals as having free will and choice, and the power to create society through their actions and interactions, rather than being shaped by society. Interactionism is the best-known theory of this type. Postmodernism also has certain features in common with action theories. See also structural theories.

alienation Where an individual or group feels socially isolated and estranged because they lack the power to control their lives and realise their true potential. Marx describes workers in capitalist society as alienated because they are exploited and lack control of the production process. See also Marxism.

anomie means normlessness. Durkheim argues that anomie arises when there is rapid social change, because existing norms become unclear or outdated, and that this is a cause of suicide. Merton's 'strain' theory argues that where individuals lack legitimate means of achieving culturally prescribed goals it results in a strain to anomie, which some resolve by adopting illegitimate means such as 'innovation' (utilitarian crime for economic gain). Other responses are retreatism, rebellion, ritualism and conformity.

asceticism Abstinence, self-discipline and self-denial. Before Calvinism, Christian asceticism was 'other-worldly' and meant renouncing everyday life to join a convent or monastery. Calvinism introduced the idea of this-worldly asceticism. Calvinists believed that God had put them on earth to glorify his name by work in an occupation, not in a monastery. For this reason, the Calvinists led an ascetic lifestyle, working long hours, shunning luxury and practising rigorous self-discipline. See also disenchantment; rationalisation.

bourgeoisie The capitalist class, the owners of the means of production (factories, machinery, raw materials, land etc). Marx argues that ownership of the means of production also gives the bourgeoisie political and ideological power. See also exploitation; ideology; Marxism; proletariat.

capitalism See Marxism.

case study Research that examines a single case or example, such as a single school, family or workplace, often using several methods or sources.

chivalry thesis, the This is the view that the criminal justice system is biased in favour of women, so that they are less likely than men to be charged, convicted or punished. It is argued that these gender differences result from male-dominated police, courts and prosecuting authorities basing their actions on a stereotype of females as incapable of serious criminality.

churches are large bureaucratic organisations, often with millions of members, run by a formal hierarchy of professional priests and claiming a monopoly of the truth. They aim to include the whole of society, but tend to attract the higher classes because they are conservative and often closely linked to the state. See also sects; denominations; cults.

civil religion A belief system that attaches sacred qualities to society itself and makes the nation-state the object of religious or quasi-religious worship. Belief and participation in the civil religion is equated with being a good citizen. Civil religion is seen as promoting social solidarity, expressed through rituals and symbols such as pledging allegiance to the flag. In America, civil religion is a faith in 'the American way of life'. See also collective conscience; functional alternatives; social integration.

class See social class.

closed-ended questions Sometimes called forced choice questions, these are questions in a survey that allow only a limited choice of answers from a pre-set list. They produce quantitative data and the answers are often pre-coded for ease of analysis. See also open-ended questions.

collective conscience, collective consciousness Terms referring to the shared norms, values, beliefs and knowledge that make social life and cooperation between individuals possible. In Durkheim's view, the collective conscience is represented in society's sacred symbols such as the religious totems of the Australian aborigines. It integrates society by giving individuals a sense of belonging to something greater than themselves. See also social integration; value consensus.

comparative method A research method that compares two social groups that are alike apart from one factor. Durkheim compared two groups that were identical apart from their religion in order to find out the effect of religion on suicide rates. The method is often used as an alternative to experiments. See also experiments.

compensators According to Stark and Bainbridge, when real rewards are scarce or unobtainable, religion compensates us by promising supernatural ones; e.g. immortality is unobtainable, but religion compensates by promising life after death. For Stark and Bainbridge, only religion provides such compensators. Non-religious ideologies such as humanism and communism do not provide credible compensators because they do not promise supernatural rewards. See also religious market theory.

content analysis A method of analysing the content of documents and media output to find out how often and in what ways different types of people or events appear. The Glasgow University Media Group (1976) used content analysis to reveal bias in how television news reported strikes.

control group In experiments, scientists compare a control group and an experimental group that are identical in all respects. Unlike the experimental group, the control group is not exposed to the variable under investigation and so provides a baseline against which any changes in the experimental group can be compared. See also experiments.

correlation When two or more factors or variables vary together; e.g. there is a correlation between low social class and low

Key Concepts

educational achievement. However, the existence of a correlation between two variables does not necessarily prove that one causes the other; it may simply be coincidence. See also experiments.

covert participant observation See participant observation.

critical criminology is a neo-Marxist approach that combines ideas from traditional Marxism and labelling theory to explain crime in capitalist society. It sees working-class crime as a conscious and often political act of resistance to the exploitation and oppression that they suffer under capitalism.

cults are loose-knit and usually small religious or spiritual groups of individuals with similar interests. Cults lack a sharply defined belief system and are tolerant of other beliefs. They are often led by 'practitioners' or 'therapists' who claim special knowledge. Many cults are world-affirming, claiming to improve life in this world. Those who take part are more like clients or customers than members of a church. See also churches; denominations; sects; new religious movements; New Age spirituality; spiritual shopping.

cultural defence Where religion provides a focal point for the defence of national, ethnic, local or other group identity in a struggle against an external force such as a hostile foreign power. For example, Catholicism in Poland was a source of national identity for many people during the communist period (1945-89), when the country was under the influence of the former Soviet Union. See also cultural transition.

cultural transition The process of moving from one culture to another. Bruce argues that religion plays an important role in cultural transition for minority ethnic groups who find themselves in a new culture, by providing support and a sense of community in a different country and culture. See also cultural defence.

culture All those things that are learnt and shared by a society or group and transmitted from generation to generation through socialisation, including shared norms, values, knowledge, beliefs and skills. See also subculture.

denominations are religious organisations that lie midway between churches and sects, e.g. Methodism. Like churches, they broadly accept society's values, but they are not linked to the state. They impose restrictions on their members (e.g. forbidding alcohol) but are not as demanding as sects. Unlike both churches and sects (but like cults), they are tolerant of other religious organisations and beliefs and do not claim a monopoly of the truth. See also churches; sects; cults.

dependency culture Where people assume that the state will support them, rather than relying on their own efforts and taking responsibility for their families. The New Right see the welfare state as over-generous, encouraging people to remain unemployed and dependent on benefits, and as responsible for the growing number of lone-parent families and rising crime rate. See also underclass.

determinism The idea that humans have no free will and that their thoughts and behaviour are shaped or caused by factors outside themselves, such as the social structure. Marxism is often accused of economic determinism – the view that the economic base shapes all other features of society's 'superstructure', such as social institutions and ideas. Determinism is the opposite of voluntarism. See also voluntarism.

deterrence See punishment.

deviance Behaviour that does not conform to the norms of a society or group. Deviance is a social construction – it is defined or created by social groups. Deviance is relative: what counts as deviant varies between groups and cultures and over time. Interactionists distinguish between primary and secondary deviance. Primary deviance refers to deviant acts that have not been publicly labelled and usually have little significance for the individual's status. Secondary deviance results from societal reaction (labelling) and may lead to the individual taking on a deviant master status, resulting in a self-fulfilling prophecy and deviant career.

deviance amplification spiral is the process whereby attempts to control deviance actually produce an increase in deviance, leading to greater attempts at control and still higher levels of deviance. For example, in a moral panic – an exaggerated over-reaction to a perceived problem – a folk devil is identified as a threat to society's values, and the media and moral entrepreneurs call for a crackdown on the problem, but this results in an increase in the scale of the problem as more individuals are publicly labelled. See also labelling; self-fulfilling prophecy.

disciplinary power According to Foucault, disciplinary power is the typical form of control in modern society. It is based on self-surveillance and self-discipline as a means of inducing conformity. Its model is the panopticon, a design for a prison in which the inmates are visible to the guards but not vice versa, so the prisoners must always act as if they are being watched, thereby turning surveillance into self-surveillance. Unlike sovereign power, which was typical of pre-modern society and sought simply to punish and control the body, disciplinary power seeks to govern the mind as well. See also punishment.

discourse Foucault sees a discourse as a set of ideas that have become established as knowledge or a way of thinking and speaking about the world. A discourse makes us see things in a particular way, so it is also a form of domination or 'power/knowledge'. A discourse is neither true nor false in any absolute sense, so there is no objective way of choosing between competing discourses. Knowledge cannot therefore be used to improve society or bring progress. See also relativism.

disenchantment The process whereby magical and religious ways of thinking are replaced by a rational mode of thought. Events cease to be explained as the work of unpredictable supernatural beings or forces. Instead, they are explained and predicted as being the result of natural forces governed by scientific laws. In a disenchanted world there is no longer any need for religious explanations. Weber sees the Protestant Reformation as beginning the process of disenchantment. See also rationalisation; secularisation.

diversity Social, cultural or religious diversity exists where people differ from one another in terms of occupations, lifestyles, beliefs etc. See also pluralism; postmodernism.

documents Public documents are produced by organisations such as governments, media etc; e.g. Acts of Parliament, school prospectuses, newspaper articles. Personal documents are created by individuals and often provide first-person accounts of events and experiences. They include diaries, letters, autobiographies etc. Both types are used as secondary sources of qualitative data in sociological research.

dramaturgical model Developed by Goffman, this interactionist approach uses analogies with drama as a framework for analysing social interaction – 'actors' carry off convincing 'role-performances' using 'props' to act out their 'scripts' etc. The model sees us actively constructing the self through impression management to manipulate the 'audience's' perception of us. See also interactionism.

empathy An understanding of how another person thinks, feels or acts, achieved by putting oneself in their place. Action theorists advocate the use of qualitative methods such as participant observation as a way of achieving verstehen or empathetic understanding. See also interactionism; objectivity; subjectivity.

Enlightenment project See modernism.

environmental crime prevention A crime reduction strategy associated with Wilson and Kelling's article, *Broken Windows*. It sees serious crime as arising out of disorder and advocates 'cracking down' on all forms of neighbourhood decline through a twofold strategy of environmental improvement and zero tolerance policing, where the police tackle proactively even the slightest sign of disorder. See also right realism.

ethics Issues of right and wrong; moral principles or guidelines. There are ethical objections to research which deceives or harms its participants or which fails to obtain their informed consent.

ethnomethodology An interpretivist approach developed by Garfinkel, it rejects the idea of an external social structure and sees society as a social construct. Although meanings are always potentially unclear (which Garfinkel calls indexicality), society's members use commonsense knowledge to achieve a sense of order (a process known as reflexivity). This is similar to the idea of typifications put forward by Schutz. See also phenomenology.

existential security theory Existential security is the feeling that survival is secure enough that it can be taken for granted. The theory is based on the view that religion arises where people lack economic security. It explains why religion has declined most in affluent societies where there is welfare provision, and why religion remains popular in poorer societies and among the poor in richer or more unequal societies. See also religious market theory; secularisation.

experiments A laboratory experiment is a test carried out in controlled conditions in an artificial setting (a laboratory), to establish a cause-and-effect relationship between two or more variables. A field experiment has the same aim but is carried out in a natural setting (e.g. a street or workplace) not a laboratory, so the researcher has less control over variables. See also control group; positivism.

experimental group See control group.

exploitation Paying workers less than the value of their labour. According to Marxists, it is the process whereby the bourgeoisie extract surplus value or profit from the labour of the proletariat. Feminists see men as exploiting the domestic labour of women. See also Marxism; feminism.

falsificationism According to Popper, falsificationism is the defining characteristic of scientific knowledge, which consists of statements that can in principle be falsified (disproved) by experiment or observation, unlike the knowledge-claims of religion, tradition or theories such as Marxism. A good theory is one that claims to explain a wide range of events and, despite being falsifiable in principle, stands up to all attempts to disprove it. Falsificationism is the opposite of verificationism – the idea that a theory can be proved true simply by gathering evidence that confirms or verifies it. See also open and closed belief systems.

feminism A sociological perspective and political movement that focuses on women's oppression and the struggle to end it.

Feminists argue that sociology has traditionally taken a 'malestream' viewpoint that ignores women. Instead, they examine women's experiences and study society from a female perspective. There are different strands of feminism, including Marxist, radical, liberal and difference or poststructuralist feminism. See also patriarchy.

folk devil See deviance amplification spiral.

Fordism A type of industrial production based on a detailed division of labour, using closely supervised, low-skilled workers and assembly-line technology to mass-produce standardised goods. Named after the manufacturing techniques first introduced by the Ford Motor Company in the early 20th century. See also alienation; post-Fordism.

function The contribution that a part of society makes to the stability or well-being of society as a whole. For example, one function of religion may be to give individuals a sense of belonging to something greater than themselves and thus integrate them into society. Merton distinguishes between manifest and latent functions. The former are the intended consequences of an institution or practice, while the latter are its unintended or hidden consequences. See also functionalism.

functional alternatives or functional equivalents are institutions that perform the same function as another institution. For example, some secular beliefs (such as political ideologies) may perform the same function as religious ones in maintaining social solidarity. See also civil religion; collective conscience; social integration.

functionalism A consensus perspective that sees society as based on shared values into which members are socialised. It sees society as like an organism, each part performing functions to maintain the system as a whole; e.g. religion, the family and education system perform socialisation functions. See also function; value consensus.

fundamentalism Religion based on an unquestioning belief in the literal truth of a sacred text. Fundamentalists believe that there is only one true view of the world, which is revealed in a sacred text, not gained through scientific enquiry or rational argument. Major examples are Protestant and Islamic fundamentalisms. See also relativism.

globalisation The idea that the world is becoming increasingly interconnected and that barriers are disappearing, e.g. as a result of instantaneous communication systems, deregulation of trade, the creation of global markets and global media and culture. Many see it as creating new risks, uncertainties and choices, and an increased rate of social change. See also postmodernity; risk society.

green crimes are crimes against the environment and the human and non-human animals within it. Primary green crimes involve the destruction and degradation of the earth's resources, including crimes of air and water pollution, deforestation, species decline and animal rights. Secondary green crime involves the breaking of laws aimed at preventing or regulating environmental disasters, such as illegal dumping of hazardous waste by organised crime.

green criminology See zemiology.

Hawthorne effect Where the subjects of research know they are being studied and begin to behave differently as a result, thereby undermining the study's validity. The term comes from Elton Mayo's studies at the Hawthorne electrical plant. See also validity.

hegemony A Marxist concept developed by Gramsci to explain how the ruling class holds the ideological and moral leadership of society, using ideas and values to prevent revolution by winning the consent of the subordinate classes to its rule. The ruling class is able to do this by controlling the institutions that produce ideas, such as the education system, religion and the media. See also ideology; Marxism.

hypothesis An untested theory or explanation, expressed as a statement. Sociologists seek to prove or disprove hypotheses by testing them against the evidence. See also experiments; falsificationism.

identity The individual's sense of self, influenced by socialisation and interactions with others; a sense of belonging to a community. Postmodernists see identity as a choice that individuals make from among different identity sources such as gender, ethnic group, religion, sexuality, leisure interests, nationality etc. See also postmodernism.

ideology Originally a Marxist idea meaning a set of beliefs that serve the interests of a dominant group by justifying their privileged position. The term usually implies that the beliefs are false or only partially true; e.g. Bowles and Gintis argue that meritocracy is a 'myth'. See also hegemony; legitimation; Marxism.

individualism The idea that the individual is more important than the group or community. In modern and postmodern society, individualism becomes more important than in traditional society and individuals' actions are influenced more by calculations of self-interest than by a sense of obligation to others. Secularisation theorists argue that individualism leads to the decline of religion by undermining its communal basis, but others argue that it has changed religion into a search for personal fulfilment. See also New Age spirituality; secularisation.

industrialisation The shift from an agricultural economy to one based on factory production. In Britain, industrialisation occurred from about the late 18th to the mid-19th centuries. Industrialisation often occurs along with urbanisation.

incapacitation See punishment.

informed consent Where those taking part in a study have agreed to do so and understand the purpose of the study, the uses to which its findings may be put, and its possible effects. See also ethics.

interactionism A perspective focusing on small-scale (micro-level) interactions between individuals and groups, rather than on the large-scale workings of society. Interactionists seek to understand the meanings that social actors give to actions and situations, usually by using qualitative research methods. See also interpretivism; labelling; self-fulfilling prophecy.

interpretivism A term covering a range of approaches including social action theory, symbolic interactionism, phenomenology and ethnomethodology. Interpretivists focus on how we construct our social worlds through the meanings we create and attach to events, actions and situations. They favour qualitative methods and see human beings as fundamentally different from the natural phenomena studied by scientists, in that we have free will, consciousness and choice. See also positivism; subjectivity.

interview schedule The list of questions to be asked in an interview. It is useful because it allows some standardisation of the interviewing process, since all interviewers will use the same questions.

interviews A method of gathering information by asking questions orally, either face-to-face or by telephone. Structured (or formal) interviews use pre-set, standardised, usually closed-ended questions producing quantitative data. Unstructured (informal or depth) interviews are more like a guided conversation and use open-ended questions producing qualitative data. Semi-structured interviews include both types of question. See also questionnaires.

knowledge claim A claim made by a belief system to know about the world, what it is like and, sometimes, how it ought to be and how we ought to act. For example, science, political ideologies and religions make knowledge claims. However, science does not make 'ought' claims, but merely claims to describe and explain the world. See also falsificationism; ideology; open and closed belief systems.

labelling is the process of attaching a definition or meaning to an individual or group; e.g. police officers may label a youth as a 'trouble maker'. Often the label is a stereotype that sees all members of a group as sharing the same attributes. The concept is widely used in the study of crime and deviance. Labelling theory uses concepts such as definition of the situation, the looking glass self and career to explain how individuals' actions and identities are shaped through the labels that are applied to them. See also deviance; self-fulfilling prophecy.

left realism regards crime as a real problem, particularly for disadvantaged groups, who are more likely to be its victims. Left realists are reformist socialists who see relative deprivation and the marginalisation of the poor as producing criminal subcultures whose members victimise other poor people. To tackle the problem of crime, they argue for structural reforms to reduce inequality and for democratic and accountable policing. See also right realism.

legitimation Justifying something by making it seem fair and natural. This is the main function of ideology. Marxists argue that institutions in capitalist society such as education, the media and religion are ideological state apparatuses whose function is to legitimate inequality.

longitudinal study Study of a sample of people (sometimes called a panel) in which information is collected at regular intervals over an extended period of time; e.g. the National Child Development Study has been running since 1958. These studies usually use questionnaires or interviews, but other methods may also be employed.

macro-level Theories such as functionalism and Marxism that focus on the large scale, i.e. on the social structure as a whole or on the relationships between social institutions like the education system and the economy. These theories see the individual as shaped by society. See also micro-level; positivism.

Marxism A conflict perspective based on the ideas of Karl Marx (1818-83). It sees society as divided into two opposed classes, one of which exploits the labour of the other. In capitalist society, the bourgeoisie (capitalist class) owns the means of production and exploits the labour of the propertyless proletariat (working class). Marx predicted that the proletariat would unite to overthrow capitalism and create a classless society. Humanistic Marxists place more emphasis on the role of class consciousness and ideas in bringing change, whereas scientific or structuralist Marxists emphasise the role of economic, political and ideological structures. See also alienation; exploitation; hegemony; ideology; modernism; polarisation.

means of production See bourgeoisie.

micro-level Theories such as interactionism that focus on small-scale, face-to-face interaction, e.g. between teacher and pupils in a classroom. These theories see individuals constructing society through their interactions. See also interpretivism; macro-level.

modernism Modernist theories (e.g. functionalism, Marxism and positivism) believe that society has a fairly clear-cut, predictable structure and that it is possible to gain true and certain scientific knowledge of how society functions. This knowledge can be used to achieve progress to a better society. The modernist notion of progress through the application of rational knowledge to social problems is sometimes referred to as the Enlightenment project. See also modernity; postmodernism.

modernity, modern society is seen as beginning with the industrial revolution. It is characterised by rapid social change, scientific and technological development, secularisation, the decline of tradition, and the bureaucratic nation-state. Modernist perspectives (such as Marxism and functionalism) seek to explain and predict its development. Beck, Giddens and others argue that in late or high modernity, many of these trends become accelerated, especially as a result of globalisation. See also globalisation; modernism; postmodernism; postmodernity; risk society.

moral panic See deviance amplification spiral.

neutralisation techniques are used by delinquents to justify their deviant behaviour (e.g. by claiming that the victim of a crime deserved it). Stan Cohen argues that states also use such techniques to justify crimes that they commit such as massacres, genocide and torture. These include denial of victim, of injury and of responsibility ('I was only obeying orders'), condemning the condemners and appeal to higher loyalty (e.g. 'the interests of national security').

New Age spirituality includes a very diverse range of beliefs and practices that have grown rapidly since the 1980s, which reject external authority and traditional sources of religion such as churches, priests and sacred texts. Spirituality refers to personal and subjective aspects of religion and the supernatural. The New Age holds the view that we can discover the truth for ourselves through experience, by following a personal spiritual path and exploring one's inner self. Increased interest in spirituality can be seen in the growth of the New Age spiritual market. Examples range from astrology to Zen Buddhism. See also new religious movements; cults; sects.

New Right A conservative political perspective whose supporters believe in self-reliance and individual choice, rather than dependence on the state. They believe in applying free market principles, e.g. the marketisation of education, and argue that generous welfare benefits encourage the growth of a criminal underclass. See also underclass; right realism.

new religious movements (NRMs) have grown since the 1960s, such as the Moonies, Scientology and Krishna Consciousness. Wallis distinguishes between three types of NRM depending on whether their attitudes to wider society are world-rejecting, world-accepting or world-accommodating. They have grown because of the marginality of some groups and individuals, relative deprivation and rapid social change. See also cults; sects; New Age spirituality.

news values are the criteria by which journalists and editors decide whether a story is newsworthy enough to make it into the newspaper or news bulletin. News values include criteria such as immediacy, dramatisation, personalisation, risk and violence. Crime often fits these criteria and is thus over-reported. Journalists' use of news values illustrates the idea that news is a social construction – something that is manufactured rather than discovered. See also social construction.

non-participant observation A primary research method where the observer records events without taking part in them; e.g. a sociologist might observe and record how gender roles influence children's play without taking part, often using a structured observation schedule.

norms Social rules, expectations or standards that govern the behaviour expected in particular situations. Norms may be formal (e.g. written laws or rules) or informal (e.g. rules of politeness). Each culture has detailed norms governing every aspect of behaviour. See also values.

objectivity The absence of bias or preconceived ideas. It implies that we can look at things as they really are and get at the truth, without our opinions or values getting in the way. Positivists believe sociology can achieve objectivity by modelling itself on the natural sciences, using methods that keep sociologists detached from their research subjects. See also positivism; subjectivity; value freedom.

official statistics Quantitative data collected by the government. They can be gathered by registration (e.g. the law requires parents to register births), by official surveys (e.g. the ten-yearly population Census) or from administrative records (e.g. of schools or courts).

open and closed belief systems Closed belief systems make knowledge claims that cannot be disproved. According to Popper, religion and Marxism are closed systems because, when challenged by contradictory evidence, they reject the evidence or have 'get-out clauses' that reinforce existing beliefs. Open belief systems make knowledge claims that are open to criticism and can in principle be falsified by testing. Popper describes science as an open belief system. See also falsificationism; knowledge claims.

open-ended questions Questions that allow respondents to answer as they wish, in their own words (e.g. 'How did it feel to be a victim of crime?'). Answers are harder to analyse because they cannot be pre-coded. See also closed-ended questions.

operationalisation The process of turning a sociological concept or theory into something measurable. For example, a sociologist studying the effect of social class on educational achievement might use parental occupation to measure the concept 'social class'.

overt participant observation See participant observation.

paradigm According to Kuhn, a paradigm is shared by members of a scientific community. It defines for them what 'normal science' is, providing them with a shared framework of basic assumptions within which to work. It tells them what nature is like, which aspects to study, the methods to use and questions to ask, and even the sort of answers they should find. Kuhn likens science under the paradigm to puzzle solving. Eventually, the accumulation of anomalies (results that the paradigm cannot account for) produces a crisis, and a scientific revolution establishes a new paradigm. See also falsificationism.

participant observation A primary research method in which the sociologist studies a group by taking a role within it and participating in its activities. It may be overt, where other participants are aware of the researcher's true identity and motive, or covert, where the sociologist's identity and purpose are kept secret.

patriarchy Literally, rule by the father. Feminists use the term to describe a society based on male domination; a system or ideology of male power over women. Child liberationists argue that children are victims of 'age patriarchy' – the domination of fathers, or adults generally. See also feminism.

Key Concepts

phenomenology An interpretivist approach developed by Schutz. He argues that we make sense of the world through shared concepts or categories called 'typifications'. Meanings are potentially unstable and unclear, but typifications clarify and stabilise them, allowing us to communicate and cooperate. In doing so, they give the world the appearance of being natural, orderly and real, but in fact it is simply a construction produced by typifications. See also ethnomethodology; interpretivism.

pilot study A small-scale trial run, usually of a social survey, conducted before the main study. Its basic aim is to iron out problems, clarify questions and their wording, give interviewers practice etc, so that any necessary changes can be made before the main study is carried out.

pluralism A pluralistic society is one with many different cultures, religions or political parties. Berger sees religious pluralism undermining religion's plausibility structure or credibility because, where there are many competing versions of the truth being put forward by different religions, people become sceptical about all of them. Berger contrasts this with how, in the Middle Ages, religion was stronger because the Catholic Church had a monopoly of religious truth and the whole society lived under a single 'sacred canopy' of shared beliefs. See also diversity; postmodernism; secularisation.

polarisation A process that results in the creation of two opposite extremes. Marx describes how in capitalist society the class structure becomes polarised into a wealthy bourgeoisie and impoverished proletariat. See also Marxism.

population In a social survey, the population (sometimes called the 'survey population') is all the members of the group in which the researcher is interested; e.g. in a study of political opinions, the population may be the entire electorate. See also sampling frame.

positivism The belief that society is made up of 'social facts' that can be studied scientifically to discover laws of cause and effect. Durkheim took official statistics on suicide as social facts and tried to produce a law explaining why suicide rates vary between groups. With such knowledge, positivists believe we can find solutions to social problems. See also comparative method; experiments; interpretivism; objectivity.

post-Fordism A type of industrial production. A highly skilled, adaptable workforce, combined with computerised technology, means that production takes the form of 'flexible specialisation', able to respond swiftly to changing consumer demands and to produce for a variety of small, customised 'niche' markets. See also Fordism.

postmodernism rejects modernism's belief in progress and its view that we can have certain, true knowledge of society that will enable us to improve it. Postmodern society is so unstable and diverse that it is now impossible to produce any absolute explanations. No one theory is truer than any other; theories such as Marxism and functionalism, as well as science, are merely 'meta-narratives' or viewpoints. See also modernism; postmodernity.

postmodernity, postmodern society Postmodernists argue that society has moved into a new era of postmodernity – a globalised, media-saturated society in which signs become 'hyper-real' simulacra with no reference to any external reality. Culture is fragmented, unstable and ever-changing, and individuals create and change their identities through consumption of signs and brands. Some Marxists see postmodernity as simply the latest phase of capitalism, in which globalisation and post-Fordist production processes permit the flexible accumulation of capital. See also modernity; post-Fordism; postmodernism.

primary data Information collected first hand by sociologists themselves for their own research purposes. Methods such as participant observation, social surveys and experiments are sources of primary data. See also secondary data.

privatisation The separation of an aspect of social life from the rest of society or the loss of its public role. For example, some sociologists argue that in modern society, religion has become privatised. Where previously religion played an important public role, influencing many areas of life such as education and the law, it is now merely a private matter of personal preference. See also structural differentiation; secularisation.

proletariat The working class in capitalist society. They own no means of production and are 'wage slaves', forced to sell their labour-power to the bourgeoisie in order to survive. See also exploitation; Marxism.

punishment Criminologists argue that punishment performs various functions. These include deterrence (either of the criminal or of others who might commit a similar crime), rehabilitation, and incapacitation (e.g. executing or jailing offenders to prevent them re-offending). Punishment may also be a form of retribution, in which society expresses its outrage and seeks vengeance against the criminal. Durkheim argues that punishment in modern society is largely restitutive, i.e. it seeks to restore the status quo, for example through compensation. See also disciplinary power.

qualitative data Information, usually expressed in words, about people's thoughts, feelings, motivations, attitudes, values etc. It is obtained from qualitative methods and sources such as participant observation, unstructured interviews, diaries and letters. It aims to give an insight into what it is like to be in another person's 'shoes'. See also empathy; interactionism.

quantitative data Information in numerical form (percentages, tables, graphs etc). Official statistics and the results of social surveys are important sources of quantitative data. See also closed-ended questions; positivism.

questionnaires Lists of questions. Written or self-completion questionnaires are widely used in large-scale social surveys, where they may be sent out and returned by post or e-mail. Questionnaires tend to use mainly closed-ended questions with pre-coded answers for ease of analysis. See also quantitative data; response rate.

rationalisation The process by which rational and scientific ways of thinking and acting gradually replace magico-religious ones. Weber argued that the Protestant Reformation in the 16th century started a process of rationalisation in the West which undermined the medieval religious worldview and played a key role in the emergence of modern society and capitalism. See also disenchantment; secularisation.

rational choice theory See right realism.

realism The view that science deals with unobservable underlying structures (such as class), in contrast to the positivist view that it only deals with observable phenomena. Realists distinguish between sciences dealing with closed systems that can be studied in the laboratory, and those studying open systems (such as society), which cannot. In criminology, left and right realist theories see crime (especially street crime) as a 'real problem' to which solutions must be found. See left realism; right realism.

reflexivity Used by Giddens to describe the situation in late or high modern society where tradition and custom no longer guide our actions. As a result, we are forced to become more reflexive – to constantly monitor, reflect on and modify our actions in the light of information about the possible risks and opportunities they might involve. Ethnomethodologists also use the term in a different sense to refer to constructing social order or making sense of reality. See also ethnomethodology; globalisation; modernity; risk society.

rehabilitation See punishment.

relativism The view that knowledge claims are not absolutely true or false, but merely true for those who believe them. The opposite of relativism is absolutism – the conviction that only one set of beliefs is true and that all others are totally wrong. Religious fundamentalists take an absolutist view that they have unique access to the truth. Critics argue that relativism is self-defeating – if no knowledge claim is absolutely true, then why should we believe relativism's claims? See also fundamentalism; pluralism; postmodernism.

reliability Research is reliable if it produces exactly the same results (a replica) when repeated using identical methods and procedures. In general, quantitative methods such as experiments and questionnaires are more reliable than qualitative methods because they use standardised procedures that are easier to replicate; e.g. a questionnaire that asks all respondents the same set of questions.

religious market theory Also called rational choice theory, this compares religious organisations with businesses competing for customers. Less popular religions decline, while others grow by offering people what they want. However, the overall demand for religion remains constant because, in this view, people are naturally religious; secularisation is only one stage in a perpetual cycle of religious decline and renewal. See also compensators; secularisation.

representative Typical; a cross-section. A researcher may choose to study a sample of a larger group. If the sample is representative, those in it will be typical of the larger group. This will allow the findings to be generalised, i.e. applied to all members of the group, not just those in the sample.

reserve army of labour A Marxist concept describing groups who can be brought into the workforce when there is a labour shortage as the capitalist economy expands during a boom, and discarded when it contracts. Women were used as a reserve army of labour during the two world wars, returning afterwards to their primary domestic role. See also Marxism.

response rate The proportion of those people included in a social survey who actually reply or respond to the questions asked. A high response rate is important to help ensure that findings are representative.

right realism sees crime as a real problem. Politically, right realists are conservatives who favour a tougher approach to crime. They reject as impractical, strategies that seek to tackle possible underlying causes of crime (such as poverty or inadequate socialisation). They see crime as a rational choice, in which criminals weigh up the risks and rewards. Right realists therefore focus on situational and environmental crime prevention strategies such as target hardening and zero tolerance policing as means of deterrence.

risk society According to Beck, in late modern society, the risks now facing humankind are increasingly human-made or manufactured risks, rather than the risks posed by nature such as famine, drought and plague to which humans were traditionally exposed. These risks are increasingly global rather than local, such as climate change, leading Beck to describe late modern society as global risk society.

role How someone who occupies a particular status is expected to act; e.g. someone playing the role of bus driver is expected to drive safely, stop for passengers, charge the correct fare etc.

sample A smaller group selected from the larger survey population to take part in a study. It may be too costly or time-consuming to study the whole population in which we are interested, so we choose a sample to study instead. See also sampling; sampling frame.

sampling The process of selecting a sample. The aim of sampling is usually to select a sample that is representative of the wider survey population, so as to allow the study's findings to be generalised. There are several types of sampling, e.g. random, stratified random, quota and snowball sampling. See also sample; sampling frame.

sampling frame The list of people from which a sample for a study is selected, e.g. a school roll could be the sampling frame for a survey of pupils. It should list all the members of the survey population that the sociologist is interested in studying, though this is not always possible; e.g. there is no complete list of all criminals (since some are not caught). See sample; sampling.

sanctions See social control.

secondary data Information collected not by sociologists themselves for their own research purposes, but by other people or organisations for non-sociological purposes. Sociologists make extensive use of this 'second hand' information because it is often free or cheap, readily available and covers large numbers. Secondary sources of data include official statistics, the media and personal documents. See also primary data.

sects are small, exclusive religious groups that expect strong commitment from their members. Sects vary considerably in terms of organisation and aims. They are often hostile to wider society and draw their members from the poor and oppressed. Others attract those seeking health, wealth and happiness in this world. Many are led by a charismatic leader. Like churches, sects claim a monopoly of religious truth. See also churches; denominations; cults.

secularisation The decline of religion; the process whereby religious beliefs, practices and institutions lose their importance or influence; e.g. fewer couples now marry in church and many people disregard religious teachings on issues like divorce, homosexuality etc.

self-fulfilling prophecy Where a prediction made about a person or group comes true simply by virtue of it having been made. For example, in predicting that some pupils will do badly, teachers treat them in line with these lower expectations. This will discourage the pupils from trying and make the prediction come true. The prediction is a form of labelling. It works by changing the individual's self-concept to bring it in line with the expectations that others have of him or her. See also interactionism; deviance.

self-report studies ask individuals to disclose the crimes or anti-social behaviour for which they have been responsible. They are often used as a corrective to official police statistics, since they can include crimes committed of which the police are unaware. However, they have their limitations; for example, they tend to focus on more trivial offences; serious offenders may also be more likely to conceal their offending. See also victim surveys.

separatism A radical feminist idea that women should organise to live independently of men as the only way to free themselves from patriarchal oppression.

situational crime prevention is a strategy for reducing opportunities for crime. It aims to manage the immediate environment of specific crimes (e.g. burglary) so as to increase the effort and risks, and reduce the rewards, of committing the crime. It often involves 'target hardening' (e.g. fitting better locks, installing CCTV) to deter criminals. Critics argue that this may lead to displacement, where criminals seek out softer targets instead. See also right realism.

social class Social groupings or hierarchy based on differences in wealth, income or occupation. Marx identified two opposed classes in capitalist society: the bourgeoisie and proletariat. Many sociologists use occupation to distinguish between a manual working class and a non-manual middle class. Some also identify an underclass beneath the working class. See also Marxism; underclass.

social construction Where something is created by social processes, rather than simply occurring naturally. For example, interpretivists argue that official crime statistics are socially constructed through the interactions of police and suspects. When something is socially constructed, it is likely to vary historically and between cultures. Social constructionists are interested in people's own definitions of situations. For example, rather than trying to find a single universal definition of religion to cover all cases, they explore what people themselves mean by 'religion'.

social control The means by which society tries to ensure that its members behave as others expect them to. Control can be formal (e.g. the law) or informal (e.g. peer pressure). Negative sanctions (punishments) and positive sanctions (rewards) may be used to encourage individuals to conform to society's norms.

social integration A socially integrated society or community is one where individuals are bound together by shared beliefs and practices. For example, shared religious rituals may remind individuals that they are part of a community to which they owe their loyalty. Taking part in such rituals strengthens a sense of belonging to the community. See also collective conscience; value consensus.

socialisation The process by which an individual learns or internalises the culture of society. Primary socialisation occurs largely within the family and involves acquiring basic skills and values, while secondary socialisation takes place through agencies such as education, religion, the workplace, media and peer groups.

social policy The actions, plans and programmes of government bodies and agencies that aim to deal with a problem or achieve a goal, e.g. preventing crime or reducing poverty. Policies are often based on laws that provide the framework within which these agencies operate. Sociologists' findings may sometimes influence social policy, but many other factors also play a part, such as political ideologies and the availability of resources.

social survey Any research method that involves systematically collecting information from a group of people (either a sample or the whole target population, e.g. the Census) by asking them questions. Usually, this involves using written questionnaires or structured interviews and standardised questions.

spiritual shopping is seen by some as a new pattern of religious participation found in late modern or postmodern society, where there is a spiritual market in which individual consumers 'pick and mix' from different religious and spiritual beliefs, practices and institutions. See also cults; New Age spirituality; postmodernity.

state apparatuses From a Marxist perspective, Althusser distinguishes between repressive and ideological state apparatuses (RSAs and ISAs). RSAs are 'armed bodies of men', such as police, prisons, the army etc, whose role is to coerce the working class into submission, while ISAs include institutions such as the media, religion and education, whose role is to persuade the working class to accept capitalist rule as legitimate. See also hegemony; ideology.

state crimes are crimes committed by, on behalf of, or with the complicity of governments or state agencies such as the police, armed forces or secret services. State crimes include genocide, war crimes, torture, imprisonment without trial and assassination of political opponents. State crimes are of concern because of the immense power of the state to do harm, and because the state can define its own harmful actions as legal because it makes the laws.

status A position in society. Ascribed status occurs where our social position is determined by fixed characteristics that we are born with and cannot normally change, e.g. gender, ethnicity or family of origin. Achieved status occurs where an individual's position is the result of their effort and ability, e.g. getting into university.

stereotype A simplified, one-sided and often negative image of a group or individual which assumes that all members of that group share the same characteristics; e.g. that all black youths are disruptive and unruly. See also labelling.

stigma A negative label or mark of disapproval, discredit or shame attached to a person, group or characteristic. The stigma is used to justify the exclusion of the individual from normal social interaction; e.g. ex-offenders may be stigmatised and excluded from jobs. See also labelling.

strain theory See anomie.

stratification The division of society into a hierarchy of unequal groups. The inequalities may be of wealth, power and/or status. Stratification systems may be based on differences in social class, ethnic group, age, gender, religion etc. Members of different groups usually have different life chances.

structural differentiation A process of specialisation where separate institutions develop to carry out functions that were previously performed by a single institution. For example, according to Parsons, religion in pre-industrial society performed educational, legal and political functions, whereas in industrial society, it comes to specialise in providing meaning and values. Structural differentiation leads to the disengagement of religion from wider society and it loses its influence over other areas of social life. See also privatisation; secularisation.

structural theories are deterministic theories that see individuals as entirely shaped by the way society is structured or organised; e.g. functionalism sees society as socialising individuals into shared norms and values that dictate how they will behave. Marxism and most types of feminism are also regarded as structural theories. See also social action theories.

subculture A group of people within society who share norms, values, beliefs and attitudes that are in some ways different from or opposed to the mainstream culture. Deviant subcultures are often seen as forming in reaction to a failure to achieve mainstream goals through the legitimate opportunity structure (e.g. education and work). In response, they substitute new, deviant goals or adopt illegitimate means of achieving legitimate goals. Many of these theories derive from anomie or strain theory. See also anomie.

subjectivity Bias or lack of objectivity, where the individual's own viewpoint or values influences their perception or judgement. Interpretivists believe sociology is inevitably subjective, since it involves understanding other humans by seeing the world through their eyes. See also empathy; interpretivism.

survey See social survey.

symbolic interactionism See interactionism.

triangulation The use of two or more different methods or sources of data so that they complement each other, the strengths of one countering the weaknesses of the other and vice versa; e.g. using both a qualitative method such as participant observation and a quantitative method such as structured interviews.

typifications See phenomenology.

underclass Those at the lowest level of the class structure; a class below the working class with a separate, deviant subculture and lifestyle, including a high rate of lone-parent families, male unemployment and criminality. See also dependency culture; New Right.

validity The capacity of a research method to measure what it sets out to measure; a true or genuine picture of what something is really like. A valid method is thus one that gives a truthful picture. Methods such as participant observation that produce qualitative data are usually seen as high in validity. See also empathy; interpretivism.

value consensus Agreement among society's members about what values are important; a shared culture. According to functionalists, it integrates individuals into society by giving them a sense of solidarity or 'fellow feeling' with others and enables them to agree on goals and cooperate harmoniously. See also functionalism.

value freedom The idea that values can and should be kept out of research. Modern positivists favour value freedom, but others argue that this is neither possible nor desirable, since values are necessary both to select a topic for research and to interpret findings. Radical sociologists reject value freedom in favour of a committed sociology in which the sociologist explicitly takes the side of the underdog.

values Ideas or beliefs about general principles or goals. They tell society's members what is good or important in life and what to aim for, and they underlie more detailed norms of conduct. Functionalists see shared values as vital in holding society together. See also functionalism; norms; value consensus.

variables Any factor that can change or vary, such as age, gender, occupation or income. Sociologists seek to discover correlations between variables, e.g. between social class and educational achievement. Laboratory experiments are occasionally used to control variables and measure their effect.

verificationism See falsificationism.

verstehen See empathy.

victimology is the study of victims. Positivist victimology aims to explain patterns in victimisation. It focuses on interpersonal violent crime, especially on how victims contribute to their own victimisation. Critical victimology sees victimisation as a form of powerlessness. It focuses on the role of structural factors such as poverty that place powerless groups at greater risk of victimisation, and on the state's role in denying the label of victim to them. See also critical criminology.

victim surveys ask individuals to say what crimes they have been victims of (usually during the past 12 months). The best known victim survey is the annual British Crime Survey. They are often used as a corrective to official police statistics, because they can reveal crimes that have not been reported to or recorded by the police. However, respondents may not report all crimes of which they have been a victim, while some crimes and some categories of victim (e.g. businesses, children) may not be covered. See also self-report studies.

voluntarism is the idea that humans have free will and can exercise choice in how they act, rather than their behaviour being determined or shaped by external forces such as the social structure. It is the opposite of determinism. See also determinism.

zemiology literally means 'the study of harms'. In criminology, it is concerned with why some harms come to be defined as crimes while others do not, even when they cause more damage than do many crimes; e.g. much environmental pollution is perfectly legal. Often such harms are committed by groups such as big business and the state, who have the power to define their actions as legal. Green criminology takes a zemiological approach and is an example of 'transgressive' criminology, i.e. it goes beyond the traditional boundaries of criminology (the study of law breaking) to study environmental harms even when they break no laws.

zero tolerance policing See environmental crime prevention.

Bibliography

Abercrombie N et al (1978; 1980) *The Dominant Ideology Thesis*, British Journal of Sociology

Adams C (2000) 'Suspect data' in King R and Wincup E (eds) *Doing Research on Crime and Justice*, Oxford University Press

Adler F (1975) *Sisters in Crime*, McGraw Hill

Adler P (1985) *Wheeling and Dealing*, Columbia University Press

Adler Z (1987) *Rape on Trial*, Routledge and Kegan Paul

Agnew R (2006) *Pressured into Crime*, Roxbury

Aldridge A (2007) *Religion in the Contemporary World*, Polity

Althusser L (1969) *For Marx*, Allen Lane

Althusser L (1971) *Lenin and Philosophy and Other Essays*, New Left Books

Amir M (1971) *Patterns of Forcible Rape*, University of Chicago Press

Ammerman N (1987) *Bible Believers*, Rutgers University Press

Ansley F (1972) cited in Bernard J (1976) *The Future of Marriage*, Penguin

Archer M (1995) *Realist Social Theory*, Cambridge University Press

Armstrong K (1993) *The End of Silence*, Fourth Estate

Armstrong K (2001) 'The War We Should Fight', *The Guardian*

Ashworth A and Redmayne M (2005) *Criminal Process*, Oxford University Press

Atkinson J (1971) 'Societal Reactions to Suicide' in Cohen S (ed) *Images of Deviance*, Penguin

Atkinson J (1978) *Discovering Suicide*, Macmillan

Atkinson J et al (1975) 'The Comparability of Suicide Rates', *British Journal of Psychiatry*

Baldwin J (2000) 'Negotiated Justice' cited in King R and Wincup E (eds) *Doing Research on Crime and Justice*, Oxford University Press

Ballard R (1982) 'South Asian Families' in Rapoport R and Rapoport R (eds) *Families in Britain*, Routledge and Kegan Paul

Bandura A et al (1963) 'The Imitation of film-mediated aggressive models', *Journal of Abnormal and Social Psychology*

Bandura A et al (1977) 'Transmission of aggression through imitation of aggressive models', *Journal of Abnormal and Social Psychology*

Barna G (2000) Church Attendance www.barna.org

Barrett M (1980) *Women's Oppression Today*, Verso

Baudrillard J (1983) *Simulations*, Semiotext

Bauman Z (1989) *Modernity and the Holocaust*, Polity

Bauman Z (1992) *Intimations of Postmodernity*, Routledge

Beck U (1992) *Risk Society*, Sage

Becker HS (1963) *Outsiders*, Free Press

Becker HS (1970), 'Whose side are we on?' in Becker HS (ed) *Sociological Work*, Transaction Books

Becker HS (1971) 'Social Class Variations in the Teacher-Pupil Relationship' in Cosin B et al (ed) *Education Structure and Society*, Penguin

Becker HS et al (1961) *Boys in White*, University of Chicago Press

Beckford J (2003) *Social Theory and Religion*, Cambridge University Press

Beechey V (1977) 'Some notes on female wage labour in the capitalist mode of production', *Capital and Class*

Bellah R (1970) *Beyond Belief*, Harper and Row

Bellah R (1996) *Habits of the Heart*, University of California Press

Bennett W et al (1996) *Body Count*, Simon and Schuster

Berger P (1969) *The Social Reality of Religion*, Faber and Faber

Berger P (1999) *The Desecularisation of the World*, William B Eerdmans Publishing

Berger P (2003) Max Weber is Alive and Well and Living in Guatemala www.economyandsociety.com

Berger P and Luckmann T (1971) *The Social Construction of Reality*, Penguin

Best L (1993) 'Dragons, Dinner Ladies and Ferrets', *Sociology Review*

Best S and Kellner D (1991) *Postmodern Theory*, Macmillan

Beyer P (1994) *Religion in Globalisation*, Sage

Bibby R (1993) *Unknown Gods*, Stodart

Billings D (1990) 'Religion as Opposition', *American Journal of Sociology*

Bird J (1999) *Investigating Religion*, Collins

Birnbaum N (1971) *Towards a critical sociology*, Oxford University Press

Black Report, The (1980), published as Townsend P and Davidson N (1988) *Inequalities in Health*, Pelican

Bloch E (1959) *The Principle of Hope*, MIT Press

Blumer H (1969) *Symbolic Interactionism*, Prentice-Hall

Bourgois P (2000) *In Search of Respect*, Cambridge University Press

Bowder B (2008) 'Sikh Girl Wins Bracelet Case', *Church Times*

Bowlby J (1965) *Child Care and the Growth of Love*, Penguin

Bowles S and Gintis H (1976) *Schooling in Capitalist America*, Routledge and Kegan Paul

Bowling B and Phillips C (2002) *Racism, Crime and Justice*, Longman

Box S (1981) *Deviancy, Reality and Society*, Holt, Rinehart & Winston

Braithwaite J (1984) *Corporate Crime in the Pharmaceutical Industry*, Routledge and Kegan Paul

Breakdown Britain (2007) www.centreforsocialjustice.org.uk

Bridgland F (2006) Europe's new dumping ground www.ban.org

Brierley P (2005) *Pulling Out of the Nosedive*, Christian Research

Brierley P (2005/08) *Religious trends*, Christian Research

British Crime Survey www.statistics.gov.uk

Bromley D and A Shupe (1980) 'The Tnevnoc Cult', *Sociological Analysis*

Brookman F (1999) 'Assessing and analysing police murder files' in Brookman F et al (eds) *Qualitative Research in Criminology*, Ashgate

Brookman F (2005) *Understanding Homicide*, Sage

Brown C (2001) *The Death of Christian Britain*, Routledge

Brown C and Gay P (1985) *Racial Discrimination*, Policy Studies Institute

Brownmiller S (1976) *Against Our Will*, Penguin

Bruce S (1995) *Religion in Modern Britain*, Open University Press

Bruce S (1996) *Religion in the Modern World*, Oxford University Press

Bruce S (2002) *God is Dead*, Blackwell

Bruce S (2003) *Politics and Religion*, Polity

Bruce S (2007) *Fundamentalism*, Polity

Bruegel I (1979) 'Women as a reserve army of labour', *Feminist Review*

Buckle A and Farrington D (1984) 'An observational study of shoplifting', *British Journal of Criminology*

Bunting M (1996) 'Finding Your Inner Cook', *The Guardian*

Burden T (1998) *Social Policy and Welfare*, Pluto Press

Butler J (1992) 'Contingent Foundations' in Butler J and Scott J (eds) *Feminists Theorize The Political*, Routledge

Cain M (1989) *Growing up Good*, Sage

Carlen P (1988) *Women, Crime and Poverty*, Open University Press

Carlen P (1997) 'Women in the criminal justice system' in Haralambos M (ed) *Developments in Sociology*, Causeway Press

Carrabine E et al (2008) *Criminology*, Routledge

Carson W (1971) 'White-Collar Crime and the Enforcement of Factory Legislation' in Carson W and Wiles P (eds) *Crime and Delinquency in Britain*, Martin Robertson

Casanova J (1994) *Public Religions in the Modern World*, University of Chicago Press

Casanova J (2005) 'Catholic and Muslim Politics in Comparative Perspective', *Taiwan Journal of Democracy*

Castells M (1998) *End of Millennium*, Blackwell

Chaiken J et al (1974) *The Impact of Police Activity on Crime*, Rand Corporation

Chambliss W (1975) 'Toward a Political Economy of Crime', *Theory and Society*

Chambliss W (1989) 'State-Organized Crime', *Criminology*

Chaves M and Gorski P (2001) 'Religious Pluralism and Religious Participation', *Annual Review of Sociology*

Chesney-Lind M (1997) *Female Offenders*, Sage

Christie N (2004) *A Suitable Amount of Crime*, Routledge

Chunn D et al (2003) *Toxic Criminology*, Fernwood Publishing

Cicourel A (1968) *The Social Organisation of Juvenile Justice*, Wiley

Clancy A et al (2001) *Crime, Policing and Justice*, Home Office

Clarke R (1980) 'Situational Crime Prevention', *British Journal of Criminology*

Clarke R (1992) *Situational Crime Prevention*, Harrow and Heston

Clarke R and Mayhew P (1988) 'The British Gas Suicide Story and its Implications for Prevention' in Tonry M et al (eds) *Crime and Justice*, University of Chicago Press

Cloward R and Ohlin L (1960) *Delinquency and Opportunity*, The Free Press

Cohen A (1955) *Delinquent Boys*, Free Press

Cohen S (1972: 1973) *Folk Devils and Moral Panics*, Paladin

Cohen S (1996) 'Human rights and crimes of the state' in Muncie J et al (eds) *Criminological Perspectives*, Sage

Cohen S (2001) *States of Denial*, Polity

Cohen S and Young J (eds) (1973) *The Manufacture of News*, Constable

Connell R (1995) *Masculinities*, Polity Press

Cooley C (1922) *Social Organization*, Scribner

Craib I (1992) *Modern Social Theory*, Harvester Wheatsheaf

Crawford A et al (1990) *The Second Islington Crime Survey*, Middlesex Polytechnic

Crockett A (2000) *Variations in Churchgoing Rates*, Oxford University Press

Cromwell P et al (1995) 'Routine Activities and Social Control in the Aftermath of a Natural Catastrophe', *European Journal of Criminal Policy and Research*

Daly M (1978) *Gyn/Ecology*, Beacon Press

Darwin C (1859: 1968) *On the Origin of Species*, Penguin

Davie G (1994) *Religion in Britain since 1945*, Blackwell

Davie G (2007) *The Sociology of Religion*, Sage

Davies P (2000) 'Doing Interviews with Female Offenders' in Jupp V et al (eds) *Doing Criminological Research*, Sage

Davis K (1961) 'Prostitution' in Merton R and Nisbet R (eds) *Contemporary Social Problems*, Harcourt Brace and Company

Dawson L (1998) 'Anti-Modernism, modernism, and postmodernism', *Sociology of Religion*

Day D (1991) *The Eco-wars*, Paladin

de Beauvoir S (1953) *The Second Sex*, Jonathan Cape

De Haan W (2000) 'Explaining the Absence of Violence' in Karstedt S and Bussman K (eds) *Social Dynamics of Crime and Control*, Hart

Delphy C (1984) 'The Main Enemy' in Delphy C (ed) *Close to Home*, Hutchinson

Denscombe M (2001) 'Uncertain identities and health-risking behaviour', *British Journal of Sociology*

Ditton J (2000) 'Crime Surveys and the Measurement Problem' in Jupp V et al (eds) *Doing Criminological Research*, Sage

Ditton J (1977) *Part-time Crime*, Macmillan

Ditton J and Duffy J (1983) 'Bias in the Newspaper Reporting of Crime News', *British Journal of Criminology*

Ditton J and Farrall S (2000) *The Fear of Crime*, Ashgate

Dobash R and Dobash R (1979) *Violence Against Wives*, The Free Press

Douglas J (1967) *The Social Meaning of Suicide*, Princeton University Press

Downes D (1999) 'Crime and deviance' in Taylor S (ed) *Sociology: Issues and Debates*, Macmillan

Downes D (2001) 'The macho penal colony' in Garland D (ed) *Mass Imprisonment*, Sage

Downes D and Hansen K (2006) 'Welfare and punishment in comparative perspective' in Armstrong S et al (eds) *Perspectives on Punishment*, Oxford University Press

Downes D and Rock P (2003) *Understanding Deviance*, Oxford University Press

Drane J (1999) *What is the New Age saying to the Church?* Marshal Pickering

Durkheim E (1893:1964) *The Division of Labour in Society*, The Free Press

Bibliography

Durkheim E (1897;1952) *Suicide: A Study in Sociology*, Routledge and Kegan Paul

Durkheim E (1915: 1961) *The Elementary Forms of the Religious Life*, Collier Books

Durkheim E and Mauss M (1903; 1963) *Primitive Classification*, Cohen and West

Dworkin A (1981) *Pornography*, The Women's Press

El Saadawi N (1980) *The Hidden Face of Eve*, Zed Books

Engels F (1895) On the History of Early Christianity www.marxists.org

Ericson R et al (1991) *Representing Order*, Open University Press

Erikson K (1966) *Wayward Puritans*, Wiley

Evans-Pritchard E (1936) *Witchcraft, Oracles and Magic among the Azande*, Oxford University Press

Farrington D and Morris A (1983) 'Sex, sentencing and reconviction', *British Journal of Criminology*

Featherstone M (1991) *Consumer Culture and Postmodernism*, Sage

Felson M (1998) *Crime and Everyday Life*, Pine Forge Press

Festinger L et al (1956) *When Prophecy Fails*, Harper and Row

Finke R (1997) 'The Consequences of Religious Choice' in Young L (ed) *Rational Choice Theory and Religion*, Routledge

Firestone S (1974) *The Dialectic of Sex*, Morrow

Flood-Page C et al (2000) *Youth Crime Findings from the 1998/99 Youth Lifestyles Survey*, Home Office

Ford J (1969) *Social Class and the Comprehensive School*, Routledge and Kegan Paul

Foucault M (1977; 1979) *Discipline and Punish*, Penguin

Freire P (1968; 1996) *The Pedagogy of the Oppressed*, Penguin

Garfinkel H (1967) *Studies in Ethnomethodology*, Prentice-Hall

Garland D (2001) *The Culture of Control*, Clarendon

Gellner E (1992) *Postmodernism, Reason and Religion*, Routledge

Gibbs J and Martin W (1964) *Status Integration and Suicide*, University of Oregon Press

Giddens A (1984) *The Constitution of Society*, Polity

Giddens A (1990) *The Consequences of Modernity*, Polity

Giddens A (1991) *Modernity and Self Identity*, Polity

Giddens A (1999) Runaway World www.bbc.co.uk

Gill A and Lundegaarde E (2004) 'State welfare spending and religiosity', *Rationality and Society*

Gill R (1988) 'Altered Images', *Social Studies Review*

Gill R et al (1998) 'Is religious belief declining in Britain?' *Journal for the Scientific Study of Religion*

Gilroy P (1982) 'The Myth of Black Criminality', *Socialist Register*

Glaser B and Strauss A (1968) *The Discovery of Grounded Theory*, Weidenfeld & Nicholson

Glenny M (2008) *McMafia*, Bodley Head

Glock C and Stark R (1969) 'Dimensions of Religious Commitment' in Robertson R (ed) *Sociology of Religion*, Penguin

Goffman E (1962; 1968) *Asylums*, Penguin

Goffman E (1963) *Stigma*, Prentice-Hall

Goffman E (1967) *Interaction Ritual*, Doubleday

Goffman E (1969) *The Presentation of Self in Everyday Life*, Penguin

Goldacre B (2008) *Bad Science*, Fourth Estate

Gordon D (1976) 'Class and the Economics of Crime' in Chambliss W and Mankoff M (eds) *Whose Law? What Order?* John Wiley & Sons

Gottfredson M and Hirschi T (1990) *A General Theory of Crime*, Stanford University Press

Gouldner A (1970) *The Coming Crisis of Western Sociology*, Heinemann

Gouldner A (1973) *Sociology: renewal and critique in sociology today*, Penguin

Gouldner A (1975) *For Sociology*, Penguin

Graham H (1983) 'Do Her Answers Fit His Questions?' in Gamarnikow E et al (eds) *The Public and the Private*, Heinemann

Graham J and Bowling B (1995) *Young People and Crime*, HMSO

Gramsci A (1971) *Selections from the Prison Notebooks*, Lawrence and Wishart

Greeley A (1989) *Religious Change in America*, Harvard University Press

Greeley A (1992) *The Catholic Myth*, Prentice Hall

Green P and Ward T (2005) 'Special Issue on State Crime', *British Journal of Criminology*

Greer G (2000) *The Whole Woman*, Anchor

Gutierrez G (1971) *A Theology of Liberation*, SCM Press

Habermas J (1987) *The Theory of Communicative Action*, Beacon Press

Hadaway C et al (1993) 'What the Polls don't Show', *American Sociological Review*

Hadden J and Shupe A (1988) *Televangelism*, Henry Holt

Halbwachs M (1930) *Les Causes du Suicide*, Alcan

Hall S et al (1978: 1979) *Policing the Crisis*, Macmillan

Hamilton M (1995) *The Sociology of Religion*, Routledge

Hammond P and Machacek D (1999) *Soka Gakkai in America*, Oxford University Press

Hanegraaff W (2002) 'New Age Religion' in Woodhead (ed) *Religion in the Modern World*, Routledge

Haney C et al (1973) 'Interpersonal dynamics in a simulated prison', *International Journal of Criminology and Penology*

Hartmann H (1979; 1981) 'The Unhappy Marriage of Marxism and Feminism', *Capital and Class*; Pluto Press

Harvey D (1989) *The Condition of Postmodernity*, Blackwell

Hawking S (1988) *A Brief History of Time*, Bantam

Haynes J (1998) *Religion in Global Politics*, Longman

Heelas P (1996) 'Detraditionalisation of religion and self' in Flanagan K et al (eds) *Postmodernity, Sociology and Religion*, Macmillan

Heelas P (2008) *Spiritualities of Life*, Blackwell

Heelas P and Woodhead L (2005) *The Spiritual Revolution*, Blackwell

Heidensohn F (1985; 1996 second edition) *Women and Crime*, Macmillan

Held D et al (1999) *Global Transformations*, Polity

Henry S and Milovanovic D (1996) *Constitutive Criminology*, Sage

Herberg W (1955) *Protestant-Catholic-Jew*, Anchor Books

Herrnstein R and Murray C (1994) *The Bell Curve*, The Free Press

Hervieu-Léger D (2000) *Religion as a Chain of Memory*, Rutgers University Press

Hervieu-Léger D (2006) The role of religion in establishing social cohesion www.eurozine.com/articles

Hill M (1983) *Understanding Social Policy*, Basil Blackwell and Martin Robertson

Hindelang M et al (1981) *Measuring Delinquency*, Sage

Hindess B (1973) *The Use of Official Statistics in Sociology*, Macmillan

Hirschi T (1969) *Causes of Delinquency*, University of California Press

Hirst P (1993) *The Pluralist Theory of the State*, Routledge

Hobbs D (1988) *Doing the Business*, Oxford University Press

Holdaway S (1983) *Inside the British Police*, Blackwell

Hollands R (2000) 'Lager Louts, Tarts and Hooligans' in Jupp V et al (eds) *Doing Criminological Research*, Sage

Holm J and Bowker J (1994) *Women and Religion*, Pinter

Hood R (1992) *Race and Sentencing*, Clarendon Press

Hopkins Burke R (2005) *An Introduction to Criminological Theory*, Willan Publishing

Horrie C and Chippindale P (2003) *What is Islam?* Virgin Books

Horton R (1970) 'African traditional thought and Western science' in Wilson B (ed) *Rationality*, Blackwell

Hough M and Tilley N (1998) *Auditing Crime and Disorder*, Home Office

Hoyle C (2007) 'Being a Nosy Bloody Cow' in King R and Wincup E (eds) *Doing Research on Crime and Justice*, Oxford University Press

Hudson B and Bramhall G (2005) 'Assessing the Other', *British Journal of Criminology*

Humphreys L (1970) *The Tea Room Trade*, Duckworth

Hunter J (1987) *Evangelicalism*, University of Chicago Press

Huntington S (1993) *The Clash of Civilizations*, Foreign Affairs

Inglehart R and Norris P (2003) *Rising Tide*, Cambridge University Press

Inglehart R and Norris P (2003) 'The True Clash of Civilizations', *Foreign Policy*

Innes M (2003) *Understanding Social Control*, Open University Press

Jackson R (2006) 'Religion, Politics and Terror', *Working Paper, University of Manchester*

Jacobs J (1967) 'A Phenomenological Study of Suicide Notes', *Social Problems*

Jameson F (1984) 'Postmodernism, or the cultural logic of late capitalism', *New Left Review*

Jewkes Y (2003) 'Policing the Net' in Jewkes Y (ed) *Dot.cons*, Willan

Jones S (1998) *Criminology*, Butterworths

Junger-Tas J (1989) 'Self-report delinquency research in Holland with a perspective on international comparison' in Klein M (1989) *Cross-National Research in Self-Reported Crime and Delinquency*, Kluwer 1989

Jupp V et al (eds) (2000) *Doing Criminological Research*, Sage

Kautsky K (1927; 1988) *The Materialist Conception of History*, Yale University Press

Keat R and Urry J (1982) *Social Theory as Science*, Routledge and Kegan Paul

Kelman H and Hamilton V (1989) *Crimes of Obedience*, Yale University Press

Kennedy D et al (2001) 'Developing and implementing operation ceasefire' in *Reducing Gun Violence*, US Dept of Justice

Kinsey R (1984) *Merseyside Crime* Survey, University of Edinburgh

Kinsey R et al (1986) *Losing the Fight Against Crime*, Blackwell

Knorr-Cetina K (1981) *The Manufacture of Knowledge*, Pergamon Press

Knorr-Cetina K (1999) *Epistemic Cultures*, Harvard University Press

Kobler A and Stotland E (1964) *The End of Hope*, The Free Press

Kuhn T (1970) *The Structure of Scientific Revolutions*, University of Chicago Press

Laidler K and Hunt G (2001) 'Accomplishing femininity among the girls in the gang', *British Journal of Criminology*

Lane C (1981) *The Rites of Rulers*, Cambridge University Press

Lash S and Urry J (1987) *The End of Organised Capitalism*, Polity

Lash S and Urry J (1994) *Economies of Signs and Space*, University of Wisconsin Press

Lea J and Young J (1984; 1993) *What is to be Done About Law and Order?* Penguin

Lea J and Young J (1996) 'Relative Deprivation' in J Muncie et al (eds) *Criminological Perspectives*, Sage

Lees S (1993) *Sugar and Spice*, Penguin

Lehmann D (2002) 'Religion and globalisation' in Woodhead L (ed) *Religions in the Modern World*, Routledge

Lemert E (1951) *Social Pathology*, McGraw-Hill

Lemert E (1962) 'Paranoia and the dynamics of exclusion', *Sociometry*

Lemert E (1967) *Human Deviance, Social Problems and Social Control*, Prentice-Hall

Lilly J et al (2002) *Criminological Theory*, Sage

Livingstone S (1996) 'On the Continuing Problem of Media Effects' in Curran J and Gurevitch M (eds) *Mass Media and Society*, Arnold

Lombroso C and Ferrrero G (1893; 2004) *Criminal Woman, the Prostitute and the Normal Woman*, Duke University Press

Löwy M (2005) Marxism and Religion www.internationalviewpoint.org

Lukes S (1975) *Emile Durkheim*, Allen Lane

Lukes S (1992) *Emile Durkheim: His Life and Work*, Penguin

Lynch G (2007) 'Understanding the Sacred', *Sociology Review*

Lynd R and Lynd H (1929) *Middletown*, Harcourt, Brace and Co

Lyon D (2000) *Jesus in Disneyland*, Polity

Lyotard J (1984) *The Postmodern Condition*, Manchester University Press

Lyotard J (1992) *The Inhuman: reflections on time*, Polity

Macpherson W (1999) *The Stephen Lawrence Inquiry*, HMSO

Maduro O (1982) *Religion and Social Conflicts*, Orvis Books

Bibliography

Maguire M (2007) 'Researching street criminals in the field: a neglected art?' in King R and Wincup E (eds) *Doing Research on Crime and Justice*, Oxford University Press

Malinowski B (1954) *Magic, Science and Religion*, Anchor Books

Mandel E (1984) *Delightful Murder*, Pluto

Mannheim K (1929) *Ideology and Utopia*, Routledge

Mannheim K (1953) 'Conservative thought' in Kecskemeti P (ed) *Essays in Sociology and Social Psychology*, Routledge

Mark Shibley (1996) *Resurgent Evangelicalism in the United States*, University of South Carolina Press

Marks P (1979) 'Femininity in the Classroom' in Meighan R et al (eds) *Perspectives on Society*, Nelson

Marler P and Hadaway C (1997) 'Testing the attendance gap in a conservative church', *Sociology of Religion*

Marsh H (1991) 'A Comparative Analysis of Crime Coverage in the United States and Other Countries from 1960 to 1989', *Journal of Criminal Justice*

Marshall G (1982) *In Search of the Spirit of Capitalism*, Hutchinson

Marshall T (1975) *Social Welfare*, Hutchinson

Martin C (2000) 'Doing Research in a Prison Setting' in Jupp V et al (eds) *Doing Criminological Research*, Sage

Martin D (1967) *A Sociology of English Religion*, Heinemann

Martin D (1990) *Tongues of Fire*, Wiley Blackwell

Martin D (1994) 'Evangelical and Charismatic Christianity in Latin America' in Poewe K (ed) *Charismatic Christianity as a Global Culture*, University of South Carolina Press

Martin D (2002) *Pentecostalism*, Blackwell

Marx K (1844; 1998) *Theses On Feuerbach*, Prometheus Books

Marx K (1846; 1970) *The German Ideology*, International Publishers

Mawby R and Walklate S (1994) *Critical Victimology*, Sage

Maynard M (1987) 'Current Trends in Feminist Theory', *Social Studies Review*

Maynard W (1994) *Witness Intimidation*, HMSO

McLaughlin E (2001) 'State Crime' in McLaughlin E and Muncie J (eds) *The Sage Dictionary of Criminology*, Sage

McRobbie A and Thornton S (1995) 'Rethinking Moral Panics for Multi-mediated Social Worlds', *British Journal of Sociology*

Mead G (1918) 'The Psychology of Punitive Justice', *American Journal of Sociology*

Melossi D and Pavarini M (1981) *The Prison and the Factory*, Macmillan

Meltzer B et al (1975) *Symbolic Interactionism*, Routledge and Kegan Paul

Merton R (1938; 1949) 'Social Structure and Anomie' in Anshen R (ed) *The Family*, Harper Brothers

Merton R (1968) *Social Theory and Social Structure*, Free Press

Merton R (1973) *The Sociology of Science*, University of Chicago Press

Messerschmidt D (1993) *Masculinities and Crime*, Rowman and Littlefield

Messner S and Rosenfeld R (2001) *Crime and the American Dream*, Wadsworth

Mestrovic S (1997) *Post-emotional Society*, Sage

Michalowski R and Kramer R (2006) *State-Corporate Crime*, Rutgers University Press

Miers D (1989) 'Legislation and the Legislative Process', *Statute Law Review*.

Miller A and Hoffman J (1995) 'Risk and Religion', *Journal for the Scientific Study of Religion*

Miller D (1997) *Reinventing American Protestantism*, University of California Press

Miller W (1962) 'Lower class culture as a generating milieu of gang delinquency' in Wolfgang M et al (eds) *The Sociology of Crime and Delinquency*, Wiley

Mitchell J (1975) *Psychoanalysis and Feminism*, Penguin

Modood T et al (1994) *Changing Ethnic Identities*, Policy Studies Institute

Moore M (2008) 'In France, Prisons Filled With Muslims', *Washington Post*

Mulkay M (1969) 'Some aspects of cultural growth in the natural sciences', *Social Research*

Muncie J (2004) 'Youth justice' in Newburn T and Sparks R (eds) *Criminal Justice and Political Culture*, Willan

Murray C (1984) *Losing Ground*, Basic Books

Murray C (1990) *The Emerging British Underclass*, IEA

Myrdal G (1969) *An American Dilemma*, Harper & Row

Nanda M (2003) *Prophets Facing Backwards*, Rutgers University Press

Nanda M (2008) *God and Globalization in India*, Navayana Publishers

Nanda M (2008) 'Rush Hour of the Gods', *New Humanist*

Newburn T and Rock P (2006) *The Politics of Crime Control*, Clarendon Press

Nichols T (1996) 'Social class' in Levitas R and Guy M (eds) *Interpreting Official Statistics*, Routledge

Nicholson L (ed) *Feminism/Postmodernism*, Routledge

Niebuhr R (1929) *The Social Sources of Denominationalism*, Shoe String Press

Noon M (1993) 'Racial discrimination in speculative applications', *Human Resource Management Journal*

Norris C and Armstrong G (1999) *The Maximum Surveillance Society*, Berg

Norris P and Inglehart R (2004) *Sacred and Secular*, Cambridge University Press

Oakley A (1972) *Sex, Gender and Society*, Maurice Temple Smith

Oakley A (1981) *Subject Women*, Penguin

Ohmae K (1994) *The Borderless World*, HarperCollins

Park R and Burgess E (1925) *The City*, University of Chicago Press

Parker H (1974) *View from the Boys*, David and Charles

Parsons T (1951; 1970) *The Social System*, Routledge and Kegan Paul

Parsons T (1955) 'The American family' in Parsons T and Bales R (eds) *Family, Socialisation and Interaction Process*, The Free Press

Parsons T (1967) *Sociological Theory in Modern Society*, Free Press

Patrick J (1973) *A Glasgow Gang Observed*, Methuen

Pawson R (1992) 'Feminist methodology' in Haralambos M (ed) *Developments in Sociology*, Causeway Press

Pearce F (1976) *Crimes of the Powerful*, Pluto

Pearson G (1983) *Hooligan*, Palgrave Macmillan

Pease K (1997) 'Crime prevention' in Maguire M et al (eds) *The Oxford Handbook of Criminology*, Oxford University Press

Pease K (2002) 'Crime reduction' in M. Maguire et al (eds), *The Oxford Handbook of Criminology*, Oxford University Press

Phillips C and Bowling B (2007) 'Ethnicities, racism, crime, and criminal justice' in Maguire M et al (eds) *The Oxford Handbook of Criminology*, Clarendon Press

Philo G and Miller D (eds) (2001) *Market Killing*, Longman

Piliavin I and Briar B (1964) 'Police Encounters with Juveniles', *American Journal of Sociology*

Pitts M and Phillips K (1991) (eds) *The Psychology of Health*, Routledge

Platt A (1969) *The Child Savers*, University of Chicago Press

Plummer K (1979) 'Misunderstanding Labelling Perspectives' in Downes D and Rock P (eds) *Deviant Interpretations*, Martin Robertson

Polanyi M (1958) *Personal Knowledge*, University of Chicago Press

Polanyi M, cited in Ben-David J (1971) *The Scientist's Role in Society*, Prentice Hall

Pollak O (1950: 1961) *The Criminality of Women*, University of Philadelphia Press

Pollert A (1996) 'Gender and Class Revisited', *Sociology*

Polsky N (1971) *Hustlers, Beats and Others*, Aldine

Popper K (1959) *The Logic of Scientific Discovery*, Hutchinson

Popper K (1965) *The Open Society and Its Enemies, Volume II*, Routledge and Kegan Paul

Poyner B and Webb B (1997) 'Reducing thefts from shopping bags in city centre markets' in Clarke R (ed) *Situational Crime Prevention*, Harrow and Heston

Pryce K (1979) *Endless Pressure*, Penguin

Punch M (1979) *Policing the Inner City*, Macmillan

Pynoos R et al (1987) 'Life threat and post-traumatic stress in school-age children', *Archives of General Psychiatry*

Ray L and Smith D (2001) 'Racist offenders and the politics of hate crime', *Law and Critique*

Redding G (1990) *The Spirit of Chinese Capitalism*, Walter de Gruyter

Reiman J (2001) *The Rich Get Richer and the Poor Get Prison*, Allyn and Bacon

Reiner R and Newburn T (2008) 'Police research' in King R and Wincup E (eds) *Doing Research on Crime and Justice*, Oxford University Press

Reinharz S (1983) 'Experiential analysis' in Bowles G and Klein R (eds) *Theories of Women's Studies*, Routledge and Kegan Paul

Reynolds L (1975) cited in Meltzer, B, Petras, J and Reynolds, L (1975), *Symbolic Interactionism*, Routledge and Kegan Paul

Rich A (1981) *Compulsory Heterosexuality and Lesbian Existence*, Onlywoman Press

Robb G (1992) *White Collar Crime in Modern England*, Cambridge University Press

Robertson R (1992) *Globalisation*, Transaction

Rock P (1979) *The Making of Symbolic Interactionism*, Macmillan

Rosenthal R and Fode K (1963) 'Psychology of the scientist', *Psychological Reports*

Rosenthal R and Jacobson L (1968), *Pygmalion in the Classroom*, Holt, Rinehart & Winston

Rosoff S et al (1998) *Profit Without Honour*, Prentice Hall

Runciman W (1966) *Relative Deprivation and Social Justice*, Routledge and Kegan Paul

Rusche G and Kirchheimer O (1939; 1968) *Punishment and Social Structure*, Russell and Russell

Rustin M (1994) 'Incomplete Modernity', *Radical Philosophy*

Said E (1978) *Orientalism*, Penguin

Sainsbury P (1955) *Suicide in London*, Chapman

Sainsbury P and Barraclough B (1968) 'Differences between suicide rates', *Nature*

Salvadori M (1989) 'Kautsky and Weber', *International Journal of Comparative Sociology*

Sampson C and Phillips A (1992) *Reducing Repeat Racial Victimization*, Home Office

Savelsberg J (1995) 'Crime, inequality and Justice in Eastern Europe' in Hagen J and Peterson D (eds) *Crime and Inequality*, Stanford University Press

Schlesinger P and Tumber H (1992) 'Crime and Criminal Justice in the Media' in Downes D (ed) *Unravelling Criminal Justice*, Macmillan

Schlesinger P and Tumber H (1994) *Reporting Crime*, Oxford University Press

Schofield M (1965) *The Sexual Behaviour of Young People*, Longman

Schramm W et al (1961) *Television in the Lives of Our Children*, Stanford University Press

Schutz A (1972) *The Phenomenology of the Social World*, Heinemann

Schwendinger H and Schwendinger J (1970) 'Defenders of Order or Guardians of Human Rights?' *Issues in Criminology*

Scott J (1990) *A Matter of Record*, Polity

Scott R (1972) 'A Proposed Framework for Analyzing Deviance as a Property of Social Order' in Scott R and Douglas J (eds) *Theoretical Perspectives in Deviance*, Basic Books

Segal L (1999) *Why Feminism?* Polity Press

Sharp C and Budd T (2005) *Minority Ethnic Groups and Crime*, Home Office

Sharpe J (1999) *Crime in Early Modern England 1550-1750*, Longman

Shaw C and McKay H (1942) *Juvenile Delinquency and Urban Areas*, University of Chicago Press

Shipman M (1997) *Limitations of Social Research*, Longman

Simmel G, cited in Wolff K (1950) *The Sociology of Georg Simmel*, Free Press

Simon J (2001) 'Fear and loathing in late-modernity' in Garland D (ed) *Mass Imprisonment*, Sage

Sissons M (1970) *The Psychology of Social Class*, Oxford University Press

Bibliography

Situ Y and Emmons D (2000) *Environmental Crime*, Sage

Skidmore W (1975) *Theoretical Thinking in Sociology*, Cambridge University Press

Sklair L (2003) 'Globalization, capitalism and power' in Holborn M (ed) *Developments in Sociology*, Causeway Press

Slapper G and Tombs S (1999) *Corporate Crime*, Longman

Smart C (1989) *Feminism and the Power of Law*, Routledge

Smith D (1990) 'The Limits of Religious Resurgence' in Sahliyeh E (ed) *Religious Resurgence and Politics in the Contemporary World*, New York Press

Smith D (2002) 'Hinduism' in Woodhead L (ed) *Religion in the Modern World*, Routledge

Smith D et al (1983) *Police and People in London*, Policy Studies Institute

Snider L (1993) 'The politics of corporate crime control' in Pearce F and Woodiwiss M *Global Crime Connections*, Macmillan

Somerville J (2000) *Feminism and the Family*, Macmillan

Soothill K and Walby S (1991) *Sex Crime in the News*, Routledge

South N (1997) cited in Carrabine E et al (2008) *Criminology*, Routledge

Sparks R (1992) *Television and the Drama of Crime*, Open University Press

Stark R (1990) 'Modernisation, secularisation and Mormon success', in Robbins T et al (eds) *In God We Trust*, Transaction

Stark R and Iannaccone L (1997) 'Why the Jehovah's Witnesses Grow So Rapidly', *Journal of Contemporary Religion*

Stark W and Bainbridge W (1985) *The Future of Religion*, University of California Press

Statistics on Race and the Criminal Justice System www.justice.gov.uk

Statistics on Women and the Criminal Justice System www.justice.gov.uk

Stewart P (2008) 'Vatican City', *Reuters*

Surette R (1998) *Media, Crime and Criminal Justice*, Wadsworth

Sutherland E (1939) *Principles of Criminology*, J P Lippincott

Swash R (2009) 'Online piracy', *The Guardian*

Sykes, G and Matza D (1957) 'Techniques of Neutralization', *American Sociological Review*

Tarling R (1982) *Unemployment and Crime*, HMSO

Tawney R (1926) *Religion and the Rise of Capitalism*, J Murray

Taylor C (1991) *The Ethics of Authenticity*, Harvard University Press

Taylor I (1997) 'The political economy of crime' in Maguire M et al (eds) *The Oxford Handbook of Criminology*, Oxford University Press

Taylor I et al (1973) *Critical Criminology*, Routledge and Kegan Paul

Taylor S (1982) *Durkheim and the Study of Suicide*, Macmillan

Taylor S (1989) *Suicide*, Longman

Thomas D and Loader B (2000) (eds) *Cybercrime*, Routledge

Thomas W and Znaniecki F (1919) *The Polish Peasant in Europe and America*, University of Illinois Press

Thomas W I (1966) 'On Social Organization and Social Personality' in Janowitz M (ed) *Selected Papers*, University of Chicago Press

Thompson EP (1977) *Whigs and Hunters*, Penguin

Thompson EP (1978) 'The Poverty of Theory' in Thompson EP, *The Poverty of Theory and Other Essays*, Merlin

Thornton D (1984) *Tougher Regimes in Detention Centres*, Home Office

Tilley N (2000) 'Doing Realistic Evaluation of Criminal Justice' in Jupp V et al (eds) *Doing Criminological Research*, Sage

Tilley N et al (2007) 'The Investigation of High Volume Crime' in Newburn T et al (eds) *Handbook of Crime Investigation*, Willan

Tombs S (2000) 'Official Statistics and Hidden Crime' in Jupp V et al (eds) *Doing Criminological Research*, Sage

Tombs S and Whyte D (2007) *Safety Crimes*, Willan

Townsend P (1979) *Poverty in the United Kingdom*, Penguin

Triplett R (2000) 'The Dramatisation of Evil' in Simpson S (ed) *Of Crime and Criminality*, Pine Forge Press

Troeltsch E (1912; 1980) *The Social Teachings of the Christian Churches*, University of Chicago Press

Tuchman G (1978) *Hearth and Home*, Oxford University Press

Vásquez M (2007) 'Sacred and Secular', Association for the Sociology of Religion

Velikovsky I (1950) *Worlds in Collision*, Macmillan

Venkatesh S (2008) *Gang Leader for a Day*, Penguin

Voas D and Crockett A (2005) 'Religion in Britain', *Sociology*

Voas D et al (2002) 'Religious pluralism and participation', *American Sociological Review*

Von Hentig H (1948) *The Criminal and His Victim*, Yale University Press

von Hirsch A (1976) *Doing Justice*, Hill and Wang

Waddington P et al (2004) 'Discretion, Respectability and Institutional Police Racism', *Sociological Research Online*

Walby S (1988) 'The historical periodization of patriarchy', *Paper presented to the BSA annual conference*

Walby S (1991) 'Post-post-modernism? Theorizing social complexity' in Barrett M and Phillips A (eds) *Destabilizing Theory*, Polity Press

Walby S (1997) *Gender Transformations*, Routledge

Walklate S (1998; 2003 second edition) *Understanding Criminology*, Open University Press

Walklate S (2000) 'Researching victims' in King R and Wincup E (eds) *Doing Research on Crime and Justice*, Oxford University Press

Walklate S (2005) *Criminology*, Routledge

Wall D (2001) 'Cybercrimes on the Internet' in Wall D (ed) *Crime and the Internet*, Routledge

Wallis R (1984) *Elementary Forms of the New Religious Life*, Routledge

Walters R (2007) 'Crime, regulation and radioactive waste in the United Kingdom' in Beirne P and South N (eds) *Issues in Green Criminology*, Willan

Walton P (1998) 'Big Science' in Walton P and Young J (eds) *The New Criminology Revisited*, Palgrave Macmillan

Watkins J (1970) 'Against "Normal Science"' in Lakatos I and Musgrave A (eds) *Criticism and the Growth of Knowledge*, Cambridge University Press

Weber M (1905; 1958; 2002) *The Protestant Ethic and the Spirit of Capitalism*, Charles Scribner's Sons

Weber M (1915; 1984) *The Religion of China*, London School of Economics

Weber M (1922; 1963) *The Sociology of Religion*, Beacon Press

Weber M (1958) *The Religion of India*, Glencoe

White R (2008) *Crimes Against Nature*, Willan

Whyte W (1955) *Street Corner Society*, University of Chicago Press

Williams P and Dickinson J (1993) 'Fear of Crime', *British Journal of Criminology*

Willis P (1977) *Learning to Labour*, Saxon House

Wilson B (1966) *Religion in a Secular Society*, C A Watts

Wilson B (1970) *Religious Sects*, McGraw-Hill

Wilson B (2003) 'Salvation, Secularisation and De-moralisation' in Fenn R (ed) *The Blackwell Companion to the Sociology of Religion*, Blackwell

Wilson B and Dobbelaere K (1994) *A Time to Chant*, Oxford University Press.

Wilson J (1975) *Thinking about Crime*, Vintage

Wilson J and Herrnstein R (1985) *Crime and Human Nature*, Simon and Schuster

Wilson J and Kelling G (1982) 'Broken Windows', *Atlantic Monthly*

Winlow S (2001) *Badfellas*, Berg

Wolfgang M (1958) *Patterns in Criminal Homicide*, Patterson Smith

Woodhead L (2002) (ed) *Religion in the Modern World*, Routledge

Woolgar S (1988) *Science: the Very Idea*, Routledge

Worsley P (1956; 1968 second edition) *The Trumpet Shall Sound*, McGibon Kee

Worsley P (1977) *Introducing Sociology*, Penguin

Wrong D (1961; 1999) *The Oversocialized Conception of Man*, Transaction

Yablonsky L (1973) *The Violent Gang*, Macmillan

Yinger M (1970) *The Scientific Study of Religion*, Macmillan

Young J (1971) *The Drugtakers*, Paladin

Young J (1997) 'Left realist criminology' in Maguire M et al (eds) *The Oxford Handbook of Criminology*, Oxford University Press

Young J (1998) 'Writing on the Cusp of Change' in Walton P and Young J (eds) *The New Criminology Revisited*, Palgrave Macmillan

Young J (1999) *The Exclusive Society*, Sage

Young J (2002) 'Crime and social exclusion' in Maguire M et al (eds) *The Oxford Handbook of Criminology*, Oxford University Press

Young M and Willmott P (1962) *Family and Kinship in East London*, Penguin

Young M and Willmott P (1975) *The Symmetrical Family*, Penguin

Youth Justice Board (2006) Anti-Social Behaviour Orders www.direct.gov.uk

Index

Index

Index

Index

Index

Index

Notes

Notes